Principles of Hydrology

FOURTH EDITION

R. C. WARD
Emeritus Professor of Geography
University of Hull

M. ROBINSON
Principal Scientific Officer
Institute of Hydrology
Wallingford

McGraw-Hill Publishing Company

London . Burr Ridge, IL . New York . St Louis . San Francisco . Auckland . Bogotá
Caracas . Lisbon . Madrid . Mexico . Milan . Montreal . New Delhi . Panama
Paris . San Juan . São Paulo . Singapore . Sydney . Tokyo . Toronto

Published by
McGraw-Hill Publishing Company
Shoppenhangers Road
Maidenhead
Berkshire SL6 2QL
England
Telephone +44 (0) 1628 502500
Facsimile +44 (0) 1628 770224
Website http://www.mcgraw-hill.co.uk

British Library Cataloguing in Publication Data

A catalogue record is available from the British Library

ISBN 0 07 709502 2

Publisher: Alfred Waller
Commissioning Editor: Elizabeth Robinson

Created for McGraw-Hill by the independent production company
Steven Gardiner Ltd TEL +44 (0) 1223 364868 FAX +44 (0) 1223 364875

McGraw-Hill

A Division of The McGraw-Hill Companies

5 4 3 2 1 IP 3 2 1 0 9

Printed and bound in Malta by Interprint Ltd

Principles of Hydrology

FOURTH EDITION

To Kay and Mary
and to
Katie and Sally Ann

Contents

Preface

Earth, the 'blue planet', has three-quarters of its surface covered by water and is the only body in the solar system on which water is known to exist in large quantities. Some of the others probably contain water, though it was not until March 1998 that the US National Aeronautics and Space Administration (NASA) confirmed that their unmanned probe, *Lunar Prospector*, had found evidence of some 300 million tonnes of water on the surface of the Moon. Although these frozen reserves may be of value to future lunar explorers, they represent only a minuscule fraction of the total volume of water on Earth (more than 138×10^9 million tonnes) and would maintain the average flow of the River Lune in north-west England for a mere 100 days.

Since ours is literally a water world, the growth of hydrology as both a practical study and a science is not surprising. Early knowledge of water developed almost exclusively through local attempts to manage and control it. However, the water which exists in such abundance on the earth is unevenly distributed in both time and space, and its circulation, closely enmeshed with the circulations of the global atmosphere and oceans, is a vital component of the earth's energy machine. Indeed much of the current impetus for the advancement of hydrology as a science comes from our increasing interest in and concern about climate variability and climate change and the associated role of the global water circulation.

Water is essential to life but excessive variations bring disasters in the form of floods and droughts and its management and appropriation have already become the source of international tension and even, potentially, of global conflict. Furthermore, as the world population continues to grow, the pressures exerted on and by water will also increase and over the next half-century increasingly large areas of the world will have insufficient water to meet their needs. Hydrology is therefore more important than ever before and certainly the need for a clear understanding of the operation of hydrological processes at all scales is significantly greater than when the first edition of this book was published more than 30 years ago.

Hydrological processes, and our improved understanding of their operation, dominate this discussion of the principles of hydrology. Although the structure of this new edition remains essentially unchanged, with chapters devoted to the major components of the hydrological cycle, the subject matter has been fully updated and the text has been largely rewritten. In addition, and by popular request, a concluding chapter on 'The drainage basin and beyond' has been added to draw together some of the ideas which are developed through the book and a selection of review problems and exercises have been added at the end of most chapters.

As in previous editions we have included a wide range of recent references, as well as some seminal historical ones, as guidance for readers who wish to follow up specific topics in more detail. Inevitably, however, our selection is a personal one and in any case represents only a minute fraction of the growing stream of publications in the relevant journals. Fortunately, access to this great body of literature, via CD ROM and the Internet, is probably easier now than at any time since *Principles of Hydrology* first appeared and it is assumed that many readers will access additional information sources, such as electronic abstracting and indexing services and online journals.

Both of us wish to thank friends and colleagues around the world who have reminded us over the years of the imperfections of earlier editions and suggested ways in which we could improve this fourth edition. We are very grateful to all who read draft versions of the manuscript and especially to Ian Calder, Duncan Faulkner, John Gash, Martin Hendriks, Duncan Reed and John Roberts whose detailed comments have done much to improve the quality of the discussions which follow. For any failings that remain, of course, we take full responsibility.

Roy Ward and Mark Robinson

CHAPTER ONE

Introduction

1.1 Water—facts and figures

Hydrology is the science dealing with the waters of the earth, their occurrence, distribution and circulation, their chemical and physical properties and their interaction with the environment. This book focuses on the *principles* of hydrology which are concerned largely with *physical hydrology*, which is sometimes known as *environmental hydrology*. In this context, water is viewed in the same way as soil, vegetation, climate or rock, as an element of the landscape to be investigated and ultimately understood by means of rigorous, scientific quantification and analysis. Water, the subject matter of hydrology, is both commonplace and unique. It is found everywhere in the earth's ecosystem and taken for granted in much of the developed world. It is, however, the only naturally occurring inorganic liquid and is the only chemical compound that occurs in normal conditions as a solid, a liquid and a gas. Its distribution over the globe is amazingly uneven.

Water plays a fundamental part in the distribution of chemicals through its central role in many chemical reactions, the transport of dissolved chemicals and the erosion and deposition of sediments. Its gaseous form, water vapour, is the principal greenhouse gas in the earth's atmosphere, an order of magnitude greater than CO_2, which is the second most important greenhouse gas (Trenberth, 1992).

About 97 per cent (depending on the method of calculation) occurs as saline water in the seas and oceans. Only the remaining 3 per cent is fresh water and of this, considerably more than one half is locked up in ice-sheets and glaciers and another substantial volume occurs as virtually immobile deep groundwater. The really mobile fresh water, which contributes frequently and actively to rainfall, evaporation and streamflow, thus represents only about 0.3 per cent (again depending on the method of calculation) of the global total. Estimated values of global water storage and fluxes are shown in *Table 1.1*. These estimates must be treated with caution because of the difficulties of monitoring and exact quantification at the macroscale. For example, the volumes of the ocean basins and of the major ice-sheets depend upon sea bed and sub-ice topography which

Table 1.1 Estimated storages of water in the hydrological cycle. Based on data from various sources, including those quoted by Speidel and Agnew (1988) and Shiklomanov (1993; 1997).

Storage	*Phase*	*Water volume* cu km × 1000	*% non-oceanic water*	*% global water*	*Typical residence time (years)*
Atmosphere	Gas	13	0.035	0.001	0.026
Land	Liquid & Solid	37 275	99.965	2.697	0.019–>4000
Oceans	Liquid & Solid	1 345 000		97.302	200–>3000
TOTAL Global water		1 382 288		100.000	
Land					
Biological water	Liquid	1	0.003	0.000	0.019
Rivers	Liquid	2	0.005	0.000	0.045
Soil water	Liquid	65	0.174	0.005	0.038–1
Inland seas, saline	Liquid	100	0.268	0.007	200
Freshwater lakes	Liquid	107	0.287	0.008	0.040–20
Groundwater, <1k	Liquid	4000	10.727	0.289	0.038–>500
Groundwater, >1k	Liquid	6000	16.091	0.434	>1000
Ice caps, glaciers	Solid	27 000	72.409	1.953	>10–>4000
TOTAL Land water		37 275	99.965		
TOTAL Non-oceanic water		37 288	100.00		

have only recently been mapped with reasonable accuracy. Reserves of deep groundwater are difficult to assess and estimates are periodically revised, usually upwards (like those of fossil fuel). Shallow groundwater storage is more accessible and mostly easier to estimate, although the proportion of usable, non-saline, water is still far from certain. Atmospheric water vapour content is normally monitored either by radio-sonde balloons released daily from just 1500 global locations or from infra-red spectrometers in weather satellites. Unfortunately, due to the presence of clouds, IR spectrometry is more difficult to interpret for the air layers closest to the earth's surface, where water vapour values are highest (Boucher, 1997).

Understandably, therefore, there is a broad range of estimates of the main global water storages, depending upon the data used and the assumptions made. Ten estimates quoted by Speidel and Agnew (1988) varied significantly in respect of water storage in the ocean basins ($1320 \times 10^6\,km^3$ to $1370 \times 10^6\,km^3$), atmospheric water vapour ($10\,500$–$14\,000\,km^3$), water storage in icecaps and glaciers (16.5–$29.2 \times 10^6\,km^3$) and groundwater (7–$330 \times 10^6\,km^3$). Similar variations were shown in other valuable reviews of global hydrological data by Shiklomanov (1993; 1997).

In the past, hydrologists have focused their attention on the relatively small amount of fresh water occurring either as rivers, lakes, soil water and shallow groundwater, or in the vegetation cover and the atmosphere. Increasingly, however, it is recognized that the oceans play a dominant role in the global water and energy budgets and that large-scale perturbations of the hydrological system may result from changes of sea surface temperature, such as those associated with El Niño, or from modifications of the thermo-haline ocean circulation which may result from the increasingly rapid break-up of major ice-sheets in both the northern and southern hemispheres. It is also important to recognize that the small volume of mobile fresh water is itself distributed unevenly in both space and time. Wetland and prairie, forest and scrub, snowfield and desert, each exhibits different regimes of precipitation, evaporation and streamflow, each offers different challenges of understanding for the hydrologist and of water management for the planner and engineer, and each poses different benefits and threats to human life and livelihood as between the developed and the developing world.

1.2 The changing nature of hydrology

Although hydrology is concerned with the study of water, especially atmospheric and terrestrial fresh water, its emphases have changed from time to time and vary from one practitioner to another. Some have discerned in such changes identifiable historical patterns or 'eras' of hydrology, with a progression, for example, from physical hydrology, through engineering hydrology, to water resources hydrology (for example Jiaqi, 1987; Kundzewicz *et al.*, 1987). Others have attempted to attribute the origins of hydrology to a particular location or country, such as Greece, Egypt, Persia, Scandinavia or South America.

From the evidence available, however, it is much more likely that, from very early times, understanding, engineering and large-scale resource development have progressed simultaneously and interdependently, especially in areas where water was a 'problem' either because of its shortage or its abundance. In Egypt, for example, the Nile flood formed the basis of successful, large-scale, agricultural irrigation for more than 5000 years and the remains of what is possibly the world's oldest dam, built between 2950 and 2750 BC, may be found near Cairo (Biswas, 1970). Again, field systems, dating from before the discovery of the New World, have been found on Columbian floodplains, where construction must have required large-scale operational effort and a high degree of social organization to take advantage of the seasonal floods (Parsons and Bowen, 1966). Indeed, the fact that water is essential to life and that its distribution and availability are intimately associated with the development of human society means that it was almost inevitable that some development of water resources *preceded* a real understanding of their origin and formation.

Archaeological discoveries and later documentary evidence emphasize the significant part played by the location and magnitude of water supplies in the lives of, for example, the Old Testament peoples, the ancient Egyptians and later the Greeks and Romans. During these periods, throughout the Middle Ages and indeed until comparatively recent times, the search continued for an explanation of springs, streamflow and the occurrence and movement of groundwater. However, the hypotheses put forward were either based on guesswork or mythology or else were biased by religious convictions; few, if any, were based on the scientific measurement of the relevant hydrological factors. And yet some of the ideas developed by the ancient writers were remarkably close to the truth as we now know it. For example, the Vedic texts in India, pre-800 BC, appear to show a clear understanding of the atmospheric portion of the hydrological cycle, with the sun breaking up water into small particles (i.e. evaporation) which are then removed by the winds before returning to the mother earth as rain (NIH, 1990). Aristotle (384–322 BC) explained the mechanics of precipitation; Vitruvius, three centuries later, recognized that springs originated from rain and snow, as did Karaji, a Persian scholar of the late tenth century, who expounded the basic principles of hydrology (Pazwash and Mavrigian, 1981). Old Norse mythology, preserved in the Edda poems of the ninth to twelfth centuries, contained remarkable insights on the physical world including a description of the hydrological cycle which showed recognition of the important roles of evaporation from the sea, condensation and cloud formation, and rainfall over the land, and of the connection between rainfall and the development of vegetation and animals (Bergström, 1989). Palissy (1510–1590) stated categorically that rainfall was the only source of springs and rivers (Biswas, 1970), although da Vinci (1452–1519), in comparison, had somewhat confused ideas about the hydrological cycle, but a much better understanding of the principles of flow in open channels than either his predecessors or contemporaries.

It was not until near the end of the seventeenth century, however, that genuine experimental evidence was used to underpin plausible theories about the hydrological cycle. The greatest advances came largely through the work of three men: Pierre Perrault and Edmé Mariotte, whose work on the Seine drainage basin in northern France demonstrated that, contrary to earlier assumption, rainfall was more than adequate to account for river flow; and the English astronomer, Edmund Halley, who showed that the total flow of springs and rivers could be more than accounted for by evaporation from the oceans. Because Perrault, Mariotte and Halley undertook hydrological research of the modern scientific type, they are regarded by many as the founders of hydrology.

In this context the science of hydrology is still a young discipline. Indeed, it was only four years before *Principles of Hydrology* was first published that the founding meeting of the 'Hydrological Group', later to become the British Hydrological Society, was held in London on 10 October 1963 (Hall, 1964). This was a seminal meeting which marked the emergence of British hydrology as a scientific, rather than an engineering, discipline, a trend greatly strengthened in subsequent years by the growing stature of the Institute of Hydrology. Throughout its development, the progress of the science of hydrology has been closely interrelated with developments, including technological advances, in other sciences (McCulloch, 1988). To a large extent this is still the case and the need for a multidisciplinary approach is certain to increase in the foreseeable future. For example, the UK Institute of Hydrology was brought together with other research institutes dealing with freshwater and terrestrial ecology and microbiology under the umbrella organization of the Centre for Ecology and Hydrology (CEH) in 1995. The following year the National Rivers Authority (NRA) was amalgamated with other government regulatory agencies dealing with water, air and land to form the Environment Agency (EA), in order to provide a comprehensive environmental body able to tackle the increasingly complex and multidisciplinary problems of environmental protection.

There are several major interdisciplinary issues which are already helping to drive hydrological science, and which will almost certainly continue to do so well into the next millennium. One is the challenge of modelling the global atmospheric and hydrospheric circulation in order to better predict the hydrological and other consequences of climate variability and climate change. Another is the need to respond to the ever increasing demands for water. These almost quadrupled from the 1940s to the 1990s (Gleick, 1998) although the earth's stock of fresh water is finite and remains relatively constant. The margin between global available stocks of fresh water and the amount used by human activities will diminish further in the future. Already ten per cent of the world's population is affected by chronic water scarcity (WMO, 1996) and this is likely to rise to one-third by about 2025 (WMO/UNESCO, 1997). There is an urgent need for a much clearer understanding of the physical, economic, social, and political consequences of large-scale water resources development and of major irrigation and flood-defence schemes which are designed to reduce the impact of drought and flood disasters.

The UN Earth Summit in 1992 highlighted the need for sustainable development, i.e. 'development that meets the needs of the present without compromising the ability of future generations to meet their own needs'. There is now an increasing recognition that water must be used more efficiently. One way is to regard water as both a natural resource and an economic commodity incurring costs of abstraction, treatment and transportation to where it is required. Thus, for example, water rights may be traded to reallocate water to higher value uses. Similarly, it makes more sense for economically wealthy, but water deficient, countries to purchase grain and other foodstuffs than to try to import vast quantities of water by major civil engineering projects.

1.3 The hydrological cycle and system

The interdependence and continuous movement of all phases of water, i.e. liquid, solid and gaseous, form the basis of the *hydrological cycle* (Figure 1.1), which has been a central concept in hydrology since very early times. Water is indestructible, so the total quantity of water in the hydrological cycle cannot be diminished as it changes from water vapour, to liquid or solid and back again. Nor can it be increased, except through the occasional release of minute quantities of fossil groundwater or possible additions from comets. Instead the processes of streamflow, groundwater flow and evaporation ensure the never-ending transfer of water between land, ocean and atmosphere, followed by its return as precipitation to the earth's surface.

Water vapour in the atmosphere condenses and may give rise to precipitation. In the terrestrial portion of the cycle not all of this precipitation will reach the ground surface because some will be intercepted by the vegetation cover or by the surfaces of buildings and other structures, and will from there be evaporated back into the atmosphere. The precipitation that reaches the ground surface may:

- be stored in the form of pools, puddles and surface water which are usually evaporated into the atmosphere quite quickly;
- be stored as snow and ice before melting or sublimation occurs, possibly after the lapse of many years or even centuries;
- flow over the surface into streams and lakes, from where it will move either by evaporation into the atmosphere, or by seepage towards the groundwater, or by further surface flow into the oceans;
- infiltrate through the ground surface to join existing soil water. This may be removed either by evaporation from the soil and vegetation cover, or by throughflow towards stream channels, or by downward percolation to the underlying groundwater, where it may be held for periods ranging from weeks to millennia. The groundwater component will eventually be removed either

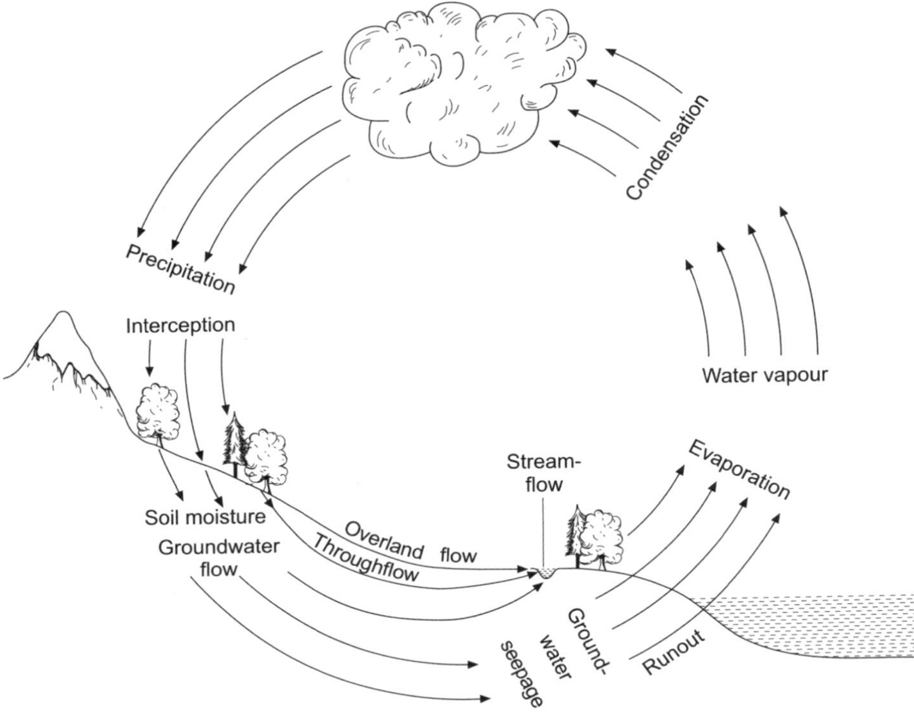

Figure 1.1 Schematic diagram of the hydrological cycle.

by upward capillary movement to the soil surface or to the root zone of the vegetation cover, whence it will be returned by evaporation to the atmosphere or by groundwater seepage and flow into surface streams and into the oceans.

The uninterrupted, sequential movement of water, implied in this simplified description of the hydrological cycle, is rarely achieved. For example, falling or newly fallen precipitation may be returned to the atmosphere by evaporation without becoming involved in streamflow, soil water or groundwater movement. Or precipitation may fall upon the oceans and be evaporated without touching the land surface at all, or it may fall upon the land and percolate to the main groundwater body within which it moves slowly towards a discharge point such as a spring, which it may not reach for centuries or even millennia. In hot deserts, rainfall is spasmodic and so too are other processes in the cycle, such as evaporation and streamflow, which can take place only for a short period during and after rainfall. Accordingly, a short burst of hydrological activity for a week or so may be followed by a long period of virtual inactivity, apart from a slow redistribution of groundwater at some depth below the surface. In cold climates the time delay between snowfall and the active involvement of the precipitated moisture, after melting, in the subsequent phases of the hydrological cycle, may range from months (seasonal snowpacks) through centuries (valley glaciers) to millennia (Antarctic icecap). Also, increasingly, the cycle is interrupted and modified by human activities.

The hydrological cycle provides a useful introductory concept and permits the relationship between precipitation and streamflow to be expressed in a very general way. It is, however, of little practical value to the hydrologist concerned with understanding and quantifying the occurrence, distribution and movement of water in a specific area, whether a small experimental plot of a few square metres or a large continent but which, for most hydrological purposes, will comprise a river basin or group of basins. In this context it is helpful to recognize that in natural conditions many rivers and streams receive water only from their own topographic drainage basin or catchment area to which the continuity equation, in the form of the hydrological or *water balance equation*, may be applied, so that:

$$\text{Inflow} = \text{Outflow} \pm \Delta\text{Storage} \tag{1.1}$$

If this equation can be solved, a quantitative assessment of the movement of water through the drainage basin becomes possible. Alternatively, each drainage basin can be regarded as an individual *system* (Figure 1.2) receiving quantifiable inputs of precipitation and transforming these, via various flows and storages, into quantifiable outputs of evaporation and streamflow. In some cases leakage from deeper subsurface water may represent either an additional input or (as shown in Figure 1.2) an additional output from the drainage basin system. Clearly each of the five storages shown also has the qualities of a system, and may therefore be regarded as subsystems of the drainage basin hydrological system.

Virtually every component of the drainage basin hydrological system may be modified by human activity (Figure 1.3). The most important of these modifications result from:

- large-scale modifications of channel flow and storage, for example by means of surface changes such as afforestation, deforestation, and urbanization, which affect surface runoff and the incidence or magnitude of flooding;
- the widespread development of irrigation and land drainage; and
- the large-scale abstraction of groundwater and surface water for domestic and industrial uses.

Other important modifications include artificial recharge of groundwater and interbasin transfers of surface and groundwater. In the future other modifications, such as the artificial stimulation of precipitation or the use of evaporation and transpiration suppressants, may become more generally important.

1.4 The nature of hydrological processes

Although the drainage basin is used as an example of a specific hydrological unit

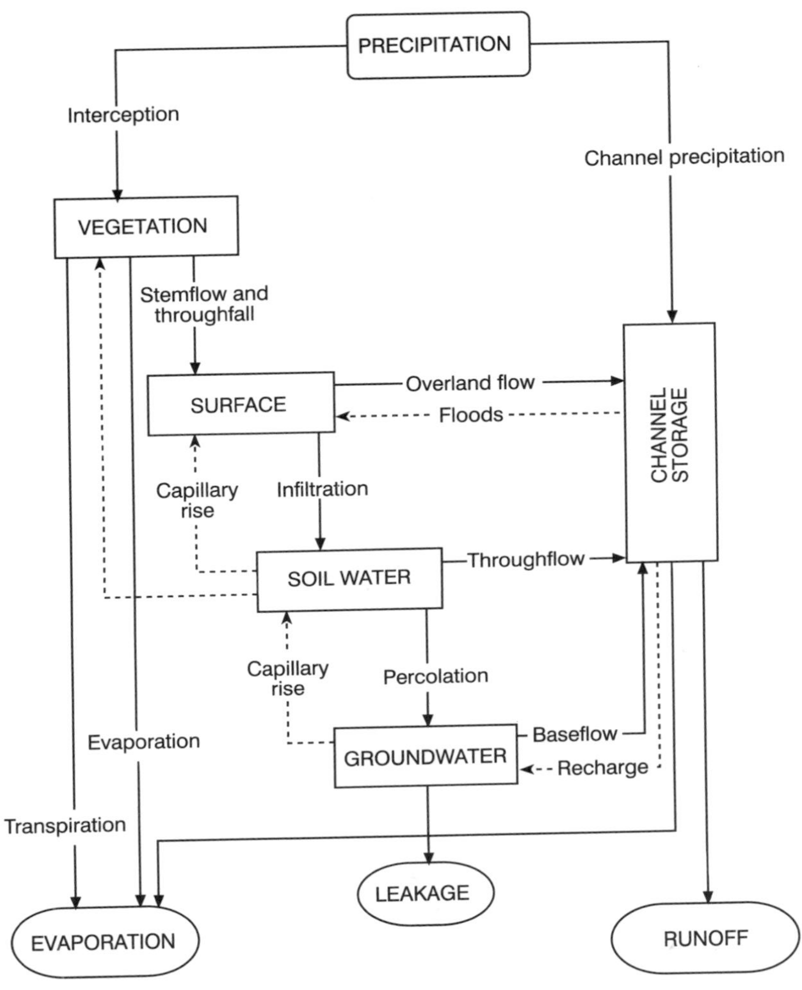

Figure 1.2 The drainage basin hydrological system (from an original diagram by Professor J. Lewin).

in the preceding section, hydrological processes are investigated over a very wide range of spatial and temporal *scales*. At one extreme, *microscale* investigations are exemplified by studies of the movement of soil solution through the interstices of the soil matrix or of the evaporation characteristics of individual plants growing in controlled environment chambers. At the other extreme, some of the emerging problems of environmental change associated with large-scale forest clearance or climate change, for example, will be resolved only by a better understanding of the hydrological system at the *macroscale*, i.e. global or regional, rather than at the *mesoscale* level of the drainage basin (see also Table 9.1).

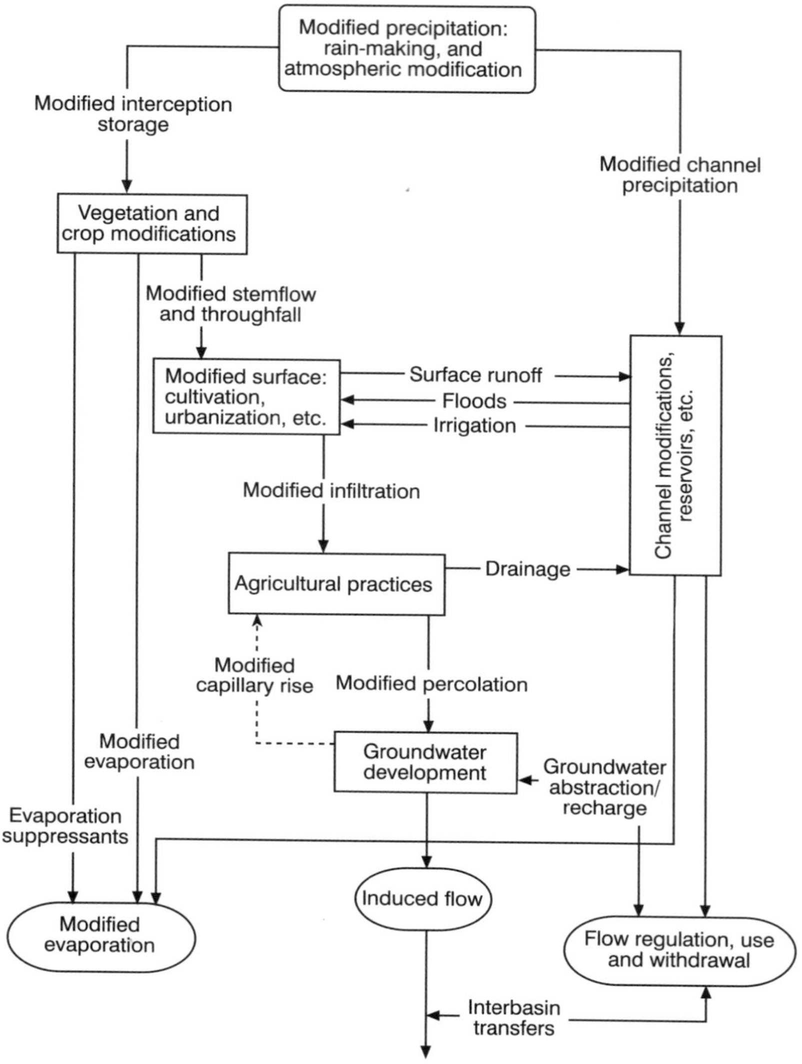

Figure 1.3 Principal areas of human intervention in the hydrological system (from an original diagram by Professor J. Lewin).

Such large-scale studies require international, as well as interdisciplinary, collaboration and depend increasingly on large data networks, on data derived from satellite-based remote sensing techniques, and on GIS and computerized databases. The two main bodies responsible for coordinating international hydrological investigations are the International Association of Hydrological Sciences (IAHS), which is part of the International Union of Geodesy and Geophysics (IUGG), and the World Meteorological Organisation (WMO), which is an agency of the UN. The first internationally coordinated programme of hydrological experiments was the IAHS International Hydrological Decade (1965–74). This was a remarkable example of international cooperation which facilitated major advances in hydrology and in the assessment of surface and groundwater resources. This was then followed by UNESCO's long-term International Hydrological Programme (IHP), which aims to find solutions to specific problems of countries in different geographical locations and at different stages of technological and economic development. Both the IAHS and the WMO, together with other agencies, are active in promoting a number of major international collaborative programmes. For example, WMO plays a major role in coordinating the international collection of hydrological data and in hydrological modelling. It also collaborates with other agencies, as in the World Climate Research Programme (WCRP) whose Global Energy and Water Cycle Experiment (GEWEX) is intended to improve understanding of evaporation and precipitation processes at a global scale (see also Section 9.4).

Implicit in these larger-scale studies is a recognition that hydrological processes form part of an *interactive* earth surface–atmosphere system. The hydrosphere, atmosphere and biosphere are interdependent components of the global system and it is therefore likely that future major advances in hydrology will be closely associated with scientific progress in our understanding of the atmosphere and the biosphere. Often in the past, hydrology has been unduly empirical and even parochial in its emphasis on problem-solving at the expense of scientific understanding and the development of theory.

As well as a greater concentration, in the future, on global-scale issues, hydrologists must also be prepared to deal more effectively than before with the enormous *spatial diversity* both at the earth's surface and in the overlying atmosphere, a diversity that exists across the entire range from micro- to macroscale occurrences. Not only do soils, geology and land use vary spatially but so also do the components of the water balance. Especially crucial is the relation between precipitation and potential evaporation, which varies enormously from one area to another *and* over time, both seasonally and in the long term. Accordingly, hydrologists must increasingly take a long-term, as well as a large-scale, view in order to meet the considerable challenges posed by, for example, the impact of climate variability and climate change on hydrological processes and on the availability of water resources.

The enormous range of scale and of spatial diversity at which hydrological processes operate poses severe problems for the physical hydrologist, not least in the sense that it is virtually impossible to argue from the particular to the general using a simple deterministic notion of causality. Arguing from Max Born's observation that 'Nature is ruled by laws of cause and laws of chance in a certain mixture', Matalas (1982) inferred that:

> ... knowing the initial conditions is not tantamount to knowing what the outcome of the experiment is to be. Thus, intuitively, probability is an intrinsic empirical property of the system.

In other words, hydrological processes may be *deterministic* (i.e. chance independent) or *stochastic* (i.e. chance dependent). All hydrological phenomena are subject to laws that govern their evolution and behaviour so that at the microscale all hydrological processes may be deterministic. However, the macroscale processes which comprise the combined effect of the individual microscopic events may be stochastic in nature. Thus the evolution of rainfall phenomena in time is stochastic in the sense that, although each micro-event is deterministic, at the macroscale present conditions do not uniquely determine future conditions; only *probabilities* of future conditions may be predicted from the present situation (Todorovic and Yevyevich, 1969).

Beven (1987) elaborated these ideas in setting out his own perception of the hydrological system as:

> . . . one of complex spatial and temporal variability of input rates, flow paths and nonlinear dynamic responses resulting from the effects of spatial variability in rainfalls, vegetation canopy, soil structure, and topography. My [perceived] model embodies the idea that preferential pathways are important in flow processes at all scales, from the microscale in soil physics, through the hillslope scale in overland and subsurface flows, to the catchment scale in expanding networks of small channels.
>
> Inherent in this perceptual model is an element of unknowability of the system resulting from heterogeneity. . . Unknowability implies uncertainty and yet hydrologists persist in using deterministic models for predicting catchment responses.

Accordingly, Beven saw the need for two developments in hydrology. First, hydrological predictions should be associated with a realistic estimate of uncertainty. Levels of uncertainty could then be used directly in the decision-making process, thereby permitting the consideration of hydrological processes that are not properly understood as well as those that are. Second, an inherently stochastic, macroscale theory is needed which can accommodate the spatial integration of heterogeneous nonlinear interacting processes, including preferential pathways, in order to provide a rigorous basis for both 'lumped' and 'physically based' predictions.

The discussions of hydrological systems and processes in the ensuing chapters of this book suggest that, although there is some way to go in both respects, hydrology has made great progress on these issues since the first edition of this book was published in 1967 and that further progress is likely in the foreseeable future. Certainly, many of the factors identified by Dooge (1988) as having hampered the development of hydrological theory in the past, for example, fragmentation of approach to the subject, failure of communication between those using different techniques, and lack of proper structures and procedures at national and international level, are rapidly receding in importance. Thus, although stochastic and deterministic approaches have been considered as rivals in the past, they are now seen to be complementary; it *is* recognized that if hydrology is to be applied effectively and economically to human needs then 'Hydrologists must learn to listen to people from other disciplines and hopefully to understand them' (Dooge, 1988). Indeed, hydrologists are increasingly working in multi-disciplinary teams with ecologists and socio-economists, as well as with civil engineers, agriculturalists and water chemists. Hydrologists now have the means, and the confidence, to work with 'real' rather than 'ideal' problem situations, and have recognized that water is important for its quality as well as for its quantity. Finally, the degree of international cooperation now in evidence, and referred to earlier in this section, is most encouraging.

This is a scientific and not an engineering text, but we should be ever mindful that hydrology is more than just an intellectual exercise. The practical and theoretical advances in hydrology, which are reflected in this book, provide an essential basis for meeting the growing challenges posed, for example, by increasing environmental pressures resulting from population growth, climate variability and climate changes, including those triggered by the 'greenhouse effect'. Such pressures have the potential to greatly affect water resources, reducing even further the already paltry per capita availability of water in many countries of Africa, Asia and the Middle East (for example, Biswas, 1996). In some countries, especially those located in downstream areas of major international river basins, there is the potential for military conflict. For example, Gleick (1993a) lists 20 countries which receive more than half their surface water from outside their national borders. Furthermore, the prolonged drought conditions in the Sahel zone of Africa after the late 1960s, together with the apparent increased severity and frequency of major flood events in many areas of the world, underline the inescapable conclusion that recent hydrological records may not be a good guide to the future unless we fully understand the hydrological processes at work. Water is our most precious resource—the original elixir of life—and for the majority of the global population a better understanding of the principles of hydrology may, literally, be a matter of life and death.

CHAPTER TWO

Precipitation

2.1 Introduction and definitions

Precipitation is a major factor controlling the hydrology of a region. It is the main input of water to the Earth's surface and a knowledge of rainfall patterns in space and time is essential to an understanding of soil moisture, groundwater recharge and river flows. Data are more readily available, for more sites and for longer periods, than for other components of the hydrological cycle. In some parts of the world precipitation data may constitute the only directly measured hydrological record (Perks *et al.*, 1996). The study of precipitation is thus of fundamental importance to the hydrologist, and this chapter concentrates on those aspects of its occurrence and distribution that are of direct relevance to the hydrologist. More detailed investigation of the mechanisms of its formation is the domain of the meteorologist and climatologist, and it is assumed that the reader will refer to standard meteorological and climatological texts for a more extensive treatment of the subject.

The meteorologist is concerned to analyse and explain the mechanisms responsible for the distribution of precipitation, an interest ceasing when the precipitation reaches the ground. The hydrologist is interested in the distribution itself, in how much precipitation occurs and in when and where it falls. Thus the hydrological aspects of precipitation studies are concerned with the form in which precipitation occurs, its variations in both space and time, and the correct interpretation and use of the measured data.

Precipitation occurs in a number of forms, and a simple but fundamental distinction can be made between liquid and solid forms. Liquid precipitation principally comprises *rainfall* and *drizzle*, the latter having smaller drop sizes and lighter intensity. In contrast to these forms, which may play an immediate part in the movement of water in the hydrological cycle, solid precipitation, comprising mainly *snow* may remain upon the ground surface for some considerable time until the temperature rises sufficiently for it to melt. For this reason solid precipitation, particularly snow, is discussed separately in Section 2.7. Hail is a rather special case since, although falling to the ground as a solid, it normally does so in temperature conditions that favour rapid melting, and so it tends to act hydrologically like a heavy shower of rain.

Other types of precipitation may be important locally. For example, in some semi-arid areas the main source of moisture may be dew, formed by cooling of the air and condensation of water vapour by cold ground surfaces at night. In coastal or mountain areas fine water droplets in low cloud or mist may be deposited directly onto vegetation and other surfaces. In practice, although it is not strictly correct, the terms 'precipitation' and 'rainfall' are often applied indiscriminately and interchangeably to any or all of these forms.

2.1.1 Water vapour

However dry the air may appear to be, it always contains some moisture as water vapour molecules. A *vapour* is a gas that is below its 'critical temperature' and so may be easily condensed or liquified by a comparatively small change in temperature or pressure. The amount of water vapour in the air varies over time and can be expressed by the *vapour pressure*, which is the partial pressure of the water vapour. This is only a very small part of the total air pressure—typically about 2.5 hPa out of a total atmospheric pressure of about 985 hPa (Trenberth, 1992).

There is a maximum amount of water vapour that the air can hold before it becomes saturated, and this increases approximately logarithmically with increasing temperature. The warmer the air the more water vapour that it can hold. Once this maximum amount is exceeded, for example by cooling, then condensation may occur. This temperature is known as the *dew point*. The degree of saturation may be expressed as the *relative humidity* of the air, which is the ratio of the actual water vapour pressure of the air to that at saturation. Since the saturation vapour pressure depends upon temperature the relative humidity falls as the temperature rises and the relative humidity increases as the air cools. At vapour pressures below the saturation vapour pressure the air is unsaturated and, if conditions are suitable (see Chapter 4), it can absorb moisture through evaporation.

The atmospheric moisture content, or humidity, may be measured by several instruments. A *dew point hygrometer* alternately heats and cools a mirror and measures the dew point temperature by noting changes in surface reflectance due to the formation of condensation. A *psychrometer* contains two thermometers, one measuring air temperature and a second kept moist by a wick connected to a water reservoir. This 'wet bulb' is cooled by evaporating water requiring latent heat of vaporization, and the temperature depression relative to the dry bulb indicates the rate of evaporation and hence the dryness of the air.

The total amount of water vapour in the atmosphere represents only a minute proportion of the world's water budget. At a given moment the atmospheric water accounts for less than 0.001 per cent of the world's total stock of terrestrial, oceanic and atmospheric water (see Table 1.1), and yet this small amount serves as a continuing source of supply in the form of precipitation. The atmospheric vapour amounts to about 25 mm of liquid water which, given the average annual precipitation over the whole globe of about 1000 mm, represents only about nine days' average supply. While the *mean* residence time is nine days, this figure hides a great variation. Some water may be carried up into the stratosphere where it could remain for up to ten years. At the other extreme, some water that is evaporated into the lower levels of a thunderstorm cloud may be precipitated out within an hour (Lamb, 1972).

The vertical profiles of air temperature and pressure exert an important influence on precipitation. The variation of air temperature with height is known as the *environmental lapse rate* (ELR). This averages a decrease of about 6°C per km, but it can vary greatly between places and through time, and this will have an influence upon the behaviour of air masses subject to a lifting mechanism. As a parcel of air ascends it becomes subject to decreasing atmospheric pressure, so it expands and cools. If there is no mixing, and hence no exchange of heat, between the ascending air and its environment (an *adiabatic* process)—which is a good approximation for many purposes—this reduction in temperature is approximately 9.8°C per 1 km, which is known as the *dry adiabatic lapse rate (DALR)*. However, if the air cools sufficiently to become saturated, latent heat of vaporization will be released as water vapour condenses into droplets. This acts to offset some of the cooling, so that the rising air cools at a slower rate, the *saturated adiabatic lapse rate (SALR)*. This is less than the DALR, typically half as much, but the exact amount is inversely dependent on temperature and air pressure. The latent heat released may thus enhance the vertical motion. If a saturated air parcel is warmer (and hence lighter) than the surrounding air, and the environmental lapse rate is greater than the SALR (or the DALR if the parcel of air is not saturated), it will continue to rise and the air is termed *unstable.* Eventually the air parcel reaches a point at which it has cooled sufficiently for cloud to begin to form. This is called the *condensation level.* The changing properties of moving air parcels may be expressed on a *tephigram* and their stability and any condensation level can be determined (Figure 2.1).

2.1.2 Clouds

A *cloud* is a mass of minute water droplets or ice crystals suspended in the atmosphere and appearing as a white or grey drifting body. Individual clouds may vary in extent from a few tens of metres to hundreds of kilometres. At any given time approximately half of the Earth's surface is covered by clouds and they have a very important effect on the radiation balance (Salby, 1992). Due to their high reflectance or *albedo* clouds reflect incoming solar radiation and re-reflect terrestrial radiation, helping to keep the Earth warm. Cloud droplet diameters are generally in the range 1–100 μm. The amount of water in a unit volume of cloud can vary greatly, but median values are about 0.1–0.2 $g\,m^{-3}$ and theoretical maximum values are about 5 $g\,m^{-3}$ (Pruppacher and Klett, 1997).

Clouds form when air becomes saturated, either by evaporation of water into

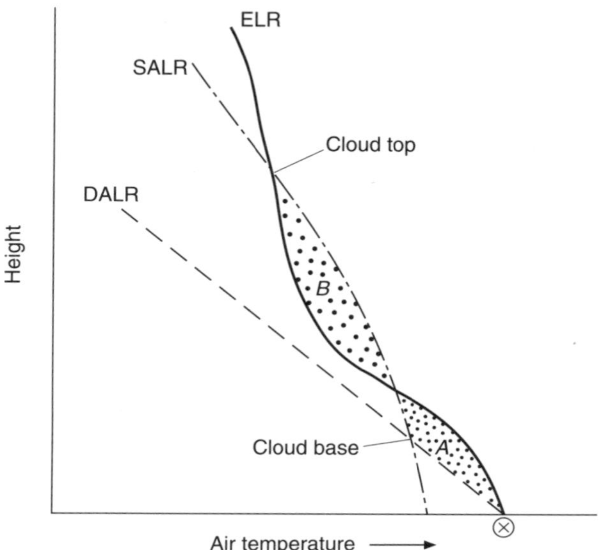

Figure 2.1 Tephigram showing the variation in air temperature with increasing height (reducing pressure). If a parcel of unsaturated air (*X*) is forced to rise it cools at the DALR until, at the dew point temperature, it becomes saturated and condensation (cloud formation) commences. With continued ascent the air will cool at the SALR. A = energy required to cause the air to rise; B = energy released from latent heat, providing buoyancy.

the air, or more commonly by cooling of the air by upward motion. Water droplets condense onto aerosol particles that act as condensation nuclei. At temperatures below freezing, water vapour molecules may be converted directly to ice crystals by sublimation. Condensation nuclei range in diameter from 10^{-4} to 1 μm, and come from various sources. These include smoke, dust, pollen and salt particles from sea spray, as well as aerosol particles created from certain chemical reactions between water vapour, oxygen, nitrogen and trace gases (SO_2, Cl, NH_3, O_3, NO_x) (Preston-Whyte and Tyson, 1988).

Although the atmosphere may have cooled sufficiently to produce clouds, precipitation will not follow unless there are suitable conditions for the growth of water droplets or ice crystals. There is still much uncertainty about the details—for example droplet growth by condensation alone is far too slow to account for raindrop occurrence within a few hours of the formation of a cloud. It is known that in warm clouds (ambient temperature above freezing) the main mechanisms for droplet growth are collision and coalescence. In cold clouds ice crystals grow more rapidly than water droplets by sublimation (water vapour condensing directly as ice onto ice crystals)—because the saturation vapour pressure over ice is lower than over liquid water—and by collision and aggregation of ice crystals.

2.2 Precipitation mechanisms

Precipitation takes place when a body of moist air is cooled sufficiently for it to become saturated and, if condensation nuclei are present, for water droplets or ice crystals to form. These processes are discussed in detail elsewhere (for example, Mason, 1971; Pruppacher and Klett, 1997), and the following is a brief summary. Air may be cooled in a number of ways, for example by the meeting of air masses of different temperatures or by coming into contact with a cold object such as the ground. The most important cooling mechanism, however, is due to the uplift of air. As air is forced to rise its pressure decreases and it expands and cools. This cooling reduces its ability to hold water until at the dew point temperature the air becomes saturated and condensation occurs.

Since cloud appearance (shape, structure, patterns and transparency) expresses air movements, different types of cloud are associated with different weather conditions. Some may be associated with dry weather or only light rain, whereas others are indicative of heavy intense rainfall. Furthermore, it is common in weather systems for several types of clouds to occur together—at different altitudes, changing through time and at different parts of the storm. This type of information has been used in weather forecasting for over 2000 years (for example NIH, 1990). The visual classification developed by Luke Howard 200 years ago (*cirrus*—fibrous, *stratus*—sheets, *cumulus*—heaped) has been incorporated with cloud height: low (< 2000 m), medium (2000–6000 m) and high (> 6000 m) into modern classification schemes, such as the International Cloud Atlas (WMO, 1975; Meteorological Office, 1982).

Low level clouds may also form due to the cooling of the lower air by a cold ground surface, leading to *fog*.

The formation of clouds does not in itself result in precipitation as there must be a mechanism to provide a source of inflow of moisture. Only when water droplets or ice crystals grow to a certain size are they able to fall through the rising air currents as precipitation. Depending upon the temperature, they may reach the ground as rain, hail or snow. Since uplift is the major cause of cooling and precipitation, the following three-way division of precipitation according to the meteorological conditions causing the vertical air motion (frontal/cyclonic, convectional, orographic) can be used in a very general way.

2.2.1 Frontal and cyclonic precipitation

Outside of the tropics, precipitation is often the result of large scale weather systems (typically > 500 km across) with precipitation occurring along the narrow boundaries, or *fronts* between the air masses, together with associated low pressure, *cyclonic*, systems where there is convergence and uplift of air. Cyclonic systems comprise air masses rotating anticlockwise in the Northern Hemisphere and clockwise in the Southern Hemisphere. In the case of frontal precipitation, warm moist air is forced to rise up and over a wedge of colder denser air. This may be either at a warm or cold front and, in broad terms, the

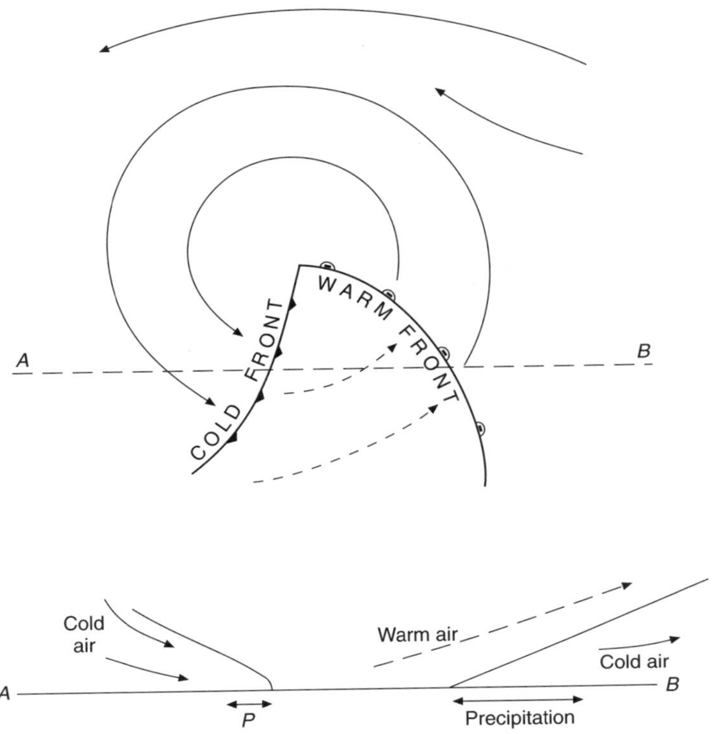

Figure 2.2 Cyclonic storm system for the Northern Hemisphere, showing the occurrence of fronts and resulting precipitation.

two may be distinguished in terms of the resulting precipitation (Figure 2.2). Cold fronts normally have steep frontal surface slopes that give rise to rapid lifting and heavy rain of short duration. In contrast, warm frontal surfaces are usually much less steep, giving more gradual lifting and cooling, leading to less intense rainfall of longer duration. Over western Europe, warm fronts are more common in winter when the westerly air moving over the Atlantic is warmer than the continental air to the east, while in summer the conditions are reversed and cold fronts are more common. In extra-tropical areas, cyclonic systems are responsible for much of the cloud cover and most of the precipitation. They usually have relatively weak vertical air motions and typically produce moderate rain intensities of fairly long duration. In tropical areas, due to the greater heating, the resulting precipitation may be much more intense, and short-lived.

2.2.2 Convectional precipitation

Convectional or convective rainfall results when heating of the ground surface causes warming of the air, and locally strong vertical air motions occur. If the air is *thermally unstable* (section 2.1.1) it continues to rise and the resulting cooling, condensation and cloud formation may lead to locally intense precipitation, but of limited duration. Such rainfall is dependent on heating, and moistening of the air from below, and is most common in tropical regions, although it occurs widely in other areas too, especially in the summer. In tropical cyclones, cloud cells may form spiralling bands around the central vortex, giving rise to prolonged heavy rain affecting large areas (Barry and Chorley, 1998).

Over warm continental interiors and tropical oceans slow-moving mesoscale convective 'systems' (or 'complexes') may produce appreciable amounts of rainfall, and in parts of central USA are responsible for a significant proportion of the summer growing season rainfall (Maddox, 1983). They comprise clusters of thunderstorm cells embedded in a much larger region of stratiform cloud shield several thousand km^2 in extent. Due to their extensive size and often long duration they can be very significant for flood hydrology (Smith and Ward, 1998). They are much rarer in maritime regions, particularly the mid-latitudes, such as the British Isles where there may be only about one per year. Nevertheless it has been suggested that such systems might have been responsible for some of the largest (and rarest) floods recorded in Britain (Austin *et al.*, 1995).

2.2.3 Orographic precipitation

Orographic rainfall results from the mechanical lifting of moist air over barriers such as mountain ranges or islands in oceans, and is analogous to warm air being forced upward at a cold front. It may not be as efficient in producing precipitation as a convective or cyclonic system, but the lifting can induce convectional instability which may be more important than the orographic uplift itself. Typically more rain falls on windward than leeward slopes, since as the air descends it warms and the cloud and rain reduces. This effect can be seen along the western coast of northern Scandinavia and in the northern and western highland areas of the British Isles. On a somewhat smaller spatial scale it is sometimes found that orographic effects may be translocated downwind, so that the largest falls are not recorded on the hill tops but some distance downwind (Chater and Sturman, 1998).

The intensity of orographic precipitation tends to increase with the depth of the uplifted layer of moist air. The vertical enhancement of precipitation has been studied using weather radar, and maps have been produced for Britain showing the amounts of enhancement of precipitation for given wind speeds and directions (Browning and Hill, 1981).

2.3 General spatial patterns of precipitation

In large storms the amount of precipitation may be several times greater than the average water content of a column of atmosphere (although in fact it could never all be precipitated out, even in the greatest storms), indicating that large-scale lateral inflows of moist air must play a key role in the distribution of precipitation.

The large variations in the amount of precipitation, both in time and in space, are of considerable interest to the hydrologist. There is, for example, a great contrast between some of the driest deserts of the world which receive rainfall perhaps only once in 20 years and places such as Bahia Felix in Chile which on average has rain on 325 days per year (van der Leeden *et al.*, 1990). The average annual precipitation over the land areas of the globe has been estimated to be about 720 mm, and may be contrasted with places such as Mount Waialeale in the Hawaiian Islands which receives about 12 000 mm annually and Cherrapunji in Assam, India, where over 26 400 mm were recorded in one year and 3720 mm fell in one four-day period (Dhar and Nandargi,1996). The magnitude of these falls emphasizes the crucial role of large-scale horizontal and vertical movements within the atmosphere in transferring large masses of moist air from areas of high evaporation to areas of high precipitation.

The great mobility of the atmosphere means that the sources of water vapour may be hundreds or thousands of kilometres from the area where that water vapour is precipitated. Consequently, it would be extremely difficult to find a link between changes in land use and changing precipitation. It has been estimated that only about 10 per cent of the total precipitation over Eurasia is recycled water that originates from evaporation from the land surface within the region (Brubaker *et al.*, 1993). The remaining 90 per cent is advected into the region from surrounding areas.

While the behaviour and pattern of individual storms may be complex and variable, broad areal patterns of precipitation exist when averaged over long periods. This is the essential difference between 'weather' as the day-to-day state of the atmosphere and 'climate', which is the normal or average course of the weather.

2.3.1 Global pattern of precipitation

The average water vapour content of the atmosphere, expressed as a precipitation equivalent, is about 25 mm. Values decline systematically from the equator to the polar regions, and also vary seasonally, increasing in summer due to greater heating and evaporation. The overall distribution of atmospheric moisture over the globe is well related to the areal pattern of evaporation and transport by winds (Peixoto and Oort, 1992). On the other hand, the pattern of world precipitation is not well related, being instead closely dependent on the processes causing precipitation, generally a vertical motion in the atmosphere which produces condensation. A review of the historical development of world precipitation maps and global water balance estimates is given by Jaeger (1983).

In broad terms, the greatest rainfalls occur in equatorial areas associated with converging trade wind systems and monsoon climates, where annual precipitation may exceed 3000 mm. High moisture contents and warm temperatures lead to abundant convectional rainfall. The lowest rainfalls, often less than 200 mm y^{-1}, are in (*a*) high latitude polar areas, due to descending air masses and the low water content of the extremely cold air, and (*b*) subtropical areas, which include many of the world's largest deserts, where high-pressure cells give rise to descending, drying air. There is a secondary precipitation maximum in the mid-latitudes (40–65°) due to the occurrence of polar fronts and associated cyclonic disturbances.

This simple general pattern is modified by a number of other factors including unexplained or random variations in the global atmospheric circulation. Evaporation from the oceans (especially subtropical oceans) is the main source of atmospheric moisture; evaporation from continents provides only a small proportion of precipitation over land (see also Table 1.1). As a result, precipitation tends to decrease with distance from the sea, resulting in areas of extremely low rainfall near the centres of most of the major landmasses. In coastal areas, precipitation is generally greater over land than over the nearby sea due to the greater mechanical and thermal overturning of the air. Mountain ranges tend to accentuate precipitation amounts, particularly in areas where the prevailing air movement is onshore.

2.3.2 Regional precipitation

When regions such as the United States, Europe or the British Isles are considered in detail, the orographic influence is far more apparent, dominating the annual and, to a lesser extent, the seasonal distributions. The pattern of precipitation across Europe (Figure 2.3 and Figure 2.4) is strongly influenced by the extensive ocean to the west, the distribution of mountains and the predominant direction of rain-bearing winds (from the west). Moist air from the Atlantic results in the highest precipitation (over 1000 mm y^{-1}) on west coasts and mountain ranges, including western parts of the British Isles, Norway, the Iberian Peninsula, the Pyrenees, Italy, the Dalmatian coast of the Balkan mountains, and the Alps. The lowest precipitation (under 500 mm y^{-1}) falls in southern and eastern areas in the lee of mountain barriers, such as Sweden and Finland downwind of the Scandinavian mountains, central and south-east Spain, north-east Italy, and eastern Greece. The lowlands of western and central Europe generally have a fairly even distribution of about 500–750 mm y^{-1}.

There is a winter precipitation maximum in western coastal areas (British Isles, Norway, north-west France) and in Mediterranean areas (Iberian Peninsula, Italy and Greece), with a summer maximum over much of central Europe due to summer heating and intensified convective activity. The climate of Europe is described fully in texts such as Wallen (1970) and Martyn (1992).

2.4 Precipitation measurement

Before dealing in detail with rainfall variations in time and space, and methods of analysing aspects of its magnitude and frequency, it is appropriate to review the

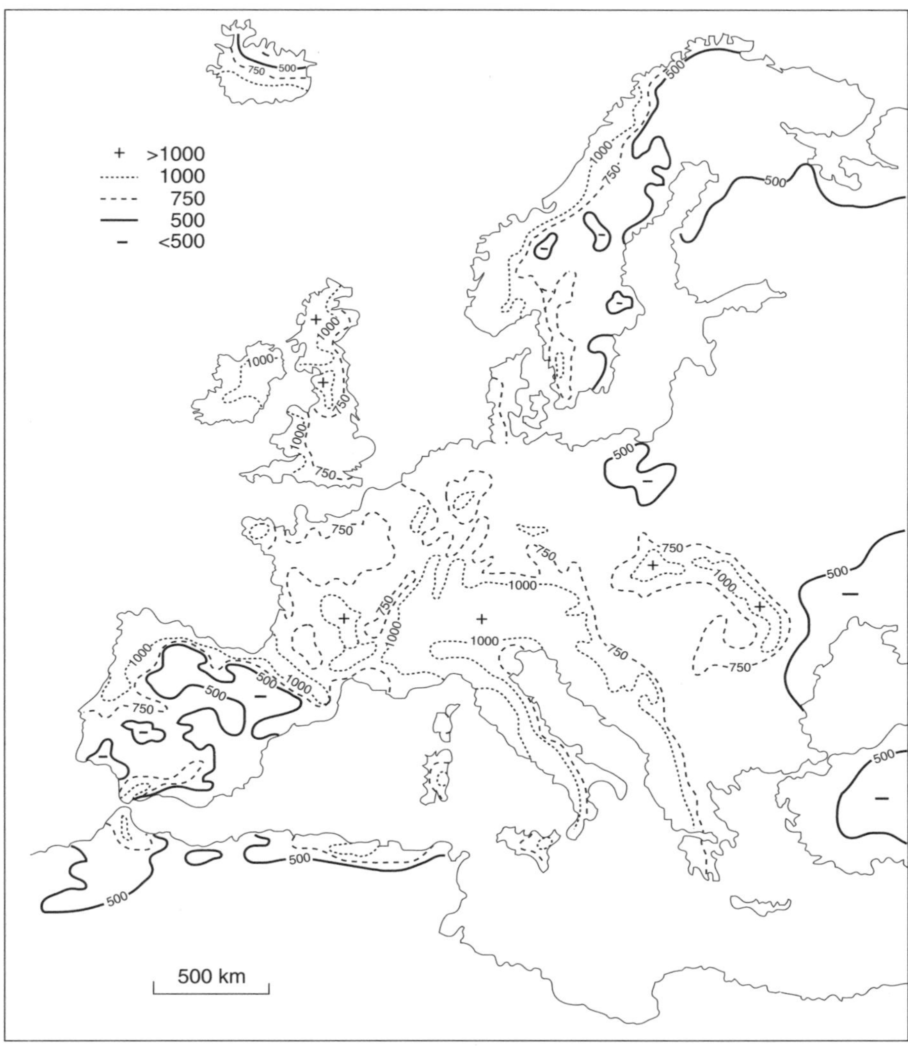

Figure 2.3 Simplified pattern of European annual average precipitation (mm).

different means of measuring and recording precipitation, and to discuss some of their problems and limitations.

Of the different forms of precipitation (rain, hail, snow, etc.) only rainfall is extensively measured with any degree of certainty. For this reason the following sections deal primarily with rainfall. Methods specifically for measuring snow are dealt with in a separate section. The measurement of rainfall comprises two aspects: first, the point measurement of rainfall at a gauge and, second, the use of the catches at a number of gauges to estimate areal rainfall.

Figure 2.4 British Isles annual precipitation (mm), 1931–60 (from an original diagram by B.W. Atkinson and P.A. Smithson in Chandler and Gregory, 1976, based on data from the UK Meteorological Office and the Eire Meteorological Service).

2.4.1 Point measurement

A raingauge is basically an open container to catch falling raindrops or snowflakes over a known area bounded by the raingauge rim. The amount of rain collected may be measured by manually emptying a *storage raingauge*, usually at daily or longer intervals, and noting the amount of accumulated water or else by using a *recording raingauge* which automatically registers the *intensity*, or rate of accumulation of rainfall. The main types of recording raingauges are either 'continuous' recorders which register changing water levels on a chart (for example the Dines siphoning raingauge) or tipping bucket raingauges which record increments, typically 0.1 to 0.5 mm, of rain. Short-period rainfall data are necessary to understand rainfall interception losses, limits to soil infiltration rates and catchment runoff hydrographs. For urban runoff studies, rainfall depths over only a few minutes' duration are necessary (for example Niemczynowicz, 1989). Guidelines on procedures for collecting and processing raingauge data are provided by Meteorological Office (1982) and WMO (1994). Gunston (1998) provides advice particularly for developing countries.

Rainfall measurement probably began over 2000 years ago in India (NIH, 1990), and the first raingauges in Europe date from about the seventeenth century (Biswas, 1970). In the 1670s, in northern France, Pierre Perrault used a raingauge to prove for the first time that the annual rainfall to a small catchment was adequate to account for the observed streamflow. Nevertheless, many problems remain in the collection and accuracy of rainfall data. The major problem of accuracy is due to wind turbulence around the gauge, which usually results in underestimates (Sevruk, 1982). This may be due both to the exposure of the site and to the type of raingauge.

Controlled experiments in wind tunnels show how the raingauge acts as an obstacle to the wind flow, leading to turbulence and an increase in wind speed above the gauge orifice. The result is that precipitation particles that would have entered the gauge tend to be deflected and carried further downwind (Robinson and Rodda, 1969; Sevruk *et al.*, 1989). This effect is much more pronounced in the case of snowfall. Errors due to turbulence increase with wind speed and with reducing drop size. Thus it may be expected that errors will be greater in temperate areas, such as Britain, than in some tropical areas, due to smaller raindrop sizes, higher wind speeds and the occurrence of precipitation as snowfall.

Raingauge measurements are sensitive to changes in the immediate environment surrounding the gauge. General advice on *raingauge siting* is provided in texts such as Meteorological Office (1982), Linacre (1992) and WMO (1994). A site should not be over-exposed to strong winds, nor should it be unduly sheltered by nearby obstacles. As a general rule the gauge should be at a distance of at least twice (and preferably four times) the height of any obstacle. But these guides also recognize that some degree of shelter is needed, as a very open site would be too exposed and subject to excessive wind effects.

The most direct way to eliminate the wind effect is to place the raingauge in a pit so that its rim is level with the ground (Stevenson, 1842; Koschmieder, 1934). If properly sited and surrounded by an anti-splash grid, this type of gauge is the most accurate measure of rain, receiving the same amount of rainfall as would have reached the ground without the gauge being present. However, this design has not been widely adopted because a pit is prone to fill with leaves or drifting snow, and on poorly drained ground it may fill with water. A more widely adopted approach is to add a shield below the rim to reduce turbulence. Different types include the rigid Nipher shield and the flexible Alter shield comprising metal strips which can move in the wind, and so restrict the accretion of snow. Such shields have, however, only been partially successful (Weiss and Wilson, 1958), and snow catches are still subject to considerable error.

Consideration of wind effects on gauge catch must be made when interpreting rainfall records. Early raingauges were often placed on a roof or a high wall to be safe from human or animal interference, thus inadvertently increasing the potential undercatch. This practice is still common in many developing countries, and so particular care must be made when interpreting such records. The first continuous record of daily rainfall in Britain, for example, was made in the seventeenth century, using a gauge on the roof of a house (Biswas, 1970; Craddock, 1976). Similarly, from 1815 to 1852 the main raingauge at Oxford University's Radcliffe Observatory was sited on a roof parapet at 7 m above the ground (Wallace, 1997). The more serious undercatches in exposed upland areas than in adjacent valleys gave the impression that rain increased as it fell through the atmosphere to lower altitudes. An extreme consequence of this belief was the abandonment in 1838 of plans to build an upland reservoir to supply water to the town of Oldham in northern England (Binnie, 1981).

Legates and Willmott (1990) used records of nearly 25 000 raingauges to compute global precipitation, and attempted to allow for gauge undercatch using correction methods devised by Sevruk (1982). They estimated that undercatches amounted to 10 per cent globally, varying from 40 per cent near the poles, due to snowfall, to under 5 per cent in the tropics. Even larger errors may occur in individual storms. The undercatch also varies between seasons, being largest in winter when drop sizes are smaller and wind velocities are higher (Rodda, 1968; Green and Helliwell, 1972) (Figure 2.5).

Over 50 different types of national precipitation gauge are currently in use, with rim heights varying from 0.2 to 2 m (Sevruk and Klemm, 1989). Some of the most widely used gauges are summarized in Table 2.1. In Britain, for example, the standard gauge has its orifice at 305 mm (one foot) above the ground. In some other European countries prone to heavy snowfall, rim heights of 1 or 2 m are adopted. This may lead to complications when comparisons are made between countries, with jumps in precipitation values at national boundaries (Groisman and Easterling, 1994). To provide a basis for comparison the World Meteorological Organization (WMO) proposed an Interim Reference Precipitation Gauge; but it, too, suffers errors from the effect of wind. In fact there are good physical reasons for the continued use of a variety of gauges; taller, wider gauges are more suitable in areas with much snow, while shorter gauges or ground level gauges are more appropriate in areas where rainfall predominates. Many countries are reluctant to change from their traditional type of gauge as this could introduce inhomogeneity into rainfall records, leading to problems in the

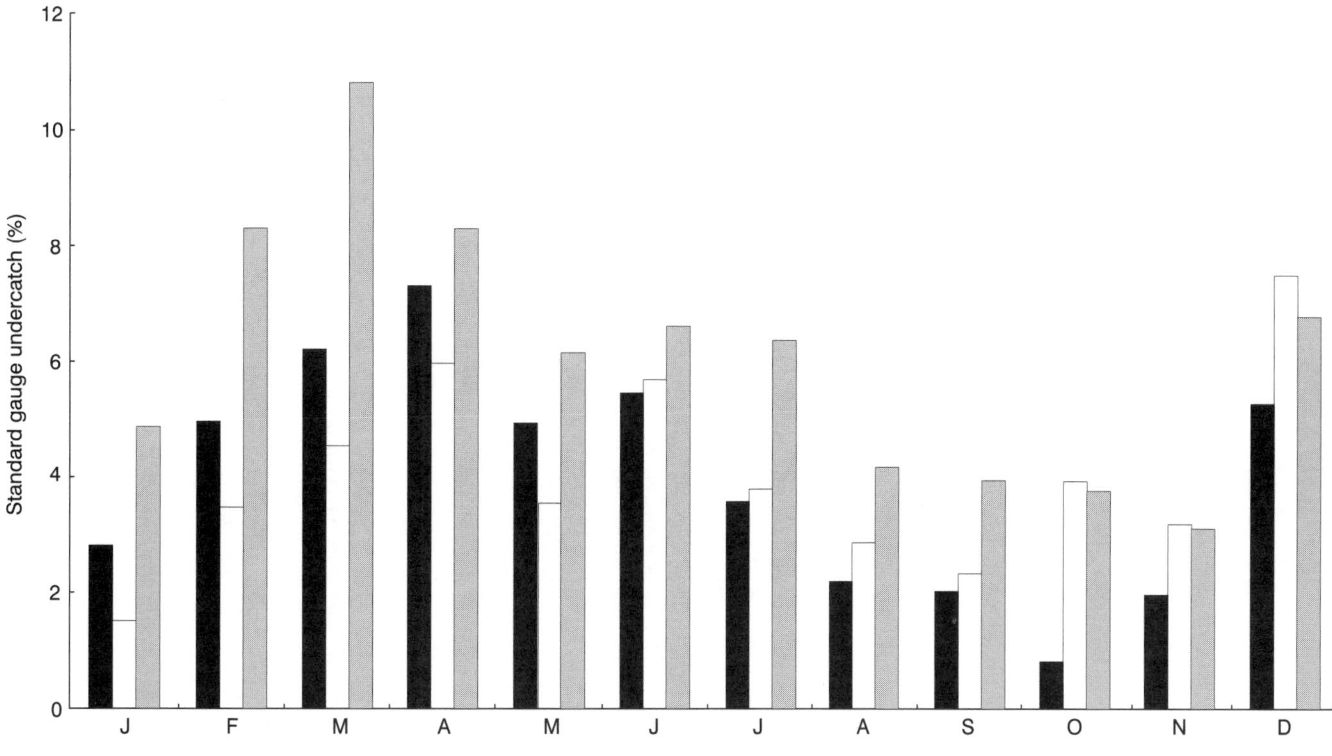

Figure 2.5 Comparison of ground level and standard height (30 cm) raingauge catches for three sites at Coalburn in northern England, 1975–92. Undercatch errors are greater in winter when wind speeds are higher, raindrop sizes are smaller and there may be snowfall. (Based on data supplied by the Institute of Hydrology)

Table 2.1 Different types of widely used storage raingauges. Based on data in Sevruk (1982) and Sevruk and Klemm (1989).

Country of origin	*Gauge name*	*Orifice area (cm^2)*	*Rim height (m)*	*Estimated number worldwide*	*Area covered (10^3 km^2)*
Germany	Hellmann	200	1.1	30 100	10 250
China	Chinese	314	0.7	19 700	10 880
UK	Mk2/Snowdon	127	0.3	17 800	10 400
Russia	Tretyakov	200	2.0	13 500	25 340
USA	Weather Bureau	324	1.1	11 300	12 560
India	Indian	200	0.3	11 000	3290
Australia	Australian	324	0.3	7600	7940
France	Association	400	1.0	3000	5000
France	SPIEA	400	1.0	1800	4710

use of such records for studies of climatic variations and in evaluating long-term average values. The addition of Alter wind shields to raingauges at sites in the western USA in the 1940s created discontinuities in the records (Groisman and Legates, 1994). Details of precipitation gauge changes in a number of countries are given by Sevruk and Klemm (1989) and Groisman and Easterling (1994).

These considerations demonstrate the crucial importance of *metadata*, records of site changes, which include instrumentation and site exposure, to be able to separate true climate trends from local site effects. Crane and Hudson (1997) provide a valuable insight into the problems of data interpretation for a climate station over a 27-year period due to site changes. Woodley (1996) describes the problems identifying and reconstructing the unrecorded changes in the data processing procedures used by the UK Meteorological Office to estimate long-term annual rainfall totals for England and Wales, and for Scotland.

Particular measurement problems

In very steep terrain, not only is rainfall spatially very variable but a standard gauge with horizontal rim will tend to undercatch precipitation in winds blowing upslope, and overcatch in winds blowing downslope. The best solution may be a ground level gauge with its rim inclined with the ground slope. The effective catch area must then be converted to a horizontal standard by dividing by the cosine of the slope angle.

About one-third of the Earth's land surfaces are covered by forests, and it is not always possible to measure precipitation in clearings. It may be necessary to install a raingauge on a tower at tree-top (canopy) level. It is possible for catches very similar to ground-level gauge values to be achieved in this way because the airflow disturbance of the gauge is similar to the roughness of the forest canopy, but this is very dependent upon the height of the gauge relative to the canopy

(Jaeger, 1985). If the gauge is too high it will experience wind induced undercatch, while if it is too low it may suffer from overcatch due to drip from adjacent branches or undercatch due to sheltering. It is difficult to define a suitable height for the gauge rim where the trees are of irregular height or the topography is uneven. Furthermore, the level of the gauge must also be regularly raised in line with growth of the trees.

Of special importance to the hydrologist is the measurement of extreme rainfall events which may be responsible for rare floods of great magnitude. Under such severe conditions, the performance of the instruments, rather than wind effects, may be the major problem (Sevruk and Geiger, 1981). Rainfall amounts may exceed the capacity of storage gauges, causing water to overflow and be lost. High intensity rainfall can cause recording gauge mechanisms to jam, or to lose accuracy due to the finite time taken for the float gauges to siphon empty ($\sim$ 10 seconds for a Dines gauge after every 5 mm of rain) or for tipping buckets to tip ($\sim$ 0.5 seconds). Calder and Kidd (1978) provide a dynamic calibration equation for tipping bucket gauges.

2.4.2 Areal rainfall

Hydrologists often need to estimate the volume of rainfall over a catchment area and require an adequate number of measurements in order to assess the spatial variation. This may be achieved with a network of raingauges alone, or by using additional information from remote sensing by weather radar or satellites.

Design of raingauge networks

A network of raingauges represents a finite number of point samples of the two-dimensional pattern of rainfall depths. The UK has one of the highest densities of storage raingauges in the world with an average of one gauge per 60 km^2 per gauge (WMO, 1995); yet the total collecting area of all the gauges in the UK is less than the size of one standard football pitch! Comparable values of the average area (km^2) per storage raingauge for a range of countries include France (110), Netherlands (130), China (470), India (790), Australia (1010), US (1040), Saudi Arabia (8140) and Mongolia (47 420).

In general, estimates of areal precipitation will increase in accuracy as the density of the gauging network increases, but a dense network is difficult and expensive to maintain. A number of general guidelines for gauge density have been produced. The World Meteorological Organization (Perks *et al.*, 1996) evaluated the adequacy of hydrological networks on a global basis for the Basic Hydrological Network Assessment Project and gave the following broad guidelines for the *minimum* gauge density of precipitation networks in various geographical regions: one raingauge per 25 km^2 for small mountainous islands with irregular precipitation; 250 km^2 per gauge for mountainous areas; 575 km^2 elsewhere in temperate, Mediterranean and tropical climates, and 10 000 km^2 for arid and polar climates.

Of course, many other factors are likely to be important, including type of topography and climate characteristics. In estimating the areal pattern of rainfall from a given gauge network, errors will occur due to the random nature of storms and their paths relative to gauges (Wiesner, 1970). The accuracy will depend on the spatial variability of precipitation; thus more gauges would be required in steeply sloping terrain and in areas prone to localized thunderstorms rather than frontal rainfall. The density of gauges required also depends upon the time scale of interest; shorter period rainfall intensities (for example, hourly) are generally much more variable than daily or annual totals.

The accuracy of areal rainfall estimation depends on both the total number of gauges and their spatial distribution. Raingauges may be sited *a priori* within a classification of 'domains' representing classes with different ranges of geographical and topographic characteristics—such as altitude, distance to the sea, ground slope and aspect—which are thought likely to influence rainfall. Alternatively, a large number of gauges may be used initially to identify the predominant areal pattern of precipitation, and the number subsequently reduced. The areal distribution of gauges might also reflect the intended use for the network; thus if the main purpose of precipitation measurement is for runoff studies, then one approach to network design would be to locate gauges in those areas that contribute most to runoff (Moore, 1987).

Kriging is a statistical method that uses the variogram of the rainfall field (i.e. the variance between pairs of points at different distances apart) to optimize the gauge weightings to minimize the estimation error. It has the advantage that it can be used to generate a map of the standard error of the estimates that indicates where additional gauges would be of most benefit. Bastin *et al.* (1984) and IH (1999) use the technique to estimate areal rainfall, to indicate the degree of redundancy in a gauge network and to identify locations where additional gauges might be most useful (Figure 2.6).

If an area has no existing gauges to indicate the spatial distribution of precipitation, it is necessary to transpose information on rainfall variations in time and space from a similar area in order to design a preliminary network. This is often the case for developing countries. In developed countries, in contrast, networks are usually in place but probably evolved in an arbitrary manner. A large number of studies have used techniques including multiple regression and kriging to quantify the statistical structure of rainfall patterns, and to identify a more effective network design (Periago *et al.*, 1998). In using any method based on the correlation between gauges it is of paramount importance to ensure the homogeneity of record of each gauge. Unrecorded changes in siting or exposure may weaken correlations between gauges, resulting in networks that are denser than necessary.

It must be remembered that there are very important non-hydrological constraints and considerations (social, economic) in determining network density. A raingauge or any other network exists to serve certain objectives. The minimum network is one that will avoid serious deficiencies in developing and

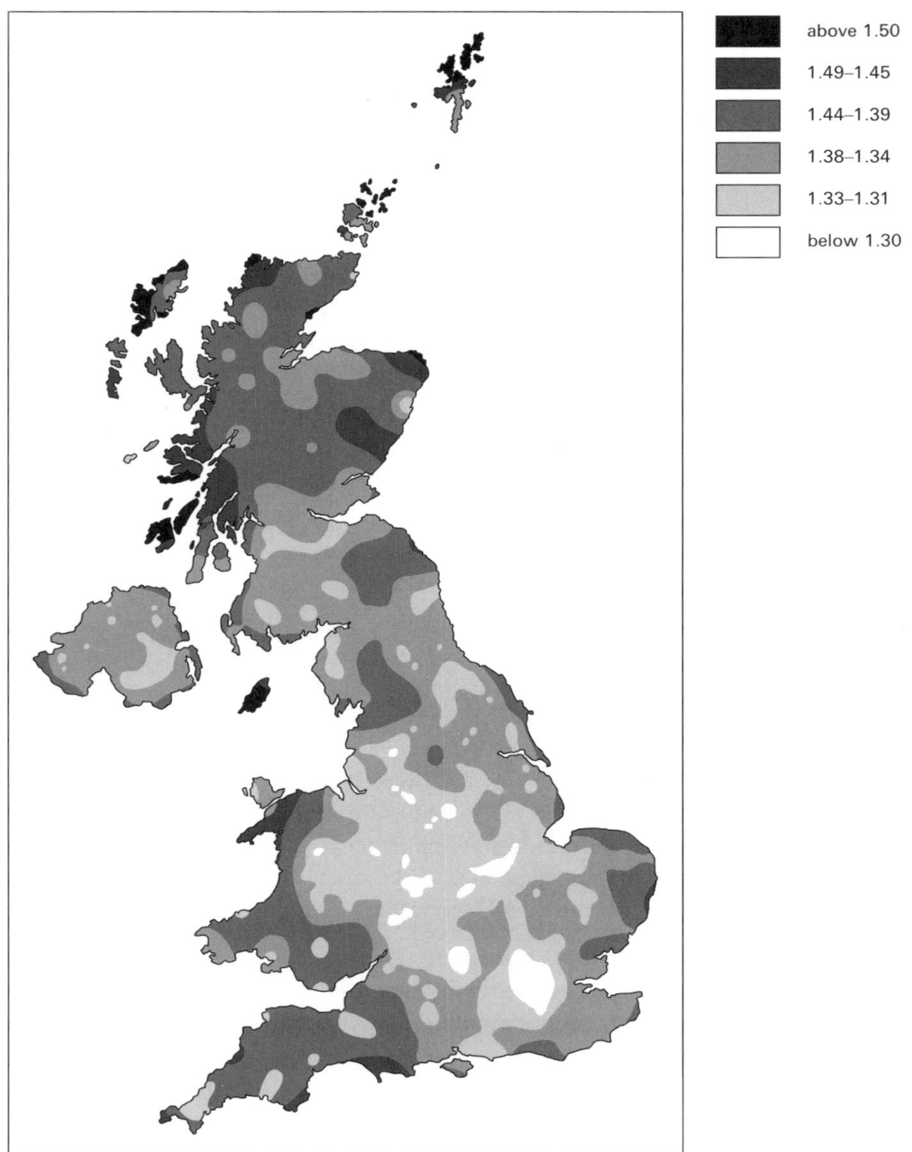

Figure 2.6 Standard deviation of estimates of one-hour median annual maximum rain depth, RMED (mm) across the UK produced by kriging. This highlights those areas where estimates are least certain and additional raingauges might be most beneficial. (Reproduced and simplified from Figure 7.5 in Vol. 2 of the *Flood Estimation Handbook*, IH, 1999.)

managing water resources on a scale commensurate with the overall level of economic development and environmental needs of the country (WMO, 1994).

Weather radar and satellites

However great the density of existing networks of raingauges, they can only give an approximation to the actual spatial pattern of precipitation. The potential of *radar* (an acronym for *ra*dio *d*etection *a*nd *r*anging) for monitoring storm rainfall patterns was first noted during the Second World War and considerable development work has been carried out in a number of countries, in particular the USA, former Soviet Union, Japan, Switzerland and the UK. The major advantage over raingauges alone is that the radar samples and averages the rainfall in a volume of many millions of cubic metres of the atmosphere (Austin *et al.*, 1995).

There are several ways of measuring rainfall using radar, including Doppler radar and attenuation, but the most widely adopted approach is based on radar echo, or reflectivity. The relation between radar reflectivity and rainfall rate is not constant, but depends on a number of factors including the concentration of drops, their size distribution and the pattern of vertical wind velocity. Marshall and Palmer (1948) analysed extensive experimental results on rainfall rates and drop size distributions, which is the basis of an empirical relation between rainfall rate, R (mm/h), and radar reflectivity, Z (mm^6/m^3) of the form: $Z = AR^B$. Values of $A = 200$ and $B = 1.6$ are most commonly used, although studies have found great variations in these parameters, with ranges in A from 70 to 500 and in B from 1.0 to 2.0 (Battan, 1973). It was this unpredictable variation in the relation between radar reflectivity and rainfall rate that for many years prevented the use of radar for quantitative rainfall measurement.

The main reasons for the variation in the relationship between radar reflectivity and rainfall (Wilson and Brandes, 1979; Collier, 1987, 1996) include:

- variations in raindrop-size distribution;
- the presence of hail, snow or melting snow. Melting snow has a much higher reflectivity than rainfall, producing an enhanced 'bright band' in the vertical reflectivity profile;
- growth or evaporation of rain below the radar beam height;
- ground echoes ('clutter') due to hills and tall buildings; and
- attenuation of the signals due to heavy rain along the beam.

The parameters of the $Z:R$ relation can vary widely, in part due to systematic differences with the precipitation type, for example, frontal storms, convective rain, orographic rain and snow (Shepherd *et al.*, 1989; Austin *et al.*, 1995). This is because of differences in their raindrop-size distribution; thus rainfall rates will be overestimated for cumulonimbus storms which have larger size drops, and underestimated for layer clouds which have smaller drops (Austin and Wickham, 1995). Snowflakes and ice crystals also produce artificially high estimates.

The major advance enabling radar to be used for quantitative precipitation estimates came from the use of measured rainfall rates for 'real time' adjustment of the $Z:R$ relation. This lumps together all sources of radar error (technological, ground clutter, $Z:R$ relation) and deals with them in a single process (Collier, 1996). Thus, the radar precipitation field is 'calibrated' or 'adjusted' by point raingauge observations, while retaining the areal pattern observed from the radar.

Calibrating raingauges can be used in real time to apply a correction factor to periods as short as hourly radar estimates. Collier *et al.* (1983) demonstrated that this factor could vary widely (but generally between 0.1 and 10) due to changes in the drop size distribution, 'bright band' enhancement due to melting snow and evaporation losses or raindrop growth below the level of the radar beam (Figure 2.7). The calibration factor can be determined in real time using telemetry gauge information, and the nature of the temporal changes in the factor can be used to automatically identify the rainfall type. For each rainfall type, Collier *et al.* (1983) identified a number of rainfall calibration domains. Correction factors based on different subsets of calibration gauges are then applied to the radar data for each domain.

Although this concept has been proposed for many years (Hitschfield and Bordan, 1954), it has required a great deal of work to implement an operational scheme. Summarizing a number of studies which differed in factors such as the summation period and the density of calibration gauges, Wilson and Brandes (1979) reported typical errors of 43–55 per cent for uncalibrated radar data. This reduced to 18–35 per cent using a single calibration raingauge and to 13–27 per cent for spatially variable calibration.

Hill and Robertson (1987) describe the operation of a weather radar system in north-west England. At this station the aerial rotates about once each minute, and in turn scans each of four elevations above the horizontal. The lowest beam is to be preferred for rainfall estimation, since there is least opportunity for raindrop growth or evaporation before reaching the ground. In practice a higher beam may be substituted on compass bearings where hills and tall structures can obstruct the beam. Three complete scans are then combined to produce 15-minute rainfall estimates. Thus, weather radar gives an integrated value over a *finite* time period, and not an 'instantaneous' value. Telemetering recording raingauges are used for automatic calibration. Radar output is produced for a 2×2 km grid within 75 km of the installation and on a 5×5 km grid for distances 75–210 km from the radar. Beyond 210 km the radar estimates are not considered to be sufficiently accurate, as the return signal becomes too weak and also because the beam becomes too high and diffuse. Weather radar calibration is discussed by Collinge (1991) and van dem Assem (1991) for situations in the UK and the Netherlands, respectively.

The techniques of radar measurement have developed enormously with hardware advances in radar technology and data processing capacity and with software developments in real-time calibration. Radar is now widely used in operational systems (Collier, 1996). At present there is a network of 15 weather

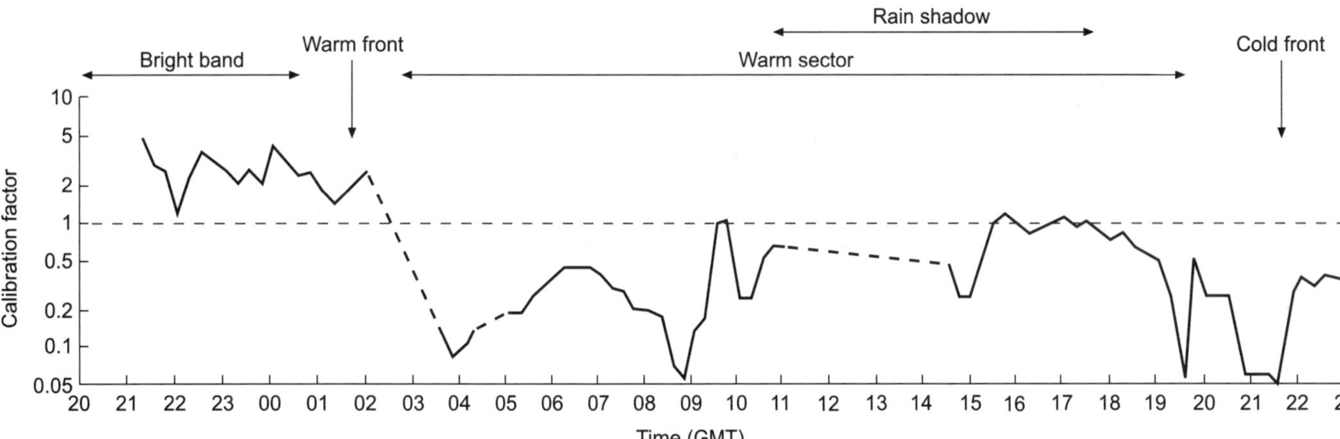

Figure 2.7 Variation in the radar rainfall calibration factor during the passage of a small depression with 'bright band' effects in advance of a warm front, 1–2 January 1981 (from Collier *et al.*, 1983).

radars over the British Isles, capable of giving rainfall estimates of high resolution (2 km grid, five minute integrations). At the European level there are about 100 operational weather radar systems (Collier and Chapius, 1990; Collier, 1995), and interest has focused on mapping quantitatively the distribution of precipitation. In the USA there is a need to give warnings for the intense storms that are more prevalent there than in Europe, and the NEXRAD (*Nex*t generation weather *rad*ar) programme (Klazura and Imy, 1993) uses approximately 140 Doppler radars to provide detailed information on wind patterns and the internal structure of storm clouds as well as precipitation estimates.

Raingauges or radar coverages are inadequate over much of the Earth's surface, comprising the oceans, most of the desert and semi-desert regions, most major mountainous regions and extensive humid regions in the tropics. Satellite techniques are the only systematic means in those areas of monitoring the movements of weather systems and to provide estimates of likely rainfall patterns. Satellites can provide spatially continuous information and, depending on the orbit, can provide complete global coverage over a period of time. Satellite techniques were first developed for convective rainfall in the tropics and subtropics, and that is where they have been most widely applied (Rango, 1994).

Satellites provide observations of clouds, not rainfall, and so cannot measure rainfall directly. Consequently, the current satellite techniques for estimating rainfall depths are not as accurate as raingauges and radar, which should be used wherever possible.

Using satellites, precipitating clouds must be inferred from cloud types and the way in which they alter through time. Rainfall rates are estimated indirectly from the albedo and radiation emissions of cloud tops, providing information on cloud extent and temperature. In practice, all operational programmes and most research using satellites for rainfall monitoring have been based on visible and infrared wavelength radiation (Barrett and Martin, 1981; Engman and Gurney, 1991). Visible radiation is most strongly related to the albedo of highly reflective surfaces such as clouds. High brightness implies a greater cloud thickness and probability of rainfall. Infrared radiation is largely dependent on temperature. Since temperature varies with altitude, this may be interpreted as indicating the cloud top height. Low temperatures imply high cloud tops and large thickness of clouds, with a greater probability of rainfall. In practice, neither bright clouds nor cold clouds necessarily produce rainfall, and the best approach is probably to use both types of information together (Browning, 1987). Rain is more likely in clouds that are both cold and bright.

A number of approaches have been developed to monitor rainfall from satellites (Barrett and Martin, 1981; Engman and Gurney, 1991; Bader *et al.*, 1995). The most important techniques include 'cloud indexing', 'life history' and 'bispectral' methods. All three methods are empirical and use coefficients calibrated against conventional weather data. Cloud indexing methods have been applied over the widest range of climate conditions. These are based on identifying cloud types and their areas, and apply a probability of rainfall to each given cloud type. Of all the available techniques, this method is the least dependent upon sophisticated hardware and software and is perhaps the most promising approach to date. However, there is still no general agreement on the best method of satellite monitoring of rainfall since the requirements for rainfall data differ so widely between users.

Although radar can be used from satellites it is not used on meteorological satellites because the background reflectivity of the Earth's surface is many times greater than that of precipitation in the atmosphere. The reflectivity of land areas is not well understood, but varies with such factors as topography, ground wetness and vegetation, while that of the oceans varies with waves on the surface.

Microwave techniques offer the greatest potential as they react directly to rainfall by emission and absorption and by scattering. Present developments use passive microwave data in conjunction with visible and infrared wavebands. Current progress appears promising and several international projects are summarized in Smith (1998).

In comparing satellite and weather radar methods for remote sensing of rainfall, Collier (1984) concluded that radar and satellite techniques are complementary. Radar is more appropriate for areas smaller than about 10 000 km^2 (the typical extent of an individual surface radar system), and unless there is a network of such radars, satellites are better for larger areas (Figure 2.8). In both cases, however, surface rainfall measurements are necessary for calibration and checking purposes.

2.5 Temporal variations in precipitation records

Variability is an intrinsic feature of the Earth's climate. Point precipitation records exhibit great variation from hour to hour, week to week and even from

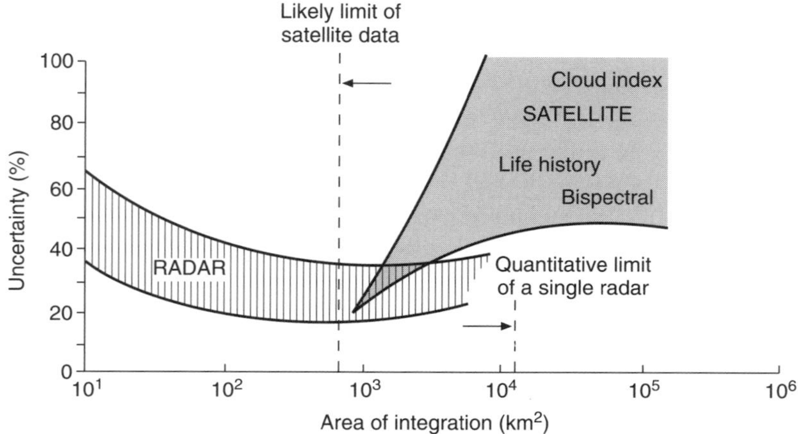

Figure 2.8 Comparison of accuracy of hourly rainfall estimates from a ground-based calibrated radar and from satellite techniques (redrawn after Collier, 1984).

year to year. This variation is far larger than that of any other component of the hydrological cycle. Evaporation, for example, is strongly related to the radiational output from the sun and the wetness of the ground, while streamflow represents a much moderated pattern of the precipitation inputs. In principle, the pattern of precipitation is deterministic, being related to the synoptic weather conditions and the properties of the air masses. Considerable advances have been made using numerical prediction methods to produce digital models of weather systems for forecasting purposes but, in practice, for hydrological purposes, the analysis of rainfall data is often based on the statistical properties of observed rainfall time series.

Variations in precipitation records may incorporate three time series components: stochastic, periodic and secular. *Stochastic* variations result from the probabilistic or random nature of precipitation occurrence, and may be so great that they effectively dominate the time series. *Periodic* or cyclic variations are related, for example, to astronomical cycles such as the diurnal and annual cycles. Finally, *secular* or long-term variations, which are often referred to as 'climatic change', may incorporate both cyclic and trend characteristics.

2.5.1 Stochastic variations

The great variability in rainfall totals can be explained by the frequency distribution of rainfall, since only a small proportion of storms or rain days in the course of a year may provide a disproportionate amount of the total rainfall (Figure 2.9). The presence or absence of only a small number of storms may therefore have a considerable effect upon the total precipitation. The variability of annual rainfalls is much greater for areas with low average annual precipitation, where rain may fall only occasionally, than for, say, equatorial regions where rain may fall on nearly every day. Thus, estimates of water resources in arid and semi-arid areas are particularly sensitive to short lengths of precipitation records (French, 1988).

In addition to rainfall amounts, the time intervals between storms are of great interest to the hydrologist, especially in the drier parts of the world. The importance of the time interval depends upon the storage capacity and the depletion characteristics of the particular system of interest, such as a column of soil or a water supply reservoir. Due to differences in the vapour inflows and the mode of uplift of the air between passing weather systems there is a tendency for rainy days to cluster in groups. This tendency for *persistence* or serial correlation has often been described using Markov chain analysis (Essenwanger, 1986).

The timing and magnitude of individual storms are largely stochastic in nature, and a number of studies have represented variables such as the time interval between storms, the storm durations and the precipitation depths by statistical frequency distributions (for example Waymire and Gupta, 1981; Mills, 1982; Essenwanger, 1986) (Figure 2.10). The pattern of rainfall during a storm, however, will be largely deterministic since it depends upon the weather

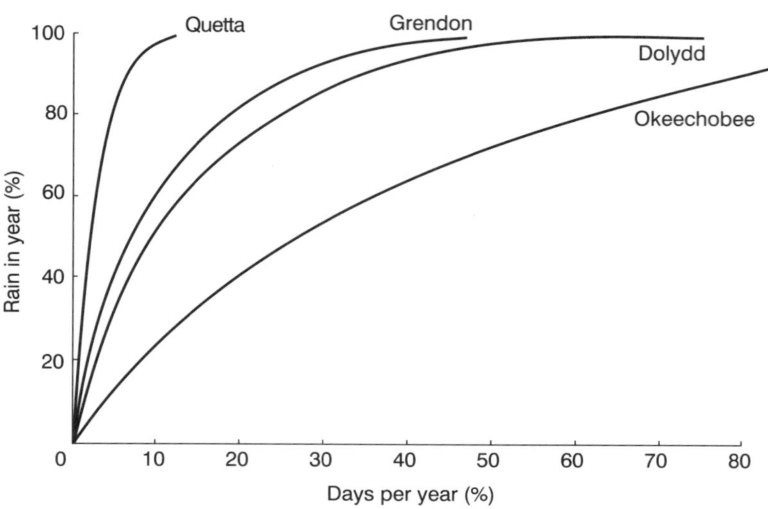

Figure 2.9 Percentage of annual rainfall occurring in a given percentage of the year for Dolydd (mid-Wales, 1780 mm yr^{-1}), Grendon (southern England, 630 mm yr^{-1}) (data 1969–81, Institute of Hydrology), and Quetta (northern Pakistan, 205 mm yr^{-1}) (data from Packman, 1987). Contrast with unusual situation at Okeechobee in coastal southern Florida where rain occurs from both synoptic disturbances and sea breezes (data 1973–76, Burpee and Lahiff, 1984).

system. Convectional rainfall is usually of higher intensity and shorter duration than rain from frontal systems. In general, convective and frontal type storms tend to have their peak rainfall rates near the beginning, while cyclonic events reach their maximum intensity nearer the middle of the storm period. The temporal profile of rainfall is almost infinitely variable, depending not only on the rainfall type, and the state of development or decay of the rainfall system as it passes over the rainfall measurement point, but also on the speed of movement of the system. If enough storms are examined for a particular site then their shapes can be summarized statistically. Extensive research carried out by the UK Meteorological Office on storm profiles for the Flood Studies Report (NERC, 1975) found great variety in shapes, and for hydrological design purposes it was decided to define storm shape in terms of the profile 'peakedness' which exceeds that of a given percentage of observed storms (Keers and Westcott, 1977).

2.5.2 Periodic variations

These are regular cyclic variations with rainfall minima and maxima recurring after approximately equal time intervals. The best known are the daily and annual cycles which give most rain over land at the warmest times of the day and during the warmest seasons—when the water vapour content of the air is high and thermal convection is strongest—and least rain around dawn and in late winter.

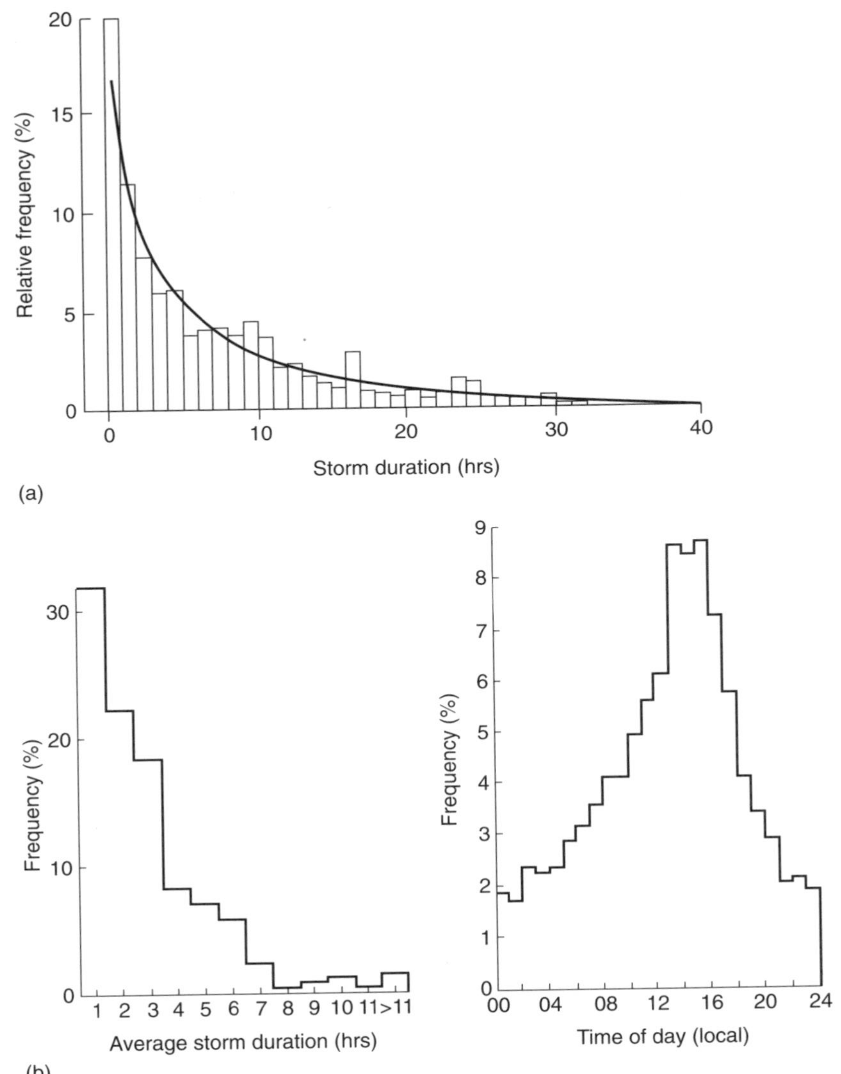

Figure 2.10 (*a*) Frequency distribution of storm rainfall duration at Ahoskie, N Carolina, May 1964 to September 1973, with a fitted Weibull probability density function (from an original diagram by Mills, 1982); (*b*) frequency distribution of storm duration and time of occurrence of rainfall during the day for a site in central Amazonia (from Lloyd, 1990).

Diurnal or within-day variations occur in areas where a large proportion of the rainfall derives from convective storms generated by local surface heating. This pattern is most often found in warm tropical continental climates although a preference for certain times of the day has been noted in many other areas

(Wallace and Hobbs, 1997). It is typified by a maximum in the afternoon, with the rainfall often accompanied by heavy thunderstorms. In Quetta in northern Pakistan, for example, 80 per cent of the annual rain falls between 1400 and 2000 hours (Rudloff, 1981). The strength of such convectional rainfall patterns will vary through the year with changes in the degree of radiant heating and convection, and variations in evaporation and hence the vapour content of the air. The pattern of an afternoon maximum may be modified by the interaction of land and sea breezes near the coast and by the effect of topography (Linacre, 1992). For most parts of the world, however, there is no systematic pattern of rainfall over the course of the day. A far more widespread cycle in rainfall patterns is that associated with the changing seasons of the year.

The annual cycle is the most obvious weather cycle and results from the regular seasonal shifts in the zones of atmospheric circulation in response to the changes in the heating patterns accompanying the migration of the zenith sun between latitudes 23° N and 23° S. Near to the equator these movements usually result in two maxima, while in tropical areas there is often a distinct summer rainfall maximum. Such changes in rainfall are most pronounced in areas on the fringes of arid zones, such as the Mediterranean region, where cyclonic depressions bring rain in the winter but the summers are typically dry. In Europe, to the north and east of the Alps, reflecting the increasing continentality, the greater proportion of rainfall occurs in the summer half-year. Over much of Asia there is a marked dominance of summer rainfall associated with the summer monsoon. The annual rainfall regimes at locations in different climatic zones of the world are described in standard climatology textbooks (for example Martyn, 1992).

One aspect of the weather that may be of particular interest to hydrologists is the occurrence of fairly regular seasonal weather sequences termed *singularities*. Examination of long weather records indicates that certain types of weather tend to occur at the same time each year with a greater frequency than expected for a random distribution (Lamb, 1972). Consequently there are certain dates when the probability of rainfall is significantly higher or lower than the average probability. The reason is that the general circulation of the atmosphere is strongest in winter, when global heat gradients are greatest, and this often results in cyclonic activity and high rainfall. Circulation strength decreases to a minimum in spring (March to May) which for many parts of north-west Europe is the period of lowest rainfall. Singularities in circulation types and rainfall regimes have also been noted in the Mediterranean region (Kutiel *et al.*, 1998). Although singularities do not provide definite forecasts, they do provide a reasonable and sound guide, with a physical basis, to periods of unsettled weather and a higher risk of extreme storm rainfalls.

2.5.3 Secular variations

There is ample evidence that climate has changed in the past, and even excluding human influences (Section 2.8) there is no reason to suppose that it will not change in the future. Nevertheless, until fairly recently hydrologists assumed the principle of stationarity—that any changes occur so slowly that the historical record is a suitable base for characterizing current and future conditions. This is of great significance to hydrology, since most design procedures (including flood estimation and water resource assessments) are based on this assumption.

Analyses of historical, botanical and palaeoclimate records indicate that parts of Europe and North America experienced a warmer climate than at present during the 'Medieval Warm Period' between the tenth and thirteenth centuries, at a time when, for example, grain cultivation in Norway extended north of the Arctic Circle. Towards the end of the thirteenth century the climate began to become colder, and in Europe the frequency of severe winters and cool wet summers increased. The period from the early sixteenth century to the mid-nineteenth century has been called the 'Little Ice Age'.

The question of whether such secular, or long-term, changes in climate are cyclic in pattern remains a controversial topic. Despite numerous attempts to detect regular periodicities, the analysis of individual annual precipitation series has generally failed to identify periodicities or trends of practical significance. It may be argued that this result should not be too surprising. Rainfall is so spatially variable that the search for cycles and trends should be based not on individual gauges but on groups of raingauges in a region.

Currie and O'Brien (1990) examined 120 long rainfall records in central USA and found evidence for cycles of about 10–11 and 20 years. They attributed these to documented changes in wind and pressure systems, and claimed that the impacts could be detected in records of crop yields. Vines (1985) found evidence of a 16-year rainfall cycle in northern Europe and a cycle of 20–22 years to the south of the Alps. Both, however, were out of phase with fluctuations in North American rainfall. Clearly, much further work will be necessary before the debate regarding the existence, or otherwise, of rainfall cycles is finally resolved. Burroughs (1992) provides a comprehensive account of the evidence for weather cycles.

Solar physicists have noted an 11-year solar sunspot cycle, with the solar radiation 'constant' greatest at the sunspot maximum, and solar magnetic reversals every 22 years, but direct links to meteorological data have remained elusive due to the great complexity of the Earth's atmospheric processes (Pecker and Runcorn, 1990).

While attempts to find generally applicable cycles of precipitation have been largely unsuccessful, investigations have demonstrated numerous examples of non-cyclic secular variations of precipitation, and some studies have considered the consequent effects on runoff. Karl and Knight (1998) analysed US daily rainfall data from nearly 200 gauges for the period 1910–96, and discussed this in relation to an observed increase in river flooding. They concluded that precipitation had increased by about 10 per cent over this period. This was partly due to an increase in the number of days in each year with rainfall, and more importantly to an increase in the frequency of very heavy falls ($>50\,\mathrm{mm\,d^{-1}}$).

In order to aid comparisons between different places, there is international agreement on the use of a standard period of record for the calculation of climatological 'normals', including precipitation. At present, this is the 30-year span 1961–90. In practice it is not always possible to use this period, but, whenever comparisons are made between areas, efforts should be made to ensure that a common time period is used. In any case average rainfall values should specify the period of record used.

Investigations have emphasized that many non-cyclic variations in precipitation are caused directly by a combination of geographical and climatological factors. Observed changes in rainfall amounts have been attributed to shifts in the global wind circulation resulting in changes in the paths of rain-bearing winds.

An increase in the vigour of the mid-latitude westerly airflow circulation from the mid-1970s has resulted in a consistent pattern of increased rainfall over the western uplands of the British Isles (Mayes, 1996). This has been associated with a general increase in flows, resulting in improved water quality of rivers due to the greater dilution of pollutants (Curran and Robertson, 1991), although there is no evidence of a national increase in the frequency of flooding (Robson *et al.*, 1998). Of particular note has been the recognition of the importance of the *El Niño* phenomenon. In some years the normally westward flow of the atmosphere and the ocean in the equatorial Pacific is reversed, increasing the temperature and the precipitation in the eastern Pacific, especially the normally dry coastal zone of Ecuador and Peru. Conversely, in the western Pacific, there may be drought in Indonesia and northern and eastern Australia. The intensity of this change varies, but it is particularly strong on average every three to eight years. This greatly modifies the energy balance of the Pacific—the world's largest ocean and a huge energy store. This is the result of the *Southern Oscillation*, a major shift in air pressure between the Asian and east Pacific regions. It has been quantified by the Southern Oscillation Index (SOI), reflecting the difference in atmospheric pressure at sea level between the central and western Pacific (Tahiti minus Darwin). There are atmospheric *teleconnections* with impacts around the world with, for example, possibly drier conditions in north east Brazil and failure of the monsoon in India and eastern Africa. It is now believed that the very strong El Niño of 1982–83, which yielded over 2000 mm of rain in six months along Peru's normally dry northern coastline, was also linked to the occurrence of droughts and wildfires in Indonesia and Australia and powerful storms in the southern USA. The global damage that winter is estimated at over US $8000 million.

Dai *et al.* (1997) examined global datasets and found evidence that precipitation in some middle latitude regions (including western and central Europe) is moderately affected by the *ENSO* (El Niño Southern Oscillation) events. Ogallo (1988) noted that there were some relationships between the Southern Oscillation and seasonal rainfall over parts of East Africa, but that some extreme wet and dry episodes appeared to be quite unrelated. There is evidence that the impact of the ENSO is felt in crop production, including grain yields in south Asia, Australia, East Africa and the North American Prairies (Hansen *et al.*, 1998).

In the Northern Hemisphere there are also important changes in the atmospheric circulation, which is characterized by the North Atlantic Oscillation Index (NAOI) defined by the atmospheric pressure difference between Iceland and the Azores (Hurrell, 1995). When the pressure gradient is stronger this results in more frequent westerly circulation types, more Atlantic frontal systems and higher rainfall.

Changes in global wind and moisture fluxes related to sea surface temperature anomalies (between Northern and Southern Hemisphere oceans) have been suggested as a possible cause of the failure of rainfall in the 1980s over the Sahel region of Africa (Folland *et al.*, 1986). More recently, rainfall has increased somewhat, although it is still lower than in the 1960s, suggesting that the variations may be random or cyclic.

2.6 Analysis of precipitation data

Several aspects concerned with the use and interpretation of precipitation data are of direct concern to the hydrologist. A basic requirement is to estimate the average rainfall over an area from a number of point measurements, or perhaps to determine the spatial pattern and movement of an individual storm, often from comparatively widely separated gauges. Hydrologists are also interested in the frequency of occurrence of rainfalls of different magnitudes, and so study the statistical properties of rainfall data. Finally, there is the special case of trying to estimate the largest rainfall that is physically possible over a given area, i.e. what is the Probable Maximum Precipitation?

2.6.1 Catchment mean rainfall

An estimate of mean areal rainfall input is a basic requirement in many hydrological applications, including water balance and rainfall–runoff studies. There are a large number of techniques that can be used to calculate areal rainfall from point measurements, including polygonal weighting, inverse distance weighting, isohyetal, trend surface analysis, analysis of variance and kriging. Singh (1989) provides a detailed discussion of 15 different methods. The selection of the most appropriate one for a particular problem will depend upon a number of factors, including: the time available and the expertise of the hydrologist, the density of the gauge network, and the known spatial variability of the rainfall field. In general, the accuracy of all the methods for estimating areal rainfall will increase with: (*a*) the density of gauges, (*b*) the length of period considered and (*c*) the size of area.

The simplest technique is to calculate the arithmetic mean of all the raingauge totals within the area of interest. This may be satisfactory for areas of flat topography with little systematic variation in rainfall and a uniform distribution of gauges. Such conditions are not generally found in practice and there is often a tendency for the distribution of gauges to mirror human populations. Thus, gauges are often most widely spaced in mountainous areas where rainfall depths and spatial variability are typically greatest.

The *Thiessen polygon* method (Thiessen, 1911) has been widely adopted as a better method for calculating areal rainfall than the mean. It allows for a non-uniform distribution of gauges by assigning 'weights' to the measured depths at each gauge according to the proportion of the catchment area that is nearest to that gauge. The method may be carried out graphically, or can be programmed for computer application by superimposing a regular grid over the area and allocating each grid point value to the nearest gauge. The resulting rainfall surface is, however, a series of polygonal plateaux with sharp steps between them. A modification is to allocate a region or 'domain' to each gauge based on physical factors such as local meteorological conditions and topography thought likely to influence rainfall (see Section 2.4.2). Voronoi interpolation (Gold, 1989) is a development of the Thiessen method and has the advantage for hydrological applications that it produces a much more realistic rainfall surface (BSI, 1996).

The *isohyetal* method is the most reliable, but subjective, of the standard methods of areal precipitation calculation (Shaw, 1994). It involves drawing *isohyets*, or lines of equal rainfall, on a map between gauges, making allowance for factors such as topography and distance from the sea. Areal precipitation is then computed by calculating the areas between the isohyets. This method uses all the data and knowledge about rainfall patterns in an area, but can involve a considerable amount of time to construct the maps.

Other methods of estimating areal rainfall overlay the area with a regular grid. Rainfall is then estimated for each grid point and these are averaged to give the areal mean. A common method for computing depths at grid points is to weight the values at the nearby gauges by the inverse square of their distance to the grid point (Essenwanger, 1986).

The preceding discussion is applicable to situations for which radar data are either not available or inappropriate. These include locations that are distant from radar installations or are very hilly (leading to obstruction of the beam), and cases where information is required over very small areas (current weather radar systems provide rainfall data on grid sizes of a kilometre or more).

2.6.2 Storm precipitation patterns

Radar provides the potential to improve the spatial (and temporal) interpolation between gauge observations and can give a detailed quantitative record of the movement of storm systems over large areas. In the absence of reliable radar estimates, storm cell movement has been studied for small areas (about 25 km^2) using dense networks of recording gauges, but it was very difficult to synchronize and validate recording rainfall data collected independently at very many sites.

An operational network of weather radars provides detailed information on storm precipitation intensities and distributions in Britain, and further integration of networks of weather radars is planned for western Europe. Figure 2.11 shows the calibrated hourly rainfall field during storms over southern England. Radar data are important for 'real-time' flood warnings and for monitoring storm cell patterns that are too small for raingauge networks. Current systems can produce a 1 km rainfall grid, and developments may soon be able to produce a 0.5 km grid at one minute resolution that will be valuable for urban flood design (Moore, 1998).

2.6.3 Rainfall statistics

The frequency of heavy rainfall is of interest to the hydrologist for a number of reasons including the design of engineered structures such as bridges, culverts and flood alleviation schemes (McCuen, 1989). In Britain, designs are commonly based on rainfall depths with a *return period* (the *average* length of time between occurrences) of between two years and 100 years. The *exceedance probability* within a time period, generally one year, is the reciprocal of the return period. Thus, a storm with a one per cent chance of occurring in any year has an annual exceedance probability of 0.01 and a return period of 100 years. The duration of the design storm rainfall that is selected will depend upon the design objectives. The critical storm duration may be several days for very slowly responding river catchments, but only a few hours for medium and small catchments. In the case of storm sewer design in fast-responding impermeable urban catchments, rainfall inputs over only a few minutes may be appropriate.

The choice and fitting of alternative frequency distributions to rainfall data are discussed in various texts (for example Sevruk and Geiger, 1981; Essenwanger, 1986), to which the reader may refer for further details.

Point rainfall frequencies

Daily read raingauge records are the most commonly analysed rainfall data, largely because of their greater availability both in terms of the number of measurement points and the length of records, compared with shorter time interval information (Sevruk and Geiger, 1981). Daily falls of given return periods may then be estimated for different durations at each site (NERC, 1975). A problem with the use of daily data is that the time interval must correspond to a standard 'rain day'. For example, in the United Kingdom, storage raingauges are traditionally read and emptied at 0900 GMT each day, and consequently the precipitation from storms which span this interval is split between two rain days. Accordingly, the maximum falls in rain day periods are smaller than the maximum falls over a 24-hour duration, on average by 14 per cent (Sevruk and Geiger, 1981) to 16 per cent (Dwyer and Reed, 1995). The use of daily totalled rainfall can be even more misleading for the estimation of

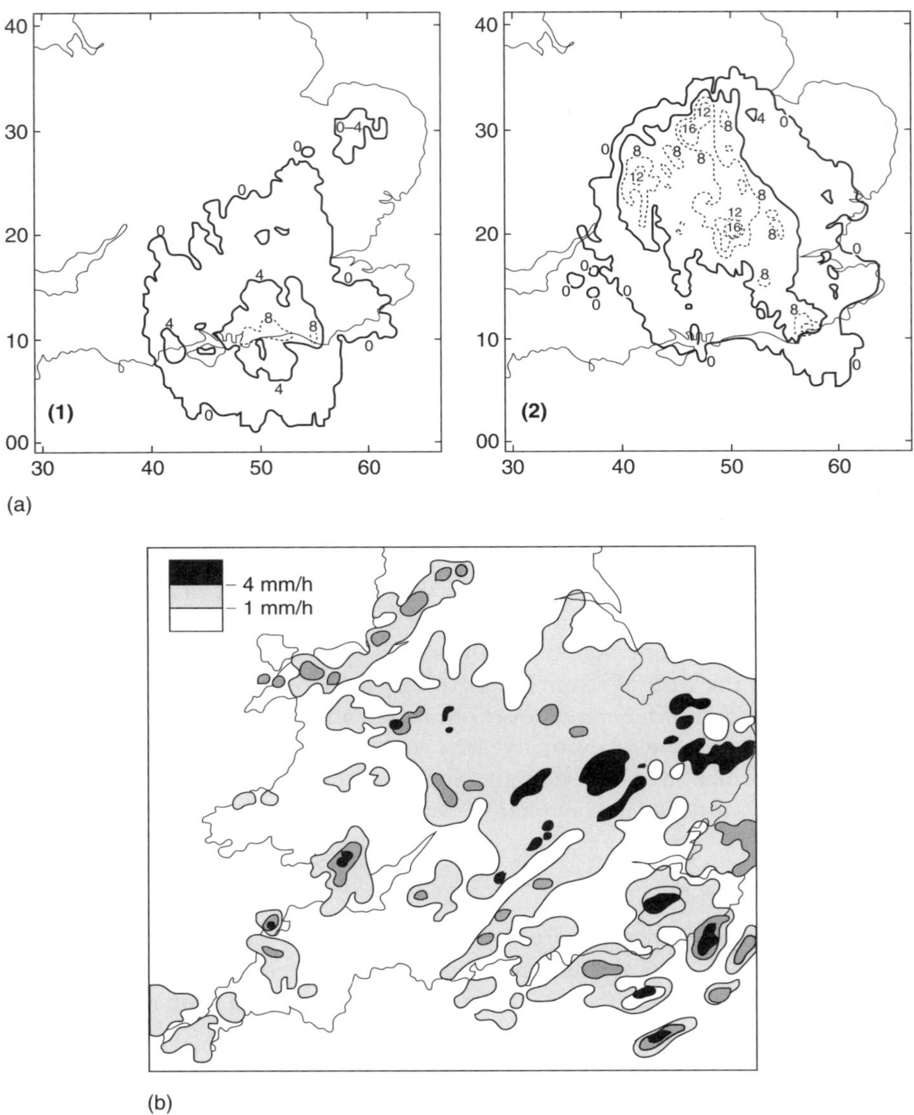

Figure 2.11 Spatial pattern of storm rainfall (mm h^{-1}) provided by weather radar. (*a*) Rainfall over southern Britain, 20 October 1987, based on one radar and five telemetry calibration raingauges for (*1*) hour ending 2100 GMT, (*2*) hour ending 2300 GMT; (*b*) composite rainfall map (mm h^{-1}) based on a network of five radars showing the rain distribution associated with a frontal system at 2030 GMT, 23 November 1984. (UK Meteorological Office. Copyright reserved. By permission of the Controller of HMSO.)

maximum short-duration intensities, since rain may only fall for a small part of the day.

Short-duration rainfall statistics have been studied by a number of investigators using data from recording raingauges. In a major national study of rainfall statistics in the 1970s the UK Meteorological Office analysed data from approximately 200 recording gauges, in addition to records from over 6000 daily read gauges (NERC, 1975, Vol. II). The UK rainfall extremes were reanalysed in the Institute of Hydrology's *Flood Estimation Handbook* (*FEH*) (IH, 1999). This benefited from a larger number of raingauges, but more importantly the FEH incorporated an additional 25 years of gauge data. This increased the number of station-years of daily rainfall data by 50 per cent, and hourly data by over 300 per cent. The procedures enable the estimation of a design rainfall from one hour to eight days duration, and a return period up to 1000 years, as well as the assessment of the rarity of observed rainfall events at any location in the UK.

The FEH rainfall frequency analysis comprises two parts. Firstly the estimation of an index variable, RMED, which is the median of the annual rainfall maxima of a given duration (and for an annual series has a return period of two years). Secondly, a rainfall growth curve is derived for the site of interest based on pooling data from all nearby gauges. This enables the index variable to be scaled up to the desired design return period. Figure 2.12 shows the computed one-hour rainfall depth of 100-year return period.

Depth–duration frequency analyses indicate that because very high rain intensities occur only rarely they contribute less overall to high annual totals of rainfall than smaller but more frequent falls. Depth–duration frequency curves vary from place to place, being steeper for areas with convectional rain than for those with predominantly frontal storms characterized by longer, less intense rainfall. For countries that do not have sufficient rainfall data to construct these curves, Bell (1969) derived generalized depth–duration frequency relations using data from a range of climatic conditions. He demonstrated a general uniformity of results for short-duration storms of less than two hours, and attributed this to the fact that these falls were mostly caused by short-duration high-intensity convective cells which have similar physical properties in many parts of the world.

Areal rainfall frequencies

For many purposes the hydrologist is interested not just in the frequency of point rainfall but also in that of the rainfall over an area. The areal rainfall can be determined from the isohyetal method by analysing a number of storms to give depth–area relationships for different durations. Several storms of similar durations should be analysed and an upper envelope curve drawn (Shaw, 1994). Curves can be drawn for a range of storm duration. Such *depth–area–duration* curves show the *maximum* observed falls for different durations over a range of areas (Figure 2.13). The construction of these curves is quite time

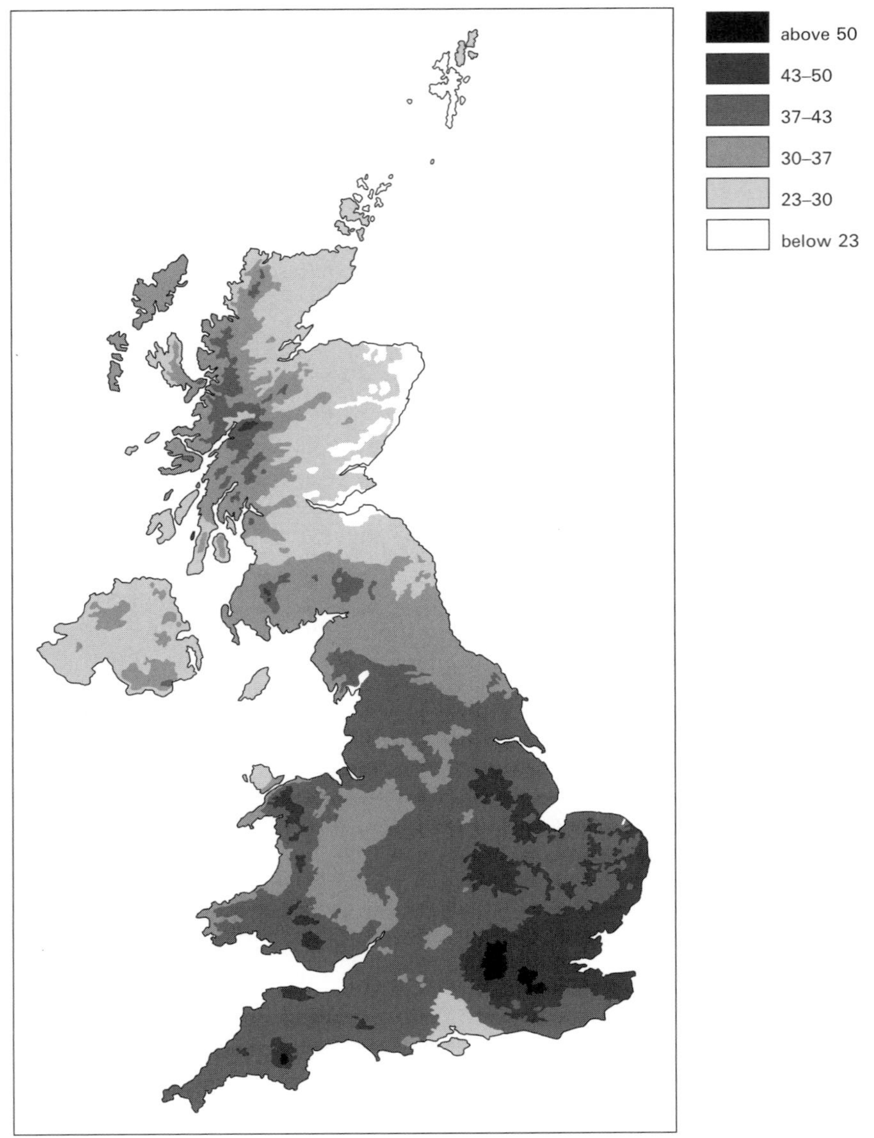

Figure 2.12 One-hour rainfall depth (mm) of 100 years return period across the UK. (Reproduced and simplified from Figure 11.6 in Vol. 2, *Flood Estimation Handbook*, IH, 1999.)

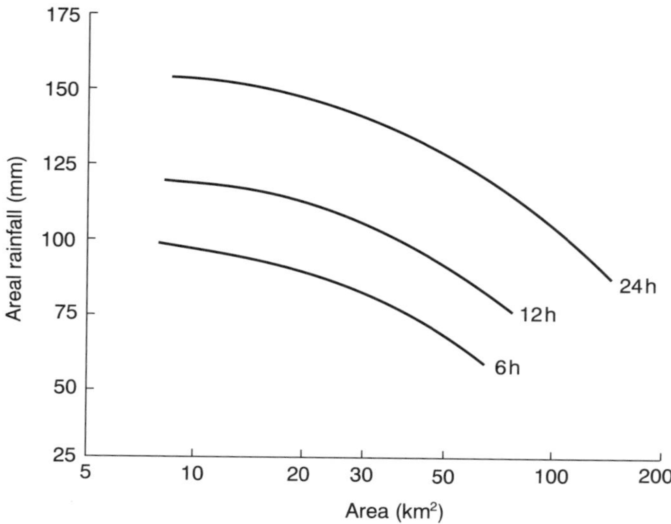

Figure 2.13 Curves showing the typical relationship between maximum storm depth, area covered and duration (from Shaw, 1994).

consuming and requires detailed rainfall data. A number of depth–area relations for regions in the USA and Europe were analysed by Court (1961) who proposed a formula for convectional storms, assuming an elliptical pattern of isohyets and a Gaussian bell-shaped cross-section. This work was subsequently supported and extended in numerous studies (Fogel and Duckstein, 1969; Huff, 1970). It must be remembered, however, that since short-duration storms tend to have steep rainfall gradients and cover smaller areas than longer-duration storms, there can be no general formula that will be applicable for all areas and for all durations (Linsley *et al.*, 1982; Shaw, 1994).

The hydrologist often needs to estimate the rainfall of a given return period over a catchment area rather than at a point. This may be obtained by applying an areal adjustment factor to a point value, since the T-year return period rain depth at a point is bound to be larger than the average rainfall of that return period over an extensive area (McCuen, 1989). The Flood Studies Report (NERC, 1975, Vol. II) applied an Areal Reduction Factor (ARF), which is defined as the ratio of the T-year rainfall over the area to the mean of the point T-year rainfall depths in the area, for a given duration (Bell, 1976) (Figure 2.14). This is a geographically fixed area relationship and the ratios are statistical averages for that area; the maximum point values at different places may come from different storms. Values of ARF are typically between 0.75 and 1, being smaller for larger areas and for shorter duration storms. According to NERC (1975) and Bell (1976), for a given storm duration this ratio appears to be constant for different return

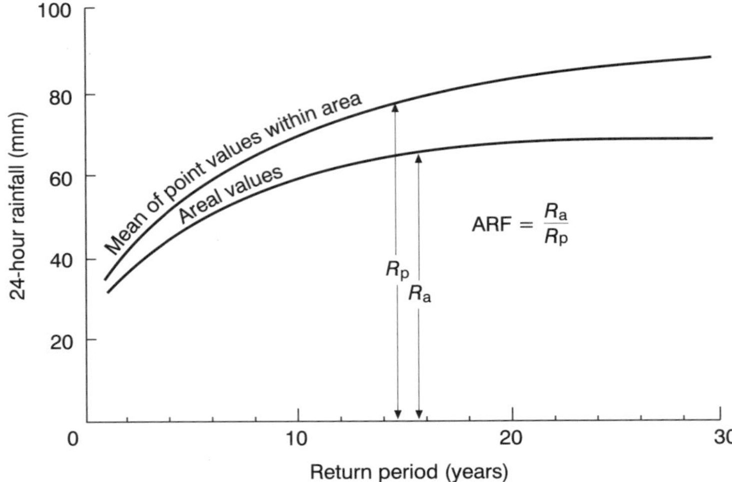

Figure 2.14 Definition of the Areal Reduction Factor (ARF) to convert point rain depths to average areal depths having the same return period (adapted from an original diagram by Bell, 1976).

periods and for different regions of the United Kingdom. More recent work, incorporating weather radar data (Stewart, 1989), has shown that, in line with studies in other parts of the world, ARFs for a given area and duration decrease slightly with increasing return period. Thus, the use of a constant value may provide an additional element of safety to designs requiring estimates of the rarest and potentially most damaging storms.

As well as being concerned with the distribution and amount of above-average rainfall, the hydrologist is also concerned with periods of *drought*. This is a sustained and regionally extensive occurrence of below-average precipitation and is not to be confused with *aridity*, which is a perennial state of water shortage. There are many different ways of defining a drought, depending on the particular purpose of study. A meteorologist may define a drought in terms of a departure from the 'normal' or average precipitation. Farmers will be more concerned with the impact upon soil water contents during the growing season, and hence on plant development and crop yield. The impact will depend upon the plant species, soil type and the stage of plant growth. Water resource managers may distinguish between groundwater droughts that are of long duration and include one or more dry winters, while surface water droughts can occur over a much shorter period (Marsh and Turton, 1996). Over 150 definitions of drought are described in the literature (Barry and Chorley, 1998), but droughts may be characterized in terms of three essential characteristics: (*a*) intensity or severity (usually measured as a departure of a climatic index from normal), (*b*) duration and (*c*) spatial extent (Wilhite, 1993). The difficulty with any drought index is to choose the thresholds that define the *onset* and the *end* of a drought. Thresholds should be linked to the impact, but are often arbitrary. However, once selected, statistical relationships between drought severity and return period can be derived from rainfall records (for example Tabony, 1977) in a similar way as for large rainfall events (Beran, 1987). Reed (1995) discusses some of the problems and limitations of current methods of drought assessment.

Determining the Probable Maximum Precipitation (PMP)

For the design of structures, such as a large dam, where failure due to an overtopping flood would have catastrophic consequences in terms of environmental or physical damage or the loss of life, it is necessary to estimate the precipitation with a very low risk of exceedance (ideally no risk of exceedance). From a consideration of the processes of precipitation generation it is generally agreed by most meteorologists that there must be a physical upper limit to the amount of precipitation that can fall on a given area in a given time. The difficulty lies in estimating that amount, as such extreme events are rarely observed and almost never measured properly. Current knowledge of storm mechanisms and their precipitation-producing efficiencies is inadequate to enable the precise evaluation of extreme precipitation, and assumptions have to be made.

The upper limit to precipitation is known as the Probable Maximum Precipitation (PMP) and has been defined as 'The greatest depth of precipitation for a given duration that is meteorologically possible for a given storm area at a particular location at a particular time of the year, with no allowance made for long-term climatic trends' (WMO, 1986). The word 'probable' is intended to emphasize that, due to inadequate understanding of the physics of atmospheric processes and imperfect meteorological data, it is impossible to define with certainty an absolute maximum precipitation. It is *not* intended to indicate a particular level of statistical probability or return period, although such associations are sometimes made. In recognition of the uncertainties in estimating PMP, yet the usefulness of such a concept, Miller (1977) called PMP a 'convenient fiction'.

There are various methods for estimating PMP (WMO, 1986) and Wiesner (1970) reviewed the basic literature and discussed the more important methods in some detail. In brief, there are two main approaches: first, the maximization and transposition of real storm events and, second, the statistical analysis of extreme rainfalls. Storm maximization and transposition is the most widely used method, and the technique involves the estimation of the maximum limit on the humidity concentration in the air that flows into the space above a basin, the maximum limit to the rate at which wind may carry humid air into the basin and the maximum limit on the fraction of the inflowing water vapour that can be precipitated. PMP estimates in areas of limited orographic control are normally prepared by the maximization and transposition of observed storms. In areas in which there are strong orographic controls on the amount and distribution of precipitation, storm models have been used for the maximization procedure for long-duration storms over large basins (Wiesner, 1970). For some large regions, PMP estimates have been made encompassing numerous catchments of various sizes, and generalized maps produced showing the regional variation of PMP for various basin sizes and storm durations. In this case the depth–area relations are storm-centred with the maximum precipitation placed in the centre of the area of interest. This is a fundamentally different case (and yielding a far more severe storm) than the statistical average approach used for ARF calculations and applicable to design storms of a specified return period.

The maximization/transposition techniques require a large amount of data, particularly rainfall data, and involve subjective decisions regarding the maximum values assigned to the meteorological factors. Austin *et al.* (1995) used weather radar data with a convective storm model to estimate PMP in a more objective manner for reservoired catchments in north west Britain.

In the absence of suitable data it may be necessary to transpose storms over very large distances despite the considerable uncertainties involved. In this case, reference to published values of maximum observed point rainfalls will normally be helpful. Worldwide maximum falls for various durations (WMO, 1986) are shown in Figure 2.15, together with maximum recorded falls in the United Kingdom.

There is a clear difference between the two curves. By comparison with the world maxima, the UK falls are rather small, having less than a third of the recorded depth for a given duration. It is to be expected that a temperate climate area would experience less intense falls than tropical zones subject to hurricanes or the monsoons of southern Asia. The maxima shown for La Réunion, a rugged mountainous island (up to 3000 m elevation) in the Indian Ocean, resulted from just two intense tropical storms, in 1952 and 1964. Thus for areas of less rugged topography and cooler climate lower values of PMP might be expected.

From an analysis of the maximum rainfall in each year at several thousand gauges, Hershfield (1961) used a general formula for the analysis of extreme value data to relate the PMP for a selected duration to the mean (X) and standard deviation (σ) of the largest falls in each year:

$$\mathrm{PMP} = X + K\sigma \tag{2.1}$$

The parameter K was originally set to 15, but this was found to vary widely between sites, and the method was subsequently modified to allow K to vary with the mean annual maximum, X, and the rainfall duration (Chow *et al.*, 1988; WMO, 1994). Although the method is somewhat crude, it has the apparent advantages that it is easy to use, it is based on observed data and—since the processes in short, intense thunderstorms are similar for different parts of the world—it could be widely applicable for such rainfall conditions. The disadvantages are that, like all statistical methods, its success depends upon the length and nature of the available record, and parameter K may depend on factors other than rainfall duration and the mean of the annual maxima. In particular, the

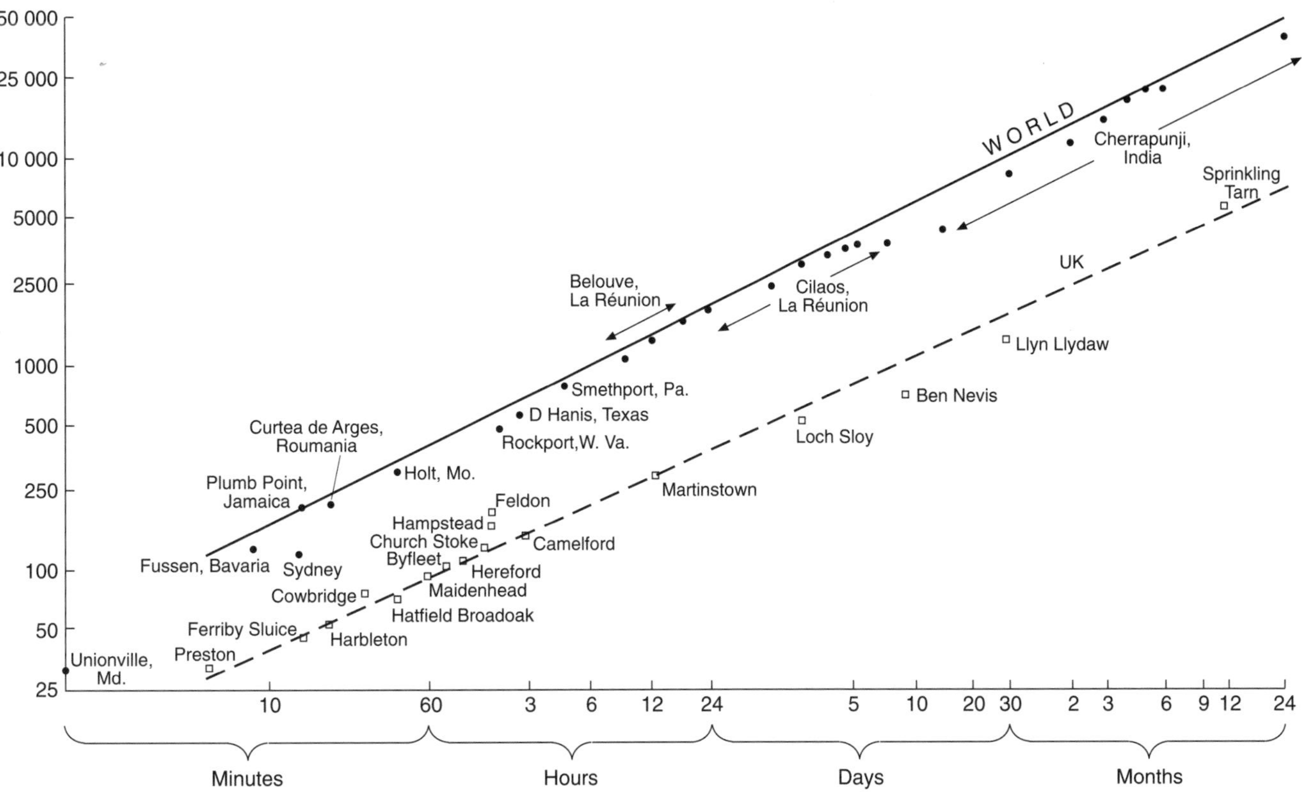

Figure 2.15 Maximum recorded storm depths of different durations across the world, and for the UK.

frequency of thunderstorms varies widely. Consequently, this 'quick' approach should be used in conjunction with other methods (Wiesner, 1970). In the final analysis, however, there is no completely objective way of assessing the level of a PMP estimate, and judgement based on an understanding of the meteorological processes is most important.

2.7 Hydrological aspects of snow

Snow and ice account for just over 75 per cent of the Earth's fresh water, although most of this is held as ice in Antarctica and Greenland, with a residence time of the order of 10 000 years. Of more relevance to the hydrologist is the fact that about 6 per cent of the global precipitation falls as snow (Kuhn, 1996). This is, of course, not evenly distributed and, for example, snow accounts for about 16 per cent of the annual precipitation in the contiguous United States (Karl *et al.*, 1993). Hydrological interest in snow is concentrated in middle and higher latitudes and in mountainous areas, although even in Britain with its mild temperate climate, flooding due in part to melting snow is a regular occurrence in upland areas (Smith and Ward, 1998).

Snow has a great hydrological importance. It has a cooling effect on climate by increasing the albedo and modifying the surface radiation balance and the near-surface air temperature, and it causes a great amount of energy to be expended on melting. Seasonal snow cover changes are known to affect global atmospheric circulation, and may have an important role influencing climatic change. In arid and semi-arid areas bordered by high mountains, including the semi-arid western United States, northern India and Iran, snowmelt is an important seasonal source of water. The presence of snow on the ground is important due to disruption of travel and commerce, and seasonal flood risk may be increased by snowmelt. In addition to providing a store of water, snow cover can serve as protective insulation for soil and crops through the winter. For these reasons the hydrologist is normally interested in a number of aspects of snowfall—*where* it falls, *how much* has fallen, and when and how rapidly *melting* of the accumulated snow occurs.

2.7.1 Distribution of snow

Seasonal snow cover extends out from the permanent ice sheets of Antarctica and Greenland, over large areas in Asia, Europe and North America. Snowfall is the predominant form of precipitation when the temperature in the lower atmosphere is below 0°C, and ground temperatures below freezing are necessary for the deposited snow to remain unmelted.

Information on the spatial distribution of snow was traditionally based on reports from observers at meteorological stations. But it is difficult to gain a broad picture of the areal extent of snow cover from such local observations.

Due to its high albedo, snow cover can be readily distinguished from snow-free ground using visible radiation reflectance. Remote sensing, from aircraft or satellites, enables the rapid mapping of the extent of snow cover over large areas. Robinson *et al.* (1993) analysed snow cover records for the Northern Hemisphere 1972–92 and found periods of greater snow extent in the late 1970s and mid-1980s with intervals of lower snow cover, and very much reduced snow cover in the 1990s, coinciding with increasing global air temperatures.

It is, however, often difficult to distinguish snow from cloud cover using visible reflectance alone, without repeated photography over time to filter out the variable cloud pattern. This can be overcome by the use of 'passive' microwave radiation emitted naturally by the Earth's surface. This can penetrate cloud cover and allow the mapping of snow extent unobstructed by weather effects. However, passive microwave data have a low spatial resolution of several tens of kilometres (Rango, 1994).

2.7.2 Amount of snowfall

It is often not sufficient to be aware of the presence of snow, and the hydrologist requires some measure of the quantity of snow. Usually of much greater importance than the depth of lying snow is the *water equivalent* of the snow, i.e. the equivalent water depth of the melted snow that is potentially available for runoff and for soil moisture replenishment.

The difficulties in measuring the amount of snowfall in gauges are even greater than those of rainfall. Snowflakes are even more prone than raindrops to turbulence around gauges, resulting in severe undercatches. Although wind effects can be greatly reduced by using wind shields around the gauges, the errors due to undercatches are often still too great to be acceptable (Weiss and Wilson, 1958; Sevruk, 1982). The WMO initiated a comparison of the catches of some of the most widely used precipitation gauges with those of a Double Fence Intercomparison Reference gauge (DFIR) comprising a Tretyakov gauge within two concentric fence shields (Goodison *et al.*, 1989). Undercatches by the standard gauges relative to the DFIR increased from only a few per cent for rain in light winds, up to 50 per cent or more for snowfall in strong winds. Eventually it may be possible to derive correction procedures to reduce the catch errors of standard gauges, but this may require detailed information including wind speed and the discrimination between 'solid' and 'liquid' precipitation.

It may be better to measure the depth of snow lying at particular locations. This may be converted to the snow water equivalent using the density of the snow. The density of freshly fallen snow varies from 0.05 to 0.20 (50 to 200 kg m^{-3}), depending on the temperature during the storm. The density increases over time due to settling and compaction under gravity as well as to any partial melting and refreezing of the snow pack, and may reach values of up to 600 kg m^{-3}. Figure 2.16 shows a long-term series of snow records.

The depth of snow may vary greatly with topography and with drifting, resulting in spatial sampling problems that are even more severe than those

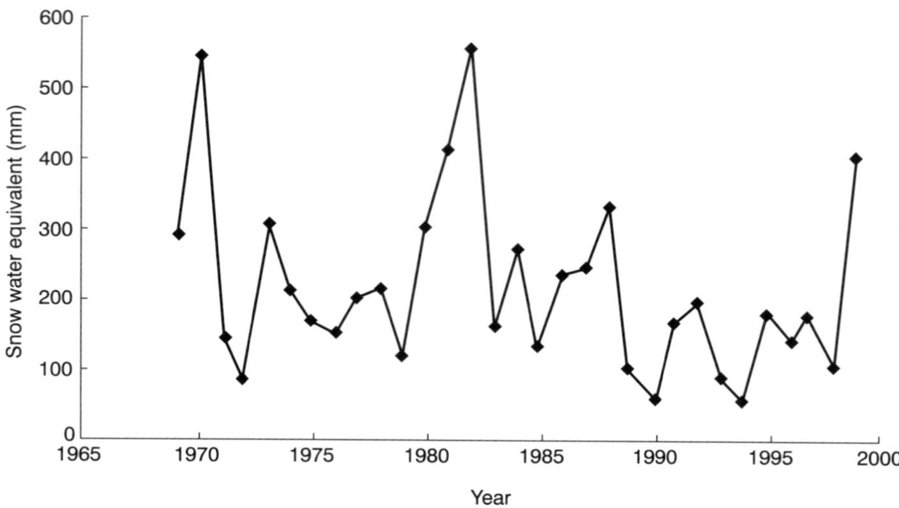

Figure 2.16 Maximum water equivalent (mm) of snow in each winter at Alptal (Switzerland), based on average figures for a 20 m long snowline, altitude 1140 m aod. (Data supplied by Swiss Federal Institute for Forest, Snow and Landscape Research, Birmensdorf.)

already discussed for rainfall. For this reason depth and density measurements may be made along predetermined snow courses selected to be representative of conditions over a wide area (US Army, 1956). Such snow courses are expensive to operate, particularly in remote terrain, and measurements generally cannot be carried out very frequently.

One solution which provides much greater time resolution information is to measure the water equivalent directly by automatically weighing the snow that falls onto a *snow pillow*, several metres in diameter, comprising a metal plate or a flexible bag filled with an antifreeze liquid. The overlying weight of snow is recorded as changes in pressure using a manometer or a pressure transducer. Choosing a representative site for the gauge is probably the most important factor to be considered. Snow pillows are widely used in the western USA, where the SNOTEL (SNOw TELemetry) network uses over 500 gauges to provide data from remote mountain basins. Results of snow pillow measurements for a site at 500 m altitude in northern England were discussed by Archer and Stewart (1995) who showed that high melt rates could take place under high wind speeds with the passage of a warm front (Figure 2.17).

The water equivalent of snow at a site may also be measured using radioactive isotopes. A gamma source and detector may be raised and lowered in separate vertical tubes through the snowpack to provide information on density changes by measuring the attenuation of the gamma emissions. Alternatively, the detector

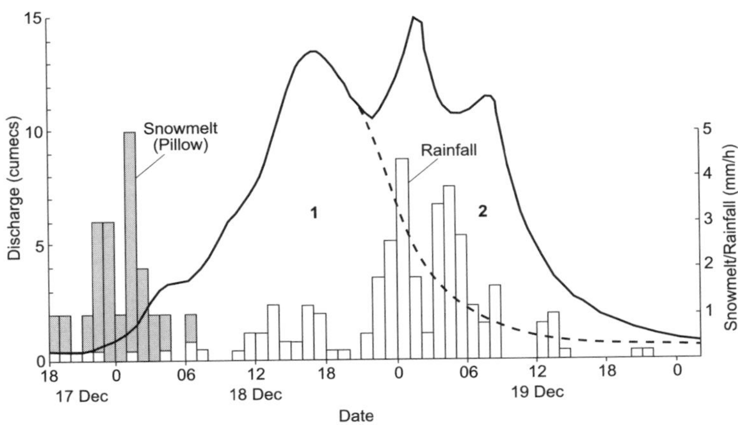

Figure 2.17 Snow pillow results showing snowmelt, rainfall and stream runoff for a small upland basin in December 1993. (*1*) = estimated snowmelt runoff (64.2 mm) and (*2*) = rainfall runoff (38.7 mm) (adapted from a diagram by Archer and Stewart, 1995).

may be positioned on the ground, beneath the snow, and the source positioned vertically above the top of the snow (Martinec, 1976). Another method to measure the water equivalent is to move a neutron probe source and counter up and down a vertical access tube to record the amount of backscatter in a manner similar to soil moisture measurements (Harding, 1986).

Point measurements can provide only limited information on the uneven areal distribution of snow cover. Areal snow water equivalents must be estimated from point values, for example by correlations with topography, altitude and vegetation parameters. Remote sensing in combination with conventional snow surveying methods offers the opportunity to obtain quantitative information on the areal distribution of snow cover. The natural radioactivity of the Earth also provides a means of measuring the snow water equivalent over large areas. Natural gamma radiation from the upper layer of the soil will be attenuated by the overlying snow. Airborne measurements carried out when snow is lying on the ground can be compared with results when the ground is snow free to provide information on the snow water equivalent (Engman and Gurney, 1991). Although it has limitations, this is by far the most widely used technique for estimating the snow water equivalent, and is used operationally in a number of countries, including the USA, the former Soviet Union, Norway and Finland (Kuittinen, 1986; Carroll, 1987). The use of microwave sensors to measure both snow depth and water equivalent appears to offer great potential, although further work is needed to develop the techniques. Tait (1998) found reasonable agreements between passive microwave measurements, obtained by satellite, with ground data obtained from snowlines in the former Soviet Union and SNOTEL data from the USA, for different land covers, terrain and snow state based on surface temperature.

2.7.3 Snowmelt

The prediction of snowmelt is of great importance in areas of seasonal snow cover where winter snow comprises much of the total annual precipitation. It is needed to estimate seasonal flood risk and, in some arid areas, to estimate the amount and timing of melt water from mountain sources for irrigation. Various approaches have been adopted, and may be grouped broadly into empirical models, using regression equations developed between snowmelt and weather variables, and conceptual models, in which the various hydrological processes are explicitly represented (Morris, 1985).

Before snowmelt can occur, a metamorphosis of the snowpack must take place. Over time the properties of a snowpack change: density increases, snow crystals become large-grained and the albedo reduces. Melting and re-crystallization are important for preparing the snowpack for melting. With the onset of warmer temperatures, meltwater from the surface layer of the snow percolates down to lower, colder layers and refreezes. This freezing releases latent heat, warming the lower layers of the snowpack and, over time, tending to equalize temperatures at 0°C thoughout the vertical profile of the snowpack. The snowpack can hold a certain amount of water in pores against gravity (usually 2–8 per cent by volume; Dunne and Leopold, 1978). When this takes place, the snowpack is said to be *ripe*: any further addition of energy will result in meltwater runoff.

The rate of snowmelt depends upon the energy exchange between the snowpack and its environment. The energy balance of an isothermal snowpack at 0°C can be written as:

$$Q_{\mathrm{melt}} = R_{\mathrm{net}} + H + LE + P + C \qquad (2.2)$$

It is the energy available for snowmelt, R_{net} is the net radiation (short and long wave), H is the convective transfer of sensible heat flux at the snow surface, LE is the latent heat flux (comprising energy gains from condensation and losses from evaporation and sublimation), P is the heat gain from warm rain, and C is the heat exchange with the underlying ground (usually very small). On an instantaneous basis the energy terms are expressed as energy fluxes per unit area ($\mathrm{W\,m^{-2}}$) and summed over a time period such as a day they are expressed as $\mathrm{MJ\,m^{-2}}$.

The complexity of the snowpack energy balance was discussed in detail in the standard work, *Snow Hydrology* (US Army, 1956). The relative importance of the various components of the energy balance is difficult to determine with accuracy and has been found to vary with time, both seasonally and diurnally, and also between days with different weather conditions. For example, in Britain, most snowmelt events occur during cloudy, windy mild weather in mid-winter when the radiation term is small (Hough and Hollis, 1997). Snowmelt is often associated with rainfall, particularly in regions with a maritime climate, although the direct warming effect of the rain is generally small—about 0.0125 mm of melt per 1 mm of rain per 1°C above zero. Rather, the main source of energy for melt is the turbulent transfer of latent and sensible heat.

Kuusisto (1986) summarized the findings of 20 studies of energy fluxes of melting snowpacks. On sunny days with little wind, net radiation may be the dominant source of energy gain. Its importance increases as the spring season advances due to increasing solar radiation as well as the decline in albedo with the ageing of the snowpack. Turbulent heat exchange (sensible heat) will dominate during the night and on cloudy days. It is greatest when there are strong, moist winds. Although dry air can cause a certain amount of evaporation (sublimation) of the snow, humid air can have a much greater effect on the snowpack since the condensation of water vapour on snow releases sufficient latent heat to melt a much larger quantity of ice.

In many situations insufficient meteorological data are available to compute the energy budget of the snowpack, and empirical methods are used to predict the magnitude and timing of snowmelt. Generally these correlations are made between snowmelt and aspects of air temperature (US Army, 1956), although it is clear from the preceding discussion that due to the variation in the relative importance of the various heat transfer processes, no single index or method of estimating snowmelt will be applicable to all areas and for all weather conditions. Zuzel and Cox (1975), in a study in Idaho, found that air temperature was the most important *single* meteorological variable in regression models of snowmelt, but that better estimates could be obtained with a *combination* of other meteorological variables, namely vapour pressure, net radiation and wind.

The simplest snowmelt models assume that melt M is a function of air temperature T_{air}:

$$M = C(T_{air} - T_{base}) \tag{2.3}$$

where C is a coefficient and T_{base} is a base temperature. Both may have to be obtained empirically for a particular area.

Snowmelt rates may differ with vegetation type, especially between forested and open sites. Forests dampen turbulent fluxes and shade direct solar radiation, although long-wave radiation is higher from the warmed tree branches. In general, rates of snowmelt on the ground are lower from forested catchments than from open ground. The role of tree canopy storage of snow is discussed in Chapter 3.

2.8 Human modification of precipitation patterns

The preceding sections have treated precipitation as a process independent of mankind, which must passively accept what nature does, or does not, provide. In fact it is now becoming apparent that human activities have an increasing ability to modify rainfall at certain scales, intentionally or otherwise.

Rain-seeding experiments have been carried out since the 1940s. Artificial nuclei, usually silver iodide, are added to clouds to encourage precipitation. Although greatly exaggerated claims were made by the early cloud-seeding experimenters, these have now largely been discredited and current claims are much more modest. While the mechanism can be observed at the local scale of individual clouds, its wider effect is less clear. There is little convincing evidence that large increases in rainfall can be produced consistently over large areas (Mason, 1975; Essenwanger, 1986).

At the regional scale there has long been controversy as to whether vegetation cover could influence rainfall via its effect on evaporation losses. In the nineteenth century, Humber (1876) attributed a period of reduced rainfall in parts of central USA to the felling of woodlands for the expansion of agriculture which was taking place at that time. Such notions were largely discounted by later research which emphasized the large-scale nature of water vapour transfer, with often great distances between the evaporation of water and its subsequent precipitation (Penman, 1963). This view may need to be modified, however, as a result of more recent studies. In the extensive tropical basin of the Amazon forest about half of the rainfall originates from forest evaporation (Salati and Vose, 1984; Shuttleworth, 1988a). Continued large-scale deforestation is likely to lead to reduced evaporation, to increased runoff and, ultimately, to reduced precipitation in that region. Similarly, it has been suggested that vegetation changes might have led to reduced rainfall over the Sahelian region of north Africa (Charney, 1975). Overgrazing would reduce the vegetation cover and expose more sandy soil, increasing the albedo of the ground surface. This in turn would lower the ground surface temperatures, reducing the likelihood of convective precipitation. Subsequent work by Sud and Fennessy (1982) gave support to this hypothesis. The Hapex–Mobilhy programme, in south-west France, showed that for a particular rain event the higher evaporation due to canopy interception from a 10–20 km wide forest area could result in nearly 30 per cent greater rainfall over farmland immediately downwind (Blyth *et al.*, 1994). Similarly, Taylor and Lebel (1998) discovered a positive feedback between antecedent soil moisture and rainfall in a semi-arid west Africa. Previous storm patterns influenced the pattern of soil moisture and hence local evaporation rates; this in turn influenced subsequent convective rainfall patterns. Rainfall patterns were observed to persist for up to a month.

At the global scale it is known that the burning of fossil fuels has caused an increase in the carbon dioxide content of the atmosphere. This is one of a number of greenhouse gases that absorb outgoing long-wave radiation from the Earth, which would otherwise be lost into space, and so will lead to a warming of the atmosphere. This may result in changes to circulation patterns, with a poleward migration of climatic zones and spatially variable effects on precipitation. The United Nations Intergovernmental Panel on Climate Change (IPCC) examined all the evidence and has concluded that 'The balance of evidence suggests a discernible human influence on climate' (IPCC, 1996). Climate change models predict that global warming will strengthen westerly circulation over the North Atlantic and Europe, with increased winter precipitation over northern and central Europe, and decreases over the Iberian peninsula (Rowntree *et al.*, 1993) (Figure 2.18). These changes could be as much as ±40 per cent from current conditions by the year 2030 in some parts of Europe, although most will be less than half this figure (Rowntree *et al.*, 1993). Summers will be hotter and probably drier. This will tend to result in greater convectional

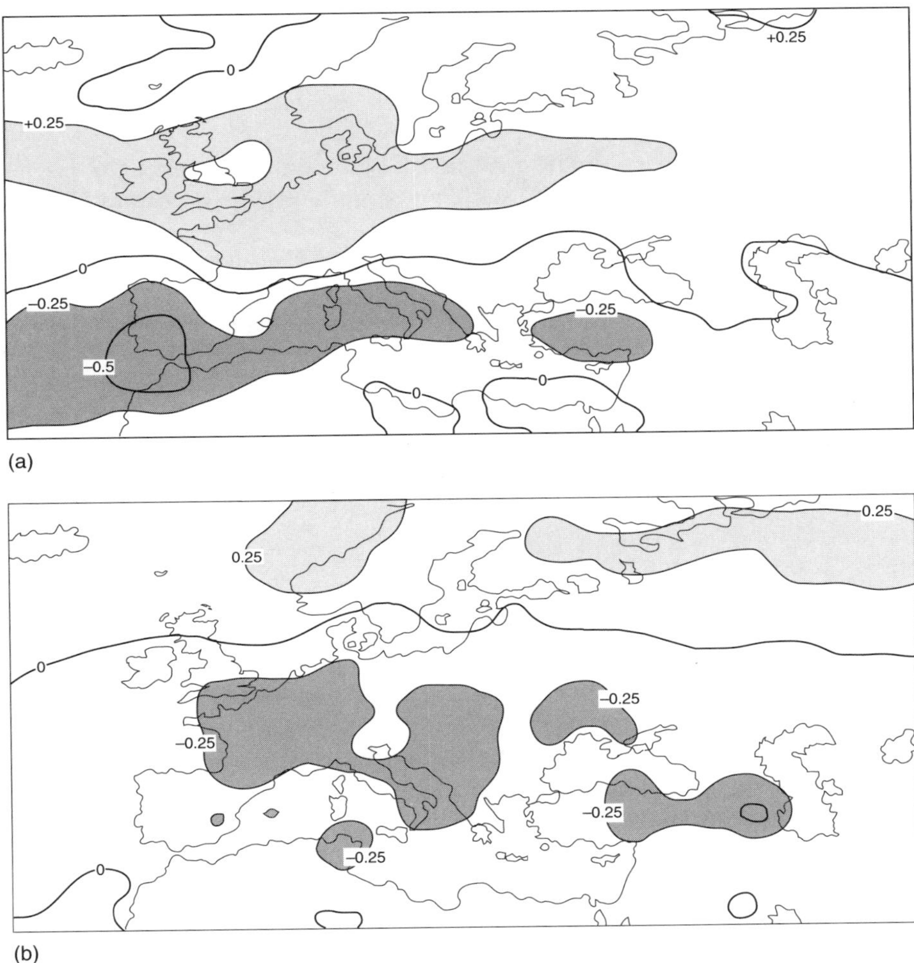

Figure 2.18 European General Circulation Model predictions of rainfall changes (mm d^{-1}) in (*a*) winter (December to January) and (*b*) summer (June to August). Shaded areas indicate changes (+ or –) greater than 0.25 (based on an original diagram by Rowntree *et al.*, 1993).

storm activity with more intense rainfall at the expense of gentler, long-duration rain. Such predictions are broadly in line with changes already noted in recent European weather patterns. Furthermore, Dai *et al.* (1997) examined global datasets and found evidence of increased precipitation in middle to high latitudes that seems to be compatible with the impacts of increased CO_2 levels noted in General Circulation Model experiments.

Such changes may have a profound impact on water resources, the environment and world food production. Hydrologists will have an important role to play in understanding and managing resources in a changing environment.

Review Problems and Exercises

2.1 Explain the importance of the very short residence time of atmospheric water for hydrology.

2.2 Discuss the principal uplift mechanisms resulting in precipitation.

2.3 What is a cloud, and why do some types produce large quantities of rain whereas others produce little or none?

2.4 Explain why over a year some areas of the world receive no rainfall while others may receive over 12 000 mm.

2.5 Discuss some of the factors to be considered when choosing a method to estimate the rainfall over an area from a number of raingauges.

2.6 Discuss the importance of real-time calibration for weather radar.

2.7 Define and distinguish the following pairs of terms: return period and exceedance probability, aridity and drought.

CHAPTER THREE

Interception

3.1 Introduction and definitions

When precipitation falls onto a vegetated surface, only a part may actually reach the ground beneath. Depending upon the nature and density of the vegetation cover a proportion of the rain may be *intercepted* by the leaves and stems of the vegetation canopy and temporarily stored on its surfaces. Some, or all, of this water may be evaporated back into the atmosphere, and so take no part in the land-bound portion of the hydrological cycle; this is termed the *interception loss*. The remaining water which reaches the ground constitutes the *net rainfall* (Figure 3.1). The bulk of this comprises *throughfall* consisting of raindrops that fall through spaces in the vegetation canopy and water which drips from wet leaves, twigs and stems to the ground surface; a generally much smaller amount of water trickles along twigs and branches to run down the main stem or trunk to the ground as *stemflow*. A forest may have a shrubby understorey vegetation which itself will also have interception and stemflow components. A layer of leaf litter on the surface of the ground may also intercept some water.

The interception process is important for a number of reasons. First, the net rainfall beneath a vegetation canopy is generally less than the *gross rainfall* falling onto the top of the vegetation canopy. In some cases the interception loss may be quite large and can have a significant impact on the water balance. Secondly, as a result of passing through a vegetation canopy the spatial variability of net rainfall is much greater than for gross rainfall. Throughfall and dripping meltwater are concentrated at the edges of the tree crowns, while concentrated drip close to the trunk and stemflow itself often result in high values of infiltration and soil moisture recharge and even the initiation of minor rills and channels in the surface. Thirdly, the passage of rainfall through the vegetation foliage may give rise to alterations in the drop size, which can have implications for soil erosion, and may also lead to significant changes in water chemistry (see Chapter 8).

Interception is discussed here, in a separate chapter to evaporation (Chapter 4), because although they have the same physics, interception loss can only occur when the vegetation canopy is wet. It is therefore much more dependent upon

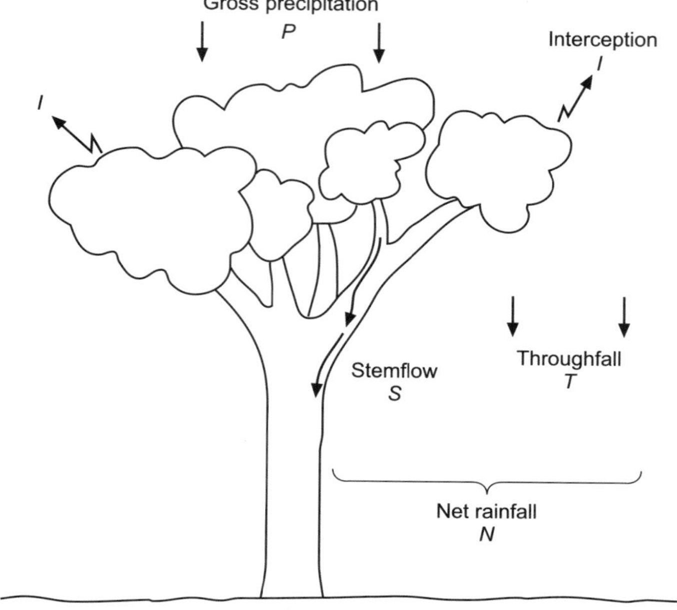

Figure 3.1 Interception loss (*I*) defined as the difference between gross precipitation (*P*) and net rainfall (*N*). Net rainfall is made up of throughfall (*T*) and stemflow (*S*).

short-term variations in rainfall, and specifically storm duration and the dry intervals between them.

3.2 Interception and the water balance

As a result of recent progress in our understanding of the mechanisms that control evaporation and transpiration from vegetation the role of interception in the water balance of catchment areas is now comparatively well understood. For many years there were two opposing views. One maintained that interception losses had no net effect on the catchment water balance, and the other that it reduced net inputs and so would diminish soil water recharge and streamflow.

Although there was considerable evidence that net precipitation under trees could be much less than in open ground (for example Horton, 1919) it was not clear if the intercepted water loss represented a real increase in evaporation. It could be argued that interception losses were balanced by a corresponding reduction in the water uptake by the vegetation, which is suppressed or ceases when the foliage is wet. In that case the overall effect on the water balance would be neutral or so small that it could be ignored. Even now, although the importance of interception is much more widely recognized, it still receives only a passing reference in some recent engineering hydrology textbooks (for example Shaw, 1994; Hornberger *et al.*, 1998). It will be shown in this chapter, however, that interception can be hydrologically very significant.

The neutral hypothesis emphasizes that interception losses are essentially evaporative; in any period of time only a certain amount of energy is available. This can be used either to evaporate water from within the leaf (transpiration), or to evaporate water from the surface of the leaf (interception). Thus, interception is at least in part balanced by a reduction in transpiration that would have occurred if it had not rained (Rutter, 1968). Early experiments on grasses using weighing lysimeters (McMillan and Burgy, 1960) indicated that there is no difference between the evaporation of wetted foliage and the transpiration of unwetted grass adequately supplied with water. They concluded that interception loss is balanced by an equivalent reduction in transpiration. Thus, interception losses are an *alternative* and not an *addition* to transpiration, and consequently would have little, if any, effect upon the water balance of a catchment area. It was argued by analogy that a similar situation would exist for forests, but it was too difficult to verify this experimentally. This hypothesis of neutral effect was undoubtedly given substantial additional credence through its support by Penman, the recognized authority on evaporation, who affirmed that 'While energy was being used up to get rid of the intercepted water, the same energy could not be used to get rid of the transpired water' (Penman, 1963).

A growing body of evidence, however, indicated that this was not the complete answer. Catchment studies in Europe and the USA indicated that forestry reduced total streamflow relative to grassland (Engler, 1919; Bates and Henry, 1928; Keller, 1988; Swank and Crossley, 1988). This was variously explained as being due to experimental errors, or to forests being able to extract greater quantities of water from the ground than shorter vegetation during times of soil water shortage. A crucial step forward in understanding was provided by Law (1958) in north west England who studied the water balance of a small (450 m^2) natural lysimeter set within a spruce forest. Measurements included both gross and net rainfall as well as surface drainage. The annual water use (gross rain minus drainage) was 50 per cent greater than that recorded at either a grass-covered percolation gauge or a nearby grass-covered catchment. Furthermore the forest water use appeared to be significantly greater than the net radiant energy available for evaporation.

This result portrayed interception, not as an alternative to transpiration, but as a net loss of water that would otherwise have been available to replenish soil and groundwater reserves or for streamflow. Fundamental questions to be answered were whether evaporation from the wetted surfaces of vegetation could take place at a significantly higher rate than the transpiration from unwetted vegetation, and whether significant evaporation of intercepted water could occur in circumstances when transpiration rates would otherwise be negligibly small, such as from wetted dead and dormant vegetation and during the winter and at night. Affirmative answers to these questions then required an explanation of the sources of energy for the additional evaporative losses.

Evidence accumulated rapidly during the 1960s, mostly from forested areas, to support the conclusion that intercepted water evaporates much faster than transpired water, and therefore much of the interception loss represents an additional loss in the catchment water balance. Rutter (1963) found that evaporative losses from cut wetted branches exceeded those from unwetted branches which lost water only by transpiration. More realistic field experiments by Rutter (1963; 1967), Patric (1966), Helvey (1967), and Leyton *et al.* (1967) indicated that during the winter period the loss of intercepted water considerably exceeded the transpiration rate *in the same environmental conditions.* Results from small catchment studies showed that substantial increases in water yield resulted from the removal of forest vegetation (Hewlett and Hibbert, 1961; Hibbert, 1967) and that decreased yields resulted from the conversion of deciduous hardwood forest to pine forest (Swank and Miner, 1968), largely as a result of interception effects.

Subsequently a combination of theoretical analysis and field data collection has confirmed that precipitation intercepted by vegetation evaporates at a greater rate than transpiration from the same type of vegetation in the same environment (Murphy and Knoerr, 1975) and that the difference may be of the order of 2–3 times (Singh and Szeicz, 1979) or as much as five times the transpiration rate (Stewart and Thom, 1973). Both Singh and Szeicz (1979) and Stewart (1977) concluded that 68 per cent of interception during daylight was additional to transpiration (i.e. 32 per cent could have been compensated for by transpiration). Pearce *et al.* (1980) found that, if account is taken of the additional water losses resulting from the existence of high night-time rates of evaporation of intercepted water, the net interception loss may be as high as 84 per cent of gross interception. Furthermore, as Pearce *et al.* (1980) observed, net interception loss will increase as the proportion of night-time rainfall duration and amount increases. This means that, in many high-rainfall areas, especially in maritime climates, where at least one-half of rainfall may occur at night, the importance of interception as an evaporative loss and the magnitude of the net loss may be greatly enhanced in relation to areas where rainfall is dominated by daytime convective activity.

In specific conditions other factors may result in additional net interception losses. For example, in some areas transpiration may be limited more by the availability of water than of energy. Then by increasing the amount of available water, interception would increase the total loss of water from a catchment area. The evaporation of water intercepted by dormant or dead, and therefore non-transpiring, vegetation and by a litter layer would certainly represent a net interception loss (McMillan and Burgy, 1960), the only factor involved in this case being the interception storage capacity and its depletion by evaporation. It was the storage aspect of interception loss that Zinke (1967) considered might play the greatest part in affecting the catchment water balance.

The primary explanation of the higher evaporation rate from wetted vegetation surfaces, and especially from wetted forest canopies, relates to the relative importance of the two main resistances imposed at the vegetation canopy on the flux of water vapour into the overlying atmosphere. This will be discussed in more detail in Chapter 4, in relation to the Penman–Monteith equation for calculating evaporation. At this stage it will be sufficient to note that the *surface resistance* is a physiological resistance, imposed by the vegetation canopy itself on the movement of water by transpiration, and the *aerodynamic resistance* is a measure of the resistance encountered by water vapour moving from the vegetation surface as wet-surface evaporation into the surrounding atmosphere. In dry conditions forest canopies probably have a slightly higher surface resistance than grass and other lower-order vegetation, but when the vegetation surfaces are wet this resistance is effectively 'short-circuited' and reduces to zero for all vegetation types (Calder, 1979). The aerodynamic resistance depends essentially on the roughness of the vegetation surface, which tends to be significantly greater for trees than for grass. The resistance to vapour flux is smaller for wetted than dry vegetation surfaces, and relatively lower still for forest compared with grasses and other short vegetation. The aerodynamically rougher canopies of forests generate more effective mixing of the air, which is the dominant transport mechanism for water vapour.

The additional energy required to maintain the higher rates of evaporative loss permitted by the dominating role of the aerodynamic resistance for wetted vegetation appears to be attributable to *advection* energy. This refers to the *horizontal* movement of energy in the atmosphere (in contrast to convection which is *vertical* movement). Rutter (1967) showed that in wet canopy conditions evaporation losses may not be controlled predominantly by the radiation balance but rather that the wet canopy acts as a sink for advected energy from the air.

Importantly, he found that when intercepted water was being evaporated the foliage was measurably cooler than the surrounding air and that the resulting temperature gradient was sufficient to yield a heat flux to supply the energy deficiency. This hypothesis was subsequently confirmed in a number of investigations, mainly of forested areas (for example Stewart and Thom, 1973; Thom and Oliver, 1977), and elaborated to the extent that it is recognized now that the advected energy may be derived either from the heat content of the air passing over the vegetation canopy (Stewart, 1977; Singh and Szeicz, 1979) or from heat stored in the canopy space and the vegetation itself (Moore, 1976). Stewart (1977) observed negative gradients of temperature and positive gradients of water vapour during wet canopy conditions. From these he was able to make measurements of evaporation at a 20-minute time scale, and noted that for 70 per cent of these periods the evaporation exceeded the net radiation, the additional energy being derived from the air passing overhead.

Additional proof of the role of advection and stored energy in promoting wet canopy evaporation was provided by Pearce *et al.* (1980) who confirmed the evidence of high evaporation rates during the night when there was no other energy source.

In this connection, it should be noted that the studies of Singh and Szeicz (1979) and Stewart (1977) were carried out in a comparatively small forested area, surrounded by farmland, where large-scale advection of 'surplus' energy was to be expected. It was possible, though, that in the case of very extensive forests, as for example on the Canadian shield or the Amazon basin, where trees extend for many hundreds of kilometres, less surplus energy may be available when large areas are wetted. Localized, thunderstorm-type wetting would, however, still permit sensible heat to be released from the dry areas to boost evaporation in the wetted areas.

Simulation of the energy exchange between the atmosphere and a vegetation surface by Murphy and Knoerr (1975), however, indicated that, in appropriate conditions, radiation balance modifications may also play a significant role. They found that the integrated effect of interception on the energy balance of a forest stand was an increase in the latent heat exchange, at the expense of the long-wave radiation and sensible heat exchange, which varied according to relative humidity and windspeed conditions. As a result they concluded that enhanced evaporation of intercepted water can occur for forests of large areal extent where horizontal advection may be negligible.

More recently, improvements in rainfall simulators and other instrumentation have enabled detailed studies of other types of vegetation cover, including grasses and agricultural crops. Finney (1984) investigated the possible paths taken by raindrops falling on Brussels sprouts, sugar beet and potatoes, i.e. they may fall between the leaves, their properties remaining unaltered; be intercepted and redirected as stemflow; be intercepted and coalesce, to fall subsequently as drip; or be intercepted and shattered by impact with the vegetation and then be redirected as small drops between the leaves. He found that as the plants matured and their interception area increased, the resulting decrease in throughfall was accompanied by an increased stemflow and leaf drip and a reduction in soil detachment except at leaf drip points.

Rainfall simulator experiments with tussock grasses showed the way in which the plant structure, with its convergent leaf arrays, directed intercepted rainfall towards the base of tussocks and sods and led De Ploey (1982) to the view that stemflow could play '. . . a major role in the process of runoff generation on slopes with steppe-like vegetation'.

3.3 Measuring interception

The most common method of measuring interception loss (I) in the field is to compute the difference between the precipitation above the vegetation layer (P) and the net precipitation below the vegetation canopy, comprising the throughfall (T) and stemflow (S). Thus:

$$I = P - T - S \tag{3.1}$$

Due to the difficulties of installing equipment underneath a vegetation canopy, this method has been used more for forest vegetation than for lower-order covers. Throughfall may be measured using funnel or trough gauges placed beneath the forest canopy and stemflow may be collected by small gutters sealed around the circumference of the trunk leading into a collecting container. Even then a number of problems may arise.

It has been found that throughfall depends upon canopy coverage and *leaf area index* (LAI), i.e. surface area of leaves (one side only)/projected crown area; whether the trees are evergreen or deciduous; and the leaf surface smoothness. Leaf shapes and orientation can concentrate throughfall at drip points. Stemflow may be influenced by branch orientation and by the roughness of the bark.

Generally, gross precipitation is measured in open areas, but sometimes this is not possible and there may be problems due to the effects of the aerodynamic roughness of the vegetation cover on the catch of the canopy-level gauges (see Section 2.4.1). Additionally there are sampling difficulties imposed by the great spatial variability of throughfall and stemflow in tropical forests (Jackson, 1975). Recent work in Amazon rainforest (Lloyd and Marques, 1988) has revealed the magnitude of the sampling problems involved due to considerable localized concentrations of throughfall in drip points (Figure 3.2). Previous estimates of interception losses for tropical forests may be in error as a result of inadequate spatial sampling (Bruijnzeel, 1990) since many early investigations did not fully appreciate the great spatial variation in throughfall necessitating a large number of randomly sited gauges, frequently relocated, to make an accurate assessment.

Stemflow on trees may be measured by sealing flexible guttering around the tree stems, and leading the water into a collecting device. Although many early studies ignored stemflow, it is now known that it can be significant for certain species, and it is particularly important for water chemistry studies due to its often high solute concentrations. There is some evidence that with increasing tree age stemflow reduces as a proportion of the gross rainfall (for example Johnson, 1990). This may result partly from their bark becoming rougher or covered with mosses and lichens and partly as older branches tend to become less steeply angled upwards.

A more satisfactory method of collecting net rainfall may be to use large sheet gauges which collect both throughfall and stemflow (Calder and Rosier, 1976; Hall and Hopkins, 1997). It may be easier to operate one large sheet gauge than a large number of throughfall and stemflow gauges. It also provides a good areal average value and there is evidence that locations with high throughfall are close to those with low throughfall, so that monitoring adjacent places is an additional advantage (Calder, 1998). However, the use of large sheets is not appropriate where information is required about the spatial variability of net rainfall, as may be the case in studies of soil moisture recharge, erosion or water quality. While they work well for dense young plantation forests, sheet gauges are problematic in other types of forest; for example they are unsuitable where there is a dense understorey vegetation, or where the trees are widely spaced and sheets have to be excessively large. Furthermore, if measurements are required over long periods the presence of the sheet may affect the tree canopy by cutting off the supply of net rainfall and litter fall to the ground.

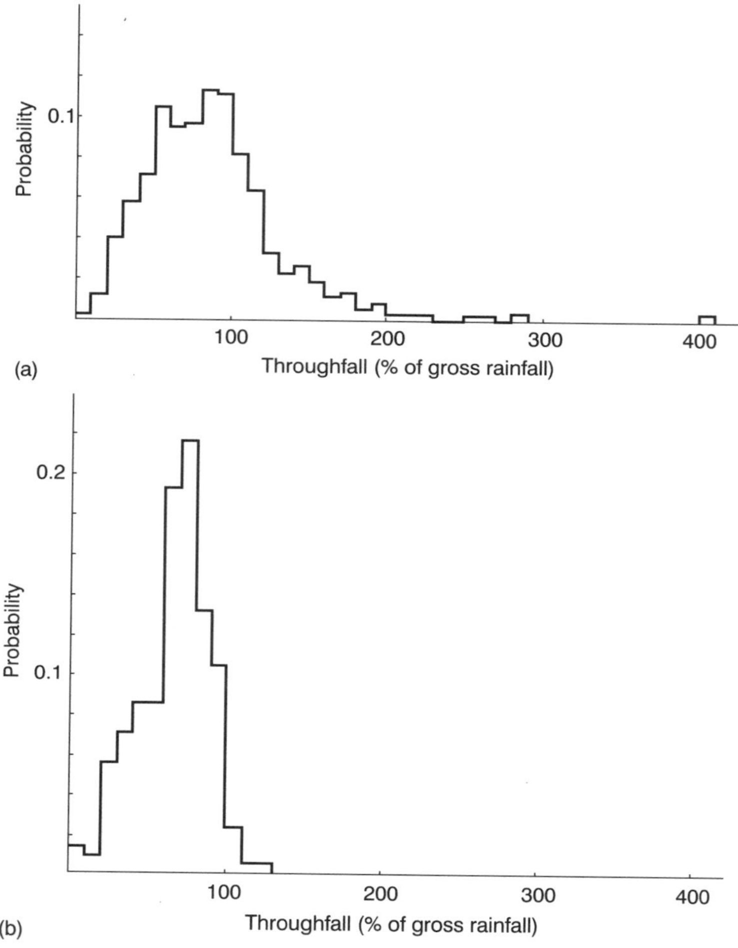

Figure 3.2 Comparison of throughfall catches in a network of collecting gauges expressed as a percentage of the gross rainfall for (*a*) tropical rain forest, (*b*) temperate conifer forest (Lloyd and Marques, 1988).

Interception studies are much more difficult for grasses and other lower vegetation for which other techniques may be possible. Small weighing lysimeters, for example, have been used to measure the wet-surface evaporation loss from heather (Hall, 1985; 1987), but care must be taken to exclude periods of transpiration loss. Corbett and Crouse (1968) devised a method for measuring grass interception losses by inserting 25 cm diameter metal collars into the soil, leaving sufficient above the ground that the soil inside the collar could be sealed by applying a latex emulsion which did not affect grass growth. A drain in the side of each collar carried combined throughfall and stemflow to a collecting container.

Water balance approaches have been used to measure indirectly the magnitude of interception loss. Some studies utilized small instrumented catchments to provide large-scale estimates of interception loss. Swank and Miner (1968), for example, reported that the effect of converting mature hardwoods to eastern white pine on two experimental catchments in the southern Appalachians was to reduce streamflow after ten years by almost 100 mm. Since most of the water yield reduction occurred during the dormant season, it was attributed mainly to greater interception loss from the evergreen pine than from the deciduous hardwoods. Increases in water yield, also attributable largely to interception effects, were reported by Pillsbury *et al.* (1962) and by Hibbert (1971), after conversion of chaparral scrub to grass.

Finally, there has been a range of approaches to quantify interception storage capacity and its individual components. The simplest approach is to plot throughfall against gross rainfall (Leyton *et al.*, 1967), and fit an upper envelope to the throughfall points. The line gives a negative intercept on the throughfall axis which represents the canopy storage capacity. However, the data usually have a large scatter due to the pattern of wetting and drying cycles within each rain event as well as the large experimental variance. An envelope tends to bias results towards points with errors in one direction. In addition there is subjectivity in excluding the smallest storms for which there was incomplete wetting of the canopy. As with the interception loss, the measurements of canopy storage and storage capacity are all expressed as equivalent depths (usually mm) per unit ground area and not as physical thicknesses of water films on the foliage.

Direct experimental approaches include wetting vegetation and measuring subsequent changes in weight as the water evaporates. This may be done for short vegetation using a weighing lysimeter (Calder *et al.*, 1984), and for trees by weighing leaves and branches and scaling up to the complete tree (Rutter, 1963; Crockford and Richardson, 1990).

Herwitz (1985) determined the interception storage capacity of tropical rainforest leaf surfaces using a rainfall simulator and the interception storage capacity of the trunks and woody surfaces by immersing bark fragments in aqueous solutions. He combined these data with measurements of the leaf area index, calculated with the help of large-scale aerial photographs, and a woody area index (WAI), i.e. woody surface area/projected crown area, to determine the total interception storage capacity. He found storage capacity values of 2–8 mm, which are much higher than the 1–2 mm generally found by in situ methods for temperate forests (Table 3.1).

Teklehaimanot and Jarvis (1991) described cutting and suspending a tree from a load cell and spraying it with water and monitoring the changes in its weight directly. Calder *et al.* (1984) used a weighing lysimeter to study the interception characteristics of a medium height vegetation, heather.

Remote sensing may also be used to measure directly the amount of water held on a whole forest canopy. Calder and Wright (1986) used gamma-ray attenuation. A transmitter and receiver were suspended from two towers, 40 metres

Table 3.1 Typical values of canopy rainfall interception capacities for different vegetation types, expressed as an equivalent water depth over the plan area of the vegetation (based on data from Rutter *et al.*, 1975; Shuttleworth, 1989; Zinke, 1967; Hall, 1985).

Vegetation	*Canopy storage capacity 'S' (mm)*		*Free fall 'p' (proportion)*	
Coniferous:				
Corsican pine (*Pinus nigra*)	1.05		0.25	
Norway spruce (*Picea abies*)	1.5		0.25	
Sitka spruce (*Picea sitchensis*)	1.7		0.05	
Douglas fir (*Pseudotsuga menziesii*)	1.2		0.09	
Deciduous:	*In leaf*	*None*	*In leaf*	*None*
Hornbeam (*Carpenus betulus*)	1.0	0.65	0.35	0.55
Oak (*Quercus robur*)	0.85	0.3	0.45	0.80
Tropical forest[1]	1.1[a]–4.9[b]		0–0.08	
Heather (*Calluna vulgaris*)	1.1		0.13	
Grasses	1.3		—	

[1] Tropical forest S values optimized using (a) Rutter model, (b) stochastic model.

apart, and were raised and lowered to allow the beam to scan across different levels in the canopy. However, for safety reasons, this could not be used for long-term unattended monitoring.

3.4 Factors affecting interception loss from vegetation

If rain falls onto a dry vegetation canopy the interception loss is usually greatest at the beginning of the storm and reduces with time. This largely reflects the changing state of the *interception storage* of the vegetation cover, i.e. the ability of the vegetation surfaces to collect and retain falling precipitation. At first, when all the leaves and twigs or stems are dry, the available storage—the *interception storage capacity*—is at a maximum, and a very large percentage of precipitation is prevented from reaching the ground. As the leaves become wetter the weight of water on them eventually overcomes the surface tension by which it is held and thereafter further additions from rainfall are almost entirely offset by the water droplets falling from the lower edges of the leaves. It is an old myth, yet one based on apparent 'common sense' that the interception capacity of trees is greater than that of shorter vegetation and grasses. Yet Table 3.1 shows that canopy storage capacities are very similar, and in fact the capacities for some grasses are higher than some forest values! However, as shown in Section 3.5.2, grass interception losses certainly will not be greater than those from the forests.

It must be remembered that condensation and raindrop formation high in the atmosphere does not necessarily mean that the air near the ground is also saturated. A considerable amount of water may be lost by evaporation from the leaf surfaces during rainfall, so that even when the initial interception storage capacity has been filled, there is some further fairly constant retention of falling precipitation to make good this evaporation loss. Indeed, during long continued rains, the interception loss may be closely related to the rate of evaporation, so that meteorological factors affecting the latter are also relevant to this discussion. While rain is actually falling windspeed is a factor of real significance. Other conditions remaining constant, evaporation tends to increase with higher windspeed, so that during prolonged periods of rainfall the interception loss is greater in windy than in calm conditions. This observation may, however, be less applicable in short-duration rainfall during which high windspeeds reduce the interception storage capacity by prematurely dislodging water collected on vegetation surfaces, and so partially outweighing the greater evaporative losses.

The duration of rainfall is another factor that influences interception by determining the balance between the reduced storage of water on the vegetation surfaces, on the one hand, and increased evaporative losses, on the other. Data collected during classic work by Horton (1919) and in numerous subsequent investigations showed that the absolute interception loss increases with the duration of rainfall, although its relative importance (i.e. interception as a proportion of rainfall) decreases. Since the amount and duration of rainfall are often closely related, many investigators have related interception losses and rainfall amount. When a storm commences, the losses are high as the initial interception storage capacity is filled; then they increase more slowly with evaporation of intercepted water during further rain as the storage capacity is replenished. Since the rate of this evaporation is generally lower than the rainfall, the relative importance of interception losses will tend to decrease as the amount of rainfall increases. This is illustrated in Figure 3.3(a), in which the *interception ratio* (i.e. interception loss/precipitation) is plotted against storm precipitation amounts in an area of tropical forest in Puerto Rico. The relationship also holds good for annual conditions, as is illustrated in Figure 3.3(b) by the graph of annual mean interception ratio against annual precipitation for a number of forest sites in the maritime climate of Great Britain. Since the average rainfall rate and the potential evaporation during rainfall are surprisingly uniform the annual ratio is fairly uniform at about 0.30–0.35 (Calder, 1990; IH, 1998).

Since the greatest interception loss occurs at the beginning of a storm, when the vegetation surfaces are dry and the interception storage capacity is large, it will be apparent that rainfall frequency, i.e. the frequency of re-wetting, is likely to be of considerably greater significance than either the duration or amount of rainfall.

Interception loss will also be affected by the type of precipitation including the size distribution of drops and particularly by the contrast between rain and snow, which will be discussed more fully at a later stage. Another important factor, which also merits a separate discussion below, is the variation of interception loss with the type and morphology of the vegetation cover.

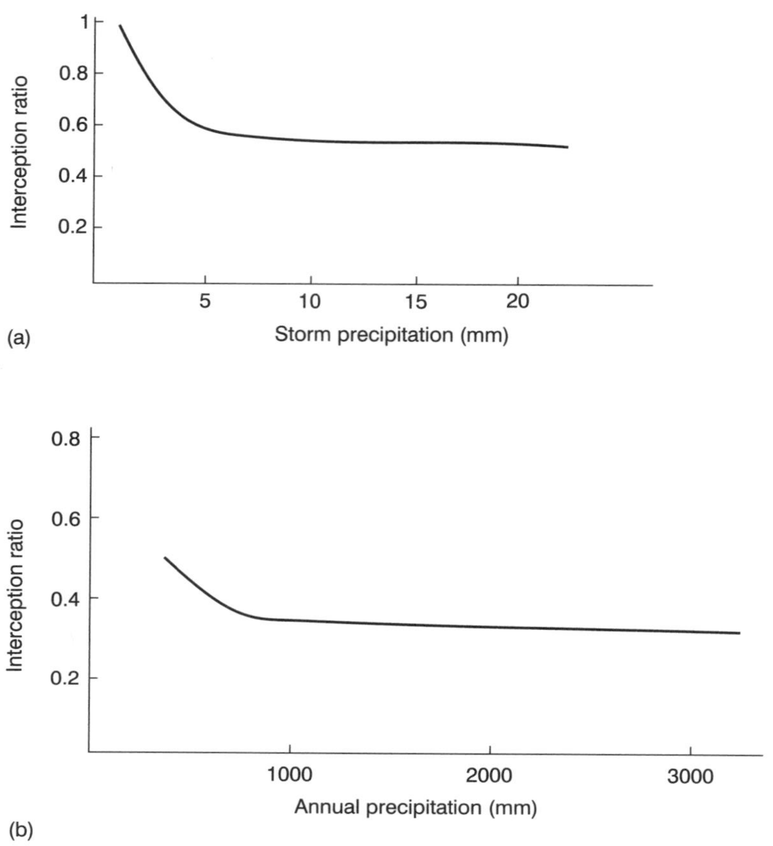

Figure 3.3 Interception ratio (loss as a proportion of rainfall) vs. (*a*) storm depth (based on data in Clegg, 1963); (*b*) annual precipitation depth (Calder, 1990).

3.5 Interception losses from different types of vegetation

On the basis of the preceding discussions it would be expected that interception losses between sites will vary in response to differences in vegetation and precipitation characteristics. The main vegetational effects relate to differences in interception storage capacity from one vegetation type to another and in aerodynamic roughness and its implications for the aerodynamic resistance and the rate of evaporation from the wetted vegetation surface. In broad terms interception losses will be greater for denser vegetation, for taller vegetation and for wetter climates. The most important precipitation characteristics are duration, frequency and intensity, as well as the precipitation type (liquid or solid), which is discussed separately in Section 3.7.

Because of the complexity of the interception process and the interrelationships between the vegetational and meteorological factors which determine the magnitude of interception losses, it is often difficult to make well-founded comparisons between published data on interception loss. It is clear, however, that in most cases, interception losses are greater from trees than from grasses or agricultural crops, although the reasons for this may vary with meteorological conditions. In the uplands of Britain, for example, where long-duration, low-intensity rain is common and vegetation surfaces are wet for considerable periods of time, there are much greater evaporation losses from trees. The reason is the much increased evaporation rate in wetted conditions (i.e. interception) due to the greater aerodynamic roughness of the trees rather than their slightly higher interception storage capacity (Calder, 1979). Interception rates for conifers in upland Britain are typically 30–35 per cent of gross rainfall due to the maritime climate of long-duration low-intensity rainfall. These losses are among the highest in the world, and it is for this reason that a substantial body of research into forest interception has been conducted in Britain.

In other conditions, however, the role of interception storage capacity in determining differences in interception loss between, say, trees and grass may be much more important. This would be the case where rainfall was frequent but short-lived with rapid drying between storms.

The values of interception loss for different vegetation covers which are quoted in this section must be interpreted, as far as possible, in the light of both the completeness of the measured data, where this is known, and also of weather conditions. For example, in some cases measurements were made of stemflow, in others an arbitrary allowance was made for this component and in still other cases it appears to have been ignored completely. Again the data presented in the literature are not always accompanied by an adequate analysis of meteorological conditions, particularly concerning the amount, duration, frequency, intensity and type of precipitation, all of which need to be known to permit a meaningful interpretation of the data.

3.5.1 Woodlands

Despite the fact that, in most cases, the leaf density is greater in deciduous than in coniferous forest, the bulk of the experimental evidence shows that interception losses are greater from the latter. Reviewing a broad range of Russian, European and American data, Rakhmanov (1966) suggested that coniferous forests, together with sparse woods and inhibited stands on peat bogs and other marshy terrain, intercept an average of 25–35 per cent of the annual precipitation compared with 15–25 per cent for broad-leaved forests. Similar values for coniferous forest interception in Britain were produced by Calder (1990), and a more recent review of European literature for broadleaf deciduous forests indicated losses of 10–30 per cent (IH, 1998). For mixed evergreen forest in South Island, New Zealand, interception losses averaged 29 per cent (Pearce *et al.*, 1982).

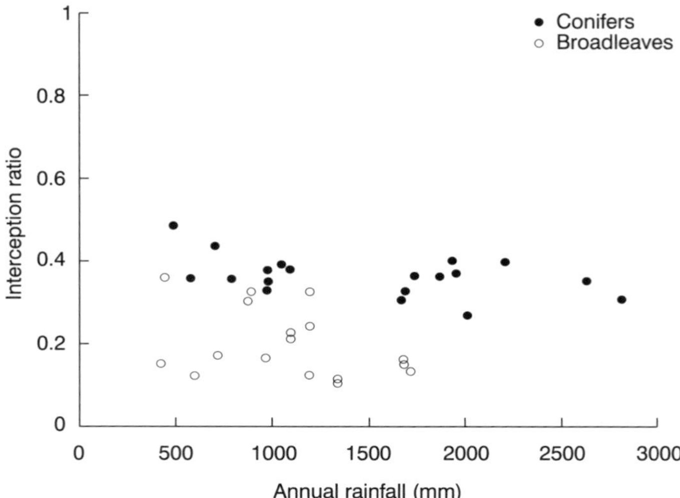

Figure 3.4 Annual interception ratios for conifers and broad-leaved trees (IH, 1998).

The contrast between broadleaf and coniferous forest is illustrated in Figure 3.4. Both types of woodland show the reduction in relative importance of interception loss as rainfall amounts increase but, over the complete range of rainfall totals, interception loss is markedly greater from the conifer forests. One of the reasons for this contrast may be that, while water droplets remain clinging to separate conifer needles, they tend to run together on the broadleaves and so drop or flow onto twigs and branches. Conifers typically have canopy storage capacities of about 1–2 mm, while broadleaf species tend to be below 1 mm (Harding *et al.*, 1992). It is also likely that the open texture of coniferous leaves allows freer circulation of air and consequently more rapid evaporation of the retained moisture. Interception losses will depend upon a number of factors including tree age and forest structure. Teklehaimanot *et al.* (1991) showed the importance of tree spacing. Interception losses decreased from 33 per cent to 9 per cent of rainfall when the spacing of Sitka spruce was increased from two to eight metres. The greater variability between the broad-leaved tree sites in Figure 3.4 is probably due to them containing a mixture of species, of different ages and with variable understorey vegetation; in contrast the conifer sites are generally even-aged, single-species plantations.

Estimates of interception in tropical forests are very variable, as a result of the spatial sampling difficulties, but are generally much lower than those reported for temperate forests. This is for three main reasons:

- the majority of tropical rainfall occurs in short-duration, high-intensity convective storms;
- the large raindrops are less effective in wetting foliage than finer drops; and

Table 3.2 Typical values of annual interception loss (% precipitation) for different forest types (based on data from Calder, 1990; Hall *et al.*, 1992; IH, 1998).

Forest type	*Annual interception* (%)
Upland conifers	30–35
Broadleaves	15–25
Tropical forests	10–15
Eucalyptus	5–15

- tropical rainforest leaves often have drip tips which concentrate throughfall which drains off as larger drops.

Recent estimates of interception losses include 9 per cent (Lloyd *et al.*, 1988) and 12 per cent (Ubarana, 1996) for rainforest in Brazil and 21 per cent for secondary forest in Indonesia (Calder *et al.*, 1986), while Asdak *et al.* (1998a) reported losses of 11 per cent for pristine unlogged forest (~ 580 trees ha^{-1}) and 6.2% for logged forest (~ 250 trees ha^{-1}) in Central Indonesia. Table 3.2 shows typical annual interception losses for four forest types.

With regard to seasonal contrasts, winter and summer interception percentages for evergreen coniferous forests appear to be about the same. Figure 3.5 shows that for a site in northern England, winter losses from spruce may be slightly higher than summer losses (Law, 1958). In contrast, it would be expected that there would be a clear seasonal difference in interception losses from

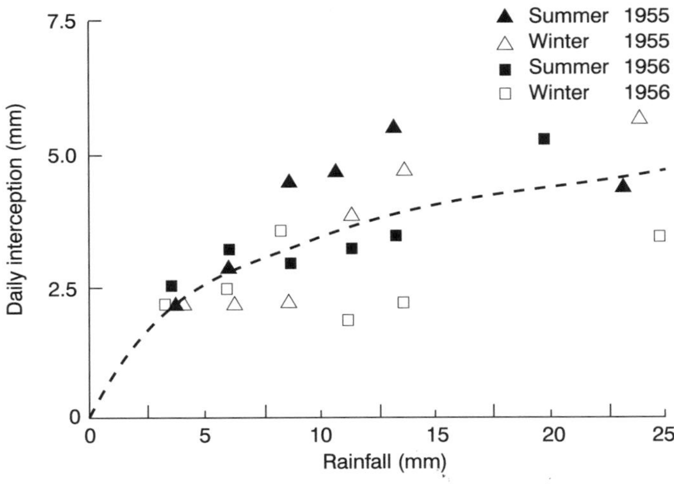

Figure 3.5 Seasonal interception losses from evergreen spruce (from an original diagram by Law, 1958).

deciduous trees, being greatest during the period of full leaf. In a review of the published literature for a number of broadleaf species, Hall and Roberts (1990) indicated a median value of canopy capacity of 0.8 mm (in leaf) and 0.6 mm (leafless). Lull (1964) quoted figures showing that when the trees were in leaf interception losses in northern hardwood and aspen–birch forests were 15 and 10 per cent respectively, whereas with leafless trees the losses were only half these amounts: 7 and 4 per cent. Similarly, Carlisle *et al.* (1965) found that the losses for oak trees were nearly 17 per cent during the vegetated summer period compared with under 10 per cent in the leafless period. However, Reynolds and Henderson (1967) found little seasonal difference in interception loss due to leaf fall. This apparently surprising result may be indicative of a number of factors. Higher rainfall intensities in summer because of convective storms may give lower interception losses. It is also to be expected that the aerodynamic roughness of the forest must change, and is probably greater in winter when the trees are bare, encouraging evaporation rates. Thirdly, as noted in Section 3.7, snow interception in the winter period may give rise to higher interception losses.

An additional important aspect of interception loss in wooded areas is that this often occurs at two or more levels within the vegetation cover. Precipitation is first intercepted by the upper canopy; some of the throughfall is then intercepted again by undergrowth, or by a layer of ground litter. Comparatively little is known about the importance of this secondary interception, although the low wind speeds in the trunk space must mean that evaporation rates are quite low. It will tend to increase with the amount of rainfall, because during light rains little or no throughfall occurs from the crown canopy, whereas during long, heavy storms throughfall will probably fill the interception storage capacity of the undergrowth or ground litter.

3.5.2 Grasses and shrubs

The total leaf area of a continuous cover of mature grass or shrub may closely resemble that of a closed canopy forest, so that the interception storage capacity may also be similar in magnitude to that of trees during the season of maximum development. Because of their higher aerodynamic resistance and shorter growing season, however, total annual interception loss from grasses is considerably less than from, say, deciduous woodland. Furthermore, in areas where grass is cut for hay or silage, or is heavily grazed in the field, interception losses are much reduced.

Kittredge (1948) found that in California undisturbed grass species intercepted 26 per cent of an 826 mm seasonal rainfall, while in Missouri, bluegrass intercepted 17 per cent of the rainfall in the month before harvesting (Musgrave, 1938). In neither case was an allowance made for stemflow. Work by Corbett and Crouse (1968), in which throughfall and stemflow were measured, showed that annual interception losses from brome grasses in southern California averaged about 8 per cent. Interception losses from mature chaparral shrub cover in southern California averaged about 13 per cent of annual precipitation. Interception experiments with cut vegetation or with artificial sprinkling have given widely divergent results. In contrast, in wet temperate areas with frequent rainfall, such as maritime western Europe, interception may provide the major part of tall grass evaporation losses, although still much less in absolute amounts than forest interception losses.

There is a paucity of data on interception by herbaceous and shrubby covers typical of the heaths and moorlands of Europe (Leyton *et al.*, 1967). This is an important omission since afforestation in such areas occurs at the expense of heather rather than grass. Measurements with raingauges placed under growing heather in Scotland (Aranda and Coutts, 1963), showed that on average 55 per cent of precipitation penetrated the canopy. Although no measurement was made of stemflow, they recognized that this might be appreciable due to the plant's multi-stemmed structure. Research by the Institute of Hydrology (Hall, 1985, 1987; Wallace *et al.*, 1982) showed that the aerodynamic resistance for heather is lower than for grass. Therefore, during wet periods interception losses from heather are likely to be much higher than those from grass. However, in dry periods transpiration losses from heather are significantly lower than those from grass, so that in regions of moderate annual rainfall ($\sim$ 1500 mm) the increased interception losses are likely to counterbalance the reduction in transpiration, in high rainfall areas interception losses will dominate and in drier areas the converse will be true.

3.5.3 Agricultural crops

Again, data on the interception loss from agricultural crops are sparse in relation to those from forested areas. Figure 3.6 shows that interception by corn, soybeans and oats increases initially with increasing crop density. After a certain coverage has been attained, however, the subsequent increase of interception is slight, indicating that the approximate average interception by fully developed oats, soybeans and corn is 23, 35 and 40–50 per cent respectively. Since no measurements appear to have been made of stemflow, these figures would have to be reduced by an appropriate amount in order to represent the true interception loss. Other observations during the growing season for the same three crops showed that interception losses were about 7, 15 and 16 per cent of the total rainfall for oats, soybeans and corn respectively (Lull, 1964). Russian experiments showed that interception by spring wheat during the growing season was about the same as, or a little less than, that by forest in leaf for the same period, amounting to between 11 and 19 per cent of the total precipitation (Kontorshchikov and Eremina, 1963).

3.6 Modelling interception

While it is much simpler to measure interception loss directly than to collect the climate and vegetation data necessary to model interception loss, modelling has a

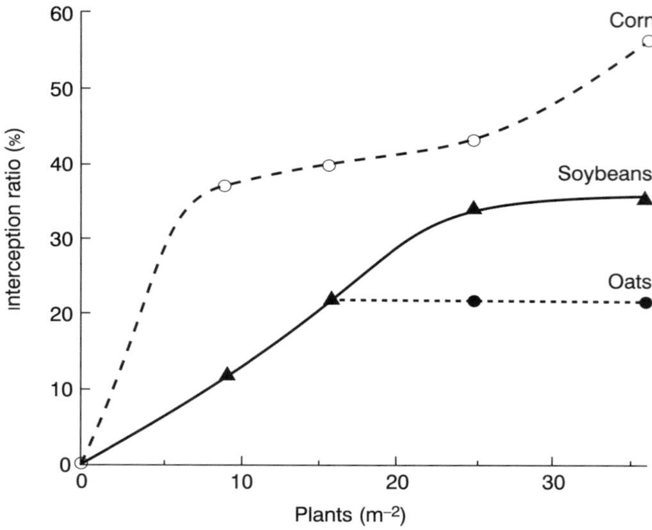

Figure 3.6 Interception loss by agricultural crops with increasing plant density (based on data from Woollny quoted by Baver, 1956).

number of advantages. First, it provides a summary of the behaviour; secondly it enables the results of one field study to be extrapolated to other areas; and thirdly it can provide insights into the process.

Various approaches to modelling interception loss have been developed, although inevitably in view of the complexity of the interception process and the difficulty of establishing precise values for the major components and influencing factors (for example canopy and stem storage capacity, drip rates, stemflow, aerodynamic resistance, evaporation rates, etc.), most of the models suffer either from over-generalization and simplification or from exacting and extensive data and processing demands.

The simplest models are those which incorporate empirical, regression-based expressions relating interception loss to gross precipitation. Horton (1919) was probably the first to propose that for storms which saturate the vegetation canopy the interception loss (I) will be equal to the sum of evaporation loss of intercepted water during rainfall and the water held on the canopy at the end of the storm (which will subsequently be evaporated)

$$I = \int_0^t E\, \mathrm{d}t + S \tag{3.2}$$

where E is the rate of evaporation of intercepted water, t is the duration of rainfall and S is the interception 'storage capacity' of the canopy, a term over which there is some confusion in the literature. Used here, it is the amount of water left on the canopy, in conditions of zero evaporation, after rainfall and drip have ceased, i.e. the minimum necessary to cover all the vegetation. This differs from its use, for example by Herwitz (1985), to signify the 'maximum storage capacity' of the vegetation canopy.

Equation (3.2) can be elaborated, by considering separately evaporation before and after canopy saturation, to give

$$I = \int_0^{t'} E\,\mathrm{d}t + \int_{t'}^{t} E\,\mathrm{d}t + S \tag{3.3}$$

where t' is the time taken for saturation of the canopy to occur.

Although Horton (1919) recognized that Eq. (3.2) was more logical, he concluded that in practice it would often be more convenient to incorporate precipitation amounts rather than precipitation duration. Accordingly, there are many empirical models of interception loss which take the general form

$$I = aP + b \tag{3.4}$$

where P is the gross rainfall on the vegetation canopy and a and b are empirically derived coefficients. Equation (3.4) can be used either to describe individual storm data or, if it is assumed that there is only one rainfall event per day, to describe daily interception loss as a function of daily gross rainfall (Gash, 1979).

Merriam (1960) incorporated an exponential expression to allow for the observed increase in storage with increased precipitation, giving

$$I = S\left[1 - \exp\left(-\frac{P}{S}\right)\right] + ET \tag{3.5}$$

where E is the mean evaporation rate during the storm, and T is the storm duration. Jackson (1975) tested several models and found that a semi-logarithmic curve fitted his data for tropical forest slightly better than other models, so that

$$I = a + b\ln\bar{P} + c\ln T \tag{3.6}$$

where a, b and c are empirical coefficients and $\bar{P}$ is the average rate of rainfall during the storm.

Useful reviews of simple models such as these were provided by Zinke (1967), Jackson (1975), Gash (1979) and Massman (1983). They stressed that, while the models are easy to use, they do not always give satisfactory quantitative results when the coefficients are derived by regression against a specific set of data and that empirical results may not be valid for similar vegetation covers at other sites.

Models that are based on more fundamental physical reasoning tend to minimize many of the weaknesses of empirical models but usually require frequent (for example hourly) data inputs for rainfall and throughfall rates and for meteorologically based estimates of evaporation. Probably the most rigorous of such models is that developed by Jack Rutter, which solves the vegetation water balance equation numerically.

The model was originally described by Rutter *et al.* (1971) and subsequently elaborated and generalized (Rutter *et al.*, 1975) as a result of work in hardwood and coniferous forest stands. It is based on describing the water storage on the vegetation canopy and stems. Intercepted rainfall is added to this store, which is then depleted by evaporation, drip and drainage. The rates of evaporation and drip are assumed to vary with the amount of water on the canopy and, accordingly, the model is designed to calculate a running balance of rainfall, throughfall, evaporation and changes in canopy and stem storage. Evaporation from the wetted vegetation surfaces constitutes the interception loss. The rate of input of water to the vegetation canopy is

$$(1 - p)R \tag{3.7}$$

where R is the rate of rainfall and p is the proportion of rain that falls through gaps in the canopy. The model assumes that when the depth of water stored on the vegetation canopy (C) equals or exceeds its storage capacity (S) evaporation will take place at the potential rate, E_p given by the Penman–Monteith equation (see Section 4.6.3). For a wet but unsaturated canopy (i.e. $C < S$) the evaporation is reduced proportionately so that

$$E = E_p \frac{C}{S} \tag{3.8}$$

Subsequently, this relationship was given observational support by Hancock and Crowther (1979), and Shuttleworth (1978) showed that it provides a theoretically reasonable description.

The rate of drip drainage from the canopy is assumed to be a logarithmic function of the degree of canopy saturation, so that

$$D = D' e^{bC} \tag{3.9}$$

where D' and b are parameters which depend upon the foliage characteristics and meteorological conditions, and may be derived from observations as described by Rutter and Morton (1977). Since this equation predicts a small but continuing drip from a dry canopy other expressions have been proposed (for example Calder, 1977; Massman, 1980).

The storage capacity of the branch/stem system (S_t) is considered to be replenished by a constant proportion of rainfall which is diverted to that part of the branch system that drains to the trunks. When the storage capacity is completely filled potential evaporation from this store takes place at a rate linearly related to the Penman–Monteith equation. When the depth of water on the branches and trunks (C_t) is less than the capacity S_t the evaporative loss from them is further scaled down by the ratio (C_t/S_t). In contrast to the expression for drip from the canopy, the drainage of water from the branches and trunks in excess of the storage capacity is assumed to be immediate.

The model was tested against observed interception losses for six forest types including both deciduous broad-leaved and evergreen coniferous species (Rutter

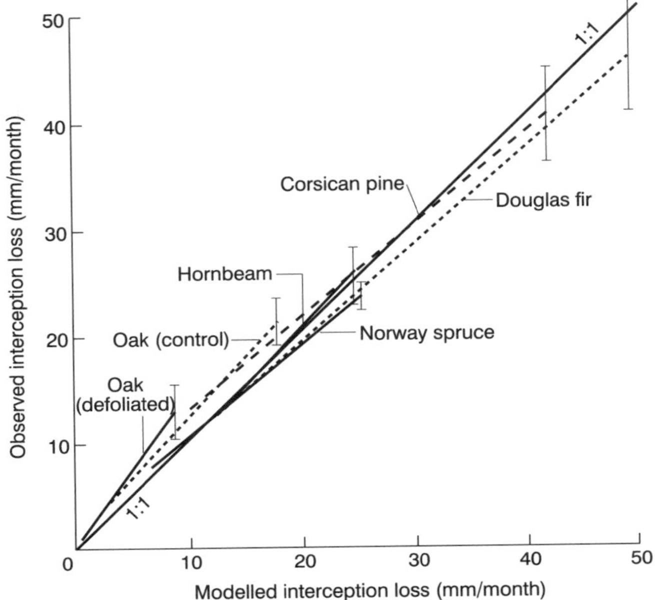

Figure 3.7 Linear regression fits of observed and modelled interception loss for six forest species. Standard deviations are shown at the right hand end of each line. (Adapted from an original diagram in Rutter *et al.*, 1975. Blackwell Scientific Publications Ltd.)

et al., 1975) and gave a very satisfactory model performnce (Figure 3.7). It was also successfully applied to other data sets (for example Calder, 1977; Gash and Morton, 1978).

The Rutter model does, however, require a great deal of data and a very short data time step and it is complex to use. As a consequence it is generally only used for research purposes. Furthermore, since it is based on keeping a running water balance, errors may accumulate over time (Calder, 1998). An alternative approach is to integrate the mass balance equation analytically. In this context one of the most satisfactory and widely used methods is the analytical model developed by Gash (1979). Despite a number of simplifying assumptions, it retains much of the physical reasoning of the more complex Rutter model. The Gash model calculates interception loss on a storm-by-storm basis and separately identifies the meteorological and biological controls of interception loss to give a framework within which results may be extrapolated more readily to other areas. The main simplifying assumptions are (Gash, 1979):

- the rainfall pattern may be represented by a series of discrete storms, separated by sufficiently long intervals for the canopy and trunks to dry;
- similar meteorological conditions prevail during wetting up of the canopy and during the storms; and

- there is no drip from the canopy during wetting up, and that within about 30 minutes of the end of rainfall the canopy storage reduces to the minimum value necessary for saturation.

A series of storms is divided into n storms which wet the canopy to saturation and m which do not reach saturation. Simplifying, the total interception loss during evaporation from a saturated canopy (from Eq. 3.3) is:

$$I = \Sigma\left[\int_0^t E\,\mathrm{d}t + \frac{E}{R}(P - P')\right] + nS \qquad \text{for } n \text{ storms} \qquad (3.10a)$$

where E and R are the mean rates of evaporation and rainfall and P' is the amount of rain necessary to saturate the canopy.

The interception loss during the wetting up of the canopy to saturation is:

$$I = n(1 - p - p_t)\,P' - ns \qquad \text{for } n \text{ storms} \qquad (3.10b)$$

where p is the proportion of rain that falls through the canopy without striking a surface and p_t is the proportion that is diverted to the trunks as stemflow.

The interception loss for m small storms insufficient to saturate the canopy is

$$I = (1 - p - p_t)\,\Sigma P \qquad \text{for } m \text{ storms} \qquad (3.11)$$

The interception loss from the trunks in q storms that fill the trunk storage, S_t, is

$$I = qS_t \qquad \text{for } q \text{ storms} \qquad (3.12a)$$

and for storms that do not fill the storage the loss is

$$I = p_t\,\Sigma P \qquad \text{for } n + m - q \text{ storms} \qquad (3.12b)$$

The total interception loss is then provided by summing the components from these individual equations (3.10–3.12).

This model was applied to data from Thetford Forest in eastern England and produced satisfactory agreement between observed and modelled interception loss (Figure 3.8). It has also been applied in evergreen mixed forest in New Zealand (Pearce and Rowe, 1981), oak forest in the Netherlands (Dolman, 1987), and tropical forests (Bruijnzeel and Wiersum, 1987; Lloyd *et al.*, 1988; Hutjes *et al.*, 1990).

Dolman (1987) compared the analytical model of Gash (1979) with a more complex numerical simulation model (Mulder, 1985) which had much greater data requirements. Both models performed equally well describing losses from an oak forest, and he concluded that the Gash model was the more appropriate for practical estimates of interception loss.

Research continues to improve both the conceptual basis and the general applicability of models of interception loss. Many of these attempts have focused upon the type of drip/drainage expression used in the Rutter model; others have attempted to simplify both the structure and the data demands of the evaporation expression.

There is little doubt that drip expressions similar to Eq. (3.9) are unsatisfactory

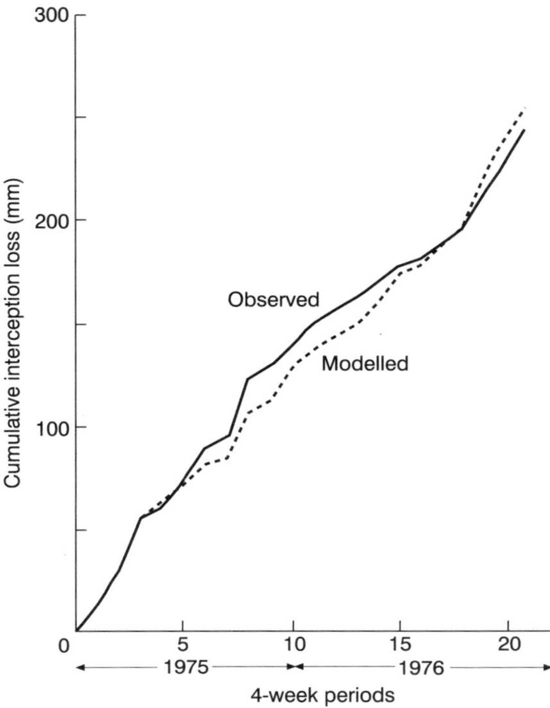

Figure 3.8 Cumulative observed and modelled interception losses for a pine forest over 21 four-week periods during 1975 and 1976 (from an original diagram by Gash, 1979).

in the sense that they assume that the drip rate is determined solely by the amount of water stored on the vegetation canopy. This means that they do not account explicitly for either the influence of rainfall rate upon the drip rate or for the physical dislodgement of previously intercepted rain by falling raindrops or for the multi-layered nature of many vegetation canopies. Accordingly, Massman (1983) proposed a model for drip rate which assumes that, after some critical amount of water has been intercepted by leaf surfaces near the top of the canopy, further interception at that level would dislodge some of the stationary droplets which would then fall out of the tree or be intercepted at lower levels. In other words, during rainfall the drip rate may be controlled by water droplets cascading through the tree, alternatively falling from and impacting on successively lower surfaces (for example Calder, 1977).

Although the Rutter model works well in temperate forests it has been noted that it is less successful in tropical forests (Calder *et al.*, 1986), although some authors have attributed this to the much greater spatial variability of the net rainfall and hence the larger sampling errors (for example Lloyd *et al.*, 1988;

Ubarana, 1996). Calder (1996) proposed a two-layer stochastic model to describe the wetting up of a tropical forest canopy. Primary raindrop sizes are related to rainfall intensity, and the size of secondary drips from the upper foliage to lower levels is characterized by the tree species from which they fall. This model takes account of the fact that in tropical forests the canopy wetting is achieved more slowly and the maximum canopy storage capacity will be lower than for temperate forests due to the larger raindrops and higher intensities that occur in intensive convective rainstorms.

Further application of the Gash model has indicated that both it and the Rutter model overestimated interception loss from sparse forests which are found in Mediterranean areas and many other parts of the non-temperate world (Gash *et al.*, 1995; Llorens, 1997). The Gash and Rutter models were reformulated and produced much improved results (Gash *et al.*, 1995; Valente *et al.*, 1997). Essentially this involved replacing the partitioning of rainfall by 'p', the free throughfall fraction (see Eq. 3.7), by partitioning the evaporation with vegetation cover. It is anticipated that the reformulated models will supersede the original versions of the Rutter and Gash models (Gash, 1998). The revised Gash model predictions of interception losses from closed canopy forests are as good as the original model (Asdak *et al.*, 1998b), while for sparse canopies it gives better predictions (Carlyle-Moses and Price, 1999).

Calder and Newson (1979) proposed a very simple model for total evaporation from conifer forests, using only annual precipitation (P) and Penman short grass potential evaporation (E_t). In essence it assumes that annual forest interception may be largely approximated as a proportion (α) of the annual precipitation:

$$I = f(\alpha P - wE_t) \tag{3.13}$$

where f is the proportion of the catchment with complete forest coverage and w is the proportion of the year when the canopy is wet (and no transpiration occurs). The E_t approximates the forest transpiration. This very simple approach was successfully extended to other vegetation types (Hall and Harding, 1993), and to a daily time step (Calder, 1990) enabling seasonal variations to be investigated. Its application to estimate total evaporation losses (interception and transpiration) is described in Chapter 4.

3.7 Interception of snow

Due to the immense experimental difficulties, the evidence concerning the interception of snow has been frequently unsatisfactory and confusing and is largely restricted to woodland vegetation. Many of the discrepancies evident in the following discussion undoubtedly result from the difficulties of measuring snowfall, particularly in view of its tendency to drift at the edge of pronounced barriers such as forests, and in forest clearings, i.e. the very locations in which measurements are normally made.

On the one hand it may be argued that evaporation of intercepted snow will be very small because the accumulation of snow on a vegetation canopy will make the surface aerodynamically much smoother. As a result, evaporation rates will be lower than from a rain-wetted canopy. In addition, snow accumulating on vegetation surfaces is prone to large-scale mass release by rainwash and sliding under its own weight, frequently aided by wind-induced movement of the vegetation, and also the smaller-scale release of snow particles and meltwater drip. Such release mechanisms mean that in many areas snow remains on the vegetation cover for only a few days before falling to the ground, so that opportunities for evaporation are small. Satterlund and Haupt (1970) recorded the weight of the snow on a suspended pine tree and collected and measured the snow and water reaching a groundsheet beneath it. They concluded that only 15 per cent of the intercepted snow was evaporated—the rest reached the ground by melting, slipping or being washed off by rain. Even when snow remains on the vegetation cover for long periods of time, the energy available for evaporation and sublimation is minimal, and in some areas, such as north-west Europe, when there is a transfer of water it tends to be to the snow cover, in the form of condensation, rather than away from it, in the form of evaporation or sublimation (Penman, 1963).

On the other hand, the water equivalent of snow stored on a forest canopy can be an order of magnitude greater than for a rain-wetted canopy. Thus there is the potential for considerably larger interception evaporation over a prolonged drying period.

Recent investigations (Nakai *et al.*, 1993; Lundberg *et al.*, 1998) have placed a much needed emphasis on the aerodynamic processes involving transport of snow through and from the forest canopy to the site of final deposition and on the energy and water fluxes above the snow cover. They have shown that the aerodynamic resistance for snow is much larger than for rain conditions. Lundberg *et al.* (1998) found an order of magnitude difference which resulted in a 2.6-fold difference in evaporation estimates using a combination equation based on the Penman equation. Gamma ray attenuation and tree-weighing experiments in Scotland (Calder, 1990; Lundberg *et al.*, 1998) showed that spruce canopies can hold in excess of 20 mm water equivalent of snow and that evaporation rates from snow-covered canopies of up to $0.56\,\mathrm{mm\,h^{-1}}$ can on occasions be as high as evaporation rates from rain-wetted canopies, especially when the snow is melting during incursions of tropical maritime air. Although sublimation rates are generally lower than evaporation rates, sublimation may be important in snow interception, as in Scottish upland coniferous forests, because of the much larger canopy capacity for snow (an order of magnitude greater than for water) and because of the long periods of subzero temperatures during which sublimation can take place. The combination of high evaporation rates, large storage capacity and sublimation effects indicates a potential for significant snow interception losses (Figure 3.9). Lundberg *et al.* (1998) suggested that at their site the total winter losses from snow intercepted on the forest canopy might be

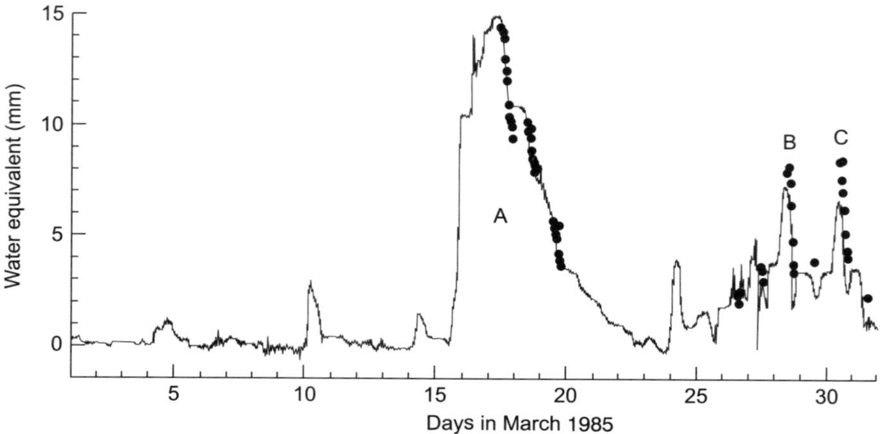

Figure 3.9 The water equivalent of snow intercepted on a forest canopy recorded by tree weighing (continuous line) and by gamma-ray attenuation (dots) for three snowfall events (from an original diagram in Lundberg *et al.*, 1998).

over 200 mm. However, there are likely to be significant variations between sites, depending not only on the climate but also on the forest characteristics. For example while the canopy snow storage capacity on the 16 m high trees at their site was over 20 mm, Nakai *et al.* (1993) reported a storage capacity of only 4 mm water equivalent for 5–7 m high trees.

3.8 Cloud water deposition

Up to this point this chapter has dealt with the evaporation of intercepted water as a loss in the effective precipitation input. There are certain circumstances where vegetation may be able to gain additional water by 'stripping' fine airborne water droplets (typically $\sim$ 10 μm radius) from mists or low cloud which would not otherwise have fallen to the ground as precipitation at that site. Consequently it would not be measured in normal raingauges (Monteith and Unsworth, 1990). This is most likely to be true in forested areas of high relief or near to coasts, where fogs or low cloud are prevalent (Kerfoot, 1968), particularly when windspeeds are relatively high. This process is also observed, however, in agricultural crops when on calm, misty mornings the accumulation of fine mist droplets on the heads of grain crops may become so heavy that the stems collapse under the load (Penman, 1967).

The main hydrological interest lies in the amount of water that is transmitted to the ground as throughfall and stemflow. Water droplets are formed on leaves, twigs and branches by impaction, and may accumulate sufficiently to fall or trickle to the ground. In the sense that this represents measurable precipitation beneath the vegetation canopy where none is recorded in the open, Kittredge

(1948) suggested that it could be regarded as 'negative interception'. Deposition of cloud or mist droplets onto vegetation is thought to be a sufficient addition to the normal precipitation to influence plant distributions along the west central coast of North America (Lull, 1964) and Chile (Kummerow, 1962).

Early studies frequently emphasized that this would be essentially an edge effect and that its importance decreases markedly away from the borders of, say, a forested plot or area of relatively taller vegetation. The border nature of the phenomenon is also apparent from results of various experiments with fog gauges which used vertical gauzes to intercept horizontally driven cloud and fog droplets (for example Nagel, 1956).

A major conceptual advance was that of Shuttleworth (1977) who showed that cloud water deposition was controlled by the same physics as interception evaporation. Rather than simply a horizontal edge phenomenon, which is limited to the first 20 m at most, he argued that it would in fact be dominated by vertical exchanges between the atmosphere and the top of an extensive vegetation canopy. Furthermore, in the same way that interception losses are greater from forests due to their greater aerodynamic roughness, so cloud water deposition amounts would be greater to forest canopies than to shorter vegetation.

Cameron *et al.* (1997) estimated cloud water deposition rates of about 0.05 mm h^{-1} to 0.8 m high tussock grass at a coastal upland site in southern New Zealand. This amounted to about 60 mm or 4 per cent of the annual precipitation. They suggested that replacement with short pasture would reduce cloud water deposition due to the lower aerodynamic conductance, while a change to forest may increase fog deposition due to enhanced turbulence. Nevertheless, the main hydrological impact overall would be enhanced forest interception loss due to the prevailing low-intensity intermittent precipitation.

The entrainment of cloud water droplets by vegetation is mainly a feature of sites where fog and low cloud are frequent due to high altitude, climate or proximity to the sea.

If the temperature falls below the dew point of the air, condensation of water vapour may occur on plant leaves and other surfaces with the formation of *dew*. This is a very different process to the entrainment of airborne particles. Monteith and Unsworth (1990) estimated that for saturated air, a typical dewfall rate would be about 0.067 mm h^{-1}, giving about 0.2–0.4 mm per night. The source of the water condensed as dew may be the atmosphere or the soil—the latter is not a net gain, but is usually the greater by a factor of about 1 : 5. Dew is therefore a very minor component of the hydrological cycle.

Review Problems and Exercises

3.1 Why was the significance of interception as net loss of water not recognized by many hydrologists?

3.2 Explain why the interception loss of forests is much greater than that from grass, although their canopy storage capacities may be very similar.

3.3 Discuss the different approaches required for measuring interception losses from grass, shrubs, open forest and close canopy woodland.

3.4 Discuss the importance of interception losses from a snow-covered forest.

3.5 Define the following terms: interception loss, net rainfall, throughfall, stemflow, canopy storage capacity.

3.6 Explain how evaporation losses can be greater than the net available radiant energy; what is the additional source of energy?

CHAPTER FOUR

Evaporation

4.1 Introduction and definitions

The term *evaporation* is used by physicists to describe the process by which any liquid is changed into a gas. For hydrologists this expression is used for the loss of water from a wet surface through its conversion into its gaseous state, *water vapour*, and its transfer away from the surface into the atmosphere. Evaporation may occur from open water (including rivers, lakes and oceans), bare soil or vegetation. In addition to the evaporation of intercepted water held upon plant surfaces, which is discussed in Chapter 3, there is also direct water use by plants termed *transpiration*. This component of evaporation comprises water taken up by plant roots from the soil which moves up the plant and thence into the atmosphere principally through the leaves. Due to the extraction of water at depth by plant roots, transpiration may continue for long after the drying out of water intercepted on vegetation foliage and held in the upper soil layer.

Although by definition evaporation includes *all* of the processes by which liquid water becomes a vapour, many American textbooks prefer to use the somewhat clumsy term *evapotranspiration* for total evaporation (for example Brooks *et al.*, 1997; Jensen *et al.*, 1990). This is to emphasize the combined processes of evaporation from soil and water surfaces plus transpiration from plants. Similarly, agriculturalists use the term *consumptive use* in order to emphasize that the necessary uptake of water by vegetation in the production of plant material represents an important 'use', rather than a mere 'loss'.

At the global scale, evaporation and precipitation are the two principal elements of the hydrological cycle. Evaporation returns to the atmosphere the same amount of water as the solid or liquid precipitation that reaches the earth's surface. Over the entire land surfaces approximately two-thirds of the precipitation is returned to the atmosphere as evaporation, making it the largest single component of the terrestrial hydrological cycle (Baumgartner and Reichel, 1975). At the global scale, land surfaces provide only a small part of the evaporated water, the bulk coming from the extensive water bodies of the seas and oceans; this has a direct impact upon the large-scale transfer of water vapour from the oceans to the continents, and hence the distribution of precipitation over land areas.

Evaporation is also very important in controlling the earth's energy budget, accounting for over 75 per cent of the net radiation reaching the earth's surface. Part of the radiation warms the atmosphere in contact with the ground by conduction and convection and is termed *sensible* heat or energy since its effect may be measured or sensed by a change in temperature; the energy used or liberated in evaporation or condensation is termed *latent* heat or energy (= hidden or not obvious) since this involves a change in state without a change in temperature. The latent heat of vaporization, λ, is $2.47\times$ MJ kg^{-1} at 10°C, and this is a very important factor in hydrological and energy budgets. The amount of energy required to change a unit volume of water into water vapour is about six times more than that needed to heat that water from 0°C to 100°C.

It is important to emphasize that there is no fundamental difference in the physics of evaporation from water, soil or plants (Shuttleworth, 1993). The only difference is in the nature of the *controls* of those surfaces. Thus, in this chapter, the evaporation process is described first, and then any important distinctions between different types of surfaces are discussed afterwards.

4.2 The process of evaporation

The physics of the evaporation process relate primarily to two aspects: (*a*) the provision of sufficient energy at the evaporating surface for the latent heat of vaporization, and (*b*) the operation of diffusion processes in the air above the evaporating surface to provide a means for removing the water vapour produced by evaporation.

In much simplified terms the evaporation process may be described as follows. The molecules in any mass of water, whether a large lake or a thin film on a soil grain, are in constant motion. Adding heat to the water causes the molecules to become increasingly energized and to move more rapidly, the result being an increase in the distance between liquid molecules and an associated weakening of the forces between them. At higher temperatures, therefore, more water molecules near the surface will be able to escape from the surface into the lower layers of the overlying air. In fact, all water surfaces are giving off water vapour to a greater or lesser extent. Similarly, however dry the atmosphere seems to be, it always contains some water vapour; the water molecules in the lower air layers are also in continual motion, and some of these will penetrate into the underlying mass of water. The partial pressure (or concentration) exerted by water vapour molecules in the atmosphere is termed the *water vapour pressure*. Partial pressures are generally used instead of concentrations so that changes in atmospheric pressure are taken into account. Water vapour pressures vary greatly, but are typically in the range 0.1 to 4 kPa, compared with the total atmospheric pressure of about 100 kPa (Oke, 1987; Trenberth, 1992).

The rate of evaporation at any given time will depend upon the balance

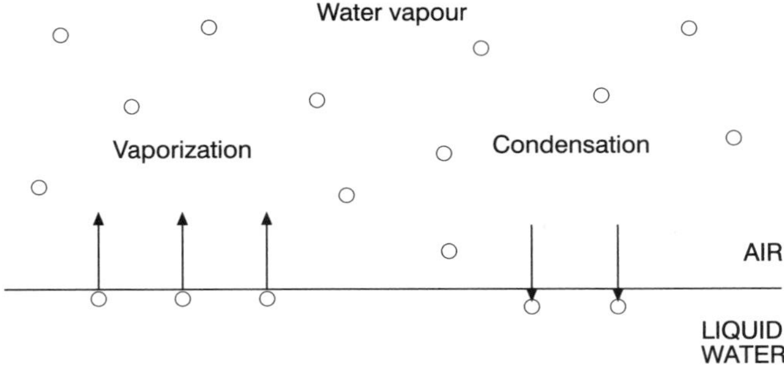

Figure 4.1 Evaporation is the net balance between the rate of vaporization of water molecules into the atmosphere, and the condensation rate of molecules from the atmosphere.

between the rate of *vaporization* of water molecules into the atmosphere and the *condensation* rate of molecules from the atmosphere (Figure 4.1). The former is determined by temperature and the latter by the vapour pressure above the surface. If more molecules are entering the air from the water surface than are returning, then evaporation is taking place; conversely if more molecules are returning to the water surface than are leaving it, condensation is said to be taking place.

In absolutely calm conditions, the net movement of water vapour molecules from an evaporating surface into the overlying air will progressively increase the water content of the lowest layers of the overlying air. This cannot continue indefinitely and eventually the vapour pressure increases until the rates of condensation and vaporization are equal, and evaporation ceases. The air is then said to be saturated. The vapour pressure exerted at saturation is called the *saturated (or saturation) vapour pressure*, SVP, and sometimes given the notation e^o. Normally, however, diffusion processes resulting from turbulence or convection mix the lowest layers with the overlying air, thereby effectively reducing the water vapour content and permitting further evaporation to take place. Warm air can hold more moisture than cold air, and the SVP increases approximately logarithmically with the air temperature having, for example, a value of 1.228 kPa at 10°C and 3.169 at 25°C.

Aristotle was the first to record that *both* the sun's heat and the wind are important in controlling evaporation, and it can be seen that for a given water surface the rate of evaporation will be controlled by a number of meteorological variables: the input of energy, the humidity of the air and the rate of movement of the air enabling the water vapour produced to move away from the evaporating surface.

Evaporation studies have centred on *thermodynamic* and *aerodynamic* approaches or a combination of the two. The former deals with the energy balance of the evaporating surface (providing the necessary latent heat), while the latter deals with the vapour flux from the evaporating surface.

4.2.1 Thermodynamic factors

The thermodynamic or energy balance approach to evaporation is concerned with estimating the latent energy available for water to change in state from a liquid to a gas. If the total amount of energy used in evaporation could be estimated, then by knowing the coefficient of latent heat it would be relatively simple to calculate the depth of water evaporated. This approach involves two main steps:

(a) determining the 'available energy' at the evaporating surface,
(b) apportioning this energy into latent and sensible heat transfers.

The application of the energy-balance approach to the estimation of evaporation from water surfaces was originally suggested by Angstrom (1920).

Of the available *net radiation*, R_n (incoming minus outgoing), some is used to heat the overlying air (H), some to heat the soil, water or vegetation surface (G), some is used for latent heat of evaporation (λE) and finally, a negligible part is used in plant growth.

An energy balance equation can, therefore, be written in the following terms:

$$R_n = H + \lambda E + G \tag{4.1}$$

where R_n may be determined using a net radiometer, and G from soil temperature measurements, but the convective sensible heat transfers (H) between the air and the water surface cannot be easily measured directly. The evaporation, E (mm), is multiplied by the coefficient of latent heat to convert it into units of energy. The second step of the energy balance approach is thus to determine the amount used in evaporation, E.

$$E = \frac{(R_n - H - G)}{\lambda} \tag{4.2}$$

Bowen (1926) proposed that the ratio of the sensible and latent heat fluxes ($H/\lambda E$), now termed the *Bowen ratio* β, may be determined from measurements of air temperature and vapour pressure at two levels, i.e.:

$$\beta = \frac{\gamma(T_s - T_a)}{(e_s - e_a)} \tag{4.3}$$

where γ is the so-called psychrometric 'constant' (which actually varies weakly with temperature), T_s is mean surface temperature, T_a is mean air temperature, e_s is saturation vapour pressure at the temperature, T_s, of the evaporating surface, and e_a is actual vapour pressure of the air at a given height (commonly one or two metres). This approach makes the assumption that the turbulent transfer coefficients of heat and water vapour by eddy diffusion are equal. Then,

$$E = \frac{(R_n - G)}{\lambda(1 + \beta)} \tag{4.4}$$

Values of β are low for areas where most radiation is used for evaporation, and

Table 4.1 Typical mean values of albedo for selected natural surfaces (based on data compiled by Lee, 1980; Brutsaert, 1982; Oke, 1987).

Surface	Condition	Albedo
Water	Zenith angle small to large	0.05–0.15
Snow	Old to fresh	0.30–0.90
Bare soil	Dark/wet to light/dry	0.05–0.35
Grass		0.20–0.30
Crops		0.15–0.25
Forest (deciduous)		0.15–0.20
Forest (coniferous)		0.05–0.15

high where water is limited and sensible heat transfer predominates. Thus, typical *average* values of β increase from 0.1 for tropical oceans and 0.1–0.3 for tropical wet jungles, to 0.4–0.8 for temperate forests and grassland and 2–6 for semi-arid areas and as high as 10 or more for deserts (Oke, 1987).

This approach demands accurate measurements of radiation, soil heat flux and vertical profiles of temperature and humidity. Although such measurements are relatively easily achieved in a research situation they impose substantial limitations for the application of the energy-balance approach to the routine calculation of evaporation.

The energy balance at the evaporating surface is materially influenced by the *albedo* of the surface, or the proportion of incoming radiation which is reflected back into the atmosphere. Typical values are shown in Table 4.1 for grass, agricultural crops and trees. It should be noted that the actual values change over time; the albedo varies with sun angle and hence the time of day, season and latitude, as illustrated in Figure 4.2. In general for a given sun angle and colour of vegetation, the albedo will be larger for tall than for short vegetation since there is more opportunity for absorption by multiple reflections within deeper canopies. The overall albedo of the earth's surface (land and oceans) is about 0.15 (the much higher planetary albedo of approximately 0.3, is due to the presence of clouds). In the absence of any information on the vegetation cover for an area, Shuttleworth (1993) recommended that the value 0.23 is used.

4.2.2 Aerodynamic factors

The aerodynamic (or vapour flow) approach deals with the upward diffusion of water vapour from the evaporating surface, and is concerned with the 'drying power' of the air, comprising its humidity and the rate at which water vapour can diffuse away from the evaporating surface into the atmosphere.

Generally speaking, the evaporation of water from a given surface is greatest in warm, dry conditions and least in cold, humid conditions, because when the air is warm, the saturation vapour pressure (e_s) of water is high, and when the air is dry,

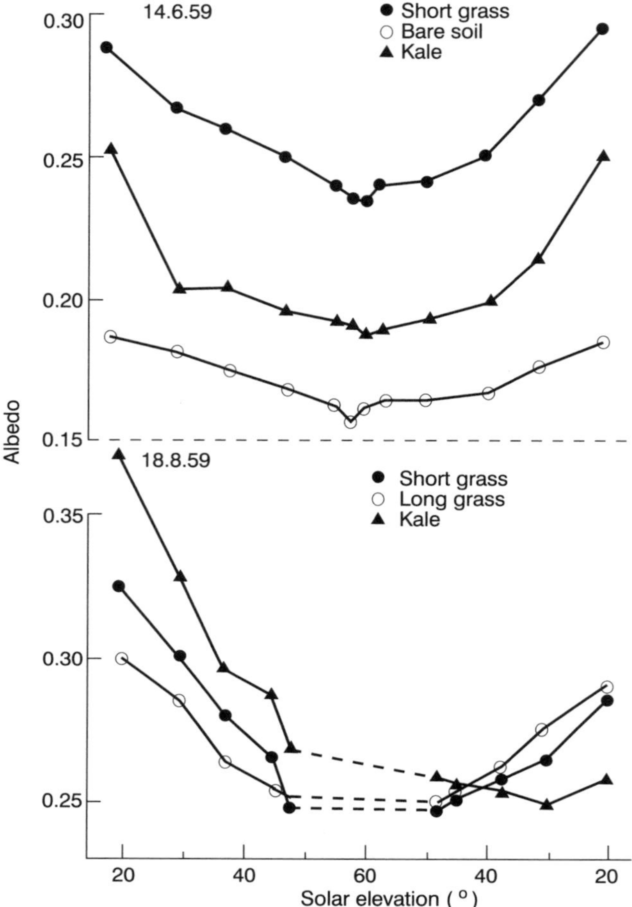

Figure 4.2 The albedo varies inversely with sun angle, here shown for three crops. Note also the enhanced albedo values after overnight dew on 18 August (based on an original diagram by Monteith and Szeicz, 1961).

the actual vapour pressure (e_a) of the water in the air is low. In other words, in warm, dry conditions the *saturation deficit* ($e_s - e_a$) is large and conversely in cold, moist conditions it is small. There is thus an underlying relationship between the size of the saturation deficit and the rate of evaporation.

Clearly, the stronger the wind, the more vigorous and the more effective will be the turbulent action in the air; and the greater the temperature difference between the surface and overlying air, the greater will be the effect of convection.

The aerodynamic approach to the evaporation from a wet surface was first expressed in quantitative terms by Dalton (1802), who suggested that if other factors remain constant, evaporation is proportional to the windspeed and the vapour pressure deficit, i.e. the difference between saturation vapour pressure at the temperature of the water surface and the actual vapour pressure of the overlying air. Dalton's law, although never expressed by the author in mathematical terms, has provided the starting point of much of the subsequent work on evaporation:

$$E = f(u)(e_s - e_a) \tag{4.5}$$

where $f(u)$ is a function of wind speed, e_s is the saturation vapour pressure at the surface, e_a is the actual vapour pressure of the free air at a reference height (commonly at 1 or 2 m).

In the lowest few millimetres of the atmosphere the air moves in straight lines or along smooth, regular curves in one direction, termed *laminar* motion. Above this layer, friction between the air and the ground surface induces eddies and whirls and air follows irregular, tortuous, fluctuating paths, termed *turbulent* motion, typified by cross-currents and gusts of wind with intervening brief lulls. This is the planetary boundary layer, where the depth and strength of turbulence are largely dependent upon the roughness of the ground surface and the strength of the wind. Convection due to frictional turbulence is the principal mechanism for transferring air properties, or *entities*, such as water vapour, momentum, heat and CO_2 through the atmosphere away from, or towards, the surface. The greater the intensity of turbulence, the more effectively are water vapour molecules dispersed or diffused upwards into the atmosphere.

The process by which these properties are transported through a fluid is known as *diffusion*. In the laminar boundary layer close to the surface vertical transfers take the form of molecular diffusion, while at a larger scale with wind blowing over a natural surface turbulent diffusion is of primary importance, and is the subject of the following discussion.

The vertical flux of any entity (s) over a vertical distance (z) is proportional to the concentration gradient (ds/dz):

$$\text{Flux} = -K\frac{ds}{dz} \tag{4.6}$$

The proportionality factor, K, is termed the turbulent transfer coefficient (or sometimes the turbulent eddy diffusivity). It is not a constant, but varies with the size of the eddies and the distance above the surface. Typical values range from about $10^{-5}\,m^2\,s^{-1}$ close to a surface up to $10^{+2}\,m^2\,s^{-1}$ well above the surface (Grace, 1983). Since its value is more dependent upon the characteristics of the turbulent motion than the particular entity being transported, micrometeorologists often use the greatly simplifying assumption, called the 'Similarity Principle', namely that the different entities are transported with equal facility, and so their K values are equal.

The turbulent mixing in the boundary layer acts to homogenize the air, since it transfers atmospheric properties (such as heat and water vapour) from places of high concentration to those of low concentration, and so acts to equalize them at all heights. Thus, water vapour added to the bottom of the boundary layer by evaporation will be dispersed and diffused upwards, under a gradient from highest moisture content of the air at the ground surface and lowest at the top of the turbulent layer. For a constant intensity of mixing, an increase in the rate of evaporation will be reflected in an increased moisture gradient in the boundary layer. Similarly, with a constant rate of evaporation, variation of moisture gradient will reflect changes in the intensity of mixing. Accordingly, it should be possible to determine the rate of evaporation from any surface by reference to the moisture gradient and the intensity of turbulent mixing. Measurements are needed of the moisture content and the windspeed at a minimum of two known heights within the turbulent layer.

The vertical flux of an entity, T, between heights a and b may also be considered in relation to a resistance to flow:

$$\text{Flux} = \frac{T_a - T_b}{r_a} \tag{4.7}$$

Where r_a is the *aerodynamic* or *boundary layer* resistance ($r_a = \int_a^b (1/K)\, dz$), which is a measure of the resistance encountered by water vapour moving from the outer surface of the vegetation cover into the surrounding atmosphere.

The degree of turbulence is closely related to wind velocity and surface roughness, although this frictional turbulence may be enhanced by convective turbulence where there is a suitable gradient in mean air temperature away from the evaporating surface.

The amount of convective mixing depends upon the *stability* of the atmosphere, which is controlled by the vertical temperature gradient of the air—the environmental lapse rate—ELR (see Section 2.1.1). If the ELR is similar to the dry adiabatic lapse rate, DALR (about 0.98°C per 100 m) a parcel of air that is transported upwards (or downwards) by turbulence will change in temperature and hence its density in a similar manner to the surrounding air. This is termed *neutral* stability and the turbulent transfer is by *forced convection*, i.e. due to external pressure gradients. These conditions tend to occur around sunset and sunrise and on dull days and cloudy nights (Grace, 1983).

On the other hand if the vertical air temperature gradient differs from the DALR, then there is an additional buoyancy-generated turbulence effect due to *free convection*. Depending upon the vertical temperature profile this may *enhance* (unstable conditions) or *reduce* (stable conditions) the amount of turbulent transfer. Under unstable conditions (ELR > DALR) a parcel of air displaced upwards cools less rapidly than the ELR and so remains lighter than its surroundings and will continue to rise. In these conditions vertical movements of eddies are enhanced. Conversely, under stable conditions a rising air parcel cools more rapidly than its surroundings and so its vertical movement is dampened.

Air stability varies diurnally; normally, the ELR increases during the day-time, reaching a maximum in the early afternoon. The associated convectional activity and the increased buoyancy of the air together reinforce the degree of turbulence and deepen the planetary boundary layer to as much as 1–2 km. At night, in contrast, the ground surface cools and lapse conditions are normally replaced by an inversion of temperature. This decreases the buoyancy of the air, damps down convectional activity and effectively suppresses the turbulent motion of the air until, on calm nights, an almost laminar flow is experienced.

4.3 Estimation of evaporation

Despite the crucial importance of evaporation in the hydrological cycle, it is inherently difficult to measure and quantify, and it remains the most difficult component of the water balance to determine with any accuracy (Oliver, 1983). Unlike some other hydrological variables, such as runoff or rainfall, which can be measured directly, evaporation is generally estimated indirectly. Some direct methods have recently been developed, and are outlined below, but they are not widely used outside of the research community.

There are two broad approaches to the measurement of evaporation (Shuttleworth, 1993). The simplest and earliest estimates involved measuring the *loss of liquid water at the surface*, while more recent and complex methods determine the vertical *flux of water vapour* (or latent heat) through the air.

4.3.1 Liquid water loss

There are several traditional methods for measuring liquid water loss (for example Shaw, 1994). Each has its limitations and disadvantages. The *atmometer* comprises a small water-filled reservoir from which water evaporates through a porous material simulating an evaporating surface. The water loss from the moist surface provides an indication of the drying power of the air, but the results are not convertible to a depth of water loss over the ground. A more useful quantitative measure may be obtained from an *evaporation pan*, a tank of water open to the air. By making regular measurements of changes in water levels and by correcting for rainfall and for any water added or removed (to maintain the water level in a certain range) the water loss due to evaporation may be derived (WMO, 1994). Due to their simplicity of manufacture and operation, evaporation pans have been widely used, and there are over 20 different designs worldwide. Some pans, including the most widely used type, the US Weather Service 'Class A' pan, stand above the ground while others are sunk in the ground with their rims a few centimetres above the surface. Unfortunately due to their small surface area (typically 1–3 m^3) all designs of pans exaggerate lake evaporation. Furthermore, this is in a non-consistent manner; not only are they subject to problems of radiation on the sides of a raised pan and variable heat flow from the ground for a sunken pan, they also suffer from advection. Consequently it is necessary to apply an empirical pan coefficient to reduce the values to match those of the surrounding lake or vegetation. The annual value of the 'Class A' pan coefficient for transfer to lakes is often assumed to be around 0.7 (Winter, 1981) but this varies enormously between years and between sites, and the variation is greater over shorter periods such as individual months (Oroud, 1998). Pans provide an even poorer indication of the evaporation from a land surface than for open water bodies, due to several differences including albedo, surface roughness, and thermal storage. Nevertheless, they are still widely used, particularly in developing countries. Doorenbos and Pruitt (1977) provide guidance for the selection of pan coefficients to estimate crop water transpiration—values range from 0.4 to 0.85 depending upon site conditions.

Another technique is to construct a water balance for a hydrologically isolated block of soil and vegetation termed a *lysimeter*. The simplest design is a drum packed with excavated soil, but this may differ substantially in behaviour from undisturbed soil and vegetation. A better situation is where a permeable soil overlies a naturally impermeable layer such as a heavy clay, allowing a wall or membrane to be installed in a trench cut down to the clay base. Evaporation may then be calculated from a mass balance of the difference between precipitation and drainage from the base of the block, together with measurements of changes in soil water storage. This approach may provide accurate measurements but it is difficult and expensive to install and maintain, may be subject to unmeasured leaks and it relies on evaporation being derived as the residual between precipitation/irrigation and drainage, each subject to measurement errors. Nevertheless, the water balance approach using carefully sited and operated lysimeters, and sometimes extended to whole catchment studies, has provided some of the most useful and validated evidence of evaporation rates and their changes due to alterations in vegetation or land use (see also Section 9.3).

There are other more specialized techniques for the measurement of transpiration. The stomatal conductance of individual leaves may be measured using a porometer, although this is notoriously labour intensive. The velocity of sap movement within individual plant stems may be measured using the heat balance and heat pulse techniques (Swanson, 1994; Smith and Allen, 1996), and the transpiration of whole plants may be obtained by the use of deuterium tracing (Calder *et al.*, 1992). All the methods suffer from the problem of extrapolating from a sample of individual trees to a whole forest stand.

4.3.2 Water vapour flow

The most fundamental approach is to measure the vertical transfer of water vapour away from the evaporating surface within the turbulent boundary layer. If the measurements are made close to the surface then the measured upward vapour flow rate is a good approximation to the surface exchange rate.

There are two basic approaches (Oke, 1987): the *profile* or *flux gradient* methods which are based on measurements of vertical *gradients*, and the *eddy fluctuation* or *eddy correlation* method which measures water vapour *flux* directly.

(a) The *profile measurement methods* rely on the assumption that over an extensive homogenous surface turbulent eddies will transfer momentum, heat and water vapour with equal facility, and so their transfer coefficients may be assumed to be equal over a given height range. This may be used in either of two ways.

First, the aerodynamic profile method measures the difference in two properties over a height range and by knowing the flux of one of them the flux of the other may be obtained. Thus by measuring horizontal windspeed at two heights and the flux of wind shear stress—and assuming an equivalent resistance to water vapour and temperature as for momentum—the latent heat flux may be obtained from measurements of vapour pressure at the same heights, and similarly the sensible heat flux by measurements of air temperature at the two levels. This approach requires accurate measurements, and in practice measurements at more than just two heights are advisable. The assumption of neutral stability (no buoyancy effects) restricts the conditions under which it may be used.

Second, the Bowen ratio or energy balance profile method makes the less restrictive assumption that the transfer coefficients of water vapour (K_v) and sensible heat (K_h) are similar, but may differ from that of momentum (K_m). Hence this approach is not restricted to neutral conditions. It apportions the available energy, R_n, between sensible and latent heat according to the ratio β:

$$Q_E = \frac{R_n - G}{1 + \beta} \tag{4.8}$$

It requires accurate measurements of net radiation, air temperature and humidity at two heights (to calculate β from Eq. 4.3), plus soil heat flux, G. It provides a more accurate measurement than the aerodynamic approach. Care must be taken over rough surfaces, such as a forest canopy; since there will be much turbulent mixing, the vertical gradients will be much smaller than over a smooth surface. Limitations on the accuracy of the instrumentation (for example temperature discrimination to 10^{-3}°C) necessitate measurements over a large height range, perhaps equivalent to the height of the forest. Problems in measuring soil heat flux were described by Passerat de Silans *et al.*, 1997).

In both of these methods flux determinations are normally applied to mean gradients over periods of at least 30 minutes duration to smooth out random fluctuations, and so they are unsuitable for situations where mean fluxes over shorter time periods are required (Monteith and Unsworth, 1990). The rate of evaporation is determined on the basis of very small humidity and windspeed differences over a narrow height range within the boundary layer. Consequently, the frequency and the accuracy of the instrumental observations must be very high.

(b) The *eddy flux* or *eddy correlation approach* is the most direct measure of water vapour flux with minimum theoretical assumptions and so is the preferred micrometeorological technique (Shuttleworth, 1993). The measurement of fluxes of water vapour (or sensible heat) in turbulent air requires the instantaneous and simultaneous measurement of vertical velocity and vapour density (or air temperature). Thus, for water vapour to be transferred upwards by turbulent air motion it is necessary that *on average* the upward moving air is moister than the corresponding down currents.

This approach was first proposed by Swinbank (1951), and experimental systems have been in existence for many years (for example Taylor and Dyer, 1958; McIlroy, 1971), but it is only since the late 1980s that developments in the necessary sensor accuracy and computing capacity have resulted in reliable systems that may be used for long periods. The UK Institute of Hydrology's Hydra (Shuttleworth *et al.*, 1988) is an eddy correlation system comprising an ultrasonic anemometer together with humidity and temperature sensors linked to a microprocessor to enable analysis of measurements as they are made in the field. This was the first compact portable instrument used in field studies around the world, using on-line digital calculation of fluxes with a low-power microprocessor. Subsequent developments include consideration of fully three-dimensional air movements to provide measurements over rough terrain, and consideration of CO_2 fluxes. Moncrieff *et al.* (1997) described a similar system based on commercially available sensors.

Such instruments must sense virtually every variation in the vertical wind velocity and the entity under study (heat or humidity), and be able to process and integrate very large amounts of data. The necessary response time depends upon the size of the eddies. Over a rough forest with large wind eddies sensors capable of operating at a frequency of 0.1–10 Hz would be adequate, whereas over a smoother surface a frequency response of 0.001 Hz might be needed (Monteith and Unsworth, 1990).

Much of the essential instrumentation for such measurements lacks standardization, is demanding in terms of maintenance and routine observing techniques and is expensive. Due to the specialist data requirements attention for routine evaporation estimates has therefore focused on ways in which evaporation may be estimated from empirical or semi-empirical models of the evaporating system, in which the model input comprises readily available, routine meteorological measurements. Modelling and estimation of evaporation, especially of total evaporation from a vegetation-covered surface, is the normal method of quantifying evaporation amounts.

Measurement representativeness

All of these approaches to the measurement of evaporation from water, soil or vegetated surfaces, together with the theoretical approaches discussed in the remainder of this chapter, suffer from the overriding problem of point sample representativeness, and most of them suffer also from the distorting effects of advection which is inversely proportional to the size of sample evaporating surface. Often, therefore, it is difficult to know what these measurements mean in terms of a valid representation of areal evaporation at a field, catchment or regional scale. However, Gash (1986) derived a simple method of estimating the areal sample of micrometeorological measurements as a function of measurement height and aerodynamic roughness.

4.4 Evaporation from different surfaces

As noted earlier, the physics of evaporation is the same regardless of the evaporating surface, but different surfaces impose different controls on the process. These differences are discussed below for three broad surface types: open water, bare soil and vegetation.

4.4.1 Open water

An open water surface is the simplest situation, with little limitation on evaporation. The supply of water is by definition, so plentiful that it exerts no limiting influence on the rate of water loss. Accordingly, evaporation rates from lakes may be very high—as much as 2000 mm yr^{-1} in some arid areas (Van der Leeden *et al.*, 1990), and this must be taken into account when, for example, planning a new reservoir since the additional loss of water from the open water surface will offset to some extent the increase in water supply from the reservoir.

The rate of open water evaporation is determined by a number of factors, both meteorological (energy, humidity, wind) and physical (especially the size of water body), in accordance with the factors outlined earlier controlling the evaporation process.

Evaporation rates broadly follow variations in radiation, modified by considerations of heat storage in the water body. Evaporation may increase as the air temperature rises, and is able to hold a larger amount of water vapour below the saturation level. Air movement is necessary to remove the lowest moist air layers in contact with the water surface and to mix them with the upper drier layers, so that the rate of evaporation is almost always influenced to some extent by turbulent air movement. In fact, the relationship between windspeed and evaporation holds good only up to a certain speed, above which further increases lead to no further increase in evaporation since evaporation is then limited by the energy and humidity conditions.

For a given water body the rate of evaporation under identical meteorological conditions may vary as a result of physical differences, the most important of which is the water surface area.

Size of water surface

As air moves from the land across a large lake there will initially be high evaporation and then as the humidity of the air increases and its temperature decreases, the rate of evaporation will decrease. The larger the lake, the greater will be the total reduction in the depth of water evaporated, although of course the total volume of water evaporated may well increase with the size of the water surface.

For an extensive water surface, such as the oceans, the humidity of the air will be largely independent of the distance it has travelled, except in coastal areas. Consequently evaporation will be uniform over extensive areas and will be closely related to the amount of heat energy available. At the other extreme, small water surfaces such as evaporation pans exert little influence on the temperature or humidity of the overlying air. The small amount of water vapour which leaves the surface, even with high rates of evaporation, is quickly diffused so that a continuous high rate of evaporation is maintained. This enhanced local evaporation has been termed the 'oasis' effect. Consequently there is an inverse relationship between the evaporation rate and the size of the evaporating surface. This difference is greatest if the humidity of the incoming air is low.

Water depth

The effect of water depth upon the seasonal distribution of evaporation may be quite considerable, due to the thermal capacity of water and to the mixing of waters. The seasonal temperature regime of a shallow lake will normally approximate closely to the seasonal air temperature regime, so that maximum rates of evaporation will occur during the summer and minimum rates during the winter. For large, deep lakes, however, there may be a time lag of several months; during the spring and summer, heat entering the water surface is mixed downward and evaporation is lower than for a shallow water body. In winter, however, the water may be warmer than the air and heat stored in the lake may be released for evaporation to take place at rates higher than would be expected from meteorological measurements. The problem of heat storage is crucial for short-term estimates, and requires regular measurements of the temperature profile of the water. Over the course of a year, however, there will be little net change in heat storage and the total annual evaporation is little altered.

Salinity

If a substance is dissolved in a liquid, the motion of the liquid molecules is restricted and the vapour pressure of the liquid is lowered ('Raoult's law'). Thus, salinity may affect evaporation rates since the SVP over saline water is lower than over pure water. Evaporation decreases by about 1 per cent for each 1 per cent increase in salinity. Accordingly, evaporation from sea water (average salinity of about 35 parts per thousand, or gram kg^{-1}), is about 2–3 per cent less than evaporation from fresh water. Although this effect is normally small enough to be discounted when comparing evaporation rates from different 'fresh' water bodies, it may be important for very saline waters, such as brackish lakes, for example the Dead Sea (Calder and Neal, 1984).

Evaporation from snow

It is now generally accepted that evaporation rates from snow-covered land are generally very low. This may be contrasted with the situation already noted for snow interception (see Section 3.7). Lying snow generally occurs at locations and times of the year when radiation inputs and air temperatures are low; furthermore, snow cover has a high albedo and a generally smooth surface which inhibits turbulent transfer of heat and water vapour (Calder, 1986). Evaporation can occur only when the vapour pressure of the air is less than that of the snow surface; evaporation from snow will cease when the dew point rises to 0°C, and as temperatures rise above freezing, the rate of snowmelt must exceed the rate of evaporation. Since approximately ten times greater energy is required to sublimate snow (change from solid to vapour) than just to melt it, the mass of water melted and available as runoff is substantially greater than the amount evaporated.

4.4.2 Evaporation from bare soils

Evaporation from a soil surface comprises the evaporation of films of water surrounding the soil grains and filling the spaces between them, and is governed by the same meteorological factors as the loss from a free water surface. However, the rate of evaporation from soils is often less than that from a free water surface under the same meteorological conditions because the supply of water in the soil may be limited by the amount of water in the soil and by the ability of the soil to transmit water to the surface. These factors are discussed in more detail in Chapter 6 (soil water) and are only briefly described here.

In semi-arid areas, with sparse natural vegetation, soil evaporation may be a major component of the total evaporation (Jacobs and Verhoef, 1997; Kabat *et al.*, 1997). In contrast, for well watered and vegetated areas, such as north western Europe, the evaporation from plants will generally provide most of the total evaporation. Exceptions include bare ploughed land and areas of immature, widely spaced crops, where evaporation from the soil surface may deplete the surface soil water and potentially affect the growth and yield of the crop.

The water content of the surface layers of bare soil exerts the most direct influence on evaporation rates. Evaporation decreases rapidly after rainfall as the surface water content falls until, with a dry soil surface, it is zero. In the absence of plant roots, the upward movement of soil water to the surface from the wet layers beneath is controlled by capillarity and will, therefore, tend to vary with soil properties. In fine-textured soil, with small intergranular pores, capillary movement may be effective over large vertical distances, such as a metre or more, whereas in coarse-textured sand it may be only a few centimetres. However, the speed of water movement tends to vary inversely with the height of capillary lift so that, in neither case where special conditions prevail, does the supply of water to the soil surface by capillary activity increase significantly the total amount of evaporation.

In areas with hot, dry, soil surfaces water vapour gradients are built up in the soil air, and water vapour may be transported up to the surface. The thickness of the evaporation zone will be greater in fine-textured soils (Yamanaka *et al.*, 1998). Soil colour will tend to affect evaporation; darker soils will absorb more heat than lighter soils and the resulting rise in surface temperature may increase the evaporation rate. The rainfall regime is also important for soil water replenishment, in just the same way as for the loss of water intercepted on vegetation foliage. On average evaporation from a soil surface will be greater if it is frequently wetted by intermittent showers than occasionally soaked by the same quantity of rain falling in a few large storms.

The most commonly used model of bare soil evaporation is that of Ritchie (1972), which comprises two phases. Following rainfall, evaporation initially proceeds at a maximum rate, and subsequently it declines as a function of time.

Remote sensing

Remote sensing has a potentially important role in providing areal estimates of evaporation for a wide range of scales from individual fields to major river basins. Evaporation cannot be directly measured by remote sensing techniques, and most current techniques combine variables that are relatively easy to measure (such as reflected solar radiation and surface temperatures) with additional ground-based meteorological measurements, in order to complete the energy balance. A review of the main approaches was given by Moran and Jackson (1991) and Rango (1994). Examples of the use of GOES imagery were discussed by Leith and Solomon (1985) and of Meteosat and NOAA thermal infrared imagery by Seguin *et al.* (1985). Figure 4.3 shows an example of daily evaporation mapping at a field/farm scale in the Netherlands which was based on infrared line scanning, reported by Soer (1980).

4.4.3 Evaporation from vegetation covers

The hydrologist's greatest interest in evaporation losses concerns those from vegetated surfaces, including agricultural crops and natural vegetation. It has been emphasized earlier that the total evaporation from vegetation comprises the *sum* of the evaporation of intercepted water from the wet surface of the vegetation (see Chapter 3) and transpiration by plants. The transpiration system provides a particular example of the evaporation process in which water is evaporated from plant tissues.

Transpiration is closely linked to *photosynthesis*, which is an essential process by which plants form carbohydrates, which are fundamental to the life of plants. For most plants the overall reaction can be written as:

$$6CO_2 + 12H_2O = C_6H_{12}O_6 + 6O_2 + 6H_2O \tag{4.9}$$

Figure 4.3 An example of daily evaporation mapping using remotely sensed crop surface temperatures for an area near Losser in the Netherlands (reproduced with permission from G.R.J. Soer, 1980, Estimation of regional transpiration and soil moisture conditions using remotely sensed crop surface temperatures, *Remote Sensing of the Environment*, **9:** 27–45, Elsevier Science Publishing Co.).

Thus, the plant takes in CO_2 from the air and combines it with water to produce carbohydrate, and O_2 is lost from the plant as a gaseous byproduct.

The photosynthetic tissue, the mesophyll, in the leaf is protected by an outer epidermis which consolidates the leaf structure and protects the inner tissues from physical damage, from attack by micro-organisms, and also from desiccation. Numerous small pores called *stomata* (singular *stoma*) on the leaf enable the diffusion of CO_2 and O_2 during photosynthesis, but they also allow the loss of water vapour from a plant.

Figure 4.4 illustrates the complexity of transpiration for a single plant in a vegetation-covered surface, and shows that it is dependent upon a sequence of water-moving processes. Soil, plant and atmosphere form parts of a continuous flowpath of varying resistances in which water moves at varying rates and undergoes both chemical and phase changes. Water at a point in the soil profile

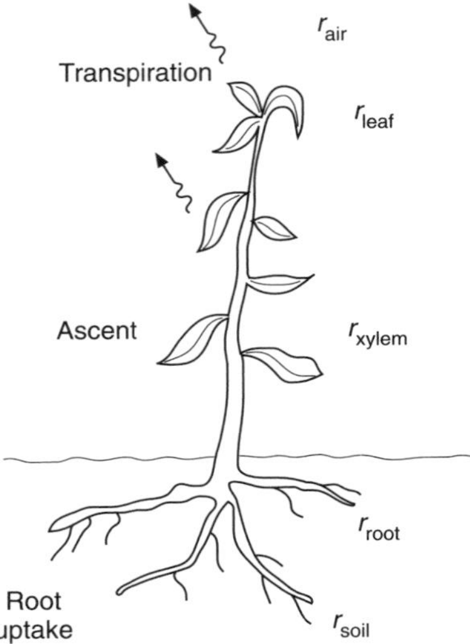

Figure 4.4 The transpiration stream for a single plant in a vegetation-covered surface, showing some of the main resistances to water movement.

moves under the influence of a moisture gradient towards the root hairs, is there absorbed and then travels up the plant stem through the *xylem*, which is a low-resistance hydraulic conductor, to the plant leaves from where it is finally vaporized in the stomatal cavities of the leaves before passing through the stomatal apertures to the atmosphere.

Transpiration—a necessary evil?

Very little of the water taken up by plant roots is actually retained for growth, most is lost in transpiration. This loss of water vapour occurs along the reverse pathway to the uptake of CO_2 in photosynthesis.

Transpiration has been called a 'necessary evil' because the assimilation of CO_2 from the atmosphere requires intensive gas exchange while the prevention of excessive water loss requires gas exchange to be kept low (Raschke, 1976). Nevertheless, transpiration is an effective way to cool a plant in hot weather (due to the heat used up in latent heat of vaporization) and the movement of water transports nutrients through the plant.

Plants can control water loss by varying the opening of the stomatal apertures. Thus, one of the consequences of water shortage in plants is a reduced uptake of CO_2, which results in a reduction in the rate of plant growth, and the need for irrigation in agricultural crops.

Cell water potentials

Cells are the basic structural elements in plants and control the fundamental plant response to water as it moves through plants. The cell wall is porous and water moves across a series of cells due to water potential gradients. This alone would be too slow to replace the water lost by transpiration, if it were not for the vital role of *osmosis*. This is the flow of water across a membrane separating two solutions of different concentrations. The *water potential*, ψ, in a plant cell may be considered as:

$$\psi = \pi + P \tag{4.10}$$

where π is osmotic potential, P is the internal cell wall pressure potential or *turgor*. At times of extreme water shortage, turgor pressure may be reduced to zero, causing the leaves to become limp or flaccid, and the plant condition may be said to be 'wilting'.

Leaves maintain a low water potential by accumulating a high concentration of salts in their cell sap, which results in a large negative osmotic potential. This is partially offset by the positive turgor potential. During active transpiration the leaf cells partially dehydrate, decreasing the turgor potential, and the cell sap concentrations increase, which in turn causes the osmotic potential to become more negative. The combined effect is to lower the water potential within the leaf cells. Thus, the loss of water vapour by transpiration from the leaves generates a reduction in the water potential, which acts as a suction force which is transmitted from cell to cell right through the system from the leaf to the root and is capable of drawing up water through even the highest trees against the force of gravity. Water potentials in plants are analogous to soil water potential discussed in detail in Chapter 6.

The flow of water from soil to leaves along a gradient of decreasing water potential, ψ, occurs against a series of resistances to movement (for example from soil to root, root to leaf, leaf to atmosphere). Each may be represented by the general transport equation:

$$\text{Flux} = \frac{\psi_1 - \psi_2}{r} \tag{4.11}$$

where r is termed the *resistance*. For a system comprising a sequence of resistances *in series*, such as a whole plant, the total resistance (R) is, by analogy with Ohm's law, simply the sum of the individual resistances (i.e. $R = r_1 + r_2 + r_3 \ldots$). In plant physiology it is often convenient to replace the resistance by its reciprocal the *conductance*, g (i.e. $g = 1/r$), since for a number of resistances *in parallel*, such as individual leaves, the overall canopy conductance is the sum of the individual conductances, (i.e. $G = g_1 + g_2 + g_3 \ldots$). Then for a given difference in water potential, the flux is directly proportional to the conductance.

Considering a *steady-state* situation the transpiration flow through the series of resistances will be equal; thus:

$$\text{Flux} = \frac{\psi_s - \psi_l}{r_p} = \frac{\psi_l - \psi_a}{r_g} \tag{4.12a}$$

$$= \frac{\psi_s - \psi_a}{r_p + r_g} \tag{4.12b}$$

where the water potential is ψ_s at the soil–root interface, ψ_l in the leaf, and ψ_a in the air; and the resistances are in the plant, r_p, and the gas phase, r_g. Although this is an over-simplification, since it assumes steady-state flow and constant resistances (conditions that seldom occur in practice), it provides a useful model of water flow in plants. By assigning reasonable values to the potentials at different points in the system, the relative importances of the different resistances in controlling the transpiration flux can be illustrated (for example Weatherley, 1976). Thus, if the soil water is at saturation (i.e. $\psi_s = 0$), the leaf water potential, $\psi_l = -2$ MPa, and the water potential of the air, $\psi_a = -100$ MPa (relative humidity $\sim$ 50 per cent), substituting these values in Eq. 4.12a indicates $r_g/r_p \sim 50$. This indicates that the resistance of the gas phase is very much larger than that of the plant, and consequently will have the controlling influence on transpiration.

Most physicists studying the transpiration process ascribed 'primary' control to the stomata, although in some conditions it is the root resistance that is the most important link in the transpiration flow. Some studies have shown that the stomatal opening is controlled by the leaf water status, while in other cases root water status appears to be the more important (Kramer and Boyer, 1995).

The factors affecting transpiration from vegetation covers are numerous and will vary in importance depending on conditions. Discussion here will concentrate on two main vegetational influences on evaporation, i.e. stomatal control and root water uptake.

Stomatal control

On average stomata occupy about 1 per cent of the total leaf area for a wide range of plant species (Monteith and Unsworth, 1990). They generally occur only on the *abaxial* surface (underside) of leaves. They may be completely absent from the upper, *adaxial*, leaf surface, especially in broad-leaved trees. Each stoma consists of a pair of elongated guard cells surrounding the stomatal aperture. The cells in the walls of the aperture are usually impregnated with water as the gases CO_2 and O_2 involved in photosynthesis can only be utilized in solution, in which state they travel within the plant by diffusion. As water evaporates from these walls the water vapour pressure in the stomatal cavity increases and diffusion of water vapour molecules takes place through the stomata into the external air.

Stomata combine an efficient means of gas exchange, needed in photosynthesis, with a means to limit the risk of damage to the plant from losing water. The size of the stomatal aperture can be varied by changes in the turgor of the guard cells. When guard cell turgor is low the pore closes. Since stomata are primarily photosynthesis structures, they are extremely sensitive to changes in light intensity. Thus, in the majority of plants there is a diurnal pattern to stomatal movements; they open during the daytime (for photosynthesis) and close at night when it is dark to avoid unnecessary water loss when photosynthesis would not be taking place. They are also sensitive to atmospheric CO_2 concentrations, opening if concentrations reduce.

The *stomatal resistance* of a leaf (r_1), is a physiological resistance imposed by the vegetation itself and is considered further in Section 4.5.1.

In general, the stomatal control of vapour diffusion is associated with the maintenance of leaf turgidity. However, the factors affecting stomatal resistance are varied and an understanding of the trigger mechanisms has emerged only slowly. These were discussed by Federer (1975) and Sharkey and Ogawa (1987), and include the pumping of potassium ions into the guard cells, the effect of carbon dioxide concentration and the role of abscisic acid. The effect of light appears to differ little among species, with stomata achieving full opening in one-tenth of full sunlight (for example Turner and Begg, 1973). On sunny days, therefore, the stomatal resistance on exposed leaves decreases rapidly at sunrise, remains at a minimum value all day if the water supply to the leaf is adequate and increases at sunset (Federer, 1975).

Physiological factors may be very important causes of interspecies variation in r_1. The low rate of transpiration from heather, for example, is caused by its large stomatal resistance ($\sim$ 50–170 s m^{-1} according to Wallace *et al.*, 1984; Miranda *et al.*, 1984). This results from the stomata occurring only on the abaxial side of the leaves in a groove lined with fine hairs, so that free movement of water vapour is impaired (Hall, 1987).

As transpiration occurs, the leaf water potential declines, thus causing increased inflow of water from regions of higher potential in the stems, roots and soil. If the soil is sufficiently moist, minimum values of resistance (i.e. maximum conductance) may be maintained throughout the day, and evaporation is controlled by meteorological factors. However, when evaporation from the leaves exceeds the rate of water supply to them through the soil–stem system, a critical leaf water potential is reached, at which stomata begin to close, thereby limiting further water loss. This critical value may depend on plant type and history and on leaf location, i.e. leaves in the upper canopy may have lower values, so that leaves in the lower canopy experience earlier stomatal closure (Stevenson and Shaw, 1971), implying a preferential water supply to the more exposed leaves in the upper canopy (Federer, 1975). The stomatal resistance increases above the minimum value and water shortage reduces actual evaporation below the potential rate via the mechanism of stomatal control. Exactly *when* this occurs is still not clear but, as Federer (1975) observed, 'It is the classic question of availability of soil water stated in terms of stomatal control'. It illustrates clearly the difficulty of distinguishing between meteorological, plant and soil influences on evaporation.

The divergence of evidence appears to be wide, ranging from work that showed stomatal control of evaporation in wet soil conditions (for example Shepherd, 1972; McNaughton and Black, 1973) to other studies in which evaporation appeared not to be reduced below the potential rate until *very* low values of soil water content had been attained (for example Veihmeyer, 1972; Ritchie, 1973). This apparently conflicting evidence was reviewed by Turner (1986).

Given that the soil–plant–atmosphere system is characterized by great variability of water content in space and time, it is perhaps not too surprising that different vegetation types, growing in different soil and atmospheric conditions, will limit evaporation at different values of soil water status. Indeed, it might be argued that much more remarkable is the similarity of transpiration from different forest species in Europe noted by Roberts (1983; 1999) and explained in terms of a possible similarity both of r_{l-min} and also of the relationship between r_l and atmospheric humidity. Roberts further suggested that similar r_{l-min} values in European forests might result from tree species being genetically adapted to similar soil water conditions.

There is also a sense in which the integration of the complex heterogeneity of, say, water potentials and surface resistances of individual leaves imposes a certain homogeneity on the system as a whole. Thus evaporation from a vegetation canopy is the sum of the evaporation losses from the much larger area of all the individual leaf surfaces. If the *leaf area index*, L, is the surface area of all the leaves in a unit area of land, and if $\bar{r}_l$ is the mean surface resistance of the leaves then the overall surface resistance of the canopy r_c (also called the *canopy resistance* or the *bulk surface resistance*) may be regarded as:

$$r_c = \frac{\bar{r}_l}{L} \tag{4.13}$$

This has been described as the 'overall physiological control of transpiration' (Lee, 1980). Since except for very sparse vegetation cover the leaf area index is usually greater than unity, the bulk stomatal resistance is generally much lower than the leaf stomatal resistance. It should be noted that while it is a commonly employed technique (for example Szeicz *et al.*, 1973), dividing the mean r_l for the canopy by the leaf area index represents a gross simplification. It makes no allowance for canopy structure and microclimatological interaction between the individual leaves, such as the reduction in radiation to the lower canopy. The relation of mean r_l to r_c is thus a 'major gap' in knowledge (Federer, 1979).

In practice, since L is difficult and laborious to calculate, the two measures of stomatal control at leaf and canopy scales are generally derived independently (Kelliher *et al.*, 1975); r_l may be obtained from porometry on individual leaves, while r_c for canopies is commonly obtained by inverting the Penman–Monteith equation (see Section 4.6.2).

There is scope for considerable inconsistency in the different terms used in the literature, and the symbols used in various publications. Table 4.2 attempts to clarify this.

Table 4.2 Nomenclature and symbols for the different resistance terms for water vapour movement used in this text. Note that there is great inconsistency in the use of these symbols: in some cases r_s is used for the canopy resistance, while in others it is used for the leaf stomatal resistance. In practice there is generally little difference in the numerical values of canopy resistance and surface resistance.

Resistance	*Description*
Aerodynamic resistance, r_a	Varies with vegetation height and wind speed.
Stomatal (or surface resistance), for individual leaves, r_l	Obtained from porometry on individual leaves.
Canopy (or bulk surface resistance), r_c	Obtained from scaling up from r_l using the Leaf Area Index.
Surface resistance, r_s	Obtained by back calculation from Penman–Monteith equation and meteorological readings. Includes non-physiological resistances (e.g. soil and litter). Thus, $r_s = r_c + r_{soil}$.

The stomatal resistance continually varies over time due to factors, especially changing light intensity. Smith *et al.* (1985) found that r_c for well-irrigated wheat varied significantly with the leaf area index and vapour pressure deficit, as shown in Figure 4.5. Similarly, Stewart (1988) derived semi-empirical relations between r_c and meteorological factors for a pine forest.

For many purposes it is the *minimum* resistance or *maximum* conductance (the inverse of resistance), rather than the average value that is of most significance when comparing transpiration of different vegetation. Table 4.3 compares average values of maximum stomatal conductance for major world vegetation types.

Root control

The preceding review of stomatal control emphasized the necessity of adequate soil–plant water supply to the leaves to maintain leaf water potential above critical levels. Indeed, traditional treatments of the subject tended to treat the roots as inert, uniform sinks for soil water, although subsequently this passivity has been questioned (Turner, 1986; Monteith, 1985).

Attention has turned to the possibility that under some situations it is the roots rather than leaves which may act as the primary sensors of water stress. It appears that a water shortage to the roots may cause changes in root metabolism, such as an increase in abscisic acid production and a disturbance in nitrate metabolism, which can send biochemical signals to the plant leaves leading to physiological changes, including a decrease in stomatal conductance and rate of photosynthesis, *regardless* of the current leaf water potential (Kramer and Boyer, 1995). Conversely, the shoots of plants in areas with adequate soil water are nevertheless often subject to water stress on sunny days, and under those conditions it seems doubtful that roots can be the primary sensors of water

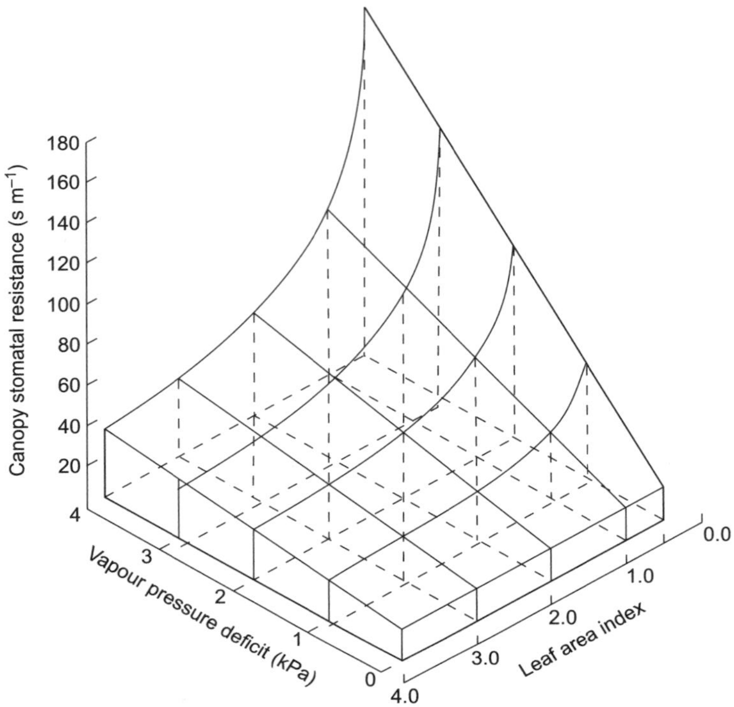

Figure 4.5 The canopy resistance of a crop varies significantly with the leaf area index and vapour pressure deficit (Smith *et al.*, 1985)

Table 4.3 Average maximum values for stomatal conductance ($mm\,s^{-1}$). (Values from Kelliher *et al.*, 1975.)

Vegetation type	*Individual leaf,* g_{max}	*Bulk vegetation,* G_{max}
Temperate grass	8	17
Cereals	11	32.5
Conifers	5.7	21.2
Deciduous	4.6	20.7
Tropical rainforest	6.1	13
Eucalyptus	5.3	17

stress. Some of the opposing arguments were presented in a series of discussion articles by Kramer (1988), Passioura (1988) and Schulze *et al.* (1988).

The uptake of water by plants during dry weather leads to a reduction in soil water around each root and a consequent fall in soil conductivity, which will considerably increase the resistance to liquid flow. The extent and efficiency of the root system should help to determine the total amount of water available to the plant cover and the rapidity with which, in drying conditions, the rate of actual evaporation falls below the potential rate (see Section 4.6.1).

Absorption of water by roots occurs along gradients of decreasing water potential in the soil to the roots, and there appear to be two mechanisms of uptake by plants (Kramer and Boyer, 1995). In rapidly transpiring plants evaporation from leaf cells decreases their potentials causing water to be drawn into them from the plant stems, in turn lowering their potentials, and 'sucking' water into the roots, which play only a relatively passive role as absorbing surfaces. In contrast, in slowly transpiring plants osmotic pressures, caused by the accumulation of solutes in the xylem sap, may cause the inflow of water from the soil and can result in such *positive* pressures that water may exude from wounds.

Considerations of rooting depth suggest that a forest will transpire more than a pasture because trees, on the whole, are more deeply rooted than grass. The relationship between root density and water uptake is, however, not as simple as this. Field experiments (for example McGowan *et al.*, 1984; McGowan and Tzimas, 1985) have shown that the capture of soil water by crop roots is not solely dependent upon root development and soil water potential, but upon the *differences* of potential that can develop between soil and root.

Measurements during and after the great British drought of 1975–6 on three consecutive crops of winter wheat grown in the same field showed that the crop with the largest root system, indeed an unusually large root system, grown in the second drought year, 1976, was the least efficient in extracting soil water and so failed to dry the soil as thoroughly as the crops in 1975 and 1977. Plant water potential data showed that this restricted use of the available soil water was associated with '. . . failure to make any significant osmotic adjustment, leading to premature loss of leaf turgor and stomatal closure' (McGowan et al., 1984). The importance of osmotic adjustment in determining the efficiency of plant water use emerged largely as a result of pioneering work by Hsaio *et al.* (1976) and Turner (Begg and Turner, 1976; Jones and Turner, 1978). The uptake by the roots may be more clearly associated with the minimum xylem potential that can develop in the root system, in response to osmotic adjustment, than with the actual root density.

4.4.4 *Soil factors*

Numerous attempts have been made to relate plant transpiration to soil water status. It will be clear, however, that the influence of soil water conditions on evaporation from vegetated surfaces is so closely linked to the vegetational 'control' exerted via the stomatal and root systems that it is very difficult to separate them. Consequently, correlations between soil water potential and evaporation have often been explored through the medium of drying curves

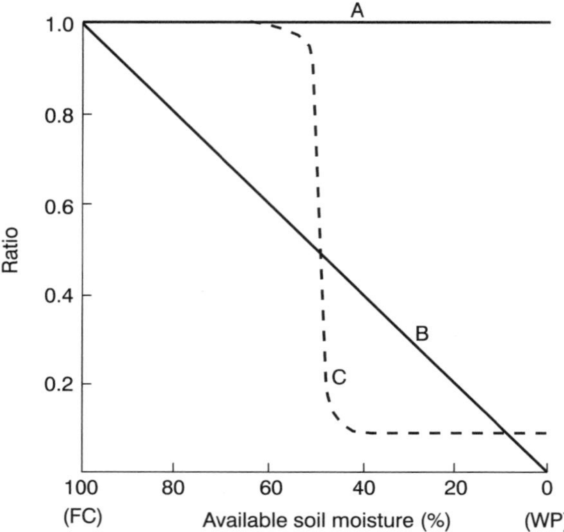

Figure 4.6 Several possible patterns of the changing ratio of actual transpiration to unstressed transpiration for vegetation as soil water availability is reduced from field capacity (FC) to wilting point (WP). See text for details.

showing the ratio of transpiration to unstressed transpiration for vegetation in conditions of reducing water availability (Figure 4.6). These represent a 'black-box' substitute for a detailed understanding of the complex soil–plant–water relationships and the necessary associated sophisticated experimental investigation of aerodynamic and physiological resistances to water movement through the soil–plant–atmosphere continuum.

Despite their obvious limitations, drying curves have enabled significant advances to be made in the understanding, measurement and modelling of evaporation from vegetated covers, and have formed the basis of many of the current operational techniques for estimating actual evaporation losses (see Section 4.6.3).

There is general agreement on the normal range in soil water contents—from the upper limit of water held at *field capacity* after initial rapid drainage ceases to the residual water held at the *wilting point* (but see also Section 6.3). The availability to plants over this range is still subject to much debate, and Figure 4.6 shows a variety of possible relationships. At one extreme (line A) is the view that transpiration continues at a maximum rate until the soil water available to the plant falls below a critical level (the wilting point) when water uptake by the roots stops (for example Veihmeyer, 1972; Veihmeyer and Hendrickson, 1955). This insensitivity to a wide range of soil water may be expected to be particularly relevant in situations where roots extend widely throughout the soil. At the other extreme many would argue that evaporation decreases throughout the range of soil moisture drying (line B), long before the wilting stage is reached, because the soil hydraulic conductivity will decrease with decreasing soil water content (see Section 6.4) (for example Thornthwaite and Mather, 1955).

Between these two extremes there are several intermediate models, one of the best known of which is that of the *root constant* proposed by Penman (1949) (line C). This may be described as the maximum soil moisture deficit below field capacity (see Section 6.3.4) that can be built up without checking transpiration. This is based on the premise that because water, on the whole, moves relatively slowly through the soil, the readily available moisture is effectively restricted to that water in the immediate vicinity of the root system (Pearl *et al.*, 1954). It will, therefore, be limited partly by the depth of the soil available and partly by the soil type, although as its name implies, Penman considered the root constant to be largely dependent upon root depth and so to be primarily a plant characteristic (Penman, 1963). The value for grass was estimated by Penman at between 70 and 120 mm, compared to as much as 250–300 mm or more for some trees. In practice, the Penman-type root constant, even for the same species growing on the same soil, is *not* a true constant but can vary significantly from year to year.

These simple models must now be viewed in the light of our better understanding of the physiology of plant–water relations and assessed accordingly.

4.5 The components of evaporation from vegetation covers

The individual components of total evaporation from a vegetation-covered surface, i.e. bare soil evaporation, transpiration and the evaporation of water intercepted by the vegetation surfaces, have been described and discussed in this and the preceding chapter. Throughout, the relationships of these principal evaporation components have been implied without directly addressing the question 'Which component is the most important?' The answer to this question clearly depends upon local conditions. Thus, in areas where the vegetation cover is dense and continuous the component of soil evaporation is the least important. More generally, it depends upon the availability of moisture for the evaporation process and specifically on whether evaporation is taking place from a wetted or a non-wetted vegetation cover.

First, it is necessary to consider the resistances that discourage that vapour flow.

4.5.1 Resistances to water vapour flux

There are two principal resistances to evaporation from vegetation: the aerodynamic (controlling interception) and the stomatal (controlling transpiration).

The aerodynamic roughness of the vegetation impacts on the role of turbulence and diffusion processes in evaporation. It commonly varies between 10 and 100 $s\,m^{-1}$, and depends solely on the *physical* properties of the vegetation cover. Vegetation height will clearly be important since the coefficient of turbulent exchange increases by a factor of over two with a change in vegetation

Table 4.4 Typical values of aerodynamic resistance and stomatal resistance (s m^{-1}). (Data from Szeicz *et al.*, 1969; Kelliher *et al.*, 1995; Miranda *et al.*, 1984; Oke, 1987; Hall, 1987.)

Land cover	*Aerodynamic resistance,* r_a	*Stomatal resistance,* r_l	*Canopy resistance,* r_c
Open water	125	0	0
Grass	50–70	100–400	40–70
Arable	30–60	100–500	50–100
Heather	20–80	200–600	60–100
Forest	5–10	200–700	80–150

height from a short cut surface at about 2 or 3 cm to 10 cm, and doubles again to a vegetation height of 90 cm (Rijtema, 1968). Similarly, the aerodynamic resistance for trees is an order of magnitude less than for grass, because trees are not only taller but also present a relatively rougher surface to the wind and so are more efficient in generating the forced eddy convection which, in most meteorological conditions, is the dominant mechanism of vertical water vapour transport (Calder, 1979).

Water vapour diffuses through the leaf stomata into the atmosphere partly in response to meteorological variables (available energy, vapour pressure deficit and windspeed), and is partly dependent on the vegetation type (stomatal conductance and the structural characteristics of the canopy which influence the aerodynamic conductance). The stomatal or surface resistance is of major importance in the evaporation process because it is usually an order of magnitude greater than aerodynamic resistance, commonly varying between 100 and 1000 s m^{-1} (Lee, 1980).

Table 4.4 shows typical values of aerodynamic and stomatal resistances and illustrates the larger aerodynamic resistance (smaller conductance) over smooth surfaces (water, short crops) than over taller, rougher vegetation. Conversely the bulk stomatal resistance is larger for forests than for shorter vegetation.

Figure 4.7 illustrates the transpiration and interception components of evaporation in terms of aerodynamic and surface resistances of two different vegetation covers. It shows calculated evaporation rates for typical meteorological conditions on a cool summer day in Britain (i.e. net radiation = 200 W m^{-2}; vapour pressure deficit = 0.5 kPa; air temperature = 10°C). Evaporation rates from grass and coniferous trees are similar in dry conditions (i.e. transpiration), but when the foliage is wet the evaporation (i.e. interception) rates differ substantially, increasing by a factor of 5–15 for the trees but by only 1.5 for grass (Calder, 1979).

Eddy diffusion is dependent on both windspeed and surface roughness, therefore r_a should be inversely related to windspeed in a predictable way, for example the line of theoretical fit in Figure 4.8. The point data for wetted grass at Wallingford and Balquhidder also shown in this diagram confirm that there is indeed an inverse relationship between r_a and windspeed but indicate that this does not take the form predicted by classical eddy–diffusion theory. Hall (1987)

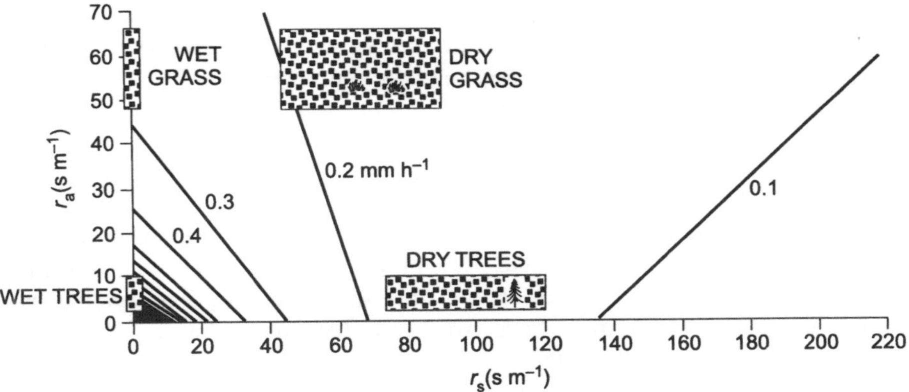

Figure 4.7 Calculated evaporation rates (mm h^{-1}) for grass and coniferous forest, as a function of aerodynamic (r_a) and surface resistance (r_s) for typical cool summer daytime conditions in Britain (based on an original diagram by Calder, 1979).

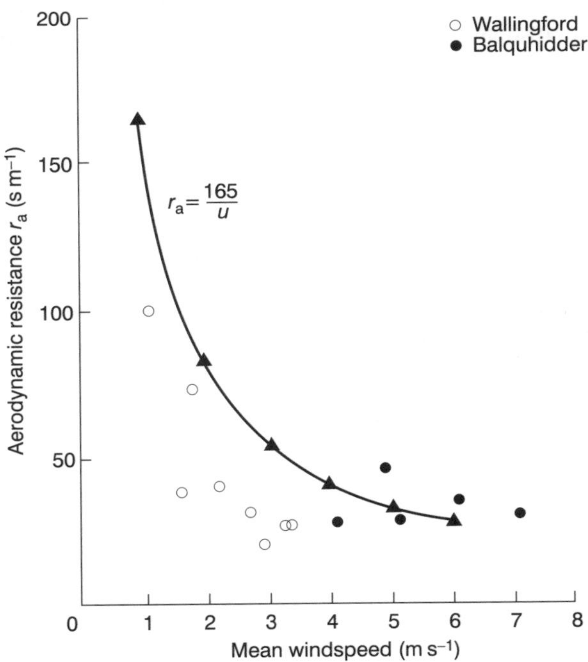

Figure 4.8 Theoretical and observed relationships between aerodynamic resistance and mean windspeed (based on an original diagram in Hall, 1987).

quoted several studies including Finnigan (1979), Denmead (1984) and Grant *et al.* (1986), which showed that large-scale turbulence in the form of intermittent energetic gusts are a major mechanism in water vapour transport and weaken the classically predicted relationship between r_a and mean windspeed.

4.5.2 Interception and transpiration

It is now generally accepted that for *tall* and *wet* vegetation the evaporation of intercepted water will normally take place at a rate much higher than transpiration by means of stomatal diffusion, i.e. that the interception component will dominate the evaporation total. Furthermore, it seems likely that the evaporation of intercepted water will be relatively more important where surface wetting by precipitation occurs predominantly at night rather than during the day (Pearce *et al.*, 1980). Even in high rainfall areas, however, vegetation surfaces are normally dry more often than they are wet, and the relative importance of interception and transpiration components over a period such as a year will reflect the relative duration of wet and dry vegetation conditions as well as the interaction of other associated soil, vegetational and atmospheric conditions. For example, Shuttleworth (1988a) reported that, in an area of Amazonian rainforest, average evaporation over two years was within five per cent of potential evaporation. However, in wet months average evaporation exceeded potential estimates by about ten per cent and fell below such estimates by at least this proportion in dry months.

Given the complexity of the processes involved, it is not surprising that the evidence varies widely even within geographically restricted areas. Table 4.5 demonstrates the importance of climate and vegetation type on the balance between the interception and transpiration components of total annual evapora-

Table 4.5 Comparison of annual precipitation (*P*), interception (*I*) and transpiration (*T*) for areas of differing climates and vegetation characteristics. Annual totals rounded to nearest 10 mm. (Based on data in Calder, 1976; Calder, Hall and Adlard, 1992; Hall, 1987; Hall and Harding, 1993; Law, 1958; Shuttleworth, 1988a.)

Site	*P (mm)*	*I (mm)*	*T (mm)*	*I/T*
UK conifers:				
Balquhidder	2500	710	280	2.5
Plynlimon	1820	520	310	1.7
Stocks	980	370	340	1.1
Thetford	600	210	350	0.6
Heather	2500	350	170	2.1
Grass	2500	200	160	1.3
Rainforest	2640	330	990	0.3
Eucalyptus (mining groundwater)	700	80	1000	0.1

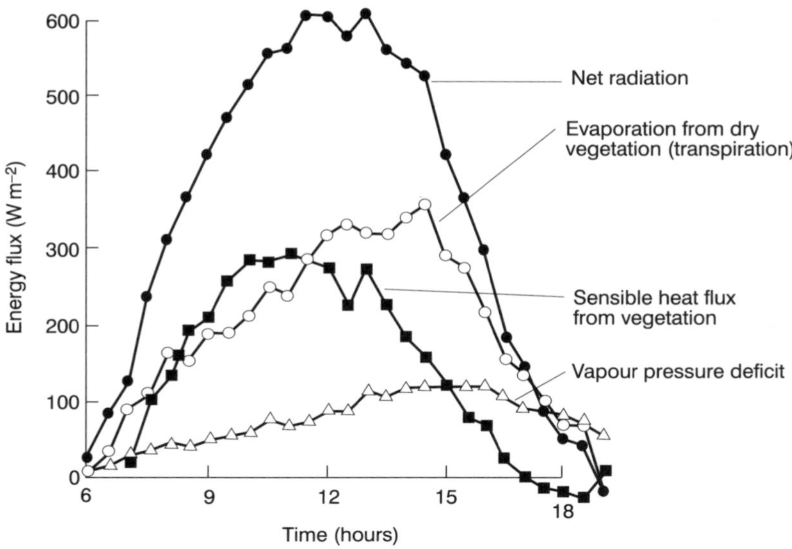

Figure 4.9 The diurnal pattern of energy budget components for a young Douglas fir forest at Blaney in British Columbia (from an original diagram by McNaughton and Black, 1973).

tion. For coniferous forested areas in Britain, for example, interception (*I*) is much greater than transpiration (*T*) for high annual rainfall areas such as Plynlimon in mid-Wales, whereas for low rainfall areas such as Thetford in eastern England, transpiration is the larger component. The difference is not just one of amount of precipitation. Comparison with the figures for the Amazon rainforest shows the importance of the rainfall regime, with rain falling in relatively few very intense convective storms, compared to the long-duration low-intensity rainfall typical of UK conditions. Differences due to vegetation type are shown for the very wet Balquhidder site in southern Scotland, where interception losses of heather are double those of grass, but still much lower than those from forests. Finally, figures are presented for a Eucalyptus forest in India where due to the highly seasonal rainfall regime the interception losses are quite modest, but total evaporation is greater than the rainfall because the Eucalyptus species there has little stomatal control, and at that particular site over the study period, the trees were effectively 'mining' soil water from a shallow-water-table.

Figure 4.9 shows the energy budget components measured for a young Douglas fir forest at Blaney in British Columbia (McNaughton and Black, 1973) and indicates that although evaporation accounted for a substantial proportion of the energy available, the sensible heat flux from the comparatively dry canopy was numerically very similar.

Figure 4.10 shows comparable data for a hardwood forest in Canada whose canopy was initially wet and then dried progressively through the day. The graphs

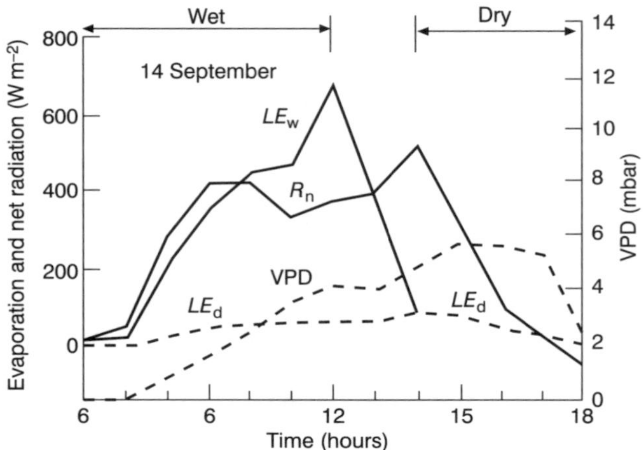

Figure 4.10 Evaporation from a hardwood forest in Canada whose canopy was initially wet (LE_w) and then dried progressively (LE_d) through the day (from an original diagram by Singh and Szeicz, 1979).

confirm the high rates of evaporation from the wetted canopy which exceed the net radiation supply at times, indicating that the wetted canopy acts as an important sink for advected energy from either the overflowing air or the canopy space itself (Singh and Szeicz, 1979).

Mixed vegetation

Except for special situations such as agricultural crops and forest plantations, vegetated surfaces usually comprise a mixture of species. One such instance is the case of forests having an understorey of shorter vegetation. In areas with an open forest and a vigorously growing understorey the non-tree component of transpiration may account for over 50 per cent of the total forest transpiration over the growing season (Black and Kelliher, 1989). The relative contributions to total forest transpiration from overstorey and understorey vegetation will change with environmental conditions. Thus, Roberts *et al.* (1980) working in a Scots pine forest with a bracken understorey, found that the bracken contributed about 25 per cent of transpiration in normal conditions; this rose to 60 per cent in very warm and dry conditions when the bracken was less affected than the pine by the large vapour pressure deficit.

Sparse vegetation

Where the vegetation cover is not continuous, however, or where it has a relatively small plant mass, evaporation comprises the sum of two components: evaporation from the vegetation and from the soil. Baumgartner (1967)

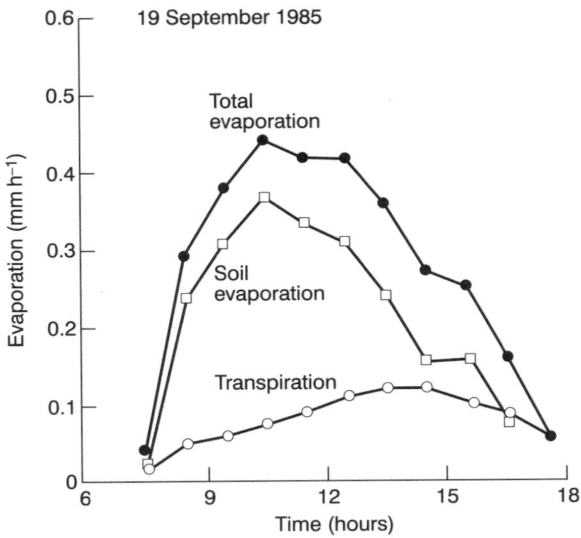

Figure 4.11 Direct soil evaporation may, after rainfall, account for twice the water loss resulting from transpiration (from Wallace *et al.*, 1989).

compared the energy balances of forest, meadow grass and cultivated crops in southern Germany and concluded that soil evaporation was inversely related to plant mass, accounting for 10 per cent, 25 per cent and 45 per cent respectively of the total evaporation loss.

Micrometeorological measurements can provide a single integrated flux, but not the individual contributions which are necessary to create accurate models for situations, such as row crops or semi-arid regions, which have large bare soil areas. Wallace and Holwill (1997) used a Bowen ratio system very close to the ground surface to obtain short-fetch-area average evaporation from just the bare soil patches in an area of 'patterned' woodland and bare soil in Niger. At their site, bare soil evaporation accounted for 28 per cent of the annual rainfall, and a higher percentage in dry years. Wallace *et al.* (1989) reported on a study of the detailed processes of evaporation from sparse dryland crops typical of those grown in many low rainfall areas of Africa and the Middle East. In these vegetation conditions, direct soil evaporation may on occasions, for example after rainfall, account for twice the water loss resulting from transpiration (see Figure 4.11). Shuttleworth and Wallace (1985) provided a framework through which measurements (or modelled values) of crop mass, stomatal and soil resistances and soil heat flux can be combined to calculate the partition of the available energy.

4.6 Modelling evaporation

Although the driving forces for evaporation are well known and relatively easy to measure (i.e. radiation, windspeed and humidity), the actual rates of evaporation are difficult either to measure or to estimate due to the complex interactions of meteorological 'demand' and surface factors controlling 'supply'. Consequently, for the routine estimation of evaporation, especially from vegetation-covered surfaces, attention has focused on empirical or semi-empirical models, in which data requirements are limited to readily available routine meteorological measurements.

4.6.1 Potential evaporation and actual evaporation

The most important simplification has undoubtedly been the development of the concept of *potential* evaporation, E_p, determined by atmospheric demand, as distinct from the evaporation that *actually* takes place, E_a. The calculated potential rate may then be reduced to yield an estimate of the actual evaporation according to the soil water content and a model, whereby inadequate soil water supply reduces evaporation below the atmospheric demand. The potential evaporation concept assumes that water is not limiting and is at all times sufficient to supply the requirements of the transpiring vegetation cover. It was defined by Thornthwaite (1944) as 'The water loss which will occur if at no time there is a deficiency of water in the soil for use of vegetation'. Subsequent modifications to this concept have limited its application to the evaporation that takes place from a continuous and unbroken green vegetation cover; for example Penman (1956) defined potential evaporation as the 'evaporation from an extended surface of short green crop, actively growing, completely shading the ground, of uniform height and not short of water'.

It is worth examining this definition more closely. The use of the term 'extended' means of sufficient extent to minimize advectional influences, 'short' excludes effects of vegetation height, 'uniform' excludes the effects of shape and roughness, and the role of soil water movement is eliminated by the term 'never short of water'. Thus defined, potential evaporation may be regarded as a climatological response, only affected by vegetation differences through albedo and stomatal control.

Clearly, such a restrictingly defined concept is likely to be of only limited practical significance, as these conditions are unlikely to be fulfilled except, perhaps, for a very large surface of close-mown grass in a humid environment. In other circumstances theoretical argument and experimental evidence indicate that the shape and height of the vegetation cover and the supply of large-scale advective energy affect the transpiration rate in such a way that, even in the humid conditions of Britain or the Netherlands, the actual rate of evaporation under these conditions of optimum water supply can exceed potential evaporation. Furthermore, it is shown in Chapter 3 that the evaporation of water intercepted on the foliage of tall vegetation may greatly exceed the rate of transpiration from the same vegetation cover. Potential values of evaporation are often not achieved because of the resistances imposed on water vapour movement through the soil–plant–atmosphere continuum.

Indeed, such are the ambiguities surrounding the various notions of a climatologically determined maximum rate of evaporation from a vegetated surface, that it may be argued that the simple concept of potential evaporation, as originally advanced by Thornthwaite and Penman, has outlived its usefulness.

While acknowledging the usefulness of potential evaporation in providing an upper limit to evaporation loss in a given environment, Lhomme (1997) outlined some of the inherent difficulties. First there is the need to provide a very precise definition of the 'ideal' surface conditions, and it is for this reason that some authorities prefer the term 'reference' evaporation (for example Shuttleworth, 1993; Allen *et al.*, 1994a, 1994b). Secondly, if the surface is sufficiently extensive to prevent any local advection, as required in the definition, then there is likely to be a feedback relationship between the evaporation process and the meteorological variable. Thus air, moving across an extensive surface adequately supplied with water, will become progressively more humid and cooler (due to latent heat of vaporization) until it reaches an equilibrium with the surface. In practice, however, potential evaporation is often calculated under conditions of water shortage at the surface, resulting in a higher air temperature (as more radiation goes to sensible heat) and a lower air humidity.

There is a range of conditions of surface wetness and/or adequate soil water supply that will permit actual evaporation to take place at a potential rate determined largely by atmospheric variables; otherwise actual evaporation will take place at a *lower* rate and may be greatly influenced by plant and soil conditions.

4.6.2 Models of potential evaporation

While many evaporation models have been developed, only a small minority are used on a routine basis. Probably the most widely used are: (*a*) the purely empirical model developed by Warren Thornthwaite, especially where data are limited, and (*b*) the physically based model of Howard Penman, especially in the form as subsequently modified and developed by John Monteith and co-workers and now known as the 'Penman–Monteith' model.

The Thornthwaite model

Thornthwaite (1948) presented a formula for estimating potential 'evapotranspiration' based on lysimeter and catchment observations in the central and eastern United States. Monthly potential evaporation (cm) is calculated as an exponential function of air temperature:

$$E_{\mathrm{p}} = 1.6\frac{10t}{I^{\mathrm{a}}} \tag{4.14}$$

where t is the mean monthly temperature (°C), I is the annual heat index (defined below) and a is a cubic function of I. The annual heat index is the sum of 12 individual monthly indices, i:

$$i = \left(\frac{t}{5}\right)^{1.514} \tag{4.15}$$

where t is the mean temperature of the month.

The only data requirements are mean air temperature and hours of daylight (to adjust for the unequal day lengths in different months). The method therefore appears to be extremely empirical and has been criticized for that reason. However, Thornthwaite's choice of an empirical model was quite deliberate, as also was his choice of mean air temperature as the main variable influencing potential evaporation (Thornthwaite and Hare, 1965). He justified the selection of mean air temperature on the grounds that there is a fixed relationship between that part of the net radiation which is used for heating and that part which is used for evaporation when conditions are suited to evaporation at the potential rate, i.e. when the soil is continuously moist (Thornthwaite, 1954). This means, in effect, that although the Thornthwaite model is empirical, it nevertheless estimates potential evaporation by an indirect reference to the radiation balance at the evaporating surface.

The Thornthwaite model was probably more widely adopted for operational use than any other, due to its modest data requirements and to its relative ease of use. The formula seems to work well in the temperate, continental climate of North America where it was derived, and where temperature and radiation are strongly correlated (for example Mather, 1954; Sanderson, 1950). In other circumstances, however, it has been less successful. It may give rise to severe underestimation of evaporation rates in dry climates (Monteith, 1985).

Over the course of a year, air temperature lags behind radiation so that temperature is not a good indicator of the energy available for evaporation. In the Netherlands, Van Wijk and de Vries (1954) noted that although November and March had similar mean air temperatures, the solar radiation was three times greater in March. Over short periods the Thornthwaite estimates may differ significantly from observed values using lysimeters, but the accuracy will increase as longer periods are considered. The method may also give poor results in areas like the British Isles, where advection effects resulting from frequent air mass changes lead to frequent rapid changes in mean air temperature and humidity, without corresponding changes in radiation. Even so, during the summer months, when E_p is of greatest significance, more stable air mass conditions tend to prevail, thereby strengthening the relationship between temperature, the radiation balance and evaporation.

It is unfortunate that the enthusiasm with which the Thornthwaite model has been adopted in so many different conditions has often been allowed to obscure his own caution that the chief obstacle to the development of a rational evaporation model 'is the lack of understanding of why [E_p] corresponding to a given temperature is not everywhere the same' (Thornthwaite, 1948).

The Penman–Monteith model

Although imposing greater data demands than the Thornthwaite approach, the Penman–Monteith evaporation model has become firmly established, not only as a routine method of quantifying evaporation but also as the basis for most of the significant conceptual advances in evaporation research that have taken place in recent decades.

Penman (1948) devised a model for potential evaporation which combined the turbulent transfer and the energy-balance approaches. This was later restated by Penman in slightly modified forms (1952, 1954, 1956, 1963). Basically, there are three equations. The first equation is a measure of the drying power of the air. This increases with a large saturation deficit, indicating that the air is dry, and with high windspeeds. The first equation is, therefore, derived from the basic pattern of the turbulent transfer approach and takes the form:

$$E_a = 0.35(e_a - e_d)\left(1 + \frac{u}{100}\right) \quad \text{mm/d} \qquad (4.16)$$

where e_a is the saturation vapour pressure of water at the mean air temperature, e_d is the saturation vapour pressure of water at the dew point temperature, or the actual vapour pressure at the mean air temperature, and u is the windspeed (miles d^{-1}) at a height of two metres above the ground surface.

The second equation provides an estimate of the net radiation (H—Penman's notation instead of the more usually used R_n) available for evaporation and heating at the evaporating surface and takes the form:

$$H = A - B \quad \text{mm/d} \qquad (4.17)$$

where A is the short-wave incoming radiation and B is the long-wave outgoing radiation, as estimated in the following expressions:

$$A = (1 - r)R_a\left(0.18 + 0.55\left(\frac{n}{N}\right)\right) \quad \text{mm/d} \qquad (4.18)$$

$$B = \sigma T_a^4(0.56 - 0.90\sqrt{e_d})\left(0.10 + 0.90\left(\frac{n}{N}\right)\right) \quad \text{mm/d} \qquad (4.19)$$

where r is the albedo of the evaporating surface, R_a is the theoretical radiation intensity at the evaporating surface in the absence of an atmosphere, expressed in evaporation units, n/N is the ratio of actual/possible hours of bright sunshine; σT_a^4 is the theoretical back radiation which would leave the area in the absence of an atmosphere, T_a being the mean air temperature in kelvin; and σ is the Stefan–Boltzman constant, and e_d is as in Eq. 4.16.

Penman assumed that the heat flux into and out of the soil, which usually represents about 2 per cent of the total incoming energy (Pearl *et al.*, 1954), is small enough to be ignored, so he simply apportioned the net radiation between heating the air and evaporation. The proportion of it used in evaporation is then estimated by combining Eqs (4.16) and (4.17) to give:

$$E = \left(\left(\frac{\Delta}{\gamma}\right)H + E_a\right) \Big/ \left(\left(\frac{\Delta}{\gamma}\right) + 1\right) \quad \text{mm/d} \tag{4.20}$$

where Δ is the slope of the saturation vapour pressure curve for water at the mean air temperature. This relationship assumes equality of the coefficients of water vapour and convective heat transfer, a requirement that is well met in windy and unstable conditions but which may be less certain in conditions of strong radiation and light winds.

The Penman equation combines two terms, namely the aerodynamic or evaporivity term E_a which describes the drying power of the air, and the energy term, H, which is an estimate of the available net radiation. The relative importance of these terms in total evaporation depends upon the dimensionless ratio Δ/γ. The value of this weighting factor varies with air temperature, for example being 1.3 at 10°C, and 2.3 at 20°C respectively (Penman, 1963). Thus, during the warm summer months, when totals of evaporation are significantly high, the net radiation term is given more weight than the evaporativity term. In humid areas, H is usually greater than E_a, and therefore H tends to be the dominant term in the equation. On the other hand, in conditions of zero net radiation, the evaporation will be determined solely by the aerodynamic term (Calder, 1990).

In its basic form, the Penman (1948) equation describes the evaporation from an open water surface, E_o. This may then be related to a vegetated surface, E_T, by the use of a coefficient, f; i.e. $E_T = fE_o$, where f for grass varies from 0.8 in summer to 0.6 in winter. Subsequently, it was shown that the potential evaporation for vegetation could be obtained directly by incorporating the reflection coefficient for an extended short green crop ($r = 0.25$) instead of that for an extended sheet of open water ($r = 0.05$).

If all or part of the available energy represented in Eq. 4.17 is measured directly then even short-period estimates of potential evaporation may be tolerably accurate. Several techniques may be employed. First, measured incoming radiation may be substituted for Eq. 4.18. A second option is to replace the whole of the expression for H, i.e. Eq. 4.17, by measured net radiation. Thirdly, in addition to net radiation, measurements may be made of the heat flow through the soil. In this way the complete energy balance is measured and errors caused by the neglect of heat storage may be obviated. The choice of options has unfortunately introduced a certain degree of uncertainty into the exact definition of the Penman equation (Calder, 1990). Robinson (1999), for example, illustrated the introduction of spurious trends into the long-term record of Penman short-grass potential evaporation at Eskdalemuir in Scotland, partly as a result of changes in the version of the Penman equation used over different time periods.

Much of the discussion of evaporation from vegetated surfaces earlier in this chapter focused on the important roles of the aerodynamic resistance and surface resistance in accounting for variations of evaporation between vegetation covers that differ in terms of wetness, structure and physiology. Neither resistance appears to be incorporated in the Penman model of the evaporation process, although interestingly Thom and Oliver (1977) showed that the wind function in Eq. 4.16 implicitly incorporates some reasonable assumption about both. The explicit incorporation of these resistances was proposed by Penman and Schofield (1951), and was subsequently presented in its most familiar form by Monteith (1965), who treated the vegetation canopy as a single extensive isothermal leaf so that:

$$\lambda E = \frac{\Delta H + \rho c(e_a - e_d)/r_a}{\Delta + \gamma[1 + (r_s/r_a)]} \qquad (4.21)$$

where ρ is the density of the air, c is the specific heat of the air and r_s is the surface resistance which combines the canopy resistance, r_c and any additional resistances, such as contributions from the soil surface; all other terms are as previously defined.

In theory this modification should permit incorporation of the important aerodynamic and physiological influences of the vegetation cover on evaporation as well as the largely meteorological influences on which the original Penman model focused. In practice, however, although the Penman–Monteith model has played a most valuable role in the development of conceptual understanding of the complex evaporation process from wetted and unwetted vegetation surfaces, it has not been used widely to determine values of evaporation. The main problem, of course, lies in the difficulty of obtaining adequate measurement of the vegetational factors, and especially of r_s (surface resistance) which is a complex function of many climatological and biological factors including radiation, saturation deficit, soil water status and biomass characteristics. This was admitted by Monteith (1985, 1995) when he noted that the model had been used mainly as a diagnostic tool for estimating canopy resistance, when the transpiration rate and the other variables are known, rather than as a prognostic tool for estimating λE when r_s is assumed.

The Penman–Monteith equation has been termed a 'big leaf' model since it is one-dimensional and assumes a bulk canopy conductance equal to the parallel sum of the individual leaf stomatal conductances. It has generally been found to work well in a wide range of studies (Calder, 1990), although in cases where the vegetation canopies are not homogeneous (for example sparse vegetation with substantial bare soil, or open forest with herbaceous plants) the one-dimensional approximation may lead to significant errors, and a dual source model (for example Shuttleworth and Wallace, 1985) is generally needed.

Much valuable research has been conducted on the dependence of r_a and r_s on environmental variables using the Penman–Monteith equation. Work in Thetford Forest, for example, showed how surface resistance values were highly dependent on the atmospheric humidity deficit and less so on the input of solar radiation (IH, 1985; Stewart, 1988). Other similar work has been done on bracken (Roberts *et al.*, 1980) and heathland vegetation (Wallace *et al.*, 1984; Hall, 1987).

Other potential evaporation formulae

Sellers (1965) compared estimates of potential evaporation including Thornthwaite and Penman with measurements from a lysimeter in eastern Australia. The Penman formula performed well, while the Thornthwaite equation grossly underestimated throughout the year.

Jensen *et al.* (1990) compared 20 equations with data from weighing lysimeters at 11 locations, and concluded that the Penman–Monteith equation performs better than the other models tested. It has been recommended as the reference standard for the estimation of crop water requirements by the Food and Agriculture Organization, the FAO (Allen *et al.*, 1994a, 1994b).

4.6.3 Temporal and spatial variations in evaporation

Annual estimates of potential evaporation have been computed for stations with long periods of data, including Penman (1948) short-grass estimates for the Radcliffe Observatory in Oxford, 1881–1966 (Rodda *et al.*, 1976) and Penman and Thornthwaite values for the Edgbaston Observatory in Birmingham, 1900–68 (Takhar and Rudge, 1970). These indicate the presence of long-term variations with, for example, a period of low annual values at both stations centred on 1930. Subsequently, Burt and Shahgedanova (1998) used air temperature data to estimate Thornthwaite values for Oxford back to 1815 but found a relatively poor agreement with 'Penman' estimates (version not specified) computed for a site outside Oxford during a recent period of record; the Thornthwaite figures lagged behind the Penman values by approximately one month.

Long-term data sets are extremely valuable, but great care must be taken to ensure their consistency—both in site and in data collection; Wallace (1997), for example, provided details of numerous meteorological instrument and siting changes at the Oxford Radcliffe Observatory; Crane and Hudson (1997) showed that siting changes can be important even outside of an urban environment; and Robinson (1999) discusses a number of general problems including changes in the frequency of observations and in the version of the E_p formula that is used.

Estimates of total evaporation and its components of transpiration and interception loss have been made for sites in Scotland, and are shown in Figure 4.12.

Knowledge of the spatial variation of potential and actual evaporation from vegetated surfaces is also of value, with applications for a variety of climatological,

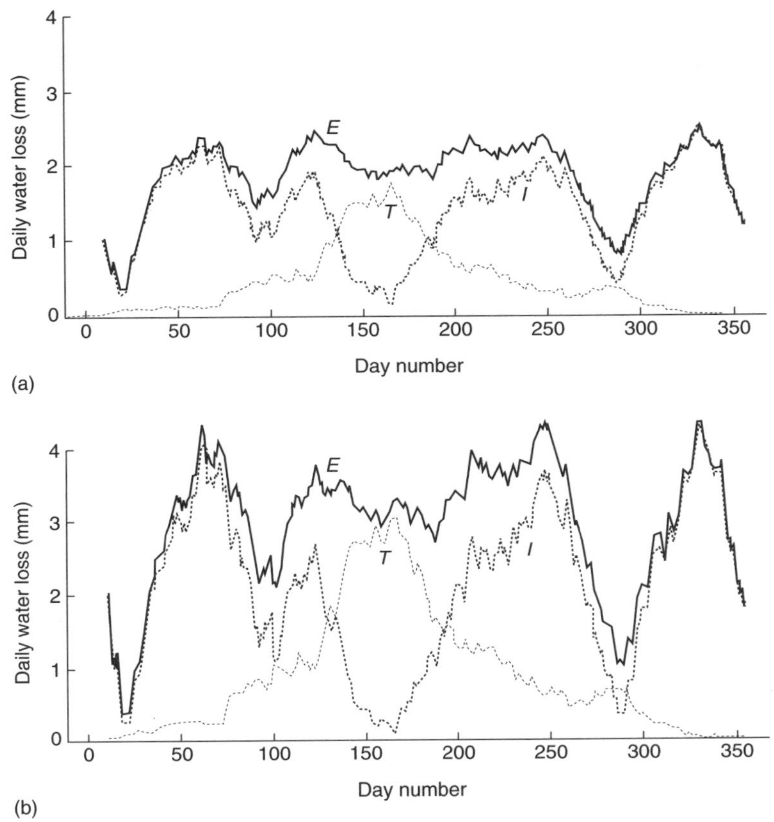

Figure 4.12 Calculated daily interception (I), transpiration (T) and total evaporation (E) from (*a*) heather and (*b*) coniferous forest (from original diagrams in Price *et al.*, 1995).

water-balance and resource evaluation purposes. Examples are shown in Figures 4.13 and 4.14. Figure 4.13 emphasizes the overriding control of available energy in determining the pattern of E_p across Europe. The comparatively regular pattern of isolines, increasing southwards, is broken only by the mountains of central and southern Europe, where relatively lower evaporation rates prevail. Figure 4.14 shows the distribution of E_p and E_a for Britain. The derivation of the E_p map, which is based on a variety of sources, was detailed by Ward (1976). The pattern of isolines shows a broad latitudinal decrease from south to north and also a marked decrease away from the coast. Both characteristics reflect the availability of net radiation, although the higher coastal values are probably also a reflection of the additional drying power associated with higher windspeeds in coastal areas. Conversely, reduced values in the main upland areas are largely

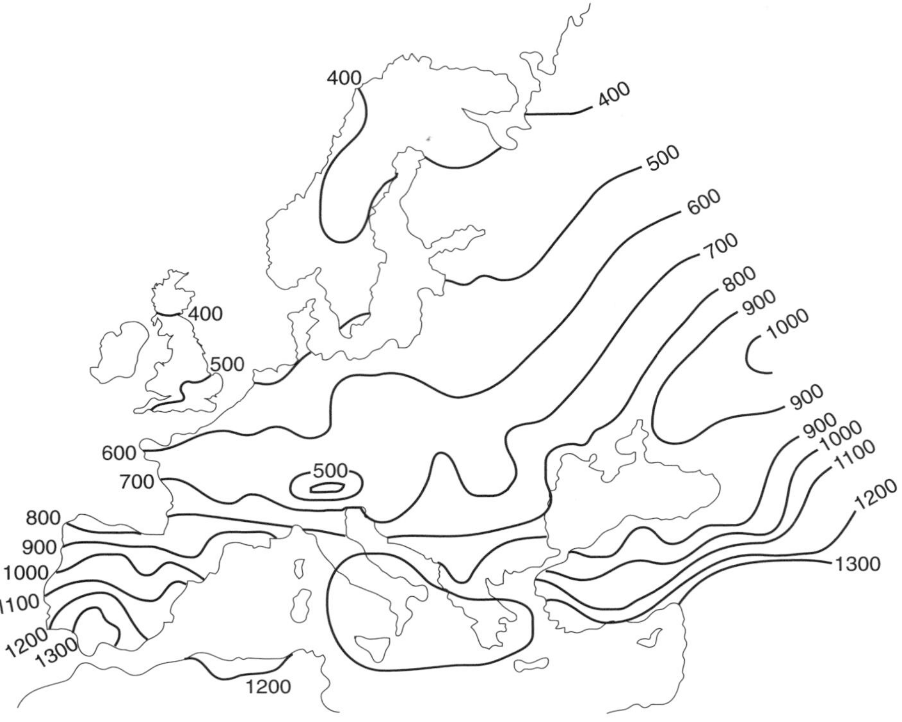

Figure 4.13 The spatial variation of mean annual Penman–Monteith potential evaporation (mm) across Europe, 1961–90 (adapted from a diagram provided by N. Arnell, University of Southampton, based on gridded climatology from the Climatic Research Unit, University of East Anglia).

associated with low radiation availability. Based on measured data from a large number of river basins, the map shows that over most of England and Wales actual evaporation values lie between 400 and 500 mm, despite the much wider variation in the potential values.

Operational use of potential evaporation models

One important prognostic use of the Penman–Monteith model has been its incorporation in the UK *M*eteorological *O*ffice *R*ainfall and *E*vaporation *C*alculation *S*ystem (MORECS). This system uses daily meteorological data to produce weekly estimates of evaporation, soil moisture deficit and effective rainfall for 190 grid squares (40 × 40 km) (Thompson *et al.*, 1981). It uses a modified version of the Penman–Monteith equation to calculate daily potential evaporation, with a soil moisture accounting system to reduce actual evaporation at times when soil water is limiting.

MORECS models soil water extraction using a two-layer water reservoir.

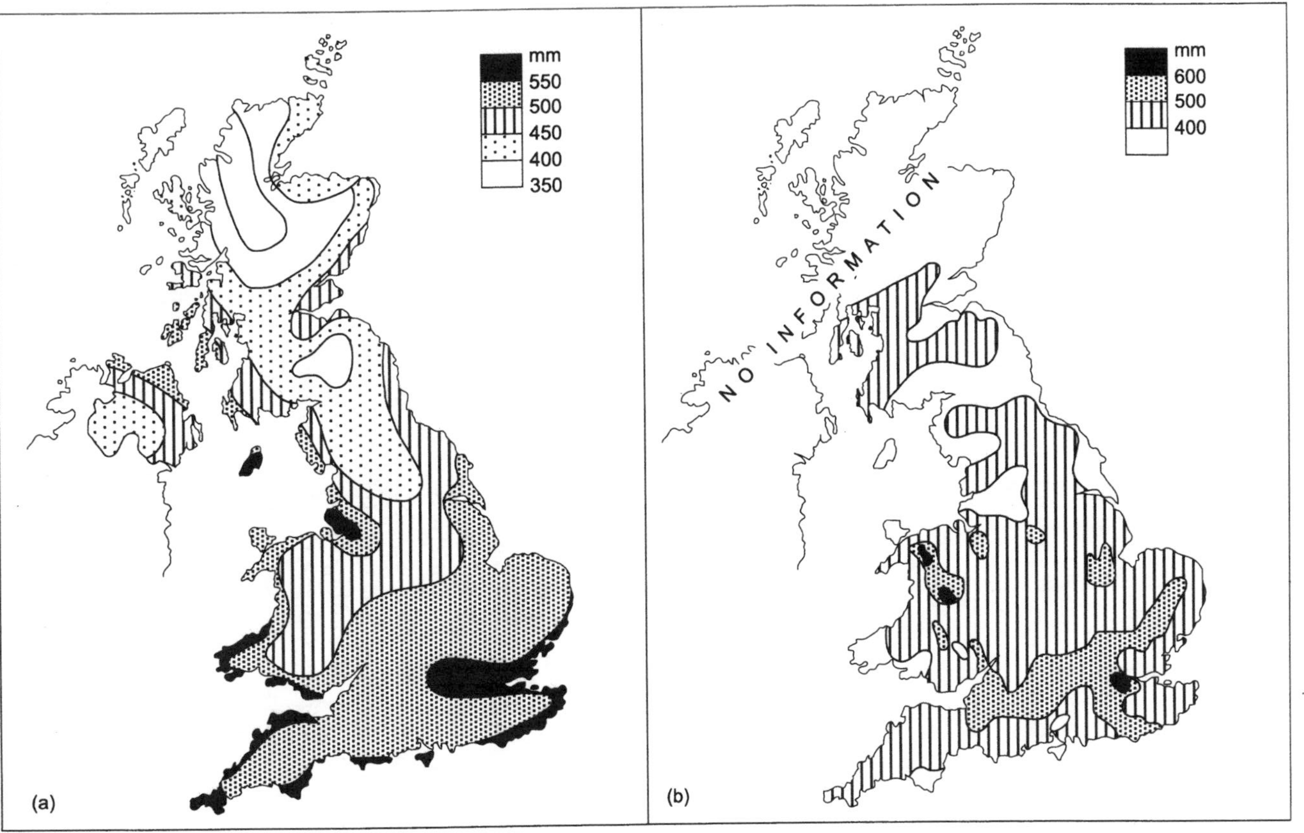

Figure 4.14 Comparison of the spatial variation over the UK of mean annual values of (*a*) Penman grass potential and (*b*) actual evaporation (based on original diagrams in Ward, 1981).

When the soil is at field capacity, layer *X* contains 40 per cent (X_{max}) and layer *Y* 60 per cent of the available soil water. When soil drying commences, water is extracted initially from layer *X* and is freely available to the vegetation (i.e. $E_a = E_p$). Subsequently water is extracted from layer *Y*, from which it becomes increasingly difficult to extract as the moisture status is reduced, and the actual evaporation falls progressively below E_p. This is achieved by increasing the canopy resistance in relation to the decrease in moisture content in *Y*. Water is extracted from *Y* only if *X* is empty, and rainfall replenishes layer *X* first, and then *Y* only when *X* is full.

Since its introduction in 1978, MORECS has undergone a number of changes, including extensive revisions in 1981 and 1983. A useful description and evaluation of the calculation of evaporation and soil moisture extraction was given by Thompson (1982), and Gardner and Field (1983) compared estimates of SMD with independent field measurements of actual soil water contents measured by neutron probe.

As Gardner and Field (1983) observed, the value of X_{max} is important (*a*) because it defines a soil moisture deficit threshold rather similar to the Penman root constant, and (*b*) because being 40 per cent of the available soil water it defines the total available water in the soil, i.e. 2.5 X_{max}. Different X_{max} values are allocated to different surface covers, ranging from bare soil to forest, and for each surface cover three values of X_{max} are used to represent soils having low, medium and high available water capacity. Thus, for grass the X_{max} values are 37.5, 50.0 and 62.5 mm, representing total available water (or maximum permitted deficits) of 94, 125 and 156 mm respectively for soils of low, medium and high water availability.

In the latest version of MORECS (Version 2.0) further improvements were made to the treatment of soils and land use (Hough and Jones, 1997). Specimen MORECS results are shown in Figure 4.15. The long-term mean monthly estimated evaporation data for two 40 km grid squares in England, taken in conjunction with the typical distribution of rainfall, indicate the close similarity between actual and potential evaporation in areas of low soil moisture deficit and the marked divergence of the two in areas of high soil moisture deficit.

Calder *et al.* (1983) compared the performance of a number of combinations of different potential evaporation formulae and different soil water depletion models relating E_p to E_a via the moisture status of the soil. The results were judged against over 3000 field measurements of soil moisture at grassland sites in the UK. They concluded that the most sophisticated models did not necessarily produce the best results. Thus, the most detailed evaporation equations did not provide better soil moisture estimates than a simple climatological mean. There was little difference between different root constant functions, and a simple linear function performed as well as mathematically more complex models. They suggested that this was the result of the conservative nature of annual potential evaporation (both spatially and temporally). Similar conclusions were reached by Andersson and Harding (1991) for grass and forest sites in Norway.

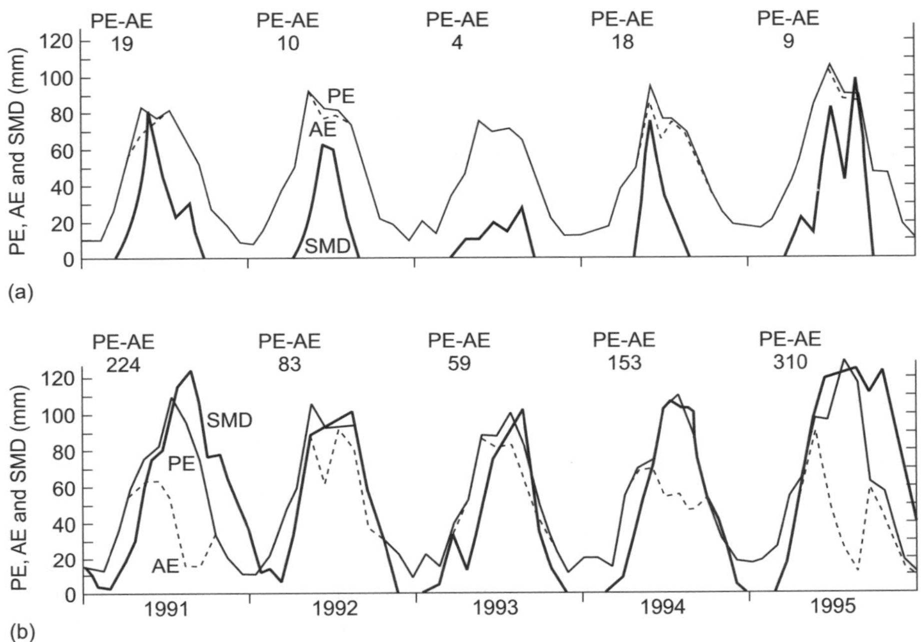

Figure 4.15 Monthly values of potential (solid line) and actual (dashed line) evaporation, and soil moisture deficit (SMD) for (*a*) MORECS grid square 55 in western Scotland and (*b*) MORECS grid square 108 in eastern England (adapted from IH/BGS, 1996 and based on data supplied by the UK Meteorological Office).

4.7 Progress in understanding evaporation processes

At the beginning of this chapter it is noted that evaporation is generally considered to be the most difficult component of the hydrological cycle to measure. From the subsequent discussions in this chapter it can be seen that there have been great advances in our knowledge of evaporation processes, and in our ability to measure or to estimate it. Nevertheless, despite this Morton (1994), in a thought-provoking paper, questioned the value of much of this work over the last four decades.

Two areas he cited for particular criticism are the physical basis for evaporation equations and the treatment of advection and atmospheric feedback.

4.7.1 Physical basis for evaporation equations

The Penman–Monteith equation is internationally accepted as the preferred method for computing potential evaporation yet, as noted above, it contains the surface resistance term, r_s which may not be known beforehand. It is assumed that r_s will be primarily dependent upon stomatal resistance, and so will reflect changes in that resistance. Morton (1985) noted, as others have before him, that there is experimental evidence to show that under certain circumstances leaf stomata may close in response to an increase in vapour pressure deficit, thus reducing evaporation (to conserve water and leaf turgor), at a time when atmospheric demand is actually increasing. This is the opposite to the expected behaviour incorporated in the Penman–Monteith equation.

4.7.2 Advection

Much of the discussion of evaporation in the literature, and including this chapter, tends to be imprecise about the role of advection. Reference, for example, was made in the definition of potential evaporation to an 'extensive' evaporating surface and to the assumption that a sufficiently extensive surface would obviate advectional effects. Implicit in such terminology is the recognition that evaporation is influenced strongly by vapour pressure deficit and that, in turn, the vapour pressure deficit is linked to the available energy and to the canopy resistance. Conceptually it is possible to move in opposite directions from this position, i.e. that potential evaporation may be viewed as both a *cause* and an *effect* of actual evaporation. Thus, as water becomes limiting, the rate of actual evaporation decreases but the potential evaporation may increase due to the rise in air temperature (as the ground warms) and the reduction in water vapour pressure.

With heterogeneous surfaces and contrasting itinerant air masses, the linkage between vapour pressure deficit, available energy and canopy resistance may be broken when air with greatly different characteristics is imported from another area. In other words, when an air mass moves across the boundary between two surfaces of different wetness a horizontal gradient of saturation deficit is produced, leading to 'advectional enhancement' (McNaughton *et al.*, 1979) if the air moves from a drier to a wetter surface and the saturation deficit increases and to advectional depression when the movement is in the opposite sense and the saturation deficit decreases. As McNaughton *et al.* (1979) observed, although 'some significant effect of advection on local evaporation rates is the rule rather than the exception', the same methods, including the Penman–Monteith model, are normally used to estimate evaporation when advective enhancement is large as at other times. In fact the use of the Penman–Monteith model would not be unreasonable if values of canopy resistance were known to sufficient accuracy. At present they are not, although research in this area continues.

With an 'infinite' rather than an extensive surface, surface exchange rates control the behaviour of the atmosphere and give rise to an 'equilibrium' evaporation rate (Shuttleworth, 1993) in which λE is nearly proportional to H. This may be stated as:

$$\lambda E_{\text{eq}} = \frac{\alpha(H\Delta)}{(\Delta + \gamma)} \tag{4.22}$$

where α is an empirical constant. Equilibrium evaporation thus represents the *lower* limit of evaporation from a wet surface. This was recognized by Slatyer and McIlroy (1961) and formalized much later by McNaughton (1976a, 1976b). Doubt persists, however, about the extent to which $\Delta/(\Delta + \gamma)$ does, in fact, represent an equilibrium rate. Priestley and Taylor (1972), in disussion of their own proposed simplification of the Penman model which eliminates the term involving windspeed and atmospheric humidity deficit, noted that the average rate of evaporation from vegetation freely supplied with water was given when $\alpha = 1.26$. The reason why this value is greater than unity has not been satisfactorily explained although the additional energy implied has been ascribed to the entrainment of relatively warm, dry air downwards through the upper surface of the planetary boundary layer (Monteith, 1985). The Priestley–Taylor equation has been widely used in areas not suffering from water stress or significant advection, but it has been found to produce serious underestimates in semi-arid areas (Gunston and Batchelor, 1983) and for forests with wet foliage (Shuttleworth and Calder, 1979).

The partitioning of the radiation absorbed by a surface between sensible and latent heat depends upon the availability of water. If the ground is drying out there will be a decrease in the amount of latent heat transfer to the atmosphere and a corresponding increase in the transfer of sensible heat. If there is no change in the prevailing air mass the atmosphere will become warmer and drier and consequently the *potential* evaporation will increase while the *actual* rate decreases. An analysis of typical British conditions showed that annual actual evaporation tends to be higher in wet years than in dry years (Penman and Schofield, 1941), due largely to differences in summer evaporation. In dry summers soil evaporation is considerably less than that from a free water surface, whereas in wet summers, when re-wetting of the soil is frequent, soil evaporation will be much higher.

Bouchet (1963) postulated that the changes to potential and actual evaporation were of equal magnitude so that the sum of actual and potential evaporation is constant, i.e. there is a complementary relationship between them.

Morton (1983, 1985) used the argument to develop the *C*omplementary *R*elationship *A*real *E*vapotranspiration (CRAE) model and used it to estimate the regional actual evaporation from estimates of potential evaporation. Early results for catchments in Ireland, Holland and North America were generally good (Morton, 1983; Brutsaert and Stricker, 1979). However, tests of the model for lowland tropical sites by the UK Institute of Hydrology (IH, 1985) were not encouraging, and Monteith (1995) suggested that the close agreement with the catchment water balance results might be a consequence of the use of empirical functions (for example for advection) to calibrate the model. McNaughton and Spriggs (1989) concluded that the CRAE model did not reflect conditions when the water supply to the soil–plant surfaces is limiting, and that although the model can work if the parameters are adjusted for the specific conditions a generally valid formulation of the model is unlikely.

Review Problems and Exercises

4.1 Define the following terms: evaporation, water vapour, latent heat, water vapour pressure, saturation water vapour pressure, and saturation deficit.

4.2 Describe the principal meteorological factors controlling evaporation from a water surface.

4.3 Explain what is meant by the Bowen ratio; what is its significance for evaporation studies?

4.4 Discuss the advantages and disadvantages of evaporation pans. Why are they still so widely used throughout the world?

4.5 Is transpiration a necessary evil?

4.6 Describe and compare the importance of stomatal and root controls on transpiration.

4.7 Define and clearly distinguish the following terms: stomatal or surface resistance, canopy or bulk surface resistance, and surface resistance.

4.8 Describe different black box models of transpiration reduction with progressive soil drying.

4.9 Discuss the importance of factors such as climate and vegetation type on the relative importance of transpiration and interception to total evaporation.

4.10 Discuss the physical basis for a definition of potential evaporation.

4.11 Explain how factors such as rainfall regime, soil moisture content and vegetation type may lead to actual evaporation rates that are: (*a*) lower than the potential evaporation rate; (*b*) greater than the potential evaporation rate.

4.12 Discuss the effect of advection on potential evaporation estimates.

CHAPTER FIVE

Groundwater

5.1 Introduction and definitions

Most of the precipitation that reaches the ground surface is absorbed by the surface layers of the soil. The remainder, once any depression storage has been filled, will flow over the surface as overland flow, reaching the stream channels quite quickly. The water that infiltrates into the soil may subsequently be evaporated, or flow laterally close to the surface as throughflow, or else it may percolate under gravity to the groundwater body.

The diagrammatic section of part of a river valley in Figure 5.1(a) shows the four main zones into which subsurface water has been traditionally classified. Precipitation enters the *soil zone* at the ground surface and moves downwards to the water table which marks the upper surface of the *zone of saturation*. Immediately above the water table is the *capillary fringe* in which almost all the pores are full of water; between this and the soil zone is the *intermediate zone*, where the movement of water is mainly downwards. These zones vary between different parts of a river basin. On the valley flanks, water drains from the soil zone proper into the intermediate zone, and may or may not eventually reach the zone of saturation perhaps several hundred metres below. In the floodplain areas, however, the capillary fringe often extends into the soil zone or even to the ground surface itself, depending on the depth of the water table and the height of the capillary fringe. Although convenient as an introduction, this classification tends to obscure the fact that subsurface water is an essentially dynamic system. As well as varying spatially within a river basin, these zones may also vary over time, as when seasonal fluctuations of the water table bring the capillary fringe up into the soil zone.

Various devices have been adopted to clarify the difference between soil water and groundwater. These include limiting consideration of the former to the surface metre or so, which contains the depth of plant roots (Shaw, 1994; Price, 1996). However, *soil water* is normally defined as the subsurface water in the zone of aeration, i.e. the unsaturated soil and subsoil layers above the water table, and *groundwater* is defined as the subsurface water in soils and rocks that are fully saturated. This distinction between saturated and unsaturated conditions is an

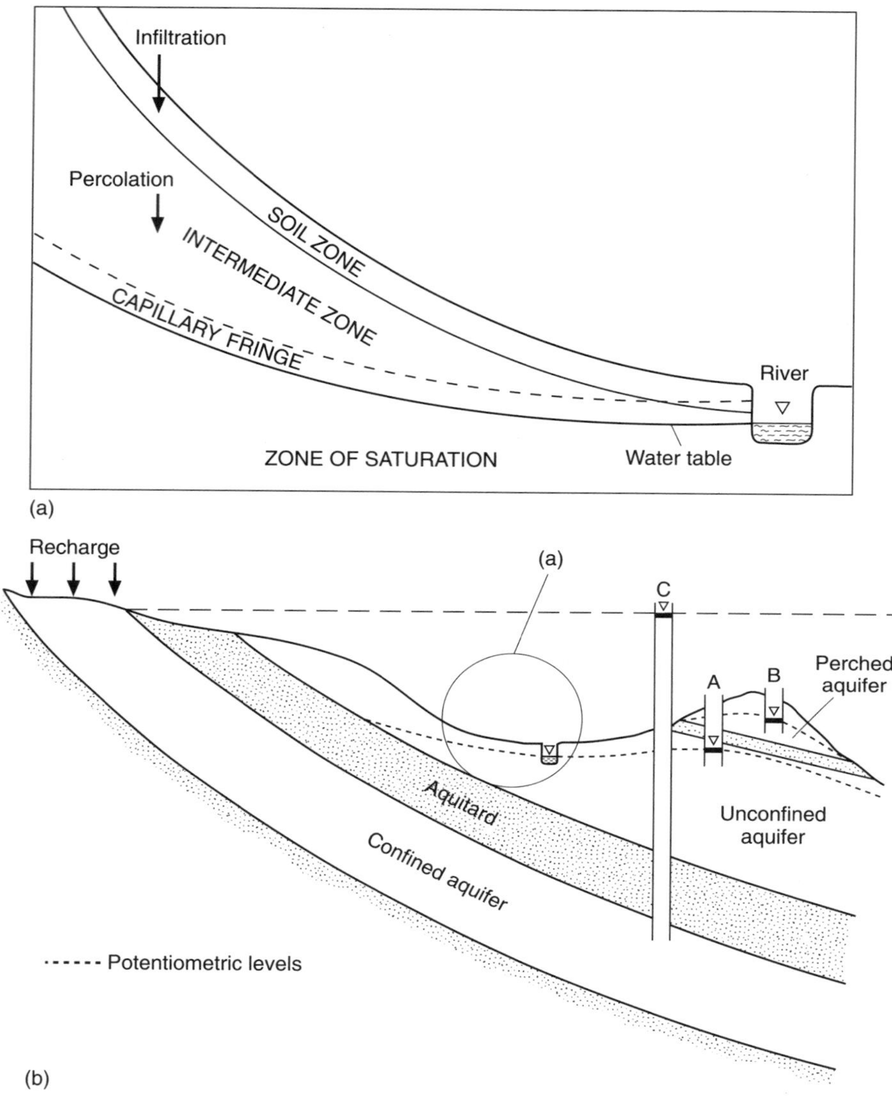

Figure 5.1 Subsurface water: (*a*) the main zones into which subsurface water has been traditionally classified; (*b*) the relationships between unconfined, perched and confined aquifers. Note that the potentiometric levels, as measured in piezometers A, B and C, may be different in each of them.

important one. In the saturated zone, the pore spaces are almost completely filled with water and the pressure of water is equal to or greater than atmospheric pressure. In the zone of aeration, the pore spaces contain both water and air and the pressure of water is less than atmospheric.

However, both saturated and unsaturated conditions are part of the continuum of subsurface water which is in a perpetual state of flux. The zone of aeration is really a transition zone in which water is absorbed, held or transmitted, either downwards towards the water table or upwards towards the soil surface from where it is evaporated. At times of prolonged or very intense rainfall, part of the soil zone may become temporarily saturated although still separated by unsaturated layers from the main groundwater below. Such transient, perched water tables may result when an impeding layer in the soil slows the drainage of infiltrating water, or when the surface layers of the soil are so slowly permeable as to result in saturated conditions. These often short-term and possibly localized areas of saturation within the zone of aeration may be very important in generating lateral flows to stream channels (see Section 7.4).

Groundwater is the earth's largest accessible store of fresh water and, excluding ice-sheets and glaciers, has been estimated to account for 94 per cent of all fresh water (see Table 1.1). Forty per cent of groundwaters is held within one km of the ground surface. The sheer size of this invisible store of water is even more strikingly illustrated by converting it to a precipitation equivalent. If distributed evenly over the entire global surface, groundwater would reach a depth of 19.6 m. Alternatively, it would cover the earth's land surfaces to a depth of 67.2 m, compared to the average annual precipitation of 0.75 m. In fact its distribution is quite variable as, for example, in the USA where the total pore space occupied by water, gas and petroleum ranges from 3 m under the Piedmont plateau to about 2500 m under the Mississippi delta (Heath, 1983). The role of groundwater as a vast regulator in the hydrological cycle can be seen from the large residence time, averaging about 300 years, although with considerable site-to-site variation. Groundwater sustains streamflow during periods of dry weather and is a major source of water in many arid regions. Due to its long residence time, areas that currently have an arid climate where there is little opportunity for water to percolate deeply, may nevertheless have significant groundwater reserves which are the result of recharge in former pluvial periods. There are, for example, enormous groundwater reserves, equivalent to over $5 \times 10^5\,km^3$ of water, under the Sahara.

Although there has been much controversy in the past regarding the source of groundwater, it is now clear that almost all of it is meteoric, i.e. composed of precipitated atmospheric moisture that has percolated downwards through the zone of aeration. Only small quantities of groundwater are derived from connate water, which originated as sea water trapped in some rocks at the time of their deposition. Valuable reviews of the development of ideas in groundwater hydrology were provided by Back and Herman (1997) and by Narasimhan (1998).

5.2 Geological background

Layers of rock or unconsolidated deposits that contain sufficient saturated material to yield significant quantities of water are known as *aquifers* and less permeable formations that transmit water more slowly than the adjacent aquifers are commonly known as *aquitards*. The terms are deliberately imprecise and indicate relative rather than absolute properties. Thus a silt bed would be an aquitard in a stratigraphic sequence of alternate sand and silt layers but, if interlayered with less permeable clay beds, the silt would be an aquifer. Most of the major aquifers are composed of *sedimentary* deposits formed from the erosion and deposition of other rocks, for example sandstones and limestones. In contrast, *igneous* and *metamorphic* rocks, formed under conditions of high temperatures and pressures, generally have few interconnected pore spaces and consequently most have only low water-bearing capacities.

The lower limit of groundwater occurs at a depth where interstices are so few and so small that further downward movement is virtually impossible. This groundwater boundary is frequently formed by a stratum of very dense rock, such as clay, slate or granite, or by the upper surface of the parent rock where the groundwater body occurs within a surface deposit of weathered material. Alternatively, the compression of strata with depth, which results from the increasing weight of the overlying rocks, means that a depth is eventually reached beyond which the interstices have been so reduced in both size and number that further water movement is effectively prevented. The depth at which this occurs will depend on the nature of the water-bearing rock, and would be shallower in a dense granite than in a deep porous sandstone. Nevertheless, the number of interstices tends generally to decrease with depth, and below about 10 km all rocks may, for practical purposes, be considered to be impermeable (Price, 1985).

5.3 Confined and unconfined aquifers

The upper boundary of the zone of saturation varies according to whether the groundwater is confined or unconfined (see Figure 5.1(b)). In the case of *unconfined groundwater*, this boundary is normally known as the *water table*, which is defined as the level where the porewater pressure is equal to atmospheric pressure.

The water table tends to follow the contours of the overlying ground surface, although in a more subdued form. Assuming a similar amount of infiltration from rainfall over both high and low ground, the amplitude of relief of the water table depends largely upon the texture of the material comprising the zone of saturation. In the case of very open-textured rock, such as well-jointed limestone, groundwater will tend to move through the interstices at such a rate that it rapidly attains a near-hydrostatic level, thus forming a more or less horizontal surface. On the other hand, with a fine-textured rock, groundwater movement will be so slow that water will still be draining towards the valleys from beneath the higher ground when additional infiltration from subsequent precipitation occurs, so that its height is built up under the latter areas. This tendency is magnified by the fact that precipitation normally increases with relief.

Perched groundwater represents a special case of unconfined groundwater where the underlying impermeable or semi-permeable bed is not continuous over a very large area and is situated at some height above the main groundwater body. Perched groundwater commonly occurs where an impermeable bed either exists at a shallow depth or intersects the side of a valley. In many areas the first unconfined groundwater encountered in drilling a borehole is of this perched type. As indicated earlier, water percolating through the zone of aeration after heavy rainfall may also be regarded as a temporary perched water body (see also the discussions of throughflow in Chapters 6 and 7).

The upper boundary of a *confined groundwater* body is formed by an overlying less permeable bed (see Figure 5.1(b)). The distinction between unconfined and confined groundwater is often made because of hydraulic differences between the flow of water under pressure and the flow of free, unconfined groundwater. Hydrologically, however, the two form part of a single, unified system. Thus, most confined aquifers have an unconfined area through which recharge to the groundwater occurs by means of infiltration and percolation, and in which a water table, as defined above, represents the upper surface of the zone of saturation. Furthermore, the confining impermeable bed rarely forms an absolute barrier to groundwater movement so that there is normally some interchange, and therefore a degree of hydraulic continuity, between the confined groundwater below the confining bed and the unconfined groundwater above it. Indeed, attention has already been drawn to the relative sense in which terms such as aquifer and aquitard must be used and to the fact that a rock forming an aquitard in one situation may form an aquifer in another.

Since the water table in the unconfined groundwater area, through which recharge takes place, is situated at a higher elevation than the confined area of the aquifer, it follows that the groundwater in the latter area is under a pressure equivalent to the difference in hydrostatic level between the two. If the pressure is released locally, as by sinking a well into the confined aquifer, the water level will theoretically rise in the well to the height of the hydrostatic head, i.e. the height of the water table in the recharge area minus the height equivalent of any energy losses resulting from friction between the moving groundwater and the solid matrix of the aquifer between the point of recharge and the point of withdrawal. The imaginary surface to which water rises in wells tapping confined aquifers is called the *potentiometric surface* (Lohman, 1972; Freeze and Cherry, 1979). This term has replaced earlier names, such as piezometric surface, and can be applied to both confined and unconfined aquifers. In practice, the elevation of the potentiometric surface is measured, not in a well, but in a *piezometer*, which is a tube having an unperforated casing except for a short length at the base. In the case of unconfined groundwater in steady-state conditions, i.e. when there is no flow, the water table and the potentiometric surface occur at the same level. In flowing unconfined groundwater, however, the elevations of the water table and the potentiometric surface will differ, hence the curvature of streamlines in local groundwater systems.

The term *artesian* has been used in different ways to describe either the confined aquifer itself, or a well that penetrates a confined aquifer, or any well producing freely flowing water up to the ground surface. Some of the classic and best-known free-flowing 'artesian' conditions are found in areas of gently folded sedimentary strata such as the type area in the province of Artois in northern France, the London Basin in England, or the great artesian basins of east-central Australia and the Great Plains of the USA. Early wells in these last two basins encountered water with sufficient initial pressure to gush more than 45 m above the ground surface, although the pressure head subsequently diminished rather rapidly (Davis and De Wiest, 1966). Artesian conditions have also been found in fissured and fractured crystalline rocks, particularly where they are overlain by relatively impervious superficial deposits. Natural artesian springs may also result from faulting in areas of folded sedimentary rocks. Artesian conditions do not always require an overlying confining bed and may occur in steep areas as a result of topographic controls (Section 5.5.4).

Categorizing groundwater as 'unconfined', 'confined' and 'perched' tends to overemphasize differences between the three types which may be difficult to recognize in practice, even in simple hydro-geological conditions. In areas of complex hydro-geology the terms become almost meaningless. However, the categories have been widely adopted in the literature and are used in this chapter as a convenient framework for the ensuing discussions of groundwater storage and groundwater movement.

5.4 Groundwater storage

Aquifers serve both as reservoirs for groundwater storage and as pipelines for groundwater movement. Because much groundwater moves so slowly and has such a long residence time in the aquifer, the storage function is often more obvious. The age of water in some aquifers in England and Libya, for example, has been estimated at more than 20 000–30 000 years (Downing *et al.*, 1977; Wright *et al.*, 1982) and in central Australia some groundwater may be 1.4 million years old (Habermehl, 1985). Clearly the accurate determination of groundwater age will be important for assessing both the resource potential of the groundwater body and also its vulnerability to pollution (Andrews, 1991). Dating methods are often based on the use of dissolved species derived either from the atmosphere or from beneath the ground surface, for example noble gases such as helium and argon.

This section considers the main features of groundwater storage, particularly the aquifer characteristics which affect it, such as porosity and specific yield and retention, and the mechanisms of storage change in both unconfined and confined aquifers.

5.4.1 Porosity

The amount of groundwater stored in a saturated material depends upon its *porosity*. This is normally expressed as the percentage of the total volume of a rock or soil which is represented by its *interstices*, or voids. While most interstices are small intergranular spaces some are cavernous. A knowledge of the nature of these interstices is clearly essential to an understanding of the storage and movement of groundwater, and several methods have been proposed to classify them. The most frequently used classification is based upon their mode of origin, and considers original and secondary interstices (Todd, 1980; Heath, 1983). *Original interstices*, as the name implies, were created at the time of origin of the rock in which they occur; thus in sedimentary rocks they coincide with the intergranular spaces, while in igneous rocks, where they normally result from the cooling of molten magma, they may range in size from minute intercrystalline spaces to large caverns. *Secondary interstices* result from the subsequent actions of geological, climatic or biotic factors upon the original rock. Faults and joints, enlarged perhaps by weathering and solution, are the most common. Such interstices are often found in old, hard, crystalline rocks which have virtually no intergranular porosity, and so play a significant role in the storage and movement of groundwater over large areas of Africa, northern North America, northern Europe and India, for example. A problem with this type of 'genetic' classification of the interstices is that the original intergranular spaces are often later modified by processes including cementation and solution. A very similar, but perhaps more appropriate, classification is, therefore, that between the primary porosity due to intergranular spaces in the soil or rock matrix (Figure 5.2(a)–(d)) and secondary porosity due to processes such as solution along joints and bedding planes (Figure 5.2(e)) or to jointing and fracturing (Figure 5.2(f)).

Confusion sometimes arises, in the case of a well-jointed rock, for example, between the porosity of the solid rock matrix (which may be very low) and the overall porosity of the whole stratum or formation that it comprises (which may be relatively high). It is important to realize that all interstices are involved in the concept of porosity, so that joints, bedding planes and fractures, including those greatly enlarged by solution and weathering, must be included as part of the total interstitial volume. This has important implications for the size of sample used in measuring porosity and hydraulic conductivity (see Sections 5.5.2 and 5.6), since the larger the sample, the more likely it is to include a large interstice, such as a joint or a fracture. Sometimes porous media contain voids that are not interconnected to other voids and which are therefore hydrologically inert. Such voids are not part of the *effective porosity*, which can be defined as the porosity that plays an active part in the storage and movement of water, and therefore are not considered further.

In analyses of aquifer systems it is common to assume that the aquifer is *homogeneous* and *isotropic*; that is that certain properties, such as porosity, have the same values in different parts of the aquifer (homogeneity) and in different

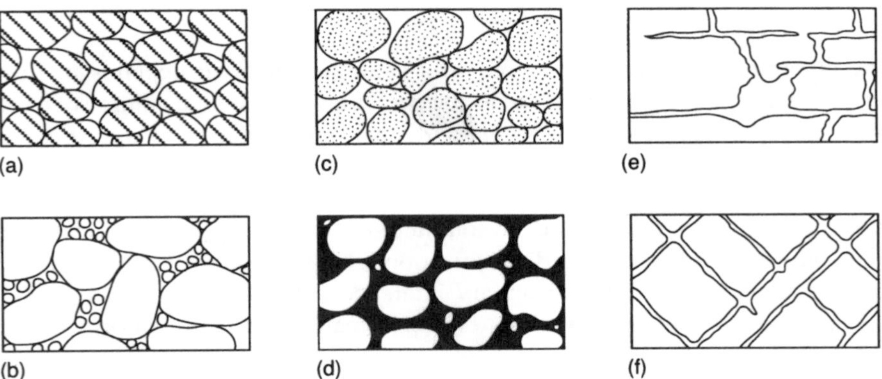

Figure 5.2 Types of interstices: (*a*) between relatively impermeable well-sorted particles, (*b*) between relatively impermeable poorly sorted particles, (*c*) between permeable particles, (*d*) between grains that have been partially cemented, (*e*) formed by solution along joints and bedding planes in carbonate rocks and (*f*) formed by fractures in crystalline rocks. (From an original diagram by Meinzer, 1923, with acknowledgements to the US Geological Survey.)

directions from the same point (isotropy). The very nature of primary and secondary geological processes means, however, that even apparently uniform deposits may have a preferred orientation of particles or fractures (anisotropy), and the stratification in most sediments often imparts a marked *heterogeneity* (Downing and Jones, 1985).

The porosity of a medium will depend upon a number of factors, including the shape, arrangement and degree of sorting of the constituent particles, and the extent to which modifications arising from solution, cementation, compaction and faulting have occurred. For example, poorly sorted material (with a large range of particle sizes) will have a low porosity since the interstices between the larger fragments will be filled with smaller particles and the porosity correspondingly reduced in comparison with material composed of uniformly sized grains. The combined effect of these various factors is illustrated in Table 5.1, which shows typical ranges of porosity for a number of different types of material. In general, rocks such as sandstone, shale and limestone have lower porosities than soils and other unconsolidated deposits. Initially it may seem strange that clay, which so often forms a barrier to water movement, has a very high porosity, while good aquifers, such as sandstone, have low to medium porosities. Further consideration, however, reveals that although porosity determines how much water a saturated medium can hold, by no means all of this water will be readily available for movement in the hydrological cycle. The proportion of the groundwater that is potentially 'mobile' will depend partly on how well the interstices are interconnected and partly on the size of the interstices and, therefore, by implication on the forces by which the water is retained in them.

Table 5.1 Typical ranges of porosity (based on data from various sources).

Material	*Range of porosity (%)*
Soils	30–65
Clay	35–60
Silt	35–60
Sand	30–50
Gravel	25–40
Siltstone	20–40
Karst limestone	5–50
Sandstone	5–30
Chalk/Oolitic limestone	5–30
Dolomitic limestone	0–50
Shale	0–15
Weathered granite	35–55
Basalt	5–35
Slate	1–5
Crystalline rocks	0–10
Fractured crystalline rocks	0–10
Granite	0–10

5.4.2 Specific yield and specific retention

Porosity determines the theoretical maximum amount of water that an aquifer can hold when it is fully saturated. In practice, however, only a part of this porosity is readily available to sustain groundwater discharge at seepages, springs or wells. This part is the *specific yield* which may be defined as the volume of water that can freely drain from a saturated rock or soil under the influence of gravity, and it is normally expressed as a percentage of the total volume of the aquifer (not just the pore space). It can be measured by a variety of methods, but well pumping tests generally give the most reliable results (Todd, 1980). The remaining volume of water (also usually expressed as a percentage of the total aquifer volume), which is retained by surface tension forces as films around individual grains and in capillary openings, is known as the *specific retention*. This term is analogous to 'field capacity' which is used when referring to soil water (Section 6.3.4), and is similarly imprecise in the sense that there is no fixed water content at which gravity drainage ceases. An extreme example of the difference between the porosity and specific yield of an aquifer is given by chalk. This is a very fine-grained limestone in which the matrix pore sizes are typically less than 1 μm and only a very small part of the pore water can drain freely under gravity (Price *et al.*, 1976). At a site in southern England, Wellings (1984a) found that the porosity of the chalk was about 30 per cent, but the specific yield was only about 1 per cent. A much larger proportion of the water was available to plants, and in the upper layers values of suction (see Section 6.3.1) in excess of 1000 kPa were recorded.

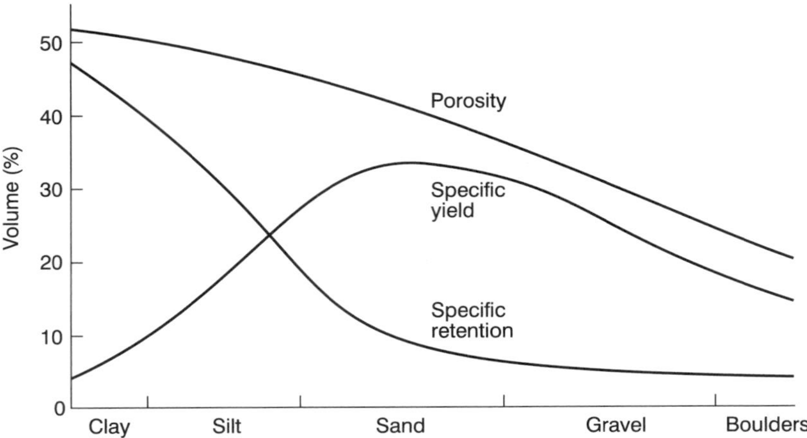

Figure 5.3 The relationship between porosity, specific retention and specific yield for different types of unconsolidated material, showing typical values which may differ significantly from values at a particular site. (From an original diagram by Eckis, 1934.)

The relationship between typical values of porosity, specific yield and retention for different types of unconsolidated material is shown in Figure 5.3. This indicates that, as the texture of the material becomes coarser, and by implication the importance of the larger interstices increases, both the specific retention and the total porosity decrease. Although clay has a high total porosity, the available water in terms of the specific yield is very small.

5.4.3 Storage change

Porosity, specific retention and specific yield control the ability of an aquifer to store and retain water, but the amount of water actually present at any one time reflects the changes of storage which are, in turn, determined by the changing balance between recharge to and discharge from the aquifer. If recharge during a given time interval exactly equals discharge, the amount of water in storage will remain constant; if recharge exceeds discharge, storage will increase while, if discharge is greater than recharge, storage will decrease. This may be conveniently expressed in the form of a simple water-balance equation:

$$\Delta S = Q_r - Q_d \tag{5.1}$$

where ΔS is the change in groundwater storage, Q_r is the recharge to groundwater and Q_d is the discharge from groundwater. A knowledge of the main components of the groundwater balance equation is normally an important prerequisite of successful attempts to develop groundwater as a resource.

The main components of recharge are:

- infiltration of precipitation at the ground surface which may result in water draining below the root zone and thus becoming potentially available for groundwater recharge;
- seepage through the bed and banks of surface water bodies such as lakes and rivers, especially in arid or semi-arid conditions, and even the oceans;
- groundwater leakage and inflow from adjacent aquitards and aquifers; and
- artificial recharge from irrigation, spreading operations, injection wells and leakage from water supply pipelines and sewers.

The main components of discharge are:

- evaporation, particularly in low-lying areas where the water table is close to the ground surface;
- natural discharge by means of spring flow and effluent seepage into surface water bodies;
- groundwater leakage and outflow through aquitards and into adjacent aquifers; and
- artificial abstraction.

The amount of water added to an aquifer by a given amount of recharge (or removed from an aquifer by a given amount of discharge) can be expressed as the *storativity*, or *coefficient of storage*, of the aquifer. Formally, this is defined as the volume of water that an aquifer takes into, or releases from, storage per unit surface area of aquifer per unit change in head. This is simply illustrated for a prism of unconfined aquifer in Figure 5.4(a). As the water table falls by 0.5 m over the prism's cross-sectional area of 10 m^2 groundwater drains from 5 m^3 (5 000 000 cc) of rock. If the amount of water draining out is 50 litres (50 000 cc) then the value of the dimensionless coefficient of storage is $50\,000/5\,000\,000 = 0.01$. In unconfined conditions the coefficient of storage corresponds to the specific yield (Section 5.4.2), provided that gravity drainage is complete, and it normally ranges from about 0.01 to 0.3 (Heath, 1983). In confined conditions (Figure 5.4(b)) no dewatering of the aquifer occurs as the potentiometric surface declines. Instead, the volume of water which is released as the potentiometric surface falls is a consequence of the slight compression of the granular structure of the aquifer and a very small expansion of the water in the aquifer (see Section 5.4.3.2). The storage coefficients of confined aquifers tend to be significantly smaller than those for unconfined aquifers, falling within the range 0.00005 to 0.005 (Todd, 1980). In other words, the potentiometric change associated with a given volume of recharge or discharge in a confined aquifer is much larger than that associated with the same volume of recharge or discharge in an unconfined aquifer.

Clearly, there are significant differences between the mechanism of storage changes in confined and unconfined conditions, and some of the more important of these differences will now be discussed.

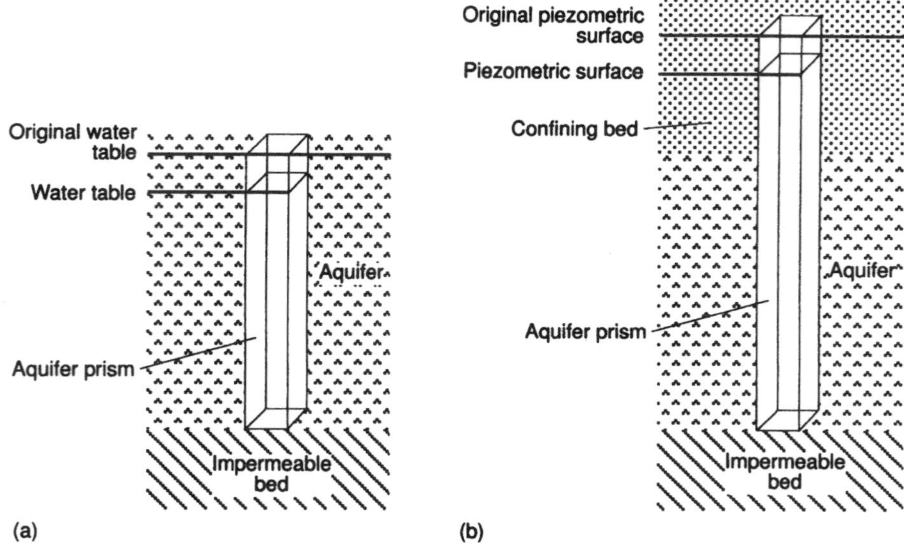

Figure 5.4 Diagram to illustrate some basic terms in the calculation of storage change in (*a*) unconfined and (*b*) confined aquifers. The aquifer prism has a cross-sectional area of $10\,m^2$ and the decline of the water table is 0.5 m. See text for explanation. (From an original diagram by Todd, 1980.)

Storage changes in unconfined aquifers

Storage changes in unconfined conditions are relatively uncomplicated and are usually reflected directly in variations of groundwater level. When recharge exceeds discharge, water table levels will rise, and when discharge exceeds recharge, they will fall. Recharge to and discharge from the same groundwater system usually occur simultaneously, so that groundwater level fluctuations reflect the net change of storage resulting from the interaction of these two components. The study and interpretation of water table fluctuations thus forms an integral part of the study of groundwater storage.

The precise hydrological linkage between a potential recharge event (for example percolating rainfall) and the consequent rise in water table level depends on conditions in the zone of aeration. Particularly important are the water content and hydraulic conductivity and the size and distribution of interstices. Apparently similar infiltration/percolation events at the ground surface can result in very different water table responses. For example, the rapid response of water table levels to precipitation, when the soil water content is high, almost certainly results from *translatory flow* (Hewlett and Hibbert, 1967). This is a displacement process which ensures that the water added to the water table during rainfall is not 'new' rainfall but previously stored rainfall that has been displaced downwards by successive bouts of infiltration (see also Section 7.4). Translatory flow

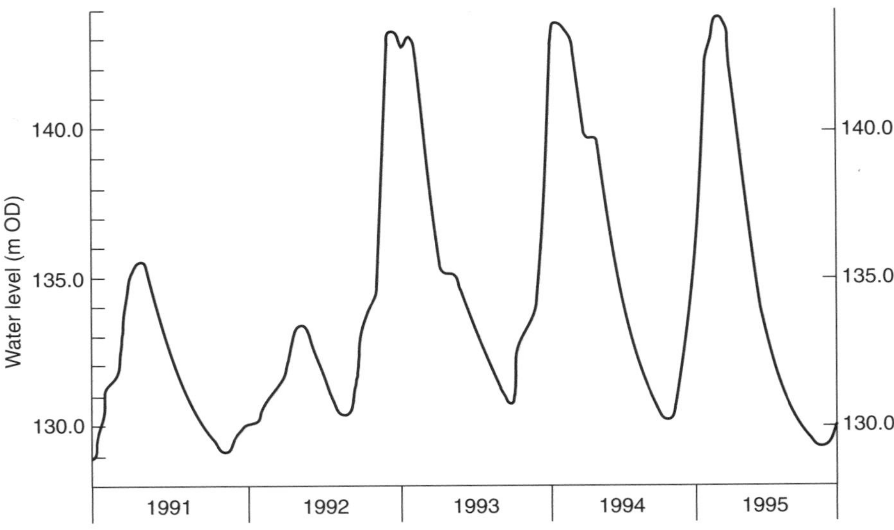

Figure 5.5 Hydrographs of groundwater level fluctuations in the chalk aquifer of southern England at Rockley, Wiltshire, for the calendar years 1991–95. (From an original diagram in IH/BGS, 1996.)

means that water tables may respond rapidly to precipitation even in low permeability material where rates of downward percolation are low. It is not effective in drier conditions, when the necessary continuity of interstitial water, from ground surface to water table, is broken. Tracer studies have shown that percolation through the zone of aeration is often spatially varied and that water may move preferentially along easier flowpaths such as cracks, fissures and decayed root channels (see Section 6.5.2 under 'Macropores'). These may be important in enabling pollutants such as fertilizers, pesticides and bacteria to bypass the filtering and purifying medium of the soil and be transmitted directly to the groundwater.

Seasonal fluctuations of water table level, reflecting as they do seasonal changes in storage and in water availability, are normally of considerable hydrological significance. In many areas, including Western Europe, high water levels occur during the winter months and low levels during the summer months, so that the hydrological year is regarded as beginning in October and ending in September. Water table levels in a chalk aquifer in southern England (Figure 5.5) are fairly typical, despite year-to-year variations. In some areas the normal climatically determined groundwater regime may be modified significantly by artificial factors such as irrigation and drainage.

Also of hydrological significance are long-term irregular or *secular fluctuations* of water table level. These are mainly associated with secular variations of rainfall (see Section 2.5.3) but may also result from changing patterns of groundwater

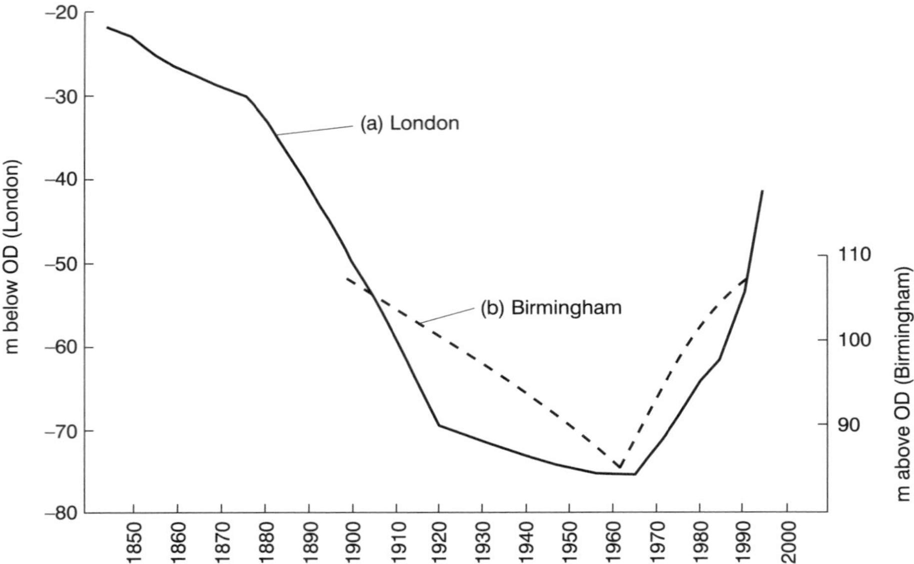

Figure 5.6 The steady decline of the water table under London and Birmingham was caused by excessive groundwater abstraction. Water levels have recovered in recent years mainly because of reduced industrial abstraction. ((*a*) is based on data in Marsh and Davies, 1983; IH/BGS, 1988, 1993, 1996; (*b*) is based on data in Lerner and Barrett, 1996.)

abstraction for industrial, agricultural and domestic purposes. Excessive abstraction over a prolonged period results in a gradual lowering of the potentiometric surface over a wide area, and this has already affected many major groundwater basins, especially in low-rainfall areas. Even in Europe significant groundwater decline has been observed around Kharkov (Ukraine), Lille (France) and in the Ruhr basin (Germany) (Arnold and Willems, 1996). In the London basin (England), continued groundwater abstraction from the 1820s caused a steady decline in groundwater levels until the 1960s. Thereafter, a rise in levels resulted from a decline in abstractions for industry and from increased leakage from the mains water supply network (Marsh and Davies, 1983) (Figure 5.6). Elsewhere in England widespread streamflow reduction has resulted from over-abstraction of groundwater from aquifers such as the chalk which extends from Yorkshire to the south coast. In many areas throughout the world groundwater abstraction has resulted in the incursion of inferior quality, saline, groundwater from adjacent aquifers or by direct seepage from the oceans into coastal aquifers (Section 5.5.8).

Short-term fluctuations of water table level, usually on a much smaller scale, are of less importance in interpreting storage changes but may provide useful hydrogeological information in particular circumstances. Thus, in many coastal and estuarine areas regular short-term fluctuations of water table level are associated with tidal movements since, if the sea level varies with a simple harmonic motion, a train of sinusoidal waves is propagated inland from the submarine outcrop of an aquifer (Todd, 1980). Investigations of this phenomenon have shown that the groundwater fluctuations are of decreased amplitude and lag behind the tidal fluctuations, the extent of the reduction and lag depending largely on distance from the sea and the ease with which groundwater can move through the aquifer. In valley bottom areas, discharge of groundwater by evaporation during the hottest part of the day may exceed the rate at which groundwater inflow from surrounding higher areas takes place and, as a result, the water table falls. During the evening and at night, the evaporation rate is much reduced, and it will be exceeded by groundwater inflow, so that the water table level will recover. This regular diurnal rhythm may be maintained for much of the summer, although it will be interrupted by periods of rainfall and reduced evaporation. If each daily drawdown exceeds the subsequent recovery, the water table level will gradually decline until it reaches a depth at which the capillary rise of water will be unable to satisfy evaporation demands at the soil surface (see also Section 6.4.4).

The relationship between storage and the level of the potentiometric surface is complicated by the fact that the latter responds to factors other than storage changes. This is most apparent in confined groundwater conditions, when variations of the potentiometric surface may result, for example, from changes of loading at the ground surface or from earthquake shocks. However, in some circumstances, unconfined groundwater may also be affected. Thus, in the late nineteenth century, Baldwin Latham found that spring flow in the chalk south of London increased with a sudden fall of barometric pressure, presumably because of a slight increase in water table level, and decreased with a rise in barometric pressure (Slichter, 1902). The magnitudes of the water table variations involved are likely to have been very small.

Maps showing the spatial change of water level over a period of time may provide valuable insights into the associated recharge and discharge. Figure 5.7 illustrates a simple derivation of the distribution of water level change from maps of initial and terminal water levels. This shows that the effects of recharge are more easily defined by the curved isopleths in the water level change map than by a visual comparison of the initial and terminal water table contours. Water level change maps may be used to calculate changes in the saturated volume of an unconfined aquifer and, if the storage coefficient is known, the actual change in groundwater storage.

Storage changes in confined aquifers

In unconfined conditions, aquifer compressibility is virtually negligible. By contrast, in confined conditions, the compressibility and elasticity of the aquifer

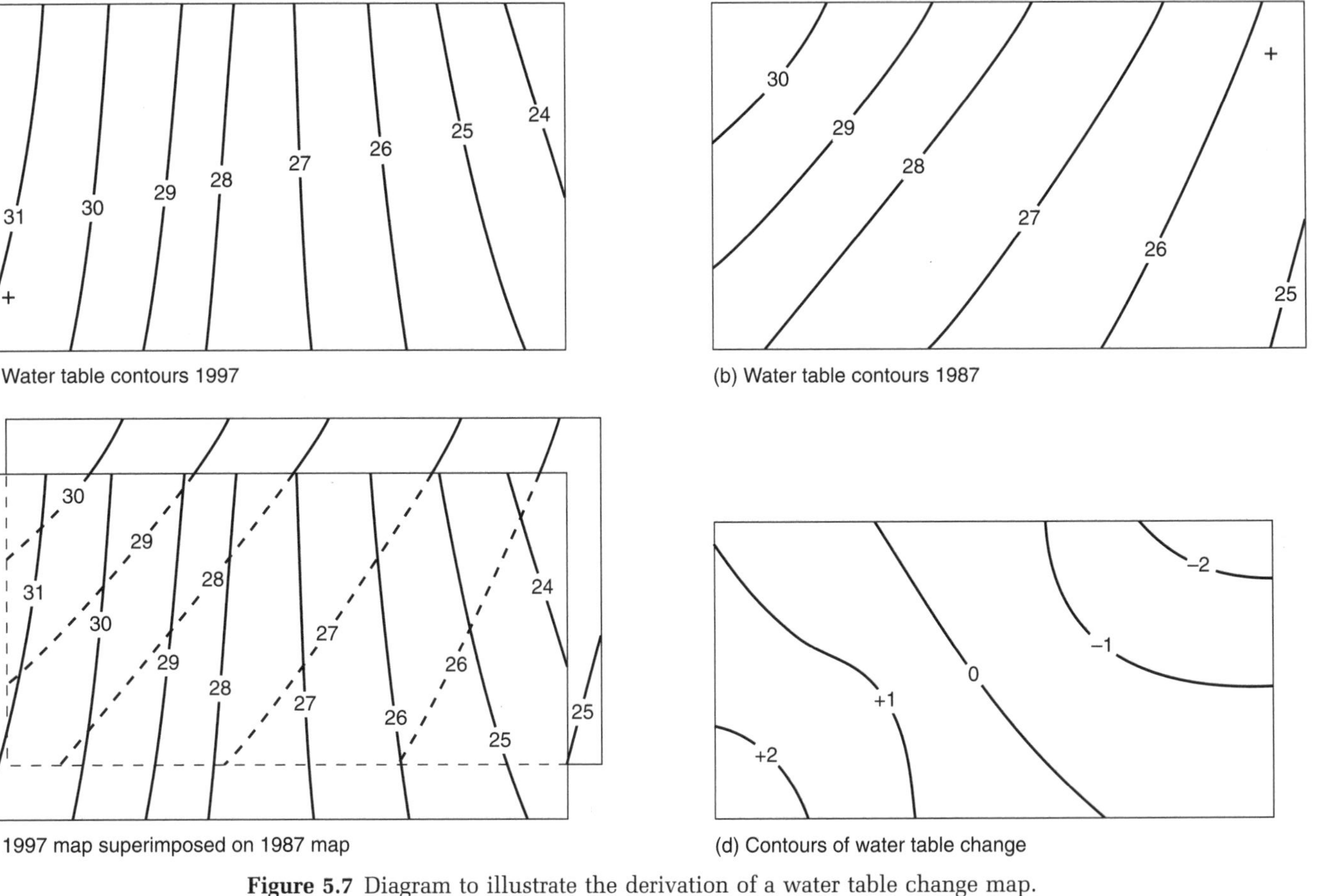

Figure 5.7 Diagram to illustrate the derivation of a water table change map.

greatly complicates the relationships between changes in potentiometric level and changes of groundwater storage.

In a confined aquifer, the total stress at a given depth is made up partly of *effective stress* (i.e. the pressure at the points of contact between individual solid particles, which is due to the weight of the overlying deposits) and partly of *neutral stress* (which is due to the pressure of the groundwater contained in the pore space of the aquifer). The neutral stress acts equally on all sides of the solid particles of the aquifer matrix and has little effect upon the overall porosity of the aquifer. However, when groundwater is removed from the aquifer the neutral stress (porewater pressure) is reduced, causing the remaining water to expand slightly. Since total stress remains the same, the effective stress (intergranular pressure) is correspondingly increased, causing the aquifer matrix to compress slightly and thereby reducing porosity. Conversely, when recharge to the aquifer occurs, neutral stress is increased, causing slight compression of the porewater and a reduction in effective stress which is accompanied by aquifer expansion and an increase in porosity. In other words, aquifer compression demands an increase in the grain-to-grain pressures within the matrix and aquifer expansion demands a decrease in the grain-to-grain pressure (Domenico, 1972). If the confined aquifer is *perfectly elastic* and the water levels in the recharge and discharge areas do not change, the original potentiometric head will ultimately be restored when discharge is followed by an equivalent amount of recharge. However, not all aquifers are perfectly elastic and especially in those having a high clay content, there may well be some permanent compaction and loss of porosity following a period of severely reduced potentiometric head.

The foregoing discussion and the earlier definition of the coefficient of storage both indicate that, for a given variation of potentiometric level, the change of groundwater storage in a confined aquifer will be small compared with that in an unconfined aquifer. Furthermore, any variation of loading on a confined aquifer may result in a fluctuation of the potentiometric surface. Such variations of loading may result from several causes, including barometric changes, variable tidal and gravitational loading and, in certain circumstances, from the occurrence of an earthquake or a nuclear explosion; in each case they may provide valuable information about the elastic and storage properties of the aquifers concerned.

With a continuing excess of discharge over recharge to a confined aquifer, the ever-increasing intergranular pressures and the resulting compression of the aquifer may ultimately result in the subsidence of the overlying ground surface. When it occurs such subsidence is normally inelastic and permanent. The ground surface has subsided as much as 10 m in countries such as Mexico, Japan and the USA (for example Johnson, 1991). Subsidence of 2–4 m has occurred at Osaka and Tokyo in Japan, Houston–Galveston in Texas and the Santa Clara valley, California (Domenico and Schwartz, 1990) and less severe but still significant subsidence in many other areas, such as Venice (Carbognin and Gatto, 1986), Bangkok (Bergado *et al.*, 1986), and Shanghai (Guangxiao and Yiaoqi, 1986). The amount of subsidence at any location depends upon the subsurface lithology, the thickness of the compressible materials and their storage characteristics, as well as upon the magnitude and duration of the decline in head. Almost all the main areas suffering from subsidence due to groundwater extraction are underlain by deposits of young, poorly consolidated material of high porosity, and much of the subsidence occurs due to compression of the clayey aquitards (Poland, 1984). Unsurprisingly, therefore, the relationship between head loss and subsidence is complex, with the main examples appearing to fall into two well-defined categories in which the ratio of subsidence to head loss is either less than 1 : 10 or more than 1 : 40 (Domenico and Schwartz, 1990).

The potentiometric surface in a confined aquifer is often smoother than the water table surface in an unconfined aquifer because local changes in head are more rapidly propagated as a recharge or discharge wave. Used carefully, however, potentiometric change maps may provide useful information about storage changes in confined aquifers.

5.5 Groundwater movement

Groundwater taking an active part in the hydrological cycle moves more or less continuously from areas of recharge to areas of discharge. Some groundwater movement is in response to a *chemical* or *electrical gradient*. For example, groundwater moves from dilute to more concentrated pore-fluid solutions, especially in clays, which tend to exhibit osmotic characteristics consistent with those of leaky semi-permeable membranes. Osmotically driven groundwater movement may play an important role in some arid and semi-arid basins. In some circumstances, however, there is clear evidence that groundwater movement in response to a solute concentration gradient is not always from the dilute solution to the more concentrated solution. In such cases the driving force seems to be the existing electrical field rather than the concentration gradient, a process which is, again, more efficient in argillaceous materials (Olsen *et al.*, 1989).

Mostly, however, groundwater movement is in response to the prevailing *hydraulic gradient*, and it is on this type of movement that the remainder of this chapter concentrates. Hydrological interest is concerned with both the speed and the direction of groundwater movement. Groundwater flow rates are very slow compared with those of surface water and are also very variable. For example, rates of groundwater movement through permeable strata in the UK range from as low as a fraction of a millimetre per day in some fine-grained pervious rocks, to as much as 5500 m day^{-1} through fissured chalk (Buchan, 1965).

The direction of groundwater movement is similarly variable since, like surface water, groundwater tends to follow the line of least resistance. Other things being equal, therefore, flow tends to be concentrated in areas where the interstices are larger and better connected, and the hydrologist's problem is to locate such areas, often from rather scanty geological information. Theoretical analyses commonly assume ideal and greatly simplified conditions, and the results from them may be difficult to apply in field conditions. For example, it is often assumed that aquifers are homogeneous and isotropic, and that groundwater flow systems are more or less complete and independent, for example bounded by impermeable beds. In most real situations, however, flow systems are bounded by semi-permeable rather than by completely impermeable beds, so that very complex and widespread systems of regional groundwater flow develop. However, simplifying assumptions are often reasonable and helpful, although it should be emphasized that important 'untypical' groundwater flow systems are found in, say, limestone and volcanic rocks where most groundwater flow occurs through the fracture systems (cf. Legrand and Stringfield, 1973; Streltsova, 1976; Price, 1987; NERC, 1991).

The direction and rate of groundwater movement in a porous medium may be calculated from the prevailing hydraulic gradient and the hydraulic conductivity of the water-bearing material, using the Darcy equation.

5.5.1 Darcy's law

Most groundwater movement takes place in small interstices so that the resistance to flow imposed by the material of the aquifer itself may be considerable. As a consequence the flow is *laminar*, i.e. successive fluid particles follow the same path or streamline and do not mix with particles in adjacent streamlines. As the velocity of flow increases, especially in material having large pores, the occurrence of turbulent eddies dissipates kinetic energy and means that the hydraulic gradient becomes less effective in inducing flow. In very large interstices, such as those found in many limestone and volcanic areas, groundwater flow is almost identical to the turbulent flow of surface water.

The law that expresses the relationship between capillary or laminar flow and the hydraulic gradient was stated by Poiseuille (1846), and is actually a special case of Darcy's law (Hubbert, 1956). Later, Darcy (1856) confirmed the application of this law to the movement of groundwater through natural materials and, for hydrologists, the law has since become associated with his name.

Darcy's law for saturated flow may be written as

$$v = -K\left(\frac{\delta h}{\delta l}\right) \tag{5.2}$$

where v is the so-called 'macroscopic velocity' of the groundwater ($\mathrm{m\,d^{-1}}$). This is not in fact a velocity but rather a 'volume flux density', i.e. a volume of flow ($\mathrm{m^3}$) through a cross-sectional area ($\mathrm{m^2}$) which contains both interstices and solid matrix. K is the saturated hydraulic conductivity and $\delta h/\delta l$ is the hydraulic gradient comprising the change in hydraulic head (h) with distance along the direction of flow (l). K is therefore also a volume flux density per unit hydraulic gradient (when the hydraulic gradient is set at one). The negative sign indicates that flow is in the direction of decreasing head. Two main components contribute to total hydraulic head (which equates with the elevation of the potentiometric surface) at a given point in the groundwater flow system. These are: (i) the

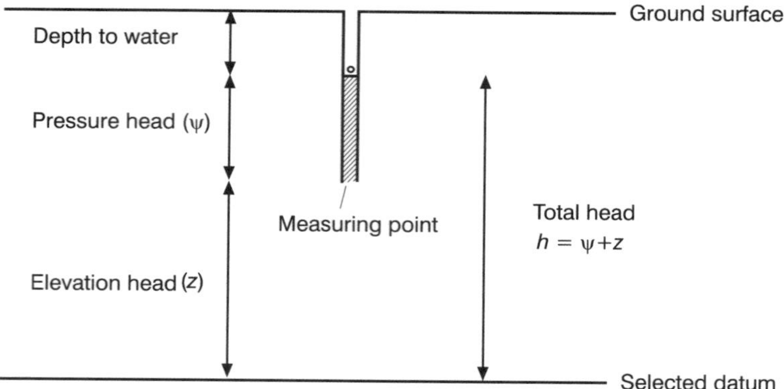

Figure 5.8 Diagram showing the elevation head (z), pressure head (ψ) and total head (h) for a specific measuring point in a groundwater flow field.

porewater pressure at that point, as measured for example in a piezometer, which determines the *pressure head*, and (ii) height above sea-level, or some selected datum, which determines the *elevation head*. The total head (h) is therefore defined as

$$h = \psi + z \tag{5.3}$$

where ψ is the pressure head and z is the elevation head above a selected datum (Figure 5.8). Both pressure and elevation are forms of potential energy, the one possessed by virtue of state and the other by virtue of position. Kinetic energy, the other energy component of fluid flow, is ignored because groundwater flow is so slow. Total head may be converted to *potential energy* (ϕ) by applying the gravitational constant so that

$$\phi = gh \quad \text{or}$$

$$\phi = \psi_{\mathrm{p}} + \psi_{\mathrm{g}} \tag{5.4}$$

where ψ_{p} is the pressure potential and ψ_{g} is the elevation potential. Using this terminology, Darcy's law states that water will move from a location where the potential energy is higher to one where it is lower. This proposition is equally applicable to either saturated or unsaturated conditions, as is shown in Chapter 6.

The *hydraulic conductivity*, K, in the Darcy equation refers to the characteristics of both the porous medium and the fluid. This is virtually synonymous with the earlier term coefficient of permeability. It should not be confused with the *intrinsic* or *specific permeability*, usually denoted as k, which depends only upon the characteristics of the porous medium itself. As indicated in the explanation of Eq. 5.2, the Darcy equation yields only an apparent velocity value, the *macroscopic velocity*, through the cross-sectional area of solid matrix and interstices. Clearly, flow velocities through the interstices alone will be higher than the macroscopic value, and since the interstices themselves vary in shape, width and direction, the actual velocity in the soil or rock is highly variable. Furthermore, due to the tortuous nature of the flow path of a water particle around and between the grains in an aquifer, the actual distance travelled exceeds the apparent distance given by the measured length of the porous medium in the average direction of flow. Thus the *effective velocity* of groundwater movement through the interstices is equal to the volume flux density (macroscopic velocity) divided by the effective porosity (Section 5.4.1). Accordingly, the Darcy equation is strictly applicable only to cases in which the cross-section being considered is so much greater than the dimensions of its microstructure that it can reasonably be regarded as uniform.

Another factor complicating the field application of the Darcy equation is that hydraulic conductivity is often markedly anisotropic, particularly in fractured and jointed rock. Furthermore, extreme flow velocities may result in deviations from Darcy's law. The effect of turbulence in modifying the relationship between the hydraulic gradient and high rates of flow has already been mentioned. At the other extreme, some investigators have claimed that in clay soils, with small pores and low hydraulic gradients, the very low flow rates are less than proportional to the hydraulic gradient (Miller and Low, 1963; Swartzendruber, 1962). A possible explanation is that much of the water in such material is strongly held by adsorptive forces and may be more rigid and less mobile than ordinary water (Hillel, 1982).

Despite concern about its strict validity (for example Davis *et al.*, 1992), the Darcy law constitutes an adequate description of the groundwater flow. It can be successfully applied to virtually all normal cases of groundwater flow and is equally applicable to both confined and unconfined conditions. An understanding of most groundwater problems demands information not only about the velocity of water movement but also about the velocity with which disturbances of head (resulting, for example, from a seismic event) are transmitted. This is usually many hundreds of times faster and is proportional to the square root of the hydraulic diffusivity (a), which is defined as

$$a = \frac{Kb}{S} \tag{5.5}$$

where K is the hydraulic conductivity, b is the saturated thickness of the aquifer and S is the coefficient of storage (Section 5.4.3 under 'Storage change'). For confined conditions, this ratio therefore depends not only on the conductivity of the aquifer material but also on its elastic properties.

By itself, the Darcy law suffices to describe only steady flow conditions, so that for most field applications it must be combined with the mass-conservation (or continuity) law to obtain the general flow equation or, for saturated conditions, the Laplace equation. A direct solution of the latter equation for groundwater flow conditions is generally not possible so that it is necessary to resort to various approximate or indirect methods of analysis, some of which are referred to later in Section 5.5.4.

5.5.2 Factors affecting hydraulic conductivity

Fundamental to the application of Darcy's law is a knowledge of the hydraulic conductivity of the saturated medium. The factors affecting hydraulic conductivity may be conveniently grouped into those pertaining to the water-bearing material itself and those pertaining to the groundwater as a fluid.

An important, though often elusive, *aquifer characteristic* concerns the geometry of the pore spaces through which groundwater movement occurs. Many studies have used an indirect approach whereby the pore space geometry is related to factors such as grain size distribution on the not always very sound assumption that there is a definable relationship between these properties and pore size distribution. Another aquifer characteristic relates to the geometry of the rock particles themselves, particularly in respect to their surface roughness, which may have an important effect on the speed of groundwater flow. Finally, hydraulic conductivity and therefore groundwater flow may be influenced significantly by secondary geological processes such as faulting and folding, which may increase or decrease groundwater movement, secondary deposition, which will tend to reduce the effective size of the interstices and the flow of water, and secondary solution in rocks such as limestone. Indeed, Heath (1982) mapped five types of groundwater flow system in the USA largely on the basis of the way in which porosity has been affected by secondary geological processes.

The chalk in England provides examples at various scales of the effect of aquifer characteristics on groundwater movement. In East Anglia, the areas of high transmissivity (the product of hydraulic conductivity and the saturated thickness of the aquifer) tend to be related to topographic valleys, which in turn are associated with fold or fault structures, or with increased fissuring. In the London Basin, compacted synclinal areas in the chalk are associated with low rates of groundwater flow compared with the more open-textured anticlinal areas (Ineson, 1963). Although tranmissivity maps are normally based on well tests or groundwater models, Bracq and Delay (1997) showed that, in Northern France, transmissivity could also be related to surface breaks of slope (lynchets) which reflect underlying vertical fracturing in the chalk aquifer.

Other studies have emphasized the role of fracture systems in determining the rates and directions of maximum groundwater flow in aquifers ranging from the karst of the Yucatan peninsula, Mexico (Steinich and Marín, 1997), to the granite of Cornwall in the south-western UK (NERC, 1991). As the scale of measurement in such rocks is increased, for example from laboratory cores, through borehole tests, to basin-wide groundwater flow, there is often an increase in the observed hydraulic conductivity (for example Garven, 1985). This is caused by the incorporation into the measurement sample of ever larger and more extensive fracture systems (see also Section 5.6 and Figure 9.2).

The effects of *fluid characteristics*, such as density and viscosity, on hydraulic conductivity tend to be rather less important than the effects of the aquifer characteristics. Certainly, in relation to normal conditions of groundwater flow, the physical properties of the groundwater are likely to be influenced only by changes in temperature and salinity. Temperature, by inversely affecting the viscosity, has a direct influence on the speed of groundwater flow. Since, however, most groundwater is characterized by relatively constant temperatures, this factor is unlikely to be important except in special circumstances.

Variations of salinity are also unlikely to be significant in normal groundwater conditions. Where saline infiltration occurs, however, hydraulic conductivities may be affected both by changes in the ionic concentrations of the groundwater and also by the chemical effect of the saline water on the aquifer material itself, particularly where this is of a clayey nature (Ineson, 1956). Increasing salinity will increase water density and so may affect hydraulic heads and gradients.

Finally, groundwater studies traditionally presuppose that hydraulic conductivity is not affected by water content, since the aquifer matrix below the water table is assumed to be saturated. Recent work has shown that for some materials, such as peat, full saturation may be prevented due to the presence of undissolved gases. In peat, methane is produced as a by-product of the microbial decay of peat in anoxic conditions and, by occupying part of the pore space, thereby reduces both water storage and hydraulic conductivity (Baird, 1997). A similar effect has also been observed in mineral soils when air is trapped in soil pores during rapid infiltration or after the sudden rise of a shallow water table.

5.5.3 Flow nets

Although groundwater flow cannot be observed directly, it is possible to make use of the relationship between flow and the hydraulic or potential gradient in order to examine two-dimensional groundwater flow indirectly by reference to the subsurface distribution of groundwater potential. Lines joining points of equal potential (ϕ) are known as *equipotentials*, and the potentiometric surface of an aquifer (confined or unconfined) above a datum plane may be contoured at regular increments of ϕ by a family of such lines. This is shown in Figure 5.9, where the equipotentials increase in value from ϕ_1 to ϕ_9. In accordance with Darcy's law, groundwater is driven along the maximum gradient of potential, i.e. perpendicular to the equipotential lines. This is depicted by the *streamlines*, which show the direction of the force on the moving water and therefore represent the paths followed by particles of water. Since at any one point the flow can only have one direction, it follows that streamlines never intersect. The network of meshes formed by the two families of equipotentials and streamlines is known as a *flow net*.

Flow nets show the direction of groundwater movement and can also be used to estimate the rate of flow, either by graphical construction or mathematically. The zone between any pair of neighbouring streamlines is known as a *streamtube*,

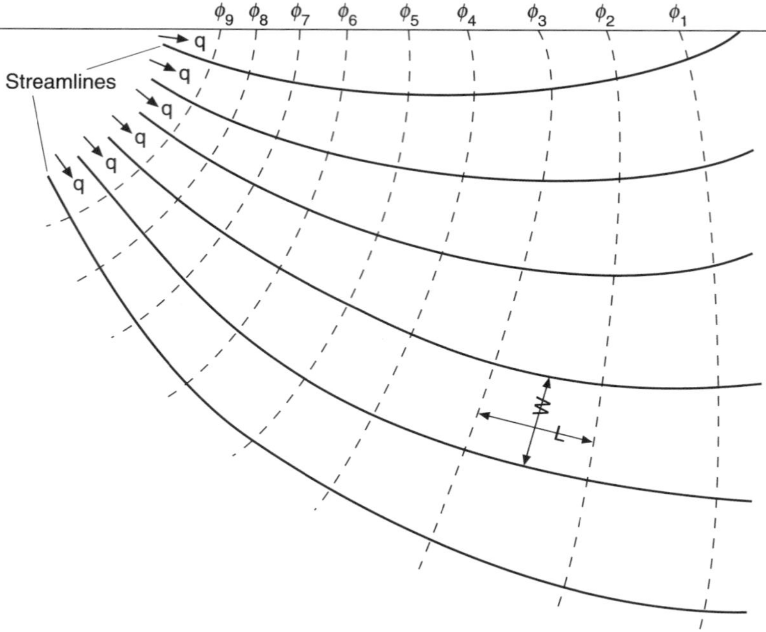

Figure 5.9 Flow net showing equipotentials (ϕ) and streamlines. Equipotentials are the contours of the potentiometric field (increasing in value from ϕ_1 to ϕ_9) and streamlines indicate the direction of groundwater flow. See text for further explanation.

and at every cross-section of a streamtube the total flow (q) remains the same. If adjacent equipotentials differ by the same increment of potential ($\Delta\phi = \phi_2 - \phi_1 = \phi_3 - \phi_2$, etc.) and the streamlines are chosen to be evenly spaced so as to give the same rates of flow in all streamtubes, Darcy's law can be applied to any of the elements of the flow net having width W and length L so that

$$q = -K\Delta\phi\left(\frac{W}{L}\right) \tag{5.6}$$

Regional and complex groundwater systems may consist of several aquifers and aquitards and therefore involve flow through both the aquifers and the confining beds. Hydraulic conductivities in aquifers are usually several orders of magnitude greater than in confining beds and so offer least resistance to flow, the result being that head loss (and hence hydraulic gradient) becomes much less in aquifers. As Figure 5.10 indicates, streamlines are refracted at the boundary between media of different permeabilities, in the direction that produces the shortest flow path through the confining bed. Streamline refraction permits the conservation of fluid mass when flow takes place across the permeability

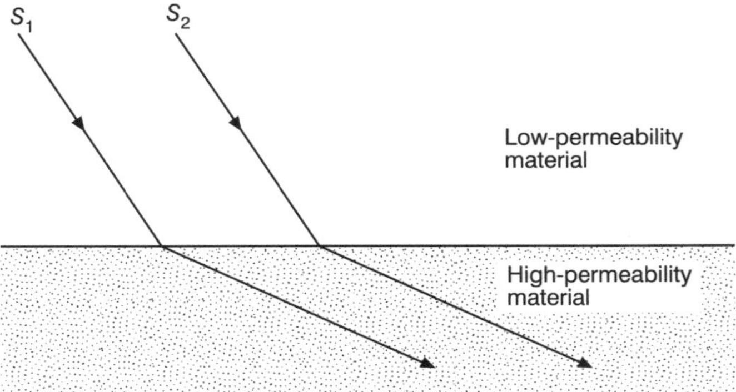

Figure 5.10 Refraction of streamlines across a boundary between two materials of differing permeability. (From an original diagram by Todd, 1980.)

boundary. Thus, in accordance with Darcy's law, other factors being equal, the higher the permeability, the smaller the area required to pass a given volume of water in a given time (Domenico, 1972). The streamlines are thus widely spaced in the low-permeability material and closely spaced in the high-permeability material.

The use of flow nets, which are commonly constructed in either a vertical plane or a horizontal plane (i.e. the potentiometric map), probably originated with Forchheimer in the nineteenth century (Maxey, 1969) but was revived again with important modifications by Hubbert (1940) and later in connection with computer models of groundwater flow (for example Tóth, 1962) and a growing interest in regional flow systems.

5.5.4 Two-dimensional groundwater flow

Groundwater flow is three-dimensional, although methods of estimating it have traditionally been simplified so as to consider it taking place in two dimensions rather than three. Such simplification was ideally suited to the use of flow nets, basic electrical analogues and parallel-plate 'Hele-Shaw' models of groundwater flow. Although it is less relevant now that affordable quasi-three-dimensional groundwater modelling packages are readily available for implementation in a Macintosh™ or Windows™-based PC environment, nevertheless the two-dimensional characterization of groundwater flow provides a useful conceptual framework for the present discussions.

Figure 5.9 is a two-dimensional potentiometric map which can be viewed as either a horizontal or a vertical section. If the equipotentials (ϕ_1 having the lowest value and ϕ_9 having the highest value) are taken to represent water table levels, Figure 5.9 could be regarded as a map, in the horizontal plane, of unconfined groundwater flow in a *non-homogeneous aquifer*. Since the change in potential between adjacent pairs of equipotentials is equal and the hydraulic gradient varies inversely with the distance between equipotentials, then if inflow for any section is just balanced by outflow, the relative steepness of the hydraulic gradient reflects the hydraulic conductivity, as indicated in Darcy's law. Thus in Figure 5.9 the hydraulic conductivity is lowest in the west of the area and increases towards the east where the equipotentials and streamlines are more widely spaced.

Alternatively, Figure 5.9 can be viewed as showing the horizontal distribution of potential in a *homogeneous aquifer*. In this case the variable spacing of the equipotentials would reflect a variation in the rate of groundwater flow, with flow decreasing eastwards in response to the decrease in hydraulic gradient in this direction.

Because of the readier availability of the appropriate data, groundwater flow is normally considered as a two-dimensional problem in the vertical rather than the horizontal plane, and in this case it is information on the rate of change of hydraulic head or potential with depth that facilitates the definition of the groundwater flow pattern. If groundwater potential increases with depth, flow will be upwards, and if it decreases with depth, flow will be downwards (Figure 5.11). In this context Figure 5.9 could be viewed as a potentiometric map in the vertical plane with the streamlines illustrating a pattern of groundwater recharge and downward movement at the lefthand side and the beginnings of groundwater discharge and upward movement at the righthand side.

Under hydrostatic conditions, there is no change of groundwater potential with depth below the water table because the increase of pressure potential (ψ_p) is exactly offset by the decrease in gravitational potential (ψ_g) (Figure 5.12). As a

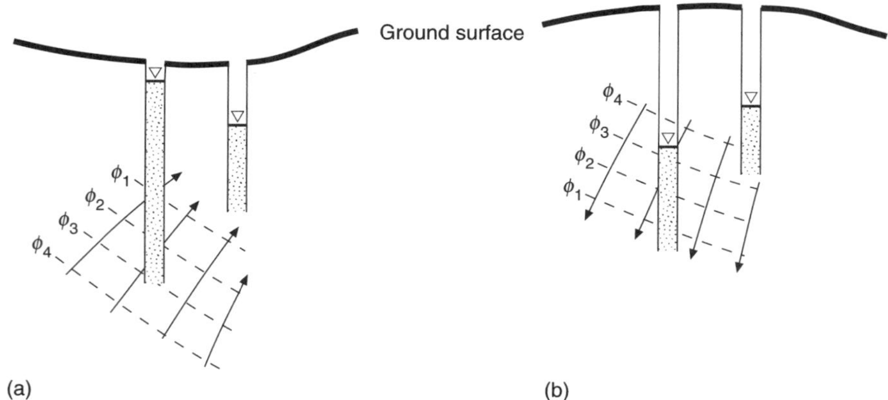

Figure 5.11 Difference in water levels in piezometers of different depths and the resulting direction of movement of groundwater in the vertical plane. The piezometers reflect an increase of potential with depth in (*a*), resulting in an upward movement of groundwater and a decrease of potential with depth in (*b*), resulting in a downward movement of groundwater. (From an original diagram by Domenico, 1972.)

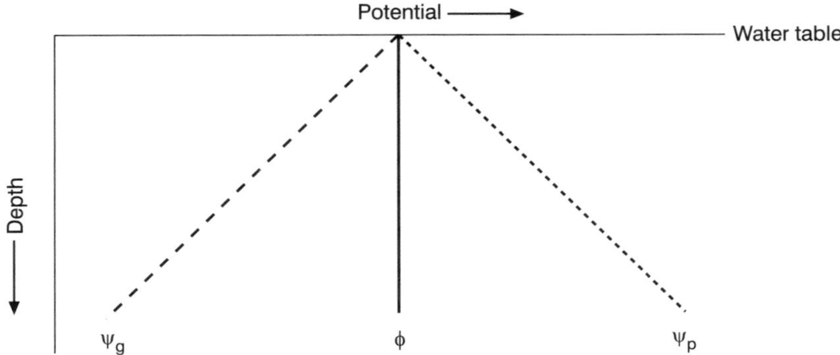

Figure 5.12 In hydrostatic conditions the increase of pressure potential (ψ_p) with depth below the water table is offset by the decrease in gravitational potential (ψ_g), resulting in no change in total groundwater potential (ϕ) with depth.

result, there is no groundwater movement in the vertical plane. However, a zero change of potential with depth is also characteristic of situations where the direction of unconfined groundwater flow is approximately horizontal. In such cases the equipotentials are approximately vertical and are labelled by the height at which they intersect the water table and the potential gradient is simply the slope of the water table immediately above the given point (Childs, 1969). This might be the situation, for example, where an extensive thin permeable bed rests on an underlying horizontal impermeable bed and is an approximation proposed by Dupuit (1863) and elaborated by Forchheimer (1914) and subsequently known as the Dupuit–Forchheimer approximation. This is an empirical approximation to the actual flow field and ignores vertical flows. In practice, however, the approach was widely used by engineers, especially before the advent of more sophisticated desk-top computer models of groundwater flow.

5.5.5 Unconfined groundwater flow—classical models

The now conventional hydrodynamic approach to the solution of groundwater problems (including the application of flow net techniques) was developed by Hubbert (1940) on the basis of the pioneering work of Chamberlin (1885) and King (1899). Hubbert's model incorporated the principal proposals of Chamberlin and King, i.e. that the water table is a subdued replica of the local topography, that topographical divides may also act as groundwater divides and that groundwater moves from topographical high areas to topographical low areas (Domenico and Schwartz, 1990). Figure 5.13 illustrates the essential features of Hubbert's presentation for a homogeneous, isotropic material. Equipotentials are shown as broken lines and the value of hydraulic head for each line is equal to the elevation of its intersection with the water table. Streamlines, indicating the groundwater flow paths, connect the source areas in which recharge is dominant

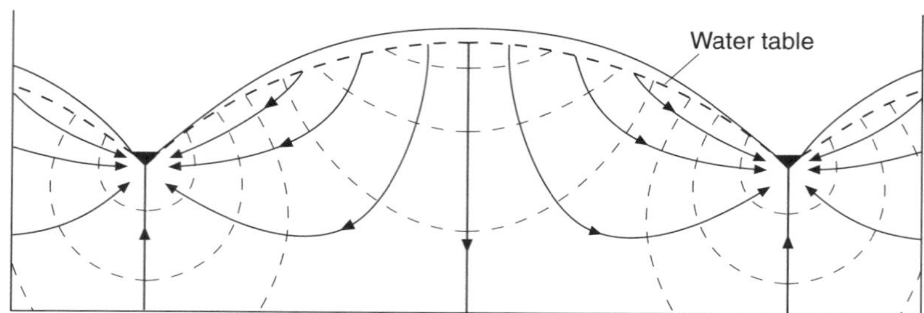

Figure 5.13 Approximate groundwater flow pattern in a uniformly permeable unconfined aquifer. (From an original diagram by M.K. Hubbert, *Journal of Geology*, **48**, University of Chicago, 1940. Used with permission of the University of Chicago Press.)

with the sinks in which discharge is dominant. Under closed conditions, groundwater flow would ultimately result in the complete drainage of water from the topographic highs and the production of a flat surface of minimum potential energy (the hydrostatic condition). This tendency, however, is counteracted by continuous replenishment from precipitation. The result of this continuous movement and renewal is the flow pattern shown whose upper surface, the water table, is a subdued replica of the topography. The source areas are the topographic highs and in this diagram the sinks are shown as streams, and each groundwater flow cell is bounded by the lines of vertical flow beneath the groundwater divides and sinks or by widely distributed impermeable beds or by both.

Tóth (1962) suggested that, whereas major streams may indeed be major groundwater sinks, as in the Hubbert model, for valleys having only low-order streams groundwater discharge is not concentrated at the stream but is broadly distributed on the down-gradient side of a midline between the valley bottom and the groundwater divide, as shown in Figure 5.14. As can be seen, the midline is an approximately vertical equipotential about which the flow pattern is broadly symmetrical, giving a central area of lateral flow where groundwater potential does not vary with depth, an up-gradient area of downward flow or recharge where groundwater potential decreases with depth and the down-gradient area of upward flow or discharge where groundwater potential increases with depth, as in Figure 5.11. Tóth's work, based on concepts first introduced by Meinzer (1917) to describe the flow system in Big Smokey Valley, Nevada, stimulated other contributions including a similar model for arid and semi-arid areas having the same three major components but differing somewhat as a result of physiographic and topographic conditions (Maxey, 1968; Maxey and Farvolden, 1965).

The unconfined groundwater models discussed above all assume that the porous medium is hydrologically isotropic and homogeneous. In many areas this may not be an unreasonable assumption. Maxey (1969) suggested, for example,

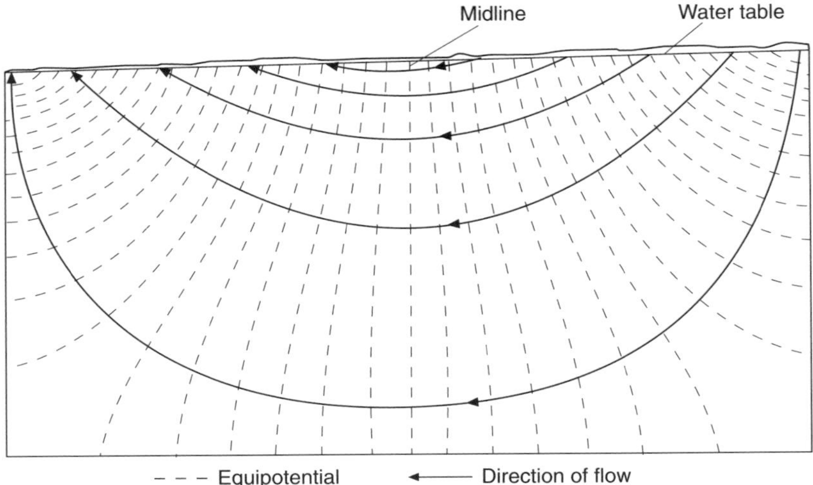

Figure 5.14 Groundwater flow pattern symmetrical about the midline between the valley bottom and the groundwater divide. (From an original diagram by J. Tóth, *Journal of Geophysical Research*, **67**, p. 4380, Fig. 3. © 1962 American Geophysical Union.)

that tectonic stresses in the Great Basin of the south-western USA have so broken up the rocks that large areas act as a single, homogeneous and isotropic hydrological unit in much the same way as a permeameter filled with sand.

5.5.6 Confined groundwater flow

At the other extreme from a homogeneous isotropic unconfined aquifer, is the situation where, with alternating beds of markedly different lithology and permeability, groundwater is confined beneath an impermeable layer and the potentiometric surface of the flow field is completely independent of surface topography and of the configuration of the water table in the upper, unconfined groundwater body. What is commonly found in actual conditions is neither a completely confined system nor a completely unconfined system, but rather a system of flow that possesses distinct characteristics of both extremes (Domenico, 1972). For example, it is noted in Section 5.3 that confining beds rarely form an absolute barrier to water movement so that there is normally some degree of hydraulic continuity. This suggests that the potential distribution with depth in a confined groundwater body is partly affected by the potential distribution of the overlying water table. Also, in an apparently unconfined situation, the flow field may possess characteristics of confinement whenever flow is refracted on emerging from a low-permeability bed, so that it proceeds almost tangentially to the lower surface of that bed. This is clearly illustrated in Figure 5.15, which represents an unconfined system with hydraulic continuity in the

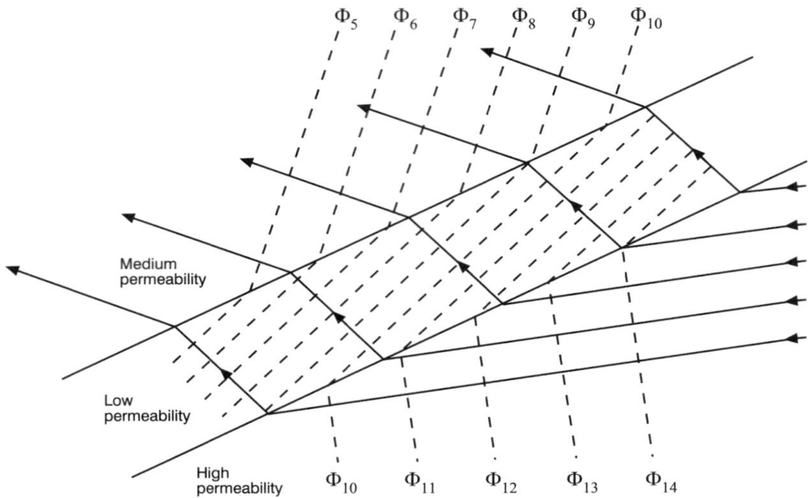

Figure 5.15 Streamline refraction in an unconfined system of permeability contrasts. (From an original diagram by M.K. Hubbert, *Journal of Geology*, **48**, University of Chicago, 1940. Used with permission of the University of Chicago Press.)

vertical direction. Streamlines in the high-permeability bed are almost tangential to the lower surface of the low-permeability bed. There is very little difference in groundwater potential along an imaginary vertical line passing through the high-permeability bed, but if this line is extended upwards, it crosses several equipotentials in the low-permeability bed and relatively few in the medium-permeability material. Thus, if a vertical well was drilled from the ground surface, there would be a large increase in potentiometric head when it first entered the high-permeability bed because static levels can establish themselves more rapidly here than elsewhere in the system. This increase in head is often attributed to confinement of water under pressure, although in reality it results from the movement of water through the low-permeability bed. In other words, the conditions implied by the term 'confinement' will arise when a unit of low permeability overlies a unit of high permeability (Domenico, 1972). The so-called artesian condition is an extreme case of this (Price, 1996).

5.5.7 Regional groundwater flow

Recognition that groundwater may vary between confinement and non-confinement as it flows through a sequence of materials having contrasting permeabilities, makes it easier to grasp the concept of 'regional' groundwater flow over substantial distances and possibly involving more than one topographic basin. The pioneering contributions of Chamberlin (1885), King (1899), Meinzer (1917) and Hubbert (1940) implicitly recognized the possibility of regional groundwater flow systems. However, significant progression of these ideas had to await the development of more powerful, computer-based modelling techniques in the 1960s when important contributions were made by a group of Canadian hydrologists including J. Tóth, P. Meyboom and R. A. Freeze.

Tóth (1962, 1963) considerably extended Hubbert's work by showing that groundwater flow patterns can be derived as mathematical solutions to formal boundary value problems. He assumed two-dimensional vertical flow in a homogeneous isotropic medium bounded below by a horizontal bed and above by the water table, which is a subdued replica of the topography. The lateral flow boundaries are the major groundwater divides. A groundwater flow system is defined as one in which any two streamlines which are adjacent at one point remain adjacent throughout the system, so that the system can be intercepted anywhere by an uninterrupted surface across which flow takes place in one direction only. Tóth (1963) recognized the three broad categories of flow system illustrated in Figure 5.16. A *local* system, which extends over distances of a few hundred metres, has its recharge area at a topographic high and its discharge area at an adjacent topographic low, and is therefore identical to the classic Hubbert model shown in Figure 5.13. An *intermediate* system, which extends over distances of a few kilometres, has one or more topographic highs and lows located between its recharge and discharge areas. Finally, a *regional* system, for example the Hungarian Basin, which may extend over hundreds of kilometres, is one where the recharge area is at the main topographic high and the discharge

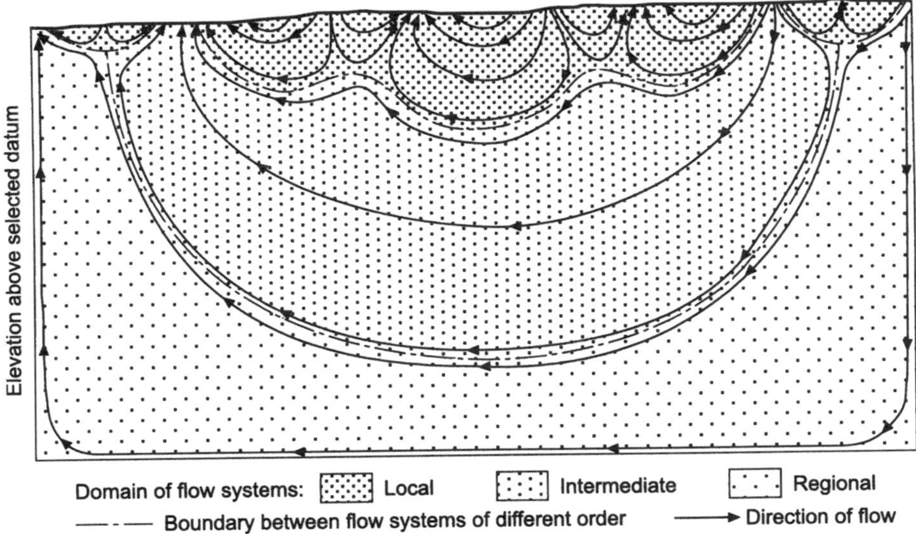

Figure 5.16 Vertical section through a large drainage basin with homogeneous geological framework showing local, intermediate and regional flow systems. (From an original diagram in Tóth, 1995.)

area at the lowest part of the basin. A helpful review of regional groundwater flow in large sedimentary basins was given by Tóth (1995, 1996).

Even in basins underlain by uniform material, topography can create complex systems of groundwater flow. Under extended flat areas, characterized by local waterlogging and groundwater mineralization from concentration of salts, neither regional nor local systems will develop (Tóth, 1963). However, regional systems will develop if local relief variations are negligible but there is a general topographic slope. With increasingly pronounced local relief, deeper local rather than regional systems will develop so that, in an area of large river valleys and steep divides, extensive unconfined regional systems are unlikely to occur. This view was extended to confined systems by Kudelsky (1990), who suggested that fold mountains are not normally catchment areas for deep artesian aquifers in neighbouring depressions, although exceptions may occur where extensive Quaternary deposits act as aquifers with outflows discharging far beyond the mountain structures. There are, nevertheless, widely held views that major mountain ranges may act as the recharge area and origin of major regional flow systems. Thus the Atlas Mountains are believed to act as source areas for the extensive groundwater systems beneath the southern Sahara desert some 1200 km to the south. Similarly, the Ogallala aquifer in northern Texas is reputed by plainsmen to be replenished by groundwater flow from the Rocky Mountains more than 500 km distant. And in the Western Ghats in India (Naganna and Lingaraju, 1990) groundwater is believed to be transported through deep-seated fractured rocks over distances of several hundreds of kilometres.

Meyboom (1963, 1967a) described a general model of groundwater flow in a prairie environment which he designated the 'prairie profile' (Figure 5.17). By definition this consists of a central topographic high bounded on both sides by

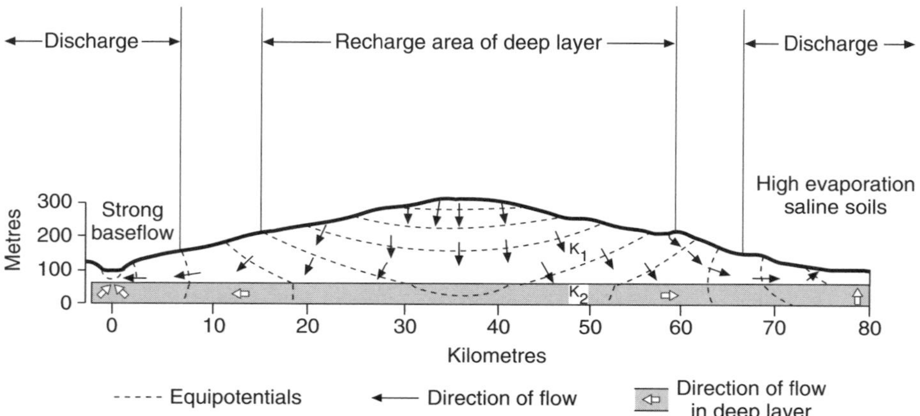

Figure 5.17 Flow patterns and areas of recharge and discharge in the prairie profile. (From an original diagram by Meyboom, 1963. Reproduced by permission of Information Canada.)

areas of major natural discharge. Geologically the profile consists of two layers of different permeability, the upper layer having the lower permeability, with a steady flow of groundwater towards the discharge areas. The ratio of permeabilities is such that the groundwater flow is essentially downwards through the low-permeability material and lateral and upwards through the more permeable underlying layer.

Since most of the natural discharge occurs by means of evaporation, Meyboom examined areas in which this component of the groundwater balance appeared to be important. He concentrated particularly on the occurrence of willow rings, areas of saline soil which occur where there is a net upward movement of mineralized groundwater, as in the major areas of regional groundwater discharge, and the occurrence of lakes and bogs and their relationship to groundwater flow (Meyboom, 1966, 1967a, 1967b).

The work of Tóth and Meyboom was itself expanded and generalized by Freeze and Witherspoon (1966, 1967, 1968) whose more versatile mathematical modelling technique was based on numerical solutions. Their model determined steady-state flow patterns in a three-dimensional, non-homogeneous anisotropic groundwater basin, with any water table configuration given knowledge of the dimensions of the basin, the water table configuration and the permeability configuration resulting from the subsurface stratigraphy. Figure 5.18 shows three potential field diagrams which demonstrate the effect of topography and geology

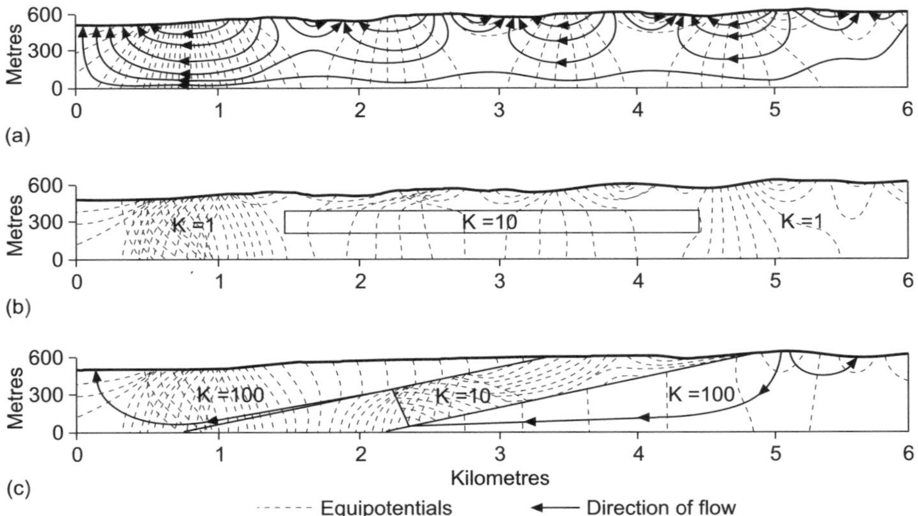

Figure 5.18 Potential field diagrams illustrating regional flow patterns: (*a*) homogeneous, isotropic medium with a hummocky water table, (*b*) as above, but with a lens of high-permeability material and (*c*) an area of sloping stratigraphy. (From original diagrams by R.A. Freeze and P.A. Witherspoon, *Water Resources Research*, **3**, p. 625, Fig. 1, p. 629, Fig. 4, p. 630, Fig. 5. © 1967 American Geophysical Union.)

on regional flow systems. The equipotential net (dashed lines) was produced from the numerical solution and the flow lines indicate the direction of flow. The water table configuration is shown by the solid line at the top of the contoured section.

Figure 5.18(a) shows the flow through a homogeneous isotropic medium in which the existence of a hummocky water table configuration results in numerous sub-basins within the major groundwater system. Figure 5.18(b) shows the effect on the potential field of a lenticular body of high permeability, given the same water table configuration as in Figure 5.18(a). In this case the flow lines are not shown although they may be readily envisaged by the reader. Finally, Figure 5.18(c) shows the regional flow pattern in an area of sloping stratigraphy. Here just two flow lines have been drawn to illustrate that the difference of a few metres in the point of recharge determines whether the water enters a minor sub-basin or a major regional system of groundwater flow.

It is usually difficult to identify, from field observations, the full continuity of regional groundwater flow which is indicated in Figures 5.16 and 5.18. Nevertheless, in many large sedimentary basins the essential elements of the flow systems described by Tóth and by Freeze and Witherspoon have been observed. Two good examples are the Surat sedimentary basin in Queensland, Australia (Figure 5.19(a)) and the sedimentary basins of southern England (Figure 5.19(b)).

The growing accessibility of greater desk-top computing power means that groundwater flow systems can now be modelled rapidly and flexibly using commercial software packages, many of which operate in a Windows™ environment. At the heart of many of these packages is the popular MODFLOW program, first developed by USGS (US Geological Survey), in which groundwater flow is simulated using a finite-difference approach. Layers of the groundwater basin can be simulated as confined, unconfined, or a combination of both. The effects on groundwater flow of wells, areal recharge, evaporation, drains and streams can also be simulated. Wang and Anderson (1995) provided a useful and comprehensive introduction to groundwater modelling.

The understanding of regional groundwater systems has also benefited from an improved understanding of groundwater chemistry and from the increasingly sophisticated use of tracers to reconstruct groundwater flowpaths (for example Wallick and Tóth, 1976). It has long been known that there is a broad correlation between the chemistry and residence time and flowpath of groundwater (see also Section 8.5.5). As groundwater moves away from the point of recharge in the outcrop area, its ionic content increases and processes of dissolution are gradually replaced by processes of ion exchange. In ideal conditions this would lead to the development of the 'Chebotarev sequence' of hydrochemical facies (Chebotarev, 1955). In this sequence shallow groundwater has a low concentration of minerals in which bicarbonate predominates and is followed by an intermediate zone of sulphate groundwater and finally a deep, highly mineralized zone of chloride groundwater. Because of the dynamic nature of groundwater systems, this ideal sequence is rarely observed. However, the underlying concept that the degree and type of mineralization of groundwater may be related to the length of flowpath and to the depth of the groundwater, provides a potentially useful means of reconstructing the flowpaths and extent of the groundwater system. For example, Smith *et al.* (1976) used ^{14}C measurements to confirm the existence of a Chebotarev-type sequence in the London Basin.

The application of groundwater chemistry to an understanding of regional groundwater flow systems advanced more rapidly in carbonate rocks, because of their relatively simple mineralogy. The approach has now also been applied to more complex silicate systems (Hanshaw and Back, 1985). De Vries and Gieske (1990) used chloride concentrations to identify sources of groundwater discharge in Precambrian rocks in Botswana and more recently, Njitchoua *et al.* (1997) used the evidence of hydrochemical facies to interpret the origin and recharge mechanisms of groundwater in a sandstone aquifer in northern Cameroon. They were able to differentiate direct infiltration of local precipitation, lateral seepage of river water and the probable upward movement of deeper, ancient groundwater. Multivariate correlation of 44 hydrochemical variables was used to interpret groundwater flow on the Greek island of Euboea (Ochsenkühn *et al.*, 1997).

As well as hydrochemical facies, a wide range of individual tracers, such as chlorofluorocarbons (CFCs), noble gases and radioelements, is now also used to investigate regional groundwater flow systems. For example, CFCs can be used as tracers to date groundwater over periods of up to 40 years and appear to estimate groundwater flow paths with a better accuracy than can be achieved by traditional hydraulic-based methods (cf. Cook and Solomon, 1997). Noble gases are dissolved by percolating water and because gas solubility is temperature-dependent, the groundwater retains a 'memory' of the climatic conditions prevailing at the time of its recharge. Radon is particularly useful in this respect (Andrews, 1991). Since its concentration in groundwater is related to the extent of rock surface per unit volume of fluid, it is greater in groundwater which has moved slowly through small interstices, such as those found in sand, than in groundwater which has moved rapidly by conduit flow through large interstices such as the fractures in limestone or granite (Figure 5.20). Radon concentrations may therefore provide useful indications of groundwater flowpath history.

Finally, regional groundwater flow systems have also been investigated by using the temperature of groundwater to trace its movement and flowpath. Static groundwater should tend towards an equilibrium temperature with the matrix rocks and therefore reflect the prevailing geothermal gradient whereby temperature increases by about 30°C for each kilometre below the ground surface. In dynamic systems, groundwater moving upwards towards the ground surface should be warmer than the surrounding matrix and groundwater moving downwards away from the surface should be cooler. Such temperature anomalies were used by Cartwright (1970) to interpret groundwater flow systems in the Illinois basin, USA, and by Kayane *et al.* (1985) in the Nagaoka plain in Japan.

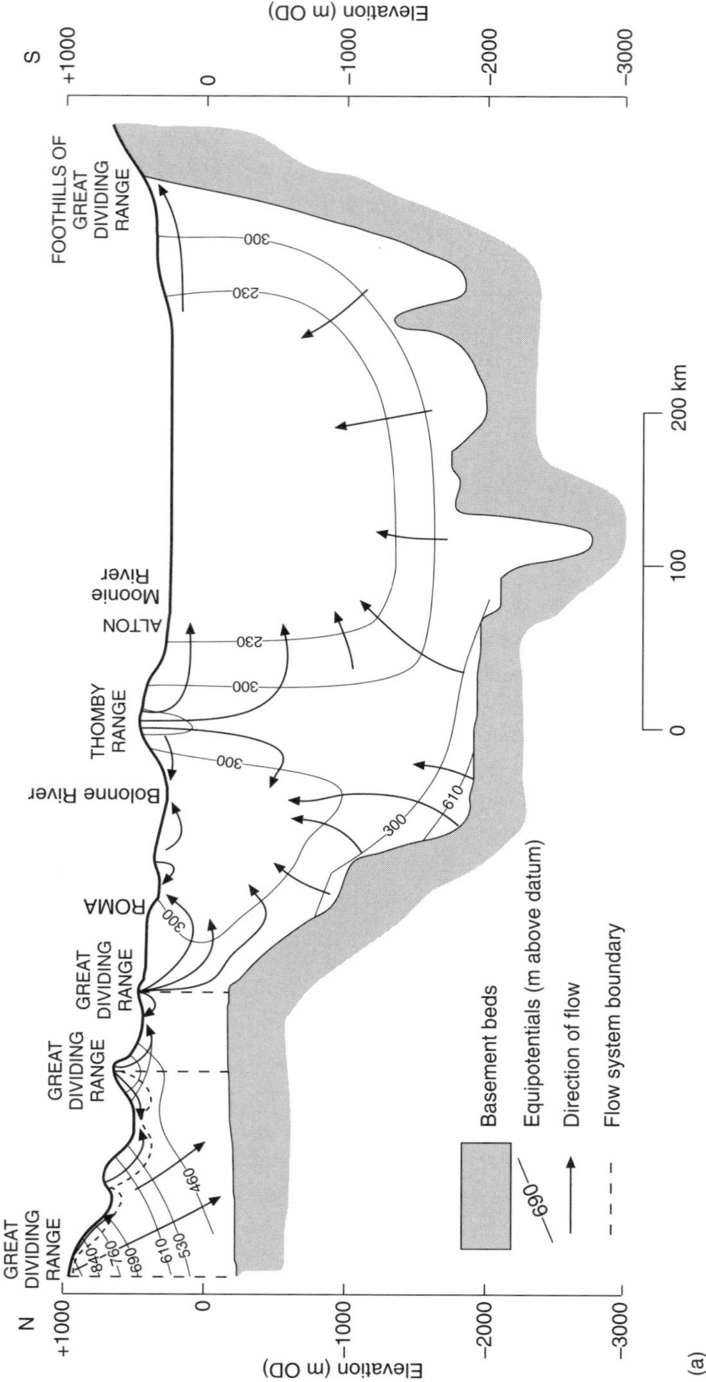
N
S
Elevation (m OD)
+1000
0
−1000
−2000
−3000
GREAT DIVIDING RANGE
GREAT DIVIDING RANGE
GREAT DIVIDING RANGE
ROMA
Bolonne River
THOMBY RANGE
ALTON
Moonie River
FOOTHILLS OF GREAT DIVIDING RANGE
840
760
690
610
530
460
300
610
300
230
0
100
200 km
690
Basement beds
Equipotentials (m above datum)
Direction of flow
Flow system boundary
(a)

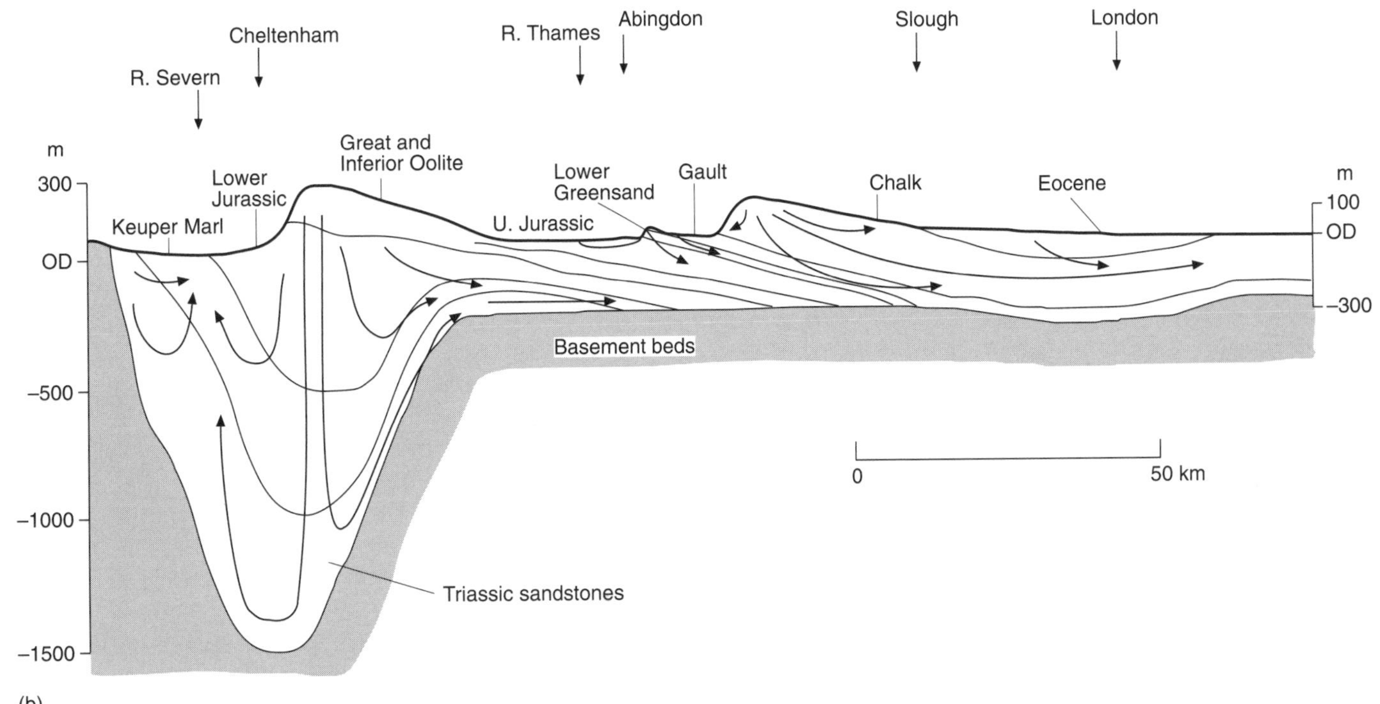

Figure 5.19 Regional flow systems in (*a*) the Surat sedimentary basin, Queensland, Australia; and (*b*) the sedimentary basins of southern England. (From original diagrams by Hitchon and Hays, 1971; and by Rodda, Downing and Law, 1976.)

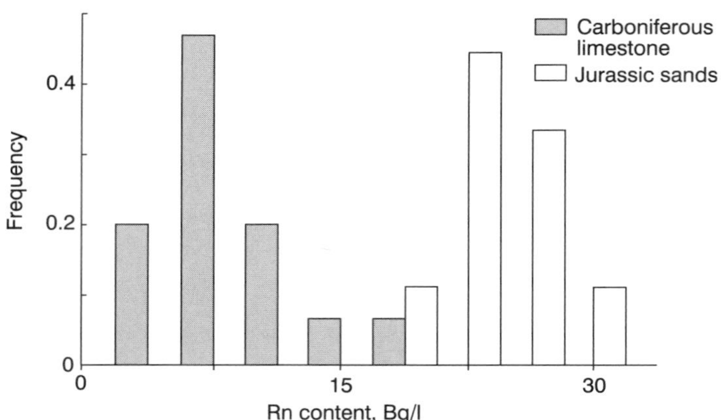

Figure 5.20 Radon concentrations in groundwater from Jurassic sands (intergranular flow; average concentration = 22 Bq/l) and carboniferous limestone (conduit flow; average concentration = 7 Bq/l). (From an original diagram by Andrews, 1991.)

Temperature anomalies may also be used in a different way to trace flow patterns in shallow groundwater systems. Here, because of seasonal differences in the temperature of recharge water, the aquifer may act either as a heat sink or a heat source. Cartwright (1974) showed that the greater the rate of groundwater flow, the greater the temperature difference between recharge and discharge zones, and that discharge areas could be identified by positive temperature anomalies in winter and negative temperature anomalies in summer.

5.5.8 Groundwater flow in coastal aquifers

The discharge of groundwater directly to the sea is believed to be small in comparison with the outflow of rivers, amounting to perhaps 5 per cent of total continental fresh water outflows (Zekster and Dzhamalov, 1981). However, its importance is almost certainly greater than this low value implies, due to the high density of human population in coastal areas and the susceptibility of coastal aquifers to degradation by salt water intrusion (UNESCO, 1987). Efforts continue, therefore, to determine fresh water discharge into the sea with ever greater accuracy (for example Roxburgh, 1985; Guglielmi and Prieur, 1997).

In coastal areas there is normally a hydraulic gradient towards the sea and the resulting seaward groundwater flow effectively limits the subsurface landward encroachment of saline water. In unconfined groundwater conditions, with a water table sloping towards sea level at the coast, the groundwater body takes the form of a lens of fresh water 'floating' on more saline water beneath. The position of the interface between the fresh and salt water was investigated independently by Badon Ghijben (1889) and Herzberg (1901). Assuming hydrostatic conditions and a negligible mixing zone the *Ghijben–Herzberg relationship* may be written as

$$h_s = \left(\frac{\rho_f}{(\rho_s - \rho_f)}\right) h_f = \alpha h_f \tag{5.7}$$

where h_s is the depth of the fresh water below sea level, ρ_f is the density of fresh water, ρ_s is the density of sea water and h_f is the height of the water table above sea level.

This equation indicates that saline groundwater is encountered, not at sea level but at a depth below sea level equivalent to α times the height of the water table above sea level, reflecting the hydrostatic equilibrium between lighter fresh groundwater and heavier saline groundwater (Figure 5.21(a)). The fresh water has a density of $1.00\,\mathrm{g\,cm^{-3}}$ and the saline water will have a density of 1.02–$1.03\,\mathrm{g\,cm^{-3}}$, depending on temperature and salinity. For $\rho_s = 1.025$ the ratio $\alpha = 40$.

In stratigraphically layered aquifers there may be more than one saline wedge. Figure 5.21(b) illustrates a simple situation in the presence of a limited semi-permeable layer and assuming steady flow and a sharp interface between fresh and saline groundwater. Collins and Gelhar (1971) noted that the saline wedge in the upper unconfined aquifer must intrude inland from the shoreline. However, the wedge in the lower aquifer may either intrude even further inland or, as shown in the diagram, may exist seaward of the shoreline if there is a sufficiently large fresh water head at the landward end of the semi-permeable layer.

The interface between saline and fresh groundwater is not as sharply defined as in Figure 5.21. Tidal fluctuations as well as variations in recharge and discharge continually disturb the balance between the fresh water and the sea water and cause the interface to fluctuate (for example Pietrucien, 1985). These fluctuations, together with the diffusion of salt water, destroy the sharp interface and create a transitional diffusion zone of brackish water instead (Stringfield and Legrand, 1971). This is well illustrated, for the Biscayne aquifer near Miami, Florida, in Figure 5.22(a).

Hubbert (1940) demonstrated that a state of dynamic rather than static equilibrium must exist at the interface or there would be no way for fresh water to discharge into the sea. Also, the depth to the interface is greater than indicated by the simple Ghijben–Herzberg relationship. For low hydraulic gradients the differences are small, but for steep gradients they may be substantial and are associated with a continual flow of salt water from the sea floor into the zone of diffusion. Only in this way can the continuous discharge of salty water from the zone of diffusion into the sea be maintained, the concentration gradient across the zone of diffusion being too weak to account for the transport of salts by means of dispersion or diffusion. Thus the salts are transported into the zone of diffusion largely by a flow of salt water with a consequent loss of head in the salt water environment (Cooper *et al.*, 1964). This is clear from the equipotentials in the Biscayne aquifer (Figure 5.22(b)) which show that negative heads, in terms of

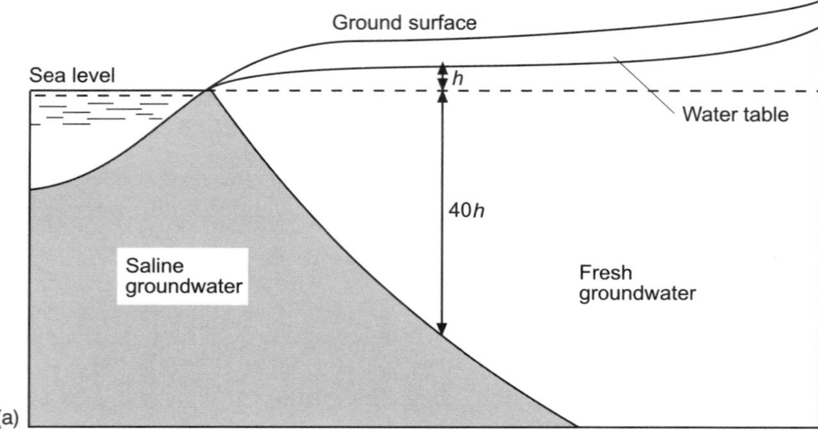

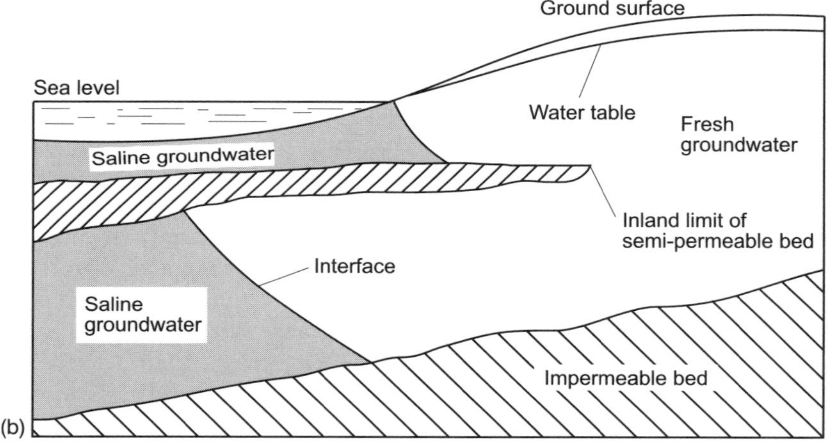

Figure 5.21 Simplified diagrams showing the Ghijben–Herzberg hydrostatic relationship in (*a*) a homogeneous coastal aquifer and (*b*) a layered coastal aquifer. (The latter is based on an original diagram by M.A. Collins and L.W. Gelhar, *Water Resources Research*, **7**, p. 972, Fig. 1. © 1971 American Geophysical Union.)

sea water densities, exist in the sea water environment. As a result, the interface between saline and fresh water will occur seaward of that estimated from the Ghijben–Herzberg relationship.

Excessive abstraction of groundwater from coastal aquifers will reduce the flow of fresh groundwater and cause a lowering of water table and potentiometric levels. In turn, this may readily lead to the incursion of saline groundwater and to the long-term contamination of the aquifer. This problem has already occurred in many areas, including the Netherlands, Spain, Israel, France, the USA, Italy and Britain (UNESCO, 1987). In some cases the existence of saline groundwater in

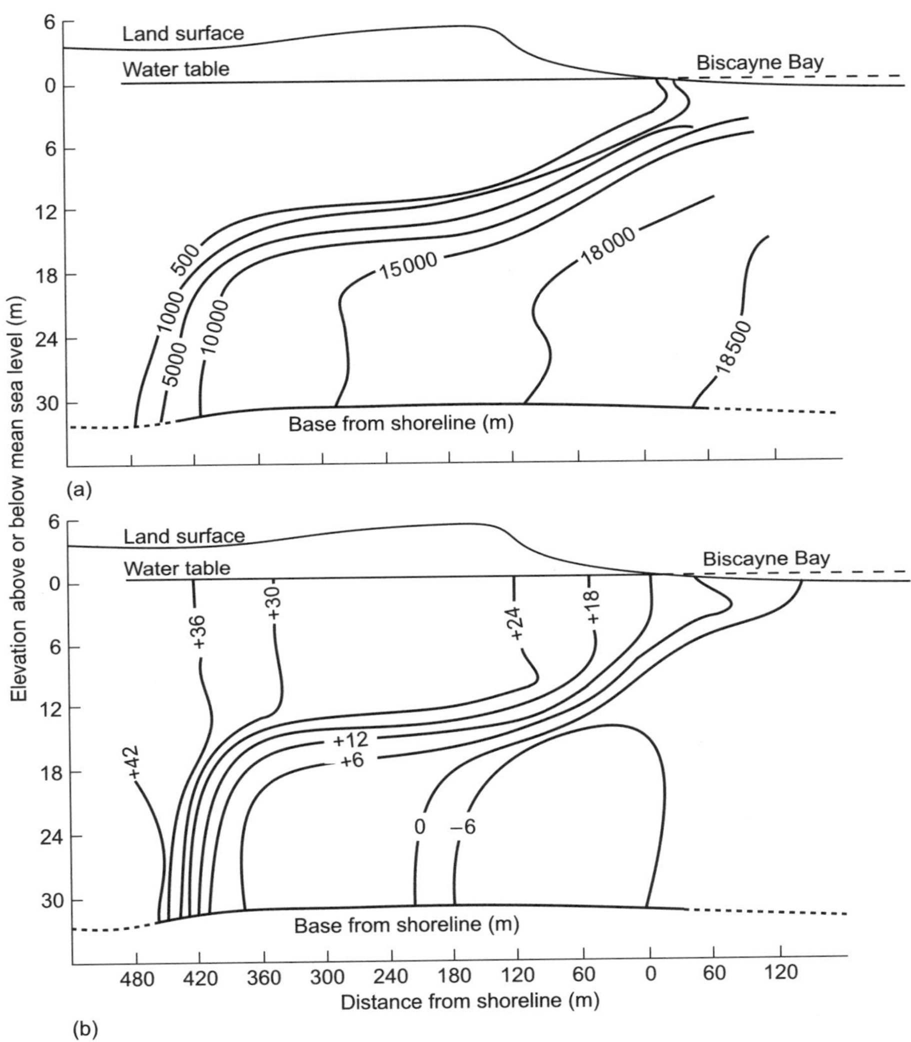

Figure 5.22 Hydrodynamic relationship between fresh and saline groundwater in the Biscayne aquifer, Florida: (*a*) isolines of salt concentration (ppm Cl^-) illustrating the zone of diffusion and (*b*) equipotential lines (cm) in the zone of diffusion (from original diagrams by Kohout and Klein, 1967, and by Stringfield and Legrand, 1969).

coastal aquifers may represent the residue of an earlier invasion of sea water, which occurred when the land was relatively lower and which now takes the form of a wedge of highly saline water beneath a superficial seaward-flowing body of fresh groundwater. The presence of saline water in the chalk along parts of the East Yorkshire, Norfolk and Suffolk coasts of England may probably be explained in this way (Buchan, 1963), as may some of the saline groundwater along the Atlantic coast of the United States (Siple, 1965).

5.6 Groundwater in jointed and fractured rocks

Despite occasional references to jointed and fractured rocks, most of the foregoing discussion of groundwater storage and movement has implied archetypal conditions of homogeneity and isotropy which are more characteristic of uniform sedimentary strata. It may be helpful, therefore, to conclude this chapter by considering briefly the particular characteristics of groundwater occurrence in jointed and fractured rocks. Together, these underlie about 40 per cent of the earth's land surface and constitute a major source of water supply in many tropical and subtropical areas (for example Wright, 1992). Outcrops of carbonate rocks in Europe cover some 3×10^6 km^2, i.e. 35 per cent of the area, but in many countries such as Germany, France, Poland, Romania and Russia, major limestone aquifers also exist beneath a thick cover of other rocks (Biondic and Bakalowicz, 1995).

Many carbonate and crystalline rock masses contain systems of faults, solution joints, or fractures. Especially at shallow depths, where these features are most frequent, the rock mass therefore consists of an assemblage of intact rock *blocks* that are separated by various features which can be generally described as *fissures*. These fissures will normally be important for groundwater storage and movement, although the significance of their role will depend partly on their contribution to total porosity and partly on the porosity and permeability of the intervening blocks. Matrix permeability may range from $\leq 0.1\,\mathrm{m\,y^{-1}}$ in dense unweathered bedrock to $\geq 1.0\,\mathrm{m\,y^{-1}}$ in soft limestone such as chalk. In addition, some of the fissures may be filled with fine deposits which are more permeable than the intervening blocks, for example in crystalline rock, or less permeable than the intervening blocks, for example in limestone. In most circumstances, however, the movement of water through the fissures will be several orders of magnitude greater than the movement of water through the block matrix. Accordingly, the classical concept of an 'aquifer', in which groundwater storage and movement are related to the formation rather than to the structures within it, is not entirely appropriate in carbonate and fractured rock. Indeed, for crystalline rock, Gustafson and Krasny (1993) suggested replacing the term aquifer by 'hydraulic conductor' which may comprise a single conductive fracture or an extensive multiple fracture zone.

In all *block-fissure systems* there is likely to be a wide range of groundwater flow rates. Where meaningful flow occurs through the blocks it will usually consist of diffuse, laminar flow in accordance with the Darcy law. Through larger, supercapillary conduits and through major fissures, flow will be rapid and turbulent and will not therefore accord with the Darcian flow model. This is illustrated for karst groundwater in Figure 5.23. A further complication of such dual-flow systems is that the relative importance of flow through the matrix of the blocks

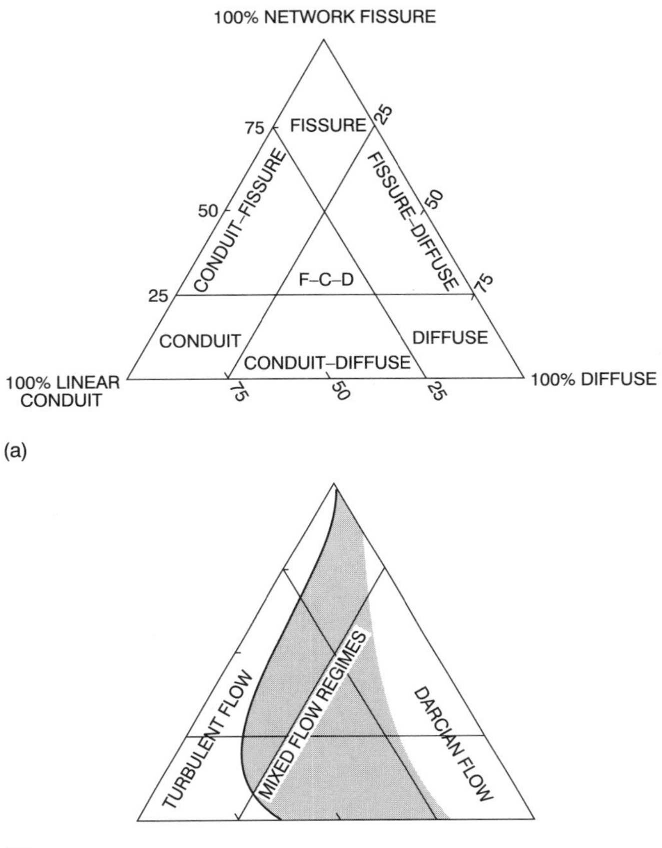

Figure 5.23 Conceptual classification of (*a*) karst aquifers and (*b*) associated modes of groundwater flow. (Based on a diagram by Atkinson, 1986.)

and through the fissures varies depending on whether the system is saturated or unsaturated. Rapid flow through the fissures predominates in saturated conditions, and slow flow through the matrix predominates in unsaturated conditions. Accordingly, there will be significant changes of groundwater flow path and travel time during periods of fluctuating water table level, particularly in more permeable rocks such as limestone and chalk. Depending on water table depth, it has been estimated that significant pesticide concentrations could reach groundwater through the chalk matrix up to 30 years after application (IH, 1997). The groundwater hydrology of Yucca Mountain in southern Nevada, USA, has been intensively studied during assessment of its suitability as a radioactive waste repository. Even so, the hypothesis that the fracture systems are barriers to water flow when the matrix rocks are unsaturated and become conduits for water flow only when the matrix is at or near saturation, thereby

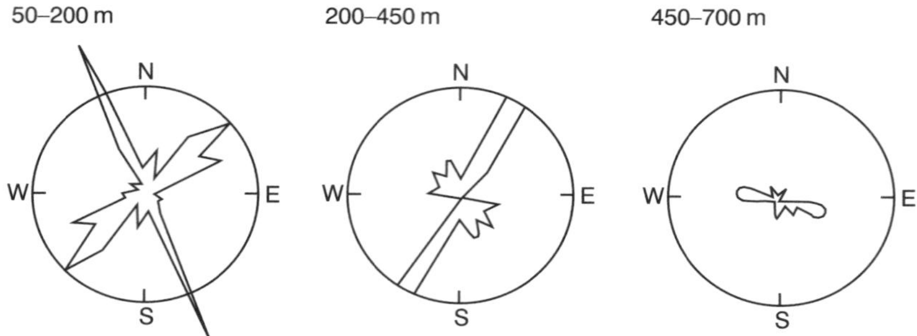

Figure 5.24 Orientation of water-conducting fractures at different depths in the Carnmenellis granite, Troon, Cornwall, UK. Most of the groundwater flow occurs through these fissures. (Based on an original diagram in NERC, 1991.)

greatly reducing groundwater travel times, has been challenged (Albrecht *et al.*, 1990). If, alternatively, water moves within fractures even at low values of matrix saturation, this would significantly reduce groundwater travel times and have profound implications for conditions within the unsaturated zone.

Apart from the effects of fluctuating water tables on groundwater movement, the orientation of fissures may itelf vary with depth, particularly in rocks such as granite (Figure 5.24). This means that the dominant direction of groundwater flow may change significantly with depth.

The mix of flow processes in block-fissure systems complicates the investigation of groundwater hydrology and may even make it difficult to define the scale of the investigation. For example, at the micro-scale, a small sample volume of fractured rock may consist entirely of solid rock or entirely of a single fracture void, resulting in the largest possible potential variation of permeability. As the sample volume is increased larger and more extensive fracture systems may be incorporated, so that there is a tendency for the observed permeability to increase (see also Section 5.5.2). In some cases, a consistent relationship between voids and solid may be reached at the meso-scale, whereby increasing the sample volume further has no further effect on the average permeability. If however the next increase in sample volume includes a major zone of fracturing this may result in a marked increase in average macro-scale permeability. Finally, at the mega-scale, a much larger sample may include many major fracture zones and again exhibit a still larger, but relatively homogeneous, permeability. In other words, the size of the sample used to determine groundwater characteristics in heterogeneous rocks should be of a comparable scale to that of the area under investigation. Since, however, all samples will contain some unrepresentative fissures, some authorities have suggested that there is no such thing as a representative sample volume (Domenico and Schwartz, 1990). And in a comprehensive review of groundwater flow in porous fractured media,

Elsworth and Mase (1993) argued that in many cases, despite the costs involved, only initial large-scale testing is likely to overcome the overt scale dependence of the geological medium. Barker (1991) provided a useful general review of flow conditions in fractured rock. Not surprisingly, however, much of the work reported in the literature concerns groundwater flow through specific fissures (for example Saxena, 1984; Cacas *et al.*, 1990; Whitaker and Smart, 1997).

Because carbonate and fractured rocks may have restricted and shallow water storage, which will tend to deplete rapidly, groundwater in such materials is usually strongly dependent on contemporary recharge (Gustafson and Krasny, 1993). However, in some areas, dating techniques have identified deeper as well as shallow flow and have also confirmed that some of the deeper groundwater must have originated during the later Pleistocene period (for example Downing *et al.*, 1977; Silar, 1990). In the case of the Lincolnshire Limestone in eastern England, groundwater movement is dominated by new water in the fissures. However, older water stored in the aquifer matrix enters the fissure system by diffusion and as a result of pressure differentials accentuated by groundwater abstraction (Downing *et al.*, 1977). Recent investigations of higher than expected low flows in rivers draining chalk catchments in southern England have indicated that these result from substantial quantities of water stored on and gradually released from the surfaces of the fissure and micro-fissure systems.

Groundwater flow systems in fractured and jointed rocks are still imperfectly understood and much work remains to be done. It is interesting to note, however, that as knowledge about groundwater in a wide range of environmental conditions continues to grow (for example Pointet, 1997), so too does the recognition that groundwater processes in 'normal' aquifers and in fissured rocks may be more similar than was once thought. This was emphasized forcibly by the editors of the 1993 Oslo Symposium on *Hydrogeology of Hard Rocks*, who noted that hydrologists:

> ... are rapidly discovering that their favourite sand or gravel aquifer is not really very homogeneous or isotropic at all, that it tends to display preferential flow pathways and macropore systems, and that it is beginning to bear a suspicious resemblance to a fractured rock system in many ways!
>
> (Banks and Banks, 1993, p. iv)

Review Problems and Exercises

5.1 Discuss the role of groundwater in the hydrological cycle.
5.2 What types of materials make good aquifers and aquitards?
5.3 Explain, with the help of diagrams, what is meant by unconfined, confined, and perched groundwater.
5.4 Define the following terms: artesian, porosity, effective porosity, specific yield, coefficient of storage.
5.5 Explain Darcy's law of groundwater flow.
5.6 Define the following terms: hydraulic gradient, hydraulic conductivity, effective velocity, equipotential, flow net, potentiometric surface.
5.7 Calculate the Darcy macroscopic velocity of groundwater flow through a sand ($K = 10\,\mathrm{m\,d^{-1}}$) when two piezometers, installed 10 m apart, give the following data (m):
Piezometer 1: $z = 0$, $\psi = 0.5$
Piezometer 2: $z = -3$, $\psi = 0.15$
5.8 Estimate the effective velocity of groundwater flow through the sand in 5.7, given that the effective porosity of the sand is 35 per cent.
5.9 Why is the water table sometimes described as a subdued replica of the surface topography?
5.10 Explain, with the help of diagrams, what is meant by regional groundwater flow.
5.11 Define the following terms: hydrochemical facies, the Chebotarev sequence, the Ghijben–Herzberg relationship.
5.12 What are the special characteristics of groundwater movement in jointed and fractured rocks?

CHAPTER SIX

Soil water

6.1 Introduction

Soil water is normally considered to include both the water contained in the soil profile itself and the subsurface water in the unsaturated subsoil layers between the soil profile and the water table (see Section 5.1). Thus defined, soil water includes all the water in the zone of aeration which may extend tens or even hundreds of metres below the ground surface. However, the ability of the shallow soil profile proper to absorb and retain moisture is generally of great hydrological importance and will therefore be the main focus of discussion in this chapter. Where soils are thin or impermeable, rainfall runs quickly off the surface, sometimes resulting in erosion, so that little moisture is held in the soil to sustain plants and animals until the next rain. Deep, permeable soils, in contrast, can absorb and store large quantities of water, providing a moisture reserve through times of drought and helping to produce a more even pattern of river runoff.

The importance of soil water is out of all proportion to its small total amount in the global water balance (Table 1.1). This is partly because the average residence time of soil water is fairly short, say three months, so that soil water is turned over four times a year. This effectively quadruples its annual contribution from 65×10^3 to 260×10^3 km^3. However, in large measure, the importance of soil water reflects its vital role as a source of water for plants. In practice, knowledge about the factors controlling water storage and movement in the soil is essential to an understanding of a wide range of processes, including not only the supply of water to plants but also the generation of runoff, recharge to underlying groundwater and the movement and accumulation of pollutants (Bear and Verruijt, 1987). As a result, possible changes in soil water status which may result from climate change, whether naturally or anthropogenically induced, are of great concern (Gleick, 1993a). Soil water is thus of interest to investigators in a number of disciplines in addition to the hydrologist, including agronomists, climatologists, foresters, geomorphologists and civil engineers.

6.2 Physical properties of soils affecting soil water

The *soil profile*, i.e. a vertical cross-section through the soil, normally comprises a number of layers or *horizons* having different physical characteristics. The nature of the soil profile depends upon a wide range of factors including the original parent material, the length of time of development and prevailing climate, as well as the vegetation and topography.

Three *phases* make up the soil system: the solid phase, or *soil matrix*, comprising the mineral and organic particles of the porous medium, the gaseous phase of the soil air and the liquid phase of the soil water. The latter is sometimes, more correctly, referred to as the soil 'solution' because it always contains some dissolved substances. The soil water system is quite complex, not least because soil properties often vary over short distances and may not remain constant through time, due to factors such as swelling and shrinking of clays, and compaction and disturbance by plants, animals and humans. For these reasons soil physicists in the past sometimes resorted to the study of 'idealized' media such as glass beads or bundles of capillary tubes. The challenge for the hydrologist, therefore, is to apply these often theoretical and laboratory-based concepts to field situations. This chapter aims to provide an introduction to some of the most important phenomena of soil water theory and their practical consequences for the hydrologist.

The amount of water that can be held in a given volume of soil and the rate of water movement through that soil depend upon both the soil *texture*, i.e. the size distribution of the mineral particles of the soil, and upon the soil *structure*, the aggregation of these particles. Water may occupy both interstructural voids and textural voids (between the particles). At high moisture contents water flow through the former may be dominant, but becomes rapidly less important as the soil becomes drier. In general, the coarser the particles, the larger will be the intervening voids and the easier it will be for water movement to take place. Thus sandy soils tend to be more freely draining and permeable than clay soils which are both slower to absorb water and slower to drain of water.

The finely divided clay material is the most important size fraction in determining both the physical and chemical properties of the soil. The sand and silt fractions mainly comprise quartz and other primary minerals that have undergone little chemical alteration while the clays, in contrast, result from chemical weathering, forming secondary minerals with a great variety of properties (White, 1987; Wild, 1988). One difference is that the clay particles comprise platey sheets and have a much higher *specific surface*, i.e. the surface area per unit volume (Brady, 1984; Carter *et al.*, 1986). Most clays have negatively charged surfaces and are balanced externally by cations which are not part of the clay structure and which can be replaced or exchanged by other cations (see Section 8.5.2). Some types of clays have only weak bonds between adjacent sheets, and the 'internal' surfaces may also be available for taking part in reactions. This is important for the retention and release of nutrients and salts. Water can enter between these sheets causing them to separate and expand. Many clay soils swell on wetting and shrink and crack on drying, which may be important for the porosity and hydraulic properties of soils.

Soil *structure* results from the aggregation of the primary particles described above into the structural units, or *peds*. These are separated from one another by planes of weakness which may also act as important flowpaths for water moving through the soil profile. The mechanics of soil structure formation and stability are very complicated and depend on a number of factors. In the surface horizon of the soil the aggregates will change over time due to weather and soil tillage, but in deeper horizons they will be more constant. Plants are very important for the structure of surface horizons since their roots bind particles to help form stable aggregates. Grass swards, for example, are particularly effective due to the high density of roots near the surface (White, 1987). Soil structure is too varied for simple geometric characterization and is usually described qualitatively in terms of form: granular, blocky, prismatic, etc., and by the degree of development, whether structureless or strongly aggregated (for example Hodgson, 1976). However, such descriptions are often only weakly related to soil hydraulic properties, especially in structured clay soils. As a result, Bouma (1981) recommended the use of tracers to characterize preferential flowpaths through the soil voids.

This broad description of the main soil properties provides a basis for subsequent sections, describing first the processes governing the storage and movement of water in idealized soil conditions (Sections 6.3 and 6.4) and then the resulting patterns of soil moisture and flow rates that are likely to be found under naturally occurring field conditions (Section 6.5).

6.3 Storage of soil water

In a seminal comment, Terzaghi (1942) remarked that if gravity were the only force acting on soil water then the soil would drain completely after each input of rain so that soil water would be found only below the water table. In such a situation, plant growth would be restricted to those areas where rainfall occurred very frequently or to locations where the water table was near to the surface. In fact soils in natural conditions always contain some water, even at the end of long dry periods lasting many months or even years. This indicates that very powerful forces are holding moisture in the soil.

6.3.1 Water retention forces

The main forces responsible for holding water in the soil are those of *capillarity*, *adsorption* and *osmosis*. Capillary forces result from *surface tension* at the interface between the soil air and soil water. Molecules in the liquid are attracted more to each other than to the water vapour molecules in the air, resulting in a tendency for the liquid surface to contract. If the pressure was exactly the same on either side then the air–water interface would be flat, but pressure differences result in a curved interface, the pressure being greater on the inner, concave, side by an amount that is related to the degree of curvature. At the interfaces in the soil pore

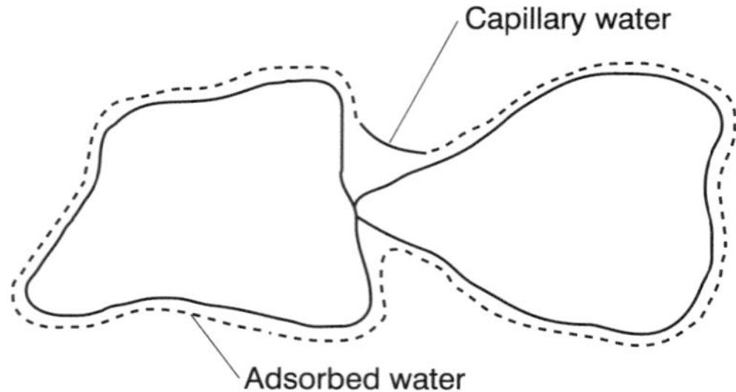

Figure 6.1 Water is held by capillary forces between the soil particles and by adsorption as a thin film of water.

space, the air will be at atmospheric pressure, but the water may be at a lower pressure. As water is withdrawn from the soil the pressure difference increases across the interfaces which become increasingly curved and can only be maintained in the smaller pores (Figure 6.1). The force with which these small wedge-shaped films of water are held will vary, in the same way the capillary rise in a glass capillary tube varies with the radius of the tube, the curvature of the surface meniscus and the surface tension of the water. For a given viscosity and surface tension, water will be held more strongly in smaller pores than larger ones. Hence as the water content of a soil reduces, the larger pores empty at lower suctions than the smaller pores.

In addition to capillary forces, soil water liquid or vapour can be adsorbed upon the surfaces of soil particles mainly due to electrostatic forces in which the polar water molecules are attached to the charged faces of the solids. Since the forces involved are only effective very close to the solid surface, only very thin films of water can be held in this way (Figure 6.1). Nevertheless, if the total surface area of the particles (i.e. the specific surface) is large, and/or the charge per unit area is large, then the total amount of water adsorbed in a volume of soil may be considerable. In the case of water vapour, adsorption may make a significant contribution to the diurnal variation of total soil water content in areas of low rainfall and large diurnal variation of air humidity (for example Kosmas *et al.*, 1998).

The magnitude of the specific surface depends upon the size and shape of the particles. Its value increases as the grain size decreases and as the particles become less spherical and more flattened. Clay size particles and organic matter contribute most to the specific surface area of a soil, with values of less than $0.1\,m^2\,g^{-1}$ for sand rising to over $800\,m^2\,g^{-1}$ for expanding layer clays such as montmorillonites (Table 6.1). This helps to explain the very strong retention of water by clays during prolonged periods of drying.

These forces of attraction between water and soil reduce the free energy of the water. This means that, in unsaturated soil, the pressure of water in the pores is negative (i.e. less than atmospheric pressure). For this reason both capillary and adsorption forces may be regarded as exerting a *tension* or *suction* on the soil

Table 6.1 Specific surface areas according to mineral type and particle size. (Based on a table in White 1987.)

Mineral or size class	*Specific surface sq m/g*
Coarse sand	0.01
Fine sand	0.1
Silt	1
Clay mineral groups	
Kaolinites	5–100
Ilites (hydrous micas)	100–200
Vermiculites	300–500
Montmorillonite	700–800

water, although their comparative importance depends upon soil texture and soil water content. Adsorptive forces are more important in clayey soils than in sandy ones and become more important in all soils as moisture content is reduced. In practice these forces are in a state of equilibrium with each other and cannot be easily measured separately. It is therefore usual to deal with their combined effect on the way in which water is held in the soil matrix, known as *matric suction* or *matric potential* (see also Section 6.3.5).

A third force which acts to retain water in the soil results from osmotic pressure due to solutes in the soil water. Although often ignored, especially in humid environments, osmotic pressure may be important when there is a difference in solute concentration across a permeable membrane. This may be at a plant root surface, making water less available to plants, especially in saline soils, or across a diffusion barrier such as an air-filled pore, by allowing the movement of water vapour, but not the solute, across the pore from the more dilute to the more concentrated solution (Hillel, 1982). In the absence of such barriers soluble ions will diffuse throughout the soil solution by virtue of their kinetic energy, resulting in a uniform concentration (Baver *et al.*, 1972).

The total suction holding water in a soil is the sum of the matric and osmotic forces. The preceding discussion has shown how these retention forces vary with moisture content. In general, soils contain a wide range of pores of varying shapes and sizes. Those with large entry channels will empty at low suctions while those with narrow channels will empty at higher suctions. The relationship between soil moisture suction and moisture content is clearly of fundamental importance to an understanding of soil water behaviour.

6.3.2 Soil moisture characteristics (retention curves)

If a slowly increasing suction is applied to a completely saturated soil, the air–water interface begins to fall below the soil surface and the matric forces of soil water retention come increasingly into effect. First, large pores will empty at low

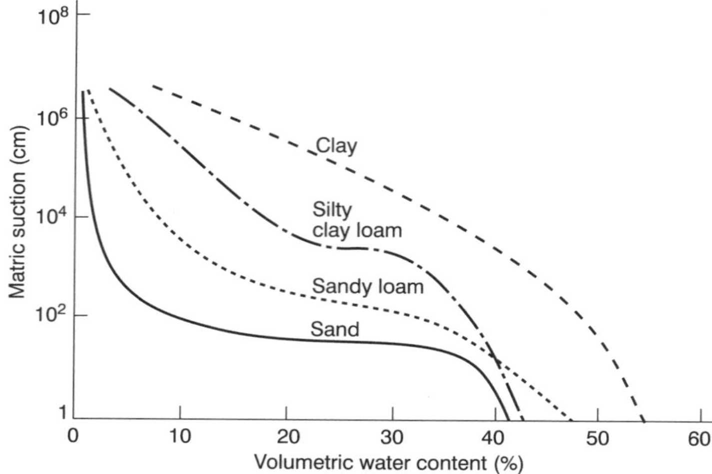

Figure 6.2 Soil moisture characteristics of different soil materials (redrawn from an original diagram by Bouma, 1977).

suctions, while narrow pores supporting air–water interfaces of much greater curvature will not empty until larger suctions are imposed.

The relationship between suction and the amount of water remaining in the soil can be determined experimentally in the laboratory using cores of soil (Klute, 1986b). The resulting function is known as the *moisture characteristic* (or *retention curve* in the case of a drying soil). Examples of moisture characteristics obtained for different types of soil are shown in Figure 6.2. The shape of the curve is related to the pore size distribution (Bouma, 1977). In general, sandy soils show a much more curved relationship than clayey soils since most of the pores are relatively large and once they are emptied there is little water remaining. Clayey soils, in contrast, have a wider distribution of pore sizes and consequently have a more uniform slope. The mechanism of water retention varies with suction. At very low suctions it depends primarily on capillary surface tension effects, and hence on the pore size distribution and soil structure. At higher suctions (lower moisture contents) water retention is increasingly due to adsorption, which is influenced more by the texture and the specific surface of the material. Due to the greater number of fine pores and the larger adsorption, clays tend to have a greater water content at a given suction than other soil types.

When an increasing suction is first applied to a saturated soil, little or no water may at first be released. A certain critical suction must be achieved before air can enter the largest pores enabling them to drain. This is called the *bubbling* or *air entry pressure*. The critical suction will obviously be greater for fine-textured material such as clays than for coarse sands with larger maximum pore sizes. However, since the latter often have a more uniform pore size, their moisture characteristics may show the air entry phenomenon more distinctly than finer-textured soils.

The fact that the suction required to drain a pore varies inversely with its radius means that the slope of the moisture characteristic, the *specific* or *differential water capacity*, can be used to indicate the 'effective' pore size distribution of the soil. If a gradually increasing suction is applied to a soil sample, then the volume of water withdrawn from the sample during each increment of suction represents the volume occupied by those pores whose diameter corresponds to that range of suction. In making such an estimate it must be remembered that at high suctions adsorptive rather than surface tension forces may predominate and that, due to the often tortuous flowpaths through the medium, not all pores of a given size will empty at the same time. A large water-filled pore may be surrounded by smaller pores, and cannot drain until these smaller pores drain first and air can pass through to the large pore. This phenomenon can lead to jumps in the water characteristic, especially at low suctions (Corey, 1977). Bouma (1977) noted that the correspondence between the 'effective' pore size distribution by this method and the size distribution obtained by micromorphological analysis of thin sections was better using the moisture characteristic obtained from a soil sample that was being wetted than from one that was being dried.

6.3.3 Hysteresis

One of the main limitations to the use of moisture characteristic curves is that the water content at a given suction depends not only on the value of that suction but also on the moisture 'history' of the soil. It will be greater for a soil that is being dried than for one that is being re-wetted (Figure 6.3). This dependence on the previous state of the soil water leading up to the current equilibrium condition is called *hysteresis*. Pores empty at larger suctions than those at which they fill, and this difference is most pronounced at low suctions and in coarse-textured soils. Hysteresis has been attributed to a number of factors, including the complexity of the pore-space geometry, the presence of entrapped air, shrinking and swelling and thermal gradients (Feddes *et al.*, 1988). Two important causes of hysteresis are the 'ink bottle' effect and the 'contact angle' effect (Baver *et al.*, 1972; Bear and Verruijt, 1987), both of which are dependent on pore behaviour. The former results from the fact that a larger suction is necessary to enable air to enter the narrow pore neck, and hence drain the pore, than is necessary during wetting, which is controlled by the lower curvature of the air–water interface in the wider pore itself (Childs, 1969). The 'contact angle' effect results from the fact that the contact angle of fluid interfaces on the soil solids tends to be greater when the interface is advancing (i.e. wetting) than when it is receding (drying), so a given water content tends to be associated with a greater suction in drying than in wetting (Bear and Verruijt, 1987). The effect of entrapped air will decrease the water content of newly wetted soil, and the failure to attain true equilibrium in experimental conditions may create or accentuate the hysteresis phenomenon. The water content at zero suction may be only 80–90 per cent of the total

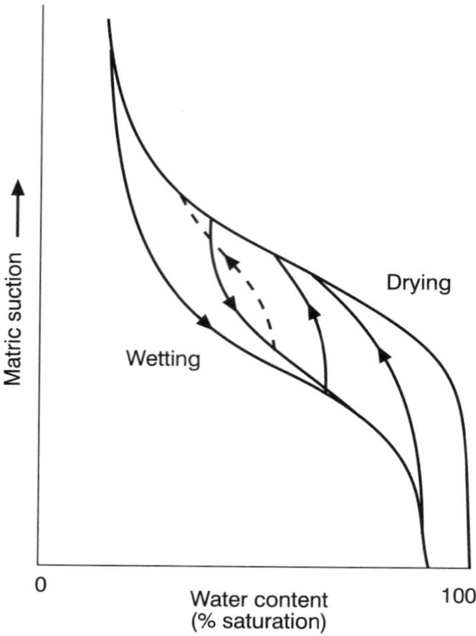

Figure 6.3 Hysteresis in the moisture characteristic, showing the main wetting and drying boundary curves and the intermediate scanning curves (redrawn after Childs, 1969).

porosity (Corey, 1977; Klute, 1986b), but may increase over time due to displacement by water flow and to the dissociation of the air into the water.

In fine-grained clay soils, wetting and drying may be accompanied by swelling and shrinkage. This leads to changes in pore sizes and the overall bulk density, and hence to a different volumetric water content at a given suction than if the matrix had remained stable and rigid. As water is withdrawn from the interstices between the plate-like particles (lamellae), the particles move closer together, thus reducing the overall volume. In some conditions it appears that as the lamellae are drawn closer together, they may reorientate themselves; on subsequent re-wetting they may not necessarily return to their original alignments, resulting in a lower volumetric water content. However, the swelling and shrinking behaviour of clay soils reflects not just their water content and suction but also the interaction of attractive and repulsive forces between the lamellae. This, in turn, is affected by the composition and concentration of the soil solution as well as by the type of clay.

A number of methods for modelling hysteresis scanning curves were reviewed by Jaynes (1985) and may be applied to soils for which the boundary wetting and drying curves are already known. In practice, however, given the many problems associated with measuring the moisture characteristic accurately, the hysteresis phenomenon is usually ignored (Beese and Van der Ploeg, 1976; Hillel, 1982). Also, although the pore size distribution is related more closely to the wetting curve (governed by the size of the pore entry channels), the drying (retention) curve is much easier to establish experimentally and is therefore used more frequently. For this reason the moisture characteristic is often referred to as the moisture retention curve.

6.3.4 Soil water 'constants'

A number of soil water constants have traditionally been used to facilitate comparisons between the hydrological status of different soils. These 'constants' are assumed to correspond to particular values of matric suction but, since the moisture characteristic curve is a continuous function, such points are plainly arbitrary and may have little intrinsic significance. Furthermore, under natural conditions rainfall and evaporation seldom, if ever, permit soil water contents to reach a state of equilibrium over the whole profile. Despite their arbitrary nature, soil water constants have long been used in solving practical soil water problems such as those concerned with drainage, irrigation and the modelling of watershed hydrology.

The 'constants' most frequently cited are the wilting point and the field capacity. The *wilting point* is defined as the minimum water content of the soil at which plants can extract water. Although this will vary between plant species and with their state of growth, the actual difference in the amount of water is quite small at such low water contents. *Field capacity* is normally regarded as the amount of water held in a draining soil after gravity movement of water has largely ceased. Although some soils continue draining for many weeks, field capacity is commonly taken to reflect the soil water content 48 hours after the cessation of a rainfall that has thoroughly wetted the soil. In practice, permeable soils will drain more rapidly than less permeable soils and achieve a state of little further moisture change more quickly and at much lower suctions (Smedema and Rycroft, 1983). It is also assumed that no evaporation losses are occurring and that the water table is sufficiently deep as to have no influence on the water content of the soil profile under consideration.

Despite such problems and limitations, soil water 'constants' are widely used (for example Rao, 1998) and the difference in moisture content between field capacity and wilting point, for instance, provides a useful approximation to the *available water capacity* for plants growing in different soils (Figure 6.4).

While these concepts are useful for making broad comparisons and generalizations, a fuller understanding of the behaviour of soil water requires consideration of the dynamic nature of the system. This needs to be based on the concepts and laws of soil physics.

6.3.5 Soil water energy (potential)

Soil water moves so slowly that its kinetic energy is insignificant. However, its potential energy, resulting from position or internal condition, is very important

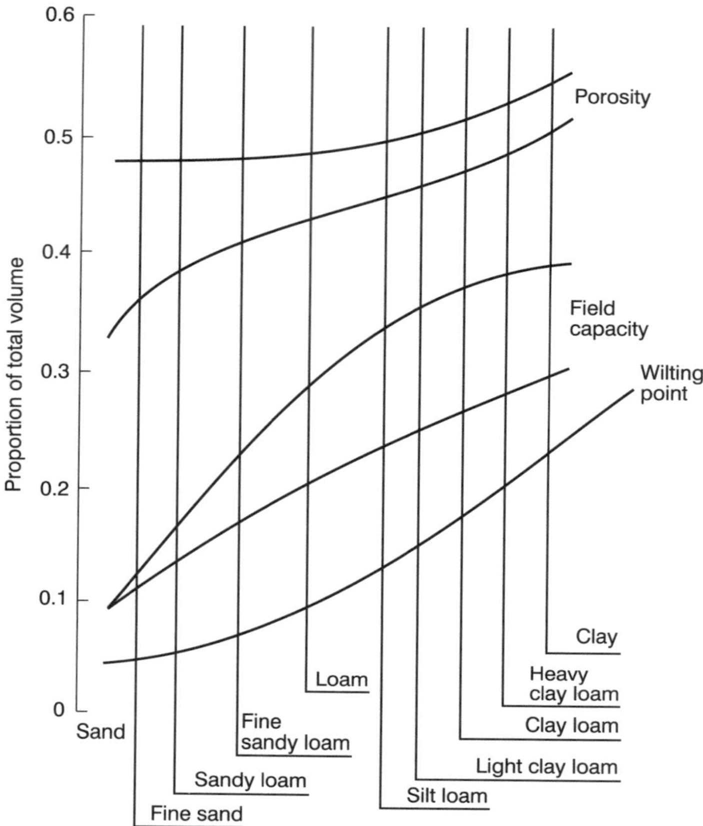

Figure 6.4 General relationship showing the total porosity, field capacity and wilting point of various soils. The volumes quoted are illustrative only, but demonstrate the increase in the available water capacity to plants (between field capacity and wilting point) from sand to clay soils. (From an original diagram in Dunne *et al.*, 1975. Blackwell Scientific Publications Ltd.)

in determining its state and movement. The term *soil water potential* describes the potential energy of soil water relative to that of water in a standard reference state. It is defined as the work per unit quantity necessary to transport reversibly and isothermally an infinitesimal quantity of water from a pool of pure water at a specified elevation (normally the soil surface) and at atmospheric pressure to a given soil water location (ISSS, 1976).

The total soil water potential (ϕ) at a given point comprises the sum of several components, of which only the gravitational potential (ψ_g), pressure potential (ψ_p) and osmotic potential (ψ_o) are usually considered:

$$\phi = \psi_g + \psi_p + \psi_o \qquad (6.1)$$

Apart from the inclusion of osmotic potential, Eq. 6.1 is, of course, identical to Eq. 5.4 for groundwater, emphasizing that the gradient of potential energy for subsurface water is continuous throughout the full depth of the unsaturated and saturated zones. Gravitational potential increases with elevation and, in the absence of strong retention forces or impeding factors, water will clearly drain downwards from higher to lower elevations. However, because of water retention forces (Section 6.3.1), pressure potential is negative in the unsaturated zone above the water table and also variable depending upon gains and losses of water due to rainfall and evaporation. Osmotic potential results from solutes in the soil water and is also negative. In dry conditions it acts to retain or draw water into the soil and therefore to lower the total potential.

Water will move from a point where the total potential energy is *higher* to one where it is *lower*. It is thus not the absolute amount of potential energy that is important, but rather the relative levels in different regions of the soil. The difference in total potential between points depends upon both differences in retention forces and also differences in elevation. These component potentials may not necessarily act in the same direction and are not necessarily equally important in causing flow.

In delineating the potential energy distribution in the saturated zone it is usual to express (the always positive) groundwater energy values in relation to an arbitrary datum level set well below the flow field under consideration (see Section 5.5.3). In studies of the unsaturated zone, however, it is more common to use the ground surface as the datum level for soil water energy values. Exceptionally, for a 'snapshot' view of the flow field, or in conditions of stable water table elevation, the water table can be used instead and has the advantage that both gravitational potential and pressure potential are zero at this datum level. However, the dynamic nature of the unsaturated flow field means that this is rarely feasible.

An example of a total energy profile, derived using the ground surface as the datum level, is shown in Figure 6.5. Osmotic pressure has been ignored, although it should be included in areas where high evaporation results in high solute concentrations in the soil water. Gravitational potential (ψ_g) declines uniformly with depth below the ground surface in both the saturated and unsaturated zones. All values are therefore negative when referred to a ground surface value of zero. Pressure potential (ψ_p) increases with depth below the water table and would eventually become positive if the diagram was extended to a sufficient depth. Above the water table the pressure potential is negative and becomes increasingly so in the plant root zone near the ground surface due to drying by evaporation. Total soil water potential (ϕ) is the sum of gravitational potential and pressure potential and in this example is therefore strongly negative at the ground surface, less negative in the moister soil layers below the root zone but then, despite increasing soil water content, becomes increasingly negative towards the water table as a result of the diminishing gravitational potential. Below the water table, conditions are identical to those in Figure 5.12, so that

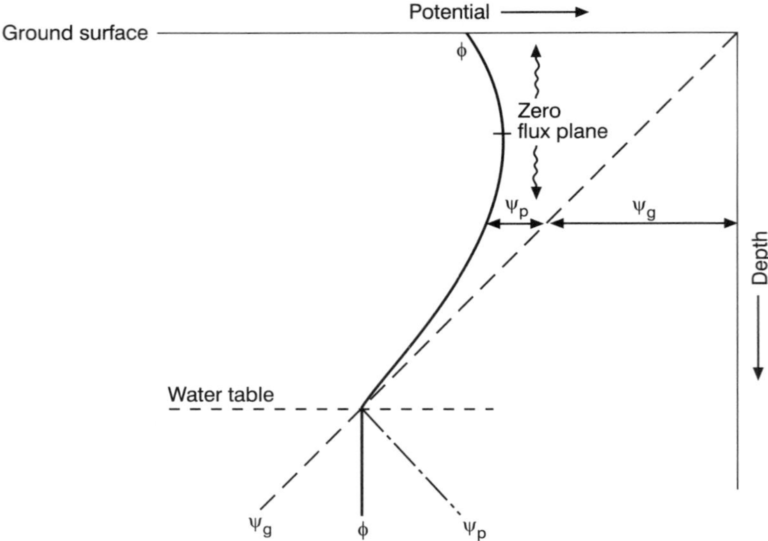

Figure 6.5 Total soil water energy profile (ϕ) below the ground surface, showing the gravitational (ψ_g) and pressure potential (ψ_p) components.

there is no change of total potential with depth because the increase of pressure potential (ψ_p) is exactly offset by the decrease in gravitational potential (ψ_g).

In the profile of total potential shown in Figure 6.5 there is one level in the unsaturated zone where there is no gradient of total potential. At this level, known as the *zero flux plane* (ZFP), there will be no vertical soil water movement. In this example, the zero flux plane divides the profile into a zone of upward flux above the ZFP and of downward flux below it. Such a *divergent* ZFP develops at the soil surface, as a result of evaporation exceeding rainfall, and moves downward into the soil during spring and summer as the profile continues to dry out. In typical British conditions, it tends to stabilize at a depth of between 1 and 6 m, depending on climate and soil conditions and the depth of the water table (Wellings and Bell, 1982). As rainfall begins to exceed evaporation in the autumn, the surface soil layers become wetter and their total soil water potential increases. This causes a new, *convergent*, ZFP to develop at the surface and then move fairly rapidly down the profile until it meets the original, divergent, ZFP. At this point both ZFPs disappear and downward drainage of soil water occurs throughout the profile during the winter months. This annual cycle of the water flux in a temperate climate soil profile is illustrated in Figure 6.6. Together with measurements of soil water content and soil water balance, such information can be used to quantify both the amounts of deep percolation downwards to the groundwater and also the upward flux due to evaporation (Bell, 1987; Moser *et al.*, 1986; Ragab *et al.*, 1997).

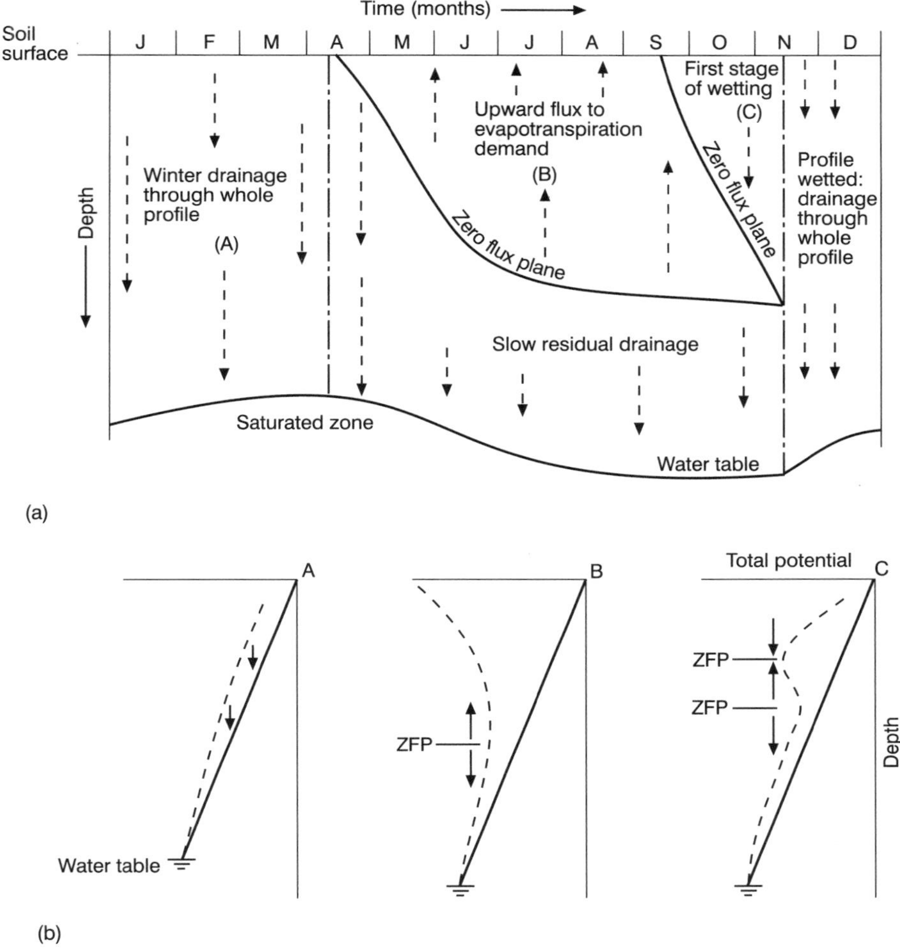

Figure 6.6 (*a*) Annual cycle of water movement and zero flux plane development in a temperate-climate soil profile (from an original diagram by Wellings and Bell, 1982). (*b*) Soil water potential profiles corresponding to times A, B and C.

Terms and units for potential energy

Potential energy (see also Section 5.5) is expressed using different systems of units:

- Energy per unit mass (ϕ)
- Energy per unit volume (i.e. pressure) (P)
- Energy per unit weight (i.e. hydraulic head) (H)

These expressions are equivalent and translate directly into one another: i.e.

$$\phi = \frac{P}{\rho} = Hg$$

$$P = \rho\phi = H\rho g$$

$$H = \frac{P}{\rho g} = \frac{\phi}{g}$$

where ρ is the density of water and g is the acceleration due to gravity.

Commonly used units of measurement for groundwater and soil water potential are:

- bars (1 bar = 0.99 standard atmosphere)
- pascals (1 newton/m^2)
- centimetres of water (cm)
- pF ($\log_{10}$ (cm)) avoids large numbers at high suctions and is used to express soil water potential.

The terms tension, suction and pressure are used interchangeably in soil water studies. Tension or suction are negative pressures (i.e. pressures that are less than atmospheric). Tension/suction is expressed as a positive quantity for unsaturated conditions (for example 100 cm). The same value expressed as a pressure would be a negative quantity (−100 cm) or could be expressed as pF = 2.0. Groundwater potential is positive and is, therefore, expressed as a pressure.

Many different symbols are used in the soil water literature and attempts to standardize them have not been successful (for example ISSS, 1976). It is necessary to understand the definition and context of symbols given in a particular text.

6.3.6 Measurement of soil water

The preceding discussions of soil water content and soil water suction imply that studies of soil moisture could be based on measurements of either soil water content or soil water potential, with conversion from one to the other by use of the moisture characteristic. In fact, errors in the measurement of the two variables, exacerbated by sampling problems and hysteresis, often encourage the direct measurement of both variables. As a result, their combined use provides a powerful approach to the study of water fluxes in unsaturated soil which are discussed in Section 6.4. Various measurement techniques are available and the following is a brief description of some of the methods used in practical field situations.

Measurement of soil water content (θ)

The standard and most widely used technique for directly measuring the water content of soil is the *gravimetric* method. This involves taking a number of soil samples of known volume by coring or augering and determining their weight loss when dried in an oven at 105°C. The methodology is laborious, time consuming and prone to errors in sampling and repeated weighings. It does not distinguish between 'structural' and 'non-structural' water; after oven-drying some clays may still contain appreciable amounts of adsorbed water (leading to underestimates of water content) while some organic matter may oxidize and decompose at temperatures as low as 50°C. For these reasons Gardner (1986) questioned the widespread and often uncritical acceptance of gravimetric values as 'correct'. The method is also destructive to the site and clearly is not suitable for a large number of repeated measurements over time.

To overcome some of these problems a number of indirect methods have been developed that, once calibrated against gravimetric samples, can be used to repeatedly make measurements more quickly, easily and with less disturbance (Schmugge *et al.*, 1980).

The *neutron probe* is the most commonly used indirect way of measuring soil water (for example Boucher, 1997). A radioactive source of 'fast' (high-energy) neutrons is lowered into a borehole in the soil, and the number of 'fast' neutrons which are slowed or thermalized by collisions with hydrogen nuclei, mainly in the soil water, is measured by a detector. The effective volume of measurement varies inversely with the water content of the soil from about a 10 cm radius for wet soil to about 25 cm in dry soil. There is a fairly linear relationship between the detector count rate and the water content, but it varies from soil to soil. The readings are usually calibrated for a given soil against the gravimetric method, but because of inherent uncertainties the neutron probe is normally used to measure moisture differences rather than absolute moisture contents.

The *capacitance probe*, which uses the dielectric constant of the soil as a measure of its moisture content, provides a non-radioactive method of measuring soil water in the field (Dean *et al.*, 1987; Bell *et al.*, 1987; Boucher, 1997). As with the neutron probe, calibration with gravimetric samples is necessary for each soil type, and the method is best suited to water content changes rather than absolute values. Due to its smaller 'sphere of influence' the capacitance probe has the potential to make measurements close to the soil surface and to study the change in water content between different horizons of a soil profile. However, its small radial penetration means that local inhomogeneities are important, and the access tube must be installed very carefully in the ground since air gaps will affect the readings. In general, the neutron probe is preferred over the capacitance probe at depths greater than 0.15 m in clays and 0.2 m in loamy soils (Boucher, 1997).

Considerable progress has been made in the application of *time-domain reflectometry* (TDR), which also determines soil water content by measuring the dielectric constant of the soil. A TDR trace is derived, using a portable cable tester, along transmission lines (rods) installed, either vertically or horizontally, in the soil profile. Early results were encouraging and had an accuracy comparable to that of gravimetric samples (Topp and Davis, 1985). Today TDR is widely accepted and used (for example Persson and Berndtsson, 1998) and has two significant advantages over the neutron probe method, namely that it is non-radioactive and can be set up for automatic, non-manual operation.

Finally, satellite-mounted *synthetic aperture radar* (SAR) has the potential to make a major contribution to the measurement of soil water content at the drainage basin scale. Like TDR, SAR determines soil water content by monitoring changes in soil dielectric properties. The equipment can operate successfully through thick cloud cover and at night and, from satellite altitude, the areal coverage is sufficiently large to smooth out localized variations of soil water content. Encouraging validation experiments have been carried out in the upper Thames basin, UK, and in Zimbabwe (IH, 1997).

Measurement of soil water suction (ψ)

Tensiometers are probably the oldest and most widely used technique for measuring matric suction. They comprise a liquid-filled porous cup connected to a pressure measuring device such as a mercury manometer or a pressure transducer. The cup is embedded in the soil *in situ*, and water can flow between the soil and cup until the pressure potential inside the cup equalizes with that of the soil water. The time taken for this equilibrium to be reached depends upon the flow rates through the cup and the surrounding soil and on the volume of water needing to be displaced to register a pressure change. Tensiometers can measure pressure heads below the water table, in which case they operate as piezometers, but are usually used to measure matric suction in the unsaturated zone. The lowest pressure that can be measured by this technique is about −800 cm (80 kPa) due to the effervescence of dissolved gases out of the water at the low pressure, making the system inoperative (Koorevaar *et al.*, 1983; Cassell and Klute, 1986). This range is adequate for many purposes, but in fine-textured soils quite a lot of water still remains available to plants at greater suctions, and in such circumstances *resistance blocks* may be useful. Two electrodes are embedded in a porous block which is buried in the soil. The matric suction in the block comes into equilibrium with that of the soil water and the resistance across the electrodes varies with the resulting water content of the block. Wellings *et al.* (1985) described the use of gypsum resistance blocks for measuring potentials as low as −15 000 cm (1500 kPa), and discussed methods of calibration, data processing and interpretation. Problems with the method include sensitivity to temperature and soil salinity, and gradual changes in block resistance over time. However, the greatest difficulty is usually in calibration and particularly in ensuring compatibility between the moisture characteristics of both soil and block. Incompatible moisture characteristics are illustrated in Figure 6.7. This

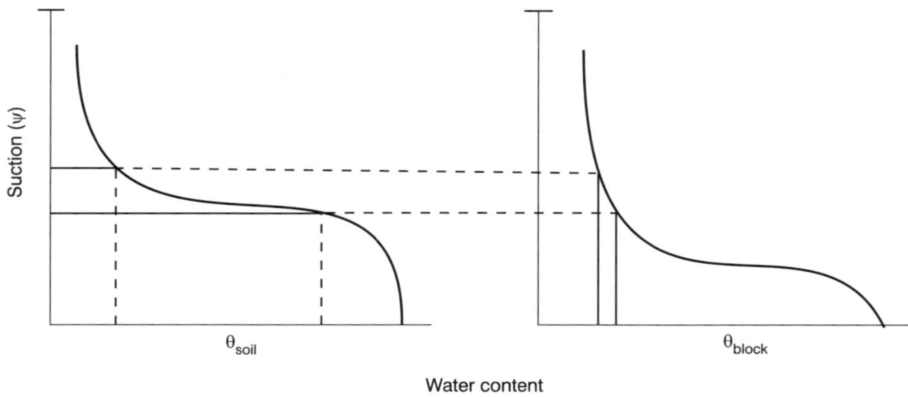

Figure 6.7 An example of incompatible moisture characteristics for a hypothetical soil and a resistance block. (See text for explanation.)

shows that in the soil a large variation of water content (θ) is associated with a much smaller variation of matric suction (ψ). In the block, however, that range of suction is associated with an even smaller range of moisture content. As a result, large variations of soil water content are reflected in only minute variations of resistance across the electrodes, making the calibration of block resistance to soil water content very difficult.

6.4 Movement of soil water

It is shown in earlier sections that soil water moves in response to a number of forces. Since gravity is not necessarily the dominant force, unsaturated flow may be in any direction. There is, however, a tendency for the main controlling forces to operate either from the ground surface (infiltration, evaporation) or from the bottom layers of the zone of aeration (groundwater recharge, capillary rise). This leads to the development of soil water potential gradients in the vertical direction, and the result is that vertical movement of soil water usually predominates. The following sections deal with the general principles of flow in the unsaturated zone and with water movement in the vertical direction—either upwards or downwards. The factors limiting the rate at which water can infiltrate into a soil are then discussed, as this controls the partitioning of net precipitation into surface and subsurface flowpaths. At the end of the chapter the roles of topography and soil layering are considered, looking at lateral soil water flow down slopes and the resulting spatially variable patterns of soil water content and movement that are observed in the field and are so important in many areas for runoff production.

6.4.1 Principles of unsaturated flow

We know that soil water will move from regions of higher total potential to regions of lower total potential (see Section 6.3.5). Because the movement of soil

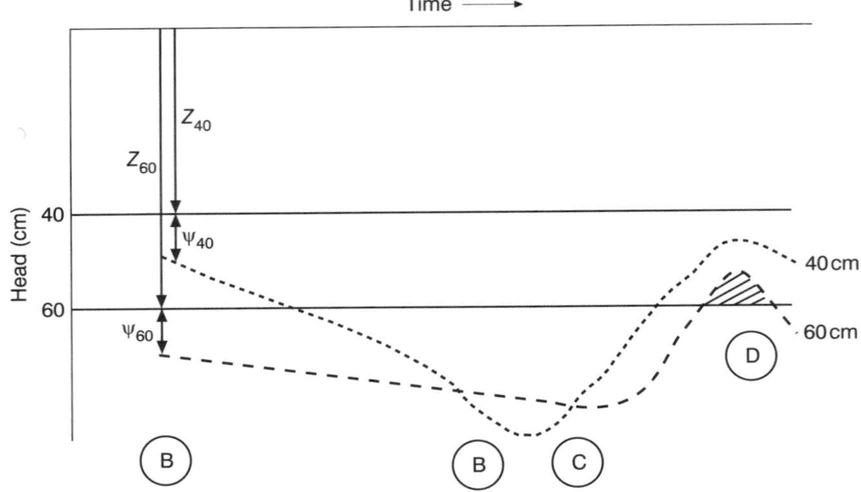

Figure 6.8 Diagram to illustrate the matric suction (ψ) and elevation (z) components of total potential (ϕ). Variations of matric suction, measured in tensiometers at depths of 40 and 60 cm below the ground surface, result in periods of downward and upward movement of soil water. (See text for fuller explanation.)

water is so slow, the kinetic energy component is ignored in stating values of total potential. For most practical purposes, therefore, the total potential (ϕ) is taken as the sum of the matric potential (suction) (ψ) and the gravitational potential (z). Using the ground surface as the datum level, the way in which the matric and gravitational potentials combine to affect water movement in a soil is simply illustrated by reference to two tensiometers at depths of, say, 40 and 60 cm (Figure 6.8). Since datum level is the ground surface and the soil is initially unsaturated, both the matric suction and elevation terms of total potential are negative. At time A, the matric suction is the same at both depths, but due to the difference in elevation, water flow in the soil layer between these points will occur downwards, from higher to lower (i.e. more negative) potential. Over time the upper soil dries more quickly than that at greater depth until, at time B, the difference in matric suction balances the elevation difference. The total potentials are the same, hence there is no flow between these depths, and the zero flux plane (ZFP) will be at some depth between them. If the upper soil continues to dry, its potential will become more negative than that of the deeper soil and upward flow will occur from 60 to 40 cm depth between times B and C. After an input of rain, the soil becomes wetter, matric suctions reduce and, in this example, the water table rises to within 60 cm of the ground surface. This is indicated by the shaded area at about time D, and demonstrates the usefulness of the pressure potential for cases where both saturated and unsaturated conditions are involved. The full annual cycle of soil water movement and ZFP depths in typical temperate climate conditions is shown in Figure 6.6.

Darcy's law (Section 5.5.1), showing that the rate of water movement through a saturated porous medium is proportional to the hydraulic gradient, is also applicable to the flow of soil water in unsaturated conditions. The Darcy equation may be simply expressed for unsaturated conditions as

$$v = -K(\theta)\left(\frac{\delta h}{\delta l}\right) \tag{6.2}$$

where v is the macroscopic velocity of water, K is the hydraulic conductivity (which, in unsaturated conditions, varies with the water content, θ) and $\delta h/\delta l$ is the hydraulic gradient comprising the change in hydraulic head (h) with distance along the direction of flow (l). As indicated earlier, the potential gradient and the resulting flow may be in any direction.

The flux calculation may be illustrated in the two simplest cases for (*a*) purely horizontal flow in the x direction, i.e. only a matric potential gradient ψ, and no gravity gradient:

$$v = -K(\theta)\,\frac{\delta\psi}{\delta x} \tag{6.3}$$

and (*b*) purely vertical flow downwards in the z direction, and with a matric potential gradient:

$$\begin{aligned} v &= -K(\theta)\,\frac{\delta(\psi + z)}{\delta z} \\ &= -K(\theta)\left(\frac{\delta\psi}{\delta z - 1}\right) \end{aligned} \tag{6.4}$$

In some situations data may be available on the gradient of soil water content rather than the gradient of potential. Soil water *diffusivity*, D (Childs and Collis-George, 1950) enables the flow equation to be transformed so that the flux is related to the gradient of water content (θ) rather than of potential. Like the hydraulic conductivity, diffusivity is also a function of water content, and the two are related:

$$D(\theta) = K(\theta)\,\frac{\delta\psi}{\delta\theta} \tag{6.5}$$

The slope of the moisture characteristic $\delta\theta/\delta\psi$ is the *specific water capacity* $C(\theta)$, so it follows that

$$D(\theta) = \frac{K(\theta)}{C(\theta)} \tag{6.6}$$

Then the relation between the flux and water content gradient is

$$v = -D(\theta)\,\frac{\delta\theta}{\delta x} \quad \text{(horizontal flow)} \tag{6.7}$$

$$v = +K(\theta) - D(\theta)\,\frac{\delta\theta}{\delta z} \quad \text{(vertical flow)} \tag{6.8}$$

The introduction of the diffusivity term is an attempt to simplify the mathematical treatment of unsaturated flow by rewriting the Darcy equation in a form analogous to equations of diffusion and heat conduction, for which solutions are readily available for a wide variety of boundary and initial conditions. The comparison is not perfect, however, since the process of soil water movement is one of convective mass flow and not one of molecular diffusion. To avoid confusion, Hillel (1982) suggested that diffusivity should be known as *hydraulic diffusivity* by analogy with hydraulic conductivity.

The application of the Darcy equation, or equations derived from it, to water movement in the unsaturated zone is subject to most of the stipulations noted in Section 5.5.1, not least in respect of its description of 'macroscopic' flow, and its restriction to steady-state situations, where the gradient and flux do not change, or change only slowly over time. Water movement may alter the gradient and the value of hydraulic conductivity and so, for field situations in which flow varies with space and time, Richards (1931) combined Darcy's equation with the continuity equation ($\delta\theta/\delta z = -\delta v/\delta z$) to yield the important non-linear equation that bears his name:

$$\frac{\delta\theta}{\delta t} = \frac{\delta}{\delta z}\left[\frac{K(\theta)}{\left(\frac{\delta\psi}{\delta z} - 1\right)}\right] \tag{6.9}$$

where t is time and flow is vertically downwards.

Water vapour will move through the soil matrix as a result of vapour pressure differences caused by variations in soil water content or soil temperature, the latter generally being more important. Water vapour will move from warm soil to cold soil, although only slowly compared with the mass flow of liquid water. The contribution of vapour flow to total soil water movement can therefore be ignored, except where soil water content is low.

Hydraulic conductivity

The hydraulic conductivity of saturated soil, like that of other saturated porous materials, depends mainly upon the geometry and distribution of the pore spaces (see Section 5.5.2). These include, not only textural voids but also macropores, such as interstructural cracks and root channels, which may greatly influence the hydraulic conductivity. This can be illustrated for a hypothetical clay soil with a *textural porosity* of 1 per cent and a matric conductivity of $0.01\,\mathrm{cm\,h^{-1}}$. Macropores, such as 1 mm wide cracks at 10 cm intervals, could develop seasonally and contribute an additional *structural porosity*.

Although this might also be only 1 per cent, its effect could be to increase the saturated hydraulic conductivity of the soil to the order of $1000\,\mathrm{cm\,h^{-1}}$ (Childs, 1969). Clearly then, even though saturated hydraulic conductivity has been correlated with soil texture and with descriptions of structure in some studies

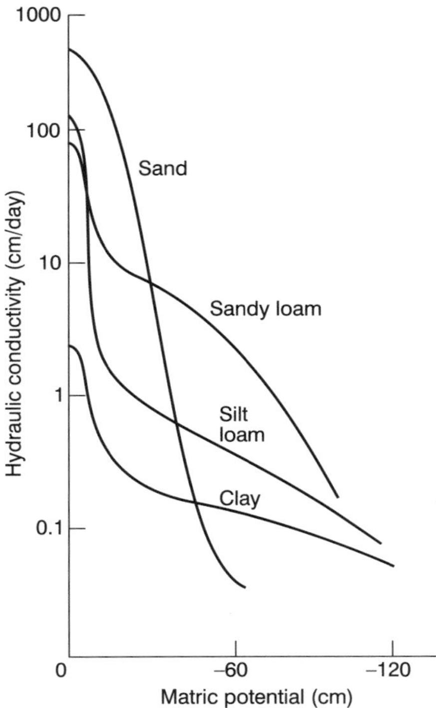

Figure 6.9 Unsaturated hydraulic conductivity ($K(\theta)$) as a function of matric potential (from an original diagram by Bouma, 1977).

(McKeague *et al.*, 1982; Rawls *et al.*, 1982), such correlations can be risky and the resulting estimates of K may be seriously in error.

By definition, the zone of aeration is not normally saturated, so that soil water movement is usually controlled by the *unsaturated* hydraulic conductivity ($K(\theta)$), which varies with moisture content (Eq. 6.2). Whereas saturated hydraulic conductivity (K) may be regarded as more or less constant for any given material, $K(\theta)$ will vary with soil water content and therefore with matric suction. Figure 6.9 shows that, for several soil types, hydraulic conductivity is largest at or near saturation and decreases rapidly with reducing water content. This reduction results from the fact that soil water movement can take place only through existing films of water on and between the soil grains. In saturated soil, all the pore spaces form an effective part of the water conducting system. In unsaturated soil, air-filled pores act as a non-conducting part of the system, reducing the effective cross-sectional area available for flow. The greater the decrease in soil water content, the greater will be the reduction in effectiveness of the conducting system and the smaller, therefore, the value of hydraulic conductivity.

The way in which $K(\theta)$ varies with soil water content is greatly influenced by the pore size distribution of the soil. In wet soils, conductivity is broadly related to soil texture, and increases as the latter becomes coarser (Figure 6.9). This is because water is transmitted more easily through large water-filled pores than through small ones. Near-saturated sand has a high proportion of large water-filled pores, so that $K(\theta)$ is larger than in clay soils. As the soil dries, the larger pores are the first to empty at low suctions, and $K(\theta)$ falls rapidly. As the suction increases and the moisture content decreases, the relationship between conductivity and texture is reversed so that, in dry conditions, clay soils are likely to have higher conductivities than loamy or sandy soils. This reflects the fact that, at high suctions, finer-textured soils have more water-filled pores and, therefore, a larger cross-sectional area through which flow can take place, than coarser soils in which only a small proportion of the pores contain water at high suctions. In shrinking soils, the increased suction that accompanies drying, reduces the size of the pores that remain full of water (Section 6.3.3), and this further helps to reduce the hydraulic conductivity.

The measurement of soil hydraulic conductivity and hydraulic diffusivity in both laboratory and field conditions is discussed in various texts (for example Burke *et al.*, 1986; Klute, 1986a). Some studies have shown that values obtained from small soil cores in the laboratory may be excessive, due to the rapid movement of water through macropores and macrovoids (for example Anderson and Bouma, 1973; Lauren *et al.*, 1988). The field measurement of $K(\theta)$ in unsaturated soils is difficult and expensive so that estimates, based on more readily available soil properties, are often used. A simple approach is that based on soil texture (for example Alexander and Skaggs, 1987). It is clear, however, that while texture is a major determinant, there are many other factors that may be important for a particular case. Better estimates of $K(\theta)$ may be expected where the moisture characteristic is available, and many studies have attempted to relate the two (for example Mualem, 1976). Ideally, predicted conductivities should be matched with measured values near saturation, although none of these methods is applicable to soils in which the hydraulic conductivity under saturated conditions is determined by water movement through macrovoids rather than through the soil matrix.

6.4.2 Infiltration of water into soils

The term *infiltration* is used to describe the process of water entry into the soil through the soil surface. The maximum rate at which water soaks into or is absorbed by the soil, its infiltration *capacity*, may in certain circumstances be very important in determining the partitioning of precipitation falling upon a catchment area. The relationship between rainfall intensity and infiltration capacity determines how much of the falling rain will flow over the ground surface, possibly directly into streams and rivers, and how much will enter the soil. Once in the soil it may move laterally as throughflow, or be retained temporarily before moving downwards as percolation or upwards by means of evaporation to the atmosphere.

Although sometimes used interchangeably, the terms *infiltration capacity* and *infiltration rate* should be differentiated since infiltration may be limited either by the capacity of the soil to absorb water, i.e. the infiltration capacity of the soil surface, or by the rate of supply of rainfall and irrigation, i.e. the infiltration rate. Use of the term infiltration rate thus indicates that infiltration is proceeding at less than the infiltration capacity. In this case, all falling rain not held as surface storage will infiltrate into the soil and there will be a direct relationship between infiltration rate and rainfall intensity. However, when rainfall intensity exceeds the infiltration capacity of the soil surface, this relationship breaks down and may, indeed, be inverted as infiltration capacity declines through a storm event. As with many of the terms which describe flow in a porous medium, both infiltration rate and infiltration capacity are volume fluxes which are usually expressed as volume flux densities. They do not, therefore, indicate the effective velocity of vertical water movement in the soil (see also the discussion of effective velocity of groundwater movement in Section 5.5.1).

Early field investigations of infiltration (for example Horton, 1933, 1939) were carried out in semi-arid areas, where it is quite common for rainfall intensity to exceed infiltration capacity, resulting in widespread surface ponding and overland flow (see Chapter 7). As a result, for many years, undue importance was attached to the hydrological role of infiltration capacity. Today, it is widely recognized that in well-vegetated areas, both temperate and tropical, most soils can absorb the rainfall of all but the most intense storms and that widespread overland flow is uncommon. Nevertheless, an understanding of the reasons for temporal and spatial variations of infiltration capacity is still important in areas where very large water inputs, such as extreme rainstorms or artificial irrigation, occur.

Infiltration capacity

The infiltration capacity of a soil generally decreases during rainfall, rapidly at first and then more slowly, until a more or less stable value has been attained (Figure 6.10). This decline of infiltration capacity is determined by a number of factors, including limitations imposed by the soil surface, surface cover conditions and the rate of downward movement of water through the soil profile.

Soil surface conditions may impose an upper limit to the rate at which water can be absorbed, despite the fact that the capacity of the lower soil layers to receive and to store additional infiltrating water remains unfilled. In general the infiltration capacity is reduced by surface sealing resulting from compaction, the washing of fine particles into surface pores and by frost (for example Poesen, 1986; Romkens *et al.*, 1990). Infiltration capacity increases with the depth of standing water on the surface, the number of cracks and fissures at the surface and the ground slope. Cultivation techniques may either increase or decrease

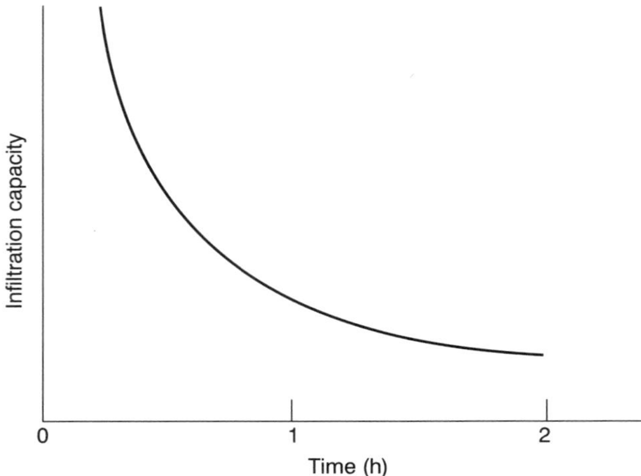

Figure 6.10 Schematic diagram showing the decline of infiltration capacity during a rainfall event.

infiltration capacity, and vegetation tends to increase the infiltration capacity of a soil by retarding surface water movement, stabilizing loose particles, reducing raindrop compaction and improving soil structure (Section 6.2). These effects are clearly demonstrated by the way in which the presence of ground litter on a forest floor normally results in higher infiltration beneath forest than beneath grass. Snow may have a similar effect to ground litter, but frozen soils and urban surfaces generally reduce infiltration capacity.

Water cannot continue to be absorbed by the soil surface at a given rate unless the underlying soil profile can conduct the infiltrated water away at a corresponding rate. The ability of a given soil to conduct water depends upon its properties, including texture and structure, and so is normally greater for permeable, coarse-textured soils than for slowly permeable clays. Other important factors include soil stratification, the initial gradient of soil water potential and the lengthening flowpaths of water as infiltration proceeds during a rainfall or irrigation event.

Soil water movement during infiltration

Soil conditions in the field are notoriously heterogeneous. In addition to the spatial variability of soil properties, there is frequently both spatial and temporal variability of soil water content, hysteresis, changes of various soil and boundary conditions over time and the existence of two- or three-dimensional flows. As a result, infiltration capacities and infiltration rates typically vary enormously in both space and time. For this reason, the development of infiltration theory was largely based on the investigation of water entry into homogeneous and some-

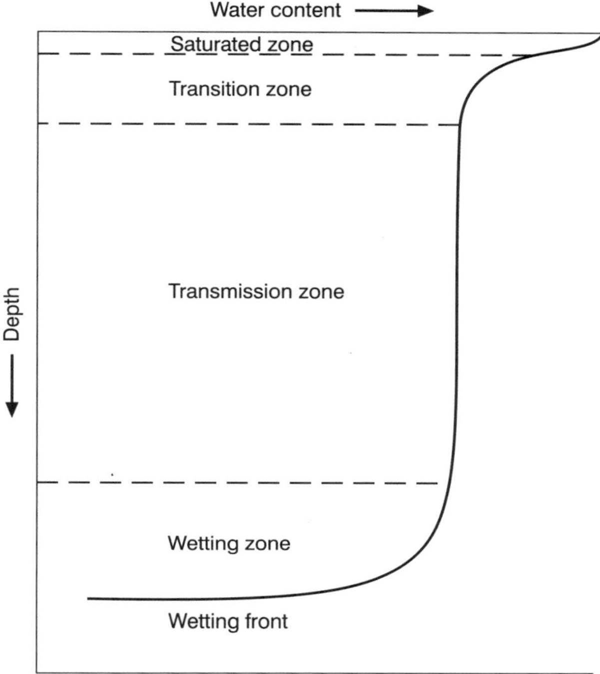

Figure 6.11 Moisture zones during ponded water infiltration (from an original diagram by G.B. Bodman and E.A. Colman, *Proceedings of Soil Science Society of America*, **8**, pp. 116–22, 1943, and adapted by permission of the publisher).

times artificial soils, assuming a uniform initial water content and the presence of ponded water at the soil surface.

Some of the classic experimental work on the entry of water into such soils (Bodman and Colman, 1943) suggested that the wetted portion of a column of soil into which infiltration is taking place comprises a number of zones, which are illustrated in Figure 6.11. The saturated zone, as its name implies, is a shallow saturated layer, a centimetre or so in thickness, at the ground surface. Immediately below this is another shallow zone, only a few centimetres in thickness, in which the water content decreases very rapidly from top to bottom and which is, therefore, known as the transition zone. Below this, again, is the transmission zone, through which water from the upper two zones is transmitted, with little or no change in moisture content, to the underlying wetting zone which, like the transition zone, has fairly steep moisture gradients and where the water content also changes appreciably with time. Finally, at the base of the wetting zone is the sharply defined wetting front, which is characterized by very steep moisture gradients and which marks the limit between the wetted soil above and the dry soil below. Provided that the supply of water to the soil surface from rainfall or irrigation continues, the wetting front advances steadily downwards into the unwetted soil as a result of the passage of water through the transmission zone.

Based on these findings, variations in the duration of surface ponded infiltration will result in variations in the depth of wetted soil rather than in continued increases in the water content of the surface layers. The only part of the soil profile in which the moisture content changes significantly with time during infiltration is the wetting zone and the wetting front. The saturated zone remains saturated, the moisture gradient in the transition zone remains fairly constant, and so, too, does the water content and matric suction in the transmission zone. As infiltration continues, the transmission zone becomes longer and the wetting zone and the wetting front move farther downwards into the soil. However, the saturation and transition zones described by Bodman and Colman have been queried as an experimental artefact resulting from looseness, structural instability or swelling of the soil at the surface (Hillel, 1982). And other investigators have found that, due to air entrapment, the surface soil generally has a water content below complete saturation and that in field soils about 8–20 per cent of the pore space is commonly occupied by air when the soil is at maximum saturation (Corey, 1977).

Similar soil water profiles, but without the saturated and transition zones, were derived from theoretical considerations by Philip (1964). Figure 6.12 shows computed profiles, during sustained surface flooding of a clay loam soil, as a function of the time since the start of infiltration. The increase in profile water over time consists mainly of an extension of the nearly saturated transmission zone. The sharp change in moisture content in the wetting zone is a consequence of the dependence of hydraulic conductivity on moisture content. From Darcy's law it is clear that a steep hydraulic gradient is necessary in this zone to achieve a flux equal to that in the (near-saturation) transmission zone.

The preceding discussion suggests that, in the early stages of infiltration into a uniformly dry soil, the matric suction gradient in the surface layer will be very steep, and is likely to be the most important factor determining the amount of infiltration and downward movement of water. Initial rates of movement are likely to be high, and the resulting rapid penetration of the moisture profile is clearly illustrated in Figure 6.12. As the wetting proceeds the transmission zone lengthens and the gravitational gradient becomes relatively more important than the matric suction gradient. The rates of infiltration and downward movement decrease until the infiltration tends to settle down to a steady, gravity-controlled rate which approximates the saturated hydraulic conductivity (Hillel, 1982).

In well-vegetated areas, the soil infiltration capacity usually exceeds the rainfall intensity. In this case, the rate of infiltration equals the rate of water supply to the soil surface so that no surface ponding occurs. Computed moisture profiles during such rainfall-limited infiltration are shown for two steady rainfall intensities in Figure 6.13. In these circumstances the surface soil does not become saturated and the moisture content increases until it reaches a value at which the

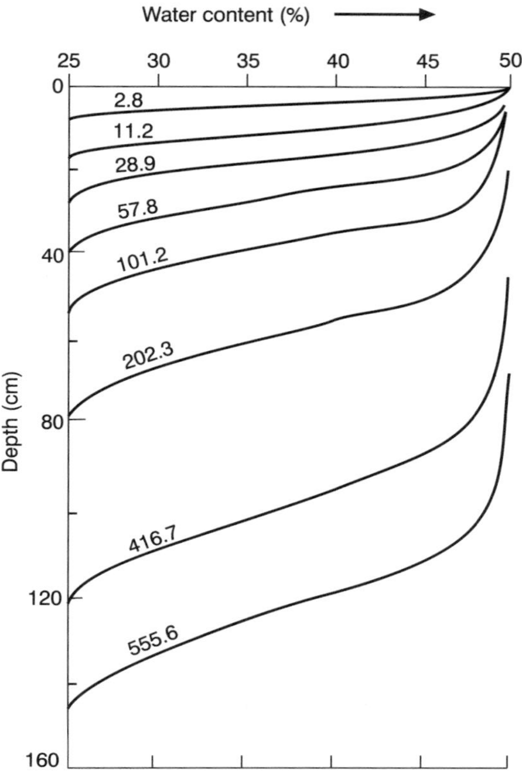

Figure 6.12 Computed soil water profiles at different times (hours) during ponded water infiltration into a clay loam soil (from an original diagram by Philip, 1964).

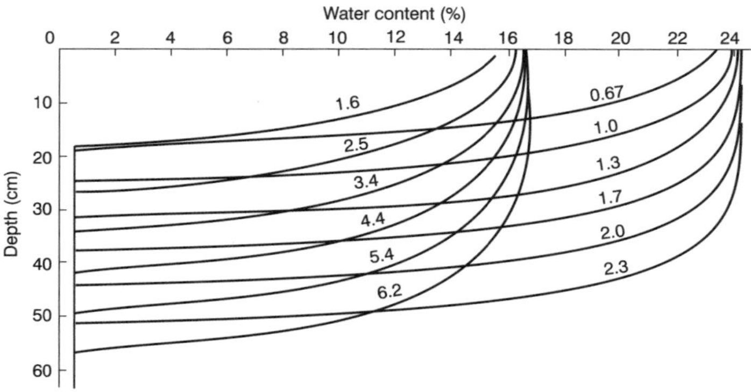

Figure 6.13 Computed soil water profiles at different times (hours) during non-ponding infiltration for constant rate rainfall intensities of 12.7 and 47.0 mm/h (after an original diagram by Rubin, 1966).

unsaturated hydraulic conductivity becomes equal to the rainfall rate. A wave of moisture percolates downwards, wetting the soil to this moisture content. Increasing the rainfall intensity results in a higher water content throughout the profile, and hence a larger conductivity. As in the ponded infiltration case, the moisture content gradient at the wetting front remains steep. Thus, although reached in different ways, the soil moisture profiles developed by both ponded infiltration and rainfall-limited infiltration are similar in shape.

Time variations in infiltration capacity

Our understanding of soil water movement during infiltration, in both ponding and rainfall-limited conditions, thus confirms that the typical curve of declining infiltration capacity over time, shown in Figure 6.10, results directly from the reduction in the gradient of water potential in the soil profile. In addition, factors operating at the soil surface, including swelling of clay particles, raindrop impact and inwashing of fine material, may also be important in the case of some clay soils or of soils with a sparse vegetation cover.

Especially for deep soils of relatively uniform texture, the high initial infiltration capacity reflects the initial steep gradient of soil water potential and the subsequent rapid fall, generally within the first hour or so of rainfall, results from the marked reduction of that gradient. This leads to a near-constant value of infiltration, driven by the gradient of gravitational potential, and closely approximating the saturated hydraulic conductivity. Where, however, the soil profile is complicated by the existence of a relatively impermeable layer at some distance below the surface, the curve of infiltration capacity versus time may show a further sudden reduction of infiltration capacity, reflecting the fact that, when the available storage in the surface soil horizons has been filled, infiltration is then governed by the rate at which water can pass through the underlying layer of lower saturated hydraulic conductivity.

Hydrologists have developed several equations to describe the variation in infiltration capacity for a uniform soil and to account for the initial rapid decrease leading to an asymptotic approach to a constant value. Most assume that, in surface ponding conditions, infiltration is a function of either the total amount of water infiltrated (i.e. storage-based) or of time (i.e. time-based). One of the earliest storage-based infiltration equations is that by Green and Ampt (1911). This identifies two flow components (Jones, 1997a). Conductivity flow A is the steady rate of flow driven by the gradient of soil water potential between the wet or flooded surface and the drier soil below. Diffusivity flow B occurs as water diffuses into the drier soil ahead of the advancing wetting front. The rate of infiltration f is given as

$$f_t = A + \frac{B}{S_t} \qquad (6.10)$$

where S_t is the volume of water stored in the depth of soil saturated by infiltration at time t, and A and B are constants for given soil texture and moisture conditions.

Although it applies best to simple sands with a narrow range of pore sizes, the equation has been widely used, not least by computer modellers, and because it is physically based, the parameters can either be evaluated experimentally from infiltration data (for example Brakensiek and Onstad, 1977) or estimated, less reliably, from basic soil property measurements (Rawls *et al.*, 1983).

The time-based equation developed by Philip (1957) is an extension of the Green–Ampt approach, which allows for a deceleration of diffusivity flow over time as the wetting front nears the water table or the base of the soil profile. The rate of infiltration is given as

$$f_t = A + \left(\frac{B}{2}\right) t^{-0.5} \tag{6.11}$$

This approach has proved useful in predicting infiltration rates for short periods of time, including the initial decline in infiltration capacity. For longer periods it is necessary to use a more complex approach based on the Richards equation (Kirkby, 1985).

The preceding discussion of the infiltration process has, for simplicity, assumed a distinct and continuous wetting front, and uniform initial soil water content. In practice these conditions are rarely, if ever, found in the field. The macropores present in most soils allow variable penetration of infiltrating water and their role in soil water hydrology is discussed further in Section 6.5. In addition, the continued movement of soil water following a period of infiltration means that a uniform soil water profile is unlikely to be present at the onset of the next infiltration event.

6.4.3 Soil water redistribution following infiltration

Continued downward movement of water, caused by the gradients of gravitational and matric potential, may continue long after infiltration at the surface ceases. During this period of soil water redistribution, the transmission zone which existed during infiltration becomes a draining zone as water moves from the infiltration-wetted upper layers of the soil to deeper, drier layers. This process is important since it controls the quantity of water retained in the plant root zone, the available air-filled porosity for subsequent storage of water in the next rainfall or irrigation event, and recharge to groundwater in the saturated zone.

The rate of soil water redistribution slows down, partly because hydraulic conductivity in the former wetted zone diminishes as a result of decreasing water content, and partly because the gradient of matric potential weakens as the soil water content becomes more uniform. The wetting front continues to move down the profile, but its advance becomes progressively slower and less distinct. After a few days the water content changes only very slowly and the soil is said to

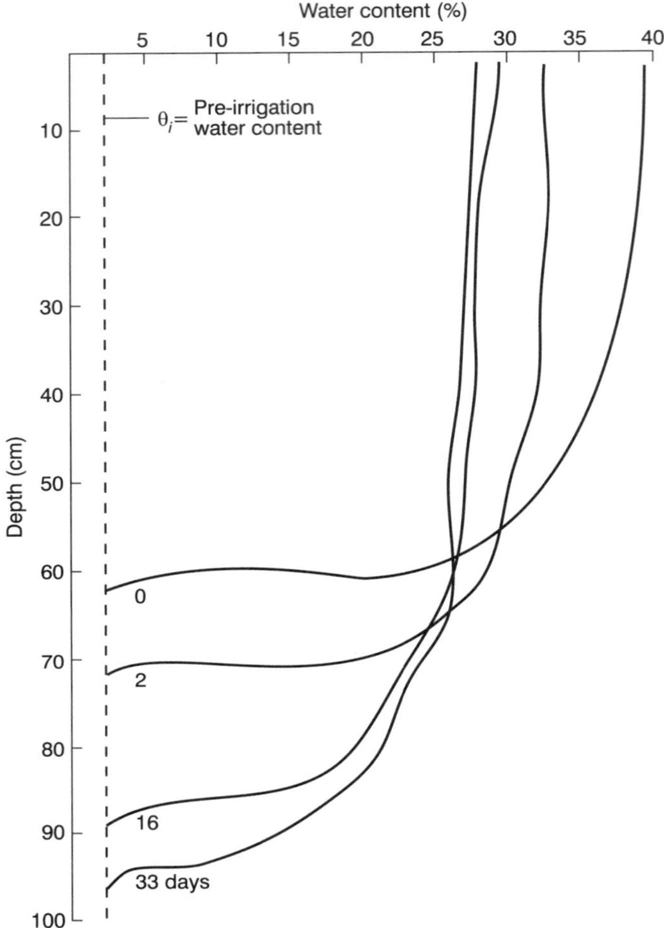

Figure 6.14 Soil water profiles during the redistribution of water in the absence of evaporation following the irrigation of a fine sandy loam soil. (From an original diagram by W.R. Gardner, D. Hillel and Y. Benyamini, *Water Resources Research*, **6**, p. 857, Fig. 3. © 1970 American Geophysical Union.)

be at 'field capacity' (Section 6.3.4). This process is illustrated in Figure 6.14 by the successive soil water profiles found in a fine sandy loam during redistribution in the absence of both evaporation at the soil surface and a water table at the base of the soil column. Since redistribution is a continuing process, there is no unique moment when field capacity is reached. Instead, field capacity is normally inferred when successive soil water profiles show little change or when the rate of change becomes less than a predetermined value.

If there were no interruptions, redistribution could theoretically continue until gravity and retention forces were in balance. Then total soil water potential would be equal at all depths and without a hydraulic gradient there would be no soil water movement. This is rarely observed in field situations either because rainfall occurs as a multiple sequence of events or because, after rainfall, evaporation from soil and plants normally dries the surface soil layers. In multiple rainfall sequences, successive inputs of new infiltration during the early stages of redistribution complicate the idealized model of soil water distribution just described. A conceptual model for infiltration in such conditions was applied to a variety of soil types by Corradini *et al.* (1997).

In the case of evaporation from the root zone and soil surface, the resulting gradient of total potential encourages the upward movement of water from the draining zone and this helps to further reduce the downward movement of water over time. Figure 6.15 shows the progress of moisture distribution in three situations: (*a*) redistribution without evaporation, (*b*) simultaneous evaporation and redistribution and (*c*) evaporation only. The curves of the simultaneous processes resemble those for redistribution alone, except for the obvious evaporation effect in the surface layers. In particular, the lower portions of the curves indicate that evaporation had little effect on the shape and rate of advance of the wetting front. In fact, evaporation appears to have reduced drainage by only about 10 per cent, even though redistribution reduced evaporation by some 75 per cent (Gardner *et al.*, 1970). This diagram also shows that the upper part of the profile, which was initially wetted during infiltration, drains monotonically, though increasingly slowly, while the immediate sublayer at first becomes wetter before eventually beginning to drain. It is in this part of the soil profile that hysteresis severely complicates attempts to measure or estimate the process of moisture redistribution. Hysteresis presents a more general problem, however, in the sense that during redistribution, as has been shown, the upper part of the profile is drying through drainage and evaporation, while the lower part is becoming wetter. The relation between water content and suction will, therefore, be different at different depths depending on the history of wetting and drying that takes place at each point in the soil (see also Sections 6.3.3 and 6.5.1).

Studies of the post-infiltration redistribution of water have often assumed deep profiles unaffected by the water table. However, in many soils the depth to the saturated zone may be fairly small, and shallow water tables may exert a considerable influence on the distribution of water in a soil profile.

6.4.4 Upward movement of soil water from the water table

Up to a certain height above the water table, capillary tension keeps the soil pores full of water. This is the capillary fringe or tension saturated zone which is of interest to the hydrologist both for its *vertical extent*, which affects the overlying soil water profile, and for the *rate of capillary flow*, which determines the ability of the soil to supply water for evaporation from the soil surface and root zone. The thickness of the capillary fringe corresponds to the air entry value, which is the

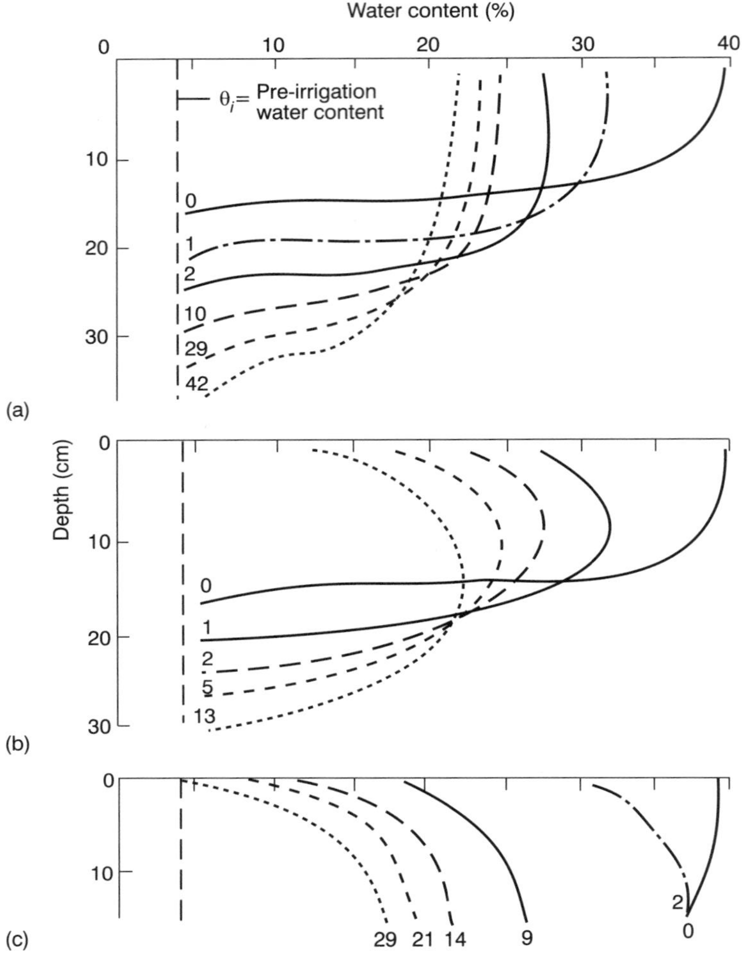

Figure 6.15 Successive soil water profiles in soil columns following an irrigation of 50 mm. Values indicate the time in days since irrigation ended. (*a*) Redistribution with no evaporation, (*b*) redistribution and evaporation, (*c*) evaporation only. (From an original diagram by W.R. Gardner, D. Hillel and Y. Benyamini, *Water Resources Research*, **6**, p. 1149, Fig. 2. © 1970 American Geophysical Union.)

suction necessary for air to enter the largest pores. This is generally greater for clays than for sandy soils but since soils contain a range of sizes of both particles and pore spaces, the height of rise will vary spatially within a given soil. In areas where the top of the capillary fringe is close to the ground surface it may play an important role in generating the quickflow component of runoff (see 'The role of groundwater' in Chapter 7), since only a small addition of water will reduce the suction to zero causing a large and sudden rise in the water table (Sklash and Farvolden, 1979; Gillham, 1984; Jayatilaka and Gillham, 1996).

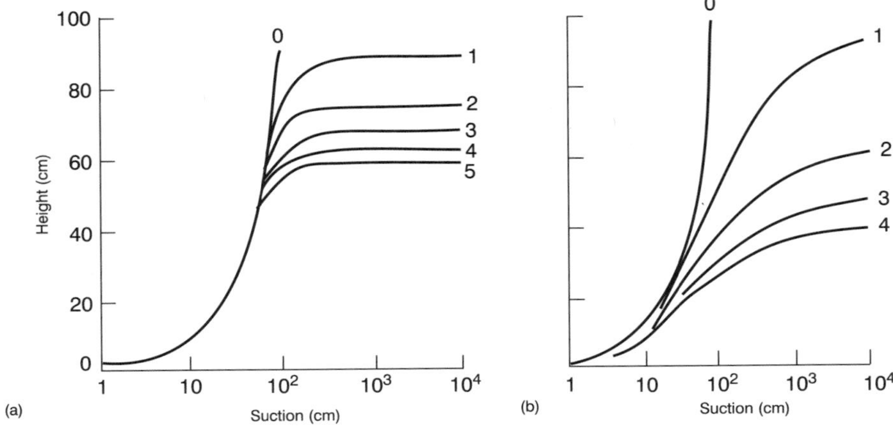

Figure 6.16 Maximum capillary flow rate (mm/day) at different heights above the water table, related to the matric suction at the ground surface for (*a*) coarse-textured and (*b*) fine-textured soils (from original diagrams by Wind, 1961).

Capillary rise also extends above the tension saturated zone by means of movement through films of water in the irregularly shaped and variously sized interparticle spaces of the unsaturated zone. The speed and direction of this movement will be largely determined by the unsaturated hydraulic conductivity and the combined gradients of matric suction and gravity. Evaporation creates a suction gradient encouraging the upward movement of water towards the soil surface or root zone. Unless the upward rate of movement can keep pace with these losses, progressively deeper layers of the soil will lose water until the rate of evaporation becomes limited.

The maximum rate of capillary rise is governed by water table depth and soil texture. Figure 6.16 compares the maximum rates of steady capillary flow at different heights in a coarse-textured and a fine-textured soil. Particularly in the coarse-textured soil, the curves become almost horizontal at higher suctions, indicating that the maximum rate of capillary flow is dependent on height above the water table rather than on the suction gradient imposed at the soil surface. The ability of the soil profile to so limit the rate of evaporation loss, through the medium of hydraulic conductivity, is a remarkable and useful feature of the unsaturated flow system (Hillel, 1982). Thus, for the soil in this example, a water table depth of 60 cm results in a maximum capillary flow of about 5 mm per day; this declines to about 1 mm per day when the water table depth is 90 cm. In the fine-textured soil the horizontal sections of the curves are not well developed, although the influence of water table depth can still be clearly seen.

Figure 6.16 suggests that, with an appropriate suction gradient, very small rates of capillary flow may occur at a considerable height above the water table. Laboratory experiments have, in fact, identified measurable movement over vertical distances of at least 7 metres (Gardner and Fireman, 1958). Especially in arid and semi-arid areas, therefore, where rates of evaporation are high, such movements may lead to damaging accumulations of salt at the ground surface, even where the water table occurs at a considerable depth (Wind, 1961). Since capillary rise may occur over a large vertical range of the unsaturated zone it is usually necessary to consider the effect of the different horizons in the soil profile upon the rate of capillary movement (Bloemen, 1980). Discussion of hydraulic conductivity in Section 6.4.1 showed that in wet conditions coarser-textured soils have a higher conductivity than clays, while in dry conditions the reverse is true. Accordingly, the highest rates of capillary rise are likely to occur in soils where the texture becomes progressively finer with height above the water table (Wind, 1961). This may be of considerable hydrological importance in areas, like the Netherlands, which have shallow water tables and where soil water movement is therefore inextricably linked with conditions in the saturated zone (for example Querner, 1997).

6.5 Soil water behaviour under field conditions

Much of the preceding discussion of soil water retention, storage and movement has been based on studies of idealized soil systems. These often involve homogeneous and sometimes artificial soils, uniform initial water content, ponded water at the soil surface and a controlled environment in which plants, evaporation losses and water table influences are usually absent and where 'rain' falls at a constant rate. In reality, the soil profile in the field is a very complex and heterogeneous system to which these restrictions and simplifications are applied only to facilitate laboratory measurements, physical experimentation and modelling. Even mathematical treatments of soil water have tended to assume considerably simplified boundary conditions (for example De Jong, 1981).

The remaining sections of this chapter are based on more realistic laboratory experiments and on actual field situations. It is hoped that they will provide at least a partial insight into some of the phenomena that are relevant to the treatment of soil water physics of a particular field site. Many of these phenomena are interrelated and have important implications for the transport of solutes (see Section 8.5.3).

6.5.1 Soil water hysteresis

Hysteresis in the relation between matric suction and soil water content (see Section 6.3.3) depends not only on whether the soil is currently being wetted or dried but also on the previous pattern of moisture changes. Although $\psi(\theta)$ hysteresis is generally ignored in soil water studies, there is growing evidence of its importance under field conditions (for example Royer and Vachaud, 1975; Beese and Van der Ploeg, 1976). In comparison with the $\psi(\theta)$ curves there generally appears to be much less hysteresis for unsaturated hydraulic conductivity, $K(\theta)$.

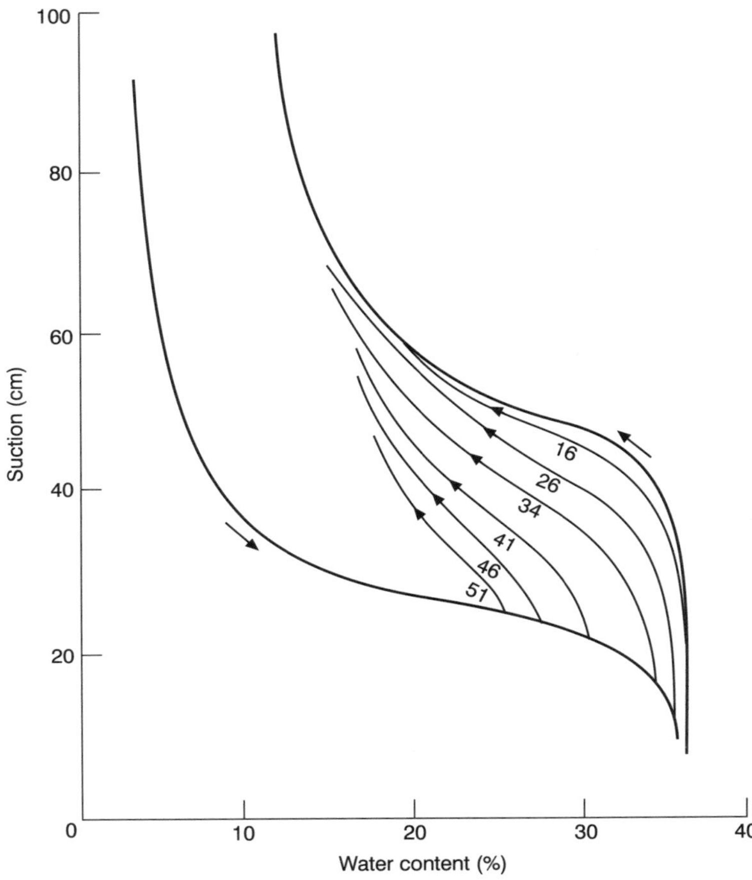

Figure 6.17 Soil water drying curves at different depths (cm) in a homogeneous soil profile (redrawn after diagrams by Vachaud and Thony, 1971).

Under natural conditions the existence of a uniform water content throughout the profile is virtually impossible, even for a homogeneous soil. Immediately after precipitation the soil surface layers will be wetter than those deeper down, while subsequent downward infiltration and redistribution, together with evaporation, will tend to dry out the surface layers so that the moisture content increases with depth. This pattern will be repeated for successive storms, their effects becoming superimposed, so that the distribution of soil water in the profile is both non-uniform and continually changing. As a result, the water content changes at different depths in the soil will follow different scanning curves (Figure 6.17). The situation will obviously be much more complicated for soils that are not homogeneous.

6.5.2 Soil heterogeneity

Depending upon the hydrological problem under study, variation in soil properties may be viewed at a number of different scales. These include areal variations across a catchment or between catchments, differences down a soil profile and differences within a small volume of soil in a single soil horizon.

Spatial variability

Soil properties tend to vary continuously over the earth's surface, with very few sharp changes. Consequently, the soil units identified by pedologists are often based on boundaries selected arbitrarily within a gradual continuum of soil characteristics. Such units are often intended primarily for agricultural use and tend to reflect features which can be readily and unambiguously noted by surveyors in the field. This means that those physical properties of most interest to the hydrologist may play only a minor role in their classification (Warrick and Nielsen, 1980). Even so, soil units may be satisfactory 'carriers' of certain types of basic data and broad groupings of soil types have been widely used in hydrology (for example Farquharson *et al.*, 1978; Bouma, 1986).

Study of a 'uniform' 150 ha field, representing just one soil series, showed very large spatial variation of some soil physical properties such as hydraulic conductivity and soil water diffusivity, which both had log-normal frequency distributions (Nielsen *et al.*, 1973). Texture, bulk density and water content exhibited much less variation and were normally distributed. Geostatistical techniques such as kriging may be used to interpolate between measured values, and the *similar media* concept has been applied by using a scaling coefficient to describe heterogeneity from site to site (Warrick and Nielsen, 1980). Hopmans (1987) provided a comparison of different scaling methods for the hydraulic properties of the soil in a research catchment in the eastern Netherlands. Price and Bauer (1984) found that small textural changes within a sandy soil gave rise to large differences in water content, with zones of preferential retention (finer texture) and preferential percolation (coarser texture) over a distance of only a few metres.

Soil layering

Many soil profiles consist of a sequence of distinctively different layers, or horizons, which are caused by natural soil forming processes. Because these horizons may differ markedly in terms of, say, hydraulic conductivity and porosity, such stratification may greatly affect the movement of water through the soil profile. In many humid areas, for example, minerals and fine particles leached from the surface soil layers are deposited at greater depths, leading to a marked decrease in the number of large pores in the zone of accumulation. In extreme cases, this deposition results in the formation of an iron pan or hard pan of near-zero hydraulic conductivity and the consequential waterlogging of the surface layers. Even without hard-pan formation, the subsoil tends to have a lower saturated hydraulic conductivity than the surface horizons. However, this is not always the case so that any soil horizon may limit the overall capacity of the complete profile to transmit water.

In general, layering of the soil profile reduces the infiltration capacity at the soil surface. In the case where a coarse layer of higher saturated hydraulic conductivity overlies a finer-textured layer, the infiltration capacity is initially controlled by the coarse layer. Once the wetting front reaches the finer layer, however, it is the latter that controls the rate of water movement and so infiltration capacity falls sharply. Then, if infiltration is prolonged, a perched water table may develop in the coarse soil immediately above the impeding layer or, in sloping terrain, throughflow may result (see Section 7.4.2 and Figure 7.6(d)). In the opposite case, where fine material overlies coarse, the infiltration capacity, although lower, is again controlled initially by the upper layer but may fall even further when the wetting front reaches the underlying coarser material. This apparently surprising effect is caused because the soil moisture suction at the wetting front is too high to allow water to enter the larger pores of the coarse material. Continued infiltration raises the moisture content in the upper layer until the matric potential has reduced sufficiently for water to penetrate the coarser layer. A layer of sand in fine-textured soil may, therefore, actually impede, rather than assist, water movement through the soil profile (Brady, 1984; Hillel, 1982).

Patterns of soil water content and soil water potential during a constant, supply-limited, infiltration into a layered soil (fine sand overlying coarse sand) are shown in Figure 6.18. The saturated conductivity of both layers was

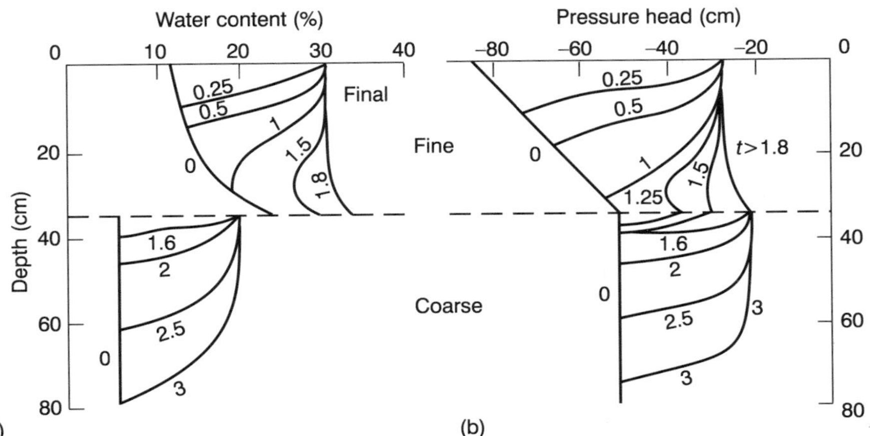

Figure 6.18 Profiles of the change with time (hours) of (*a*) water content and (*b*) suction during a constant rate of water application to a layered soil (redrawn after diagrams by Vachaud *et al.*, 1973).

considerably greater than the rate of application of water (Vachaud *et al.*, 1973). Since water transfer occurs between the two layers, the soil water potential must be continuous across the boundary because any pressure discontinuity would imply an infinite hydraulic gradient (Corey, 1977). Similarly, the flux must be equal across the boundary. The sudden jump in moisture content, in contrast, results from the difference in the moisture characteristic of the two materials. As infiltration continues, the wetting front moves down and the water content of each layer increases until its hydraulic conductivity becomes sufficient to carry the flow (see Section 6.4.2 under 'Time variations in infiltration capacity').

Outside the humid regions, climate also broadly determines the sequence of horizons in the soil profile. Where evaporation exceeds precipitation the net upward movement of water and solutes may result in surface deposition and the formation of a crusted or indurated surface layer. Indurated layers, which are widespread in Africa and Australia, may also result from compaction by raindrops or from the breakdown of soil aggregates during wetting. Even a thin surface crust can considerably impede infiltration (Ben-Hur *et al.*, 1985; Poesen, 1986; Romkens *et al.*, 1990). A similar effect is found in high latitudes, and in some high altitude areas, where frozen soils may impede infiltration and the movement of water through the soil profile. The effect of frozen soils on the rate of infiltration depends largely on the soil water content at the time of freezing. The wetter the soil is when freezing takes place the greater the number of ice-blocked pores and the lower the rate of infiltration, so that, when a saturated soil freezes, its intake rate will be virtually zero.

Macropores

One of the main reasons why water in natural soils does not always move in the manner predicted from Darcy's equation is that, in certain circumstances, water movement may be dominated by flow through a few large openings or voids rather than by the bulk flow through the microstructural interstices of the soil matrix. These large openings include structural cracks and fissures and quasi-cylindrical voids caused by earthworms and other burrowing creatures, and by the decay of plant roots. Increasingly, they have become known as *macropores* although, given their typical size range, the term *mesopores* would be more generally appropriate. Interconnected, supercapillary interstices with diameters greater than about 30 μm can significantly increase the rate of soil drainage and may even allow sufficient flow velocity to result in some erosional smoothing (Jones, 1997a). Larger interstices are even more effective in these respects and some workers have proposed a lower limit for macropores of 60 μm. Others have related the threshold for macropore flow to capillary tension rather than to pore diameter. Thus Beven and Germann (1982), in a seminal review of the influence of macropores on the flow of water through soils, proposed a soil water potential of 0.1 kPa, which is equivalent to pores larger than about 3 mm in diameter. Jones

(1997a) included soil pipes in a consideration of macropores, thereby considerably extending their size range.

The inclusion of soil pipes usefully underlines the fact that, whether defined by pore diameter or by capillary tension, the hydrological influence of macropores depends much more upon their interconnectivity and continuity than upon their abundance since, in most cases, macropores are likely to comprise only 1 or 2 per cent of the bulk soil volume. Their hydrological role will also vary with soil water content and potential. For example, when the soil is drier than Beven and Germann's proposed threshold potential of 0.1 kPa, which will be the majority of the time for most soils, rapid water flow through macropores will not take place. In other words, their role and importance in infiltration and redistribution of water in the soil profile is largely confined to periods of heavy rainfall or artificial irrigation. In these circumstances, when the rate of water supply exceeds the infiltration capacity of the adjacent soil peds, water will flow through the macropore system to reach the subsoil rather than moving down the profile as a well-defined wetting front. This was demonstrated by Blake *et al.* (1973), who applied 50 mm of tritiated water to the surface of a dry clay soil (Figure 6.19). They found that tritium concentrations were much higher on the faces of the cracks than within the soil peds. A further example of the way in which the pattern of wetting of the soil profile is altered when macropores allow infiltration directly from the surface to the subsoil, was provided by Hodnett and Bell (1986). Working on a swelling clay soil in central India, they found that the monsoon rains led to initial saturation at about 1.6 m depth rather than the 'classic' pattern of saturation from the surface downwards (Figure 6.20).

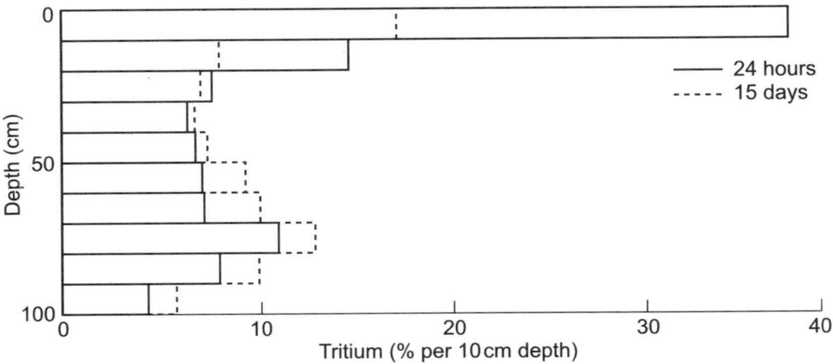

Figure 6.19 Distribution of tritium down the soil profile at 24 hours and 15 days after application at the ground surface (reproduced from G. Blake, E. Schlichting and U. Zimmermann, *Proceedings of Soil Science Society of America*, **37**, 1973, pp. 669–72 by permission of the Soil Science Society of America, Inc.).

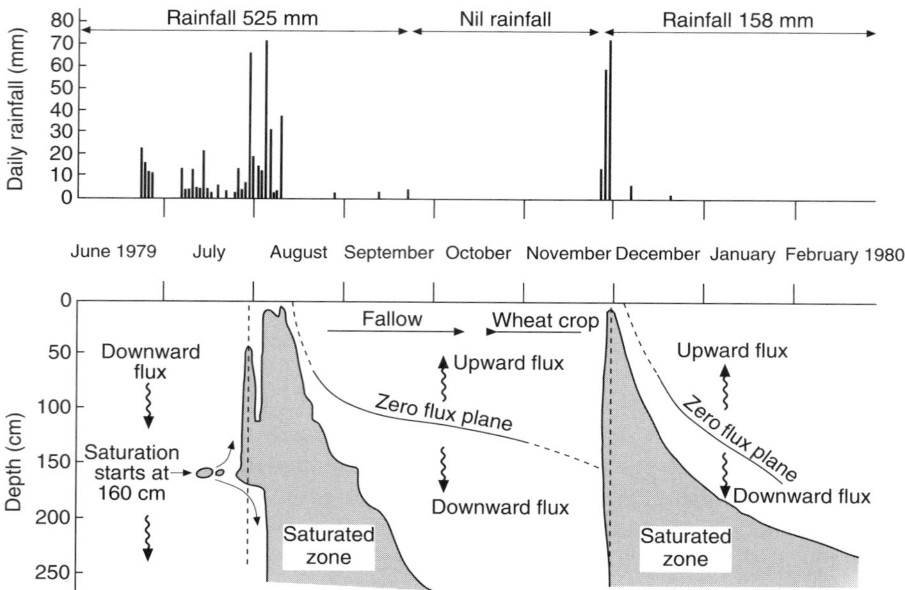

Figure 6.20 Annual cycle of water movement in a swelling clay soil in India, showing the development of saturated conditions starting at 1.6 m depth due to infiltration down shrinkage cracks. (From an original diagram by Hodnett and Bell, 1986. Blackwell Scientific Publications Ltd.)

Rapid, preferential movement of water through the soil profile, which typifies macropore flow, may have a number of hydrological consequences:

- Macropores may considerably increase the infiltration capacity of soils and help to reduce the incidence of overland flow.
- Water flowing through macropores will bypass, and so fail to wet, the soil matrix and this may mean that less water is available in the surface layers for plants.
- Macropore flow may allow deep percolation and recharge to groundwater, even when the overlying soil is dry. This is especially likely where macropore continuity extends through the full depth of the soil profile, as for example when shallow clay soils are fully penetrated by shrinkage cracks (Hodnett and Bell, 1986).
- Since macropore flow does not pass through the natural filtration and purification of the soil matrix, it may lead to contamination of groundwater supplies.
- In some soil and slope conditions, especially during heavy rainfall, macropore flow may play an important role in the development of throughflow, which moves laterally at shallow depths below the ground surface (see also Section 7.4.2).

The continuity of macropores is very important for flow processes which are consequently less well developed where most macropores have closed bottom ends and so fill up with water during rainfall, than where most are connected to large air-filled cavities such as soil pipes, animal burrows or artificial drains. Also, the hydrological importance of macropores is likely to vary over time. For example, seasonal variations may be significant, especially in shrinking soils. Robinson and Beven (1983) found that, in a clay soil exhibiting seasonal shrink–swell, flows from artificial drains were much more responsive to storms in summer, when the ground was dry and cracked, than in winter when the topsoil was close to saturation. Similarly, observations on the Keuper formation in Luxembourg (Hendriks, 1993) showed that direct runoff during summer storm events was higher from forested catchments than from grassland and arable catchments. This was because of the greater development, under forest, of macropores such as shrinkage cracks and animal burrows. Again, macropore flow tends to dominate soil water flow processes during, and shortly after, rainfall but becomes less important than matrix flow during the subsequent period of redistribution.

It is now well established that the presence of interconnected macropores means that soil water behaviour cannot be adequately described by equations based on Darcy's law, since the necessary assumptions of homogeneous soil hydraulic properties and a well-defined hydraulic gradient will no longer apply (Beven and Germann, 1982; Feddes *et al.*, 1988). However, the very irregular hydraulic gradients observed during infiltration by macropore flow (for example De Vries and Chow, 1978) and the generally variable nature of macropore flow systems means that the search for an appropriate model of soil water behaviour in such conditions is still very much at the research frontier (for example Villholth *et al.*, 1998; Villholth and Jensen, 1998). Some valuable pioneering work on flow modelling in macropore systems was done by Germann (1990) and studies, using laboratory columns, have been conducted on the hydrological role of artificial macropores in a sandy loam (Buttle and Leigh, 1997). But a great deal of further work will be necessary before a full understanding is developed of macropore flow systems and their role, not only in surface and groundwater hydrology but also in respect of water quality issues relating to, say, the leaching of nitrates and other constituents from agricultural land and as an aggravating factor in the drainage of acid rain (Jones, 1997a).

6.5.3 Topography

Up to now discussion of soil water behaviour has considered predominantly vertical movement in an implicitly horizontal soil profile. In such conditions, soil water behaviour is likely to be dominated by soil properties but this is less likely to be true for sloping ground, where it may be more closely correlated to topography. In particular, ground slope influences the magnitude, speed and direction of lateral flows (for example throughflow) in the soil, and this tends to promote large-scale spatial variations in soil water content within drainage basins and especially a downslope increase of soil water content.

Downslope water movement may be particularly marked in layered soils, where water tends to be deflected 'downdip' at horizon boundaries, particularly where there are large permeability contrasts between horizons (Warrick *et al.*, 1997). However, tracer studies have confirmed the importance of flow parallel to the soil surface, even in permeable stony soils, providing the angle of slope is sufficiently great (for example Buchter *et al.*, 1997). Soil scientists have, in fact, traditionally recognized a 'hydrologic sequence' of progressively deteriorating drainage condition downslope (Cruikshank, 1972; White, 1987). Both topographic and soil maps may therefore provide hydrologists with a useful starting point in the study of soil water distribution within a catchment area (for example Bouma, 1986).

The changing patterns of soil water suction and flow in a uniform hillslope soil profile, during the course of a storm, are shown, in a generalized form, in Figure 6.21. Initially the soil water state is close to complete gravity drainage (*a*) and suction increases with elevation, approximately balancing the gravity potential, except near the base of the slope, where there is some saturated lateral flow. Once rain begins (*b*), the surface layers of the soil become wetted and suction is reduced. Then percolation wets deeper layers (*c*) and the saturated layer begins to grow as it is fed by unsaturated vertical and lateral flows. After the end of rainfall (*d*), drainage of water from upper to lower layers continues, with drying of the upper layer and further expansion of the saturated conditions. The extent of this saturated zone at the base of the slope is an important factor in the generation of storm runoff (Section 7.4). Finally, with continued drainage of soil water after the storm, the soil water pattern reverts to that of the initial state (*a*).

Simple two-dimensional studies of downslope soil water movement provide a useful starting point for the explanation of soil water distribution in catchment areas. However, they normally fail to incorporate the effects on soil water distribution of flow convergence caused by slope curvature. The links between flow convergence and surface saturation are discussed in the context of runoff generation in Section 7.4.2. At this point it is sufficient to note that slope concavities, in both plan and cross-section, have long been recognized (for example Kirkby and Chorley, 1967) as a cause of flow convergence which may lead to soil water flows that exceed the transmission capacity of the soil profile. Slope concavities tend, therefore, to be associated with high soil water contents (for example Zaslavsky and Sinai, 1981), especially in steeply sloping terrain, and in extreme cases the 'surplus' water tends to move towards the soil surface, causing surface saturation. Similar effects occur in areas of thinner soil (see also Figure 7.6). An example of the changing spatial pattern of soil water distribution, including areas of surface saturation, on a hillside was determined by Anderson and Burt (1978) from measurements of pressure potential at a grid of points (Figure 6.22). Similar distributions of soil water on hillslopes were observed by

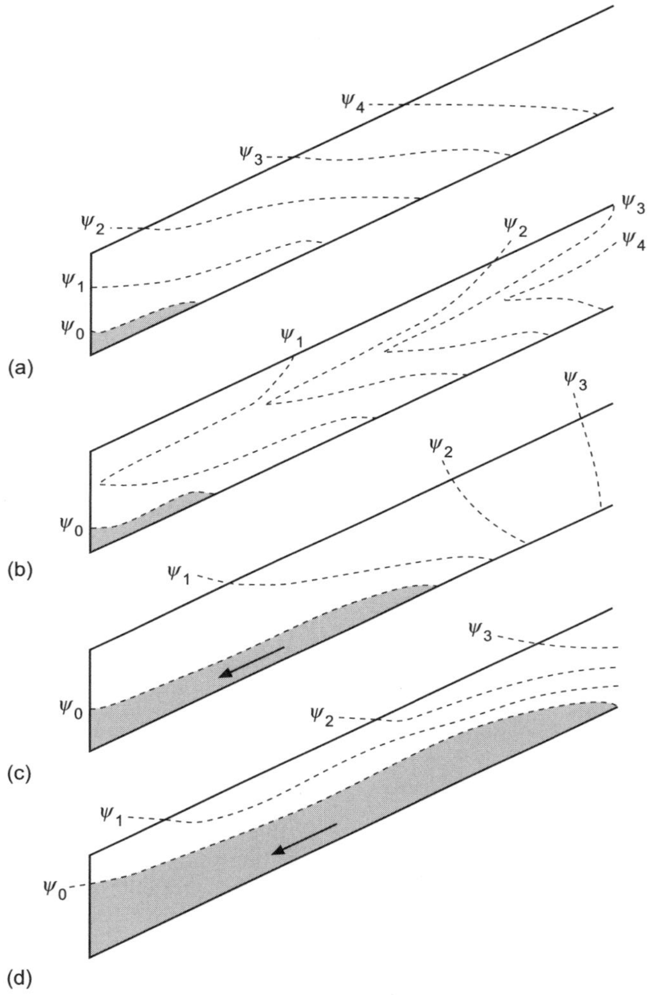

Figure 6.21 Generalized pattern of pressure potential in a straight hillslope. See text for details (redrawn after an original diagram by Weyman, 1973).

Dunne (1978) and were generated from a computer model by O'Loughlin (1981).

High soil water contents, including areas of surface saturation, are also often observed close to stream channels. These moister conditions are typically associated with a slope-foot concavity but may sometimes reflect the presence of a water table maintained at shallow depth by the level of water in the adjacent channel. Additional elevation of riparian water table level may result from a zero pressure outflow boundary condition whereby water can only flow out from a soil

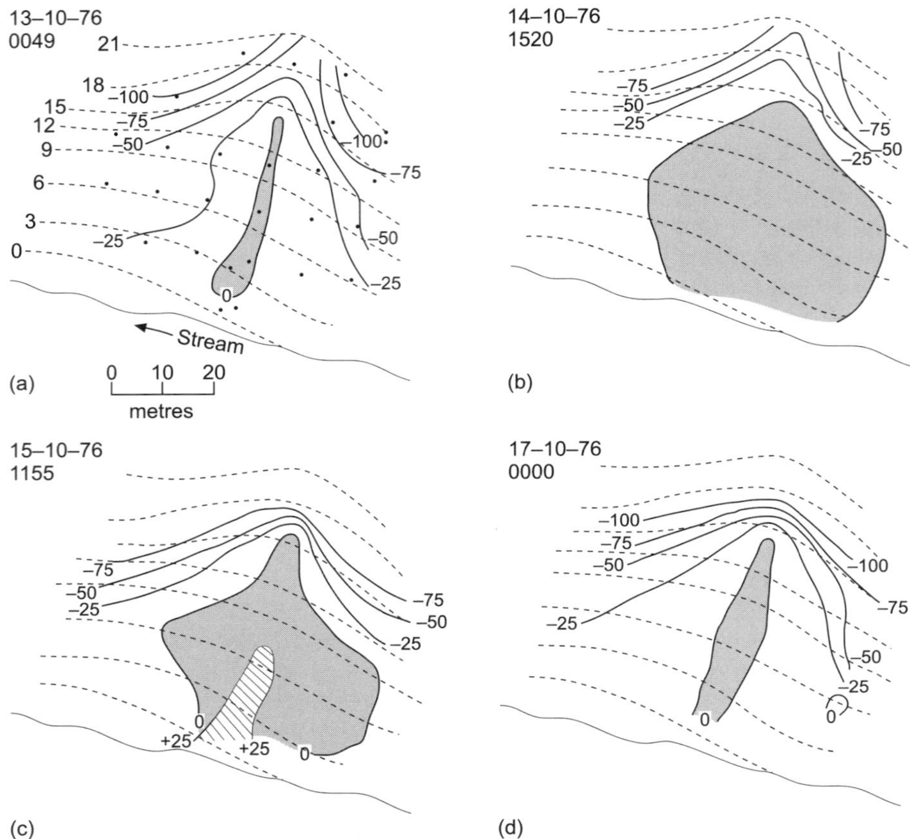

Figure 6.22 Pattern of soil water pressure potential (cm), measured at 60 cm depth, over a hillside for one storm: (*a*) prior to rainfall, (*b*) near end of rain, (*c*) at stream hydrograph peak, (*d*) two days after storm. (From an original diagram by Anderson and Burt, 1978, by permission of John Wiley and Sons Ltd.)

through seepage faces, such as channel banks, field drains or even large macropores, if the soil water pressure exceeds atmospheric pressure (Freeze and Cherry, 1979). This 'boundary effect' elevation of the water table is especially marked at times of baseflow between storms (Troendle, 1985) and, although long recognized (for example Richards, 1950), has often been subsequently ignored (for example Anderson and Burt, 1977).

The topography of a catchment area, especially through the effects of slope gradient and concavity on the discharge and seepage of subsurface water, may therefore impose some element of order and predictability on an otherwise heterogeneous spatial distribution of soil water content. In general, however, and particularly in flat areas or areas of gentle relief, soil water patterns are usually difficult to predict and even to observe (for example Baird, 1997; Ragab and Cooper, 1993a and 1993b; Youngs, 1991). In many areas soil water content is modified by human activity, including the drainage and irrigation of agricultural land. Natural vegetation and soil properties may provide useful indicators of the extent of saturated conditions (Dunne *et al.*, 1975) and remote sensing techniques (Schmugge *et al.*, 1980) provide a means of studying spatial variations over large areas.

6.5.4 Groundwater recharge

The component of groundwater recharge that results from the infiltration of precipitation or irrigation at the ground surface (see also Section 5.4.3) is a soil water process, since water recharging the saturated zone must first traverse the unsaturated zone as infiltration and percolation. Accordingly, improved understanding of the principles and mechanisms of soil water movement have greatly facilitated efforts to estimate groundwater recharge (for example Lerner, 1997). Early attempts to do so were largely based on the assumption that groundwater recharge could be estimated simply from a knowledge of the texture and saturated hydraulic conductivity of the overlying soil.

In idealized conditions, a process of displacement occurs whereby the water that is added to the water table during rainfall is not 'new' rainfall but previously stored rainfall that has been displaced downwards in the zone of aeration by successive bouts of infiltration (Horton and Hawkins, 1965). This *piston flow* process is also sometimes referred to as *translatory flow* (see also Section 7.4). It is a major factor in explaining the often rapid response of water tables to precipitation, even in low-permeability material, especially when the soil water content is at field capacity or wetter. One result of translatory flow is that deep water table levels may respond rapidly to precipitation even when percolation rates are very low (for example Bonell *et al.*, 1983; Bengtsson *et al.*, 1987).

However, laboratory and field observations, including tracer studies (for example Gee and Hillel, 1988; De Vries and Gieske, 1990), have shown that infiltration to the water table is often isolated both in space and time and that very small differences in water table depth, soil matric potential, hydraulic conductivity and water content can result in large differences in groundwater recharge (for example Freeze and Banner, 1970). Furthermore, as shown in Section 6.5.2, in many soils there are preferential flowpaths through an interconnected macropore system. These may be important, especially in near-saturated conditions, in enabling pollutants such as fertilizers, pesticides and bacteria to bypass the filtering and purifying medium of the soil and be directly transmitted down to the groundwater. However, detailed measurements in the chalk aquifer in southern England (Wellings, 1984a, 1984b) showed that, even in the presence of macropore systems, the predominant movement of water and solutes towards the water table was through the matrix.

6.5.5 Human influences

Human influences can alter soil water conditions in a large number of ways, ranging from irrigation schemes, which considerably increase the amount of water entering the soil, to the construction of large impermeable surfaces in urban areas, which prevent water from infiltrating into the soil beneath. These effects, which are described in engineering and agricultural texts, are outside the scope of this chapter. Accordingly, only a brief account of a few examples is given below.

Agricultural practices have the most widespread effect on soil water conditions. Irrigation and artificial drainage are used throughout the world as a means to increase crop production (Framji *et al.*, 1982). Agricultural drainage schemes comprise open ditches or subsurface pipes (Smedema and Rycroft, 1983; Farr and Henderson, 1986). These are deeper and closer together than the natural stream channels, so increasing the hydraulic gradient in the soil and lowering the water table more rapidly between storms than would otherwise occur. A detailed account of the distribution and purpose of field drainage in England and Wales, the most intensively drained part of Europe, was given in Robinson and Armstrong (1988).

Tillage and cultivation operations may also alter the movement and distribution of soil water. Ploughing increases the pore spaces in the upper soil (Kuipers and van Ouwerkerk, 1963) and may encourage lateral flow in the topsoil, with less downward flow into the subsoil (Goss *et al.*, 1978). It has been shown by tracer studies that ploughing disrupts the vertical continuity with pores in the soil below (Quisenberry and Phillips, 1976; Douglas *et al.*, 1980). Infiltrating water was found to penetrate to greater depths on land that had not been ploughed.

A change in agricultural land use from grassland to arable cropping may also affect interception and evaporation losses, especially if the arable farming leaves the soil bare at times of the year. Heavy rainfall on land with little vegetation cover may lead to crusting and sealing of the soil surface, reducing infiltration. Forestry may have a large effect on interception and evaporation losses, causing soils under trees to be much drier than under other types of vegetation (see Chapters 3 and 4). In areas where the natural water table is close to the ground surface, groundwater abstraction may lower the water table, causing significant drying of the soil and a reduction in plant growth (Van der Kloet and Lumadjeng, 1987). The most extreme case of human influence on soil water conditions, however, is perhaps found in areas of steep topography, where deforestation and bad farming practices lead to accelerated erosion and may, in severe cases, ultimately result in the complete destruction of the soil.

Review Problems and Exercises

6.1 Why is the importance of soil water described as being 'out of all proportion to its small total amount'?

6.2 Describe the hydrological role of the following: soil matrix, soil texture, soil structure, specific surface.

6.3 Define the following terms: surface tension, adsorption, matric potential, moisture characteristic.

6.4 Explain the causes and the hydrological significance of hysteresis.

6.5 Explain the role of total potential in soil water movement.

6.6 What are the main problems in soil water measurement?

6.7 Explain the difference between saturated and unsaturated hydraulic conductivity.

6.8 Describe the process of infiltration and the main attempts to model it mathematically.

6.9 What are the main factors affecting the redistribution of soil water after infiltration has ceased?

6.10 To what extent has the development of soil water theory been adversely affected by its failure to account for the heterogeneity of soil conditions in the field?

6.11 Discuss the role of macropores in soil water movement.

6.12 Discuss ways in which an improved understanding of soil water movement has helped attempts to estimate groundwater recharge.

CHAPTER SEVEN

Runoff

7.1 Introduction

Runoff or streamflow comprises the gravity movement of water in channels varying in size from those containing the smallest ill-defined trickles to those containing the largest rivers such as the Amazon, the Congo, and the Yangtze. As well as *streamflow*, runoff may be variously referred to as stream- or river *discharge*, or *catchment yield*.

At a general level the relationship between streamflow and precipitation can be expressed in terms of the continuous circulation of water through the hydrological cycle. More specifically, we can recognize that in simple situations, where topographic and groundwater basins coincide, each river receives water only from its own drainage basin or catchment area. Each catchment can, therefore, be regarded as a system receiving inputs of precipitation and transforming these into outputs of evaporation and streamflow. Allowing for changes of storage within the system, input must be equalled by output. In all but the driest areas, output from the catchment system is continuous but the inputs of precipitation are discrete and often widely separated in time. As a result, the annual hydrograph typically comprises short periods of suddenly increased discharge associated with rainfall or snowmelt and intervening, much longer, periods when streamflow represents the outflow from water stored on and below the surface of the catchment and when the hydrograph takes the exponential form of the typical exhaustion curve (see Figure 7.14).

Units of runoff

Runoff is normally expressed as a volume per unit of time. The *cumec*, i.e. one cubic metre per second ($m^3\ s^{-1}$), and *cumecs per square kilometre* ($m^3\ s^{-1}\ km^{-2}$) are commonly used units. Runoff may also be expressed as a depth equivalent over a catchment, i.e. millimetres per day or month or year. This is a particularly useful unit for comparing precipitation and runoff rates and totals since precipitation is almost invariably expressed in this way. Alternative runoff expressions still found in the literature include millions of gallons per day (m.g.d.) and, particularly in American irrigation literature, acre-feet, i.e. the volume of water cover that would cover one acre to a depth of one foot.

7.2 Quickflow and delayed flow

The immediacy of streamflow response to a rainfall event indicates that part of the rainfall takes a rapid route to the stream channels (i.e. *quickflow*); equally, the subsequent continuity of flow through often prolonged dry weather periods indicates that another part of the rainfall takes a much slower route as *delayed flow*, which is more usually referred to as *baseflow*. These two components of flow are apparent in rivers of all sizes. However, in large river systems lag effects, both within and outside channels, and the multiplicity of flow contributions to the main channel from numerous tributary streams complicate interpretation of the hydrograph response of major rivers to precipitation. Accordingly much of the initial discussion of runoff processes in this chapter attempts to explain the response to precipitation of *headwater streams* draining catchment systems that are comparatively small and simple.

In such situations the response of catchments to precipitation is often very rapid but is rarely the same, i.e. the proportion of precipitation that appears quickly as streamflow under the storm hydrograph differs from storm to storm. Figure 7.1 shows graphs from a pioneering paper by Ramser (1927), which emphasize the immediacy and the variability of streamflow response to precipitation in a small catchment, and which, because rainfall and streamflow are plotted on the same scale, also emphasize the low percentage of rainfall that appears as quickflow under the storm hydrograph. Although, on a small scale, the exact percentage varies with precipitation characteristics and catchment conditions, it is estimated that globally an average of 36 per cent of the total precipitation falling on the land areas reaches the oceans as runoff. Of this amount, quickflow accounts for about 11 per cent and delayed flow accounts for the remaining 25 per cent of precipitation.

7.3 Sources and components of runoff

The variable response of streamflow to precipitation, both spatially and with time, reflects the contrasting flowpaths of precipitation towards the stream channels. Figure 7.2 shows that precipitation may arrive in the stream channel by a number of flowpaths: direct precipitation onto the water surface; overland flow; shallow subsurface flow (throughflow); and deep subsurface flow (groundwater flow). Accumulations of snow will, upon melting, follow one of these four flowpaths.

These terms are used widely and relatively unambiguously in the literature. Persistent misuse of other terms such as surface runoff and direct runoff has resulted in unnecessary confusion and ambiguity, and accordingly Figure 7.3

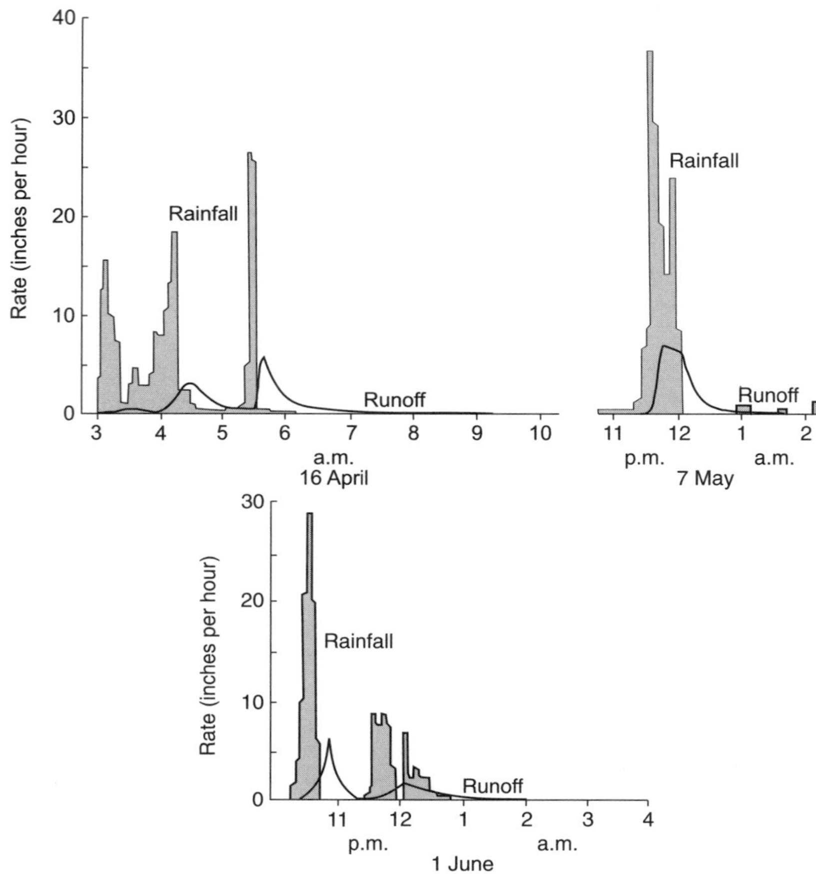

Figure 7.1 Graphs of rainfall and runoff for three storm events in Tennessee, USA (from original diagrams by Ramser, 1927).

attempts to provide a consistent and logical terminology. This shows that surface runoff is the part of total runoff that reaches the drainage basin outlet via overland flow and the stream channels, although it may in some circumstances also include throughflow that has discharged at the ground surface at some distance from the stream channel. Subsurface runoff is the sum of throughflow and groundwater flow and is normally equal to the total flow of water arriving at the stream as saturated flow through the channel bed and banks. Quickflow, or direct runoff, is the sum of channel precipitation, surface runoff and quick throughflow, and will represent the major runoff contribution during storm periods and most floods. It will be observed that quickflow and surface runoff as defined above are not synonymous.

Baseflow or delayed runoff is the sustained component of runoff which continues even through dry weather periods. It is normally regarded as the

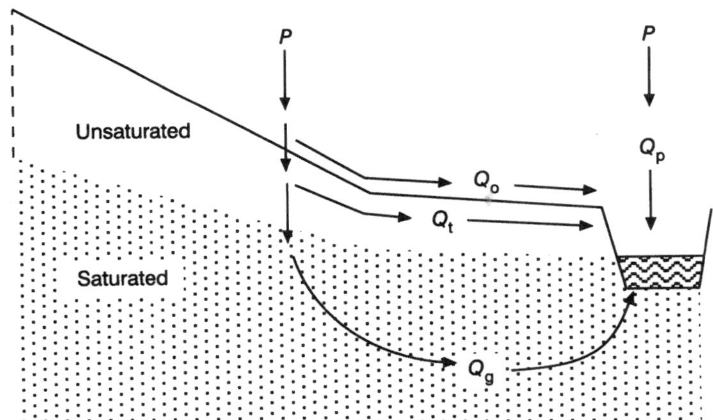

Figure 7.2 Flowpaths of the sources of streamflow: Q_p is direct precipitation onto the water surface, Q_o is overland flow, Q_t is throughflow and Q_g is groundwater flow.

sum of groundwater runoff and delayed throughflow, although some hydrologists prefer to include the total throughflow as illustrated by the broken line in Figure 7.3. Again baseflow and groundwater flow, as defined above, are not synonymous; indeed, in some steep mountain drainage basins, baseflow may consist almost entirely of unsaturated lateral flow from the soil profile (see 'The role of throughflow' later in this chapter).

The relative importance of these sources of runoff may vary spatially, depending upon drainage basin characteristics, such as soil type and the nature and density of the vegetation cover, and upon precipitation conditions. In addition, the importance of individual runoff sources may vary with time, for example over a period of years or seasonally, and may also change quite dramatically during an individual storm or sequence of rainfall events in response to variations of infiltration capacity, water table levels, and surface water area.

7.3.1 Channel precipitation (Q_p)

The contribution of precipitation falling directly on to water surfaces is normally small simply because the perennial channel system occupies only a small proportion (1–2 per cent) of the area of most catchments. Even so, for small precipitation events, channel precipitation may be the *only* component of the hydrograph. The channel system is more extensive where catchments contain a large area of lakes or swamps and in these circumstances Q_p will tend to be a more dominant component of runoff. In addition, Q_p will increase significantly during a prolonged storm or sequence of precipitation events, as the channel network expands (see Section 7.4.2), and may temporarily account for 60 per cent or more of total runoff in some small catchments (for example Rawitz *et al.*, 1970).

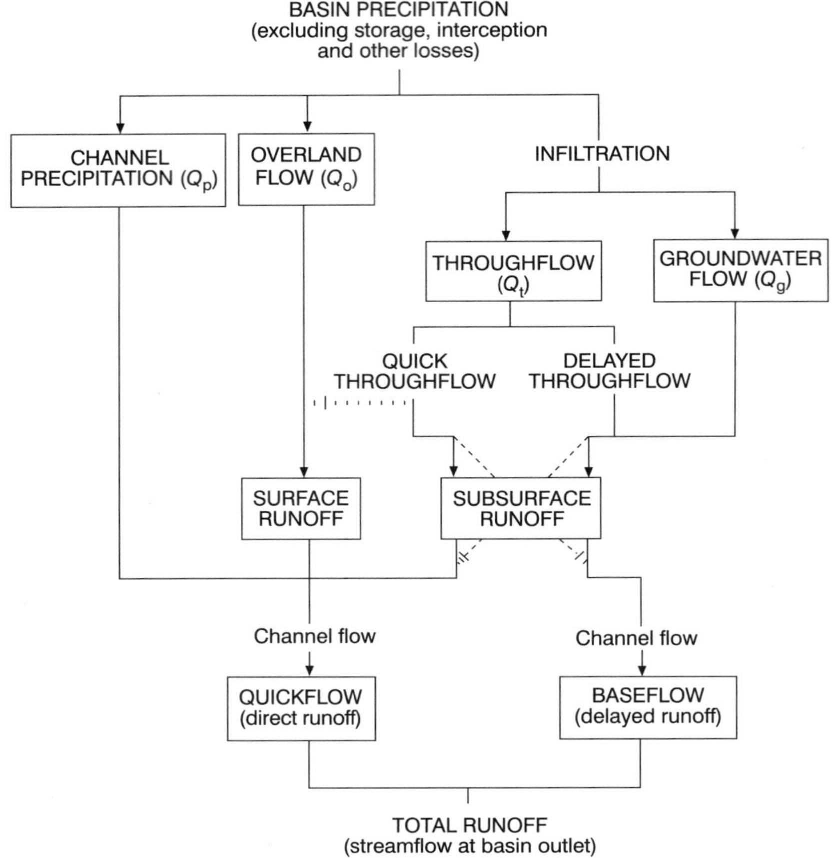

Figure 7.3 Diagrammatic representation of the runoff process.

7.3.2 Overland flow (Q_o)

Overland flow comprises the water that flows over the ground surface to stream channels either as quasi-laminar sheet flow or, more usually, as flow anastomosing in small trickles and minor rivulets. One cause of Q_o is the inability of water to infiltrate the surface as a result of a high intensity of rainfall and/or a low value of infiltration capacity. Ideal conditions are found on moderate to steep slopes in arid and semi-arid areas. Here, vegetation cover may be sparse or non-existent, exposing the surface to raindrop impact and crusting processes. As a result it has been suggested that virtually all runoff in such areas occurs in the form of overland flow (Abrahams *et al.*, 1994). Other conditions in which Q_o assumes considerable importance involve the hydrophobic nature of some very dry and sodic soils, the deleterious effects of many agricultural practices on infiltration capacity, and freezing of the ground surface. In humid areas, vegetation cover is thicker and more substantial and because of the high value of infiltration which characterizes most vegetation-covered surfaces, overland flow is a rarely observed, even in tropical rainforest (for example Anderson and Spencer, 1991).

However there are many areas, both humid and sub-humid, where the effects of topography or the nature of the soil profile facilitate the rise of shallow water tables to the ground surface during rainfall or throughflow events. In such conditions the infiltration capacity at the ground surface falls to zero and *saturation overland flow* (Q_o(s)) results (see Section 7.4.2).

7.3.3 Throughflow (Q_t)

Water that infiltrates the soil surface and then moves laterally through the upper soil horizons towards the stream channels, either as unsaturated flow or, more usually, as shallow perched saturated flow above the main groundwater level, is known as throughflow. Alternative terms found in the literature include *interflow*, *subsurface stormflow*, *storm seepage* and *secondary baseflow*. Throughflow is liable to occur when the lateral hydraulic conductivity of the surface soil horizons greatly exceeds the overall vertical hydraulic conductivity through the soil profile. Then, during prolonged or heavy rainfall on a hillslope, water will enter the upper part of the profile more rapidly than it can drain vertically through the lower part, thus accumulating and forming a perched saturated layer from which water will 'escape' laterally, i.e. in the direction of greater hydraulic conductivity.

In the absence of artificial disturbance, such as surface compaction, the situation described above is the one most commonly found. Even in a deep relatively homogeneous soil profile, hydraulic conductivity will tend to be greater in the surface layers than deeper down in the profile, thereby encouraging the generation of throughflow. Still more favourable conditions exist when (i) thin permeable soil overlies impermeable bedrock, (ii) the soil profile is markedly stratified, or (iii) an ironpan or ploughpan occurs at a short distance below the surface. There may be several levels of Q_t below the surface, corresponding to textural changes between horizons and to the junction between weathered mantle and bedrock. In addition, there is evidence that water may travel downslope through macropores and macrofissures (see the heading 'Macropores' in Section 6.5.2) and that, in some circumstances, soil biological activity may play an important role in runoff generation (Bonell *et al.*, 1984) as well as in drainage basin erosion (Jungerius, 1985).

These various mechanisms of throughflow formation result in different rates of water movement to stream channels. Accordingly, it is sometimes helpful to distinguish broadly between 'quick' and 'delayed' throughflow (see Figure 7.3). However, apart from flow through interconnected macropores, the very rapid arrival of throughflow at stream channels, which has been observed by some investigators, is likely to result from 'piston displacement' (see 'The role of throughflow' in this chapter). Some throughflow does not discharge directly into the stream channel but surfaces at some point between the catchment divide and the stream, before continuing to flow over the surface to the stream. This component probably should be considered as subsurface runoff, although it is sometimes regarded as an addition to overland flow and surface runoff, as indicated by the heavy-dotted line in Figure 7.3.

The role of Q_t in total runoff is discussed in more detail in subsequent sections of this chapter, although it is interesting to note at this stage that experimental evidence has long indicated that it may account for up to 85 per cent of total runoff (Hertzler, 1939).

7.3.4 Groundwater flow (Q_g)

Away from the relatively steeply sloping terrain of the headwaters, where subsurface runoff is dominated by throughflow, most of the rainfall that infiltrates the catchment surface will percolate through the soil layer to the underlying groundwater and will eventually reach the main stream channels as groundwater flow through the zone of saturation. Since water at depth can move only very slowly through the ground, the outflow of groundwater into the stream channels may lag behind the occurrence of precipitation by several days, weeks or even years. Groundwater flow tends to be very regular, representing as it does the outflow from the slowly changing reservoir of moisture in the soil and rock layers. In certain circumstances, however, groundwater may show a rapid response to precipitation. Indeed, the 'piston displacement' mechanism (discussed in 'The role of throughflow') frequently results in a rapid response of groundwater flow to precipitation during individual storm periods, and especially on a seasonal basis, and this is represented by the fine-dotted line in Figure 7.3. Since this can operate only in moist soil and subsoil conditions, however, the replenishment of large moisture deficits created particularly during summer conditions may result in a considerable lag of groundwater outflow after precipitation during and immediately following prolonged dry periods. In general, Q_g represents the main long-term component of total runoff and is particularly important during dry spells when surface runoff is absent.

7.4 Event-based variations

The nature of streamflow response to precipitation at varying time scales (for example single precipitation event, seasonal, annual) is determined by the precise way in which the various sources and components of runoff combine in specific circumstances. It has long been recognized that the balance between quickflow and baseflow is the essential determinant of hydrograph shape. However, only gradually has improved field evidence confirmed the relative importance of the individual components of quickflow and baseflow shown in Figures 7.2 and 7.3. Early attempts to explain the variation of streamflow with time, especially through a precipitation event, concentrated almost exclusively on the overland flowpath. Later work clarified the varied nature of overland flow and showed that throughflow and even groundwater flow may also play an important part. Many hydrologists have contributed to our present understanding of the runoff process but two principal pioneers, whose work has proved to be seminal, were R.E. Horton and J.D. Hewlett. It seems appropriate, therefore, to discuss runoff variations in the light of their individual contributions.

7.4.1 *The Horton hypothesis*

Horton (1933) proposed quite simply that the soil surface partitions falling rain so that one part goes rapidly as overland flow to the stream channels and the other part goes initially into the soil and thence either through gradual groundwater flow to the stream channel or through evaporation to the atmosphere. The partitioning device is the infiltration capacity of the soil surface which was defined as '. . . the maximum rate at which rain can be absorbed by a given soil when in a given condition'.

Figure 7.4 indicates that, during that part (t) of a storm when rain falls at a rate (i) that is greater than the rate (f) at which it can be absorbed by the ground surface, there will occur an excess of precipitation (P_e) which will flow over the ground surface as overland flow (Q_o). No overland flow will occur if the rainfall intensity is lower than the infiltration capacity; instead the infiltration that takes place will first top up the soil water reservoir until the so-called moisture capacity is attained, after which further infiltration through the ground surface will percolate to the groundwater reservoir thereby increasing the groundwater flow (Q_g) to the stream channel.

Horton (1933) suggested that infiltration capacity (f) passes through a fairly definite cycle for each storm period (see also Section 6.4.2). Starting with a maximum value at the onset of rain, f decreases, rapidly at first, as a result of the

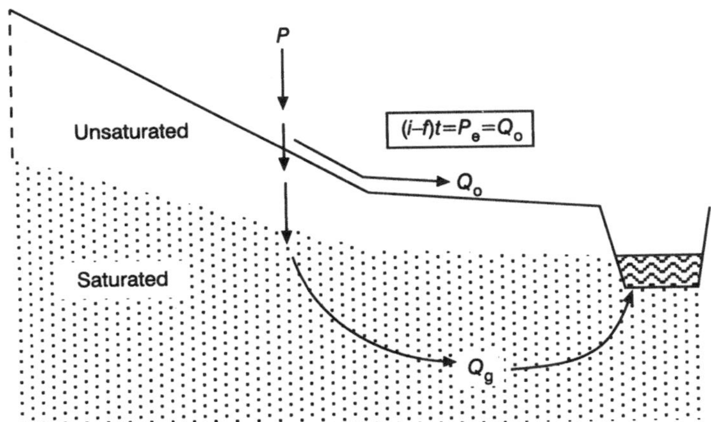

Figure 7.4 The response of streamflow to precipitation: the Horton hypothesis.

compaction of the soil surface by falling raindrops, colloidal swelling of the soil, which closes sun-cracks and other interstices, and the clogging of interstices by the inwashing of fine particles. After the initial rapid decline, infiltration capacity becomes stable or declines only very slowly for the remainder of the storm and begins to recover immediately after the end of the storm. He maintained that this cycle of infiltration capacity resulted from the operation of processes '. . . confined to a thin layer at the soil surface'. Numerous field experiments have subsequently confirmed the general shape of the infiltration capacity curve, but have shown that the rapid decline of infiltration capacity also results from factors acting *within* the soil profile, especially the lengthening flowpath of percolating rainfall, the initial moisture gradient and variations of hydraulic conductivity with depth.

Ideal conditions for the generation of 'Horton overland flow' are found where bare soil is exposed to raindrop impact, as in arid and semi-arid areas such as those in the southwestern USA where Horton carried out his investigations (see Section 7.3.2). Even here, however, overland flow is generated by only a small proportion of rainfall events. Furthermore, its occurrence is spatially variable within a catchment, and tends to be concentrated where soil crusting occurs. This was demonstrated for the Loess Plateau of China by Zhu *et al.* (1997) and for the Sahel region of Niger, where low-infiltration surface crusts develop, even on cultivated deep sandy soils, resulting in significant amounts of overland flow (Rockström and Valentin, 1997). In parts of the Negev Desert, Israel, where sodic soils crust easily during rainfall, often only the first few millimetres of rainfall are able to infiltrate through cracks, etc., before the crust begins to shed water with about the same efficiency as an asphalt road surface (Van der Molen, 1983).

In summary, the possible implications of the infiltration capacity cycle for short-term variations of runoff are as follows. Rain of high intensity may generate precipitation excess and therefore overland flow throughout a storm, although rarely over more than limited areas of the catchment; rain of moderate intensity will not generate overland flow until the initially high infiltration capacity has declined; and rain of low intensity may fail to generate overland flow at all. Furthermore, since infiltration capacity is likely to show a continued decrease through a sequence of closely spaced storms, we would expect a given amount of rainfall falling late in the storm sequence to generate more overland flow and therefore a greater streamflow response than the same amount of precipitation falling early in the storm sequence.

7.4.2 The Hewlett hypothesis

Hewlett proposed (Hewlett, 1961a; Hewlett and Hibbert, 1967) that over much of a catchment area, even during intense and prolonged precipitation, all precipitation infiltrates the soil surface (Figure 7.5(a)). Infiltration and throughflow within the soil profile cause rising water tables to saturate the ground surface, first in the shallow water table areas immediately adjacent to stream channels (Figure 7.5(b)) and subsequently in the lower valley slopes. In these

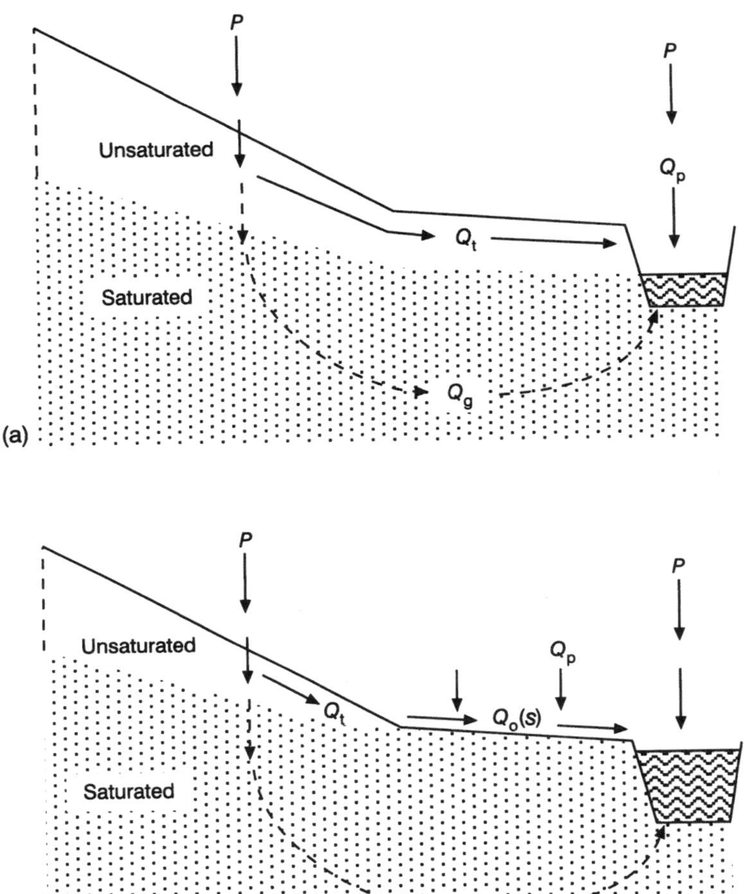

Figure 7.5 The response of streamflow to precipitation: the basic Hewlett hypothesis. (*a*) flowpaths in the initial stages of rainfall; (*b*) flowpaths in the later stages of rainfall.

surface-saturated areas infiltration capacity is zero so that all precipitation falling on them, at whatever intensity, is excess precipitation (P_e) or overland flow, which we can term *saturation overland flow* ($Q_o(s)$), in contrast to the *infiltration-excess overland flow* (Q_o) envisaged by Horton. According to Hewlett, only the saturated areas of the catchment act as a source of quickflow; all other areas of the catchment absorb the rain that falls and either store it or transfer it beneath the ground surface. Note also that the source area for quickflow is of variable size, growing as rainfall proceeds.

In one of those interesting coincidences which seem to characterize scientific progress, similar ideas were advanced independently in France by Cappus

(1960). Additionally, Hewlett's hypothesis was contemporaneously supported by growing evidence of the pattern of subsurface water movement through valley slope profiles. This was generalized by Tóth (1962) in his midline model (see Figure 5.14) which shows infiltration and downward percolation in the upper slope, horizontal water movement through the middle slope material and upward movement near the base of the slope, reflecting the prevailing pattern of pore-water pressure. In such situations the increase of pressure potential with depth in the lower slopes facilitates rapid saturation of the surface layers when even modest quantities of water are added to the soil profile by infiltration or shallow throughflow. This possibility had been anticipated two decades earlier by Vaidhianathan and Singh (1942) and its physical basis was later described in detail by Gillham (1984).

Disjunct source areas

Although Hewlett originally implied that variable source areas would be contiguous with the stream channels, later work showed that areas of saturation overland flow may also occur widely within a catchment area, often in locations far removed from the stream channels. Furthermore, if such disjunct areas have effective hydrological connections with the valley bottoms or lower slopes they, too, may contribute quickflow to the stream channel. Apart from areas where crusting, compaction, sparse vegetation cover or thin, degraded soils (all frequently the result of human interference), result in infiltration–excess overland flow, *disjunct source areas* of quickflow often occur where *flow convergence* leads to surface saturation and saturation overland flow. Three typical locations for flow convergence, shown in Figure 7.6, are:

(a) slope concavities in plan where convergence leads to subsurface flow rates that may exceed the transmission capacity of the porous medium and lead, therefore, to the emergence of flow at the soil surface in the central areas of the concavities;
(b) slope concavities in section where, assuming uniform hydraulic conductivity throughout the section, subsurface flow rates will be directly proportional to the hydraulic gradient so that water will enter a concavity from upslope areas more rapidly than it can leave downslope; and
(c) areas of thinner soil whose water holding and transmitting capacity is low.

Slope concavity is more easily assessed than soil depth, both in the field and from maps and aerial photographs. Inevitably, therefore, much attention has been devoted to its effects on quickflow generation. Zaslavsky and Sinai (1981) presented field measurements of soil water concentrations in concave areas for European locations, including their own results for a site near Beer-Sheba, Israel, and O'Loughlin (1981) used computer models to demonstrate that the size of saturated zones on undulating hillslopes depends strongly on topographic convergence or divergence. Others have emphasized the relationship of dynamic

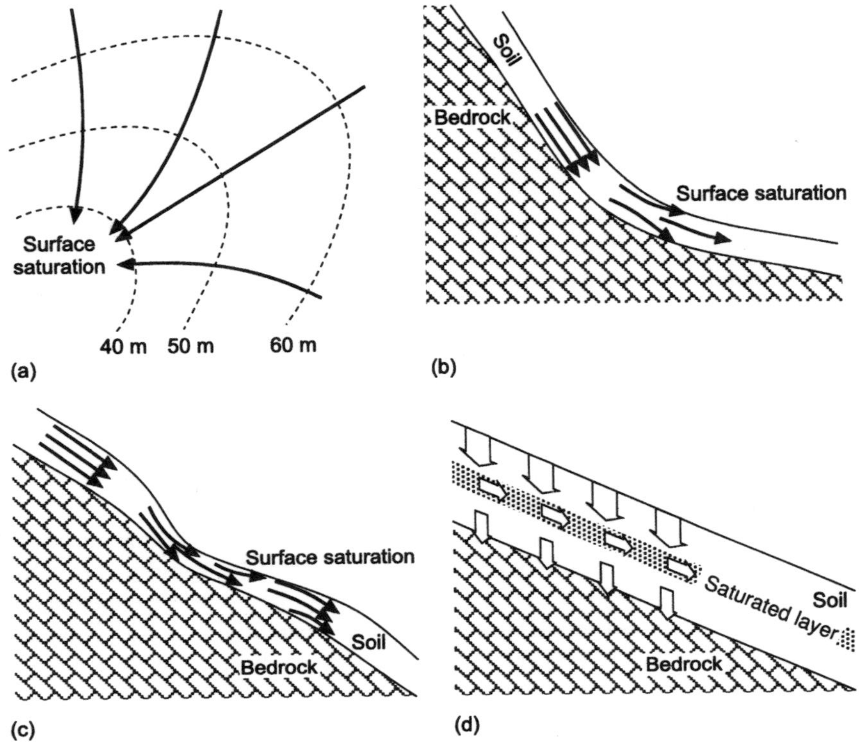

Figure 7.6 The principal locations of flow convergence in catchment areas.

quickflow-contributing areas to geomorphological structure (Beven and Wood, 1983) and to vegetation (Gurnell *et al.*, 1985) and Van de Griend and Engman (1985) discussed their identification by field survey and remote sensing techniques.

A fourth type of flow convergence, illustrated in Figure 7.6(d), occurs as water percolates vertically through a soil profile. Partly because of the reduced hydraulic gradient as the flowpath of the percolating water lengthens and partly because most soils, whether layered or not, exhibit a reduction of hydraulic conductivity with depth, rates of percolation decrease with depth, leading to the development of a layer, or layers, of temporary saturation. This accumulation of subsurface water normally moves downslope as throughflow before the build-up of saturation reaches the soil surface. In flat areas, however, or in sloping areas having very high rainfall amounts and intensities, saturation overland flow will be produced. This is most likely where an impeding layer occurs at shallow depths in the soil profile, as in the pseudo-gley soils of central Europe, or with high-intensity tropical rainfall (for example Bonell and Gilmour, 1978).

Hydrological linkages

The existence of convergence-induced disjunct variable source areas effectively extends the Hewlett concept of runoff generation, in the manner proposed by Jones (1979), provided that satisfactory *hydrological linkages* allow the rapid transmission of water between disjunct areas and the stream channels. Various linkage mechanisms have been proposed. An overland flow connection was favoured by Engman and Rogowski (1974) where a disjunct upslope source area is associated with thinner soils. Those who have walked the moors and fells of upland Britain in typical weather conditions may recognize here an illustration of observed reality. These are often areas where the combination of heavy rainfall and shallow soils of variable depth exemplify the conditions described by Engman and Rogowski.

Where soils are thicker or of more uniform depth, or where vegetation cover is denser, other linkage mechanisms are likely to prevail. Increasing recognition of their widespread occurrence has led to further consideration of the role of macropores and macrofissures (see Chapter 6). Early recognition that turbulent flow through large, quasi-cylindrical conveyances, such as animal burrows or decayed root channels, could lead subsurface stormflow rapidly through the slope material was provided by Hursh (1944) for the southern Appalachians, USA, and was confirmed much later for a forested catchment in Luxembourg by Bonell *et al.* (1984). However, biotic voids have been regarded by some hydrologists as 'pseudo-pipes' in contrast to the more widespread and hydrologically important pipes formed by hydraulic and hydrological processes (Jones, 1981). These latter types are found in a wide range of locations (cf. Jones, 1981; Jones and Crane, 1984; Tanaka, 1982; Tsukamoto *et al.*, 1982; Walling and Burt, 1983; Hendriks, 1993) and appear to increase the quickflow contributing area to as much as two or even five times that identified from surface contours (Jones, 1987, 1997b). Apart from pipe networks, other interlinked systems of macrofissures (as discussed in Chapter 6) may be capable of delivering quickflow to stream channels.

The high velocity of conduited, macropore subsurface flow suggests that the water arriving in the stream channel by this route will be 'new' water, i.e. water added by the current storm, rather than 'old' water, i.e. water that was stored in the catchment prior to the current storm event. However, tracer experiments in a variety of environments (for example Villholth and Jensen, 1998; Villholth *et al.*, 1998) confirm that the hydrological efficiency of macropore systems varies with factors such as changes in soil water status and soil structure which influence the exchange of water between the soil matrix pore space and the macropore systems. Accordingly, field results, even from the same locations, may seem inconsistent, though many appear to support Hewlett's view that 'old' water dominates the storm runoff hydrograph, even in areas where the existence of macropores is well established. This was demonstrated by Sklash *et al.* (1986) and Pearce *et al.* (1986) for catchments in New Zealand in which earlier analyses by Mosley (1979) had, in contrast, suggested that 'new' water dominated the storm runoff.

The role of throughflow

The preceding discussion of variable source areas and the ways in which these may be linked to the channel network must not be allowed to obscure the fact that, except in some arid and semi-arid areas, most of the water arriving at the stream channels (including some part of the quickflow component) has travelled below the ground surface as *throughflow* (Q_t) and *groundwater flow* (Q_g). The importance of these two flowpaths, once thought to be too slow and indirect to influence the short-term response of streamflow to precipitation, largely reflects the anisotropic nature of the hillslope soil profile and its effect on water movement.

The 'thatched roof' analogy of Zaslavsky and Sinai (1981) (see Figure 7.7) helps to explain the anisotropic hillslope soil profile and the way in which this encourages throughflow more or less parallel to the slope surface. No hydrologist, having measured the infiltration characteristics of bundles of straw, would recommend their use as a roofing material. And yet, even in the heaviest rain, the building remains dry, no water runs over the thatch as 'overland' flow, there is no 'groundwater' flow into the roof void and no evidence of zones of 'temporary saturation', i.e. all the rainfall is evacuated along the narrow layer of the thatch

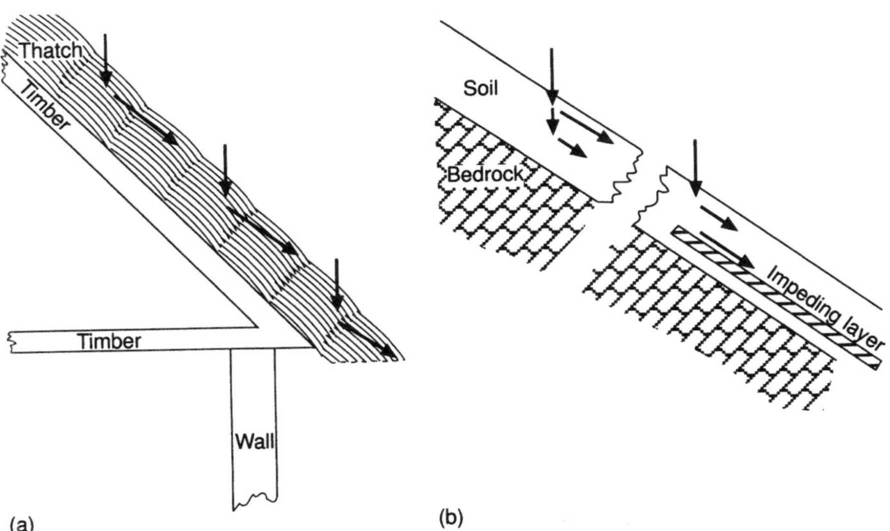

Figure 7.7 The thatched roof analogy of water movement through a hillslope soil profile showing schematic flowpaths through (*a*) a thatch and (*b*) a sloping soil profile with and without an impeding layer.

itself (Figure 7.7(a)). The thatched roof works because the alignment of the straw imparts a preferential permeability along the stems and because the roof has an angle of slope; it would not work if the straw bundles were placed vertically or if the roof were flat. In the case of the soil on a hillslope (Figure 7.7(b)), we know that, whether or not an impeding layer exists beneath the surface, there is normally a preferential hydraulic conductivity through the more open-textured upper layers parallel to the surface. As with the thatched roof, this may enable the sloping soil profile to dispose of rainfall without generating either overland flow or groundwater recharge.

Hewlett's experiments with sloping soil models (for example Hewlett, 1961b; Hewlett and Hibbert, 1963) indicated water flowpaths resembling those of a thatched roof, and led Hewlett (1961a) to prepare the diagram shown in Figure 7.8. Hewlett shows no overland flow and no deep groundwater recharge, implying that all rainfall infiltrates and is then transmitted through the soil profile. Note that the infiltrating rainfall contributes preferentially to storm flow, with upslope rainfall recharging the soil water store in preparation for succeeding days and weeks of baseflow whereas downslope rainfall and channel precipitation provide most of the storm flow. Although some reinterpretation is now appropriate, this intuitive diagram undoubtedly represents one of the single most important conceptual advances in the history of hydrology.

Initially, Hewlett found it difficult to explain how throughflow, having a maximum rate of movement of 5–6 m d^{-1}, could reach the stream channel

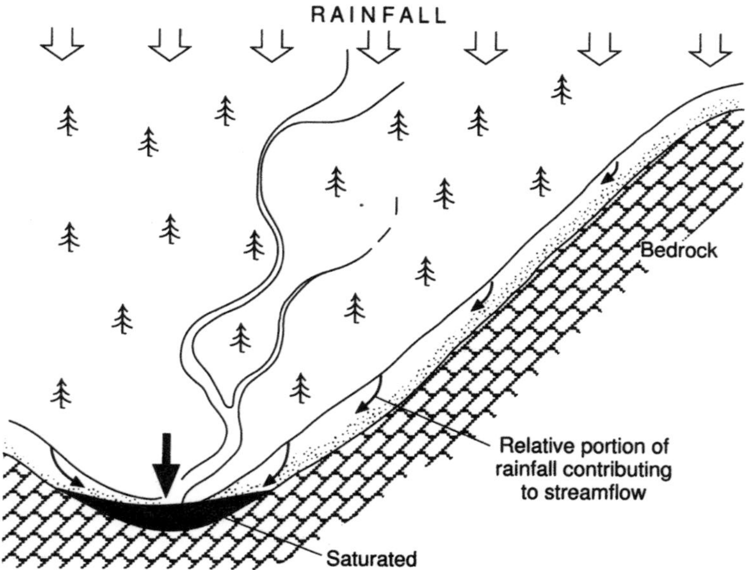

Figure 7.8 The relative contributions of rainfall to streamflow (from an original diagram by Hewlett, 1961a).

quickly enough to contribute to the storm hydrograph. Two relevant factors are indicated in Figure 7.8, which implies that: (i) most of the throughflow contribution comes from the lower slopes, closest to the channel, and (ii) expansion of the riparian area of surface saturation, as rainfall proceeds, shortens the effective flowpath for throughflow from more distant parts of the slope. Ultimately it was recognized that, in certain circumstances, soil water can move by a process of 'piston displacement' or 'translatory flow', whereby each new increment of rainfall displaces all preceding increments, causing the oldest to exit simultaneously from the bottom end of the hillslope profile.

This process had been confirmed by Horton and Hawkins (1965) in laboratory experiments. Tritium-tagged water was added to the top of a vertical column of moist soil which was then subjected to successive irrigations of simulated rainfall. Ignoring the effects of dispersion, each new rainfall caused a downward displacement of the tagged water and a corresponding outflow of untagged water from the bottom of the soil column. Eventually, after sufficient irrigations, the tagged water itself emerged. Regarding the soil profile as an inclined column receiving inputs of rainfall, Hewlett and Hibbert (1967) adduced the displacement process to explain why each input of rainfall could be accompanied by a virtually instantaneous outflow of subsurface water at the slope foot. Subsequent confirmation of the important contribution of pre-event water to the storm hydrograph has come from the gradual accumulation of field evidence across a wide range of catchment conditions (Buttle, 1994). In one example, detailed field measurements of soil water hydraulic properties and water chemistry formed the basis of successful attempts to model the displacement process on Mediterranean hillslopes (Taha *et al.*, 1998).

A weakness of this explanation is that a given input will result in an equivalent output only if the available moisture storage capacity within the soil system is already filled or nearly full. In drier conditions rainfall inputs and/or displacements will be used to 'top up' the soil water store rather than to maintain the chain of displacements. This means that the mechanism will be most effective after a period of rain and/or on the lower (i.e. moister) slopes, thereby confirming the intuitive reasoning of Hewlett's original diagram.

Hewlett and Hibbert sought further confirmation of the dominant role of throughflow from the sloping soil models referred to earlier. A sloping soil block was thoroughly wetted, covered to prevent evaporation and then allowed to drain, during which time the outflow was measured continuously. The outflow pipe established a free water table, which was used as the zero datum for all measurements, and below it a saturated wedge. The soil moisture and outflow data were interpreted as showing that unsaturated drainage from the soil mantle was alone sufficient to account for the entire recession limb of the storm hydrograph in steep forested headwater catchments and that the saturated wedge was not of itself a source but rather a conduit '. . . through which slowly draining soil moisture passes to enter the stream' (Hewlett and Hibbert, 1963). Two decades later Boughton and Freebairn (1985) presented recession data from five small agricultural catchments in south-east Queensland, Australia which showed that rates and sources of throughflow evident in the recorded hydrographs were possible in the plough depth of the soil.

The role of groundwater

Although Hewlett and Hibbert's conclusions about the role of the saturated slope-foot wedge were correct for the conditions being investigated, the relationship between the saturated and unsaturated flow components of hillslope hydrology is partly a function of slope angle. Hewlett (1982a) provided a succinct summary as follows (our italicization):

> The steeper the soil body is inclined, the greater will be the contribution of unsaturated flow to sustained outflow. In flat basins, groundwater storage represents a large percentage of total storage; in steep basins, the soil moisture store is much the larger one. *In the long run, the water will come from where the water was.*

In one sense this simply restates the long-established view that in highly permeable catchments and in the lowland areas of larger drainage basins, groundwater is the major component of streamflow. However, in such areas the magnitude of the groundwater contribution often appears to diminish the response of rivers to precipitation. By contrast, the concern in this section is with the situation where groundwater may make a major contribution to the storm hydrograph in a wide range of hydrogeological and relief conditions and where the response of rivers to precipitation is both rapid and pronounced. Hursh and Brater (1941) had indeed advocated such a role for groundwater near the stream channels, although it was much later that widespread field evidence, often based on tracer measurements, was used to show that groundwater can be a major and active component of storm runoff (for example Pinder and Jones, 1969; Dincer *et al.*, 1970; Martinec *et al.*, 1974; Sklash and Farvolden, 1979). This was illustrated specifically by O'Brien (1977), who found that groundwater accounted for 93 per cent of annual streamflow from two wetland catchments in Massachusetts, and by Zaltsberg (1987) who showed that groundwater contributed about 30 per cent of summer stormflow in the Wilson Creek basin in Manitoba.

Where shallow water tables are prevalent, groundwater and surface water are inevitably closely interlinked. Accordingly, in countries like The Netherlands, the important role of groundwater in runoff generation has long been recognized (for example De Vries, 1976; Ernst, 1978) and runoff has been studied using combined groundwater and surface water models (for example Querner (1997). Interestingly, a groundwater-based concept of 'variable source areas' was introduced by De Zeeuw (1966), apparently unaware at the time of Hewlett's pioneering work. He argued that, in The Netherlands, the response of drain and ditch flow to precipitation depends on the number of drains and ditches that are deep enough to cut the water table and that will, therefore, receive the more rapid field (i.e. local) discharge compared with the slower seepage (i.e. regional) groundwater flow. As groundwater levels rise, so more drains and ditches receive the quicker local flow.

In other circumstances, the ability of groundwater to contribute significantly to the storm hydrograph appears to reflect the formation of a *groundwater ridge* adjacent to the stream channel, as illustrated in Figure 7.9(b). Such a feature was identified by Ragan (1968) and Hewlett (1969) who referred to '. . . an ephemeral

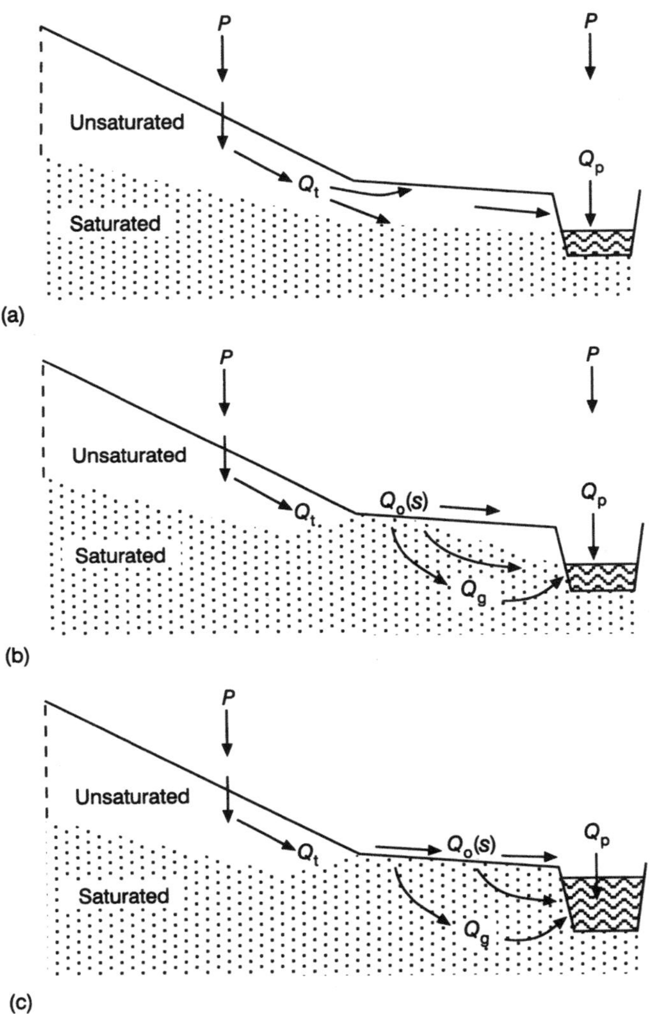

Figure 7.9 The response of streamflow to precipitation: an integrated view. Q_t includes both matrix flow and macropore flow. See text for explanation.

rise in the groundwater table' near the stream channel which '... helps produce the storm hydrograph'. Later, Sklash and Farvolden (1979) used field evidence and computer simulation to show that the formation of a groundwater ridge, together with the resulting steepened hydraulic gradient and increased groundwater discharge area, was capable of producing large groundwater contributions to the stream channel.

Two factors encourage the formation of a groundwater ridge close to the stream channel. First, the favourable gradient of moisture potential in the lower-slope areas, which was discussed in the opening paragraphs of Section 7.4.2, means that comparatively modest inputs of infiltration cause rapid increases of moisture potential in the surface layers (for example Abdul and Gillham, 1984). Secondly, the lower valley sides are often concave in profile and are therefore zones of convergence in which subsurface flow lines not only emerge at the ground surface, leading to surface saturation, but are also deflected downward (see Figure 7.9(a)), leading to concentrated groundwater recharge (Zaslavsky and Sinai, 1981).

Figure 7.9 thus serves to summarize the Hewlett hypothesis of runoff formation. Water from rainfall and snowmelt infiltrates the slope surface and moves as *throughflow* (including macropore flow) in the slope mantle (*a*). Convergence and infiltration in the lower-slope areas leads to surface saturation *and* groundwater recharge which will create both an *overland flow* and a *groundwater* contribution to the storm hydrograph (*b*), with the groundwater ridge merging eventually in some locations into a wider riparian area of surface saturation (*c*) which, with further rainfall, may extend onto the lower slope.

7.4.3 Exceptions to the Hewlett hypothesis?

The strengths of the Hewlett hypothesis are:

- it accommodates a broad diversity of field observations of runoff;
- it realistically incorporates important dynamic aspects of the runoff process, for example the inherently nonlinear effect of a variable source area; and
- it appears to accommodate the entire range of runoff processes from 'Horton' overland flow (including the extreme case of the car-park hydrograph) to the deep porous basin having stable channel length, in which total runoff is derived almost entirely from subsurface flow components.

In other words, the infiltration–excess overland flow described by Horton could be considered as an example of saturation overland flow in conditions where infiltration rates are so much lower than rainfall intensities that vertical flow convergence results in rapid surface ponding. However, some hydrologists prefer to treat it as a 'different' process in those environmental conditions where infiltration rates are exceptionally low or rainfall intensities exceptionally high. Two environments for which 'exceptional' conditions are commonly believed to prevail are arid/semi-arid and tropical rainforest areas.

As noted in Section 7.3.2, sparsely vegetated arid and semi-arid slopes would appear to offer ideal conditions for the generation of infiltration–excess overland flow, especially where surface crusting occurs. Experimental evidence which seems to confirm this was presented for the Walnut Gulch experimental area in Arizona, USA (Abrahams *et al.*, 1994), for a tropical semi-arid area of gently sloping terrain in Queensland, Australia (Bonell and Williams, 1986) and for many soil types in the Mediterranean area (Morin and Jarosch, 1977). In such areas infiltration rates drop rapidly during rainstorms and runoff contains virtually no subsurface or throughflow components. Crust formation on predominantly sodic soils largely explains the rapid drop in infiltration rate and results in hydraulic conductivity at the surface being several orders of magnitude lower than that in the subsurface horizons (Morin *et al.*, 1981; Agassi *et al.*, 1985).

In contrast, other field evidence suggests that 'Horton' overland flow may not be common in all arid and semi-arid conditions. For example, in hydrological investigations extending over several decades in steeply sloping drainage basins in the semi-arid southwest of the USA, widespread overland flow was not observed. And again, field experiments in Spain showed that quickflow resulted, not from infiltration–excess overland flow but from profile-controlled saturation overland flow (Scoging and Thornes, 1979).

Tropical rainforest environments, commonly associated with high rainfall intensities, also appear to offer conditions conducive to the formation of infiltration–excess overland flow. However, widespread field evidence, succinctly reviewed by Bruijnzeel (1990) and Anderson and Spencer (1991), confirms that the infiltration capacities of forest soils are generally high, largely because of the presence of a litter layer. As a result, infiltration–excess overland flow is a rare phenomenon, only occurring where bare soil is exposed by litter removal, treefall, or landsliding, or where stemflow (see Chapter 3) augments the flow of water adjacent to the base of tree trunks. On the other hand, saturation overland flow appears to be much more common. For example, in a small tropical catchment in Brazil, Nortcliffe and Thornes (1984) showed that quickflow is almost entirely the result of saturation overland flow from floodplain areas immediately adjacent to the stream channel. This result was later confirmed for a similar catchment by Hodnett *et al.* (1997). And in northern Queensland, Australia (Bonell *et al.*, 1983), where highly transmissive surface soils are underlain at shallow depth by a relatively impermeable subsoil, widespread saturation overland flow results when daily rainfalls, commonly exceeding 250 mm, cause a perched water table to rise to the surface (Figure 7.10(a)).

More generally, field evidence has confirmed that, as in temperate areas, there is a full range of runoff flowpaths on forested slopes in tropical areas and that the dominance of flow at different levels on or below the surface depends very much on the nature of the substrate (Figure 7.10). Indeed, Cassells *et al.* (1985) considered that the major significant difference between runoff processes in temperate and tropical forest catchments is that, in the latter, wet areas are

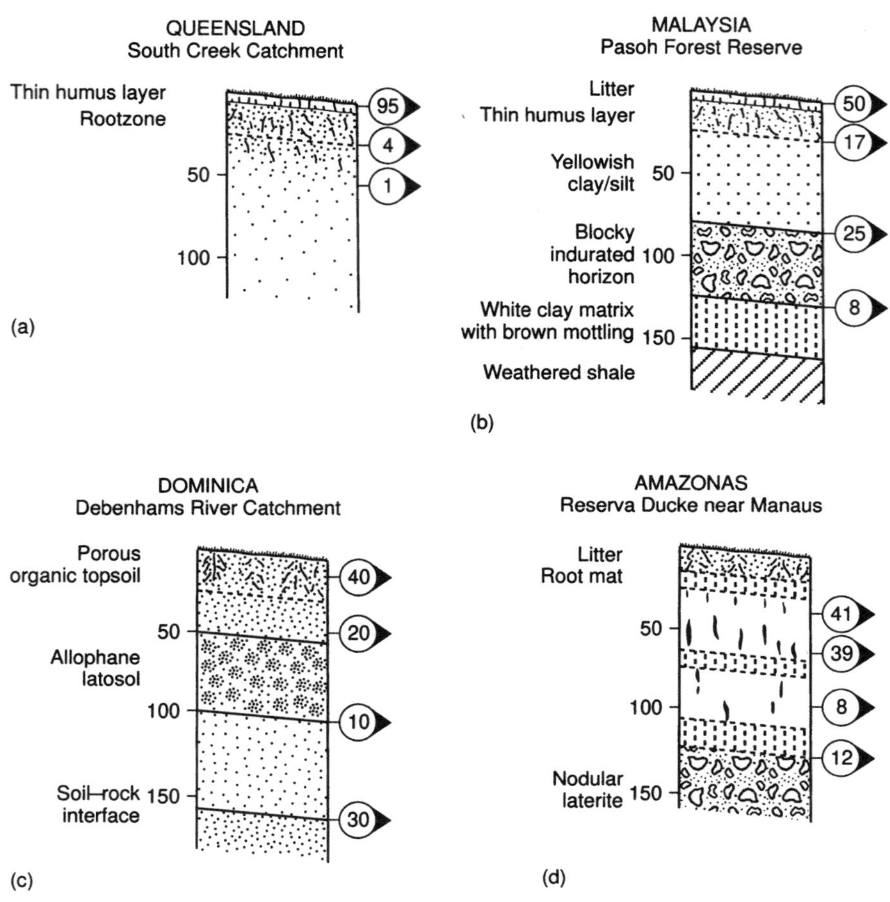

Figure 7.10 Runoff flowpaths at four tropical rainforest sites (from an original diagram by Douglas and Spencer, 1985). See text for explanation.

widespread throughout the catchments during storm events rather than being concentrated in riparian areas. Because of the high wet-season soil water contents such areas can redevelop almost instantaneously with the onset of intense storms. As a result of surface outflows from these widespread areas, quickflow inevitably accounts for a large proportion of total streamflow.

These findings suggest that neither arid/semi-arid nor rainforest conditions constitute genuine exceptions to the Hewlett hypothesis of runoff generation. Instead, they seem to confirm the intuitive conclusion that, in general, slope, slope material and slope vegetation are in equilibrium such that precipitation is normally able to infiltrate the ground surface. Only where one or more of these factors has been drastically modified, usually by human activity or during the course of 'catastrophic' meteorological events, is widespread overland flow generated. Were this not so the entire land surface would be scarred by gullies. The concept of variable (or partial) source areas is an attempt to reconcile the absence of widespread overland flow with the spatial variability of channel flow (for example Huff *et al.*, 1982) and the rapid response of most streams to precipitation by postulating that over-the-surface movement of water is restricted to limited areas of a drainage basin.

7.4.4 Hydrograph separation

The shape of the runoff hydrograph resulting from a precipitation, or melt, event is determined by the relative proportions of quickflow and delayed flow arriving at the stream channel and by the speed of arrival of each individual runoff component. The preceding discussion has shown that, even in simple headwater catchments, the precise contribution of the individual components may vary from storm to storm depending, for example, on the size and location of quickflow contributing areas and on whether throughflow contributes primarily to quickflow or delayed flow. In larger catchments hydrograph response to precipitation is complicated further by the coalescence of tributary stream hydrographs and by the attenuation of the combined hydrograph as it moves down the main channel. Clearly, therefore, early attempts to analyse the hydrograph by genetic separation of flow components, on the basis that overland flow would arrive most rapidly at the stream channel, throughflow next, and groundwater flow at the slowest rate, were unlikely to be very successful. And yet 'hydrograph analysis' is a potentially valuable investigatory and management tool which allows notional separation of the volume of discharge under the hydrograph into a quickflow and a delayed flow component.

For headwater and other relatively simple catchments, current hydrograph separation techniques rely largely on an arbitrary division between quickflow and delayed flow which is based simply on the time of arrival of water at the stream channel. A widely used approach is that proposed by Hewlett and Hibbert (1967) in which quickflow is separated from delayed flow by a line of constant slope ($0.000\ 546\,\mathrm{m^3\,s^{-1}\,km^{-2}\,h^{-1}}$ or $0.0472\,\mathrm{mm\,d^{-1}}$) projected from the beginning of a stream rise to the point where it intersects the falling limb of the hydrograph (Figure 7.11). This slope value was chosen because it exceeded the normal diurnal fluctuation of flow, gave a relatively short time base to the largest single-peaked hydrographs in the study area and permitted large storms separated by a period of about three days to be calculated as separate events. This technique has been applied successfully to many areas, using appropriate values for the slope of the line of separation.

Other, even more arbitrary, graphical separation techniques are illustrated in Figure 7.12. For example, quickflow and baseflow may be separated by drawing a straight line from the sharp break of slope X where discharge begins to increase to a selected point (Z) on the recession limb of the hydrograph. Point Z may be

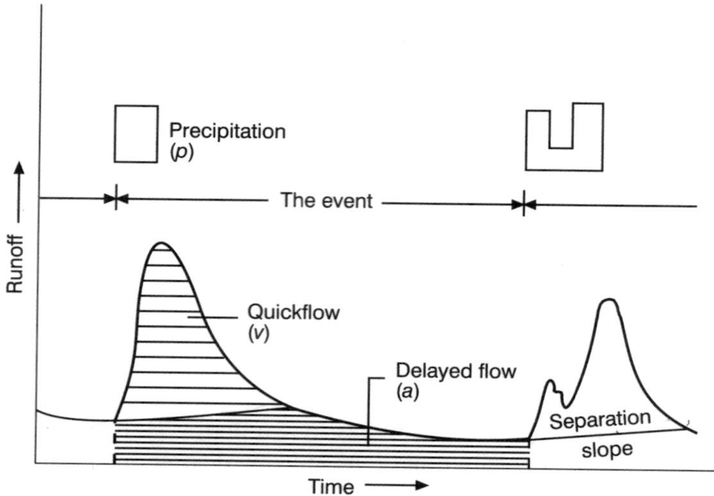

Figure 7.11 Hydrograph separation into quickflow and delayed flow using a constant separation slope of 0.000 546 $m^3\,s^{-1}\,km^{-2}\,h^{-1}$ or 0.0472 $mm\,d^{-1}$. (From an original diagram by J.D. Hewlett and A.R. Hibbert, in *Forest Hydrology*. © 1967, Pergamon Press Ltd.)

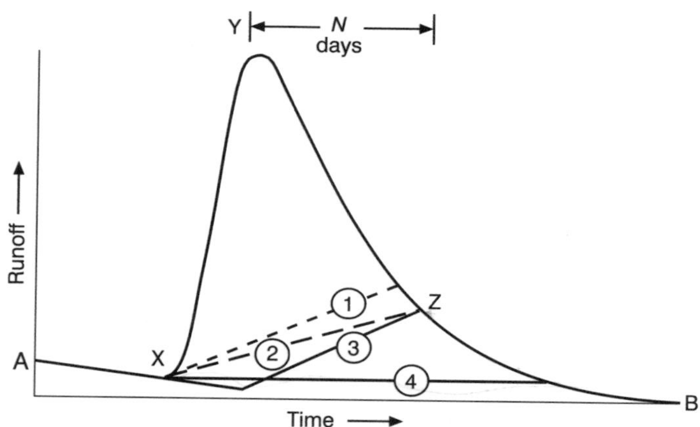

Figure 7.12 Other methods of hydrograph separation. See text for explanation.

located at the point of greatest curvature near the lower end of the recession limb (line 1) or at a given time interval (*N*) after the occurrence of peak flow (line 2), where *N* tends to vary with catchment size. Alternatively, the pre-storm baseflow recession curve (AX) may be projected forwards in time to a point beneath the peak of the hydrograph and then connected by another straight line to the arbitrarily chosen point Z (line 3). Finally, the simplest approximation is that of a horizontal line drawn from point X to its intersection with the recession limb (line 4).

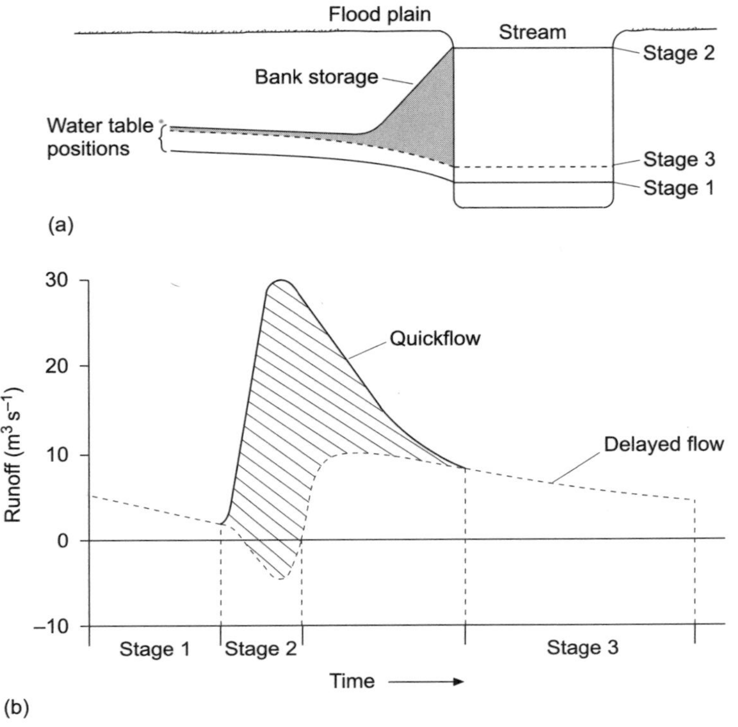

Figure 7.13 Diagram to illustrate (*a*) the process of bank storage; and (*b*) its influence on the separation of quickflow and delayed flow.

As upstream runoff peaks move down-channel into the lowland reaches of river basins, where floodplains are normally well developed, a significant proportion of the quickflow volume may be temporarily retained in the floodplain material. This *bank storage* mitigates the height of the peak and extends the time base of its hydrograph (for example Neuman and Witherspoon, 1970; Whiting and Pomeranets, 1997). Figure 7.13 shows that, with the arrival of the runoff peak, water level in the channel increases from stage 1 to stage 2 resulting in the flow of water from the channel into the adjacent floodplain. This bank storage begins to drain back into the channel as the peak passes and the channel water level falls to stage 3. In these circumstances a straight-line separation between quickflow and delayed flow is clearly inappropriate.

Because the quality of water may reflect its flowpath to the stream channel (for example Section 5.5.7 and Chapter 8) attempts have long been made to separate the components of the hydrograph on the basis of either ionic composition or water temperature. The use of conductivity, as a surrogate for ionic concentrations, has met with variable success (for example Nakamura, 1971; Anderson and Burt, 1982; Calles, 1985). Generally improved results have come from the analysis of specific ionic constituents (for example Duysings *et al.*, 1983; Laudon and Slaymaker, 1997) and of stable isotopes of the constituents of the H_2O molecule, such as hydrogen isotope deuterium (D) and oxygen isotope oxygen-18 (^{18}O) (Loye-Pilot, 1990). The latter, in particular, have been used successfully to identify old and new water contributions to streamflow on the basis that new water (rain or snowmelt) and old water (soil water and groundwater) have distinct isotopic signatures (for example Rodhe, 1981; Sklash *et al.*, 1986; Buttle, 1994; Kubota and Sivapalan, 1995; Taha *et al.*, 1998). Between storm events the stream comprises baseflow which carries the isotopic signature of old water. During runoff events, however, the isotopic character of the stream is diluted by the addition of new water (see also the section 'The role of throughflow' earlier in this chapter).

7.5 Daily flow variations

Variations of runoff with time are often studied using flow values for calendar time intervals (days, weeks, months, years) rather than for runoff events of non-uniform duration. In the case of major continental rivers, where the passage of flood peaks through the system may take several months, weekly flow values are usually suitable. For small drainage basins, such as those of the British Isles, which respond rapidly to precipitation/melt events, hydrographs of daily flow values may be more appropriate. The three examples in Figure 7.14 illustrate a range of flow conditions from the flashy behaviour of the Dee, with its dominant quickflow component, to the subdued behaviour of the Avon, with its very large delayed flow (or baseflow) component. Flow conditions in the Thames are clearly intermediate in character.

This long-term relationship between quickflow and delayed flow provides a basis for classifying streams as ephemeral, intermittent or perennial. *Ephemeral* streams consist solely of quickflow and therefore occur only during and immediately after a precipitation/melt event. There are usually no permanent or well-defined channels and the water table is always below the bed of the stream. Ephemeral streams are typical of arid and semi-arid areas, where they are characterized by large transmission losses. This means that runoff peaks, generated by storm rainfall, diminish rapidly downstream as they are absorbed by the dry stream beds. For example, only about 15 per cent of the runoff entering the channels of Walnut Gulch, Arizona, actually leaves the catchment as streamflow (Renard, 1979). In some areas of inland drainage the percentage is even lower and may diminish to zero for particular precipitation events. *Intermittent* streams, which flow during the wet season and dry up during the season of drought, consist mainly of quickflow but delayed flow makes some contribution during the wet season, when the water table rises above the bed of the stream. A particular case occurs in high latitude areas when flow ceases as subsurface water freezes during the winter. *Perennial* streams flow throughout the year because, even during the most prolonged dry spell, the water table is always

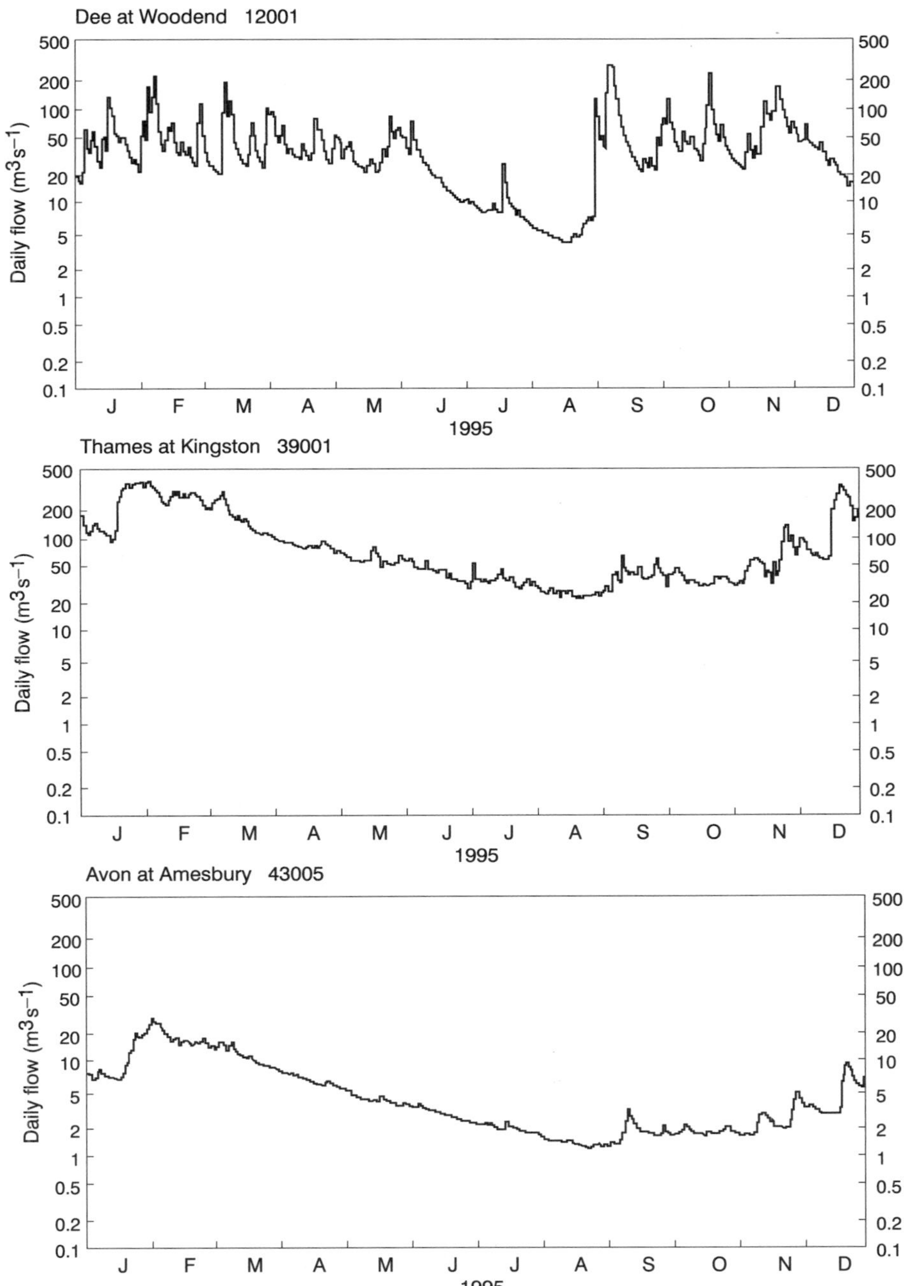

Figure 7.14 Hydrographs of daily flow for three British rivers, i.e. the Dee, Thames and Avon (redrawn from one of the standard retrieval options offered by the National Water Archive, Institute of Hydrology, Wallingford, OX10 8BB).

above the bed of the stream, so that groundwater flow can make a continuous contribution to total runoff. Rarely is it possible to classify the entire length of a stream under only one of these three headings. A chalk bourne, for example, is normally intermittent in its upper reaches but perennial farther downstream; many other streams are ephemeral in their upper reaches but intermittent downstream.

The contrasting contributions of quickflow and delayed flow to total runoff, so clearly illustrated by the hydrographs of daily flow in Figure 7.14, reflect the integrated operation of a wide range of topographical, pedological, vegetational and geological factors that condition the runoff processes described earlier in this chapter. The extremes of flow associated with a flashy stream and the more muted variations of a stream dominated by delayed flow may be quantified and compared more conveniently if the daily flow values are arranged according to their frequency of occurrence and plotted as a *flow-duration curve*. This is a curve showing the percentage of time that specified flows are equalled or exceeded during a given year or period of years. Flow-duration curves for UK rivers included in the National Water Archive are available as one of several data-retrieval options (for example IH/BGS, 1998). For ease of comparison a flow-duration curve may be plotted in dimensionless form (Figure 7.15), by dividing the daily discharge values by the average daily discharge value for the period under study. The technique thereby combines in one curve the entire range of stream flows, although not arranged chronologically, and the shape and slope of the curve reflect the complex combination of hydrological and catchment factors that determine the range and variability of stream discharge.

Flow-duration curves that slope steeply throughout (for example Tees and Tamar in Figure 7.15) denote highly variable flows with a large quickflow component, and gently sloping curves (for example Ver) indicate a large delayed flow component. In particular, the slope of the lower end of the flow-duration curve may reflect the perennial storage in the drainage basin, such that a flat lower end indicates a large amount of storage.

Because the slope of the flow-duration curve is a useful measure of streamflow variability, various descriptive slope indexes have been derived. For example, the US Geological Survey has long related the flow available 50 per cent of the time to the flow available 90 per cent of the time (Searcy, 1959). For a wide range of British rivers, the mean daily flow is exceeded 30 per cent of the time and the modal flow is exceeded 70 per cent of the time, and Hall (1968) suggested that the ratio of mean and modal flows could be related to geological and other drainage basin characteristics. For 58 widely distributed British rivers the median 30 : 70 per cent ratio was found to be 2.6 (Ward, 1981) with 32 rivers having 30 : 70 per cent ratios of 2–2.99, 12 falling into each of the adjacent classes, i.e. 1–1.99 and 3–3.99, and the remaining two having ratios greater than 4.0. Flow-duration curves representative of the largest group (2–2.99) are those for the Hull, Wharfe and Severn in Figure 7.15, which can, therefore, be considered as 'typical' British rivers. Low values are exemplified by the Ver (1.79) and high

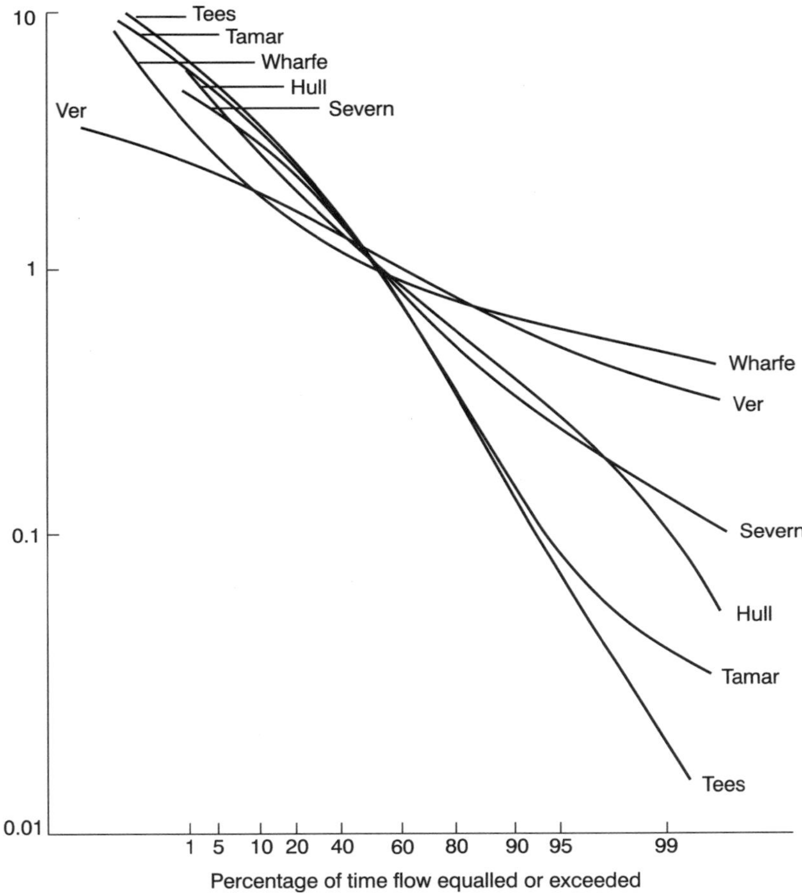

Figure 7.15 Dimensionless flow-duration curves for selected British rivers.

values by the Tamar (4.32) and the Tees (4.42). In contrast the median 30 : 70 per cent ratio for the coastal rivers of northern New South Wales, Australia, is 4.4 with a range from 2.8 to 8.4, and for rivers in the Murray–Darling basin the median value is 6.7 with a range from 4.7 to 13.0. For the same Australian rivers the median 50 : 90 per cent ratios are 5.1 for the coastal rivers and 18.2 for those of the Murray–Darling basin (Ward, 1984).

7.6 Seasonal flow variations

The hydrographs in Figure 7.14 illustrate that individual, event-based variations of flow may, in total, define a broadly seasonal pattern. This seasonality, often known as the river *regime*, becomes much clearer when hydrographs are plotted for weekly or monthly data, averaged over a period of 20–30 years, and comparisons between rivers are facilitated if the data are plotted in dimensionless form, for example, as a ratio of the mean annual flow. River regimes are driven largely by climate (see Figure 7.16) and in Britain, for example, are a reflection of the balance between rainfall and evaporation.

Many small rivers exhibit comparatively *simple regimes* having one period of high water and one period of low water each year. Such regimes may result from the spring/summer melting of snowpacks or glaciers followed by a period of near-zero flow during the winter months when temperatures are low and icemelt is negligible. Alternatively, where rainfall is evenly distributed throughout the year, low flow coincides with the peak of evaporation during the summer months and high runoff values occur during the winter months when evaporation is small. By contrast, in tropical areas evaporation tends to be high throughout the year, so that the rainfall distribution is the main determinant of river regimes, with high runoff occurring during the wet season.

River regimes characterized by four distinct hydrological phases through the year, i.e. two low flow and two high flow periods, were defined by Pardé (1955) as *Complex I regimes*. In Europe the first high runoff period, resulting perhaps from snowmelt, may occur in spring and then be followed by a period of low runoff. Later in the year, a second period of high water levels and runoff may occur in the summer as a result of, say, convectional rainfall over a 'continental' area, or in the autumn as a result of Mediterranean storms, or in the winter as a result of an excess of rainfall over evaporation in an oceanic area. Complex I regimes may have as many as six hydrological phases.

Large rivers may flow through several distinct relief and climatic regions and may receive the waters of large tributaries which themselves flow over varied terrain. As a result, the regimes of such rivers tend to change with distance downstream. Rivers exhibiting these *Complex II regimes* (Pardé, 1955) normally have simple or complex I regimes in their headwater reaches but downstream are gradually influenced by a variety of factors such as snow or glacier melt, rainfall and evaporation regimes. These different inflows may either reinforce the trends found in the headwater regime or may cancel each other out. Two European examples are shown in Figure 7.17. The Rhine is typical of rivers that are meltwater streams in their headwater reaches, but which become increasingly influenced downstream by a single type of rainfall regime. At Kehl, the Rhine has a simple meltwater regime with a summer maximum; after the confluence of the Neckar at Frankenthal, the slightest signs of a winter rainfall peak become apparent, and this feature is further strengthened after the confluence of the Main at Mainz. The entry of another large tributary, the Moselle, considerably alters the regime again so that, at Coblenz, the runoff peak attributable to the excess of winter rainfall over evaporation almost equals the summer meltwater peak. Finally, at Emmerich, on the Dutch border, the winter oceanic rainfall regime has become the dominant factor and the contribution of meltwater now gives rise only to a secondary peak in the summer months.

The Rhône is an interesting example of rivers that are influenced upstream by

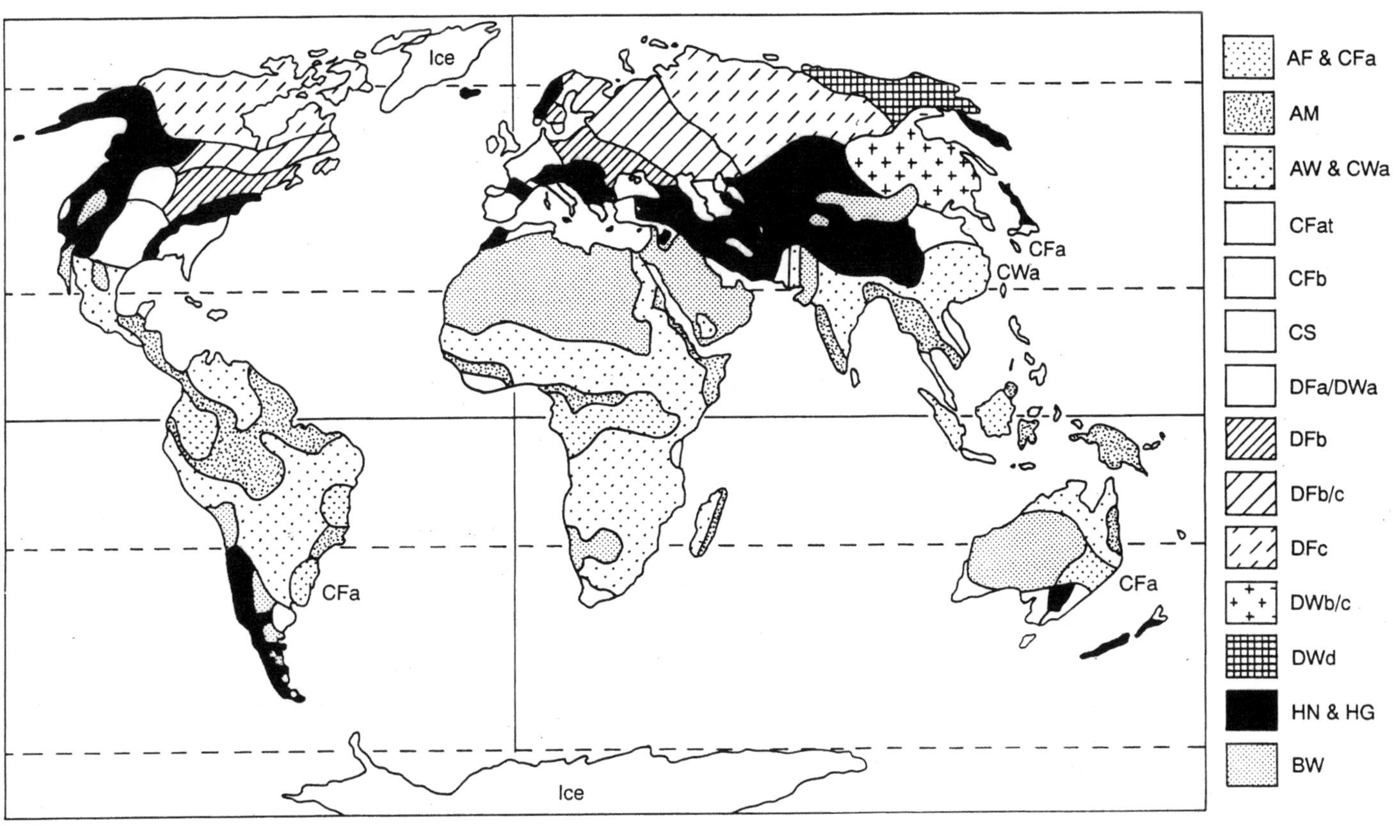

Figure 7.16 World distribution of characteristic river regimes based on the climatic terminology of Koppen. HN and HG refer to mountain river regimes which are shown where the scale permits; BW denotes desert and other dry areas where streams cannot originate (from an original diagram by Beckinsale, 1969).

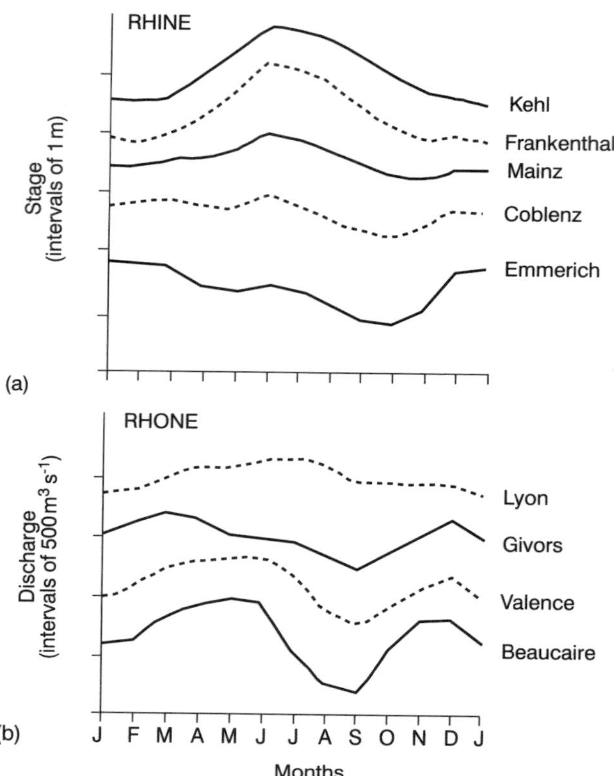

Figure 7.17 Regimes of (*a*) the Rhine; and (*b*) the Rhône (from original diagrams by Pardé, 1955).

meltwater and downstream, by at least two types of rainfall regime. At Lyon, a glacier melt summer maximum is apparent, but at Givors, below the confluence of the Saône, an oceanic rainfall-evaporation regime becomes dominant. Farther downstream, however, the influx of water from the Isère, above Valence, re-establishes the dominance of the meltwater peak, although there is still a secondary winter maximum. Finally, in the lower reaches, as at Beaucaire, a Mediterranean rainfall regime is superimposed upon all this, resulting in a rapid increase of runoff in the autumn.

Because *British rivers* are short, most have 'simple' rainfall-evaporation regimes with summer minima and winter maxima. Figure 7.18 shows that the timing of these runoff extremes is successively delayed towards the south and east. This spatial variation reflects both the pattern of evaporation and also the greater water-holding capacity and therefore later release of baseflow from the sedimentary rocks of the English plain. On a smaller scale, this geological influence means that there are similar contrasts in the timing of minimum flows between 'chalk' and 'clay/urban' catchments in south-east England (Marsh, 1988). Some rivers in the north and west tend towards a 'complex I' regime, with a period of high water in both summer and winter. This additional hydrological phase appears to result from a combination of geological and climatological factors, including spring snowmelt and reduced summer evaporation. Monthly mean flows for UK rivers are available in the form of computer graphs or data tabulations as one of the many retrieval options offered by the IH National River Flow Archive (for example IH/BGS, 1998).

In the past, river regime graphs have been used in a rather simple, descriptive way. Increasingly, however, it is recognized that their dependence on climate means that they could also be used as an analytical tool for monitoring the changes in flow seasonality, both in time and space, which result from underlying environmental changes, particularly climate changes. Krasovskaia (1997), for example, used an objective, entropy-based grouping of monthly flow series to discriminate flow regime types and illustrated the outcome for a number of Scandinavian rivers.

7.7 Long-term variations of flow and flow variability

By definition river regimes are an expression of seasonal conditions averaged over many years. Since similar seasonal patterns tend to occur in both wet and dry years, regime graphs may imply a stability of long-term runoff which is misleading. The variability of annual runoff values not only reflects closely the variability of precipitation but is also approximately inversely related to the annual total (see Figure 7.19).

Accordingly, there is a marked contrast in the variability of runoff between humid and dry areas and this is illustrated by comparisons between rivers in Britain, the semi-arid Karoo region of South Africa and the Murray–Darling basin in south-eastern Australia for periods varying between 30 and 110 years. Coefficients of variation of annual flow are, respectively, 0.29 and 0.20 for the Thames and the Severn, 0.89 for six Karoo rivers (Gorgens and Hughes, 1982), and 1.30 and 1.46 respectively for the Barwon and the Darling. With such a high degree of variability several centuries of flow data would be necessary in order to derive satisfactory estimates of mean flow conditions. Indeed, in such circumstances, the concept of 'average' flow conditions becomes relatively meaningless, as is further illustrated in Figures 7.20 and 7.21. The bar graphs emphasize the great variability of flow from year to year, especially in the case of the Barwon and Darling, and also illustrate the alternation of sequences of wet and dry years and their contrasting relative importance in the two areas. For example, the Barwon and Darling (Figure 7.20) are characterized by sustained periods of low flow interspersed with shorter periods of high flow, whereas the Thames and Severn (Figure 7.21) are characterized by long periods of medium to high flow and shorter intervening periods of low flow. This bunching or grouping of wet and dry conditions has been referred to as 'persistence' or the 'Hurst phenomenon', and is an important complicating factor in the stochastic variation of precipitation

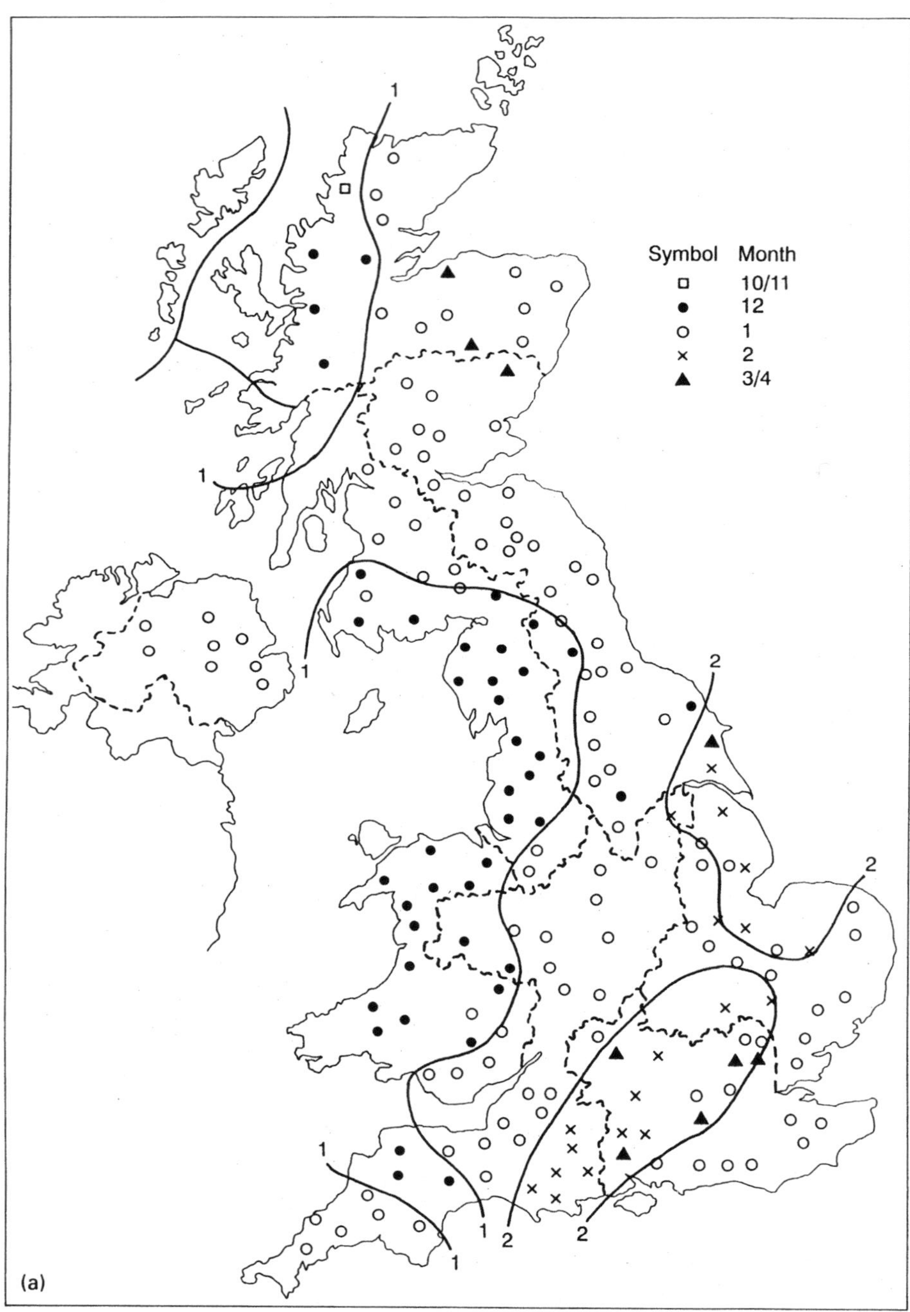

Figure 7.18 Maps showing the timing of (*a*) maximum monthly runoff; and (*b*) minimum monthly runoff in Britain (from an original diagram by Ward, 1981).

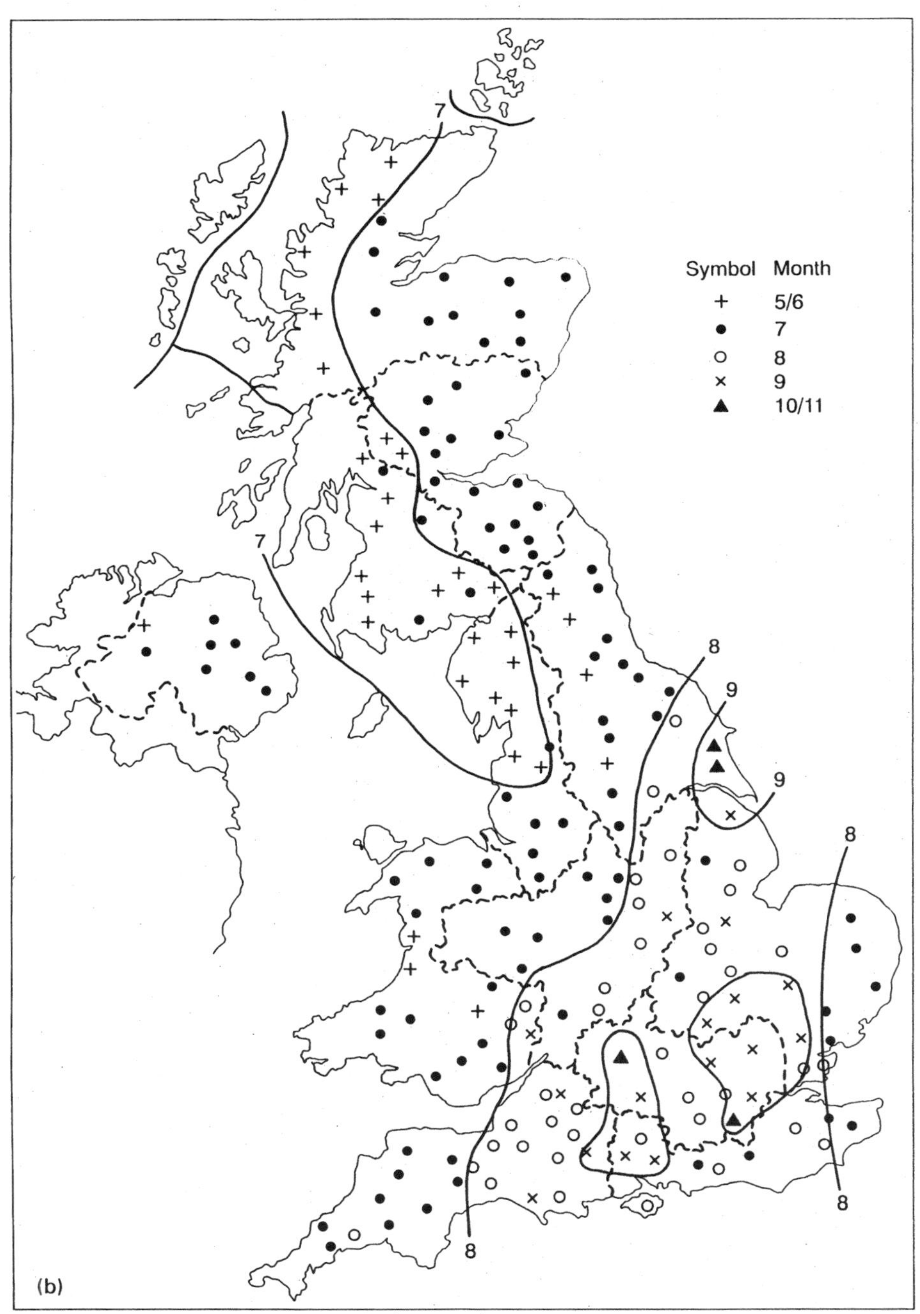
Symbol Month
+ 5/6
• 7
○ 8
× 9
▲ 10/11
7
7
8
9
9
8
8
8
(b)

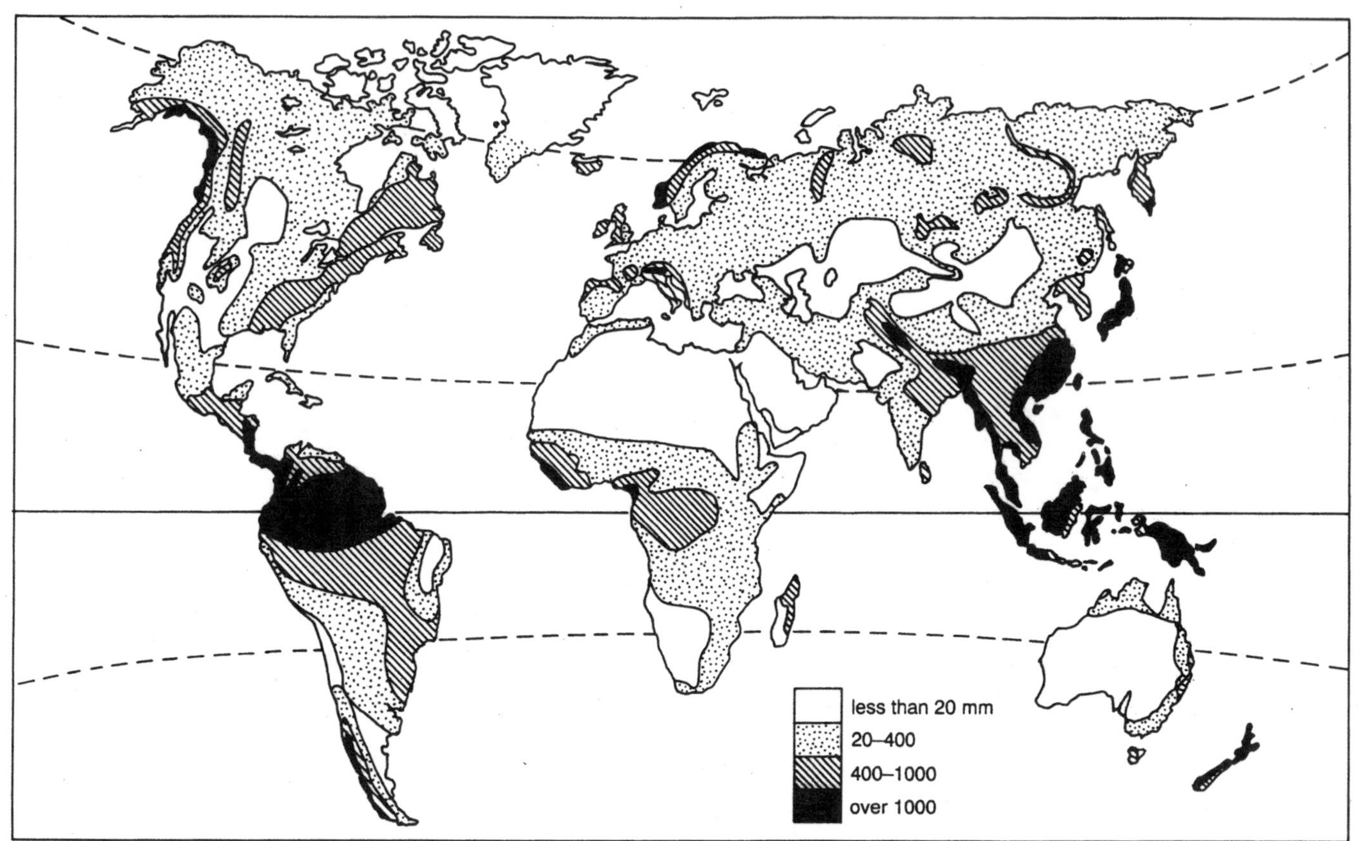

Figure 7.19 Simplified world map of mean annual runoff. (From an original map by M.I. Lvovich, *Transactions of American Geophysical Union*, **54**, p. 34, Figure 1. © 1973 American Geophysical Union.)

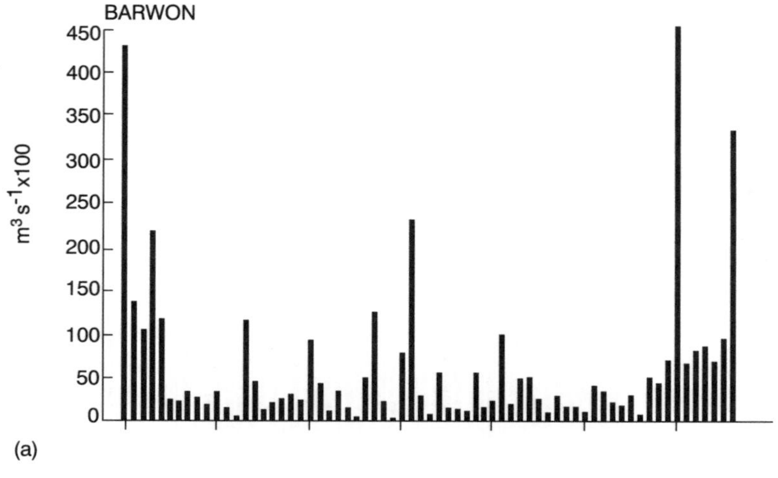

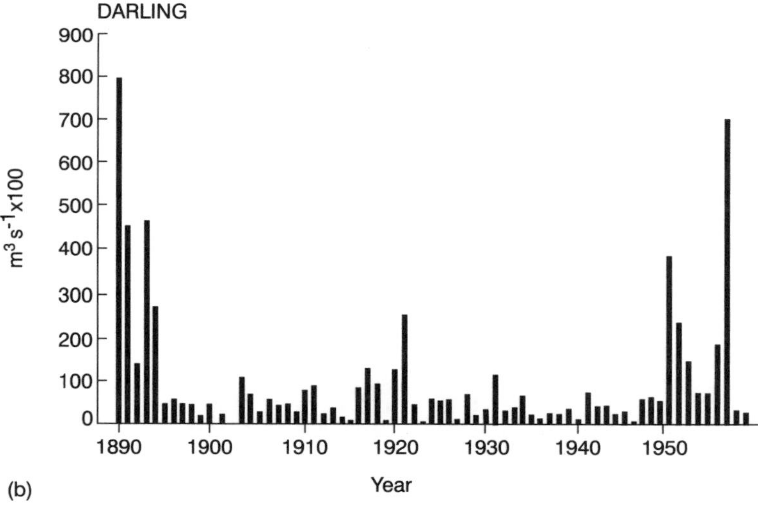

Figure 7.20 Bar graphs of annual flow for (*a*) the Barwon and (*b*) the Darling rivers in Australia.

driving the runoff process. Furthermore, the Hurst coefficient, which indicates the tendency towards persistence, itself appears to vary with time.

For most areas of the world, flow records are much shorter than those for the Thames or Darling, which exceed 100 years. The opportunities for identifying trends in the variation of runoff with time are therefore extremely limited. However, for some areas there have been comparatively successful reconstructions of runoff from the very much longer records of precipitation. Eleven-year

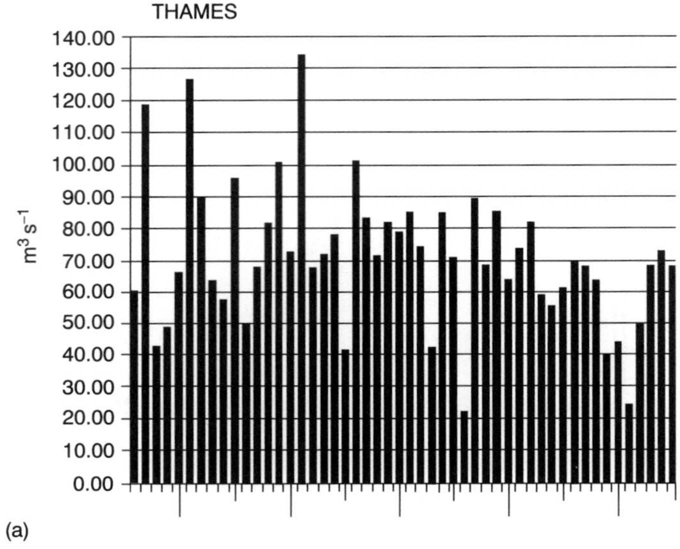

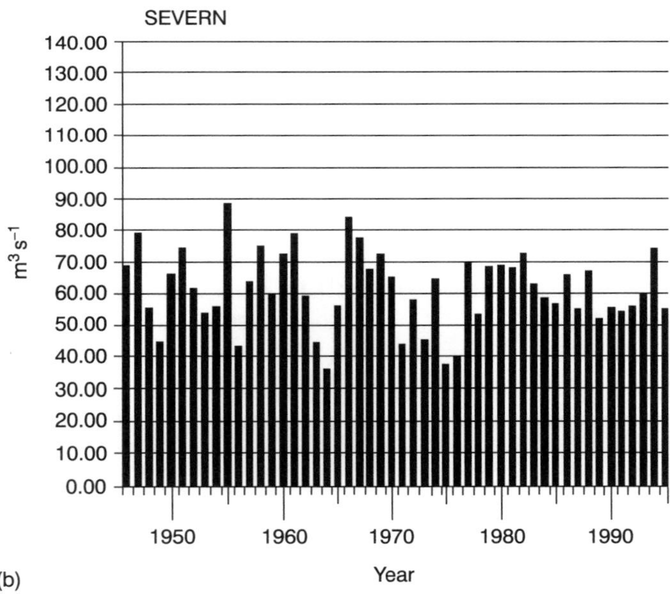

Figure 7.21 Bar graphs of annual flow for (*a*) the Thames and (*b*) the Severn in Britain, 1935–95.

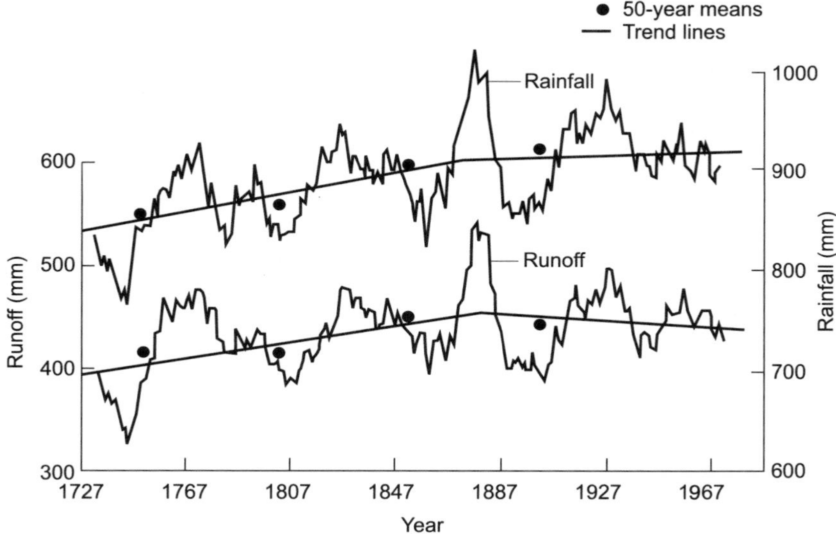

Figure 7.22 Eleven-year running means of rainfall (top) and runoff for England and Wales, 1728–1976, with 50-year means and estimated trend lines (based on data presented by Rodda *et al.*, 1978, and Marsh and Littlewood, 1978).

running means of reconstructed runoff values for England and Wales for the period 1728–1976 (Marsh and Littlewood, 1978) are shown in Figure 7.22, together with those for mean annual rainfall (Rodda *et al.*, 1978). The graphs emphasize the alternation of wet and dry periods already evident in Figures 7.20 and 7.21. Superimposed on this pattern are the 50-year means and long-term trend lines. Although the 249-year mean runoff value is 435 mm, the five successive 50-year means (49 years for the final period) are 413, 417, 453, 447 and 443 mm, indicating either a slight upward trend through the period of record or, as the trend lines suggest, possibly a period of about 150 years in which there was a clear upward trend followed by a period of about 100 years, since the late 1870s, in which there has been a scarcely discernible downward trend. After the mid-1970s runoff variability was significantly greater than average. However, during this period runoff was greater than average, especially in Scotland, and within-year variability was characterized by lower low flows and higher high flows, if not by an increased frequency of major floods (Marsh, 1988).

7.8 Extremes of runoff

To some extent persistence accentuates the contrast between the extremes of flow illustrated in Figures 7.20 and 7.21. Flood conditions resulting from a given precipitation event may be more severe if that precipitation event occurs at the end of a long sequence of such events. Low flow or drought conditions will certainly intensify as the preceding dry period is prolonged. Thus in many parts of England and Wales the extreme low flows recorded in August 1976 came at the end of the driest 17-month period thus far recorded. Similar low-flow conditions recurred between 1988 and 1992 (see Figure 7.35). However, the comparisons between extreme high and low flows should not be pursued too far since although extreme low flow events are indeed dependent on antecedent conditions, extreme flood events are much more directly dependent on the severity of the causal precipitation/melt event. Severe floods can, and of course frequently do, occur in deserts and other persistently low rainfall areas.

Limitations of space mean that floods and droughts are discussed only briefly in the following paragraphs. For a more detailed treatment, the reader is referred to books on floods such as Smith and Ward (1998) and White and Watts (1994).

7.8.1 Flood flows

Flood peaks are generated in river channels by a variety of causes (see Figure 7.23), including storm surges in estuaries, the failure of dams and embankments, and landslides. Most river floods, however, result directly or indirectly from climatological events such as excessively heavy and/or excessively prolonged rainfall. In cold winter areas, where snowfall accumulates, substantial flooding usually occurs during the melt season in spring and early summer, particularly when melt rates are high. Floods may also result from the effects of rain falling on an already decaying and melting snowpack. An additional cause of flooding in cold winter areas is the sudden collapse of ice jams, formed during the break-up of river ice.

Flood intensifying factors

As the lower part of Figure 7.23 shows, floods may be modified by a number of factors. These can operate either to ameliorate or to intensify flooding although, for the sake of brevity, only the latter function is considered in the ensuing discussion. For example, river floods may be intensified by factors associated either with the catchment itself or with the drainage network and stream channels. Most of these operate to increase the volume of quickflow and to speed up its movement. Few of these factors operate either uni-directionally or independently. Area, for example, is fundamentally important in the sense that the larger the catchment, the greater is the flood produced from a catchment-wide rainfall event. However, when the rainprint of the storm covers only part of the catchment, the attenuation of the resulting flood hydrograph, as it moves through the channel network to the outlet, is greater in a large catchment than in a small one. Again, basin shape and the pattern of the drainage network combine to influence the size and shape of flood peaks at the basin outlet as shown in Figure 7.24. Some of the most complex relationships, those between the variable

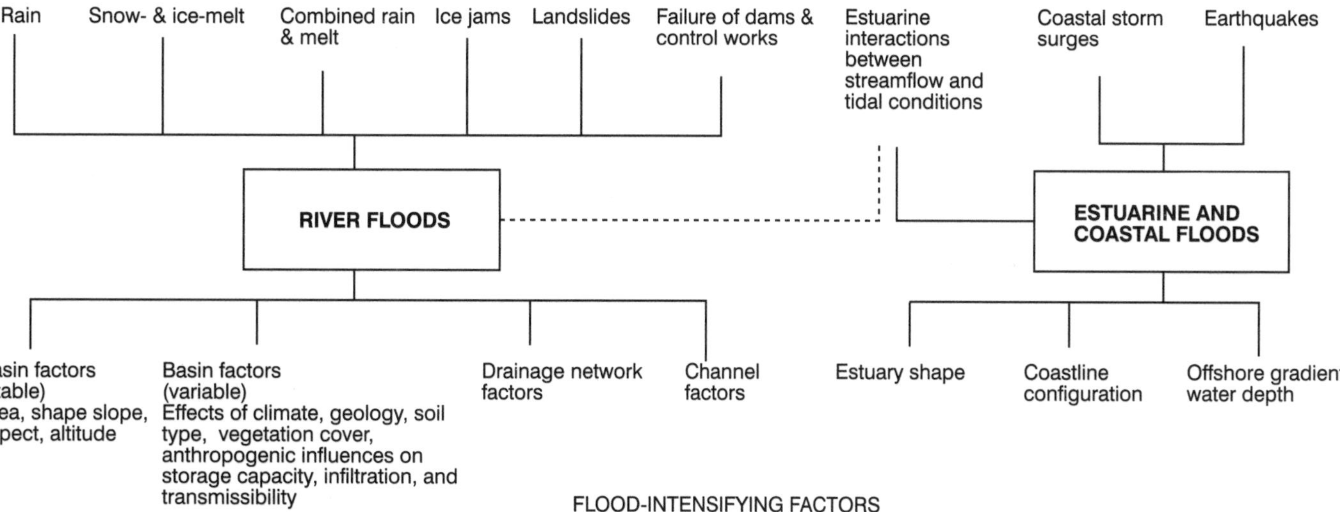

Figure 7.23 Causes of floods and flood-intensifying factors.

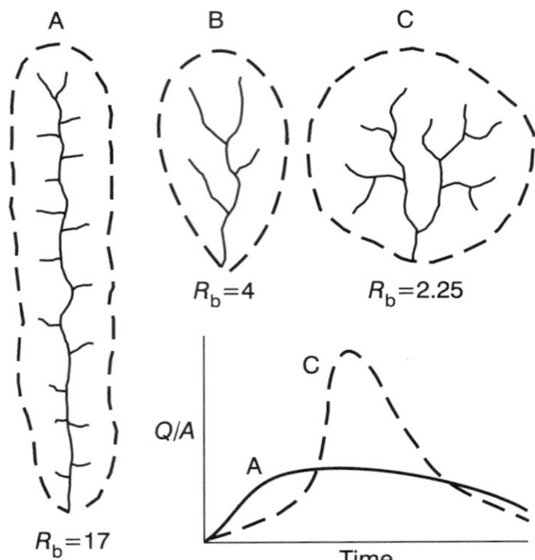

Figure 7.24 Relations between catchment shape, bifurcation ratio (R_b) and the shape of the flood hydrograph (from an original diagram by Strahler, 1964).

basin factors, have a significant influence on three important hydrological variables, i.e. water storage, infiltration, and transmissibility.

Water storage in the soil and deeper subsurface layers may affect both the timing and magnitude of flood response to precipitation, with low storage often resulting in rapid and intensified flooding. High infiltration values allow much of the precipitation to be absorbed by the soil surface and may thereby reduce catchment flood response, depending on the extent and growth of areas of saturation overland flow and on subsurface transmissibility; low infiltration values encourage infiltration–excess overland flow leading to rapid increases in channel discharge (see also Section 7.4).

Human influences

Human activity (for example urbanization, forestry, and agriculture) frequently acts as a flood-intensifying factor by modifying key hydrological variables such as water storage, infiltration, and transmissibility.

The extent to which flood characteristics are modified by *urbanization* depends very much on the nature of the modified urban surface, the urban hydrological system, and climate. Urban surfaces are less permeable than most of the surfaces which they replace. As a result they are effective source areas for quickflow and their flood hydrographs tend to have both higher and earlier peaks (Figure 7.25), reflecting the greater volume of quickflow and its rapid movement across the urban surface. Accordingly, urbanization tends to increase downstream flood peaks and volumes. However, much depends on the permeability contrast between an urbanized area and the pre-urban surface, so that flood conditions

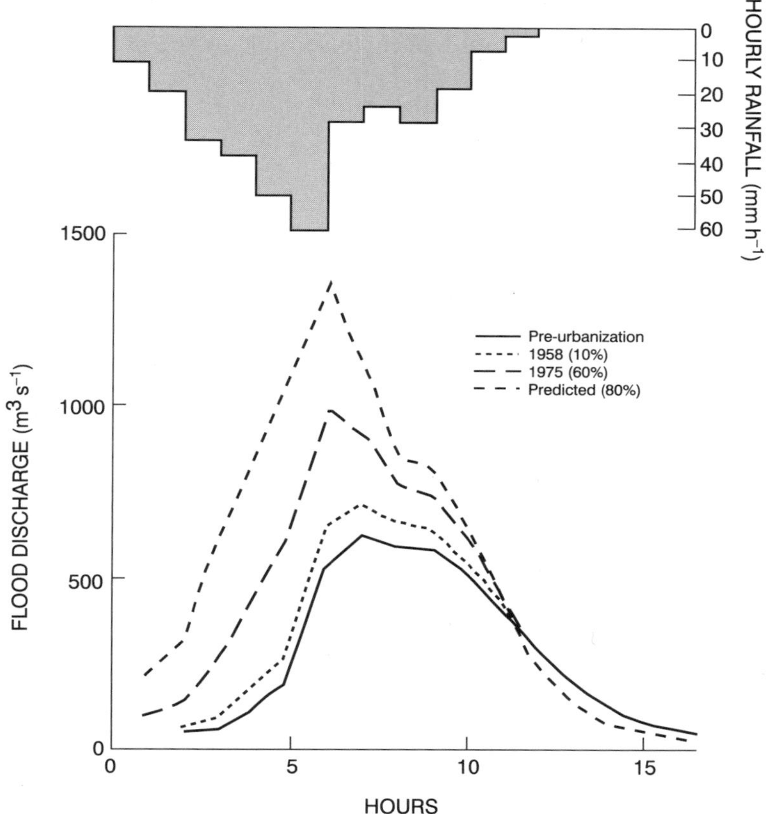

Figure 7.25 Flood hydrographs reflecting the spread of urbanization (shown as percentage of basin urbanized) in western Tokyo, Japan (from an original diagram by Yoshimoto and Suetsugi, 1990. Reproduced by permission of IAHS Press).

are exacerbated more by the urbanization of a high infiltration, sandy area than by the urbanization of a low infiltration clay area. The additional quickflow produced by urban surfaces is routed through stormwater systems many of which, like those in the UK, are old and unable to cope with high-magnitude events. As a result, stormwater surcharges are common and may lead to widespread flooding.

Generally, the influence of urbanization is smaller in winter than in summer and in wet climates than in dry ones. It specifically reduces with the severity of the flood-producing event in the sense that, after prolonged and heavy rainfall, the infiltration characteristics of urban and saturated non-urban surfaces are very similar.

The role of *forestry* in modifying river basin flood hydrology remains a controversial topic in the light of proposals to double the forested area in

England, largely by the creation of new 'community' forests in central England (MAFF, 1994), or the afforestation likely to accompany the growth of set-aside agriculture in the European Union, or the deforestation which has already occurred in the foothills of the Himalayas.

Afforestation is generally thought to reduce peak flows, although temporary increases of flooding may initially result from forest road construction or from pre-planting drainage. Deforestation may intensify river flooding by: adversely affecting soil structure and volume; reducing infiltration rates, either through the effects of diminished root mass or by facilitating the development of concrete as opposed to granular frost; and reducing water storage, either in the soil profile or within the canopy. However, these influences are normally significant only during frequent low-magnitude storms. Their effect during increasingly severe flood-producing storms diminishes as prolonged heavy rainfall and/or melting fills available storage and creates widespread conditions of surface saturation and zero infiltration. Accordingly, their effects are also insignificant where initial storage values are low, for example swamplands and steep slopes with shallow soils, which produce rapid quickflow whether forested or not (Hewlett, 1982b). Furthermore, the effect on the flood hydrograph of an additional volume of quickflow diminishes with distance down the channel system, so that headwater deforestation becomes less significant as the flood peak moves downstream. These are important factors in high-rainfall areas such as the Himalayan foothills of the Indian sub-continent where forest clearance for agriculture has frequently been blamed for increased flooding many hundreds of kilometres downstream. Examination of several decades of hydrological data led Hofer (1993) to conclude that there is no evidence that flooding on the Gangetic plain has increased.

The substantial growth in the area of drained agricultural land, for example in Europe, which occurred after 1939, generated interest in the effects of *agricultural drainage* on flood hydrology. However, early work failed to recognize either the inadequacy of much of the available data or the importance of soil type. It is now clear (for example Robinson, 1990; Robinson and Rycroft, 1999) that the drainage of heavy clay soils, which are prone to prolonged surface saturation in their undrained state, generally results in a lowering of large and medium flood peaks, as drainage ameliorates their naturally 'flashy' response by greatly reducing surface saturation. On more permeable soils, which are less prone to surface saturation, the effect of drainage is usually to accelerate the speed at which water follows subsurface flowpaths, thereby tending to increase flood flows.

Spatial patterns of flooding

Although floods at any location in a river system are a function of the floods generated in the catchment upstream of that point, the relationship between flood behaviour in headwater catchments and the flood behaviour of the entire river basin is often complex. The downstream flood hydrograph differs from the upstream flood hydrograph for the same event, partly because of lag and routing effects, partly because of the changing nature of the basin geology, physiography and climate from headwaters to outlet, and partly because of scale effects.

Scale effects are important in relation to both catchment conditions and precipitation inputs and frequently restrict our ability to generalize from existing flood data and to predict flood occurrence and distribution. The fact that floodpeak discharges tend to increase downstream when measured absolutely (i.e. $m^3\,s^{-1}$) but decrease downstream when expressed as specific discharge (i.e. $m^3\,s^{-1}\,km^{-2}$) in part reflects a mismatch between the scales of catchment and precipitation event. In other words, large catchments normally have a lower specific discharge than small catchments partly because the flood-producing precipitation event is smaller than the total catchment area. In small catchments the precipitation event is often at least as large as the area of the catchment, thereby encouraging high specific flood discharge. It follows, therefore, that a large basin subjected to a macro-scale precipitation event, such as a major tropical storm (see Table 3.1), should generate a higher specific discharge than when it is subjected to a meso- or micro-scale precipitation event.

From the preceding discussions of runoff processes and flooding, one might expect the flood-producing potential of each river basin and sub-catchment to be distinctively different. However there is some evidence of a spatial dimension to river flooding on a scale larger than that of a river basin. This can be illustrated for the UK by two frequently used flood indexes, which are mapped in Figure 7.26. The first is an index of flood potential in the form of an estimate of mean annual flood (Figure 7.26(a)) and the second is an indication of flood experience during the period of recorded flow data in the form of the highest instantaneous gauged discharge (Figure 7.26(b)).

The best estimate of mean annual flood (BESMAF) was derived by extending the recorded flood experience by correlation with nearby flood records (NERC, 1975). When such extension was not possible the arithmetic mean of annual maximum floods was used or, when the period of record was too short, some other technique was employed, for example the use of a peak-over-threshold series. For ungauged catchments equations were developed relating the mean annual flood to several catchment characteristics. The pattern of isopleths drawn through the BESMAF values shows a marked gradient from specific discharges exceeding $1.50\,m^3\,s^{-1}\,km^{-2}$ in the north and west to values well below $0.25\,m^3\,s^{-1}\,km^{-2}$ in the south and east (Figure 7.26(a)).

Despite the difference in cartographic presentation, a comparison of BESMAF with the distribution of highest instantaneous gauged discharges, averaged for each hydrometric area (Figure 7.26(b)), reveals a striking similarity. In both cases it should be noted that the comparatively low values of flood flow per unit area over south-eastern England may be misleading in the sense that they are, to some extent, compensated by the large area of the catchments concerned. The highest instantaneous gauged discharge for the Thames at Kingston, for example, is

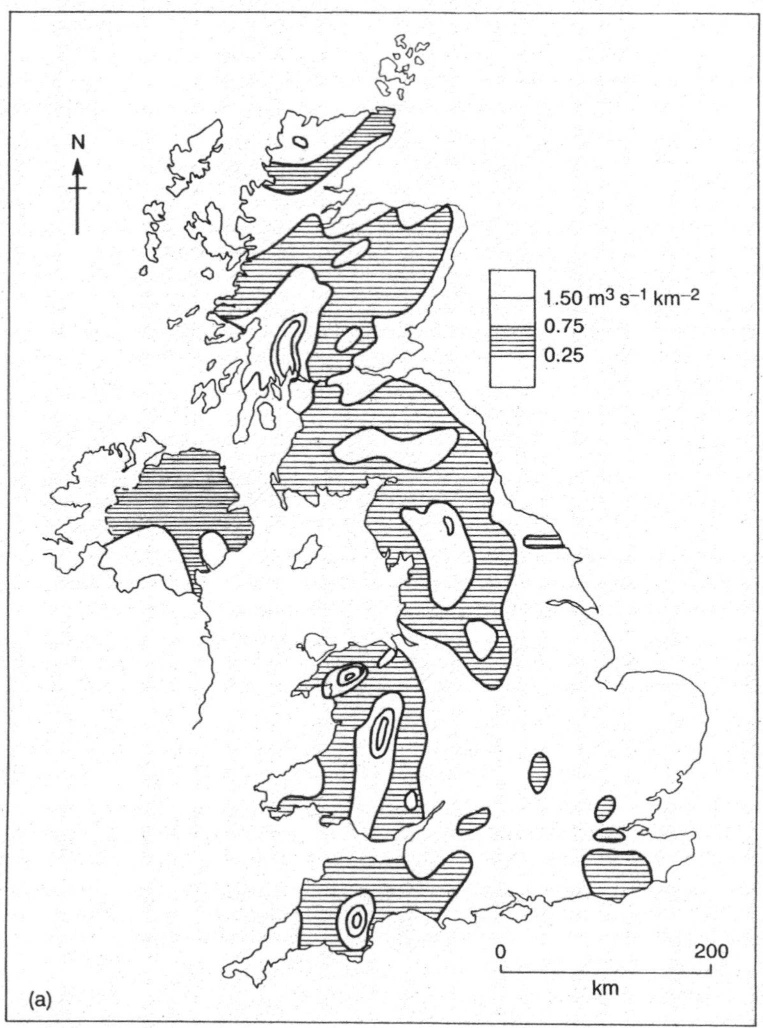

Figure 7.26 Selected flood discharge characteristics for the UK: (*a*) BESMAF (best estimate of mean annual flood) values (from an original diagram in NERC, 1975); (*b*) peak flows for the period of record for hydrometric areas (based on data in IH/BGS, 1998).

approximately $1060\,\mathrm{m^3\,s^{-1}}$, which exceeds that for the Tees at Broken Scar of $710\,\mathrm{m^3\,s^{-1}}$ or for the Clyde at Blairston of $666\,\mathrm{m^3\,s^{-1}}$.

The *Flood Studies Report* (NERC, 1975) generalized the relationship between mean annual flood ($\bar{Q}$) and the flood of a given return period (Q_T) for each of the defined regions shown in Figure 7.27. The factor by which the mean annual

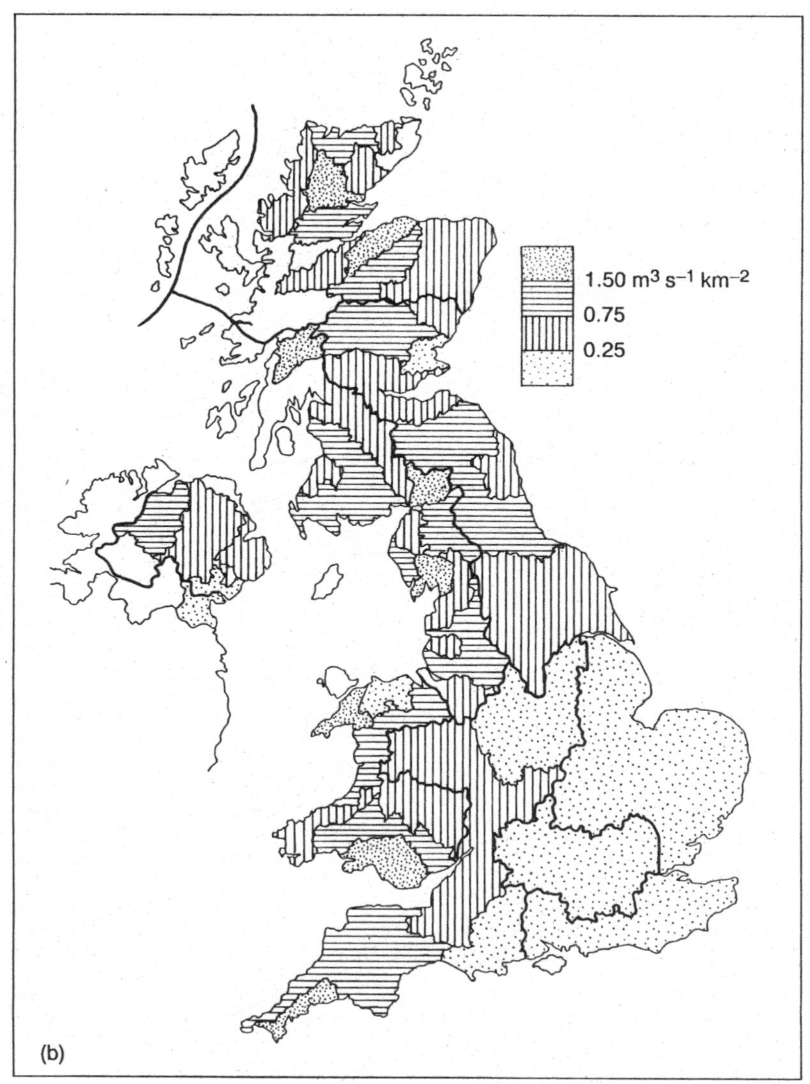

flood value is multiplied to obtain Q_T for selected return periods is set out in Table 7.1. Thus Figure 7.27 and Table 7.1 may be used in conjunction to obtain approximate values of floods having those specified return periods. Subsequent analyses of European data (IH, 1987) confirmed that, in areas having the same flood-producing mechanism, it is possible to 'pool' or average flood frequency curves so as to produce inter- as well as intra-national comparisons (Figure 7.28). The *Flood Estimation Handbook*, which is due to succeed the *Flood Studies Report* in the UK, adopts a more sophisticated approach in relating flood hydrology to

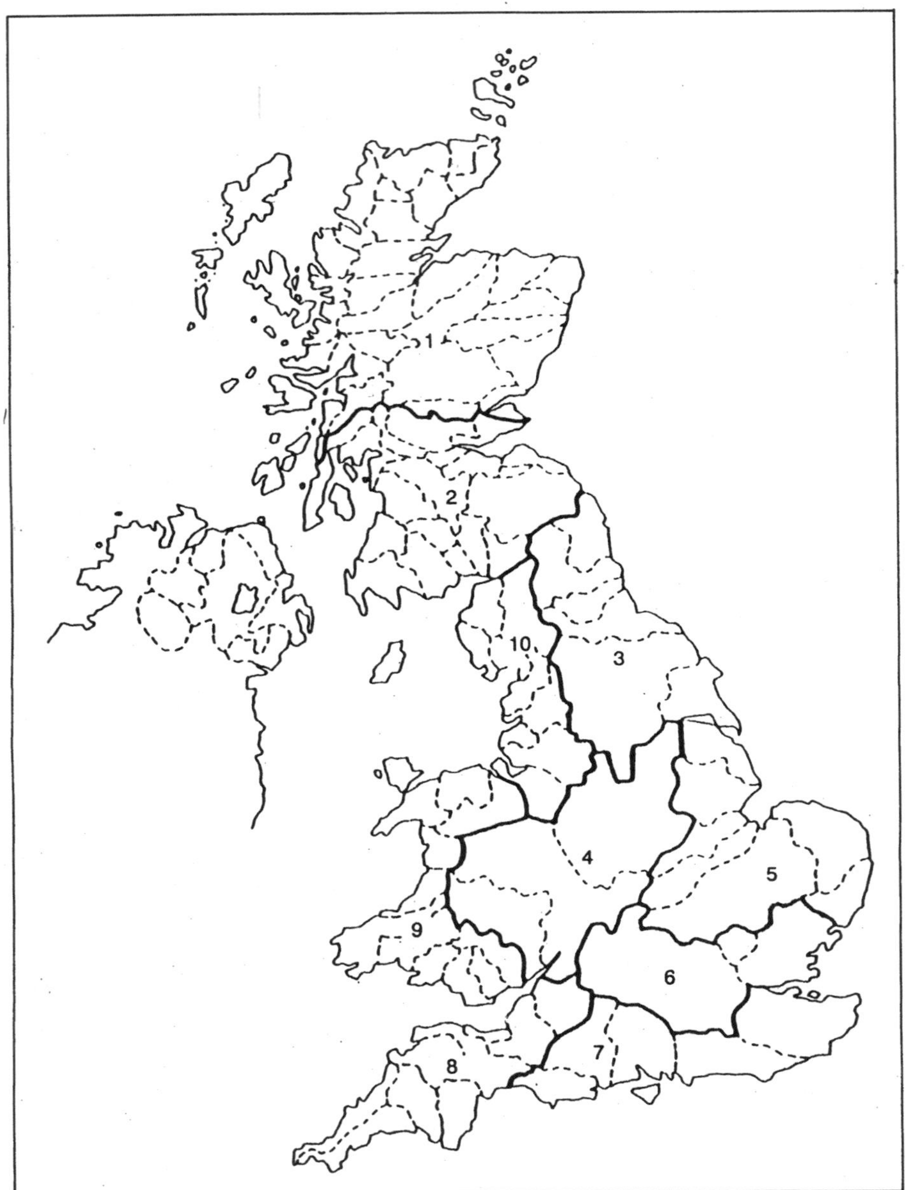

Figure 7.27 Regions defined in the UK *Flood Studies Report* (NERC, 1975).

catchment characteristics. This is achieved largely by using indicators such as stream length, stream density and slope gradient which can be derived from digital terrain models and other increasingly accessible digitized and gridded data which were not available at the time of the earlier report.

Table 7.1 Mean annual flood multipliers for deriving Q_T for selected return periods (from data in NERC, 1975).

Region	*Return period*						
	2	*5*	*10*	*25*	*50*	*100*	*200*
1	0.90	1.20	1.45	1.81	2.12	2.48	2.89
2	0.91	1.11	1.42	1.81	2.17	2.63	3.18
3	0.94	1.25	1.45	1.70	1.90	2.08	2.27
4	0.89	1.23	1.49	1.87	2.20	2.57	2.98
5	0.89	1.29	1.65	2.25	2.83	3.56	4.46
6/7	0.88	1.28	1.62	2.14	2.62	3.19	3.86
8	0.88	1.23	1.49	1.84	2.12	2.42	2.74
9	0.93	1.21	1.42	1.71	1.94	2.18	2.45
10	0.93	1.19	1.38	1.64	1.85	2.08	2.32
Great Britain	0.89	1.22	1.48	1.88	2.22	2.61	3.06
Ireland	0.95	1.20	1.37	1.60	1.77	1.96	2.14

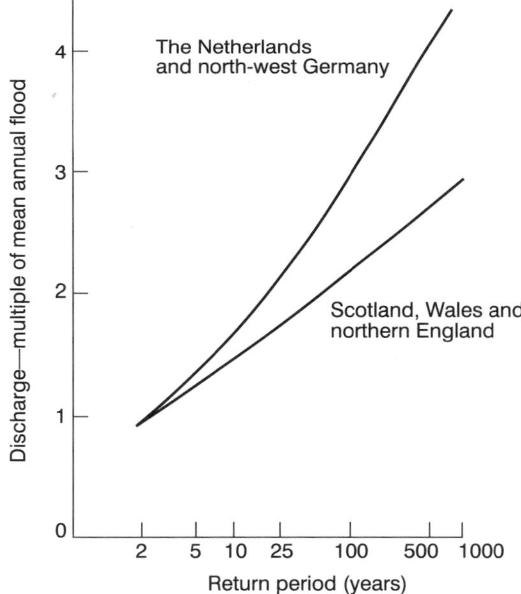

Figure 7.28 Average flood frequency curves for selected European areas (from an original diagram in IH, 1987).

7.8.2 *Low flows*

At the other extreme, the problems posed by low flows, although different, are equally varied and severe. Low flows not only reduce the amount of water available for supply but also lead to water quality degradation, as the diluting and reaerating capability of streams and rivers is reduced. This, in turn, leads to the aesthetic degradation of the affected channel reach. In contrast to flood flows, however, hydrologists were slow to develop adequate methods for estimating low-flow characteristics or even to standardize low-flow definitions.

Low-flow definitions

There is, for example, no low-flow equivalent of the Probable Maximum Flood. The probable *minimum* flow that can be experienced is obviously zero but in most small catchments and many larger ones (cf. the Darling River draining an area of 570 000 km^2 at Menindee) zero flows occur frequently, and it is then the *frequency* of zero flows that is the more useful index of low-flow conditions. In virtually all rivers, of course, the problems associated with low flows are manifest long before a flow of zero is attained, and are intensified as the duration of a given low-flow discharge is prolonged. Hydrologists are therefore concerned primarily with defining selected critical low-flow discharges and with identifying the duration and frequency of spells of low flow.

Pirt and Douglas (1982) noted several flow conditions that can be defined as 'low'. One is the lowest flow ever experienced, a condition that was closely approached over much of southern and central England in the late summer of 1976 and again on several occasions between 1988 and 1992. A more usual measure, however, is the 95 per cent exceedance flow (Q95), i.e. the flow that plots at the 95 per cent position on a flow-duration curve and is therefore exceeded 95 per cent of the time or on average on all but 18 days of the year.

In contrast to high flows, low flows occupy the lower part of a continuous or quasi-continuous storage depletion curve for a river basin (for example Demuth and Schreiber, 1994; Moore, 1997). Low flows are, therefore, prolonged rather than instantaneous and the daily flow interval is less appropriate than a period flow interval of, say, seven days or ten days. Thus in the Institute of Hydrology's *Low Flow Studies Report* (IH, 1980) equations were derived for estimating Q95(10), i.e. the 95 percentile 10-day flow.

Alternative flow *frequency* characteristics may be used rather than flow-duration characteristics to define low-flow conditions. The *Low Flow Studies Report* used the mean annual minimum 10-day flow, MAM(10), although an older and apparently more useful measure (Pirt and Douglas, 1982; Pirt and Simpson, 1982) is the condition defined by Hindley (1973) as Dry Weather Flow (DWF), i.e. the mean annual minimum 7-day flow. This is approximately the driest week in the average summer and is exceeded from 89 to 93 per cent of the time depending on the type of catchment (Pirt and Douglas, 1982). DWF has a return period of 2.33 years (Q7, 2.33) but in the USA it is the 10-year return period 7-day flow (Q7, 10) which is the most widely used index of low flow (ASCE-TASK, 1980). Some analyses have been based on very extreme flows, cf. the 7-day 20-year flow (Q7, 20), but few gauging stations are designed to measure extreme low flows and so recorded data may be subject to large measurement errors (Pirt, 1983). Loganathan *et al.* (1985) assessed various frequency analysis methods as applied to low-flow data for streams in Virginia, USA, and Gottschalk *et al.* (1997) described an interesting approach in which recession analysis was used to derive low-flow distribution functions.

Residual flow diagrams

In comparison with flood flows, low flows may be substantially affected by human activity, especially the discharge of effluents into stream channels and the abstraction of water from stream channels for supply purposes. In both cases the added or extracted water may represent a very large percentage of the natural flow and must therefore be taken into account if analyses of low-flow data are to shed light on natural low-flow processes. Lloyd (1968) suggested the residual flow diagram as a simple graphical method of accounting for artificial interference with low flows, and the technique was subsequently also advocated by Pirt (Pirt and Douglas, 1982; Pirt, 1983).

A residual flow diagram (RFD) separates streamflow at any point into its natural and artificial components. In Figure 7.29, for example, distance downstream is shown on the vertical axis and flow on the horizontal axis. Natural runoff is shown to the left of the vertical axis and the artificial flow component to the right, so that total flow is represented by the distance between the natural and artificial lines, for example $A'A''$. If the artificial line crosses the central axis this indicates that total flow at that point is less than the natural flow would have been in the absence of human interference. Thus in the hypothetical example shown in Figure 7.29 the river consists of natural flow only in reaches 1 and 2, with a natural tributary entering in reach 2. The first artificial component is shown in reach 3, representing perhaps industrial effluent or compensation water from a reservoir. In reach 4 abstraction of water for supply depletes the total flow and reduces natural flow below its 'untouched' level. A major tributary enters in reach 5 and since it contains both natural and artificial flow components both sides of the RFD are affected. Another tributary enters in reach 6, but in this case abstraction has taken place from the tributary as indicated by the reduced artificial component, and finally in reach 7 there is a large increase in artificial flow in the main stream.

A residual flow diagram can be constructed for any selected flow condition, for example Q7, 2.33 or Q7, 10, and then used as the basis for investigating low-flow hydrology, particularly in terms of catchment controls. For example, the portion to the left of the central axis represents only the natural runoff of the main stream and its tributaries. It is, therefore, possible to divide the net addition to natural runoff between any two points on the main stream by the contributing catchment area and so calculate the natural runoff yield per unit area or natural runoff coefficient. This was done for contributing subcatchments within the Severn–Trent basin by Pirt and Simpson (1982) and the coefficients mapped as in Figure 7.30. Using relevant geological and topographic information it was then possible to interpolate runoff coefficients for ungauged catchments and to provide a first

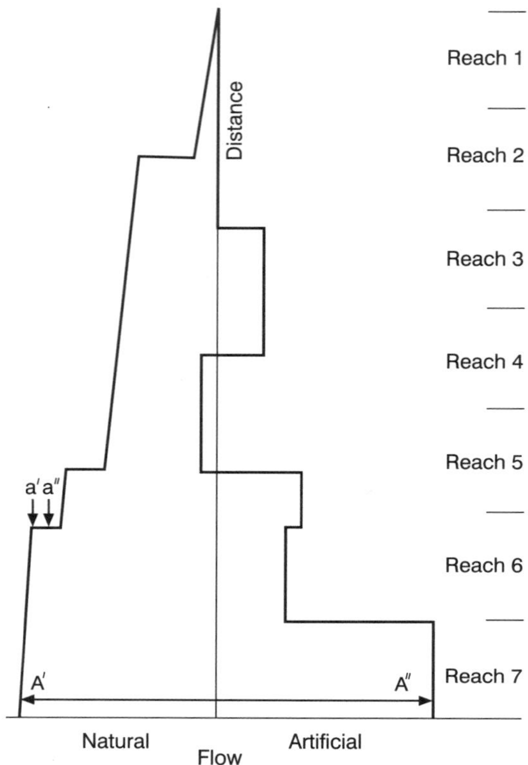

Figure 7.29 A simplified residual flow diagram (from an original diagram by Pirt, 1983).

estimate of Q7, 2.33 for any ungauged point solely from a knowledge of catchment area.

Factors affecting low flows

In broad terms low flows are determined by the balance between precipitation and evaporation and are therefore particularly susceptible to persistence when this results in the bunching of a sequence of dry years. Within a drainage basin experiencing essentially uniform climatological conditions, however, such as that of the Trent shown in Figure 7.30, other more local or catchment controls play a significant role in determining the detailed pattern of low-flow variation. Inevitably, since low flows comprise baseflow, subsurface factors such as soil and geology are likely to play an important part. For example, Figure 7.31 shows the dimensionless annual minimum series for two catchments. The strong control of geology is clearly identified, with groundwater discharge in the chalk catchment sustaining low flows even in extreme droughts, whereas low flows

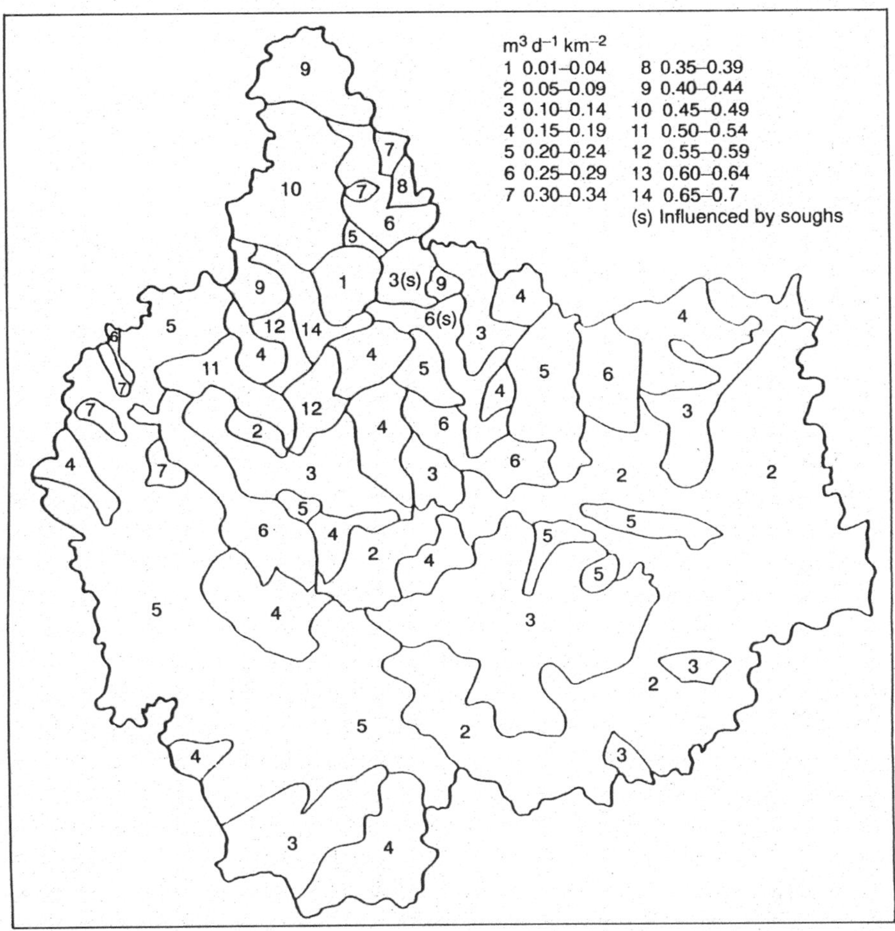

Figure 7.30 Runoff coefficients for the dry weather flow condition in the Trent basin, UK (from an original diagram by Pirt, 1983).

from the clay catchment are at very low rates throughout the range of flow magnitudes. A similar contrast is shown by the flow-duration curves in Figure 7.32, which show that for a given geology the steepness of the curves is associated with soil winter rainfall acceptance potential. Pirt and Douglas (1982) and Pirt and Simpson (1982) developed methods for extrapolating the RFD/runoff coefficient analysis, discussed in the preceding subsection, in order to quantify geological influences on low flows.

It was acknowledged that although RFD and runoff coefficient maps relate to only one specified flow condition, for example Q7, 2.33, many users would prefer to compare the data to another statistic, for example Q7, 10 or Q7, 20. This was

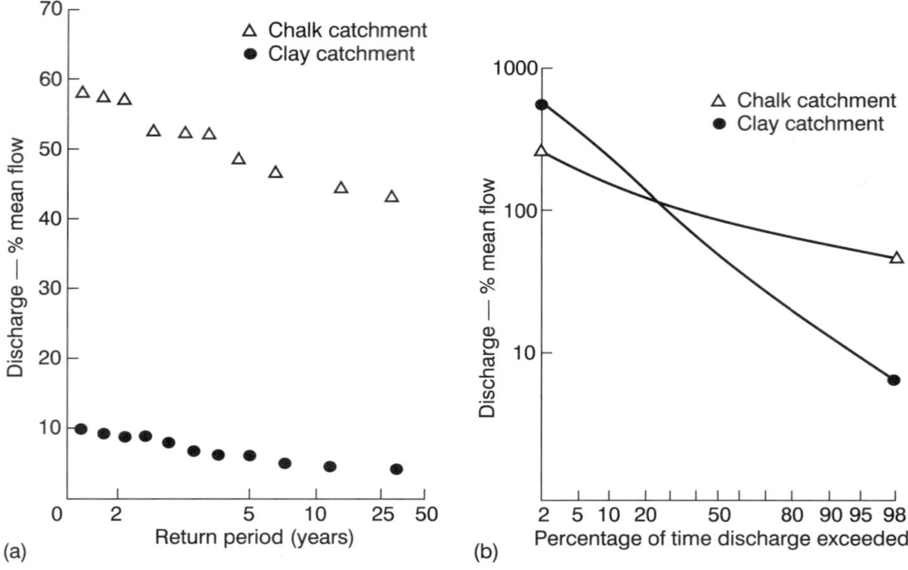

Figure 7.31 (*a*) Annual minimum series; and (*b*) flow duration curves for clay and chalk catchments (from original diagrams in IH, 1987).

done in two ways. In the first approach a family of naturalized flow-duration curves were normalized by dividing by area (km^2) and mean annual effective rainfall (m), and the variations between them were found to depend almost entirely on catchment geology and soil. The various curves were then averaged to provide a set of master curves relating to specific geological and soil types using the NERC *Flood Studies Report* soil index (NERC, 1975), as in Figure 7.32 for Carboniferous rocks. These can then be used to derive flow-duration curves for ungauged catchments for which area, effective rainfall, geology and soil type are known, by selecting the appropriate master curve, multiplying a number of points on the curve by effective precipitation and catchment area, and finally adjusting for any artificial effects.

In the second approach multiple regression analysis of eight catchment variables produced an equation to predict the difference (Q_{diff}) between the discharge per unit area for Q7, 2.33 and that for Q7, 20, and thus the slope of the normalized flow-frequency curve. Flow-frequency curves for ungauged catchments can then be developed from the map of runoff coefficients (Figure 7.30) by multiplying the relevant runoff coefficients by catchment area. This gives the 2.33-year flow which is then plotted on Gumbel probability paper. Q_{diff} is calculated using the equation referred to above and is subtracted from the 2.33 flow value to give the value of Q7, 20 which is plotted at the 0.95 probability position on the Gumbel paper. A straight line drawn through the two points then permits either the interpolation of 7-day flows having intermediate return periods

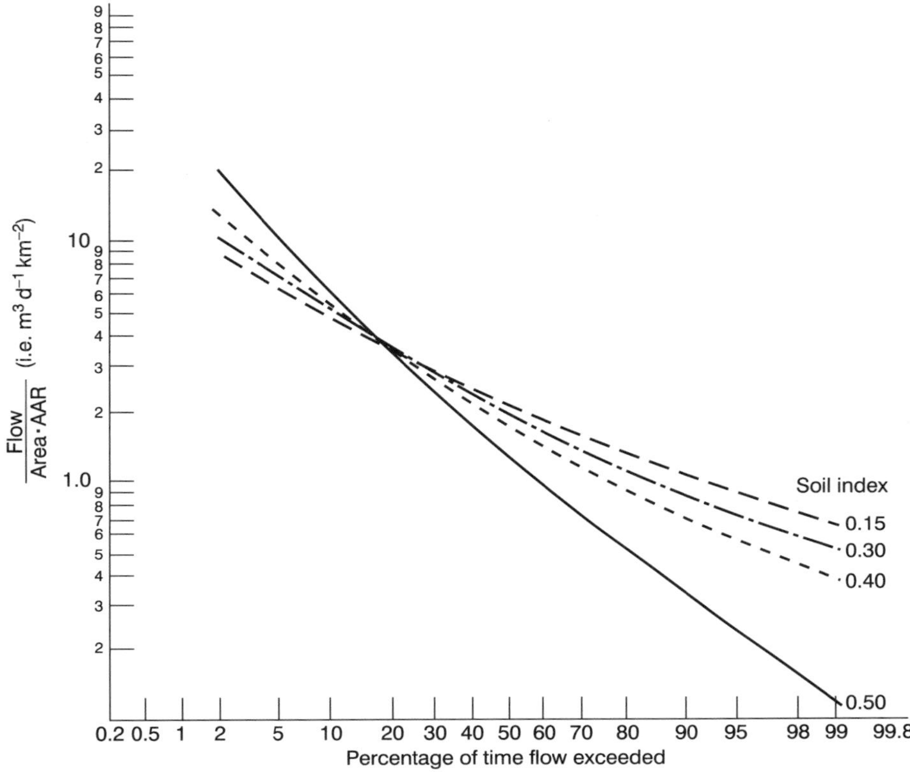

Figure 7.32 A set of normalized flow duration curves for Carboniferous rocks. See text for explanation (from an original diagram by Pirt, 1983).

or extrapolation to higher return periods. Examples of such plots for the Henmore Brook at Ashbourne and the River Sence at Blaby are shown in Figure 7.33, together with comparative plots derived from measured data. The results indicate that good estimates of flow-frequency curves can be obtained in this way for ungauged sites provided that maps of DWF runoff coefficients are available (Pirt and Simpson, 1982).

An alternative approach to the study of the low-flow characteristics of British rivers was the development of the baseflow index (BFI) (for example Beran and Gustard, 1977). BFI is an index of hydrograph behaviour which is related to catchment geology, so that a high BFI (close to 1) reflects a baseflow-dominated regime, while a low BFI indicates a 'flashy' regime dominated by quickflow. A stream network map of BFI for Scotland, at a scale of 1 : 62 500, was derived to estimate low-flow statistics at ungauged sites (IH, 1985). Figure 7.34 shows low-flow regions in the UK based on estimates of Q95(10) determined from values of BFI and either annual average precipitation (SAAR) or main stream length (L)

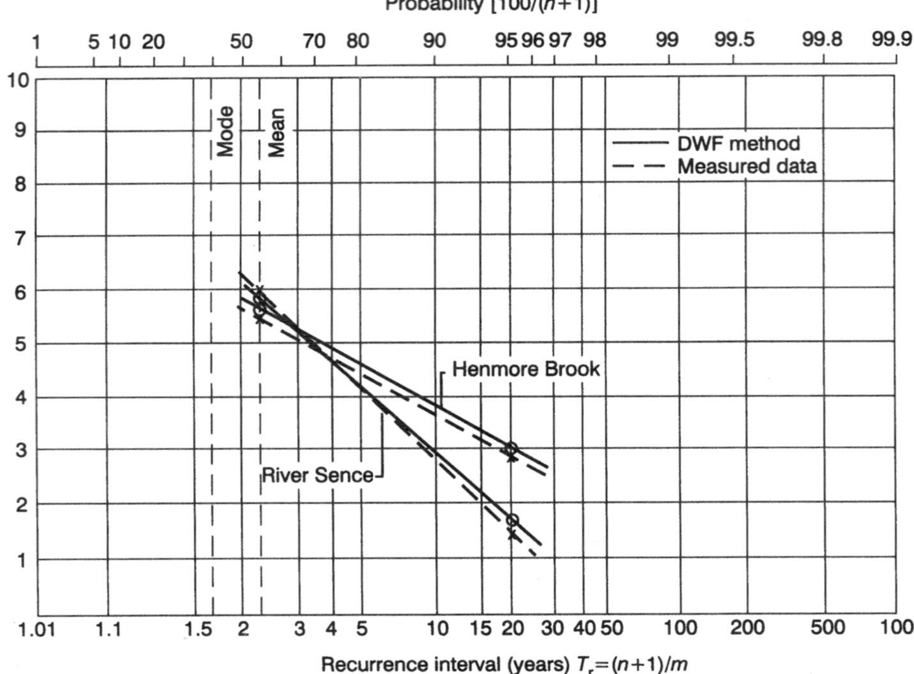

Figure 7.33 Comparisons of estimated and observed flow-frequency curves for gauging stations at Ashbourne and Blaby (based on data in Pirt, 1983).

(IH, 1980). Relationships between soil type and low-flow parameters, such as BFI and MAM (10), were discussed for the UK and continental Europe by Gustard *et al.* (1992) and Gustard and Irving (1994).

Patterns of low flow in Britain

The running means of runoff for England and Wales (Figure 7.22) illustrate a variability that, although modest in comparison with that of runoff in many semi-arid areas, nevertheless reflects an alternation of lengthy periods of high and low flow. In recent times, the most significant periods of below-average runoff occurred for about 25 years commencing around 1885 and for a shorter duration in the 1930s and 1940s. Since then periods of low flow have been less sustained but sometimes quite dramatic in their impact.

The 1975–76 drought, in particular, which provided a major stimulus to low-flow studies (for example Doornkamp *et al.*, 1980; IH, 1980), resulted in runoff values less than 40 per cent of the long-term mean over much of southern England (Figure 7.35(a)). Another significant drought event occurred in the UK in 1984 (Harrison, 1985; Marsh and Lees, 1985), despite rainfall in the 1980s being higher than for any decade since 1900. Then, during the period 1988–92,

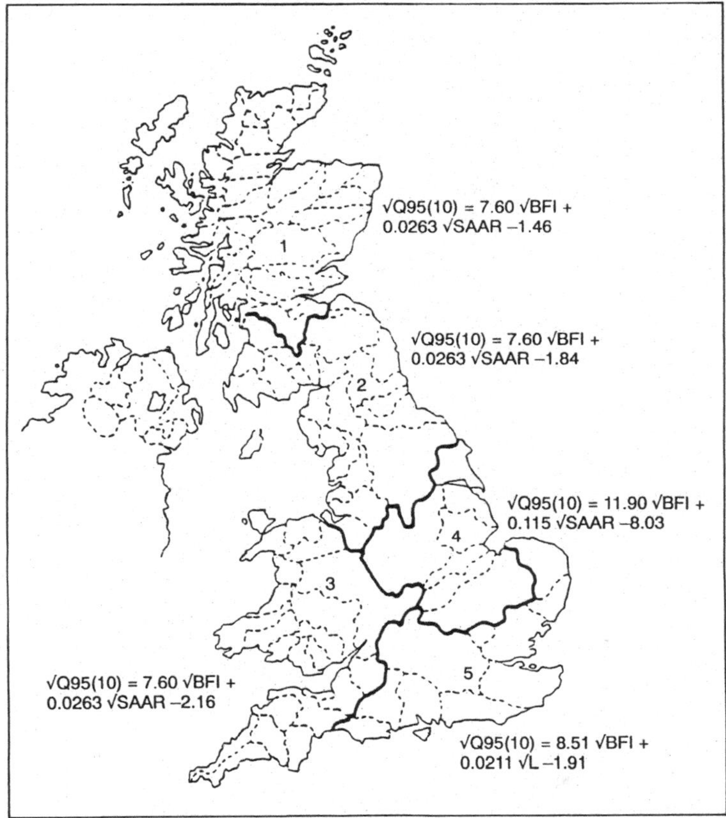

Figure 7.34 Low-flow regions as defined by IH (1980).

there occurred a drought that was, in places, as severe as the 1975–76 event (Figure 7.35(b)). Certainly, the two-year period beginning in July 1990 produced runoff totals in parts of lowland England that were lower than any previously registered (Marsh *et al.*, 1994). The 1988–92 drought also affected large areas of continental Europe, and by late 1990 more than 3000 km of rivers had dried up in southern France and low flows were causing irrigation problems from Hungary to Spain.

7.9 Runoff from snow-covered areas

Most of the land surface polewards of 40° of latitude in the northern hemisphere has a significant seasonal snow cover in most years. Polewards of 50° of latitude seasonal snow cover tends to occur every year and over large areas the snow cover is permanent. Elsewhere, extensive snow cover is associated largely with high-altitude areas. Runoff from permanently or seasonally snow-covered areas differs from rainfall-driven runoff in several important respects. For example, the low-

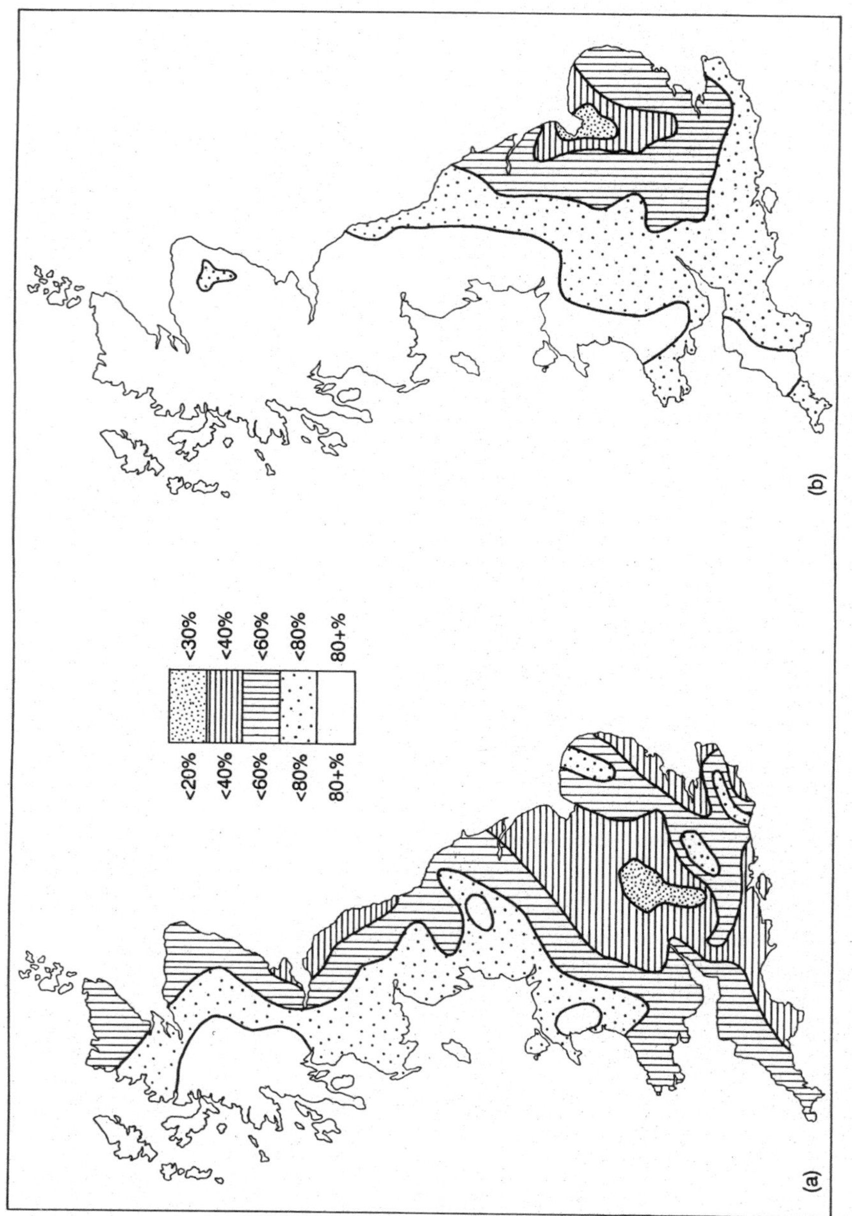

Figure 7.35 Runoff in Britain expressed as a percentage of the long-term average: (*a*) 1975–76 (from an original diagram in Ward, 1981); and (*b*) Sep. 1990–Aug. 1992 (from an original diagram in Marsh *et al.*, 1994).

flow period often coincides with the period of maximum precipitation and high flow is associated with the usually drier period of maximum melt. Furthermore, streamflow from a snow-covered catchment reflects not only the complex interaction of factors discussed earlier but also the effects of additional factors, of which the most important are (*a*) the water equivalent of the snowpack, i.e. how much water would be released if the snowpack melted completely; (*b*) the rate of melting; and (*c*) the physical characteristics of the snowpack, for example ice-banding, differential compaction, ripeness, etc.

The spatial variation of each of these factors, together with the spatial variability both of melt-season rain falling upon the snowpack and also of sub-snowpack terrain conditions, combine to create an enormously complex runoff system which may look deceptively simple when viewed from an aircraft or a space satellite. Despite continued advances in instrumentation and remote sensing, as well as in our understanding of the physics of snowmelt, there remain considerable uncertainties about the estimation of snowpack water equivalent, the quantification of energy exchanges and snowmelt in the snowpack, and the relationship between snowpack properties and water movement.

7.9.1 Snowpack water equivalent

One of the major challenges in snow hydrology is the estimation of snowpack water equivalent and its spatial variation within a catchment area. A fundamental problem is that of adequate sampling, since snowpacks tend to exhibit much more spatial variability than an equivalent fall of rain because of the differential effects of drifting, compaction and partial melt (for example Barry, 1983; Ferguson, 1985; Rango, 1985) (see also Section 2.7.2). Even in areas of modest snowfall, temporal and spatial variations may be significant. For example, in the Cairngorms, Scotland, maximum water equivalent has been shown to vary from around 50 mm in mild winters to 200 mm in more severe ones and to vary from a few millimetres in one part of a catchment to more than 2000 mm elsewhere (Soulsby *et al.*, 1997).

Traditional methods of measurement, using pressure sensing devices such as snow pillows or metal pressure tanks, although still a valuable source of data, are gradually being replaced by remote sensors and digital terrain models. These are particularly successful in mapping the areal extent of the snowpack over large areas on a periodic, repeating basis (for example Van de Griend and Engman, 1985; Rango *et al.*, 1990). However, areal extent, although a partial indicator of future snowmelt runoff, is less useful than information on the snowpack water equivalent which is a function also of snowpack quality and depth.

Two examples illustrate the nature of the progress which is being made. Kuittinen (1989) estimated water equivalents in Finland by establishing a relationship between snow-free areas and the water equivalent of the remaining snow-covered areas. Satellite imagery was then used to measure snow-free areas. Water equivalent was also inferred from the ratio between gamma emission from bare ground and the emission from snow-covered ground and was checked periodically by field measurement. And Rango and van Katwijk (1990) described a method of estimating snowmelt runoff for a mountain catchment in Colorado, USA. A 'family' of snow-cover depletion curves was developed, which covered a range of areal snow water-equivalent values at the beginning of the melt season in each of three elevation zones. Satellite measurements of snow cover were used to select the appropriate snow-cover depletion curve for the melt season in question. Runoff estimates were updated with weekly observations of actual runoff and air temperature.

7.9.2 Energy exchange and snowmelt

Snowmelt is the result of many different processes which result in a net transfer of heat to the snowpack (see also Section 2.7.3). The principal energy-balance fluxes involved are solar radiation, long-wave radiation (especially at night), sensible heat transfer from the air to the snow by convection and conduction, and latent heat transfer by evaporation and condensation (and occasionally rain) at the snow surface. Conductive heat flow from the ground to the base of the snowpack is of comparatively minor importance, but together with the penetration of short-wave radiation into the top few centimetres of the snowpack and the much deeper penetration of rainfall, it exemplifies the partially distributed nature of snowmelt energy sources. Nevertheless, as Colbeck *et al.* (1979) emphasized, meltwater is predominantly generated at the snowpack surface, and this has been confirmed by sequential density profiles of melting snowpacks.

In forested areas, or other situations where the vegetation cover protrudes through the snowpack, the energy exchange is very much more complex than in the open bare snow situation and many of the relevant components, for example radiative and sensible heat transfer and evaporation, are almost impossible to measure accurately. Even in situations away from the complicating effects of vegetation, energy flux measurements can be made only 'at-a-point'. As a result, estimates of runoff or soil water status involve large-scale extrapolation of these point measurements. A further complication results because snow covers which look alike may produce widely different streamflow contributions from a given energy input because of the amount by which the snowpack temperature falls below the melting point (0°C).

Baseline conditions for snowmelt calculations assume: (*a*) the latent heat of ice is 3.35×10^5 J/kg (80 cal/g); (*b*) the snow is pure ice; and (*c*) the snow temperature is 0°C. Often, however, especially in the winter months, snowpack temperatures are well below 0°C so that initially heat is required to raise the temperature to melting point. Until that temperature is reached no meltwater runoff occurs. On the other hand, during the melt season the snowpack may not only be isothermal at 0°C but may also contain some liquid water in the interstices of the ice matrix up to a water content equivalent to the retention capacity (cf. 'field capacity') of the snowpack, i.e. the snowpack is 'ripe'. Liquid

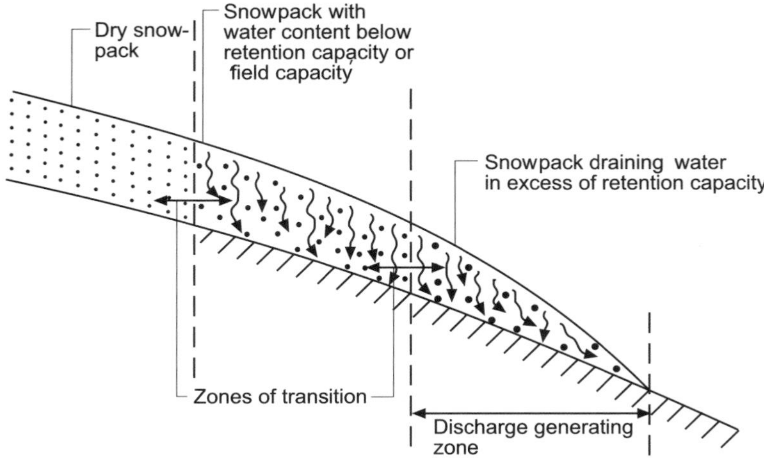

Figure 7.36 Typical distribution of snowpack conditions in a mountainous area (from an original diagram by Van de Griend, 1981).

water in excess of the snowpack's retention capacity drains through the pack as gravity flow.

Figure 7.36 suggests that in mountainous areas these different snowpack conditions are distributed in relation to elevation. In snowpack areas in plains, however, the distribution of ripe and unripe snow is much less predictable. In either situation it will be clear that when a snowpack containing liquid water is melted, the liquid water is also released, resulting in a total outflow from the snowpack which exceeds that derived simply from energy-balance considerations.

It has been suggested that in extreme circumstances snowpack 'collapse' may occur where an ultra-ripe snowpack, comprising a blend of ice matrix, snow and the maximum possible amount of liquid water, is subjected to rapid thaw conditions, for example sudden temperature rise plus heavy warm rainfall. Then the matrix of the snowpack may rupture sending a slush flow or slush avalanche, i.e. a cascade of snow, ice and water downslope to the channel system (for example Washburn, 1980; Hestnes, 1985; Onesti, 1985).

7.9.3 Snowpack properties and water movement

The rate at which meltwater, generated near the surface of a snowpack, can move through the pack to the underlying ground surface and thence to the channel system is greatly affected by the structure and stratification of the snowpack. Most snowpacks develop a layering of less permeable ice strata within the generally more permeable snow matrix. According to Colbeck *et al.* (1979), this layering arises from the sequential nature of snow deposition and/or the preferential retention and refreezing of water in fine-grained layers such as wind crusts. The layers divert the percolating meltwater so that complicated flowpaths develop which not only delay and diffuse the outflow of meltwater but also greatly increase the storage capacity of the snowpack (for example Singh *et al.*, 1997).

During the initial stages of infiltration, if the retention or 'field' capacity of the snowpack is not exceeded, no meltwater runoff occurs at all. Subsequently the downward movement of the wetting front into a naturally stratified snowpack is accompanied by delays and ponding at the ice layers and the development of flow fingers which eventually penetrate to the base of the snowpack (Wankiewicz, 1978; Colbeck, 1975, 1979; Marsh and Woo, 1984, 1985). These flow fingers, which can also be caused by the impact of intense rain on the snow surface (Singh *et al.*, 1997), continue to act as zones of higher permeability after snowpack ripening has occurred. Thus, from the early stages of melting and even where a large portion of the snowpack remains 'unripe', rapid flowpaths for meltwater may be opened up.

Similarly, beneath the snowpack, the initial routing of meltwater early in the melt season is through a saturated layer overlying the soil surface. McNamara *et al.* (1998) described the way in which such surface-saturated areas serve as source areas for quickflow in small catchments in northern Alaska. As meltwater channels at the base of the snowpack develop further, a more rapid drainage of the snowpack occurs because the flowpath length for meltwater has been greatly reduced. Colbeck *et al.* (1979) observed that as a result of flow finger development through the pack and melt channel development beneath the pack, a snow-covered catchment '... makes a gradual transition from snow-controlled to terrain-controlled water movement'. The runoff process in a snow-covered catchment thus often involves a gradual transition from snow-controlled water movement to terrain-controlled water movement (Colbeck *et al.*, 1979) as flow fingers gradually develop through the pack and as meltwater channels and areas of surface saturation develop at the base of the pack.

7.9.4 Runoff from glacierized areas

In high mountain areas, a further meltwater dimension to runoff variations is contributed by the presence of glaciers, whose hydrological importance is widely acknowledged (for example IAHS, 1973, 1975, 1982; Young, 1985; Gurnell and Clark, 1987). As in snow-covered areas, the hydrology of glacierized basins is, to a large extent, thermally controlled. The interaction between variations in energy supply and variations in precipitation amounts and type (rain or snow) leads to variations either in the production of meltwater or in the storage of ice and snow within the drainage basin. Changes in the balance between meltwater production and storage from year to year mean that annual total runoff may be greater than or less than annual precipitation. In other words, glacierized basins, like those with permanent snow covers, may experience changes in snow and ice storage between years.

As well as snow and ice storage, however, *liquid* water may be stored within glaciers and in marginal lakes alongside them. Furthermore, the changing morphology of the glacier ice matrix within which water flows and is stored and the dynamic interaction between the glacier ice and the liquid water stored within it, complicate further the variations of runoff from glacierized basins. Runoff from such areas is also characterized by outburst floods, created by the sudden release of large quantities of water stored within, under or alongside glaciers.

Characteristics of glacier runoff

Glacier runoff is thus characterized by two main components, i.e. a *periodic*, thermally driven meltwater regime, which produces distinctive diurnal and seasonal variations of flow, and an *aperiodic* component, which results from the occurrence of either extreme meteorological events or sudden releases of water from the glacial drainage system. In addition, *long-term* runoff variations may reflect aspects of climatic variation and climatic change.

Figure 7.37 shows the expected diurnal cycle of meltwater runoff. It also illustrates, however, that during the first part of the melt season there is an increasing 'baseflow' component of runoff upon which this diurnal cycle is superimposed. Rothlisberger and Lang (1987) suggested that baseflow from glacierized basins comprises groundwater runoff, runoff from water-filled cavities within the ice, runoff from the melt-fed firn water aquifer in the accumulation area of the glacier and regular drainage from lakes. They further suggested that the diurnal 'quickflow' component whose variation is superimposed upon that of baseflow, consists of the rapidly draining component of that day's meltwater, i.e. meltwater draining supra- and sub-glacially from the lowest parts of the basin and meltwater from the snow-free part of the glacier which drains via short conveyances to the main subglacial conduits.

The *seasonal variation* of runoff defines a classically simple regime (see Section 7.6). An increase of discharge during the summer broadly reflects the seasonal increase of available melt energy, although the detailed timing of flow variations also reflects the progressive development of the glacier drainage system during the ablation season and the build-up of baseflow from storage, as described above.

Aperiodic variations of runoff from glacierized basins are exemplified by unusually high flood discharges resulting from (*a*) periods of very rapid melt over a week or more, which permit high rates of baseflow as well as of quickflow, (*b*) the occurrence of extreme high-intensity rainfall, especially late in the afternoon when meltwater runoff is at a maximum, or (*c*) sudden releases of water ('jökulhlaup' is the Icelandic term) which has either been held in storage within the glacier, or as surface lakes on or adjacent to the ice, or has been dammed back by ice in tributary valleys. In some cases the flood outburst appears to be triggered when meltwater behind the glacial dam reaches a critical elevation. Then, if meltwater generation is similar from season to season,

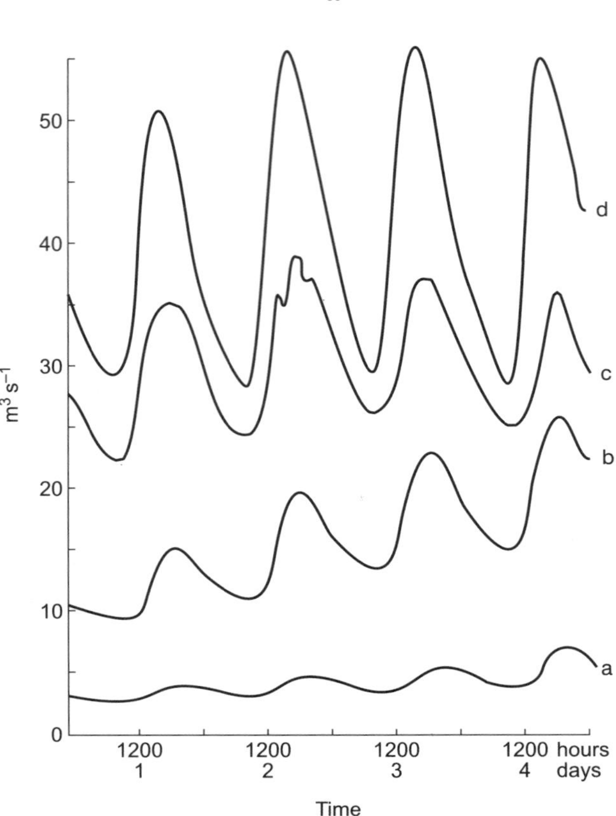

Figure 7.37 The runoff hydrograph of a glacierized basin, the Matter-Vispa, during four periods in 1959: (*a*) 17–20 May, (*b*) 14–17 June, (*c*) 23–26 June and (*d*) 19–22 July (from an original diagram by Elliston, 1973).

jökulhlaup recurrence may take on a quasi-periodic annual or biennial pattern which may be so regular that its date can be predicted (for example Bezinge, 1987; Konovalov, 1990). Glacier outburst floods are a seasonal characteristic of most high mountain regions. In the European Alps it has been found that 95 per cent of them occur from June through September (Tufnell, 1984).

Finally, *long-term variations* of glacier runoff, which result mainly from long-term changes of climate, are an amalgam of conflicting influences. Periods of persistently warmer summer weather result in increased ablation and high runoff values, whereas a series of cool summers favours increased storage and low runoff. However, continued ice removal causes shrinkage of the lower sections of glaciers, and since these are the zones of highest melt rate, their progressive disappearance results in a corresponding loss of potential for meltwater yield (Rothlisberger and Lang, 1987). Martinec and Rango (1989) modelled the influence of global warming in mountainous areas in Canada, the USA and Switzerland and suggested that the main effects on peak flows would come from earlier melting in the spring. Such melting would occur when runoff losses were smaller and would result in an increased seasonal runoff volume of the order of 10 per cent. With an air temperature increase of 2°C, modelled summer flood peaks in the Himalaya of central Nepal more than double if the glacier-covered area remains constant, and increase by about 30 per cent if there is a concomitant reduction in the glacier-covered area (Fukushima *et al.*, 1991).

Review Problems and Exercises

7.1 Describe the various processes which generate streamflow and the circumstances in which one or another of them may become dominant.

7.2 Explain the difference between 'infiltration–excess' overland flow and 'saturation' overland flow.

7.3 Outline the role of the following in the generation of quickflow: convergence; macropores; throughflow; groundwater ridge.

7.4 With reference to Figures 7.11–7.13, discuss whether hydrograph separation is a valid exercise.

7.5 To what extent are there distinctive runoff-producing conditions in semi-arid and tropical rainforest areas?

7.6 Define the flow duration curve and explain what information it may yield on drainage basin characteristics.

7.7 In the light of growing information about climate variability and climate change, discuss the following concepts: river regimes; mean annual flow; the 100-year flood.

7.8 Define the following terms: annual maximum series; partial duration series; return period; dry weather flow; residual flow diagram.

7.9 Outline the main causes of river floods.

7.10 Discuss the influences of geology and climate on the generation of low-flow conditions.

7.11 Compare the movement of water through a snowpack and through a soil profile.

7.12 Explain what is meant by the following: water equivalent of a snowpack; snowpack energy balance; a 'ripe' snowpack; glacier runoff.

CHAPTER EIGHT

Water quality

8.1 Introduction and definitions

The preceding chapters in this book deal with the storages and fluxes of the substance 'water' through the hydrological cycle, but little mention is made of the nature of the water. Indeed, except in specific areas where soil erosion is severe, or where salinization occurs, it is only comparatively recently that hydrologists have paid much attention to the characteristics of water (Hem, 1985). There is now, however, a growing awareness among hydrologists of the importance of *water quality*, including both *chemical* characteristics, due to dissolved material, and *physical* characteristics, such as temperature, taste and suspended solids. Given the increasing usage and pollution of water sources by human activities, it may be argued that the problems of water quality are now often more difficult and demanding than those of water quantity. Water quality research is now one of the most rapidly expanding aspects of hydrology (Andrews and Webb, 1987). In many areas of the world the use of water is limited more by its quality than by its quantity.

Information on, and control of, water quality is of great importance for a wide range of purposes, including water supply and public health, agricultural and industrial uses. Water quality is also important to preserve aquatic habitats for fish and invertebrates, birds and mammals. There is thus a pressing need to monitor and control the ever-increasing human impact on water chemistry through various forms of pollution.

In principle, evaporation provides a source of pure (distilled) water for precipitation, which then becomes increasingly concentrated with dissolved material as it moves through the atmosphere and in subsequent stages of the hydrological cycle as it comes into contact with organic matter, soil and rock material. In fact no waters are free from human influences—even Arctic precipitation contains constituents discharged into the atmosphere. There remains a great deal to be learned about the chemistry of these natural processes, as well as the mechanisms and pathways of solute fluxes. The hydrologist studying the rates and pathways of water movement is thus placed in a unique position to help find solutions to these problems.

This chapter provides a brief overview of general principles and discusses a number of selected aspects of this important area of research; further details can be found in specialist books (for example Stumm and Morgan, 1996). Before turning to the water quality processes at different stages of the hydrological cycle, the properties of water and the nature of chemical reactions are reviewed.

8.1.1 Properties of water

Water occupies a central role in the transport of chemicals around the surface of our planet. Although its appearance is bland and pure water is almost colourless, tasteless and odourless, it has certain properties that make it unique. Water is a *chemical compound* of two commonly occurring *elements*, hydrogen (H) and oxygen (O), but differs in behaviour from most other compounds to such an extent that it has been called a 'maverick' compound (Leopold and Davis, 1970). One of the most unusual characteristics is that under normal climatic conditions it is commonly found in all three *phases*: solid (ice), liquid and gas (water vapour). Changes of phase (melting and freezing, evaporation and condensation) absorb or release more *latent heat* than most other common substances; water also has an extremely high *specific heat capacity*—the amount of energy required to increase water temperature by one temperature unit. Together these account for why water acts as a cushion against extremes of temperature. Many of its physical and chemical properties are unusual, but of most importance for water quality studies is the fact that virtually all substances are *soluble* to some extent in water. The water *molecule* (H_2O) is strongly attracted to most inorganic substances (including itself). It is, in fact, practically impossible to produce and store absolutely pure water (Lamb, 1985).

The unusual properties of water can be accounted for by its molecular structure. Each water molecule comprises two *atoms* of hydrogen attached to one oxygen atom by a very strong and stable mechanism, involving sharing a pair of electrons, known as a *covalent bond*. The two hydrogen atoms are not on diametrically opposite sides of the oxygen atom but at an angle of 105° apart (Figure 8.1(a)). This produces a bipolar molecule, equivalent in effect to a bar magnet, with an unbalanced distribution of *electrical charge*: the oxygen atom on one side of the molecule has a negative charge while the side with the two hydrogen atoms has a positive charge. As a result of this *electrostatic* effect, adjacent water molecules tend to interact by a process known as *ionic* or *hydrogen bonding* (Figure 8.1(b)). It is the combined strength of these two types of bond that accounts for the unusually large latent and specific heat capacity of water. It is also responsible for water's cohesive nature and large surface tension which enables it to 'wet' surfaces and move through materials such as soils and plant stems by capillarity.

These properties account for the solubility of many materials in water. The atoms in many substances are held together not by strong covalent bonds but by weaker electrostatic attraction. These bonds may be weakened further by the

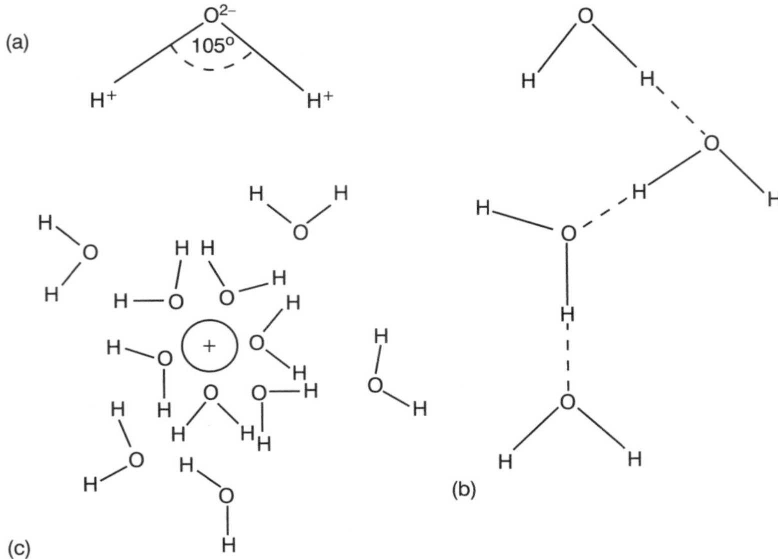

Figure 8.1 Structure of water: (*a*) water molecule comprising one oxygen atom and two hydrogen atoms (protons); (*b*) hydrogen bonding between molecules; (*c*) hydration 'shell' of water molecules surrounding a cation in solution.

bipolar water molecules which act to cancel out some of the electrostatic attraction and enable the atoms to move apart as separate electrostatically charged atoms or groups called *ions*—positively charged *cations* and negatively charged *anions*. When these ions become surrounded by water molecules and have little direct influence on each other, the substance is said to be *dissolved* (Figure 8.1(c)). The liquid (in this case, water) is called the *solvent* and the dissolved solid is called the *solute*. The mixture of solvent and solute is called a *solution*. This chapter is concerned with *aqueous solutions*, in which water is the solvent. Most inorganic compounds dissociate into ions when they dissolve in water, although there may be some interaction between oppositely charged ions to form *complex ions*. Organic compounds occur in solution as unchanged molecules (Hem, 1985). The powerful solvent action of water is vital for plant and animal life as it provides the medium for the transport of chemicals and nutrients. In that sense it may be considered to be the original 'elixir of life' (Lamb, 1985). However, this same solvent action also works to transport harmful pollutants and toxic substances through the environment.

8.1.2 Water quality characteristics

The notion of 'water quality' comprises consideration of many different factors. Commonly quoted *determinands* include physical characteristics such as colour, temperature, taste and odour, as well as chemical characteristics such as acidity, hardness, and the concentrations of various constituents including nitrates, sulphates and dissolved oxygen and man-made pollutants including pesticides and herbicides. There is no simple measure of the purity of water, and the term 'quality' only has meaning when related to some specific use of water. Thus, the concentration of total dissolved material in raw sewage is similar to that in many groundwater supplies used for drinking water—both are about 99.9 per cent pure water (Tebbutt, 1977)—but they are obviously very different in other respects!

There are many texts that detail analytical procedures for the evaluation of different aspects of water quality to which the interested reader may refer (for example DOE, 1972; Clesceri *et al.*, 1989). It is outside the scope of this chapter to deal with them in detail, but a limited number of aspects will be outlined which are of importance for discussions in subsequent sections in which the data and results from the completed analyses are discussed. For many purposes it is not the total amount of a particular element that may be of interest but the chemical form in which it occurs. Thus, for example, nitrogen may occur in a number of *species*, including organic nitrogen, ammonia (NH_3), nitrite (NO_2) and nitrate (NO_3), and these may have very different effects on the suitability of the water for different uses.

Methods of chemical analysis are available to identify and measure the concentrations of many elements and compounds in water. The most commonly used unit for expressing the concentration of dissolved constituents is as the weight of solute per unit volume of water, for example milligram per litre ($mg\,l^{-1}$). For some purposes the weight of solute per unit weight of solution is used, measured most often as parts per million (p.p.m.). For most practical purposes the two systems yield the same numbers; however, for highly mineralized water with solute concentrations greater than $7000\,mg\,l^{-1}$ a density correction should be used to convert between the two. For the calculation of the masses of substances involved in chemical reactions the concentrations may be expressed in *moles* per litre, where a mole of a substance is its atomic or molecular weight in grams. For thermodynamic calculations, described later, *chemical activities* rather than concentrations are used. A correction factor, or activity coefficient, usually represented as γ_i, is applied to the concentration values to allow for non-ideal behaviour of ions in solution. Its value is unity for ideal conditions; for dilute solutions (less than $50\,mg\,l^{-1}$ of dissolved ions) the coefficient is generally > 0.95, which is similar to the measurement error of concentrations, but at high concentrations (for example $500\,mg\,l^{-1}$) for ions with a large charge, or *valency*, it may be as low as 0.7 (Hem, 1985).

For many purposes it is useful to express chemical species by their *equivalent weight*. This is the molecular weight of the ion dissolved in water, divided by the ionic charge. Concentrations are often expressed in units of milliequivalents per litre ($meq\,l^{-1}$) or as $mg\,l^{-1}$. Table 8.1 gives the chemical formulae of many of the common ions in solution, which are discussed in this chapter, and conversion factors between the different methods of expressing concentration. In any

Table 8.1 Names and formulae of some common chemical species showing their electrical charge (valency), formula weight and conversion factor to equivalent weight units. The concentration ($mg\,l^{-1}$) divided by the final column equivalent weight (formula weight/valency) gives milliequivalents per litre (based on data in Hem, 1985).

Name	*Species*	*Formula weight (approx.)*	$mg\,l^{-1}$ *to* $meq\,l^{-1}$
Aluminium	Al^{3+}	26.9	8.994
Ammonium	NH_4^+	18.0	18.037
Bicarbonate	HCO_3^-	61.0	61.013
Calcium	Ca^{2+}	40.1	20.040
Carbonate	CO_3^{2-}	60.0	30.003
Chloride	Cl^-	35.4	35.448
Hydrogen	H^+	1.0	1.008
Hydroxide	OH^-	17.0	17.007
Iron (ferrous)	Fe^{2+}	55.8	27.925
(ferric)	Fe^{3+}	55.8	18.615
Magnesium	Mg^{2+}	24.3	12.152
Nitrate	NO_3^-	62.0	61.996
Nitrite	NO_2^-	46.0	45.998
Phosphate	PO_4^{3-}	95.0	31.656
Orthophosphate	HPO_4^{2-}	96.0	47.985
	$H_2PO_4^-$	91.0	96.993
Potassium	K^+	39.1	39.093
Silica	SiO_2	60.1	—
Sodium	Na^+	23.0	22.988
Sulphate	SO_4^{2-}	96.1	48.031

solution the overall number of positive and negative electrical charges must be equal to maintain electrical neutrality, i.e. the total $meq\,l^{-1}$ of cations must equal the total $meq\,l^{-1}$ of anions. This requirement of *electroneutrality* is useful for checking the accuracy of the determination of ionic concentrations and for ensuring that all of the significant ionic species in a solution have been accounted for. Some ions, however, such as silica (SiO_2), do not have a charge, and therefore an equivalent weight cannot be computed.

An aspect of water quality which is of great importance, since it affects many chemical reactions, is the *acidity* of the water (Drever, 1988). Whether or not solutes are present in water, some of the water molecules will dissociate into hydrogen (H^+) and hydroxyl (OH^-) ions. Since the resulting concentrations of H^+ ions are very low, they are expressed in terms of the pH, or negative $\log_{10}$ of the H^+ ion activity, i.e.

$$\mathrm{pH} = \log_{10}\frac{1}{[\mathrm{H}^+]} \tag{8.1}$$

The square brackets denote chemical activities in moles per litre. Values of pH less than 7 (10^{-7} moles/litre of H^+ ions) are said to be acidic, while those above 7 are *alkaline*. A pH of 7 at 25°C is said to be *neutral* but as hydrogen ion behaviour is temperature dependent, this value decreases somewhat with increasing temperature. Waters that are uninfluenced by pollution generally have pH values of between 6 and 8.5 (Hem, 1985). This may appear a small variation but it should be remembered that since pH has a logarithmic scale, a change of one unit corresponds to a ten-fold change in H^+ ion concentration.

The term 'acidity' applied to aqueous solutions may also be defined as the ability to react with OH^- ions, and this may be determined by titration with an alkali (Stumm and Morgan, 1996). It is a function of a number of solute species (including, for example, iron) and is not simply related to the H^+ concentration. In contrast, the 'alkalinity' of water (i.e. its ability to react with H^+ ions) can usually be identified with the concentration of CO_3^{2-} and HCO_3^- ions (Hem, 1985). The 'strength' of an acid refers to the extent to which it dissociates in solution.

To understand the chemical processes in natural waters that affect the composition of water and to make quantitative statements about them requires the application of certain fundamental concepts, of which some of the most useful are the principles of chemical thermodynamics.

8.2 Processes controlling the chemical composition of water

Chemical processes in natural waters are principally concerned with reactions in relatively dilute aqueous solutions; these are usually *heterogeneous* systems comprising a liquid phase with either or both a solid and a gaseous phase. Due to the great complexity of natural water systems it is usual to employ simplified models to illustrate the principal regulatory factors controlling the chemical composition of natural waters. Many reactions are *reversible*, being able to proceed in both directions, and in practice a dynamic equilibrium will be established between the two opposing reactions. The behaviour of such reversible reactions may be studied using the principles of *chemical thermodynamics*. This enables the likely direction of a reaction over time to be determined and the final equilibrium solute concentrations in the water to be predicted (Sposito, 1981; Stumm and Morgan, 1996). The final products of an *irreversible* reaction will be determined by the quantities of the reactants available.

The solution of gaseous carbon dioxide in water is a reversible reaction producing carbonic acid (H_2CO_3), and may also form the ions HCO_3^- and CO_3^{2-}:

$$CO_2(g) + H_2O \rightleftharpoons H_2CO_3\,(aq) \tag{8.2}$$

$$\upharpoonleft\!\downharpoonright$$

$$HCO_3^- + H^+ \tag{8.3}$$

$$\upharpoonleft\!\downharpoonright$$

$$CO_3^{2-} + 2H^+ \tag{8.4}$$

The second and third steps produce hydrogen ions (H^+) and will alter the pH of the solution. Letters used in brackets in this chapter indicate the physical state of the substance: g = gaseous, aq = aqueous species occurring in solution as written and c = crystalline solid.

Similarly, a solid may dissolve in water; an example of this is calcite ($CaCO_3$) which occurs in many carbonate rocks:

$$CaCO_3\,(c) + H^+ \rightleftharpoons HCO_3^- + Ca^{2+} \tag{8.5}$$

Depending upon the pH of the water there may be subsequent interactions between the dissolved carbonate species, i.e.

$$HCO_3^- \rightleftharpoons CO_3^{2-} + H^+ \tag{8.6}$$

or

$$HCO_3^- + H^+ \rightleftharpoons H_2CO_3 \tag{8.7}$$

The *equilibrium constant* (K) of a reversible reaction has a constant value for a given combination of reactants and products at a given temperature. Experimentally obtained values at standard temperature (usually 25°C) are available in the chemical literature. Alternatively, the equilibrium constant of a reaction may be calculated from the Gibbs free energy (Drever, 1988), using published values (for example Woods and Garrels, 1987).

The solution of $CaCO_3$ in water may be used to illustrate the use of these principles to give the final equilibrium values of a set of reactants. The equilibrium constant is calculated from the ratio of the activities of the products divided by the activities of the reactants, i.e. for the reaction given in Eq. (8.5),

$$K = \frac{[Ca^{2+}][HCO_3^-]}{[CaCO_3(c)][H^+]} \tag{8.8}$$

where K for this reaction has a published value (Jacobson and Langmuir, 1974) of 81. The activity of a solid (here $CaCO_3$) is taken as unity, so the equation becomes

$$81 = \frac{[Ca^{2+}][HCO_3^-]}{[H^+]} \tag{8.9}$$

Therefore, given measurements of the pH, solution temperature and concentrations of calcium (Ca) and bicarbonate (HCO_3^-) it is possible to say whether the system is in equilibrium. If the quotient is less than the equilibrium constant, K, the water may dissolve more calcite (assuming the solid is present); if it equals K the water is at equilibrium (the concentrations will not change unless outside influences alter, for example temperature); or if it is greater than K the solution is supersaturated and will precipitate calcite. The fact that the final equilibrium condition depends upon the amounts of the reactants and products is known as the law of *mass action* (Schnoor, 1996). It does not provide quantitative

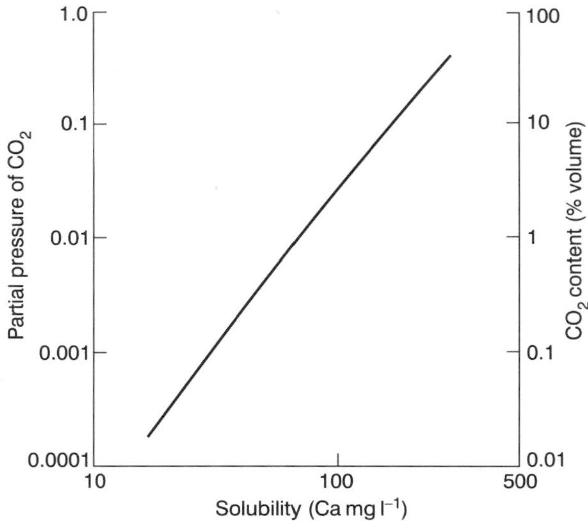

Figure 8.2 Solubility of $CaCO_3$ in water at 25°C (expressed as mg l^{-1} of Ca) for different atmospheric partial pressures of CO_2.

information on the *rate* of a reaction, although in general the further it is from equilibrium the faster it may be.

For a chemical in gaseous form the *partial pressure* is used in such calculations. This is the proportion (by volume) of the particular gas, multiplied by the total pressure (measured in atmospheres).

More complex reactions may be dealt with by combining several equilibrium equations; for example, the dissolution of CO_2 in water produces H^+ and HCO_3^- ions, which are a reactant and product respectively of the dissolution of calcite. Adding the equations for these two reactions (Drever, 1988) enables the solubility of calcite to be expressed as a function of the partial pressure of CO_2 (Figure 8.2).

In practice there are many limitations to the application of thermodynamic procedures in real world situations since, outside the chemistry laboratory, there are likely to be exchanges of energy and reactants with the surrounding environment and equilibrium is not attained. The extent to which natural water systems are in chemical equilibrium is not well known. It is more likely to be attained in aquifer systems, where the rate of movement is relatively slow and residence times are long, than for rapid near-surface flows.

Nevertheless, the principles have proved very useful for indicating the direction and the maximum extent of reactions and are widely adopted. Thermodynamics has been called 'One of the most useful tools in physical chemistry' (Alberty, 1987). A number of computer programs are available to facilitate the calculations of equilibrium conditions (Nordstrum *et al.*, 1979; Truesdell and Jones, 1974).

The rate of different chemical reactions can vary enormously: some reactions are so rapid that equilibrium can be attained almost immediately, while others are so slow that an equilibrium may not be achieved before environmental conditions alter. While thermodynamics deals with equilibrium states, *chemical kinetics* is concerned with the mechanism and rate of operation of chemical changes and with the factors controlling the reaction rate (Stone and Morgan, 1990; Schnoor, 1996). For a reversible reaction the ratio of the forward and backward reaction rates equals the equilibrium constant. Many reversible reactions involve a sequence of intermediate steps, some rapid, some slow. Kinetics can identify the slowest or limiting change that determines the overall rate of the reaction (Drever, 1988; Stumm and Morgan, 1996). Thus kinetics is a more fundamental science than thermodynamics, but due to the great complexities it is much less well understood, and thermodynamic principles are much more generally used.

In addition to these chemical considerations of the thermodynamics and kinetics of reactions, hydrology plays an important role in determining solute composition and concentrations. Apart from snow and ice, and with the exception of some deep groundwater systems, water is generally in continual movement. Its velocity, and hence residence time, will strongly influence whether or not the water attains a chemical equilibrium for a particular reaction. Many reactions are *diffusion controlled* (Alberty, 1987), i.e. their rate constants are controlled by the physical speed at which reactants can diffuse together, rather than by the rate of chemical reaction at a point. Furthermore, the dynamic nature of flow, particularly in the soil zone, means that in periods between storms pore water solute concentrations may increase as minerals are dissolved, but are then flushed out by new waters in the next storm. Thus the flushing frequency and interstorm period may be important variables.

Succeeding sections of this chapter deal in turn with particular aspects of water quality pertaining to different components of the hydrological cycle. These discuss first the composition of precipitation and then the water quality behaviour and changes as the water passes through soils and groundwater, ending with the mixture of chemicals found in rivers and lakes. Both natural and man-made sources are considered, as it may often be difficult or impossible to separate the two. Finally, the relation between water quality and the characteristics of the region or catchment area is discussed.

8.3 Atmospheric solutes

At the moment that a droplet is formed in the atmosphere the water is very pure, but its chemistry will alter rapidly due to conditions both within the cloud and in the atmosphere between the cloud layer and the earth's surface. Particulate material may act as nuclei for raindrop formation (Section 2.1), determining its initial chemical composition, and as the precipitation moves through the atmosphere it will accumulate further particulates by entrainment and various gases in the atmosphere will dissolve in the droplets. The particulates in the atmosphere originate from a wide variety of sources including ash from volcanoes and power stations and wind-blown dust. Of particular importance as cloud condensation nuclei are *aerosols*. These are very small particles (less than 1 μm) which may be liquid or solid material and originate from the land or sea, or from chemical reactions in the atmosphere.

The removal of gases and particulates is a very complex process, which is discussed in detail elsewhere (for example Fowler, 1984). Note, however, that this natural 'scrubbing' of the atmosphere by precipitation is a major means by which the air is purged of materials that might otherwise accumulate to reach dangerous concentrations (Lamb, 1985). The removal of particulates from the atmosphere by heavy rain or snowfall often gives rise to a period of much improved visibility.

The oceans comprise about 70 per cent of the earth's surface, and sea salts are a major source of dissolved material in precipitation. Sea-water droplets become entrained in the atmosphere when waves break and are carried upwards by turbulence, becoming increasingly concentrated as their water evaporates. This may continue until just a solid particle is left, carried in the wind until it is dissolved in rain. The supply of sea salt to the atmosphere varies with meteorological conditions and the state of the sea surface. Skartveit (1982), for example, found a close relation between the concentration of sea salt in the precipitation of a coastal area and the windspeed over the sea.

A number of studies have mapped the concentrations of the dissolved elements in precipitation (Hingston and Gailitis, 1976; Munger and Eisenreich, 1983) and have demonstrated a decline with distance inland from the coast in those elements, including Na^+, Cl^-, Mg^{2+} and K^+, which are derived from marine sources (Figure 8.3(a)). In contrast, the solutes in precipitation falling in inland areas are derived predominantly from terrestrial sources, and include Ca^{2+}, NH_4^+, SO_4^{2-}, HCO_3^- and NO_3^- (Cryer, 1986). These comprise substances from natural sources such as gases from plants and soils and wind-blown dust and, in addition, oxides of sulphur and nitrogen produced by the burning of fossil fuels and from industrial and vehicle emissions. As a consequence of the difference between terrestrial and marine solutes, there are differences in the relative amounts of ions, for example the ionic ratio Na^+/Cl^- increases with distance from the ocean due to Na enhancement from terrestrial sources, for example dust (Figure 8.3(b)). The ratio of Na/Cl concentrations ($mg\,l^{-1}$) in sea water is about 0.56 (or about 0.85 using equivalent weight units).

The relative concentrations of different marine-derived ions in precipitation are not necessarily the same as in sea water due to a number of processes causing *fractionation* and enrichment. Certain substances in the sea, such as iodide, are attracted to the organic microlayer on the ocean surface and are then lost in greater proportions to the atmosphere. Rising bubbles tend to retain ions with larger charge/mass ratios, ejecting them into the atmosphere on bursting at the surface. Sodium, chloride and sulphate, in contrast, occur naturally in similar proportions in precipitation as in the oceans, although concentrations are smaller than in sea water by at least a factor of 1000. The ratio of Cl^- to SO_4^{2-} in rainfall

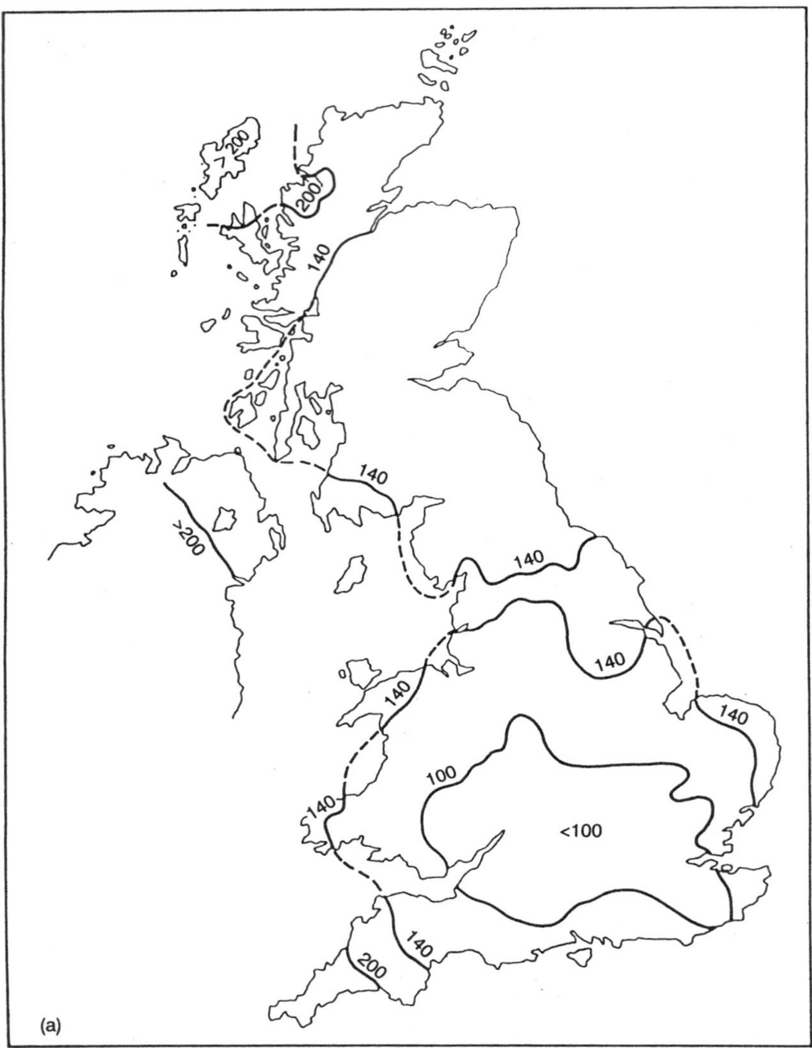

Figure 8.3 (*a*) Mean concentration of chloride ($\mu eq\,l^{-1}$) in precipitation over the UK in 1986 (data from Warren Springs laboratory); (*b*) ratio of Na/Cl concentrations ($mg\,l^{-1}$) in precipitation over the conterminous USA July 1955–June 1956 (redrawn from an original diagram by Junge and Werby, *Journal of Meteorology*, 1958. By permission of the American Meteorological Society).

may be compared to that in the oceans to determine the 'excess' input of sulphate to the atmosphere (i.e. above that from natural marine sources), assuming that all the Cl^- in a rainwater sample is of the marine origin. Table 8.2 shows data, assembled by Meybeck (1983) from various sources, to compare the chemistry of

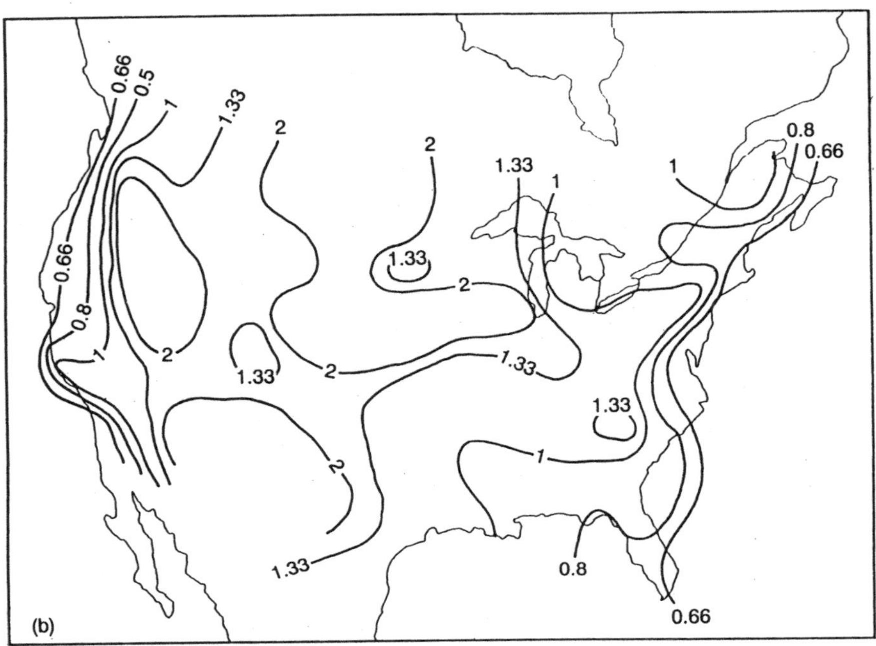

Table 8.2 Comparison of chemical composition of ocean water and precipitation showing the ratio of the concentrations of different ions to that of Cl^- (equivalent weight units), absolute Cl^- concentrations and mean annual precipitation.

	Ca^{2+}	Mg^{2+}	Na^+	K^+	SO_4^{2-}	Cl^- ($mg\,l^{-1}$)	Rain ($mm\,y^{-1}$)
	(ratio to Cl^-)						
a) World							
Ocean water	0.037	0.19	0.85	0.018	0.10	19 300	—
Ocean precipitation	0.160	0.24	0.86	0.021	0.30	4.0	—
b) Inland sites							
French pre-Alps	7.4	0.95	1.15	0.90	4.90	0.6	1380
Arid central Asia	1.1	0.24	0.80	—	0.68	39.0	150
W. Ontario	2.2	0.94	0.83	0.33	3.0	0.35	790
Central Amazonia	0.16	0.17	0.90	0.07	0.74	0.49	2250
c) Heavily polluted							
Rouen, N. France	—	—	0.74	0.13	13.7	5.0	450

ocean water with that of precipitation under different influences. The concentrations of ions (in equivalent weight units) are compared to that of Cl^- as the reference element. While there is enrichment of some species in the oceanic precipitation, major changes are evident for the inland sites (> 100 km from the coast). The calcareous rocks of the French pre-Alps, for example, provide Ca^{2+} and Mg^{2+}, and soil dust in arid areas provides ions such as Ca^{2+} and SO_4^{2-}. The industrial town of Rouen shows the effect of pollution, including SO_2 gas, resulting in very high SO_4^{2-} levels in the rain.

In recent years considerable concern has arisen about the possible effects of the large number of polluting substances emitted into the atmosphere by human activities. These *anthropogenic* materials comprise both particulates and gases, and while many are naturally occurring constituents even in 'unpolluted' atmospheres, some of the substances may be harmful if present in high enough concentrations. Appreciable amounts of pollution in precipitation began to occur in the nineteenth century during the Industrial Revolution. Peat soil profiles near industrial towns in northern England contain widespread accumulations of soot and heavy metals within the layers formed in the last two hundred years. This pollution and the associated gases (which are not retained in the peat record) are thought to have been responsible for major changes in natural vegetation species at that time over extensive areas of the Pennine uplands of Britain (Ferguson and Lee, 1983).

Not surprisingly, early concern about atmospheric pollution was centred on the clearly visible depositions of particulates, rather than the dissolved material in precipitation, leading many countries to introduce smoke abatement legislation such as *Clean Air Acts*. As long ago as the mid-nineteenth century, however, Smith (1852) discovered that higher concentrations of sulphuric acid were found in precipitation nearer to the industrial town of Manchester in northern England. The term *acid rain* was probably used for the first time in the 1870s (Smith, 1872). In the 1950s Gorham (1958a, 1958b) showed evidence of links between atmospheric pollution and the acidity of precipitation and surface waters in small pools; however, the significance of this work was not recognized by other workers at that time.

It was not until the late 1960s that a direct link between 'acid rain' and damage to the environment was first identified by Odén, who pointed to declining fish populations in Scandinavia as a consequence of the acidification of freshwater rivers and lakes (Havas, 1986). Since that time acidification of fresh waters has been observed in other parts of the world, particularly in Europe and in eastern North America (Rhode, 1989), and it has been found to affect forests, crops and soils (Cresser and Edwards, 1987; Innes, 1987). Natural acid deposition, for example from volcanic gases, is of minor importance in comparison with anthropogenic sources. Atmospheric pollutants in snowpacks are released on melting, but due to the enrichment of solute in the first meltwaters (fractionation) the severity of the acidity of the early snowmelt waters is intensified (Brimblecome *et al.*, 1985).

Sulphuric acid accounts for about 60–70 per cent of the mean annual acidity of precipitation in north-west Europe and North America, and most of the rest is due to nitric acid (Fowler *et al.*, 1982; Seip and Tollan, 1985). The primary chemical pollutants are sulphur dioxide (SO_2) and nitrogen oxides NO and NO_2

(often referred to together as NO_x) which are produced by the burning of fossil fuels. These undergo oxidation in the atmosphere, to sulphuric acid (H_2SO_4) and nitric acid (HNO_3), in a number of complex reactions, involving sunlight, moisture, oxidants and catalysts, that are still not well understood. Many of the reactions involve photochemical oxidants, including ozone (O_3), the hydroxyl radical (OH^-) and hydrogen peroxide (H_2O_2).

The reactions in very simplified form may be viewed as:

$$NO + O_3 \rightarrow NO_2 + O_2 \tag{8.10a}$$

$$NO_2 + OH^- \rightarrow HNO_3 \rightarrow NO_3^- + H^+ \tag{8.10b}$$

$$SO_2 + O_2 \rightarrow SO_3 \xrightarrow{H_2O} H_2SO_4 \rightarrow SO_4^{2-} + 2H^+ \tag{8.10c}$$

Sulphuric acid is the main cause of acid deposition because sulphur is emitted in much larger quantities than nitrogen, and the sulphuric acid molecule in solution releases two H^+ ions whereas nitric acid releases one (Swedish Ministry of Agriculture, 1982). There is, however, evidence that as sulphur emissions in the UK decline as part of the UK pollution reduction policy, the relative importance of nitrogen emissions for acidification is increasing (DETR, 1997).

Although the term 'acid rain' is widely used it is a misleading name (Seip and Tollan, 1985), and phrases such as acid input or acid deposition are more accurate and are to be preferred. Due to the dissolution of atmospheric CO_2 even pure water has an 'acidic' pH of about 5.6 (UNEP, 1995) i.e. well below the neutral pH 7. This value has been used as the reference level for distinguishing 'natural' from polluted 'acid' rain. However, other natural materials, including dissolved aerosols and volcanic gases, can also influence the pH, resulting in still lower values. Furthermore, while rain is usually the most important mechanism by which atmospheric water transfers pollutants to the ground it is not the only one. In some areas snow is an important component of precipitation, while in upland and coastal areas frequent cloud or mist can provide a significant contribution to acidification. The fine water droplets of mist and cloud may contain much higher concentrations of acid than the larger drops of rain (Bator and Collett, 1997). As a result, the deposition of these fine droplets may cause a proportionately much more important chemical input than the quantity of water deposited would suggest. This so-called *occult* deposition occurs much more efficiently on aerodynamically rough surfaces such as tall vegetation, in exactly the same way that such surfaces have greater interception losses due to the enhanced air turbulence.

The forms of *wet deposition* (rain, snow and mist) are efficient processes for removing material from the atmosphere, but are restricted to the times when condensation and precipitation occur. Wet deposition may be highly 'episodic'. For example, in one year about 30 per cent of the total deposition of H^+ ions at Goonhilly in south-west England took place on only five rainy days (Watt Committee on Energy, 1984). As well as large total rainfall on these days, the concentrations of pollutants were very high, the air masses having moved to the site after stagnating for some time over areas of high emissions. The importance of weather type and wind direction in determining the ion content of precipitation was discussed by Davies *et al.* (1991) and Metcalfe *et al.* (1995). Appreciable acid deposition also takes place by means of the *dry deposition* of gases and aerosol particles onto the surfaces of soils, plants and water bodies. The main process is by the absorption of gases, such as SO_2 and NO_2, rather than particles (Cape *et al.*, 1987), and will depend upon the chemical and physical affinity of each gas for a particular surface (Fowler, 1984). In contrast to the episodic nature of wet deposition, this is a continuous process, although the rate of deposition may fall as the collecting surface approaches 'saturation' (Fowler and Cape, 1984). Subsequent oxidation to SO_4^{2-} and NO_3^- takes place on the soil and vegetation surfaces when they are wetted by rain or dew. In addition, gases may also pass into the plant stomata and be metabolized.

The relative importance of dry and wet deposition varies with factors such as geographical location and season (due to differences in the amounts of rainfall and of artificial emissions). In general, dry deposition dominates close to emission sources and wet deposition is more important at greater distances. Before discussing deposition rates in more detail it is necessary to consider briefly some of the difficulties encountered in the measurement or estimation of the different processes.

The different forms of acid deposition have created great problems in the design of measurement devices (Barrett, 1987). The majority of the available measurements are from bulk collectors—storage raingauges collecting precipitation, and any dry deposited material on the gauge funnel that gets washed in. As well as the problems of assessing the point depth and areal variability of the rain, which were discussed in Chapter 2, there are water quality problems. Apart from obvious sources of contamination, such as bird droppings, the dry deposition rates of gases and aerosols on the raingauge surface may be very different from that occurring on adjacent soils and vegetation. For this reason 'wet only' collectors with a movable cover that is opened when a sensor detects rainfall may be used, but they are expensive, and prone to miss the early part of the rain, which often has the highest solute concentrations.

Dry deposition of gases and particulates is extremely difficult to measure. Deposited particulate matter has been measured by the use of air filters, and the deposition rate of gases may be inferred from their decrease in concentration near to the ground level. Gas deposition depends on the physical and chemical properties of the gas, and the type and roughness of the surface, and may vary with temperature and the presence of moisture on the surface (Fowler, 1984).

It has been found that pollutants may be carried many hundreds of kilometres in the atmosphere before being deposited. Dry deposition usually occurs within two or three days and is greatest close to the source of emission, while if the pollutants remain longer in the atmosphere there is greater opportunity of being oxidized to sulphuric and nitric acids; these acids are then dissolved in precipitation. This may be demonstrated by comparing the nature of deposition occurring in an industrial country such as Britain with a predominantly rural country such as Sweden. In Britain as a whole, dry deposition of acidity exceeds that by wet deposition, and 75 per cent of the deposited sulphur originates from British pollutant sources (Barrett, 1987). Sweden, in contrast, has much less industry of its own, but it is downwind of a number of industrialized countries. Consequently, it is found that wet deposition of acidity predominates, and only 20–25 per cent of the sulphur deposited derives from Swedish sources (Swedish Ministry of Agriculture, 1982).

The pattern of acid deposition is, however, not simply related to the distribution of sources. In Britain, for example, while the largest inputs by dry deposition are in the industrial parts of the country, the largest loads of wet deposition are in fact upwind of the emission sources (Fowler *et al.*, 1985). These are the remote uplands of the north and west country where, despite low concentrations of H^+ ions in the rain, the total input is greatest due to the high rainfall amounts (Figure 8.4; compare with Figure 2.4). In remote areas such as these and parts of Scandinavia where wet deposition predominates and precipitation is high, there may be an appreciable contribution to acid deposition from very distant sources, either from Europe or from North America (Watt Committee on Energy, 1984).

The relative importance of wet and dry deposition will be influenced by local factors including topography and the prevailing meteorological conditions, but in general terms the ratio of dry/wet deposition declines systematically from about 10 close to pollution sources to < 1 for areas over 300 km away (Fowler, 1984). Even in remote areas, however, dry deposition is still a significant contributor to the total deposition.

Acid deposition causes the acidification of soils and waters if the neutralization of the acids by weathering is too slow (Stumm and Morgan, 1996). The sensitivity of a particular catchment to acid deposition depends on a variety of factors, including the geology, soils and land use; this is discussed further in Sections 8.5 and 8.6, particularly in terms of the concept of a 'critical load'. The areas where damage is most severe are not necessarily those receiving the greatest deposition of acidity.

8.4 Interception and evaporation

It is known that different land uses affect the water budget of an area. Chapter 3 presents the results of studies showing much higher evaporation losses from forests than from grassland due to the greater interception losses of the taller and aerodynamically rougher trees. This loss will act to increase the solute concentrations of the remaining water reaching the forest floor as throughfall or stemflow, although it will not affect the solute loads. Vegetation can, however, also directly influence the total amount of solutes reaching the ground in several ways. It is shown (Section 3.8) that trees provide efficient collecting surfaces for

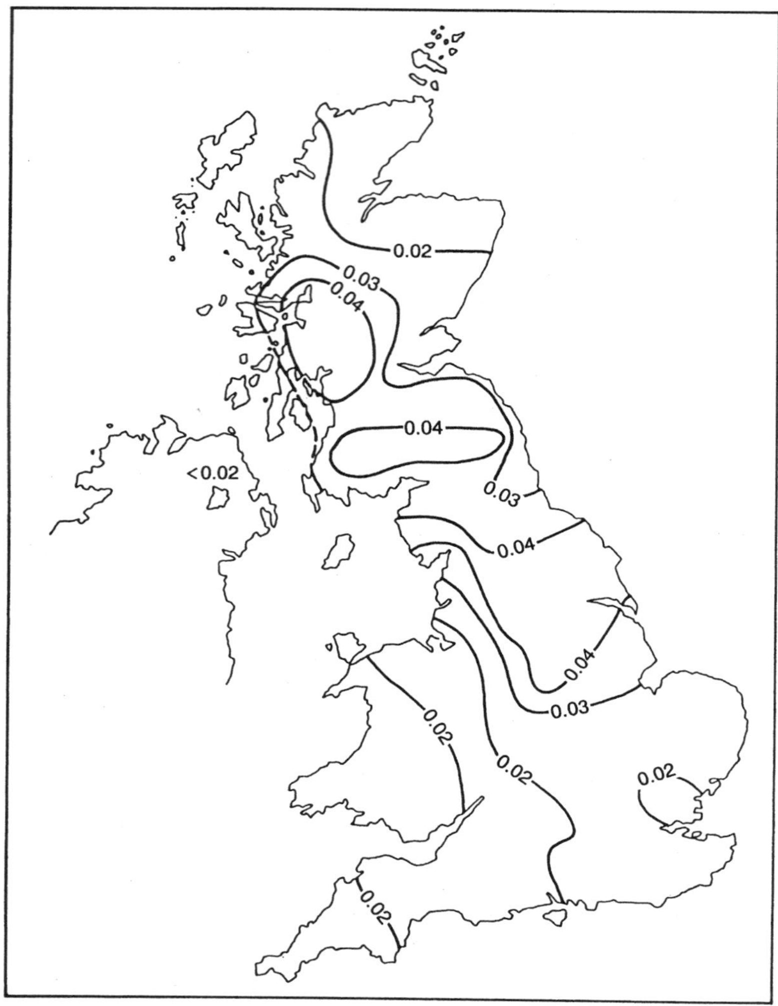

Figure 8.4 Wet-deposited acidity in the UK in 1986 ($g\,H^+\,m^{-2}\,y^{-1}$). (Data supplied by Warren Springs Laboratory.)

the deposition of fine mist or fog droplets, which may have much higher concentrations of solutes than rainfall. They may also receive deposition of particulate materials, which are subsequently dissolved in rain to reach the ground as *washoff*. In addition, trees may absorb gases into their leaves by stomatal uptake and this material, together with nutrients translocated from their roots and exuded on the leaves, may be transferred to rainwater running over them, as *crown leaching*. In a study of water chemistry changes in the canopy of a coniferous forest in northern Britain, Cape *et al.* (1987) found that the sulphate loads in the rainfall above the trees amounted to only 30 per cent of that reaching the ground via throughfall and stemflow. They concluded that the bulk of this gain was due to leaching of SO_4^{2-} from the foliage and that this material originated from gaseous SO_2 taken up by stomata and from particles containing SO_4^{2-} which had been deposited externally on the vegetation.

The view that trees may filter pollutants from the air was developed by Mayer and Ulrich (1974), who suggested that the enhancement in chemical fluxes between the rain above the tree canopy and the throughfall (and stemflow) beneath was equal to the dry deposition of particles and gases as well as occult deposition by mists. It is very difficult, however, to separate the *net gain* of atmospheric material by wet deposition and the washoff of dry deposition, from the *recycling* of materials by crown leaching (Miller and Miller, 1980). While increases in acidity under coniferous forests have been noted in many studies (Cape *et al.*, 1987; Skeffington, 1987), this is not always the case, and some investigators have found little difference in acidity between precipitation and throughfall (Miller, 1984; Reynolds *et al.*, 1986). Several studies of throughfall under different tree species have found greater acidity under conifers than under hardwoods, which may be due to more efficient 'filtering' of atmospheric pollutants by the former and the greater cation exchange capacity of the latter (Joslin *et al.*, 1987). As rainwater passed through the canopy of a deciduous forest in the north-eastern USA, there was a large increase in solute concentrations and much of the acidity was neutralized (Bormann and Likens, 1994). Increasing acidity of rainfall will tend to accelerate the leaching of many cations from the foliage and this exchange of H^+ for cations can, in some cases, result in the rainwater becoming progressively less acid as it passes through the tree canopy (Watt Committee on Energy, 1984). Such neutralization of acid inputs will, nevertheless, still result in acidification of the overall soil–plant system as these cations are ultimately derived from the root zone and will be lost in drainage water.

The pattern of chemical input to the ground surface under trees is likely to be very spatially variable. If the canopy is discontinuous there will be direct incident precipitation between the tree crowns and enhanced input of leached material under the canopy. Stemflow may provide high solute concentrations in water to a very localized zone immediately surrounding the base of each tree trunk. The role of vegetation in water chemistry does not end when the water reaches the ground due to the intimate role of vegetation in soil chemical systems, involving organic matter and nutrient cycling, as well as in physical processes including soil structure that affect soil water movement.

8.5 Soil water and groundwater

Before discussing the water quality processes operating in these subsurface zones it is necessary to give some attention to the nature of the media in which the water resides and through which it passes, since they may provide important sources of, and sinks for, solutes. The relative abundance of the elements in the surface layers of the earth is determined by the composition of the earth's crust; the materials in the rocks and soils derive directly or indirectly from rock minerals formed originally under conditions of extreme heat and temperature, and which are found in *igneous* and some *metamorphic* rocks. Cooling magma formed *primary minerals* such as feldspars, quartz and micas. Apart from quartz, which is very resistant, these are however, unstable at the earth's surface, and are prone to chemical alteration to more stable *secondary minerals*, such as clays and iron oxides. In addition, the operation of biochemical processes forms new minerals such as calcite. About 75 per cent of the land surface of the globe comprises these reworked sedimentary rocks, which are much more important for holding and transmitting water than the relatively impermeable and low-porosity igneous and metamorphic rocks.

8.5.1 Weathering of rocks

Approximately 99 per cent by weight of the earth's crust comprises just eight elements: 47 per cent oxygen (O), 28 per cent silicon (Si), 8 per cent aluminium (Al), 5 per cent iron (Fe), 3.5 per cent calcium (Ca), 3 per cent sodium (Na), 2.5 per cent potassium (K) and 2 per cent magnesium (Mg). The chemicals are combined into minerals, which have a definite chemical composition. The concern of the hydrologist centres on the weathering of these minerals to make substances available to go into solution and the behaviour of the soil and rock systems in retaining, cycling and leaching these chemicals.

Interest in rock weathering has been given a tremendous impetus by the development of the *critical load* concept, which has come to dominate European legislation on air pollution (Nilsson and Grennfelt, 1988). This may be defined as 'The maximum deposition of a given compound which will not cause long-term harmful effects on ecosystem structure and function, according to present knowledge'. In other words it is a threshold deposition rate that ecosystems can tolerate without long-term damage. This means that acid inputs should not exceed within-soil alkalinity production—essentially the production of base cations by mineral weathering. Sverdrup and De Vries (1994) described one approach to calculating critical loads. In practice there are many difficulties in applying the concept (Schnoor, 1996). For example, which pollutants are the most critical, and how do they interact to cause ecological damage? Which elements of the environment are we trying to protect—the most sensitive lake in a region or a lesser target so that some resources may be lost?

The most effective mechanism of chemical weathering is the action of rainwater, containing dissolved acids, on rock minerals. The main source of natural acidity in the environment is provided by the solution of CO_2 in water to form carbonic acid (H_2CO_3). This dissociates in water (Eqs 8.2 to 8.4) to form bicarbonate, and to a lesser extent carbonate, ions and generates H^+ ions:

$$\begin{array}{l} H_2O + CO_2 \rightleftharpoons H_2CO_3 \rightleftharpoons H^+ + HCO_3^- \\ \qquad\qquad\qquad\qquad\qquad\qquad\quad \upharpoonleft\downharpoonright \\ \qquad\qquad\qquad\qquad\qquad\qquad CO_3^{2-} + H^+ \end{array} \tag{8.11}$$

The CO_2 is dissolved from the atmosphere but, due to plant root respiration and the decay of organic matter, the concentration of CO_2 in the air in soil pores may be 100 times greater than that in the atmosphere. This results in a much higher concentration of carbonic acid in the soil water than is found in surface water such as rivers and lakes. In most humid areas other, stronger acids may also be important, including very dilute H_2SO_4 and HNO_3, as well as organic acids formed from decaying vegetation.

The major mechanism of mineral weathering is by *acid hydrolysis*, whereby H^+ ions replace cations in the mineral, leading to an expansion and decomposition of its silicate structure. An example of such chemical action is the weathering of the mineral orthoclase feldspar, found in igneous rocks, to the clay mineral, kaolinite:

$$\underset{\text{(primary mineral)}}{\underset{\text{Feldspar}}{2KAlSi_3O_8(c)}} + \underset{\text{Acid}}{2H^+(aq)} + 9H_2O \rightleftharpoons \underset{\text{(secondary mineral)}}{\underset{\text{Kaolinite}}{Al_2Si_2O_5(OH)_4(c)}} + \underset{\text{(in solution)}}{4H_4SiO_4(aq) + 2K^+(aq)} \tag{8.12}$$

Although chemically a reversible reaction, in practice it is essentially irreversible because the feldspar cannot be reconstituted to any significant extent without imposing very great temperatures and pressures. The silica and potassium are removed in solution to groundwater and to streams, pushing the reaction to the right, and kaolinite clay accumulates as part of the soil mantle. Such secondary minerals do not necessarily represent the final weathering products since they are only stable within certain pH limits and may, under suitable conditions, undergo further chemical weathering to even more stable chemical forms. Another example of mineral weathering is given by Eq. 8.5 which describes the chemical solution of calcite (a major constituent of limestones). The rate of weathering, and the resulting concentrations of solutes in streams and underground waters for a given reaction, will depend on a number of factors including the temperature and the flux of water. In general, reaction rates speed up with increasing temperature, and rates of weathering and leaching in the tropics are several times greater than in temperate areas. Tropical soils have much higher clay contents (often 60 per cent or more) than temperate areas (for example 35 per cent clay is considered high in Britain), and some authors have invoked this much stronger weathering history to explain why the solute loads of streams in the tropics are much lower than those in temperate regions (Nortcliffe, 1988). Geographical differences in rock type may, however, be more important in accounting for these differences (Walling and Webb, 1983). The rate of weathering will also be affected by the flux of water, removing products in solution and bringing new water into contact with the minerals. In some cases the rate of dissolution may reach an upper limit, governed by surface chemical processes.

The rate of supply of minerals by chemical weathering of rocks is fairly slow, and if there was no mechanism for retaining the substances that are in solution they would be quickly washed out in drainage water. Such mechanisms do exist, however, and are closely related to the operation of biological processes and have an important control over short-term solute dynamics.

8.5.2 Adsorption and exchange reactions

When plants colonize the weathered rock debris they have a direct physical effect by controlling the removal of particulate weathering products by erosion, and they also result in a number of chemical changes. Plants take atmospheric gases into their foliage and dissolved minerals into their root systems and return chemicals to the soil as crown leaching (see Section 8.4) or as leaf litter and other partially decomposed plant remains, known as *humus*. The humus combines with the soil clays to form colloidal complexes which have extremely large areas per unit weight. Their surfaces have electrical charges which enable them to attract and *adsorb* a 'swarm' of dissolved ions (Figure 8.5). This electrostatic attachment of adsorbed ions is sufficiently weak for them to be easily exchanged for other ions in solution. The exchange of ions between the soil exchange surfaces and the soil solution is a continuous process. The rate of exchange is generally rapid and, following a change in the composition of the soil solution, requires only a few minutes for a new equilibrium to be established between the adsorbed ions and those in solution. The amount of a given ion that is adsorbed depends upon the abundance of the different ions in solutions, the

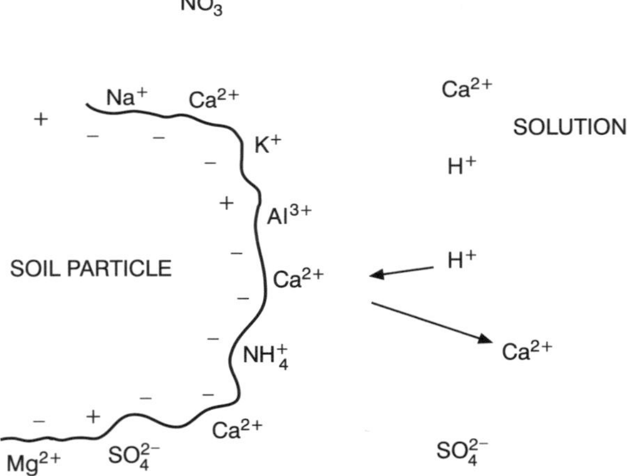

Figure 8.5 Ion exchange between cations in solution and cations adsorbed on soil particles.

ion exchange capacity of the clay or humus and the relative strength of adsorption of the various ions.

With the exception of kaolinite (which has the fewest surface charges), the clay and humus surfaces have more negative than positive charges and consequently attract more cations than anions (Plant and Raiswell, 1983). The *cation exchange capacity* (CEC) measured in meq per 100 g or centimole/kg (cmol kg^{-1}) varies from about 10 for kaolinite to 100–150 for montmorillonite, and organic colloids have capacities of 200 or even more. Values of CEC for topsoils typically range from about 5 cmol kg^{-1} for sandy soils up to 50 cmol kg^{-1} for a heavy clay with a high organic matter content. The relative strength of adsorption of the different ionic species increases with their charge and decreases with their hydrated ion radius (i.e. the charged ion surrounded by a 'shell' of polar water molecules). Thus for *equal* concentrations of ions in solution (in equivalent weight units) the relative strength of adsorption of cations is:

$$Al^{3+} > H^{+} > Ca^{2+} > Mg^{2+} > K^{+} > NH_4^{+} > Na^{+}$$

The capacity of a given exchange surface for holding cations is not constant, but varies with the pH of the solution. As acidity increases, for example due to the accumulation of organic matter, there is an increase in the number of H^+ ions in solution. These H^+ ions are strongly adsorbed onto the exchange surfaces and consequently will displace some of the previously adsorbed cations—excepting Al which is too strongly held. Increasing acidity also increases the rate of Al supply to solution from mineral weathering. Since there is a dynamic equilibrium between the adsorbed Al and that in solution some of this Al is adsorbed on the surfaces as Al^{3+} or Al-hydroxy ($Al(OH)_x$) ions. The H and the Al ions tend to dominate acid soils, and both contribute to H^+ concentrations in solution—the H ions directly and the Al ions indirectly by hydrolysis, releasing H^+ ions:

Increasing pH

$$Al^{3+}\,(aq) + H_2O \rightleftharpoons Al(OH)^{2+}\,(aq) + H^{+} \tag{8.13a}$$

$$Al(OH)^{2+}\,(aq) + H_2O \rightleftharpoons Al(OH)_2^{+}\,(aq) + H^{+} \tag{8.13b}$$

$$Al(OH)_2^{+}\,(aq) + H_2O \rightleftharpoons \underset{\text{Gibbsite}}{Al(OH)_3\,(c)} + H^{+} \tag{8.13c}$$

Under low pH conditions Al becomes soluble in the form of Al^{3+} and Al hydroxy cations which are very strongly adsorbed on exchange surfaces. At higher pH conditions these Al ions react with OH^- ions to form insoluble $Al(OH)_3$, making the exchange surfaces available to other cations. In contrast to Al and H these *base cations*, which principally comprise Ca, Mg, K and Na, act to neutralize acidity and dominate the CEC in neutral and alkaline soils. In acid soils, Al and H tend to be the dominant cations due to their greater adsorption by the soil, while Ca, Mg, K and Na are leached out in solution. The percentage of the CEC accounted for by base cations is known as the *base saturation*, and acid soils which are therefore poor in these plant nutrients have a low base saturation. The leaching of these cations depends both upon the equilibrium between the cations in solution and on exchange surfaces, and also on the presence of a *mobile anion*, such as SO_4^- or NO_3^-, which is not itself readily retained on soil surfaces or taken up by plants and can transport the released cations from the soil in solution (for example as $CaSO_4$ or $MgSO_4$) in drainage water. Anions may also be adsorbed on soil particles, but to a much lesser extent than cations. The 'mobile' sulphate anion, for example, may be adsorbed by some soils but there is evidence that under high atmospheric deposition rates of sulphate, SO_4^{2-} 'saturation' of the soil may result (Cresser and Edwards, 1987). Once this happens, further sulphate inputs can percolate freely through the soil.

The ions adsorbed on the exchange surfaces are, like those in solution, largely available to plants and micro-organisms. Although the exact biochemical processes are not yet fully understood, it is well established that plants can take up, or absorb, ions selectively, and that different plant species have different nutrient requirements. The uptake of these ions must not disturb the overall charge neutrality within the plant, however. Thus the roots must excrete H^+ ions if there is an excess cation absorption, or HCO_3^- or OH^- ions if anion absorption predominates. Plants can thus directly influence the pH and the ionic composition of the soil water around their roots. Important ions for plant nutrition include the cations K, Ca, Mg and Na, and the anions phosphorus (P), nitrogen (N) and sulphur (S). The concentration of these ions in the soil solution consequently varies systematically over a growing season, becoming depleted as the plants take up nutrients, and then increasing again over the winter period, or when there is no crop.

From the preceding discussion it will be evident that the pH of the soil solution has a very important effect on the way in which substances are gained (by mineral weathering), retained (by ion adsorption or plant uptake) or lost from the soil (dissolved in drainage water). The soil solution 'acidity', defined in terms of its ability to neutralize OH^- ions, is related to the concentration of H and Al ions. This can be considered to comprise two forms: an *active acidity* due to the H^+ (and Al) ions in solution and a much larger *reserve or exchange acidity* comprising the H and Al ions adsorbed on exchange surfaces. The reserve acidity is very much larger than the active form, being about 10^3 times greater in sandy soils and about 10^5 times greater for a clay soil with a high organic matter content. Since the active and reserve acidities are in a dynamic equilibrium any change in the concentration of the H^+ ions in solution (for example an increase caused by acid deposition from the atmosphere or a reduction due to adding lime to farmland) will tend to be balanced by the adsorption or release of adsorbed H^+ ions. Thus any pH change in the soil solution following the addition of an acid or base will be negligibly small until there has been a significant change in the (much larger) reserve of adsorbed ions. Most natural waters exhibit this resistance to change of the pH which is known as *buffering* (Stumm and Morgan, 1996). It is therefore important to distinguish between intensity factors (pH) and capacity factors, i.e. the total acid or base neutralizing capacity. The buffering capacity of a soil is related to its cation exchange capacity and is important in determining the effect on a soil of external inputs of water and solutes. Thus, for example, the soils and surface waters of Scandinavia and eastern North America have been greatly affected by atmospheric acidification because they have lime-poor bed-rocks that are very resistant to weathering and provide only small amounts of base cations (Swedish Ministry of Agriculture, 1982). Similarly, in Britain the upland soils of the north and west, which have developed on igneous rocks, low in cations, are more susceptible to acidification by atmospheric deposition than the soils of lowland, eastern Britain where, although the total deposition is greater, the soils have a much higher content of exchangeable cations (Catt, 1985). By the same token, of course, the pH of these poorly buffered upland soils could in theory be relatively easily increased by the application of lime. Different buffering mechanisms correspond to broad soil pH ranges. In neutral and slightly acid soils $CaCO_3$ is an efficient buffer (Eqs 8.5 to 8.7). Aluminium is a major source of buffering in the pH range 4–5 (Eqs 8.13a to 8.13c), while in very acid soils, pH <3.5, iron oxides control the pH.

Once in solution the movement of solutes may be influenced by a number of processes, both physical and chemical, and these are discussed below.

8.5.3 Solute movement in soils and groundwater

Materials dissolved in water will be transported by the flow of that water, but they will rarely travel at exactly the same rate. Movement of a solute species depends on three mechanisms: advection, dispersion and reaction (Freeze and Cherry, 1979; Wang and Anderson, 1982). The mass flow of water will carry solutes by *advection* (sometimes also called *convection*) which, in the absence of other processes, results in chemicals being transported at the same rate as the macroscopic velocity of the water. The velocity of solutes will, however, in practice vary from this rate due to *hydrodynamic dispersion*, leading to a range of velocities. This results from two processes: mechanical dispersion and molecular diffusion, which are similar in effect, and in consequence are generally considered together. Mechanical dispersion is a consequence of the complexities of the pore system of the medium through which the water is moving. Flows are faster through large pores than through small pores, and across the middle of pores than near the pore walls. Flows also vary due to the tortuosity of pore networks, with flows in some pores at an angle to the mean direction of water flow (Figure 8.6). Molecular diffusion is much smaller and results from the random, thermal-kinetic motion of molecules, and occurs regardless of whether or not there is net water movement. Both mechanical dispersion and molecular diffusion cause a movement of solute from areas of high to low concentration, and this response to concentration gradients makes the solute species become more diffuse with time. The resulting intermixing of chemicals between the moving 'mobile' water in the larger pores and the largely 'immobile' water held in

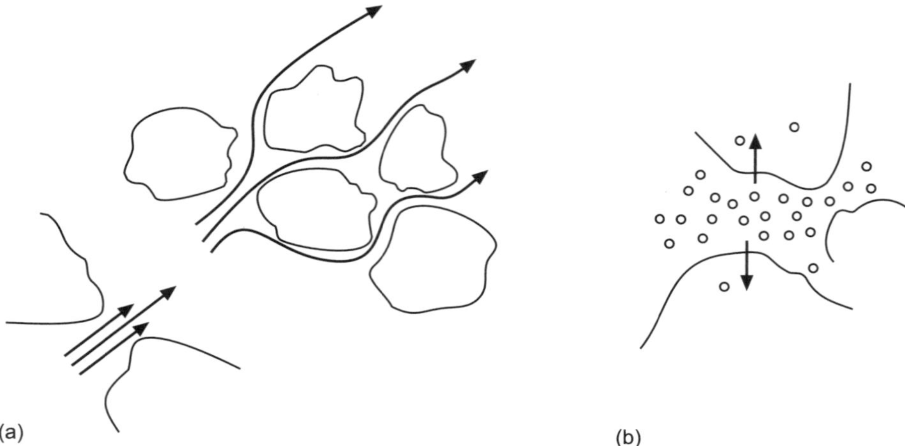

Figure 8.6 Dispersion of a solute in porous media: (*a*) mechanical dispersion; (*b*) molecular diffusion.

finer pores of the matrix can influence the overall rate of transport of solutes (Van Genuchten and Wierenga, 1976).

Changes in solute concentrations may also take place due to *chemical reactions*. These may be with the solid matrix of the medium or between dissolved substances or, in the unsaturated zone, between the solution and the gas phase. Many different chemical and biochemical reactions can occur, including oxidation, reduction, solution and precipitation, but of the most general importance is the ion exchange process of *adsorption*.

The effects of these processes on the movement of a solute species through a porous medium may be presented in graphical form as a breakthrough curve (BTC). Figure 8.7 shows such curves for the simplest case of a non-reactive tracer (of concentration C_o) continuously added to steady, saturated, downward flow through a column of a porous, uniform medium. As the tracer replaces an existing solution (tracer concentration zero), there is an increase in the concentration of the tracer in the outflow (C). Advection alone results in a simple 'piston flow' displacement of the existing solution by the new solution with a sudden, step-like change (line a) in the proportion of new solution in the outflow C_e ($= C/C_o$) (Figure 8.7). This moves at the average linear velocity of the water. Hydrodynamic dispersion (line b) results in some of the tracer moving faster, and some slower, than this velocity. With increasing flow distance from the tracer input this spread of the concentration profile due to dispersion becomes greater.

For groundwater systems the adsorption reactions are normally very rapid relative to the flow velocity and an equilibrium state is usually assumed between the solute species in solution and adsorbed on solid particles (Freeze and Cherry, 1979). In this situation the relation between the concentration of a solute species adsorbed per unit weight of a particular medium and the concentration in

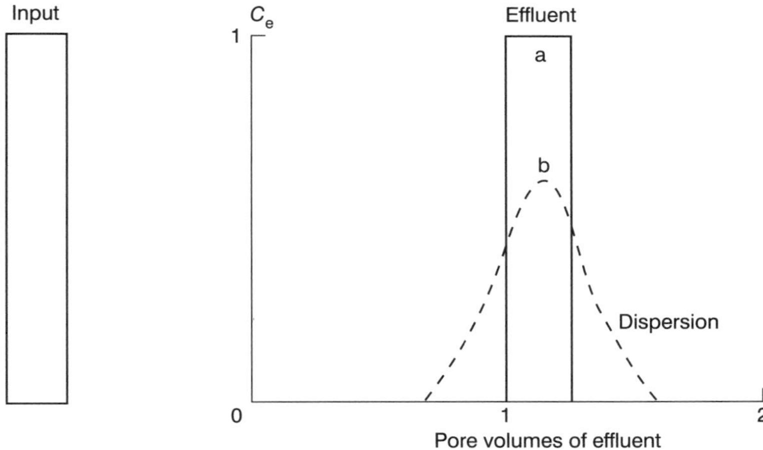

Figure 8.7 Schematic breakthrough curves resulting from piston-type displacement of a pulse input of solute.

solution at a given temperature can be described by the *adsorption isotherm* (Stumm and Morgan, 1996). From this 'partitioning' of the chemical between solid and liquid phases a retardation factor can be calculated to describe the delay in solute movement due to adsorption (Van Genuchten and Wierenga, 1976; Smettem, 1986). The effect of greater adsorption is to alter the time distribution of a pulse of tracer, reducing the average rate of movement (shifting the BTC to the right) and making the concentration curve more asymmetrical (Figure 8.8).

The displacement process may be described by the convective-dispersion equation for one-dimensional, steady-state, uniform flow in a homogeneous saturated medium as

$$\frac{\delta C}{\delta t} = \underset{\text{Dispersion}}{D\frac{\delta^2 C}{\delta Z^2}} - \underset{\text{Convection}}{V\frac{\delta C}{\delta Z}} \left[+ \underset{\text{Sorption}}{\frac{\rho\,\delta S}{n\,\delta t}}\right] \tag{8.14}$$

where the third term is an extension to account for the gain or loss of the solute by reaction. C is the concentration of the solute species under consideration, Z is the distance along the flow line, t is the time, D is the coefficient of hydrodynamic dispersion and V is the average flow velocity; ρ and n are the bulk density and porosity of the medium and S is the mass of the chemical adsorbed per unit mass of solid. If the adsorption rate is slow compared to the flow rate, $\delta S/\delta t$ can be estimated from reaction kinetics.

In some soils and rocks macrovoids can act as conduits for the rapid movement of water and solutes. Such channels may include shrinkage cracks and root channels in soils (see the section 'Macropores' in Chapter 6) and fracture lines and jointing in rocks (see Section 5.6), and, under certain circumstances, enable flows to effectively bypass the soil or rock matrix.

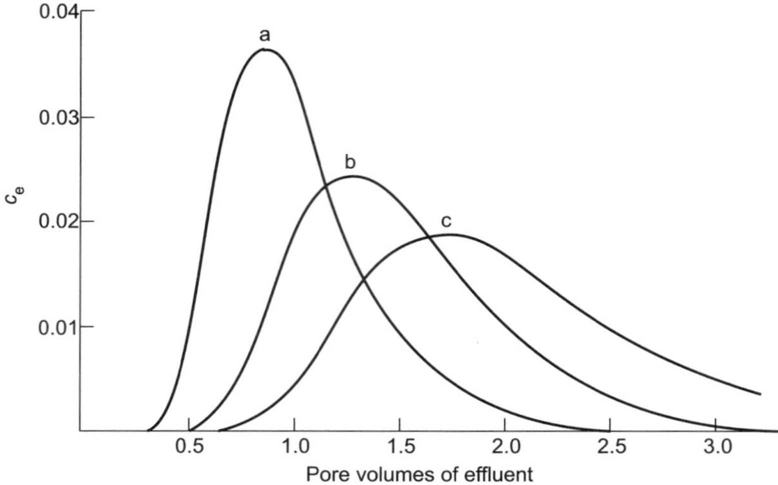

Figure 8.8 Schematic solute breakthrough curves showing the effect of increasing adsorption of the solute by the medium (curves a to c). (Redrawn from an original diagram by Smettem, 1986. By permission of J. Wiley and Sons Ltd.)

Schematic breakthrough curves are shown in Figure 8.9 for media with different ranges of pore sizes. For simplicity, adsorption and dispersion effects are ignored. The rate of inflow is sufficiently great for preferential flow to be generated in the larger pores. This pattern may be contrasted with the classical infiltration equations developed by soil physicists (Section 6.4.2) which deal with ideal situations of a homogeneous medium (uniform pore size) and a uniform initial moisture content. In the case of preferential or bypass flow, the water does not come into chemical equilibrium with the soil as it can only react with the soil mass by lateral diffusion. The obvious consequence is that greater amounts of dissolved chemicals will pass unchanged through the medium to underlying layers and to receiving water bodies. Macropores may be important in the contamination of groundwater since, under high surface inputs of water, they enable solutes to bypass the natural purification actions in the soil matrix and penetrate beyond the reach of plant roots. In areas subject to 'acid rain', bypass flow through the soil will react less completely with the soil buffering processes, and this may result in greater acidity of the water in rivers and lakes.

In a study of nitrate losses under arable (winter wheat) cultivation Smettem *et al.* (1983) observed high concentrations early in the winter period which could not be accounted for by normal convective–dispersive flow. They attributed this to bypass flow with nitrate moving in the larger, water-filled pores. Very high stream nitrate losses in runoff were recorded immediately after the application of nitrogen fertilizer (due to bypassing), but only a month later the nitrate had relocated in the immobile water in small pores in the soil peds and was 'protected' from leaching by subsequent bypass flow.

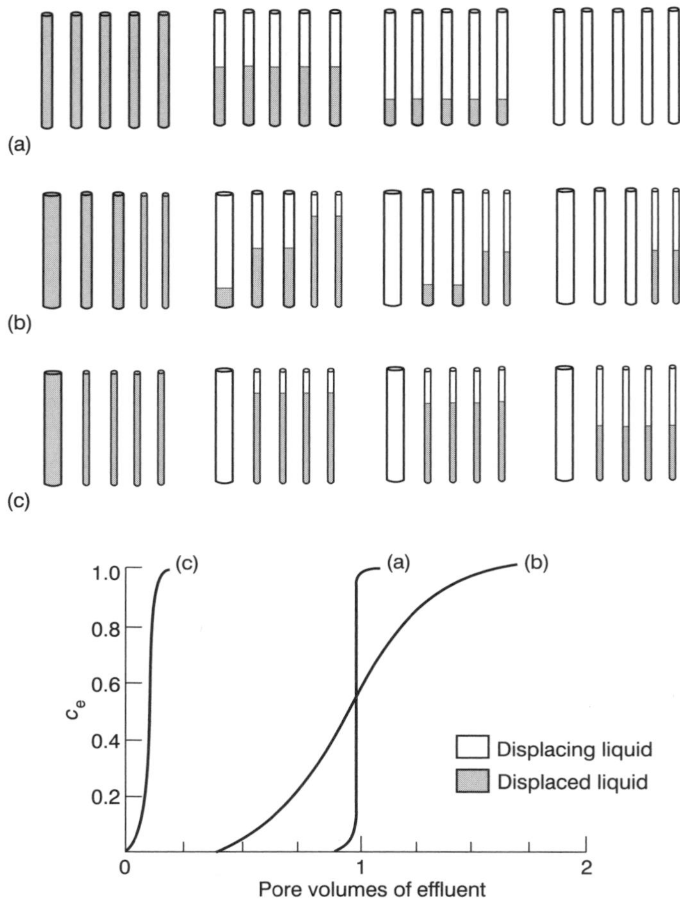

Figure 8.9 Breakthrough curves for a continuous input of solute: (*a*) piston-type displacement; (*b*) a medium with a limited range of pore sizes; (*c*) a medium with bypass flow through interconnected macropores (from an original diagram by Bouma, 1981).

Further work is needed, however, to elucidate the factors controlling the generation of macropore flow and the resulting solute travel time distributions in such situations. Macropore flow results in an early rise in the BTC while adsorption on the solid phase and solute diffusion from mobile to immobile water zones will cause a delay. Subsequent desorption and diffusion back to the mobile flow zone will both give rise to a long tail to the BTC. Due to the complexity of these effects and to the generally unknown extent of the spatial variability of soil structure at the field scale, a 'black-box' transfer function, analogous to the 'unit hydrograph' approach in catchment rainfall-runoff studies, has been used to model the solute travel time distribution BTC (Jury, 1982). A number of studies have found that the pore water velocities may be approximated by a log-normal frequency distribution.

In field situations it is often unlikely that an equilibrium will be reached between the concentration of the solute and the soil matrix due to the sorption rate being much slower than the rate of change of the solute concentrations. This will be the case for situations with (*a*) rapid and varying soil water fluxes, (*b*) varying solute concentrations and (*c*) slow adsorption rates. The relative importance of these factors will vary between sites where different hydrological processes are operating as well as between different chemicals at the same site.

Much of the available information on adsorption rates has been derived from laboratory experiments, often dealing with homogeneous solutions or well-stirred suspensions, and may give very different results to those encountered in field situations. The soil solution is not always well mixed, resulting in local concentration gradients, and it may in practice be very difficult to separate out the effects of the chemical processes from those of diffusion (Skopp, 1986). In addition to adsorption, other processes which may be occurring at the same time include precipitation or solution, degradation, volatilization and oxidation. The great complexity of the solute–water–soil system creates great problems in investigating solute movement and concentration changes, and Travis and Etnier (1981), in a review paper, suggested that we may never achieve a full understanding and ability to make quantitative predictions. Nevertheless, significant progress has been achieved and some broad generalizations regarding surface and shallow subsurface solute processes in storm events can be made.

Subsurface flows will have a much greater opportunity for reactions with the solid phase than flow over the ground surface. Consequently, subsurface flows may carry much higher concentrations of solutes than overland flow (Hubbard and Sheridan, 1983). Overland flow will, however, take up organic chemicals from leaf litter and vegetation matter (Bache, 1984), and on poorly vegetated sloping sites the erosion of soil particles (and any adsorbed chemicals) may occur. The distinction between subsurface and surface flow chemistry is not necessarily clear cut, however, since infiltrating water must pass through the surface organic layers, and subsurface lateral flow may subsequently re-emerge at the ground surface further downslope as 'return flow'. The chemical and physical properties of different soil horizons may also give rise to different solute concentrations in the water following different flowpaths. Whitehead *et al.* (1986) used a simple two-compartment soil model, with an upper layer representing a thin acidic organic soil overlying a more alkaline mineral subsoil, to investigate the effect of changes in flowpaths on stream chemistry. Stream storm runoff was very acid, whereas the baseflow in dry weather periods was much less acid and had lower Al levels since a greater proportion of the flow was moving through the subsoil and undergoing acid buffering. In such areas artificial drainage to encourage percolation into the deeper, less acid soil horizons may help to improve the water quality of the streams. Such a management practice will not necessarily be effective at other sites and indeed in some situations deep drainage may increase stream Al and H^+ concentrations (Bache, 1984; Cresser and Edwards, 1987). Knowledge of soil processes, including adsorption, can be used to limit the loss of agricultural chemicals into the streams by discouraging their application close to streams. The intervening 'buffer' strips act to filter out the chemicals (Hall *et al.*, 1983). Similarly, by applying liquid chemicals at low intensities it will be less likely that bypass flow in macropores will be generated, so that chemicals will pass slowly through the soil matrix and have a greater opportunity to be adsorbed.

8.5.4 Tracers

The direction and speed of water movement may be studied by 'labelling' the water by adding a tracer. This should move as part of the water flow and it is therefore important to select one which is unreactive. Thus, cations are not good tracers due to exchange reactions. Certain anions are also unsuitable; for example phosphate (PO_4^{2-}) undergoes a variety of reactions. Sulphate (SO_4^{2-}), nitrate (NO_3^-) and chloride (Cl^-) are generally considered to be 'mobile' (or 'conservative'), being adsorbed little on solids and travelling at more nearly the same speed as the water. Of these, Cl^- is the most widely used although even it is not ideal due to *anion exclusion*. Since soil surfaces generally have a net negative charge the Cl^- anions are repelled and become concentrated in the faster moving flow in the middle of the pores (Marshall *et al.*, 1996). Thus, Gvirtzman *et al.* (1986) found that Cl tracer moved faster than the average water movement, given by tritiated water.

A wide range of substances has been used as tracers, including salts, fluorescent dyes and radioisotopes. A detailed discussion of their relative advantages and disadvantages has been given by various authors (for example Atkinson and Smart, 1981; Moser *et al.*, 1986). One important group of tracers are *isotopes*, which are atoms of a given element that have a different atomic mass but the same chemical properties, and may be used to 'label' chemical species in solution. They may be either *stable isotopes* or *radioisotopes*.

Tracers can be used in a number of ways. Some of the earliest work, for example, used dyes to study conduit flowpaths in limestone terrain. Tracers have also been used in a long-standing debate concerning the relative importance of matrix and fissure flow in the unsaturated zone of chalk aquifers. Since its intergranular pores are exceedingly small it was widely assumed that downward flow is dominated by movement in the fairly frequent joints and fissures. In a classic study, Smith *et al.* (1970) examined the tritium profile of pore water in the unsaturated zone. Tritium T, or ^3H, is an isotope of hydrogen that occurs naturally in small concentrations in rainfall, but very much larger concentrations occurred due to thermo-nuclear weapon tests in the atmosphere after 1952 with peak values in 1963–64. They concluded that about 85 per cent of the percolating water was as intergranular seepage moving by piston displacement at about $0.9\,m\,y^{-1}$. This, at first, surprising result has important water supply implications with potentially large quantities of recent man-made pollutants in slow but steady movement downwards to the water table. Subsequently, however, Foster (1975) argued that the observed tritium profile could alternatively have been produced by flow through the fissures if allowance is made for diffusion of tritium from the joint water into the pore water in the matrix. Later work by Wellings and Cooper (1983) and Price (1987), using measurements of both matric potentials and solute movement, suggested that different processes may be operating at different locations and in different strata. Where the matrix permeability is sufficiently high fissure flow does not occur; where matrix permeability is much lower, or infiltration rates are very large, water cannot enter the matrix fast enough and fissure flow can occur.

Wright *et al.* (1982) compared the ratio of the radioisotope ^{14}C, produced naturally by cosmic radiation interaction with atmospheric nitrogen, to the stable isotope ^{12}C in the carbonate dissolved in groundwater and rainfall. They used the known rate of decay of ^{14}C to date the large groundwater reserves under the Libyan desert and concluded that these were largely derived from recharge in a much more rainy period some 15 000–35 000 years ago.

8.5.5 Chemical evolution of groundwater

Since the kinetics of mineral weathering are often slow, it is unlikely that thermodynamic equilibrium with the flowing water will be reached in the soil zone. In large groundwater systems, however, residence times are much longer and as water moves through the medium equilibrium may be progressively established.

In areas of groundwater recharge there is a net transfer of mineral matter from the soil zone to the underlying saturated zone. As this groundwater moves along flow lines to discharge areas, its chemistry will be altered by the minerals with which it comes into contact.

As groundwater moves through the system it will normally dissolve further material from the matrix rocks and the concentration of total dissolved solids will increase. Some materials may be precipitated out due to changes in temperature and pressure affecting their solubility or to reactions with ions dissolved from the matrix forming new insoluble compounds.

In a classic study of the chemical changes in groundwater as it moves from areas of recharge to areas of discharge, Chebotarev (1955) studied over 10 000 Australian groundwater samples and found a progressive evolution in the dominant anion species with increasing travel distance and age:

$$HCO_3^- \rightarrow SO_4^{2-} \rightarrow Cl^-$$

This sequence is determined by mineral availability and solubility (Freeze and Cherry, 1979). In broad terms, minerals which dissolve to release Cl^- (for example halite) are more readily soluble than those releasing SO_4^{2-} (for example gypsum and anhydrite), which are in turn more soluble than those releasing HCO_3^- (for example calcite and dolomite). Thus Cl^- and, to a lesser extent, SO_4^{2-} may have been largely leached from the recharge zone of a groundwater system. Furthermore, HCO_3^- enters the groundwater system in recharge zones from the dissolution of CO_2 from the atmosphere and the soil air.

While this chemical sequence is a useful conceptual model, these changes cannot be defined quantitatively to particular ages or distances, and it is rarely observed in its entirety due to the often dominant effects of the local physical environment. Thus some waters may not evolve past the HCO_3^- or SO_4^{2-} stage, while if the water comes into contact with a highly soluble mineral such as halite it may evolve directly to the Cl^- stage. Many sedimentary deposits are not homogeneous, but comprise assemblages of minerals, and one of the most important factors controlling the chemistry of their groundwater is the order in which the minerals are encountered by the flowing water. Thus the chemical reactions in one stratum, changing the ionic composition and the pH of the water, will influence the reactions in subsequent strata (Freeze and Cherry, 1979). In a heteroeneous aquifer system flow will occur predominantly in the more permeable strata, and the mineral composition of these layers, rather than the composition of the whole aquifer, will be the main factor influencing water chemistry. Furthermore, there may be great differences between the solutes in the different strata. Cation changes also occur along groundwater flow lines, although due to cation exchange reactions, the pattern is much less clear than that outlined by Chebotarev for the anions, but as a broad generalization Ca and Mg are replaced by Na (Price, 1996). Discussions of groundwater evolution in sandstone and in chalk aquifers were given by Edmunds *et al.* (1982) and Ineson and Downing (1963) (see also Section 5.5.7).

8.5.6 Presentation of water chemistry data

It is often useful to summarize and display data on the chemical composition of groundwater, for example to study changes along a flow line, or to detect mixing of waters of different compositions. There are many different ways of presenting the data, and some of the most important and commonly used were summarized by Hem (1985). The most widely adopted system is the trilinear diagram attributed to Piper (1944) and used for the major ion composition. Groundwater is characterized by three cation constituents: Ca^{2+}, Mg^{2+} and Na^+ plus K^+, and three anion constituents: HCO_3^-, SO_4^- and Cl^-. The trilinear diagram (Figure 8.10) combines three plotting fields. The cation and anion compositions are plotted in the left- and righthand triangles respectively (expressed in equivalents per litre). The intersection of the rays projected from the cation and anion plotting points onto the central field represents the overall major-ion character of the groundwater. The values given are the relative rather than absolute concentrations, and since the latter are important in many situations, it is common to plot in the central field not a point but rather a

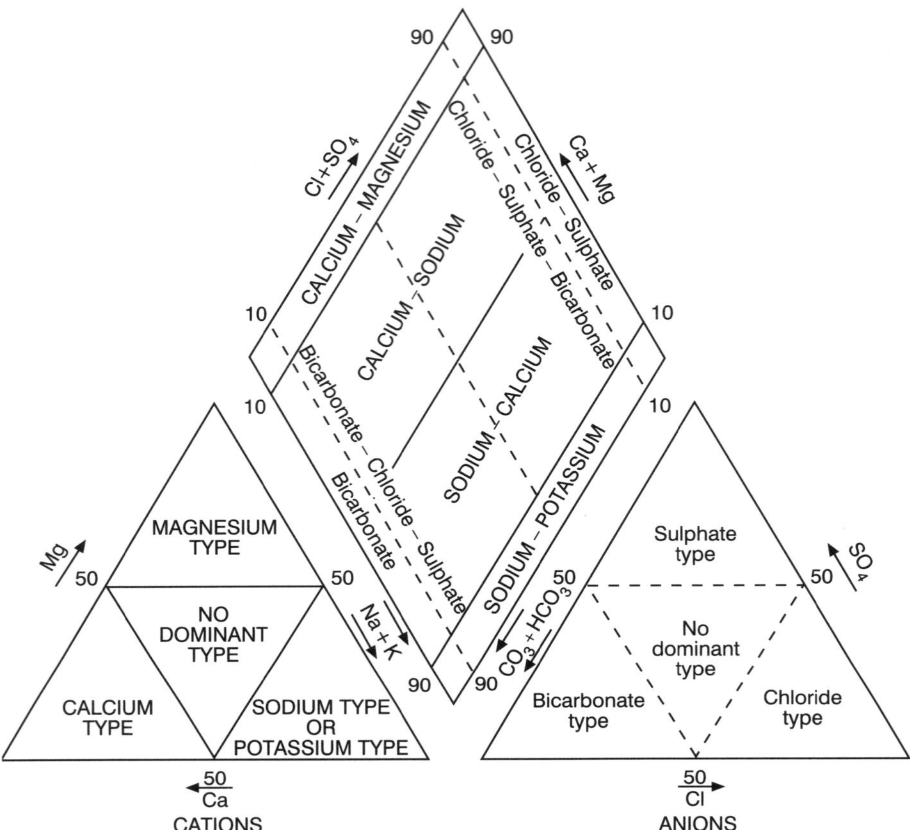

Figure 8.10 Trilinear diagram used to represent the chemical composition of groundwater. See text for details. (From an original diagram by Davis and De Wiest, 1966.)

circle centred on that point whose area is proportional to the total dissolved concentration of the water (Hem, 1985). This type of presentation is useful for describing differences in chemistry of water samples and it can be extended to give identifiable categories or *facies*, based on the concept of the composition of groundwater tending towards equilibrium with the matrix rocks through which it is flowing. The hydrochemical facies represent the observed spatial pattern of solute concentrations in the groundwater which results from the chemical processes operating, the rock types and the flowpaths in the region.

8.6 Runoff

Surface waters, comprising rivers, streams and lakes, are almost always a mixture of waters from different sources. They receive varying inputs from overland flow, throughflow and baseflow, which due to their very different flowpaths and residence times, have different solute and sediment loads. These waters are then mixed together in the channel and routed downstream. In addition to such *non-point* sources, there are *point sources* of pollution entering the river system as industrial waste discharges and effluent from sewage treatment works.

The following sections deal with the water quality changes and processes occurring within stream channels and lakes and then look at the water quality of a watercourse in the context of the overall catchment, in terms of its precipitation chemistry, mineral weathering, vegetation and land use.

8.6.1 Processes in stream channels

A number of changes may occur when water from the soil zone or groundwater enters a stream channel. These include physical, chemical and biological processes which result, perhaps most obviously, in changes in water temperature, dissolved oxygen and the ability to transport solid particles. Solute concentrations may increase due to the solution of materials in the stream bed and banks. In semi-arid areas, in particular, solute concentrations increase as stream water volume is depleted by evaporation.

The solute composition of water flowing into stream channels will be related to the flowpaths and residence times of that water in the soil and groundwater systems. Thus baseflow in streams during periods of dry weather is likely to be composed of water that has been in contact with mineral material for some time and as a result has a higher solute concentration than flows in storm periods which have had a much shorter period of contact with the vegetation and soil material. As a consequence, solute concentrations in river water are generally found to be inversely related to flow rates (Walling and Webb, 1986). In fact some studies have used this to develop chemical means of apportioning a stream flow hydrograph into 'baseflow' and 'stormflow' components.

As noted in Section 8.5, subsurface waters may contain much higher concentrations of CO_2 than atmospheric levels due to biological activity. When such waters enter stream channels there is a rapid 'degassing' of CO_2 to levels that are much closer to atmospheric values. This leads to the consumption of H^+ ions and a consequent raising of the pH (Eqs 8.2 to 8.4) and may result in the precipitation of $CaCO_3$ (Eqs 8.5 to 8.7) as well as certain ions that become less soluble in less acid conditions. An example of the latter is the increasing insolubility of aluminium in less acid water.

There may also be interactions between the solutes entering the channels and sediments in the channel. Pollutants may be adsorbed by stream sediments and then carried with the sediments as they move through the river system, or may be deposited for a considerable time on the beds of lakes and rivers, or on flood plains during times of overbank flooding. In some cases these reactions with the sediments may be irreversible, for example caesium-137 becomes fixed between the lattice plates of illite, while in other cases the effect is simply to introduce a time delay before the adsorbed materials are released back into solution. The study of sediment movement and storage is important, both in its own right, in relation to problems of land erosion and sedimentation of channels and lakes, and also for the fate of adsorbed hazardous or toxic substances.

A crude, but convenient, classification of the sediment movement in a river is into *suspended load*, comprising the finer particles which are held in the flow by turbulence, and *bed load*, comprising the coarser particles which move by sliding, hopping or rolling along the stream bed. In practice there is no clear division between the two modes of transport, and particles that may move as bed load in times of low flow may be carried as suspended sediment in times of high flow.

The mechanism of sediment movement and the transporting capacity of given flow conditions are discussed in various texts on hydraulics and fluvial geomorphology (for example Bogardi, 1974; Richards, 1982). Rating curves between flow and sediment discharge are commonly used in sediment yield studies as a means to interpolate between the often infrequent sediment measurements. Hydraulic factors control the sediment transport capacity of a stream and so are most appropriate for *alluvial rivers*, which have beds and banks formed of river-deposited material that can be transported by high flows. Many rivers are non-alluvial and the discharge of sediment loads, and in particular that of the finer suspended load, is controlled more by the quantity and timing of the supply of sediment into the stream than by the capacity of the flow to transport it. In such rivers, although there may be a positive relation between flow and sediment load (the higher flows can move larger particles and storm erosion supplies new sediment to the channels), the relationship between flow and sediment discharge may be very poorly defined (Figure 8.11). Improved estimates of sediment loads may be obtained by the use of separate rating curves for different seasons and for rising and falling river levels. Ideally, however, sediment sampling should be sufficiently frequent to define the variations over time. Turbidity meters provide one means of achieving a detailed picture of temporal variations without excessive expense and sampling frequency, but are not suitable for all situations.

The situation is further complicated by the fact that solute and sediment travel at different speeds in a river and both move more slowly than the rate of propagation of a flood wave (Glover and Johnson, 1974). Furthermore, the distributed nature of river networks results in the complex mixing of inputs from various tributaries.

The natural pattern of sediment and solute behaviour in a river is therefore best understood in terms of the characteristics of, and processes operating in, the drainage basin as a whole. This is discussed in Section 8.6.3, but first attention must be paid to the study of point source inputs into a river network which may be viewed in terms of the processes operating within the channels. Point inputs to stream channels may have some important consequences; an example, which is of fundamental biological importance, is the role of certain types of organic waste, such as sewage and animal wastes, in consuming dissolved oxygen.

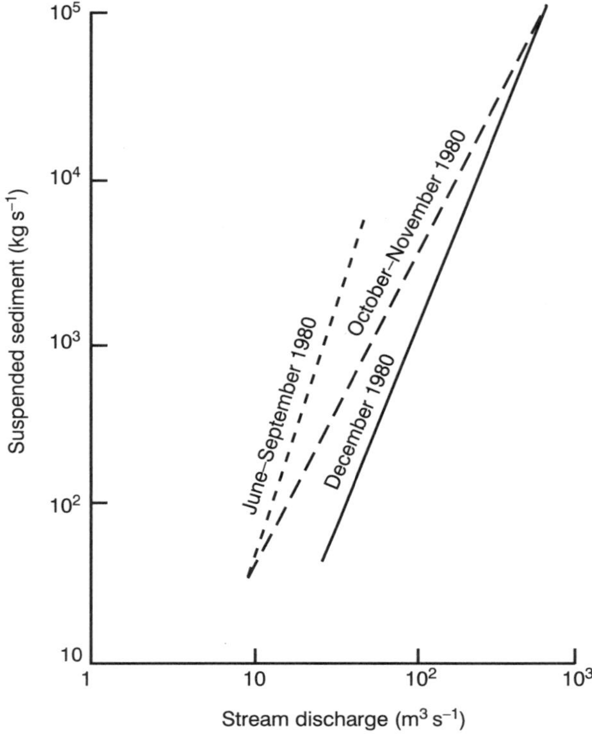

Figure 8.11 Suspended sediment–discharge relations for the Toutle River, Washington, showing the impact of the Mount St Helens volcano eruption in May 1980, depositing enormous quantities of easily erodible sediment. Previously stream sediment loads had been negligible. (Redrawn from an original diagram by Nordin, 1985. By permission of J. Wiley and Sons Ltd.)

Oxygen is critical for aquatic life, and when large amounts of biodegradable materials enter a stream or lake, their chemical and microbial breakdown consumes appreciable amounts of oxygen, hence reducing the concentrations available to aquatic life. In a well-aerated turbulent stream dissolved oxygen concentrations may be close to saturation, about $10\,\mathrm{mg\,l^{-1}}$. Low concentrations ($< 3\,\mathrm{mg\,l^{-1}}$) may be harmful to fish (UNEP, 1995) and, if the dissolved oxygen becomes exhausted, further decomposition will occur by means of anaerobic processes, which generally produce noxious odours (Lamb, 1985).

The pollutant 'strength' of an effluent, i.e. its potential for removing dissolved oxygen, is measured in terms of its *biological* or *biochemical oxygen demand* (BOD). This is a laboratory-derived measure of the consumption of oxygen under standard conditions, usually at 20°C over a period of five days. Details of the method of determination are given in standard texts. While five days is too short for some resistant chemicals, such as those found in wood pulp wastes, for which

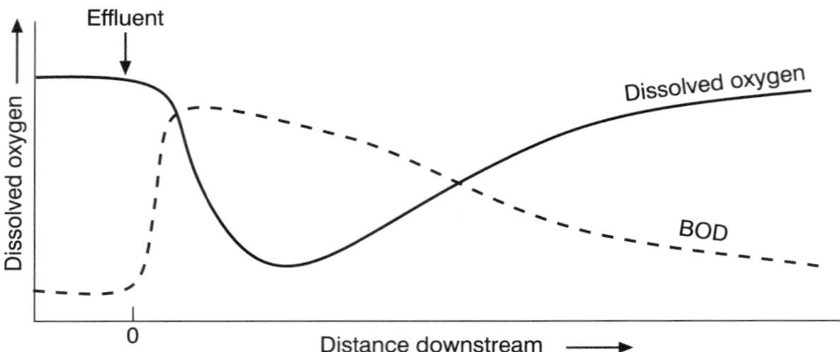

Figure 8.12 Dissolved oxygen 'sag' curve and biochemical oxygen demand (BOD) in a river resulting from the input of an organic effluent.

a 20-day BOD is often used, it is sufficiently long for the majority of the oxygen demand for domestic sewage and many industrial wastes. Even so, the necessity of at least a five-day delay may be unacceptable for some purposes, such as monitoring the performance of a treatment plant, and the quicker measure of *chemical oxygen demand* (COD) can provide a value in a couple of hours, which can then be related by an empirical relation for the site to BOD (Lamb, 1985). Figure 8.12 illustrates a typical dissolved oxygen 'sag' curve due to the deoxygenation and subsequent recovery after the addition of organic effluent to a stream from a single outfall point. This curve represents the balance between the rate of consumption of oxygen (which progressively declines as the waste is broken down) and the replenishment of oxygen, mainly by solution from the atmosphere. The rate of reoxygenation increases with the severity of oxygen depletion and the turbulence of the water and reduces with increasing water temperatures. Since the rate of reoxygenation is much slower than that of depletion, the minimum levels of dissolved oxygen may occur some distance, perhaps many kilometres, downstream of the effluent outfall. The magnitude of oxygen sag will depend on the flow in the river, to dilute the effluent, so that any problems of low oxygen levels will be particularly critical at times of low flow in warm weather.

8.6.2 Lakes

The discussion of water quality changes in open water bodies has, so far, centred on changes in channels containing flowing water. It is appropriate at this point to briefly discuss the properties of lakes, which generally tend to reduce the wide variations in water quality of the rivers entering them. Due to their reduced water velocity and turbulence, lakes may cause important differences in water quality. Much of the sediment and organic matter entering with river water may settle out, reducing turbidity, and allowing sunlight to penetrate further, which in turn allows more photosynthesis and a richer growth of plants and algae. Under natural processes this gradual accumulation of organic matter will eventually result in the infilling of the lake and creation of a peat bog. The rate of this aquatic plant growth may be limited by a shortage of dissolved nutrients, of which phosphorus and nitrogen seem to be the most important (OECD, 1986). Increased levels of these nutrients are released into streams by man from agricultural fertilizers and domestic sewage, and by removing the natural limits to aquatic plant production this may result in excessive growth of algae and/or other aquatic plants, termed *eutrophication*. This can cause problems for water supply abstractions by affecting the taste and smell and cause filtration problems. In some cases it may result in severe oxygen depletion when the plants die, and can lead to the death of fish and other aquatic life.

One important aspect of some lakes is *thermal stratification*. This is a consequence of water being at its maximum density at 4°C. In deep lakes or reservoirs there may be little mixing of the surface layer of water with that below during most of the year. In summer the surface waters are warmer and less dense than the water below and in winter the surface water may be colder and more dense. As a result, the surface layer (or epilimnion), which may be some 5–8 metres deep, has a high dissolved oxygen content, abundant sunlight and a rich plant life, while in contrast the deeper water (or hypolimnion) is insulated from direct contact with atmospheric oxygen and so may have little or no dissolved oxygen and receives less sunlight. Under these conditions the accumulation of decaying organic matter, sinking down from the surface, leads to stagnant conditions. In the deep water of lakes, phosphate and silica may be released into solution, and ammonia and other gases produced from the biological decay. These two layers of the lake water may remain distinct until with the onset of cold winter weather the surface water cools and becomes denser, allowing mixing of the layers by wind action. This 'overturn' of the lake water may occur over only a few hours, and the outflow of the bottom stagnant water may cause serious reductions in the dissolved oxygen levels both within the lake and in streams flowing from it. The sudden upwelling of nutrients from the bottom to the surface can also result in algal blooms.

8.6.3 Catchments

The foregoing sections discuss the main processes controlling the water chemistry of the different components of the hydrological cycle. The following sections give a few examples of how the water quality at the outlet of a catchment can be interpreted as the integration of these processes. These discuss the influence on water quality of geology, climate and human activities, including the use of chemicals such as fertilizers and pesticides, and detail the main water quality characteristics of a number of British rivers.

Geology

Since weathering reactions and their soluble products will be largely determined by the minerals available, it is to be expected that the natural composition of stream solutes will be primarily determined by the soil type and the underlying geology. On a global scale, about 60 per cent of the total natural dissolved load of rivers is derived from rock weathering (Walling and Webb, 1986). The rest comes mainly from the dissolution of atmospheric CO_2 (to form HCO_3^-) and from sea salts.

A number of studies have shown the importance of lithology on stream chemistry. Miller (1961) found that solute concentrations in streams draining sandstone catchments were 10 times higher than in those draining quartzite, and he attributed much of the difference to the dissolution of thin limestone beds in the sandstones. Johnson and Reynolds (1977) found lower solute concentrations in streams draining granite catchments than in those draining mixed metamorphic sedimentary rocks. In a study of major ions and total dissolved solids in 56 single bedrock-type catchments across the USA, Peters (1984) concluded that lithology was a major factor determining dissolved loads, with the highest values in streams draining limestone basins.

Table 8.3 shows typical stream solute concentrations that have been reported in the literature, arranged into broad classes by rock type. Igneous rocks are generally rather impervious and their minerals are resistant to weathering; they generally have the lowest solute concentrations while sedimentary rocks commonly give higher values (but this is very dependent upon their mineral composition). Streams on metamorphic rocks tend to have solute concentrations that are intermediate between igneous and sedimentary rocks, depending on the original material and the degree of alteration. Precipitates such as limestone (mainly $CaCO_3$) and dolomite ($CaMg(CO_3)_x$) generally have much higher concentrations, while evaporates such as halite (NaCl) and anhydrite ($CaSO_4$), which are derived from soluble minerals deposited by evaporation of water, may produce the highest concentrations of dissolved solids. In areas where rock weathering is very slow the stream solutes may be strongly dependent upon atmospheric inputs (Bormann and Likens, 1994; Reid *et al.*, 1981).

Rates of chemical weathering cannot be considered in isolation from physical weathering since the latter is necessary to expose fresh rock material to attack

Table 8.3 Solute concentrations in streams in catchments underlain by different rock types.

Rock type	*Total dissolved solids* ($mg\,l^{-1}$)	*Principal ions*
Igneous and metamorphic	< 100	Na, Ca, HCO_3
Sedimentary (detrital) *	50–250	Variable
Limestone and dolomite	100–500	Ca, Mg, HCO_3
Evaporites	< 10 000	Na, Ca, SO_4, Cl

* Very variable depending on composition.

(Drever, 1988). Thus, solute loads may be higher from steep or poorly vegetated areas where physical erosion continually removes the solid weathering products. In many situations the subsurface waters pass through several different rock strata, so the controls on the resulting chemical composition of the surface waters may be very complex.

Stream sediment yields in western Europe are generally low (<10 tonnes $km^{-2} y^{-1}$), with the highest yields observed in south east Asia (>500 tonnes $km^{-2} y^{-1}$) due to a combination of heavy rainfall, steep slopes and readily erodible soils (UNEP, 1995).

Climate

The water quality of streams depends on a number of interrelated environmental factors, but in general terms the most important natural factor, along with geology, is climate.

The most important control on the speed of chemical weathering is the availability of liquid water. Temperature is less crucial, and while weathering reactions are faster at higher temperatures this may be offset by less rapid exposure of bedrock by physical erosion due to a denser vegetation cover. In a classic study, Langbein and Schumm (1958) demonstrated that mechanical erosion declined with increasing mean annual rainfall as a result of the greater vegetation cover protecting the ground surface from erosion.

In a study of annual flow and solute data for nearly 500 catchments in which pollution was relatively limited, Walling and Webb (1983) found clear evidence that *loads* increased with annual runoff, although this was at a slower rate than the increase in flows, so solute *concentrations* actually decreased. There was a great deal of scatter in the solute/runoff relationships, due largely to differences in catchment lithologies. They could not make 'positive' suggestions regarding the climatic controls on solute loads due to differences in the predominant rock types in different climate zones. Thus, for example, temperate regions have a greater abundance of sedimentary rocks while tropical areas have predominantly crystalline (igneous and metamorphic) rocks.

Human impacts

In recent years human activities have had an increasing effect on the water quality of all the components of the hydrological cycle. This has been both through the addition of chemicals (whether into the atmosphere, onto the land or directly into watercourses) and by the alteration of catchments by land-use changes. The following discussion is by no means comprehensive, since limitations of space prevent a full treatment of all the many influences and interactions. It is intended, therefore, to indicate some of the processes involved and some of the management options available, by reference to the examples of chemical fertilizers and pesticides on farmland and to the planting of some agricultural land for commercial forestry.

Fertilizers are applied to the land to correct nutrient deficiencies limiting plant growth. They are particularly important for arable crops since nutrients are removed when the crops are harvested. The main fertilizers in use supply nitrogen (N), phosphorus (P), potassium (K) and sulphur (S).

In recent years there has been a great deal of concern regarding the possible links between nitrates in water and health risks to humans, including stomach cancer and infant methaemoglobinaemia (WHO, 1996). The European Union has specified a maximum admissible NO_3 concentration of $50\,mg\,l^{-1}$ ($= 11.3\,mg\,l^{-1}$ N as NO_3) in drinking water. Over the 40-year period 1940–80 there was an eight-fold increase in the use of fertilizer nitrogen in the UK as part of an overall intensification of agricultural production (DOE, 1986), and this was one of the principal causes of increases in the nitrate levels in British rivers. From the 1980s onwards, applications of nitrate fertilizer stopped increasing and concentrations in natural waters also appeared to level off (Addiscott, 1996). Although it may be argued that this is too simplistic a picture, and that other nitrate sources result from land drainage, sewage effluent and atmospheric deposition, budgeting studies confirm that in rural areas agriculture is the main source of nitrate in river water (Burt and Johnes, 1997). It has been estimated that European agriculture is responsible for 60 per cent of the riverine flux of nitrogen to the North Sea and 65 per cent of the total atmospheric nitrogen loading (Ongley, 1996).

Soils naturally contain a large amount of nitrogen, most of which is held in the humus-rich surface horizons. This is, however, largely unavailable to plants (and to leaching) and only slowly becomes available by a two-stage process comprising decomposition (mineralization) to ammonium (NH_4^+) and then oxidation (nitrification) to NO_3^- by soil bacteria. As noted earlier, NO_3 is a 'mobile' anion which is not adsorbed by the soil and will move with the water flux, but in the upper soil layers it is taken up by plants. Nitrogen fertilizer is generally applied to crops in spring or early summer when plant growth is rapid, and the crops are subsequently harvested in late summer. This is reflected in the seasonal pattern of nitrogen concentrations in the stream water draining an intensively farmed arable catchment (Figure 8.13). Nitrate leaching losses are greatest in the winter when plant uptake is minimal, and lowest in the summer when the plants are growing rapidly. The late spring peak values correspond to the 'flushing' of nitrogen by the first big storm after the fertilizer application, and this has also been observed in other studies (Roberts, 1987).

In catchments where the dominant source of nitrate is sewage effluent the seasonal pattern of concentrations is reversed, with the fairly constant input of effluent undergoing greater dilution by the generally larger flows of river water in winter (Roberts and Marsh, 1987). The LOIS Project (Land Ocean Interaction Study) provides a large-scale multidisciplinary study of UK river inputs to the North Sea. This included major ions, nutrients, trace metals, pH, alkalinity and

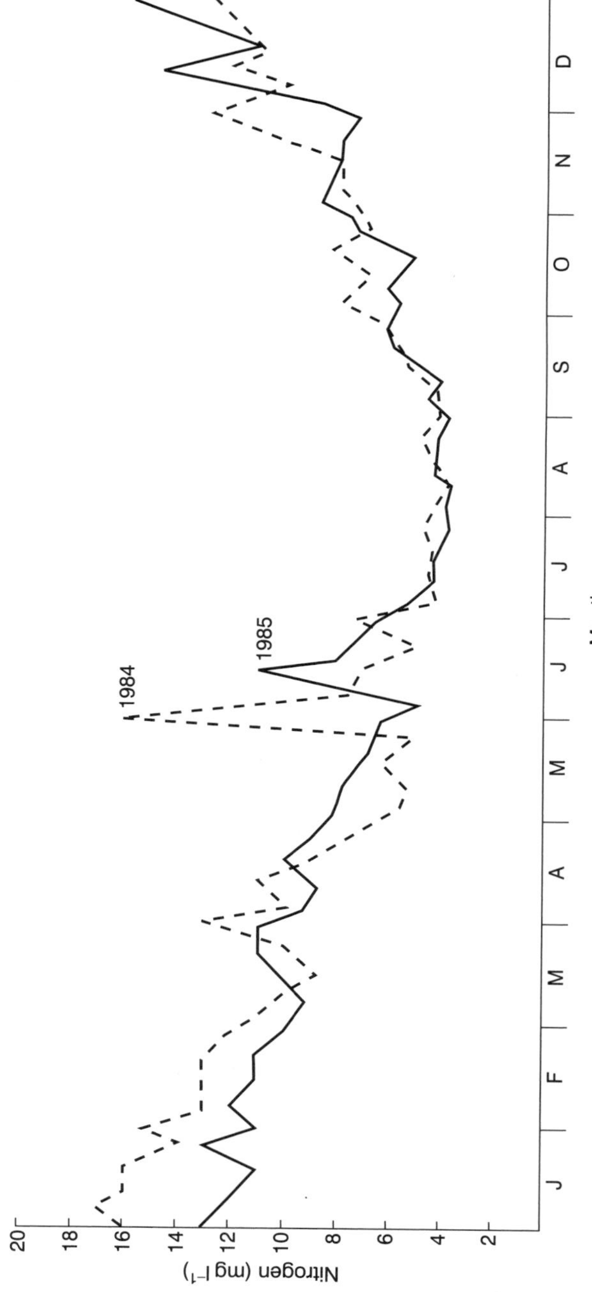

Figure 8.13 Seasonal pattern of nitrate concentrations (mg l^{-1}) for the River Stour at Langham in south east England in 1984 and 1985 (data from the Environment Agency, Anglian Region).

suspended solids (Leeks *et al.*, 1997). Variations in water quality were shown to be related to regional differences in geology, climate, land use and population density (Robson and Neal, 1997).

Agricultural practices will also affect the rate of loss of nitrate from farmland. Ploughing leads to aeration of the soil and greater mineralization and nitrification, and in the case of ploughing up of old grassland it can result in an increase in the release of nitrogen over a number of years. Similarly, artificial drainage will increase nitrate leaching and will also alter the flow paths by diverting some of the leachate from downward movement towards the groundwater to lateral flow in pipes discharging into streams (OECD, 1986).

There has also been concern regarding the increasing concentrations of nitrate found in groundwater supplies. Foster and Young (1981) studied pore water nitrate levels in the unsaturated zone of the chalk aquifer in Britain. Cores were drilled at 60 locations and the interstitial water was extracted by centrifuge. Nitrate concentrations were found to be closely related to the history of agricultural practice on the overlying land. Thus, all sites under arable farming had NO_3^--N levels $> 11.3\,mg\,l^{-1}$ and many had over double this figure, while under permanent unfertilized vegetation, such as rough grassland and woodland, concentrations were much lower, i.e. generally less than $5\,mg\,l^{-1}$ and often less than $1\,mg\,l^{-1}$. Values beneath fertilized grassland were intermediate between these land-use categories, i.e. generally in the range 5–$10\,mg\,l^{-1}$. Water in the underlying saturated zone was generally 10–$15\,mg\,l^{-1}$ under arable crops (cf. 20–$30\,mg\,l^{-1}$ in the unsaturated zone above). This suggests that as this water moves downwards to the water table nitrate concentrations in the groundwater will continue to increase for some years, even if no further fertilizer is applied.

While much attention has been given in recent years to the loss of nitrates from agricultural land, much less is known about the leaching of *pesticides* (literally meaning 'killer of pests'). In temperate climate areas the most commonly used pesticides are *herbicides* to kill weeds while in tropical areas *insecticides* have revolutionized health and life expectancy by controlling insects which are the principal vectors of disease. However, while it has been claimed that pesticides have saved over one hundred million lives in developing countries widespread concern has arisen, especially in developed countries, regarding their environmental effects. Pesticides may accumulate in the food chain and so pose a threat to fish, birds and mammals, and this has led to a long-standing debate about whether they are 'lifesaving chemicals' or the 'elixirs of death' (Harding, 1988).

Pesticides comprise an enormous range of both naturally derived and synthetic chemical compounds, designed to be toxic and persistent (stable), to protect against pests, disease and weeds. Over 500 pesticides are licensed for use in the UK. Since 1940 there has been a dramatic increase in the use of pesticides; virtually all UK agricultural and horticultural crops are treated (OECD, 1986).

Due to their potential environmental damage there has been a change from the persistent organochlorine pesticides to less persistent chemicals which will degrade, by chemical hydrolysis or bacterial oxidation, over a few months rather than years. These newer compounds are, however, generally more soluble in water, posing the risk of contamination of groundwater and surface water. The fate of an applied chemical in the soil depends upon its partitioning between the soil particles and the soil solution (Lawrence and Foster, 1987).

As with fertilizers, pesticides are particularly prone to leaching in solution in the first couple of weeks after application, before processes such as degradation, adsorption and volatilization make the residues unavailable (Burgoa and Wauchope, 1995). At present, the European Union has adopted an arbitrary standard for pesticides in drinking water of $0.1\,\mu g\,l^{-1}$ for each pesticide, regardless of toxicity. In Britain the most commonly used herbicide is *isoproturon* (Eke *et al.*, 1996), which is used to control weeds in cereal crops. Its high usage and predominantly autumn application results in its contaminating surface and groundwaters. In several studies concentrations greater than $10\,\mu g\,l^{-1}$ have been recorded in streams during storms that occurred within a few days of its application (Harris *et al.*, 1991; Johnson *et al.*, 1994). Williams *et al.* (1995) noted that pesticide transport to streams was increased by bypass flow through structural cracks in a heavy clay soil. Garmouma *et al.* (1998) related the varying pattern of herbicide concentrations in the streams of four catchments in northern France to differences in application rates and weather conditions, land use and soil types.

Since the mid-1980s there has been a growing awareness of potential problems to the aquatic environment caused by *endocrine disrupters* in domestic sewage and industrial effluents. These include the main active component of the oral contraceptive pill and can interfere with the endocrine (hormonal) system of plants and animals which controls a wide range of physical processes including metabolism, growth and reproduction. Effects include a high incidence of intersexuality (hermaphrodite) condition in fish downstream of sewage treatment works (Jobling *et al.*, 1998; Routledge *et al.*, 1998). Given the increasing number of substances with endocrine disrupting properties (from antifouling paint to some detergents) there is a large potential for ecological damage.

There are many different types of land-use change and disturbance to catchments resulting from man's activities which may alter the water quality of streams. With overproduction of certain food products and reforms to the Common Agricultural Policy (CAP) in Europe there has been a move to encourage the planting of forestry on former agricultural land. This may benefit the environment, for example by locking up carbon in the plant material and so helping to reduce 'global warming', and by providing a land use that is less dependent upon the application of chemicals.

However, as was shown earlier, forests may alter water quality both directly through the increased 'capture' of atmospheric pollutants and indirectly due to increased evaporation losses and hence an increase in the solute concentrations. Forestry management practices will also affect water quality. Pre-planting drainage and cultivation can release sediments into stream systems (Robinson and Blyth, 1982) and drainage of organic soils increases aeration and may result in substantial losses of nutrients including nitrate and ammonium. If the land is of poor quality, fertilizers such as phosphorus and potassium may be used and herbicides are sometimes necessary to control competing weeds when the young trees are first becoming established. Felling of the forest for timber will also affect stream water quality, with an increase in nitrates in streams draining felled areas (Bormann and Likens, 1994). This is a result of the decay of the organic debris, the soil disturbance caused by harvesting machinery and the lack of any plants to take up the released nutrients.

Water quality modelling and management

As demand for water resources increases and the variety of pollutants becomes more diverse, there is an increasing conflict between the use of rivers for water supply and as 'sewers' for disposing of industrial and domestic effluent. It has been estimated that in the UK, 30 per cent of all drinking water is of a recycled nature (Lester, 1990). Considerable effort has been applied to developing techniques to improve decision-making in water quality problems, and mathematical models can be used to assess alternative control measures to operate water and wastewater treatment facilities. Such models may be used to develop alternative operating rules in river basin management to take into account factors such as flood control, water supply, sewage disposal, fisheries, recreation and amenity activities. There are many different types of mathematical models used for water quality management (for example review by Whitehead, 1984).

Information on common water quality determinands in British rivers is analysed and collated as part of a national network of 'harmonized monitoring' sites (IH/BGS, 1996). Table 8.4 gives data from a subset of 16 catchments showing median values of samples taken at approximately two-week intervals over a 20-year period. Differences between the sites can be related to differences in catchment characteristics. The Nene and Stour, for example, contain much intensively farmed (and fertilized) land, with high rates of nitrate-nitrogen loss. In contrast the Exe, Carron and Spey have only poor farmland, so the water is of high quality with low solute concentrations and a high level of dissolved oxygen. The Trent and Aire are examples of catchments with large inputs of industrial effluent and domestic sewage, and as a result have high concentrations of orthophoshate, chloride, NO_3-N and BOD. The Avon has an intensively farmed catchment and a high sewage effluent input which together give a median NO_3-N level close to the EU limit of $11.3\,\mathrm{mg\,l^{-1}}$.

8.7 In conclusion

The quality of water is of great importance in determining the uses to which the water can be put. Increasing demand for water and increasing sources of pollution (amounts and types) mean that there is greater potential for environ-

Table 8.4 Median values of selected determinands in river water for the 20-year period 1975–94 (data in IH/BGS, 1996). Units are $mg\,l^{-1}$, unless otherwise specified.

River, location	*pH units*	*Conductivity* ($\mu S\,cm^{-1}$)	*Suspended solids*	*Dissolved oxygen*	*BOD O*	*Ammoniacal nitrogen N*	*Nitrate N*	*Orthophosphate P*	*Chloride Cl*	*Alkalinity* $CaCO_3$
Trent, Nottingham	7.8	904	14	10.2	3.0	0.25	8.6	1.50	99	163
Aire, Fleet	7.5	680	17	8.0	7.0	1.49	4.9	1.08	77	126
Avon, Evesham	8.0	937	16	11.0	2.7	0.16	10.4	1.60	74	199
Nene, Wansford	8.0	955	14	10.6	2.7	0.13	9.4	0.98	76	209
Stour, Langham	8.2	911	10	10.9	2.1	0.07	7.2	0.59	68	250
Thames, Teddington	7.9	587	13	10.0	2.3	0.23	7.1	1.08	42	190
Gt. Stour, Horton	7.9	698	7	10.9	2.3	0.12	6.2	0.93	53	223
Almond, Craigehall	7.7	595	10	9.7	2.9	0.95	3.7	0.45	61	120
Ribble, Samlesbury	7.8	407	8	10.2	2.4	0.15	3.4	0.31	30	120
Itchen, Gatersmill	8.1	492	8	10.6	1.8	0.09	5.3	0.35	22	239
Axe, Whitford	8.0	393	6	10.9	1.6	0.06	3.6	0.23	23	140
Dee, Overton	7.2	164	4	11.1	1.1	0.03	1.0	0.05	18	25
Leven, Linnbrane	7.1	68	3	11.0	1.8	0.02	0.3	0.01	10	15
Exe, Thorverton	7.5	163	5	11.2	1.6	0.05	2.3	0.08	17	38
Carron, New Kelso	6.7	42	1	11.3	0.9	0.01	0.1	0.01	10	5
Spey, Fochabers	7.1	77	2	11.4	0.9	0.02	0.3	0.01	10	25

mental damage than ever before, and emphasizes the need for public and political pressure to protect and manage our common resource. Climate change may lead to longer summer periods of low flow in rivers which will reduce the dilution of pollutants.

In scientific terms the study of water quality is more than simply an 'add-on' to our existing knowledge of water quantity fluxes and stores. The use of tracers, both natural and artificial, can provide very revealing information on the flow-paths of water, and the use of natural tracers such as ^{18}O has led to a questioning of some of the traditional hydrological theories of storm runoff generation. Water quality can also affect the behaviour and movement of subsurface water and high solute concentrations can lower the evaporation from water bodies as a result of the reduced saturation vapour pressure (Section 4.4.1 under 'Salinity'). Increasingly the hydrologist must consider both the quantity and the quality of water, and in the future the latter may pose the greater challenges.

Review Problems and Exercises

8.1 Discuss the reasons for the growing importance of water quality compared to water quantity.

8.2 Why has water been described as a maverick compound? Compare its properties to those of some other commonly occurring substances.

8.3 Define the following terms: atom, molecule, ions, solvent, moles, valency, acidity, strong acid.

8.4 How are the techniques of chemical thermodynamics and kinetics used in the study of chemical processes in natural waters?

8.5 Describe the various processes by which acid deposition occurs, and discuss the problems of their measurement.

8.6 Explain the importance for acidification processes of the following: base cations, cation exchange capacity, mobile anions, active acidity and buffering capacity. Discuss the concept of critical loads; in what situations may this approach not be appropriate?

8.7 Define and distinguish the following terms: advection, dispersion, convection, reaction and adsorption.

8.8 Discuss the likely differences in chemical and sediment loads of waters that have travelled via different flow pathways.

8.9 Discuss the challenges inherent in modelling the solute–water soil system.

8.10 Contrast the arguments that pesticides are 'elixirs of death' or 'lifesaving chemicals'. Discuss the importance of a proper hydrological understanding of the pathways and residence times of water movement, in any strategic planning to minimize environmental damage from the use of pesticides and nitrate fertilizers in a predominantly agricultural catchment.

CHAPTER NINE

The drainage basin and beyond

9.1 Introduction

The unity of the hydrological cycle is introduced in Chapter 1 and is emphasized frequently in the descriptive analyses of individual processes and of water quality in succeeding chapters. Intentionally, however, Chapters 2 to 8 pursue an essentially thematic approach, focused largely on the particular components of precipitation, interception, evaporation, groundwater, soil water, runoff and water quality. In this final chapter the approach adopted is one of *synthesis*, in an attempt to illustrate the interaction between hydrological processes within a coherent spatial framework.

In the past, the drainage basin has normally been selected as the most obvious and convenient spatial unit for such integrative and synthesizing studies. As noted in Chapter 1, each drainage basin acts as an individual hydrological system, receiving quantifiable inputs of precipitation which are transformed into flows and storages and into outputs of evaporation and runoff. As a result, the drainage basin is the most commonly used unit for modelling hydrological processes, for water balance studies, for chemical budgets and for examining human impacts on hydrological systems. Small experimental drainage basins, in particular, have made an important contribution to hydrology for more than 100 years. Significant examples include the basin experiments at Emmental, Switzerland (established in the 1890s), Wagon Wheel Gap, USA (1900s), Coweeta, USA (1930s), Cathedral Peak, RSA (1940s) and Plynlimon, UK (1960s). The drainage basin is also the natural geomorphological unit for the operation of fluvial and some fluvio-glacial processes and, because of the close links between the development of fluvial geomorphology and hydrology, this has further strengthened the role of the drainage basin approach in hydrology.

In both the hydrological and geomorphological sense drainage basins are dynamic rather than static entities. The processes of fluvial geomorphology shape the landforms over and through which the water moves. In so doing they significantly influence hydrological features such as stream channels, soil profiles and water-table depths. In this sense, as shown in Figure 9.1, geomorphological activity exerts a feedback on the hydrology that drives it

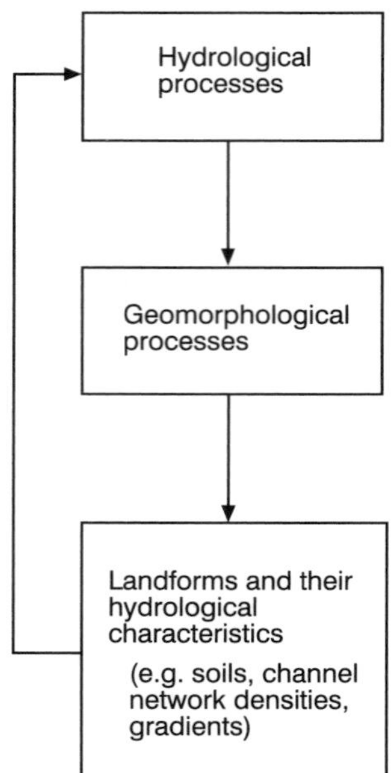

Figure 9.1 Feedback in the relationship between the processes of hydrology and fluvial geomorphology (from an original diagram in NRC, 1991).

(NRC, 1991). Recognition of the dynamic nature of, and feedback between, drainage basin systems was taken a stage further in the 'fluvial hydrosystem' approach (Amoros and Petts, 1993; Petts and Amoros, 1996), which attempts to consolidate hydrology, geomorphology and ecology by viewing fluvial systems as interdependent combinations of the aquatic and terrestrial landscapes (Petts and Bradley, 1997). One of the key concepts of the fluvial hydrosystems approach is that the size and nature of the drainage basin changes continuously from headwaters to mouth as, for example, flow regime, sediment load and water temperature are affected by increased drainage area and by reduced gradient and altitude. *Ph*ysical *Hab*itat *Sim*ulation (PHABSIM) (Bovee, 1982) is now a widely adopted methodology for relating these changing physical conditions to the habitat preferences of individual species.

Increasingly it is recognized that, however large the drainage basin, its scale may nevertheless be too small for the effective study of many environmental processes. For example, recognition of the global-scale impact of climate variations, such as the short-term increases of sea-surface temperature (SST) associated with El Niño–Southern Oscillation (ENSO) events, which were once regarded as a local or regional phenomenon, has reawakened interest in the global nature of the hydrological circulation (see also Section 2.5.3). Much work still needs to be done to clarify the reasons for such temperature changes and the linkages, or teleconnections, between ENSO events and other, longer-term variations of SST resulting from variations of ocean circulation and vertical mixing processes over time scales of a decade or longer. For example, SST anomalies may trigger both flood-producing rainfalls in the Sahel region of West Africa and intense hurricane activity in the eastern USA, enabling the latter to be predicted from knowledge of the former (Gray, 1990). El Niño SST anomalies also appear to be responsible for a significant part of the annual variations of precipitation and river discharge in Florida, USA (Sun and Furbish, 1997).

Similarly, it is now clear that major point sources of pollution may have continuing and widespread impacts on the global atmosphere. And summer thunderstorms over the Great Plains of the USA, once attributed to quasi-random convection cells, are now seen to result from the development and circulation of large disturbances, known as mesoscale convective complexes (MCCs), which may cover areas exceeding 50 000 km^2 (for example Maddox, 1983). Much work remains before the full hydrological effects of MCCs are clarified. Finally, extensive forest clearance in the Amazon basin, which once contained about 50 per cent of the world's tropical rainforest, is blamed for perturbations of rainfall and streamflow many thousands of kilometres away (Mitchell *et al.*, 1990).

Interest in the global scale operation of hydrological processes has come about largely from the growth of interest in global climate change, particularly concern about the possibility of global warming, but also partly because of the availability, through satellite-based remote-sensed data, of key hydrological information at a global or major regional scale (for example Engman and Gurney, 1991). Such data are usually much better suited to large-scale spatial integration, particularly since the technology underpinning their collection may permit rapid assimilation of the data into regional, continental, or even global GIS and database systems (for example Kovar and Nachtnebel, 1996).

The growing interest in the operation of hydrological processes at the global or major regional scale emphasizes the extraordinary range of spatial scale embraced by hydrology (see Table 9.1). Hydrogen bonding at the molecular scale is

Table 9.1 Spatial scales in hydrology (from a table in Dooge, 1988).

Class	*System*	*Typical length (m)*
MACRO	Planetary	10 000 000
	Continental	1 000 000
	Large basin	100 000
MESO	Small basin	10 000
	Sub-catchment	1000
	Catchment module	100
MICRO	Elementary volume	0.1
	Continuum point	0.000 01
	Molecular clusters	0.000 000 01

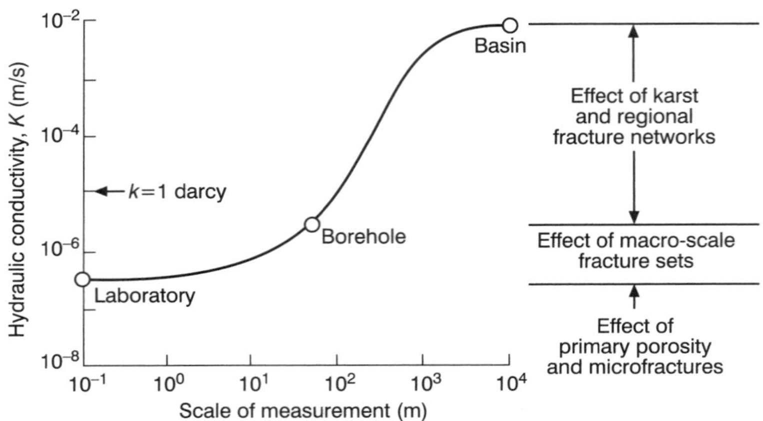

Figure 9.2 Effect of scale on the measured hydraulic conductivity of carbonate rocks in central Europe (from an original diagram in Garven, 1985).

fundamental and facilitates the three-phase existence of water. Many of the classical hydrological theories (for example for the free flow of surface water and for saturated and unsaturated subsurface flow) were developed at the highest of the micro-scales shown in Table 9.1 (Dooge, 1988). Currently, the majority of hydrological studies are at the catchment or sub-catchment scale (Baird, 1997) and therefore fall into the highest of the meso-scale and the lowest of the macro-scale classes in Table 9.1. Global hydrology would focus interest on the highest spatial category. It would also further exacerbate scaling problems in the transfer of theory and of data from one spatial scale to another. It has proved difficult to apply relationships developed at the laboratory scale to spatial units the size of even a small drainage basin. An alternative approach would be to validate laws governing drainage-basin response at the macro-scale and then attempt to disaggregate the results in order to make them applicable at the meso-scale (Dooge, 1988). At the simplest level, even basic data may be difficult to extrapolate from one spatial scale to another. This is illustrated most clearly by measurements of hydraulic conductivity. Figure 9.2 shows values for carbonate rocks in central Europe, with the open circles denoting average permeability. Values increase with the scale of measurement, largely because of the incorporation into the sample volume of increasingly large and even more extensive fracture systems. The issue of scale has been regarded as one of the major unresolved problems in hydrology (NRC, 1991; Sivapalan and Kalma, 1995).

Already these introductory comments have touched upon issues and problems about each of which entire books have been written. Discussion in the remainder of this chapter is thus necessarily selective and concentrates briefly on hydrological modelling at the drainage basin scale, water balance studies of selected drainage basins, and the emergence and likely future development of global hydrology. In these ways we hope to reinforce our view that, although the principles of hydrology may be conveniently taught and studied in a thematic, analytical way, their application to the solution of water-based problems is best achieved through integrated, synthetic studies at a wide range of scales.

9.2 Drainage basin models

Hydrologists have long regarded the development of models which accurately represent drainage basin hydrology as an important test of their understanding of hydrological processes. All too often, however, such models are more successful in hindcast than in forecast mode. And rarely are they applicable with equal success to other drainage basins than the one for which they were developed. As a result there are numerous drainage basin models. Some of these have a value for limited and specific purposes but are of little general hydrological interest. Some are simple black box models which may give a 'correct result' for a chosen hydrological variable, for example runoff, for a particular period of time but may give a poor prediction for other variables. Others are more sophisticated and attempt to reproduce some of the complexity represented by spatial variations of precipitation and drainage basin characteristics. However, the quality of the data used and of the model structure are often more important ingredients for success than model complexity (for example Gan *et al.*, 1997). Underlying, and indeed undermining, all attempts to produce the definitive model is an enigma of the drainage basin itself: large-scale system response (for example the stream hydrograph resulting from a given rainfall) is so simple that it is almost impossible to reconcile with the small-scale spatial complexity which defies description and experimental study at the basin scale (Beven, 1987).

In some circumstances, the ideal drainage basin model would work equally successfully in real time and indeed, many such models have been developed for flood-forecasting purposes. Some of these were reviewed by Smith and Ward (1998). However, in the case of models developed for other specific purposes, real-time operation may be a less important criterion than other relevant factors. Indeed, one of the reasons for the great variety of drainage basin models is that most have been developed for specific predictive purposes rather than for the more fundamental purpose of scientific investigation of hydrological processes. Another reason is that models have been developed to accommodate a wide range of hydrological data availability, from the large ungauged drainage basin with no precipitation data, at one extreme, to the continuous monitoring of many hydrological variables in a small, intensively instrumented, experimental basin, at the other.

9.2.1 Types of drainage basin model

This plethora of models may be broadly categorized in a number of ways. For example, *deterministic* models simulate the physical processes operating in the drainage basin to transform precipitation into evaporation or runoff, whereas *stochastic* (probabilistic) models take into consideration the chance of occurrence or probability distribution of the hydrological variables. Again, *conceptual* models are based on limited representation of the physical processes acting to produce the hydrological outputs, for example the representation of a drainage basin by a cascade of stores (Figure 1.2), while *physically based* models are based more solidly on an understanding of the relevant physical processes. Models may also be *linear* or *non-linear* in either the systems theory or statistical regression sense. Perhaps the most important difference is that between *lumped* and *distributed* models. This depends on the extent to which the spatial distribution of hydrological variables within the basin is considered either in a probabilistic or in a geometrical sense.

In recent years there has been increasing emphasis on the development of *physically based distributed* models. The rationale behind this development is that a model that treats the drainage basin as a spatially variable physical system is intrinsically more realistic and has significant theoretical advantages that make it more useful, over a wider range of applications, than other types of model. However, spatial variation in such models is necessarily a highly simplified representation of actual drainage-basin heterogeneity and is normally achieved by applying mathematical equations of hydrological processes to each intersection of a grid laid over the drainage basin. At best it is then assumed that the parameters governing these processes change smoothly between intersections; at worst that they apply equally to the surrounding area and are therefore discontinuous at the grid mesh boundaries. There are also problems of physical scale (for example Sivapalan and Kalma, 1995) and grid size. Change these and totally different 'surfaces' of interpolated values appear, which are related only at the points common to the generation of each surface (Eeles *et al.*, 1990).

In some respects the distributive mechanism means that the distributed model is essentially a 'lumped' model at the grid scale. More significant perhaps is the concern that, in many distributed models, the equations used to describe hydrological reality at the grid element scale are themselves incorrect, for example the application of Darcy's law to undisturbed soil conditions (Beven, 1996). Also, there have been very few attempts to validate distributed models, even apparently successful ones such as SHE and IHDM, through the prediction of internal hydrological state variables. Beven (1996) described work by Jensen *et al.* (1993), on MIKE-SHE estimates of hydraulic conductivity, as one of the few published studies '. . . in which model predictions are compared with internal state measurements within the flow domain'.

Physically based distributed models are both complex and demanding in terms of data input and computer capacity so that simpler, lumped models, which average and aggregate for the entire catchment, may often be preferred. An alternative approach, of intermediate complexity, is based on probability-distributed models. Instead of taking account of the actual spatial configuration of hydrological variables over a basin, models based on the probability distributed principle consider only the frequency of occurrence of hydrological variables of certain magnitudes over the basin without regard to the geographical location of a particular event. Moore (1985) described *probability distributed models* based on infiltration capacity and on storage capacity.

Simpler models (for example lumped, conceptual, or partially distributed) have been shown to give an adequate empirical fit to the observed behaviour of particular drainage basins (cf. Robinson and Sivapalan, 1995) and are therefore widely used in hydrological investigations. Such models have certainly dominated the trend towards PC-based, desk-top computer modelling procedures, whose popularity owes much to the fact that their operating routines and graphical output are familiar and user-friendly. The nature of these models means, however, that their parameters must generally be calibrated from existing discharge records and in most cases this limits their general applicability and transferability (Becker and Pfuetzner, 1990).

An interesting and well-known example is provided by HYRROM (Hydrological Rainfall Runoff Model) (Blackie and Eeles, 1985). This is a conceptual rainfall-runoff model, developed by the UK Institute of Hydrology and found to have wide applicability. The program is easy to use and requires little understanding of the computer operating system or the structure of the data files. Output is in the form of colour screen graphics which can be copied to a plotter or graphics printer if required.

In HYRROM, flows are predicted using a simple representation of the physical processes which govern water movement within the drainage basin (Figure 9.3). The model incorporates interception, soil water, groundwater and runoff stores,

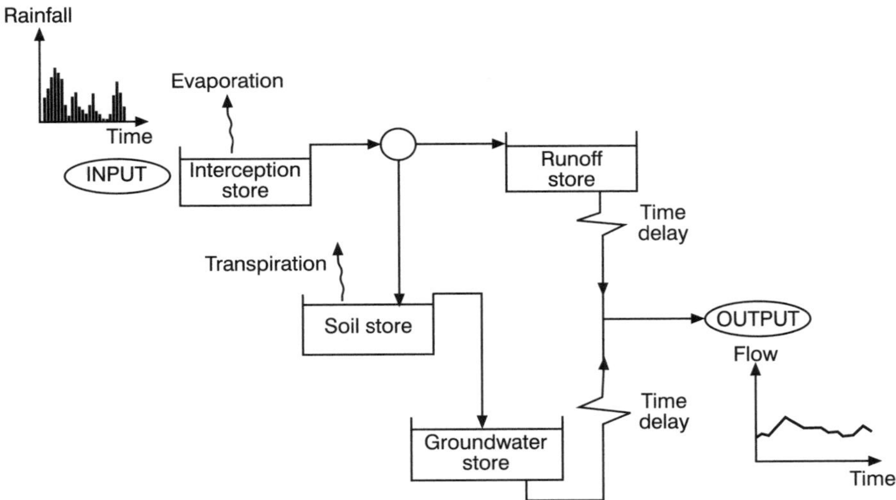

Figure 9.3 The structure of HYRROM (Hydrological Rainfall Runoff Model) designed to run on IBM and IBM-compatible PCs (from an original diagram by the Institute of Hydrology, Wallingford, Oxon, OX10 8BB, UK).

Table 9.2 The adjustable parameters in HYRROM and their permissible ranges (from a table in Watts, 1997).

Parameter	*Description*	*Range allowed*
SS	Size of the vegetation interception and surface detention store (mm)	$0 < x < 5$
RC	Surface runoff partitioning factor	$0 < x < 1$
RDEL	Routing store delay (days)	$x > 0$
RX	Routing store index	$x > 1$
RK	Routing store factor	$0 < x < 1$
FC	Penman open water evaporation factor	$0.3 < x < 1$
GDEL	Groundwater store delay (days)	$x > 0$
GSP	Groundwater store index	$x > 1$
GSU	Groundwater store factor	$x > 30$

and includes some representation of the losses due to evaporation. It can be calibrated manually by the user or automatically using a built-in optimization routine. Nine of the parameters in the model can be adjusted (see Table 9.2); the remainder are preset.

9.2.2 Stanford Watershed Model (SWM4)

One of the best known of the early conceptual drainage basin models is the Stanford Watershed Model (SWM) whose pioneering version, SWM1, was published in 1960 as a rainfall-runoff model. This was rapidly developed to model total drainage basin response, rather than simply storm runoff, and emerged as SWM4 in 1966. The model, described in detail by Crawford and Linsley (1966) and more recently by Viessman and Lewis (1996), uses a soil moisture accounting procedure and represents hydrological processes within the drainage basin through storage and routing functions (Figure 9.4). A system of quasi-physical equations is used to keep a running account of all water entering the basin as precipitation, stored within the basin hydrological system, and leaving as hourly runoff or evaporation. Each input of water is accounted for until it evaporates, infiltrates to groundwater or enters a stream channel. The model then routes the runoff from the point of entry into the channel to some specified downstream location. Fleming (1975), an enthusiastic proponent of SWM4, listed the data needed to model daily streamflow, together with the 34 parameters which describe the physical characteristics of the basin (25 if snowmelt is not included). These parameters can be varied by a slight adjustment of the input data in order to study the effect of different basin characteristics on runoff and other specific aspects of basin hydrology.

Despite its early pioneering status, SWM4 is a very sophisticated conceptual model, in which hydrological processes retain a correct relationship to each other

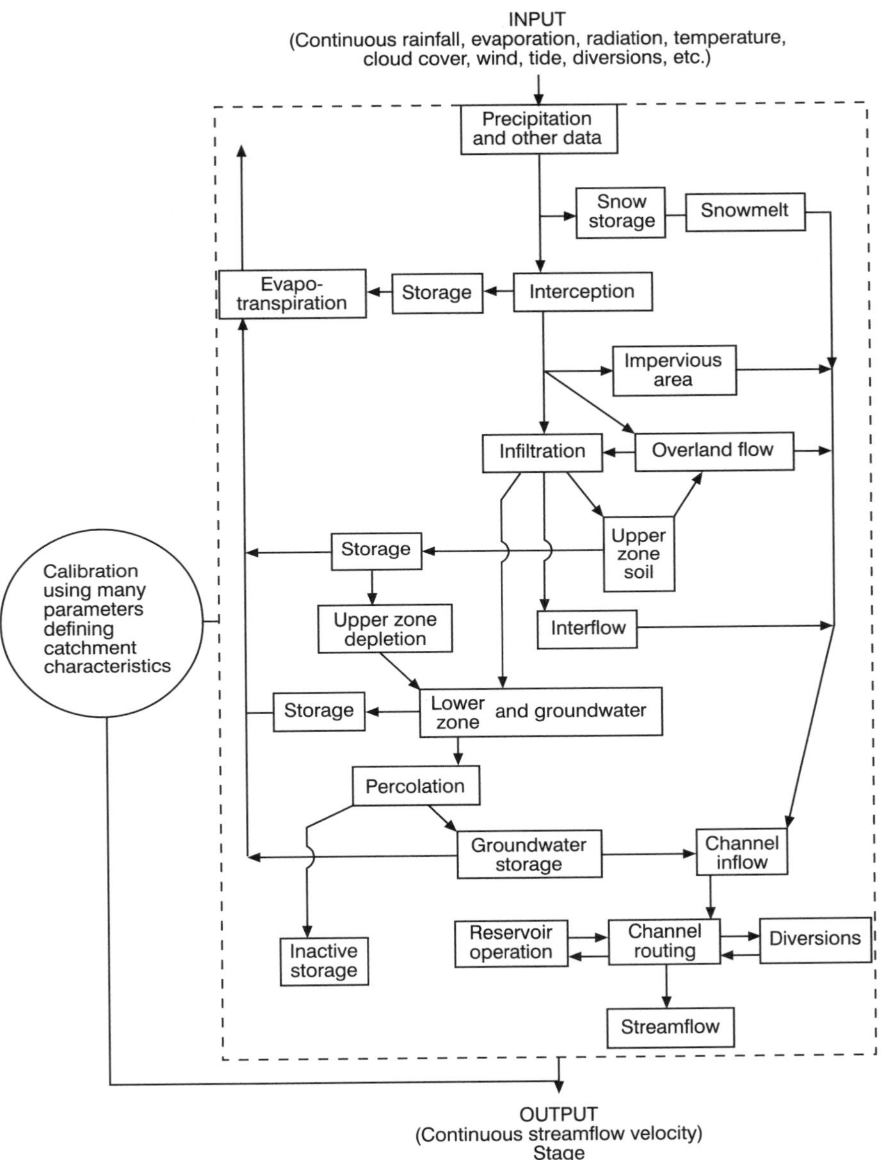

Figure 9.4 The structure of the Stanford Watershed Model IV (from an original diagram by Fleming, 1975).

and in which empirical rules, albeit of a fairly simple linear kind, allow the modeller to represent evaporation and quickflow generation in a quasi-spatially variable way. Not surprisingly, the model and its derivatives are still in widespread use.

9.2.3 SHE (Système Hydrologique Européen)

An important example of a new generation of physically based distributed models is the Système Hydrologique Européen (SHE). This is really a modelling framework, rather than a model, whose flexible system architecture is designed to allow the integration of new versions of component models and provides the potential for a continuous upward development path for the system (O'Connell, 1991). SHE was developed collaboratively by the UK Institute of Hydrology (IH), the Danish Hydraulic Institute (DHI) and the Société Grenoblois d'Étude et d'Applications Hydrauliques (SOGREAH). IH developed the interception, evaporation and snowmelt components, DHI the saturated and unsaturated flow components and SOGREAH the overland and channel flow components. The motivation to develop SHE came from the perceived failure of existing models to represent the impact of human activity on drainage basin flow, water quality and sediment transport regimes (O'Connell, 1991).

Hydrological processes are modelled using either a finite difference approach or research-based empirical equations. The model structure, shown diagrammatically in Figure 9.5, is based on dividing the drainage basin spatially into a grid of up to 2000 squares, with a column of up to 30 horizontal layers at each grid square. Given that data limitations prevent this high level of differentiation being attained at the present time, appropriate parameters and data are specified individually for each grid square used, including surface elevation, vegetation

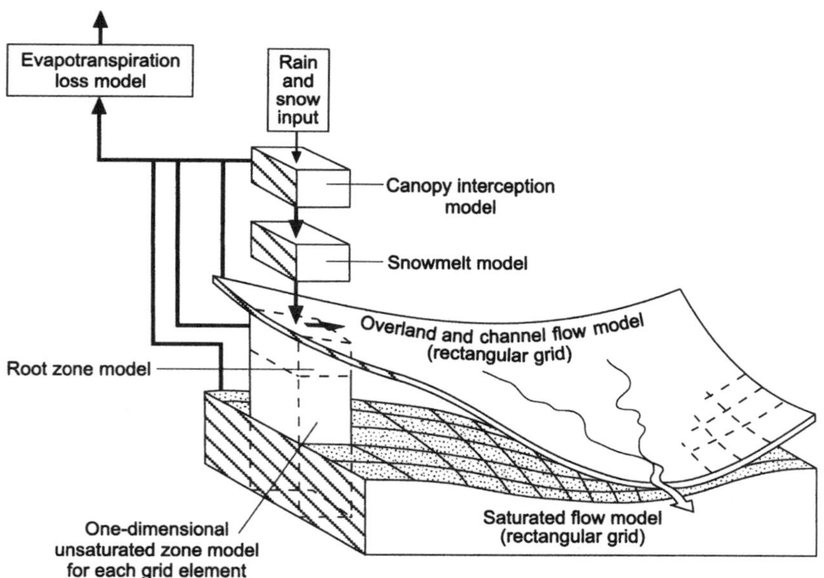

Figure 9.5 The structure of the Système Hydrologique Européen (SHE) (from an original diagram in Abbott *et al.*, 1986).

and soil properties, meteorological data, channel and surface flow resistance data, impermeable bed levels and potentiometric surface levels. Surface and subsurface flow conditions are developed by the model for each grid square, thereby permitting investigation of local hydrological variations. The two-dimensional surface water and groundwater flow components are linked by a simplified one-dimensional flow component in the unsaturated zone. Interception is estimated using the Rutter accounting procedure but evaporation may be estimated in several ways, including the Penman–Monteith equation, depending on the available data. Flow in the unsaturated zone is estimated by the one-dimensional Richards equation and in the saturated zone by the two-dimensional Boussinesq equation. Snowmelt is determined from an energy budget approach and overland and channel flow from simplifications of the St Venant equations.

An advantage of the model is that it uses parameters that have some physical significance and can be estimated from drainage basin characteristics. Also, full parameterization means that SHE is regionally transferable, and can be applied even in ungauged river basins, although computer demands are very high (Becker and Pfuetzner, 1990). Moreover, the distributed nature of the model allows the possibility of calibration for the entire basin based on comparisons between modelled and observed hydrographs at several points within it (IH, 1985). The model has been applied to catchments in a wide range of environments, including Europe and New Zealand (for example Lumadjeng, 1989; New Zealand Ministry of Works and Development, 1985). Such field testing has highlighted model weaknesses and has contributed to further model refinement, as evidenced in the several versions of the model that have been described to date (for example Abbott *et al.*, 1986; Bathurst *et al.*, 1995; Refsgaard and Storm, 1995; Jayatilaka *et al.*, 1998).

9.2.4 TOPMODEL (topography-based hydrological model)

Despite the terminology used, it is clear that models such as SHE are not 'physically based' in the true sense of that description. For example, the equations used are gross simplifications of actual hydrological processes and small-volume physics is applied to model grid squares of 250 m or 500 m on a side. Beven (1991) illustrated the problem by reference to modelled estimates of capillary potential:

> What does a grid element average capillary potential mean over an area of 250 by 250 m? It is not a physical variable in the sense that we can measure it. How can we compare it with a tensiometer measurement within the grid square which may have a zone of influence of a few cm^3 [?] Worse still, what does a grid square average capillary potential *gradient* mean when it is calculated from nodes 0.05 m apart in the vertical for an area of 62 500 m^2 [?].
> p. 378

And yet the discussions of hydrological processes in this book repeatedly confirm the existence of clear spatial patterns, especially those influencing the variable source areas for quickflow, which arise mainly from topographic variability and the influence of gravity on hillslope water movement. TOPMODEL represents an attempt to improve hydrological predictions by incorporating such spatial patterns into a *semi-distributed conceptual model*, though in a parsimonious way with a limited number of parameters.

The model combines the spatial variability of source areas with the average response of the basin soil-water storage (Beven and Kirkby, 1979), thereby minimizing the number of model parameters and the field data input. TOPMODEL uses readily available topographic data, together with a limited amount of soil data, and since all the model parameters can be obtained by direct measurement, the model should be applicable to ungauged basins of up to 500 km^2, where a forecast of the hydrological response is required and where only rainfall and evaporation data are available (Beven *et al.*, 1984). Numerous improvements and refinements have been incorporated since the model was first developed (for example Hornberger *et al.*, 1985; Sivapalan *et al.*, 1987; Holko and Lepistö, 1997; Saulnier *et al.*, 1997).

A fundamental assumption is that the water table follows the topography, allowing flow to be estimated using topography as a surrogate for hydraulic gradient. In this way, the drainage basin may be subdivided into several relatively homogeneous subcatchment units, each modelled separately and with their simulated discharges being routed individually through the channel to the basin outflow. The model parameters, summarized in Table 9.3, are physically based in the sense that they can be obtained directly from field measurements. The main features of TOPMODEL (shown schematically in Figure 9.6) are an interception store (S_1), a near-surface infiltration store (S_2), and a variable contributing area which varies with the average subsurface store (S_3) and is the major source of overland flow.

Table 9.3 Summary of model parameters used in TOPMODEL (from a table in Beven *et al.*, 1984).

Symbol	*Description*	*Calibration*
S_D	Maximum interception storage	Sprinkling infiltrometer
S_c	Maximum infiltration store level	Sprinkling infiltrometer
i_0	Constant infiltration rate	Sprinkling infiltrometer
OFV	Overland flow velocity parameter	Sprinkling infiltrometer
FC	Field capacity	Sprinkling infiltrometer
m	Subsurface flow parameter	Dilution gauging and soil water analysis
q_0	Subsurface flow parameter	Dilution gauging and soil water analysis
λ	Subcatchment topographic constant	Topographic analysis
CHA	Channel velocity parameter	Dilution gauging
CHB	Channel velocity parameter	Dilution gauging

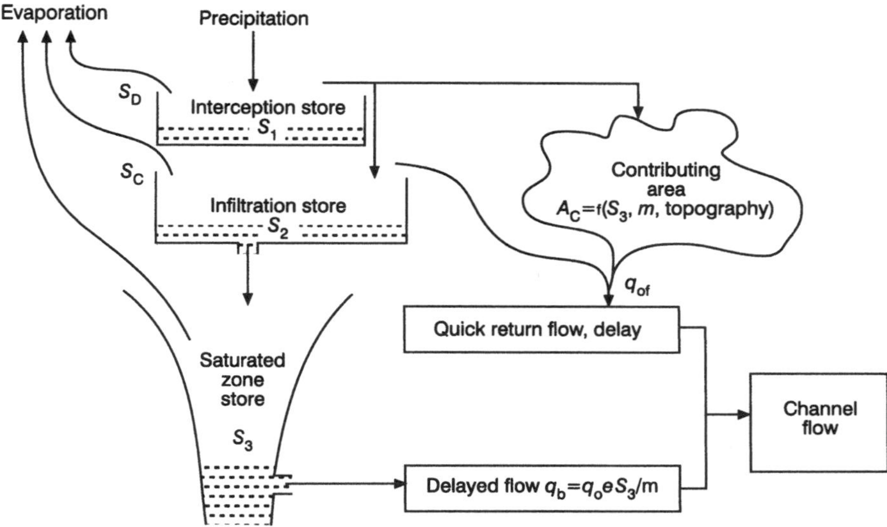

Figure 9.6 The structure of the TOPMODEL subcatchment model (from an original diagram in Beven, 1977).

Undoubtedly, one of the reasons for the success of TOPMODEL is that it is one of the more readily understood distributed models, so that comparisons between model output and drainage basin reality can genuinely be used to test the validity of the hydrological concepts used. This is illustrated at a simple level by the fact that TOPMODEL can predict the geographical location of areas of saturated or near-saturated soil which can easily be verified in the field (Beven, 1991).

9.3 Water balance studies of selected drainage basins

Solving the water balance equation for a specified unit (for example plot, hillslope segment or drainage basin, of whatever size) is a fundamental test of the hydrologist's ability to make accurate assessments of each component flux and storage in the hydrological system. Failure to resolve the water balance, especially for large drainage basins and quasi-continental areas, severely diminishes the potential contribution of hydrology to the solution of current major problems such as the causes and impacts of climate change, the impact of large-scale human activity like deforestation, and the development of successful and reliable models of the general atmospheric circulation. Given an adequate understanding of hydrological processes, it should be possible to quantify each aspect of the drainage-basin water balance, from the initial inputs of solar radiation and precipitation to the ultimate outputs of evaporation and runoff.

However, it is clear from the thematic discussions in this book that our understanding of hydrological processes is still incomplete, our ability to quantify fluxes and stores is often rudimentary, and our understanding of the linkages between processes, particularly at the continental and global scales, is often uncertain and in any case still needs much refinement. Moreover, the components of the water balance equation may vary between drainage basins and may also vary with time for a given drainage basin. It is understandable, therefore, that Klemes (1988) described the water balance equation as:

> ... one of the most challenging Rubik Cubes of nature, one in which the 'squares' change colours, shapes and sizes as they are being moved around by the different forces, and in which even the structural setup changes with time ... p. 20.

The way in which environmental conditions may determine the number of component variables in the water balance equation is illustrated by the inclusion, or otherwise, of the atmospheric water vapour flux. For many drainage basins, particularly small ones, the water balance may be adequately defined in terms of the terrestrial components of the hydrological cycle, as shown in Figure 9.7(a). These are the inputs of precipitation and groundwater flow, the outputs of evaporation, runoff and groundwater flow, and the changes in water storage (principally groundwater and soil water) within the drainage basin. For larger drainage basins it may be necessary to take account of the water vapour fluxes in the atmosphere above the drainage basin, as shown in Figure 9.7(b), either

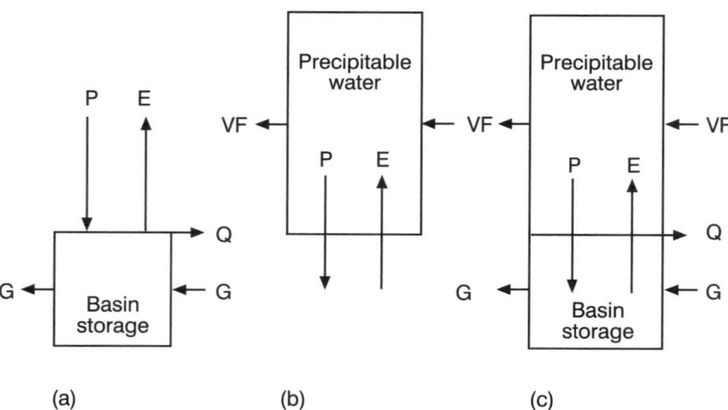

Figure 9.7 Components of the water balance: (*a*) terrestrial; (*b*) atmospheric; and (*c*) combined atmospheric and terrestrial (from an original diagram in Oki *et al.*, 1995).

because basin evaporation contributes significant amounts of water vapour to the local precipitation process, or because the amounts of water vapour entering and leaving the atmosphere above the drainage basin by advection are very different. Then the combined water balance components, for the drainage basin and its overlying atmospheric block, are those shown in Figure 9.7(c).

Other major differences in water balance components may result simply from the lack of reliable data. Indeed, the solution of the *complete water balance equation* is often only possible in small experimental basins, where a full range of relevant hydrological measurements is made. In such cases closure errors are normally small. In other cases it may be possible to solve only a *partial water balance equation*, often with significant closure errors, although this may have value if it helps to illustrate major discrepancies and draw attention to the need for additional specific data. For extensive drainage basins in areas of low and sporadic rainfall, accurate data on all aspects of the water balance may be very difficult to obtain. As a result, closure errors are normally very large, and in these cases the main function of the water balance calculations may be to emphasize the sparsity of knowledge and understanding about drainage basin hydrology.

The four examples which follow have been selected to illustrate the effects of data availability, drainage basin size and water balance complexity on the character, usefulness and applications of water balance calculations.

9.3.1 Catchwater Drain, Yorkshire, UK

When small experimental drainage basins are intensively instrumented for hydrological research purposes it may be possible to solve the complete water balance. Indeed, this is normally an early priority in order to assess the validity of the database and the hydrological integrity of the experimental basin. In such cases, not only are continuous short-interval data available for precipitation, evaporation and runoff, but also detailed data are available from which short-term changes of soil water and groundwater storage may be estimated.

A pioneering example in the UK was the Catchwater Drain in East Yorkshire. This small ($16\,km^2$) drainage basin experiment was established in the early 1960s by the University of Hull in order to investigate the hydrological characteristics of boulder clay (for example Ward, 1967). Precipitation and streamflow were measured continuously, hourly evaporation was calculated from meteorological data, and groundwater storage was estimated from a network of observation wells. Soil water storage, the least satisfactory data set, was determined from tensiometer measurements.

Water balance calculations were carried out, for time intervals ranging from three years to ten days, using the following equation:

$$P - Q - E - \Delta G - \Delta S = 0 \tag{9.1}$$

where P is precipitation, Q is streamflow, E is evaporation, and ΔG and ΔS are, respectively, changes of groundwater and soil water storage. These calculations

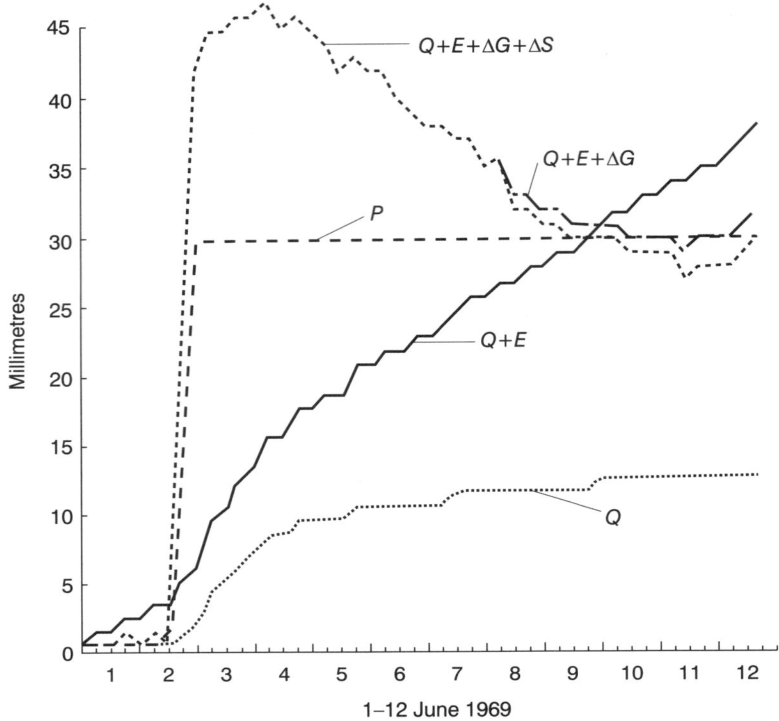

Figure 9.8 Mass curves of principal water balance components for the Catchwater Drain, Yorkshire, during a storm period in 1969.

showed consistently small residuals and were interpreted as confirming the accuracy of the data and the hydrological independence of the defined drainage basin (for example Ward, 1972). A further illustration was provided by hourly data for one storm period. Mass curves of the principal water balance components for the period 1–12 June 1969 are shown in Figure 9.8 which indicates that Eq. 9.1 solves without residual, i.e.

$$29 - 12 - 25 + 6 + 2 = 0 \qquad (9.2)$$

The mass curve of precipitation reflects a single fall of 29 mm of rain which fell in a brief period during the night of 2–3 June. The resulting mass curve of runoff (12 mm) reflects a typical sharp-peaked hydrograph with steep rising limb and shallower falling limb. Evaporation losses were 25 mm and occurred fairly uniformly through the period, so that by the end of the final day the mass ($Q + E$) curve exceeded the P curve by 8 mm, an amount which was precisely accounted for by a 6 mm net decrease of groundwater storage and a 2 mm net decrease of soil water storage.

These satisfactory water balance results formed the basis for the development of a conceptual model of the Catchwater Drain basin. In the early years of the experiment there was very close agreement between modelled and measured runoff but this relationship deteriorated with time. Further investigation showed that the deterioration resulted from changes in the hydrological behaviour of the basin, as a result of land drainage and residential building development (for example Robinson *et al.*, 1985). Thus the knowledge, derived from the early water balance calculations, that all measurements were being made properly and accurately, enabled the subsequent model to be used with confidence as a diagnostic tool to identify changes in drainage basin hydrology.

9.3.2 River Thames, UK

The Thames above Kingston, London, drains a very much larger area of 9948 km^2. The drainage basin comprises a wide range of Jurassic and younger sedimentary rocks, with several important clay vales. Major groundwater storage in the chalk and oolitic limestone is largely responsible for the sustained baseflow which characterizes this river. Topography and land use are diverse and there is extensive urbanization, especially in the downstream parts of the basin. The water balance is significantly affected by human activity. Substantial amounts of water are withdrawn for agricultural, domestic and industrial purposes, although patterns of use have changed; industrial withdrawals in the London region, for example, have decreased in recent years, resulting in a significant increase in water table levels (see the section 'Storage changes in unconfined aquifers' in Chapter 5).

In such circumstances measured values of runoff, which are available from 1883, are no longer appropriate for use in water balance calculations. Instead it is necessary to calculate 'naturalized' runoff values, which take into account all the artificial factors which affect the measured flow values. In the case of the Thames, these include:

- reservoir storage, which diminishes river flows when the reservoirs are supplied from the drainage basin above the gauging station at Kingston;
- river regulation, especially by releases of water pumped from groundwater storage in the upper part of the basin;
- abstraction of water for public water supplies;
- abstraction of groundwater for direct supply and for river regulation;
- effluent return, especially outflows from sewage treatment works;
- industrial and agricultural abstractions which result in a net reduction of natural flow.

Naturalized flow values are available for the Thames basin from the National Water Archive (for example IH/BGS, 1996). In this example, monthly values of naturalized flow, together with those for measured flow and rainfall, and estimated average values of actual evaporation for the period December 1993 to December 1995, are used to solve a partial water balance equation:

$$P - (Q + E) = 0 \tag{9.3}$$

where P is precipitation, Q is runoff and E is actual evaporation. Precipitation and runoff are the measured values published by the National Water Archive; actual evaporation values are the estimated long-term monthly means, based on MORECS data (see the section 'Operational use of potential evaporation models' in Chapter 4), so that identical values are used for both years. Values of groundwater and soil water storage are not available.

The use of long-term averages for actual evaporation and the absence of data on storage means that the monthly residual values of Eq. 9.3 are unlikely to be zero. However, provided that the measured values are accurate and the estimated values are reasonable, the pattern of cumulative monthly residuals should reflect patterns of total storage which are consistent and relatively stable from one year to the next. Cumulative monthly water balance residuals, using measured flow data, are plotted in Figure 9.9(a). Not surprisingly, this pattern is unstable, with a dominance of positive values and an increase from year to year in the year-end (December) values (60 mm in 1993; 139 mm in 1994; 185 mm in 1995). However, when the naturalized flow values are substituted in Eq. 9.3 (see Figure 9.9(b)), there is a much better balance between positive and negative cumulative residuals and the year-end values are much more stable (55 mm in 1993; 65 mm in 1994; 38 mm in 1995).

Because of the amount of work involved in calculating naturalized flows, these data are routinely available for only a few rivers. As a result, water balance calculations are normally performed using measured flow data. But as this example illustrates, even a partial water balance exercise can reveal the extent to which measured flow values have been affected by 'other' factors and serve as a caution against their continued use.

9.3.3 Murray–Darling basin, Australia

Australia is a dry continent, over most of which the annual balance between precipitation and potential evaporation is heavily in deficit. Only in a discontinuous and comparatively narrow coastal fringe, accounting for a little over one-third of the total landmass, is annual rainfall sufficiently high to promote coordinated river systems whose waters reach the sea. More than half the continent drains internally. The remaining 13.8 per cent consists of the hydrologically hybrid Murray–Darling basin, which has an integrated or co-ordinated internal drainage system with an external outlet for about 40 per cent of its discharge (Warner, 1977). This low external streamflow results partly from the adverse natural balance of evaporation and precipitation and partly from the fact that the Murray–Darling basin includes 75 per cent of the total irrigated area of the continent and has a higher percentage of its surface and groundwater resources in use than does any other river basin in Australia (Stewart *et al.*, 1990).

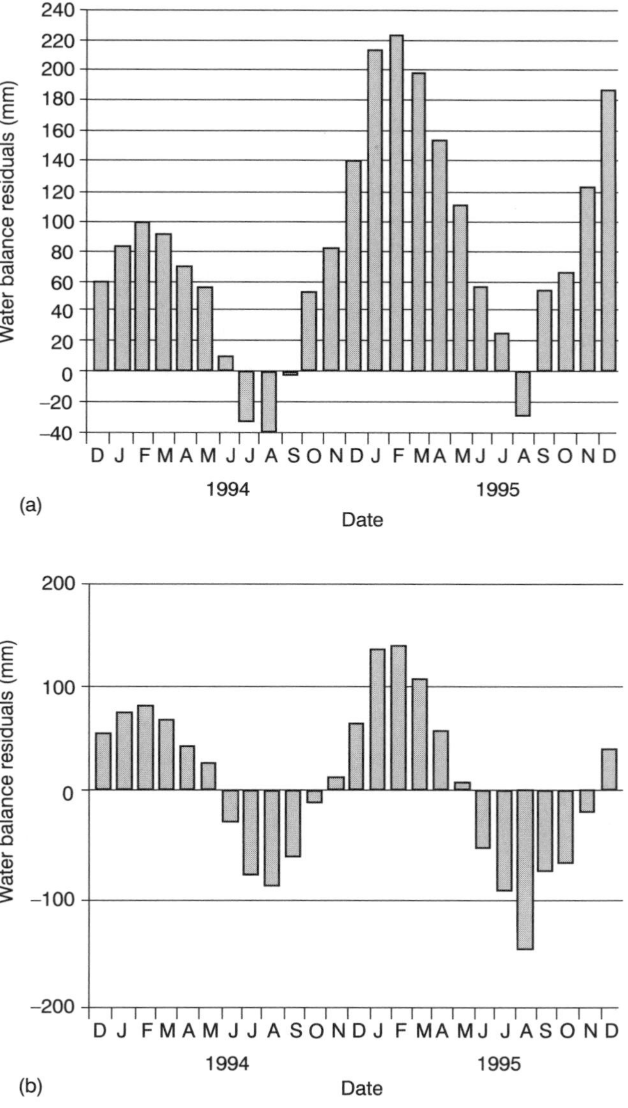

Figure 9.9 Monthly water balance residuals (mm) for the partial water balance of the Thames basin above Kingston, December 1993 to December 1995: (*a*) using measured flow values; (*b*) using naturalized flow values (drawn from data in IH/BGS, 1994; 1995; 1996; 1998).

The basin is of major socio-economic importance to Australia because of its important role in irrigated agriculture; at the same time, the high level of water use means that it is very vulnerable to climate change and climate variability.

Understandably, therefore, accurate information on the water balance has long been regarded as of fundamental hydrological significance as a means of assessing present resources and also as a means of estimating the hydrological impacts of past and likely future climate changes. And yet the size and geographical complexity of the Murray–Darling basin mean that even the major elements of the water balance are very difficult to determine.

The total area of the basin is 1 057 000 km^2, of which 647 000 km^2 is drained by the Darling River, more than 2700 km in length. Much of the Murray–Darling basin consists of extensive flat plains of sand or fine alluvium, with large areas of floodplain deposits which were laid down by intermittent flooding over long periods of time. Land surface elevations in such areas range from about 150 m in the north to close to sea level in the south. The basin is fringed by the higher land of the Barrier Range (up to 300 m) in the west and the Great Dividing Range in the north and east, which rises to more than 1300 m in the Carnarvon Range in the north, to more than 1500 m on the New England tablelands in the east and to more than 2000 m in the Snowy Mountains of Victoria in the south.

This pattern of relief is only partially reflected in the distribution of annual precipitation. About 80 per cent of the basin has an annual precipitation of under 600 mm, with less than 300 mm over extensive areas in the west and up to 1600 mm in very limited areas of the Snowy Mountains headwaters of the Murray River. Although values of annual potential evaporation are very high, ranging from more than 2000 mm in the north-west to about 1000 mm in the south-east, actual evaporation losses are constrained by water availability and therefore reflect more closely the spatial distribution of annual precipitation. Annual values range from more than 600 mm in the eastern highlands to 200 mm at Broken Hill in the west. Given the broad spatial distributions of precipitation and evaporation, it follows that annual runoff will be very low over most of the Murray–Darling basin, with higher values along the eastern and southern fringes. Indeed the western half of the basin has a mean annual runoff of less than 10 mm; the eastern and southern upland areas generate more than 100 mm and within them there are restricted areas generating more than 500 mm. Only in the Snowy Mountains do annual values in excess of 1000 mm occur.

Typical annual water balance diagrams are shown for three contrasting locations in the Murray–Darling basin in Figure 9.10. These diagrams emphasize that, on average, over most of the basin, precipitation is almost wholly accounted for by evaporation, leaving little surplus water for the generation of runoff. Even in some of the wetter headwater areas, for example of the Murray River (Figure 9.10(a)), the runoff coefficient is only 0.22; over most of the basin runoff coefficients are less than 0.05 (USSR IHD Committee, 1979). However, it is emphasized in Section 7.7 that in semi-arid areas average hydrological data have only limited usefulness. For example, the coefficient of variation of annual flow for the Darling is 1.46, compared with 0.29 for the Thames in England and 0.89 for six Karoo region rivers in South Africa (Gorgens and Hughes, 1982). This high degree of variability means that several centuries of flow data would be necessary in order to derive satisfactory estimates of mean flow conditions.

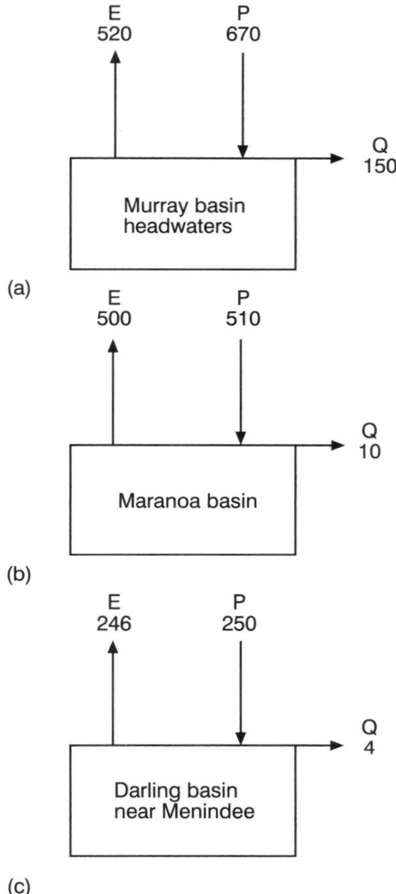

Figure 9.10 Annual water balance diagrams for three locations in the Murray–Darling basin, Australia: (*a*) Murray basin near Albury; (*b*) Maranoa basin; and (*c*) Darling basin near Menindee (based on data in USSR IHD Committee, 1979).

Again, even at Menindee, where the Darling River drains an area of 570 000 km^2, zero monthly flows occur frequently. In other words, over much of the Murray–Darling basin, surpluses of water for groundwater recharge or for runoff generation are available only sporadically, tend to be spatially concentrated in the eastern and southern highlands and, in the case of runoff peaks, take many months to travel down major rivers such as the Darling, during which time they undergo further losses. Massive water resource exploitation is therefore heavily dependent upon surface storage of water and upon the enormous reserves of groundwater associated with the Great Artesian basin and the Murray basin. There is also, understandably, concern about how an already 'fragile' water balance may be affected by climate change. Stewart *et al.* (1990) considered three methods of determining the impact of climate change on precipitation in the Murray–Darling basin and concluded that, ultimately, the most promising involves the use of general circulation models. However, they emphasized the need for the output from these to become more appropriate at the regional (i.e. large drainage basin) scale. They also called for the increased evaluation of historical and palaeohydrological data, such as lake levels, to assist in the interpretation of hydrological response to past climate change and thereby improve the ability to predict hydrological response to climate changes that may occur in the future.

9.3.4 The Amazon

The drainage basin of the Amazon river is a major focus of hydrological interest for several reasons. Its gigantic size of 4 640 000 km^2 (60 per cent of the area of Australia) and its high average annual rainfall of nearly 2000 mm mean that hydrological processes operate at a quasi-continental scale; for example, the river contributes nearly 10 per cent of the world's total runoff. In addition, the basin contains the world's largest area of rainforest which has been subjected in recent years to massive clearance operations, often involving burning, which are intended to facilitate the expansion of large-scale, extensive agriculture. More important still is that several studies have confirmed the significance of precipitation recycling within the Amazon basin.

Precipitation over an area derives partly from water vapour formed by local evaporation and partly from water vapour which moves into the atmosphere above that area by means of horizontal advection (see also Section 2.3). *Precipitation recycling* is defined as the contribution of evaporation within an area to precipitation in that same area and may be expressed as a recycling ratio ρ, i.e. the fraction of precipitation which is contributed by local evaporation (Eltahir and Bras, 1994). This ratio is a function partly of the size of the area concerned. At one extreme, $\rho = 1$ for the entire earth; at the other extreme, it is likely that $\rho = 0$ for a given point on the earth's surface since the effect of horizontal wind advection makes it improbable that a water molecule evaporated from that point will subsequently be precipitated at the same point. Between these two extremes, ρ will depend mainly on the size of area and to a lesser extent on the vigour of the evaporation–rainfall process.

Accordingly, it would be expected that a large equatorial drainage basin, like that of the Amazon, would have a large precipitation recycling ratio. This was confirmed in studies by Brubaker *et al.* (1993) and Eltahir and Bras (1994) which calculated $\rho = 0.25$–0.35, depending on the source of vapour flux data. In other words, at least one-quarter of all precipitation falling on the Amazon basin is derived from local evaporation. In such circumstances, the simple terrestrial water balance (Figure 9.11(a)) does not give an adequate indication of drainage basin hydrology. Although the input of precipitation (1950 mm) is balanced by

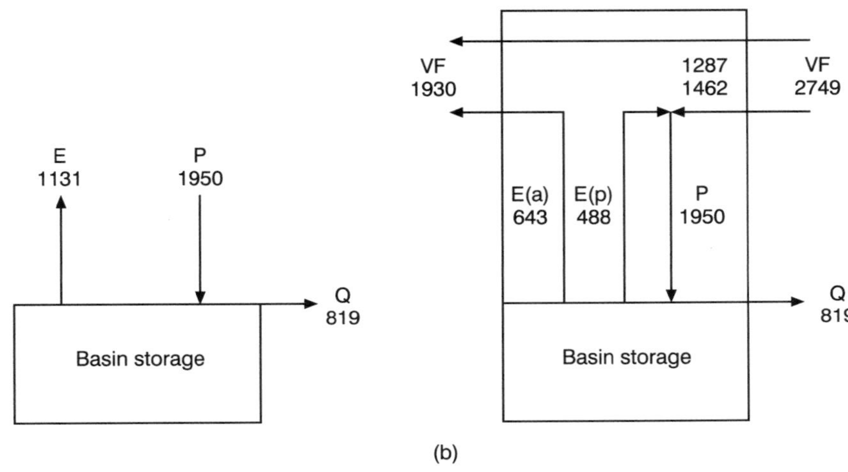

Figure 9.11 Components of the water balance in the Amazon basin (annual values in millimetres): (*a*) terrestrial water balance; and (*b*) combined atmospheric and terrestrial balance, illustrating the role of precipitation recycling (based on data in Eltahir and Bras, 1994).

the combined outputs of evaporation (1131 mm) and runoff (819 mm), the relationship between evaporation and precipitation is not apparent unless the combined terrestrial and atmospheric water balance is considered (Figure 9.11(b)). Then it is clear that 43 per cent (488 mm) of the evaporation from the drainage basin returns to the drainage basin as precipitation, contributing 25 per cent of the water vapour used in the precipitation process.

The hydrological significance of water vapour recycling on this scale, particularly in terms of its implications for the impacts of land-surface changes, may be considerable. For example, in a drainage basin where virtually none of the precipitation results from 'local' evaporation, even large-scale deforestation may have no significant impact on drainage basin hydrology. In the (hypothetical) situation where all precipitation derives from local evaporation, changes of vegetation cover or other land-surface characteristics would be expected to have a significant effect on drainage basin hydrology and climate. A high estimate of precipitation recycling, as in the Amazon basin, may not be conclusive evidence of a major role for land-surface hydrology, but it certainly suggests a strong potential for that role (Eltahir and Bras, 1994) and a need for concern about the likely hydrological and climatological effects of large-scale rainforest destruction. Similar concern about the potential hydrological impact of surface changes should also be evoked for other areas where estimates of precipitation recycling are high, including the Sahel zone of Africa where Brubaker *et al.* (1993) estimated $\rho = 0.35$. Moreover, where precipitation recycling has been determined on a monthly basis, strong annual cycles have been apparent, with the range of monthly values exceeding the mean of those values for Eurasia and Africa and attaining at least 75 per cent of the mean for North America and South America (Brubaker *et al.*, 1993). In other words, in most areas there are some periods of the year when land-surface changes are likely to have significant hydrological impacts.

9.4 Beyond the drainage basin: global hydrology

Earlier discussion in this chapter has illustrated that, however appropriate and useful the drainage basin is for a wide range of hydrological investigations, there are many purposes for which it is too small a unit of study. Increasingly, the major hydrological problems being faced are of a regional, continental, or global nature. A simple illustration is provided by the vapour flux figures shown in Figure 9.11. These indicate that the Amazon basin is a sink for water, since more water vapour enters than leaves the atmosphere over the basin. Indeed the magnitude of vapour flux convergence over the Amazon basin was emphasized by the observation of Keller (1984) that the annual precipitation over the basin equals the entire global atmospheric water content at any one moment! Since the Amazon basin is not the only regional sink for water vapour, it follows that other extensive areas of the earth's surface must act as net sources of water vapour. In the tropics and sub-tropics, for example, the distribution of water vapour is generally consistent with the distribution of surface temperature over the ocean and of vegetation type over the land. Dodd and James (1996) noted that high values occur in regions to which water vapour is supplied by the large-scale atmospheric circulation; low values are associated with regions from which water vapour is removed by advection. In extra-tropical areas, however, the water vapour flux is influenced more by transient eddies associated with storm tracks and by enhanced evaporation where cold air breaks out over warm oceans.

The location, role and inter-relationships between global sources and sinks of water vapour constitute emerging and important issues in modern hydrology, not least because information on vapour flux convergence and divergence provides a valuable contribution to water balance studies. The potential for using vapour flux data in terrestrial water balance calculations has long been recognized (for example Starr and Peixoto, 1958), although progress was delayed by the sparsity of upper air soundings. However, good quality data sets, prepared by the European Centre for Medium-Range Weather Forecasts (ECMWF) in connection with numerical forecasting procedures, became available after 1980 (Oki *et al.*, 1993; Oki *et al.*, 1995) and greatly facilitated the identification and quantification of the net sources and sinks for water vapour on a global scale. Certainly, the use of ECMWF data in global water balance calculations was described as 'rather encouraging' (Dodd and James, 1996). Considerable impetus was given to progress in this area by initiatives such as WMO's Global Energy and Water Cycle Experiment (GEWEX), and the Hydrological Atmospheric Pilot Experiment (HAPEX) (for example Askew, 1991; Shuttleworth, 1988b), although it is clear that a great deal of further work and development remains to be done.

9.4.1 The global water balance

Despite the ever-changing global distribution of water vapour, evaporation, precipitation and runoff, and the associated changes in soil water and groundwater storage, the global water balance is, in effect, a closed system. Virtually no water is lost from the system and the occasional releases of fossil groundwater, or possible additions of water from comets, are minute. Furthermore, over quite short periods of time, the input of water vapour into the atmosphere by evaporation is wholly accounted for by the condensation–precipitation process. Thus described, the global water balance is very simple. However, quantifying it has proved a difficult and elusive task. Many estimates have been made, all of which differ and the earliest of which were based on sparse and often inadequate data. Of the relatively recent attempts, the most widely accepted are probably those of Lvovitch (1973), Baumgartner and Reichel (1975) and especially Shiklomanov (1993, 1997). Useful summaries of world water balance data were also presented by Speidel and Agnew (1988).

Estimates of the main fluxes in the global water balance, based on a number of sources, are summarized in Table 9.4 and Figure 9.12. These estimates are

Table 9.4 Estimated annual fluxes in the global water balance. (Based on data from Speidel and Agnew, 1988 and other sources; see text for further details.)

Flux	*Oceans (cu km)*	*Land (cu km)*	*Global total (cu km)*	*Oceans (mm)* *	*Land (mm)* *	*Global total (mm)* *
Precipitation	385 000	111 100	496 100	1066	746	973
Evaporation	−424 700	−71 400	−496 100	−1176	−480	−973
Runoff (river flow, direct groundwater flow, icemelt)	39 700	−39 700	0	110	−267	0
Net inland advection of water vapour	−39 700	39 700	0	−110	267	0
TOTAL	−39 700	39 700	0	−110	266	0

* These figures are calculated on the basis that total land area is 148 904 000 sq km and total ocean area is 361 110 000 sq km, i.e. 29.2 per cent and 70.8 per cent respectively of the global surface.

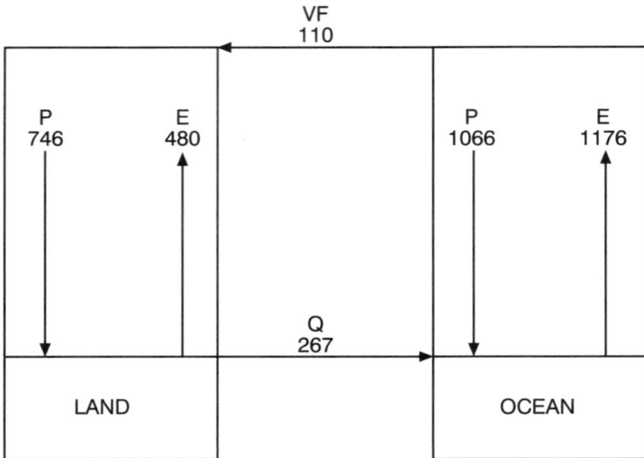

Figure 9.12 Global water balance: average annual fluxes. Values are expressed in mm precipitation equivalent. See also Table 9.4 in which these fluxes are expressed both in terms of precipitation equivalent and as volumes (i.e. precipitation equivalent depth multiplied by total land or ocean area) (based on data in Speidel and Agnew, 1988 and other sources).

illustrative, reflecting as they do a wide range of values for each water balance component. For example, the precipitation and evaporation estimates presented by Speidel and Agnew (1988) varied by 29 per cent and the estimates of runoff to the oceans varied by 40 per cent. Such uncertainty about the magnitude of major fluxes of water and energy makes it difficult to identify and interpret global change within the hydrologic, atmospheric and oceanic systems or to predict the likely impact of that change upon human beings and their activities. Hopefully, reduced levels of uncertainty will result from initiatives such as GEWEX. The net inland advection of water vapour, illustrated in Table 9.4 and Figure 9.12, involves a sometimes complex interchange of water vapour between ocean and land areas. A significant quantity of water vapour generated by land evaporation is precipitated over the oceans and an even greater quantity of water vapour generated by ocean evaporation is precipitated over the land.

The compensating advective flux of liquid water from the land to ocean poses problems because two of the components (direct groundwater flow into the ocean and icemelt) are difficult to quantify. Although the third main component, streamflow, is much larger and easier to monitor, its uneven distribution, both spatially and seasonally, complicates the assessment of its role in the global water balance. For example, streamflow into the oceans is concentrated at a relatively small number of locations, with the 20 largest rivers accounting for nearly one third of the total global flow from land to ocean. Again, some continents are bigger sources of water than others; Asia and South America together contribute 59 per cent of the global flow from land to oceans and despite its overwhelming size (about $181 \times 10^6\,km^2$) the Pacific Ocean receives only 31 per cent of the water leaving the land areas each year whereas the Atlantic Ocean (about $82 \times 10^6\,km^2$) receives 49 per cent.

These inequalities, together with seasonal variations of runoff, both within climatic regions and between the northern and southern hemispheres, mean that river and direct groundwater flow only partially account for the return advective water flux from land to ocean. The remainder takes place via ocean currents, which redistribute not only the excess runoff received by some ocean basins compared with others, but also imbalances between ocean evaporation and precipitation. For example, the Atlantic Ocean has a deficit in the annual precipitation–evaporation balance which is not made up by the inflow of land water. The remaining difference is compensated by flow from the Arctic and Pacific oceans, which have a surplus in the precipitation–evaporation balance (Speidel and Agnew, 1988).

9.4.2 Challenges in hydrology

Uncertainty about the magnitude of the main elements in the global water balance is largely a reflection of a number of underlying and fundamental problems, including inadequate measurement and estimation techniques, the spatial heterogeneity of hydrological systems and difficulties associated with transferring both hydrological measurements and our understanding of hydrological processes from one scale to another. To a certain extent these problems are inter-related and there is already evidence, for example, that those involving measurement and hydrological heterogeneity may be yielding as a result of continuing improvements in data collection by remote sensing.

However, at perhaps the simplest level, that of *data reliability*, the fact remains that our basic inventory of global water is still incomplete. Shiklomanov (1997) moved us closer to an agreed total of global water but, as preceding discussion has illustrated, there is less agreement about the quantities associated with individual elements of the global water balance. It is not, at the moment, possible to make reliable measurements at the regional or continental scale of precipitation, evaporation or soil water. Moreover, new discoveries of water are still occasionally reported, as in the case of the huge sub-ice Lake Vostok in Antarctica (Ellis-Evans and Wynn-Williams, 1996).

It is not surprising, therefore, that the attention of hydrologists and climatologists is focusing increasingly on ways to improve large-scale and global hydrological data. For example, a major IAMS/IAPSO symposium on global and regional water and energy cycles at Melbourne, Australia, in 1997 considered four complementary issues: experimental water and energy cycles within international observational programmes; the impact of land surface on climate; water vapour and climate; and radiation and climate. And of the five IAHS workshop sessions at the XXIInd General Assembly of the IUGG at Birmingham, England, in 1999, one was concerned with global databases, specifically with bringing together users of the

> ... rapidly growing number of large-scale biophysical data sets for synthesis studies of the terrestrial water cycle and ... water resources assessment. (IAHS, 1997)

Another, designed as a contribution to the GEWEX Model Parameter Estimation Experiment (MOPEX), was to examine the regionalization of parameters of hydrological and atmospheric land-surface models.

Earlier discussions of hydrological modelling emphasize the problems caused by the *heterogeneity* of hydrological systems and the potential contribution of distributed modelling techniques to the solution of these problems. For larger drainage basins, and certainly for regional and continental areas, the data complexity associated with spatial heterogeneity is probably capable of resolution only through spatially distributed models which are capable of handling data generated by satellite sensors and pre-processed through GIS. However, further problems then arise through the need to interpolate hydrological data to grid networks. This has traditionally been easier in the case of precipitation, and to a lesser extent of evaporation. In these cases spatial distributions have usually been derived in the first place from a network of point observations, and variation with distance from the point of observation, and therefore the correlation structure of the hydrological component, are quite well understood. In the case of runoff, however, such assumptions may not be valid since correlation is dependent on the absolute positions of points in a river system and not only on the relative distances between points. Accordingly, Gottschalk and Krasovskaia (1994) examined different approaches for stochastic interpolation of runoff to a regular grid network.

Probably the most vexatious of the current problems in hydrology are related to issues of *scaling* (for example Feddes, 1995). Specifically, is it possible to transpose findings reliably from one scale of hydrological investigation to another? Scale issues in hydrological modelling were the focus of an international workshop (Kalma and Sivapalan, 1995) and were the subject of the keynote address on the 'global hydrological processes' theme at the BHS international conference on hydrology in a changing environment (Wheater and Kirby, 1998). For obvious reasons, the problem addressed is normally that of upscaling, i.e. whether we have the understanding to transpose from small scale to large scale, especially to the global scale (for example Stewart *et al.*, 1996: Vörösmarty *et al.*, 1998). Basically this relates to the issues raised in earlier discussion of Table 9.1, i.e. that much of the development of hydrological theory has been based upon observation and experimentation at the micro- and meso-scale. Increasingly, however, the problem is couched in terms of downscaling. In large measure this derives from the growing use of global climate models, especially in relation to studies of climate change and of the hydrological impacts of climate change. Hydrologists are now interested in the extent to which GCM output may be downscaled for use in drainage basin investigations. Pilling *et al.* (1998), for example, described a globally applicable methodology for downscaling daily precipitation and evaporation values at the drainage basin scale from airflow circulation patterns obtained from the Hadley Centre's second-generation ocean–atmosphere GCM. Encouraging results were also reported by Beaumont *et al.* (1995), who used Meteosat meteorological data as an input to modelling the water balance of the Ivory Coast on a 25 km grid.

These are important challenges which demand an urgent and effective response if hydrology is to link productively with current and growing interests in global climate, climate change and GCMs (for example Wilkinson, 1993). This point was emphasized by Watts (1997), who argued that:

> The ultimate scope of hydrological models extends to the development of global circulation models representing the entire hydrosphere. These are being used to predict the impact of climatic change on regional weather and hydrology.

Wilby (1997) went further still in suggesting that hydrology is in danger of being marginalized by other geophysical disciplines unless it can demonstrate a unique contribution to the growing knowledge database and suggested that the emphasis should be '... on solving the water balance equation ... at a global or regional scale'.

9.4.3 Hydrology in the global village

Numerous examples in this chapter, and elsewhere in the book, illustrate that hydrology is studied, and hydrological processes operate, in the 'global village'. Evaporation from one country contributes to precipitation in another. Pollution in the headwaters of an international river may impact upon the economy of other countries in the lower part of the basin. In other words, it becomes ever clearer that decisions on water management (for example irrigation, river abstraction, or river diversion) or on the management of other resources which impact upon hydrological processes (for example deforestation), must in future be made with the fullest possible understanding of their potential global impact.

There have been major water management proposals in the last few decades which, if implemented, could have had significant adverse effects on an international scale. For example, the North American Water and Power Alliance (NAWAPA) proposals, once described as 'plumbing on a continental scale' (Simons, 1969), envisaged controlling the major western rivers from the Yukon to Mexico, using a major dam in the Rocky Mountain trench. Subsequently, there were Russian proposals to divert the flow of some of the major northward-flowing rivers such as the Ob-Irtysh, Yenisey, Pechora and Northern Dvina (Micklin, 1981). In the case of the Ob-Irtysh, this would have been achieved by constructing a large dam just below the confluence of the two rivers and leading the water 2600 km southward to the Amu Dar'ya for use in regional irrigation projects in the Aral–Caspian basin. The resulting changes of salinity in the Arctic Ocean would almost certainly have had significant ecological and climatological repercussions on a global scale. But in the event, economic and then political obstacles conspired to prevent further development of the proposals. Similar, global concern also accompanied more recent proposals to dam the Chang (Yangtze) River at the Three Gorges, Sanxia, China. However, despite extensive criticism on several grounds, including the loss of agricultural land and ecological and geomorphological degradation both upstream and downstream of the dam site, work is now well advanced on the dam which will eventually create a reservoir 600 km in length.

Such concerns are understandable in the light of channel and other geomorphological changes which followed the construction of the Aswan High Dam on the River Nile and of the widespread and adverse ecological effects which have already resulted from some of the river diversions which *have* been carried out in the former USSR. For example, almost all the waters of the Amu Dar'ya and Syr Dar'ya rivers, which formerly drained to the Aral Sea, were diverted to irrigate cotton and other crops. This resulted in the drying out of the Aral Sea, whose surface area diminished by 40 per cent between 1926 and 1990 and whose salinity increased by some 300 per cent (Gleick, 1993b), and a subsequent collapse of fisheries and of the regional economy.

Macro-scale projects of this type may, in any case, become less important as the potential of *'virtual water' trading* becomes more clearly understood. This approach regards water as one of a number of goods to be traded and recognizes that, in some situations, it may be both easier and more environmentally friendly to move grain and other foodstuff into an area rather than develop capital-intensive programmes of crop irrigation. This is likely to be especially true of many arid and semi-arid areas, where the disbenefits of irrigation, especially salination, have long been recognized. Indeed, virtual water trading is already a reality in the Middle East and North Africa region which has effectively run out of water. By 1980, about 20 per cent of the region's water needs were being delivered as 'virtual water', i.e. as water embedded in water-intensive commodities such as wheat (Allan, 1997).

The research strategy of the British Hydrological Society (BHS, 1994) identified the global environment as one of its three recommended programme areas. Within that area, four issues of 'global hydropolitics', i.e. problems involving the global community rather than individual nations, were listed as follows:

- transboundary problems, including atmospheric and aquatic pollution and the sharing of water resources;

- the need for better institutional frameworks to support the assessment and implementation of appropriate water management strategies;
- better flow monitoring networks to support international action in fostering 'drought preparedness centres'; and
- dryland degradation, which remains a key interdisciplinary challenge across many countries.

These ideas were refined in discussion at the BHS international conference on Hydrology in a Changing Environment and incorporated into the 'Exeter Statement' (BHS, 1998) to be presented at the 1999 Inter-Government Conference on Hydrology in Geneva.

Harbingers of some of the current issues in 'global hydropolitics' have been seen in problems relating to the management of water in large international river basins. A well-known example relates to disputes between the USA and Mexico which arose from water exploitation in the Colorado River basin. Vidal (1995) listed other major rivers which are the source of potential conflict, even water wars, between two or more nations, including the Brahmaputra, Ganges, Indus, Jordan, Mekong, Nile, Rio Grande, Tigris/Euphrates and Zambezi. In many cases tensions have arisen as a result of ill-judged actions and policies which have themselves been based on an incomplete understanding of drainage basin hydrology. Not surprisingly, therefore, attempts to improve the understanding of hydrological processes and of the potential role of hydrology in the solution of such problems, continues to be the focus of a great deal of international activity (for example Van de Ven *et al.*, 1991; Biswas, 1996).

Epilogue

Although macro-scale issues are likely to dominate the future of hydrology in the early decades of the new millennium, many hydrological problems will continue to be approached and solved at the meso- or even micro-scale. Some of the hydrological processes which are currently attracting increasing attention are regionally circumscribed but global in their impact; cryohydrology, especially the interactions of snow and ice on macro-hydrological processes, falls into this category (for example Jones *et al.*, 1994; Tranter *et al.*, 1999). Other growth areas in hydrology are quasi-global in their distribution but essentially localized in their impact; the important area of urban hydrology falls into this category (for example Ellis, 1999). These and many other issues will continue to focus the attention of hydrologists on the important inter-relationships between processes operating at very different spatial (and temporal) scales. In turn, it is hoped that such activity may resolve some of the current difficulties of upscaling and downscaling hydrological processes.

It is more than 30 years since the first edition of this book was published. During that time the greatest advance in hydrology has undoubtedly been its growth in stature as a science. In the early 1960s hydrology was still largely the preserve of engineers, both civil and agricultural, for whom it will continue to provide an important framework of theories and methods for solving specific problems. However, we believe that the future of hydrology lies in its potential role as a scientific discipline and in its closer integration with other disciplines. Much of the impetus for such a development has been, and will probably continue to be, provided by the resurgence of interest in climate variability and climate change, particularly in respect of possible anthropogenic influences on climate, and by an expansion of computing power, undreamt of 30 years ago, which has permitted the development and rapid running of GCMs. But if hydrology is to fulfil its scientific potential, it will have to mature as a discipline. This point was made effectively and succinctly by Chahine (1992):

> In the short span of about 10 years, the hydrological cycle has emerged as the centrepiece of the study of climate, but basic changes are still required in this field. Hydrological science must adjust itself to become a discipline not unlike atmospheric science or oceanography. Rather than fragmented studies in engineering, geography, meteorology and agricultural science, we need an integrated program of fundamental research and education in hydrological science.

We believe this is a realistic assessment for the future of hydrology and that such a development would greatly strengthen its ability to grapple with macro-scale problems other than those involving climate variability and change.

Review Problems and Exercises

9.1 Outline the main problems of modelling drainage basin hydrology.

9.2 Explain what is meant by the following descriptions of drainage basin models: conceptual; lumped; physically based distributed; probability distributed.

9.3 Critically evaluate the hydrological assumptions incorporated into one well-known drainage basin model.

9.4 Explain the potential hydrological value of solving accurately the water balance equation of a drainage basin.

9.5 Outline some of the factors which have contributed to the growing interest in global hydrology.

9.6 Comment on the view (expressed in this chapter) that 'macro-scale issues are likely to dominate the future of hydrology'.

References

Abbott, M.B., J.C. Bathurst, J.A. Cunge, P.E. O'Connell and J. Rasmussen (1986) An introduction to the European Hydrological System—Système Hydrologique Européen 'SHE' 2. Structure of the physically based, distributed modelling system, *J. Hydrol.*, **87:** 61–77.

Abdul, A.S. and R.W. Gillham (1984) Laboratory studies of the effects of the capillary fringe on streamflow generation, *WRR*, **20:** 691–8.

Abrahams, A.D., A.J. Parsons and J. Wainwright (1994) Resistance to overland flow on semiarid grassland and shrubland hillslopes, Walnut Gulch, southern Arizona, *J. Hydrol.*, **156:** 431–46.

Addiscott, T.M. (1996) Fertilizers and nitrate leaching, in R.E. Hester and R.M. Harrison (eds) *Agricultural chemicals and the environment*, Issues in environmental science and technology, No. 5. Royal Society of Chemistry, London.

Agassi, M., J. Morin and I. Shainberg (1985) Effect of raindrop impact energy and water salinity on infiltration rates of sodic soils, *Proc. SSSA*, **49:** 186–90.

Alberty, R.A. (1987) *Physical chemistry, 7e*, J. Wiley and Sons, New York, 934 pp.

Albrecht, K.A., D.F. Fenster and S.G. Van Camp (1990) Reducing groundwater flow model uncertainties at Yucca Mountain, in *Calibration and Reliability in Groundwater Modelling*, IAHS Publ. No. **195:** 301–9.

Alexander, L. and R.W. Skaggs (1987) Predicting unsaturated hydraulic conductivity from soil texture. *J. Irrig. Drainage Engg.*, **113:** 184–97.

Allan, J.A. (1997) *'Virtual water': A long term solution for water short Middle Eastern economies?*, Paper presented at the British Association Festival of Science, Leeds, 9 September.

Allen, R.G., M. Smith, A. Perrier and L.S. Pereira (1994a) An update for the definition of reference evapotranspiration, *International Commission for Irrigation and Drainage*, **43:** 1–34.

Allen, R.G., M. Smith, L.S. Pereira and A. Perrier (1994b) An update for the calculation of reference evapotranspiration, *International Commission for Irrigation and Drainage*, **43:** 35–92.

Amoros, C. and G.E. Petts (eds) (1993) *Hydrosystèmes Fluviaux*, Macon, Paris.

Anderson, J.L. and J. Bouma (1973) Relationships between saturated hydraulic conductivity and morphometric data of an argillic horizon. *Proc. SSSA*, **37:** 408–13.

Anderson, J.M. and T. Spencer (1991) Carbon, nutrient and water balances of tropical rain forest ecosystems subject to disturbance, *MAB Digest*, 7, UNESCO, Paris, 95 pp.

Anderson, M.G. and T.P. Burt (1977) A laboratory model to predict the soil moisture conditions on a draining slope. *J. Hydrol.*, **33:** 383–90.

Anderson, M.G. and T.P. Burt (1978) The role of topography in controlling throughflow generation, *Earth Surf. Processes*, **3**: 331–4.

Anderson, M.G. and T.P. Burt (1982) The contribution of throughflow to storm runoff: an evaluation of a chemical mixing model, *Earth Surf. Proc. and Landforms*, **7:** 565–74.

Andersson, L. and R.J. Harding (1991) Soil moisture deficit simulations with models of varying complexity for forest and grassland sites in Sweden and the UK, *Water Resources Management*, **5:** 25–46.

Andrews, E.D. and B.W. Webb (1987) Emerging issues in surface water quality research, *IASH Publ.*, **171:** 27–33.

Andrews, J. (1991) Noble gases and radioelements in groundwater, *NERC News*, January, pp. 19–24.

Angstrom, A. (1920) Applications of heat radiation measurement to the problems of evaporation from lakes and the heat convection at their surfaces, *Geografisca Ann.*, **2:** 237–52.

Aranda, J.M. and J.R.H. Coutts (1963) Micrometeorological observations in an afforested area in Aberdeenshire: rainfall characteristics. *J. Soil Sci.*, **14:** 124–33.

Archer, D. and D. Stewart (1995) The installation and use of a snow pillow to monitor snow water equivalent. *JIWE(M)*, **9:** 221–30.

Arnold, G.E. and W.J. Willems (1996) European groundwater studies, *European Water Pollution Control*, **6:** 11–18.

ASCE-TASK (1980) Characteristics of low flow, *Trans. ASCE, J. Hydraul. Div.*, **106(HY5):** 717–31.

Asdak, C., P.G. Jarvis, P. van Gardingen and A. Fraser (1998a) Rainfall interception loss in unlogged and logged forest areas of Central Kalimantan, Indonesia. *J. Hydrol.*, **206:** 237–44.

Asdak, C., Jarvis, P.G. and P. Van Gardingen (1998b) Modelling rainfall interception in unlogged and logged forest areas of Central Kalimantan, Indonesia. *Hydrology and Earth System Sciences*, **2:** 211–220.

Askew, A.J. (1991) Climate and water—a call for international action, *Hydrol. Sci. J.*, **36:** 391–404.

Atkinson, B.W. and P.A. Smithson (1976) Precipitation, in T.J. Chandler and S. Gregory (eds), *The Climate of the British Isles*, Longman Group Ltd, London, pp. 129–82.

Atkinson, T.C. (1986) Soluble rock terrains, in P.G. Fookes and P.R. Vaughan (eds), *A Handbook of Engineering Geomorphology*, Surrey University Press, pp. 241–57.

Atkinson, T.C. and P.L. Smart (1981) Artificial tracers in hydrology, in C.R. Argent and D.J.H. Griffin (eds), *A survey of British hydrogeology 1980*, The Royal Society, London, pp. 173–90.

Austin, G.L. and P.G. Wickham (1995) Radar imagery: basic principles. In M.J. Bader, G.S. Forbes, J.R. Grant, R.B.E. Lilley and A.J. Waters (eds), *Images in Weather Forecasting*. Cambridge University Press, pp. 50–61.

Austin, B.N., I.D. Cluckie, C.G. Collier and P.J. Hardaker (1995) *Radar-based estimation of Probable Maximum Precipitation and Flood*, Meteorological Office, Bracknell, 124 pp.

Bache, B.W. (1984) Soil–water interactions, *Proc. Phil. Trans. Roy. Soc. London, B*, **305:** 393–407.

Back, W. and J.S. Herman (1997) American hydrogeology at the millennium: An annotated chronology of 100 most influential papers, *Hydrogeology J.*, **5:** 37–50.

Bader, M.J., G.S. Forbes, J.R. Grant, R.B.E. Lilley & A.J. Waters (1995) *Images in Weather Forecasting*. Cambridge University Press, 499 pp.

Badon Ghijben, W. (1889) Nota in verband met de voorgenomen putboring nabij Amsterdam (Notes on the probable results of the proposed well drilling near Amsterdam), *Tijdschrift van het Koninklijt Inst. van Ingenieurs*, The Hague, pp. 8–22. Quoted by Todd (1980).

Baird, A.J. (1997) Continuity in hydrological systems, in R.L. Wilby (ed), *Contemporary Hydrology*, Wiley, Chichester, pp. 25–58.

Banks, S. and D. Banks (1993) Editors' Preface, in *Hydrogeology of Hard Rocks*, Memoirs of the XXIVth Congress, Int. Assoc. Hydrogeologists, Oslo, iii–iv.

Barker, J.A. (1991) Transport in fractured rock, in R.A. Downing and W.B. Wilkinson (eds), *Applied Groundwater Hydrology*, Clarendon, Oxford, pp. 199–216.

Barrett, C.F. (Chairman) (1987) *Acid deposition in the United Kingdom 1981–1985*, 2nd Report of the UK Review Group on Acid Rain, Warren Spring Laboratory, Stevenage, 104 pp.

Barrett, E.C. and D.W. Martin (1981) *The use of satellite data in rainfall monitoring*, Academic Press, London, 340 pp.

Barry, R. G. (1983) Research on snow and ice, in *Contributions in hydrology, US National Report 1979–1982, 18th General Association, IUGG, Hamburg*, American Geophysical Union, Washington, D.C., pp. 765–76.

Barry, R.G. and R.J. Chorley (1998) *Atmosphere, weather and climate*, Routledge, London.

Bastin, G., B. Lovert, C. Duque and M. Gevers (1984) Optimum estimation of the average areal rainfall and optimal selection of rain gauge locations, *WRR*, **20:** 463–70.

Bates, C.G. and A.J. Henry (1928) Forest and streamflow experiment at Wagon Wheel Gap, Colorado. *Monthly Weather Review*, Supplement 30, pp. 1–79. US Dep. Agriculture Weather Bureau.

Bathurst, J.C., J.M. Wicks and P.E. O'Connell (1995) The SHE/SHESED basin scale water flow and sediment transport modelling system, in V.P. Singh (ed), *Computer Models of Watershed Hydrology*, Water Resource Publications, Colorado, 563–94.

Bator, A. and J.L. Collett (1997) Cloud chemistry varies with drop size, *JGR*, **102:** 28071–8.

Battan, L.J. (1973) *Radar observation of the atmosphere*, University of Chicago Press, Chicago, 324 pp.

Baumgartner, A. (1967) Energetic bases for differential vaporization from forest and agricultural lands, in W.E. Sopper and H.W. Lull (eds), *Forest hydrology*, Pergamon, Oxford, pp. 381–9.

Baumgartner, A. and E. Reichel (1975) *The World Water Balance*, Elsevier, Amsterdam. Translated by R. Lee.

Baver, L.D. (1956) *Soil physics, 3e*, John Wiley and Sons, New York.

Baver, L.D., W.H. Gardner and W.R. Gardner (1972) *Soil physics, 4e*, John Wiley and Sons, New York, 498 pp.

Bear, J. and A. Verruijt (1987) *Modelling groundwater flow and pollution*, D. Reidel Publishing Co., Boston, 414 pp.

Beaumont, M.J., A. Wilmshurst and E.C. Barrett (1995) Development of a surface water balance model for West Africa using Meteosat data inputs, *Annales Geophysicae*, **13:** C537.

Becker, A. and B. Pfuetzner (1990) Larger-scale hydrological modelling for regional transferring of hydrological information, in M.A. Beran, M. Brilly, A. Becker & O. Bonacci (eds), *Regionalization in Hydrology*, IAHS Publ. No. **191:** 61–68, IAHS Press, Wallingford.

Beckinsale, R. P. (1969) River regimes, in *Water, earth and man*, R. J. Chorley (ed), Methuen, London, pp. 455–71.

Beese, F. and R. R. van der Ploeg (1976) Influence of hysteresis on moisture flow in an undisturbed soil monolith, *Proc. SSSA*, **40:** 480–4.

Begg, J.E. and N.C. Turner (1976) Crop water deficits, *Advances in Agronomy*, **28:** 161–217.

Bell, F.C. (1969) Generalized rainfall–duration–frequency relationships, *Proc. ASCE, J. Hydraul. Div.*, **95 (HY1):** 311–27.

Bell, F.C. (1976) *The areal reduction factor in rainfall frequency estimation*, Report 35, Institute of Hydrology, Wallingford, 58 pp.

Bell, J. P. (1987) *Neutron probe practice*, Report 19, 3rd edn, Institute of Hydrology, Wallingford, 51 pp.

Bell, J. P., T. J. Dean and M. G. Hodnett (1987) Soil moisture measurement by an improved capacitance technique, II. Field techniques, evaluation and calibration. *J. Hydrol.*, **93:** 79–90.

Bengtsson, L., R.K. Saxena and Z. Dressie (1987) Soil water movement estimated from isotope tracers, *Hydrol. Sci. J.*, **32:** 497–520.

Ben-Hur, M., I. Shainberg, R. Keren and M. Gal (1985) Effect of water quality and drying on soil crust properties, *Proc. SSSA*, **49:** 191–6.

Beran, M. (1987) Data collection and use for modelling, simulation and forecasting of drought, *Water Supply*, **5:** 11–21.

Beran, M.A. and A. Gustard (1977) A study into the low-flow characteristics of British rivers, *J. Hydrol.*, **35:** 147–52.

Bergado, D.T., A.S. Balasubramanian and W. Apaipong (1986) Fluid monitoring of subsidence effects at AIT campus, Bangkok, Thailand, *IAHS Publ.*, **151:** 391–404.

Bergström, J. (1989) Incipient earth science in the Old Norse mythology, *Geologiska Föreningens i Stockholm Förhandlingar*, **111:** 187–91.

Beven, K.J. and M.J. Kirkby (1979) A physically-based variable contributing area model of basin hydrology, *Hydrol. Sci. Bull.*, **24:** 43–69.

Beven, K. (1987) Towards a new paradigm in hydrology, in *Water for the future: hydrology in perspective*, IAHS Publ. **164:** 393–403, IAHS Press, Wallingford.

Beven, K. (1991) Spatially distributed modeling: Conceptual approach to runoff prediction, in D.S. Bowles and P.E. O'Connell (eds), *Recent Advances in the Modeling of Hydrologic Systems*, Kluwer, Dordrecht, 373–87.

Beven, K.J. (1996) A discussion of distributed hydrological modelling, in M.B. Abbott and J.C. Refsgaard (eds), *Distributed Hydrological Modelling*, Kluwer, Dordrecht, 255–78.

Beven, K. J. and P. Germann (1982) Macropores and water flow in soils, *WRR*, **18:** 1311–25.

Beven, K. and E. F. Wood (1983) Catchment geomorphology and the dynamics of runoff contributing areas, *J. Hydrol.*, **65:** 139–58.

Beven, K.J., M.J. Kirkby, N. Schofield and A.F. Tagg (1984) Testing a physically-based flood forecasting model (TOPMODEL) for three UK catchments, *J. Hydrol.*, **69:** 119–43.

Bezinge, A. (1987) Glacial meltwater streams, hydrology and sediment transport: the case of the Grande Dixence hydroelectricity scheme, in *Glacio-fluvial sediment transfer*, A. M. Gurnell and M. J. Clark (eds), Chichester, Wiley, pp. 473–98.

BHS (1994) *Sustainability in a Changing World: the key role of hydrology*, The National Research Strategy of the British Hydrological Society, The Society, London, pp. 18.

BHS (1998) The Exeter Statement, *Circulation, Newsletter of the British Hydrological Society*, **59:** 1–3.

Binnie, G.M. (1981) *Early Victorian water engineers*, Thomas Telford Ltd, London, 310 pp.

Biondic, B. and M. Bakalowicz (eds) (1995) *Hydrogeological Aspects of Groundwater Protection in Karstic Areas*, COST action 65, Final Report, Directorate-General XII Science, Research and Development, European Commission, Luxembourg.

Biswas, A.K. (1970) *History of hydrology*, North-Holland Publishing Co., Amsterdam, 336 pp.

Biswas, A.K. (1996) Water for the developing world in the 21st century: Issues and implications, *ICID Journal*, **45:** 1–12.

Black, T.A. and F.M. Kelliher (1989) Processes controlling understorey evapotranspiration, *Proc. Phil. Trans. Roy. Soc. London, Series B*, **324:** 207–31.

Blackie, J.R. and C.W.O. Eeles (1985) Lumped catchment models, in M.G. Anderson and T.P. Burt (eds), *Hydrological Forecasting*, Wiley, Chichester, pp. 311–45.

Blake, G., E. Schlichting and U. Zimmermann (1973) Water recharge in a soil with shrinkage cracks. *Proc. SSSA*, **37:** 669–72.

Bloemen, G.W. (1980) Calculation of steady state capillary rise from the groundwater table in multi-layered soil profiles, *Zeitschrift für Pflanzenernährung und Bodenkunde*, **143:** 701–19.

Blyth, E.M. and A.J. Dolman (1994) The effect of forest on mesoscale rainfall: an example from HAPEX-MOBILHY, *J. Appl. Met.*, **33:** 445–54.

Bodman, G. B. and E. A. Colman (1943) Moisture and energy conditions during downward entry of water into soils. *Proc. SSSA*, **8:** 116–22.

Bogardi, J. (1974) *Sediment transport in alluvial streams*, Akademiai Kiado, Budapest, 826 pp.

Bonell, M. and D.A. Gilmour (1978) The development of overland flow in a tropical rainforest catchment, *J. Hydrol.*, **39:** 365–82.

Bonell, M. and J. Williams (1986) The generation and redistribution of overland flow on a massive oxic soil in a eucalypt woodland within the semi-arid tropics of north Australia, *Hydrol. Processes*, **1:** 31–46.

Bonell, M., D. S. Cassells and D. A. Gilmour (1983) Vertical soil water movement in a tropical rainforest catchment in northeast Queensland, *Earth Surf. Proc. and Landforms*, **8:** 253–72.

Bonell, M., M. R. Hendriks, A. C. Imeson and L. Hazelhoff (1984) The generation of storm runoff in a forested clayey drainage basin in Luxembourg, *J. Hydrol.*, **71:** 53–77.

Bormann, F.H. and G.E. Likens (1994) *Pattern and processes in a forested ecosystem*, Springer, New York, 226 pp.

Boucher, K. (1997) Hydrological monitoring and measurement methods, in R.L. Wilby (ed), *Contemporary Hydrology*, Wiley, pp. 107–49.

Bouchet, R.T. (1963) Evapotranspiration réelle et potentielle, signification climatique, *IAHS Publ.*, **62:** 134–42.

Boughton, W. C. and D. M. Freebairn (1985) Hydrograph recession characteristics of some small agricultural catchments, *Australian J. Soil Res.*, **23:** 373–82.

Bouma, J. (1977) *Soil survey and the study of water in the unsaturated soil*, Soil Survey Paper 13, Netherlands Soil Survey Institute, Wageningen, 106 pp.

Bouma, J. (1981) Soil morphology and preferential flow along macropores, *Agric. Water Manag.*, **8:** 235–50.

Bouma, J. (1986) Using soil survey information to characterize the soil-water state, *J. Soil Sci.*, **37:** 1–7.

Bovee, K.D. (1982) *A guide to stream habitat analysis using the Instream Flow Incremental Methodology*, Instream Flow Information Paper, 12, FWS/OBS–82/26, Office of Biological Services, US Fish and Wildlife Service, Fort Collins, CO.

Bowen, I.S. (1926) The ratio of heat losses by conduction and by evaporation from any water surface, *Physical Review*, **27:** 779–87.

Bracq, P. and F. Delay (1997) Transmissivity and morphological features in a chalk aquifer: a geostatistical approach of their relationship, *J. Hydrol.*, **191:** 139–60.

Brady, N. C. (1984) *The nature and properties of soils*, 9th edn, Macmillan Publishing Co., New York, 560 pp.

Brakensiek, D. L. and C. A. Onstad (1977) Parameter estimation of the Green and Ampt infiltration equation, *WRR*, **13(6):** 1009–12.

Brimblecome, P., M. Tranter, P.W. Abrahams, I. Blackwood, T.D. Davies and C.E. Vincent (1985) Relocation and preferential elution of acidic solute through the snowpack of a small, remote, high altitude Scottish catchment, *Ann. Glaciol.*, **7:** 141–7.

Brooks, K.N., P.E. Ffolliot, H.M. Gregersen and L.F. DeBano (1997) *Hydrology and the management of watersheds*, Iowa State University Press, Ames, 502 pp.

Browning, K.A. (1987) Towards the more effective use of radar and satellite imagery in weather forecasting, in V.K. Collinge and C. Kirby (eds), *Weather radar and flood forecasting*, John Wiley and Sons, Chichester, pp. 239–69.

Browning, K.A. and F.F. Hill (1981) Orographic rain, *Weather*, **36:** 326–9.

Brubaker, K.L., D. Entekhabi and P.S. Eagleson (1993) Estimation of continental precipitation recycling, *J. Climate*, **6:** 1077–89.

Bruijnzeel, L.A. (1990) *Hydrology of Moist Tropical Forests and Effects of Conversion: A state of knowledge review*, Free University, Amsterdam, 224 pp.

Bruijnzeel, L.A. and K.F. Wiersum (1987) Rainfall interception by a young Acacia auriculiformis plantation forest in west Java, Indonesia: application of Gash's analytical model. *Hydrological Processes*, **1:** 309–319.

Brutsaert, W.H. (1982) *Evaporation into the atmosphere—theory, history and applications*, D. Reidel Publishing Co., Dordrecht, 299 pp.

Brutsaert, W.H. and H. Stricker (1979) An advection–aridity approach to estimate actual regional evapotranspiration, *WRR*, **15:** 443–50.

BSI (1996) *Guide to the acquisition and management of meteorological precipitation data: Areal rainfall*, British Standard 7843: Section 2.4. British Standards Institution, London.

Buchan, S. (1963) Geology in relation to groundwater, *JIWE*, **17:** 153–64.

Buchan, S. (1965) Hydrogeology and its part in the hydrological cycle. Informal discussion of the Hydrological Group, *Proc. ICE*, **31:** 428–31.

Buchter, B., C. Hinz and J. Leuenberger (1997) Tracer transport in a stony hillslope soil under forest, *J. Hydrol.*, **192:** 314–20.

Burgoa, B. and R.D. Wauchope (1995) Pesticides in runoff and surface waters, in T.R. Roberts and P.C. Kearney (eds) *Environmental behaviour of agrochemicals*, J. Wiley and Sons, Chichester, pp. 221–55.

Burke, W., D. Gabriels and J. Bouma (eds) (1986) *Soil structure assessment*, A. A. Balkema, Rotterdam, 92 pp.

Burpee, R.W. and L.N. Lahiff (1984) Area average rainfall variations on sea breeze days in S. Florida, *Mon. Wea. Rev.*, **112:** 520–34.

Burroughs, W.J. (1992) *Weather cycles: real or imaginary?* Cambridge University Press, Cambridge.

Burt, T.P. and P.J. Johnes (1997) Managing water quality in agricultural catchments, *Trans. IBG*, **22:** 61–68.

Burt, T.P. and Shahgedanova, M. (1998) An historical record of evaporation losses since 1815 calculated using long-term observations from the Radcliffe Meteorological Station, Oxford, England. *J. Hydrol.*, **205:** 101–11.

Buttle, J.M. (1994) Isotope hydrograph separation and rapid delivery of pre-event water from drainage basins, *Progress in Physical Geography*, **18,** 16–41.

Buttle, J.M. and D.G. Leigh (1997) The influence of artificial macropores on water and solute transport in laboratory soil columns, *J. Hydrol.*, **191:** 290–314.

Cacas, M.C., E. Ledoux, G. de Maisily and B. Tillie (1990) Modelling fracture flow with a stochastic discrete fracture network: Calibration and validation, 1. The flow model, *WRR*, **26:** 479–89.

Calder, I.R. (1976) The measurement of water loss from a forested area using a 'natural' lysimeter, *J. Hydrol.*, **30:** 311–25.

Calder, I.R. (1977) A model of transpiration and interception loss from a spruce forest in Plynlimon, central Wales. *J. Hydrol.*, **33:** 247–65.

Calder, I.R. (1979) Do trees use more water than grass?, *Water Services*, **83:** 11–14.

Calder, I.R. (1986) The influence of land use on water yield in upland areas of the UK, *J. Hydrol.*, **88:** 201–11.

Calder, I.R. (1990) *Evaporation in the uplands.* J. Wiley, Chichester, pp. 148.

Calder, I.R. (1996) Rainfall interception and drop size—development and calibration of the two layer stochastic interception model, *Tree Physiology*, **16:** 727–32.

Calder, I.R. (1998) Personal communication, University of Newcastle upon Tyne.

Calder, I.R. and C.H.R. Kidd (1978) A note on the dynamic calibration of tipping bucket gauges, *J. Hydrol.*, **39:** 383–6.

Calder, I.R. and C. Neal (1984) Evaporation from saline lakes: a combination approach, *Hydrol. Sciences J.*, **29:** 89–97.

Calder, I.R. and M.D. Newson (1979) Land use and upland water resources in Britain—a strategic look. *Water Resources Bull.*, **15:** 1628–39.

Calder, I.R. and P.T.W. Rosier (1976) The design of large plastic sheet net rainfall gauges. *J. Hydrol.*, **30:** 403–5.

Calder, I.R. and I.R. Wright (1986) Gamma ray attenuation studies of interception from Sitka spruce: some evidence for an additional transport mechanism. *WRR*, **22:** 409–17.

Calder, I.R., R.L. Hall and P.G. Adlard (1992) *Growth and water use of forest plantations*, John Wiley, Chichester, 381 pp.

Calder, I.R., R.J. Harding and P.T.W. Rosier (1983) An objective assessment of soil water deficit models, *J. Hydrol.*, **60:** 329–55.

Calder, I.R., I.R. Wright and D. Murdiyarso (1986) A study of evaporation from tropical rain forest—West Java. *J. Hydrol.*, **89:** 13–31.

Calder, I.R., R.L. Hall, R.J. Harding and I.R. Wright (1984) The use of a wet-surface weighing lysimeter system in rainfall interception studies of heather (Calluna vulgaris). *J. Climate and Applied Met.*, **23:** 461–73.

Calder, I.R., G.S. Kariyappa, N.V. Srinivasulu and K.V. Srinivasa Murty (1992) Deuterium tracing for the estimation of transpiration from trees, 1. Field calibration, *J. Hydrol.*, **130:** 17–25.

Calles, U.M. (1985) Deep groundwater contribution to a small stream, *Nordic Hydrol.*, **16:** 45–54.

Cameron, C.S., D.L. Murray, B.D. Fahey, R.M. Jackson, F.M. Kelliher and G.W. Fisher (1997) Fog deposition in tall tussock grassland, South Island, New Zealand. *J. Hydrol.*, **193:** 363–76.

Cape, J.N., D. Fowler, J.W. Kinnaird, I.A. Nicholson and I.S. Paterson (1987) Modification of rainfall chemistry by a forest canopy, in P.J. Coughtrey, M.H. Martin and M.H. Unsworth (eds), *Pollutant transport and fate in ecosystems*, British Ecological Society Special Publication 6, pp. 155–69.

Cappus, P. (1960) Etude des lois de l'écoulement, application au calcul et à la prévision des débits, *La Houille Blanche A*, Jul-Aug: 493–520.

Carbognin, L. and P. Gatto (1986) An overview of the subsidence of Venice, *IAHS Publ.*, **151:** 321–8.

Carlisle, A., Brown, A., H.F. and E.J. White (1965) The interception of precipitation by oak (*Quercus petraea*) on a high rainfall site. *Quarterly Journal of Forestry*, April, pp. 140–3.

Carlyle-Moses, D.E. and A.G. Price (1999) An evaluation of the Gash interception model in a northern hardwood stand. *J. Hydrol.*, **214:** 103–10.

Carroll, T.R. (1987) Operational airborne measurement of snow water equivalent and soil moisture using terrestrial gamma radiation in the United States, *IAHS Publ.*, **166:** 213–23.

Carter, D. L., M. M. Mortland and W. D. Kemper (1986) Specific surface, Ch. 16 in *Methods of soil analysis, 1. Physical and mineralogical methods*, A. Klute (ed), 2nd edn, ASA/SSSA, Madison, Wis., pp. 413–23.

Cartwright, K. (1970) Groundwater discharge in the Illinois basin as suggested by temperature anomalies, *WRR*, **6:** 912–18.

Cartwright, K. (1974) Tracing shallow groundwater systems by soil temperatures, *WRR*, **10:** 847–55.

Cassell, D. K. and A. Klute (1986) Water potential, tensiometry, Ch. 23 in *Methods of soil analysis, 1. Physical and mineralogical methods*, A. Klute (ed), 2nd edn, ASA/SSSA, Madison, Wis., pp. 563–96.

Cassells, D. S., D. A. Gilmour and M. Bonell (1985) Catchment response and watershed management in the tropical rainforests in north-eastern Australia, *Forest Ecology and Management*, **10:** 155–75.

Catt, J. (1985) Natural soil acidity, *Soil Use and Management*, **1:** 8–10.

Chahine, M.T. (1992) The hydrological cycle and its influence on climate, *Nature*, **359:** 373–80.

Chamberlin, T.C. (1885) The requisite and qualifying conditions of artesian wells, *US Geological Survey 5th Annual Report*, pp. 131–73.

Charney, J.G. (1975) Dynamics of deserts and drought in the Sahel, *QJRMS*, **101:** 193–202.

Chater, A.M. and A.P. Sturman (1998) Atmospheric conditions influencing the spillover of rainfall to lee of the Southern Alps, New Zealand, *Int. J. Climatology*, **18:** 77–92.

Chebotarev, I.I. (1955) Metamorphism of natural water in the crust of weathering, *Geochim. Cosmochim. Acta*, **8:** 22–48, 137–70, 198–212.

Childs, E.C. (1969) *An introduction to the physical basis of soil water phenomena*, John Wiley and Sons Ltd., London, 493 pp.

Childs, E.C. and N. Collis-George (1950) The permeability of porous materials. *Proc. Phil. Trans. Roy. Soc., London, A*, **201:** 392–405.

Chow, V.T., D.R. Maidment and L.W. Mays (1988) *Applied Hydrology*, McGraw-Hill Book Co. New York, 572 pp.

Clegg, A.G. (1963) Rainfall interception in a tropical forest. *Caribbean Foresters*, **24:** 75–9.

Clesceri, L.S., A.E. Greenberg and R.R. Trussell (1989) (eds), *Standard methods for the examination of water and wastewater, 17e*, Joint publication of: American Public Health Association, American Water Work Association, and Water Pollution Control Federation, Washington, D.C.

Colbeck, S.C. (1975) A theory for water flow through a layered snowpack, *WRR*, **11:** 261–6.

Colbeck, S.C. (1979) Water flow through heterogeneous snow, *Cold Regions Science Technology*, **3:** 37–45.

Colbeck, S.C., E.A. Anderson, V.C. Bissell, A.G. Crook, D.H. Male, C.W. Slaughter and D.R. Wiesnet (1979) Snow accumulation, distribution, melt and runoff, *EOS*, **60:** 464–71.

Collier, C.G. (1984) Remote sensing for hydrological forecasting, in J.C. Rodda (ed), *Facets in hydrology*, vol. II, John Wiley, New York, pp. 1–24.

Collier, C.G. (1987) Accuracy of real-time radar measurements, in V.K. Collinge and C. Kirby (eds), *Weather radar and flood forecasting*, John Wiley and Sons, Chichester, pp. 71–95.

Collier, C.G. (ed) (1995) *Weather radar systems*, Report EUR 16013 EN, European Commission, Brussels, 814 pp.

Collier, C.G. (ed) (1996) *Application of weather radar systems, 2e*, John Wiley and Sons, Chichester.

Collier, C.G. and M. Chapius (eds) (1990) *Weather radar networking*, Kluwer Academic Publishers, Dordrecht, 580 pp.

Collier, C.G., P.R. Larke and B.R. May (1983) A weather radar correction procedure for real time estimation of surface rainfall, *QJRMS*, **109:** 589–608.

Collinge, V.K. (1991) Weather radar calibration in real time: prospects for improvement, in I.D. Cluckie and C.G. Collier (eds), *Hydrological applications of weather radar*, Ellis Horwood, London, 25–42.

Collins, M.A. and L.W. Gelhar (1971) Seawater intrusion in layered aquifers, *WRR*, **7:** 971–9.

Cook, P.G. and D.K. Solomon (1997) Recent advances in dating young groundwater: Chlorofluorocarbons, $^{3}H/^{3}He$ and ^{85}Kr, *J. Hydrol.*, **191:** 245–65.

Cooper, H.H., F.A. Kohout, H.R. Henry and R.E. Glover (1964) Sea water in coastal aquifers, relation of salt water to fresh groundwater, *USGS Wat. Sup. Pap.*, 1613C, 84 pp.

Corbett, E.S. and R.P. Crouse (1968) Rainfall interception by annual grass and chaparral ... losses compared. *Research Paper PSW–48*, US Forest Service, Berkeley.

Corey, A. T. (1977) Mechanics of heterogeneous fluids in porous media, in *Water Resources Publications*, Fort Collins, Colo., 259 pp.

Corradini, C., F. Melone and R.E. Smith (1997) A unified model for infiltration and redistribution during complex rainfall patterns, *J. Hydrol.*, **192:** 104–24.

Court, A. (1961) Area-depth rainfall formulas, *JGR*, **66:** 1823–31.

Craddock, J.M. (1976) Annual rainfall in England since 1725, *QJRMS*, **102:** 823–40.

Crane, S.B. and J.A. Hudson (1997) The impact of site factors and climate variability on the calculation of potential evaporation at Moel Cynnedd, Plynlimon, *Hydrology and Earth System Sciences*, **1:** 429–45.

Crawford, N.H. and R.K. Linsley (1966) *Digital Simulation in Hydrology: Stanford Watershed Model IV*, Tech. Rept. No. 39, Dept. Civ. Engg., Stanford University, Stanford, CA, 210 pp.

Cresser, M. and A. Edwards (1987) *Acidification of freshwaters*, Cambridge University Press, Cambridge, 136 pp.

Crockford, R.H. and D.P. Richardson (1990) Partitioning of rainfall in a eucalyptus forest and pine plantation in southeastern Australia, III. Determination of the canopy storage capacity of a dry sclerophyll eucalypt forest. *Hydrol. Processes*, **4:** 157–67.

Cruikshank, J.G. (1972) *Soil geography*, David and Charles, Newton Abbot, 256 pp.

Cryer, R. (1986) Atmospheric solute inputs. In Trudgill, S.T. (ed) *Solute Processes*, J. Wiley and Sons, New York, pp. 15–84.

Curran, J.C. and M. Robertson (1991) Water quality implications of an observed trend of rainfall and runoff, *JIWE(M)*, **5:** 419–24.

Currie, R.G. and D.P. O'Brien (1990) Deterministic signals in precipitation records from the American Corn Belt, *Int. J. Climatology*, **10:** 179–89.

Dai, A., I.Y. Fung and A. D. Del Genio (1997) Surface observed global precipitation variations during 1900–88, *J. Climate*, **10:** 2943–62.

Dalton, J. (1802) Experimental essays on the constitution of mixed gases, *Manchester Literary and Philosophical Society Memo.*, **5:** 535–602.

Darcy, H. (1856) *Les fontaines publiques de la ville de Dijon*, V. Dalmont, Paris.

Davies, T.D., S.R. Dorling, C.E. Pierce, R.J. Barthelmie and G. Farmer (1991) The meteorological control on the anthropogenic ion content of precipitation at three sites in the UK: the utility of Lamb weather types, *Int. J. Climatology*, **11:** 795–807.

Davis, P.A., N.E. Olague and M.T. Goodrich (1992) Application of a validation strategy to Darcy's experiment, *Adv. in Water Res.*, **15:** 175–80.

Davis, S.N. and R.J.M. De Wiest (1966) *Hydrogeology*, John Wiley and Sons, New York, 463 pp.

De Jong, R. (1981) *Soil water models, a review*, Contribution 123, Land Resource Research Institute, Ottawa, Canada, 39 pp.

De Ploey, J. (1982) A stemflow equation for grasses and similar vegetation. *Catena*, **9:** 139–52.

De Vries, J.J. (1976) The groundwater outcrop-erosion model: evolution of the stream network in The Netherlands, *J. Hydrol.*, **29:** 43–50.

De Vries, J. and T.L. Chow (1978) Hydrologic behaviour of a forested mountain soil in coastal British Columbia, *WRR*, **14:** 935–42.

De Vries, J.J. and A. Gieske (1990) A simple chloride balance routing method to regionalize groundwater recharge: a case study in semiarid Botswana, in M.A. Beran, M. Brilly, A. Becker & O. Bonacci (eds), *Regionalization in Hydrology*, IAHS Publ. No. 191, 81–9.

De Zeeuw, J.W. (1966) *Hydrograph analysis of areas with prevailing groundwater discharge*, Veenman and Zonen, Wageningen (with English summary).

Dean, T.J, J.P. Bell and A.J.B. Baty (1987) Soil moisture measurement by an improved capacitance technique, I. Sensor design and performance, *J. Hydrol.*, **93:** 67–78.

Demuth, S. and P. Schreiber (1994) Studying storage behaviour using an operational recession method, in P. Seuna, A. Gustard, N.W. Arnell and G.A. Cole (eds), *FRIEND: Flow regimes from international experimental and network data*, IAHS Publ. No. 221, IAHS Press, Wallingford, 51–9.

Denmead, O.T. (1984) Plant physiological methods for studying evapotranspiration: problems of telling the forest from the trees, *Agric. Water Management*, **8**(1)**:** 67–89.

DETR (1997) *Acid deposition in the UK, 1992–94*, Department of the Environment, Transport and the Regions, London.

Dhar, O.N. and S. Nandargi (1996) Which is the rainiest station in India – Cherrapunji or Mawsynram?, *Weather*, **51:** 314–15.

Dincer, T., B.R. Payne, T. Florkowski, J. Martinec and E. Tongiori (1970) Snowmelt runoff from measurements of tritium and oxygen-18, *WRR*, **6:** 110–24.

Dodd, J.P. and I.N. James (1996) Diagnosing the global hydrological cycle from routine atmospheric analyses, *QJRMS*, **122:** 1475–99.

DOE (1972) *Analysis of raw, potable and waste waters*, Department of the Environment, London, HMSO, 305 pp.

DOE (1986) *Nitrate in water*, Pollution Paper 26, Report by the Nitrate Coordination Group, Department of the Environment, London, 101 pp.

Dolman, A.J. (1987) Summer and winter rainfall interception in an oak forest. Predictions with an analytical and a numerical simulation model. *J. Hydrol.*, **90:** 1–9.

Domenico, P.A. (1972) *Concepts and models in groundwater hydrology*, McGraw-Hill, New York, 405 pp.

Domenico, P.A. and F.W. Schwartz ((1990) *Physical and Chemical Hydrogeology*, John Wiley, New York, 824 pp.

Dooge, J.C.I. (1988) Hydrology in perspective, *Hydrol. Sci. J.*, **33:** 61–85.

Doorenbos, J. and W.O. Pruitt (1977) *Guidelines for predicting crop water requirements*, Irrigation and Drainage Paper 24, Food and Agriculture Organisation (FAO), Rome.

Doornkamp, J.C., K.J. Gregory and A.S. Burn (eds) (1980) *Atlas of drought in Britain 1975–6*, Institute of British Geographers, London.

Douglas, I. and T. Spencer (1985) Present-day processes as a key to the effects of environmental change, in I. Douglas and T. Spencer (eds), *Environmental Change and Tropical Geomorphology*, Allen and Unwin, London, 39–73.

Douglas, J.T., M.J. Goss and D. Hill (1980) Measurements of pore characteristics in a clay soil under ploughing and direct drilling, including the use of a radioactive tracer (^{114}Ce) technique, *Soil and Tillage Research*, **1:** 11–18.

Downing, R.A. and G.P. Jones (1985) Hydrogeology—some essential facets, in *Hydrogeology in the service of man*, Memoirs of the XVIIIth Congress, Int. Assoc. Hydrogeologists, 1–16.

Downing, R.A., D.B. Smith, F.J. Pearson, R.A. Monkhouse and R.F. Otlet (1977) The age of groundwater in the Lincolnshire Limestone, England and its relevance to the flow mechanism, *J. Hydrol.*, **33:** 201–16.

Drever, J.I. (1988) *The geochemistry of natural waters, 2e*, Prentice-Hall, Englewood Cliffs, New Jersey.

Dunne, T. (1978) Field studies of hillslope flow processes, in M.J. Kirkby (ed), *Hillslope Hydrology*, Wiley, Chichester, pp. 227–93.

Dunne, T. and L.B. Leopold (1978) *Water in environmental planning*, Freeman, San Francisco, 818 pp.

Dunne, T., T.R. Moore and C.H. Taylor (1975) Recognition and prediction of runoff-producing zones in humid regions, *Hydrol. Sci. Bull.*. **20:** 305–26.

Dupuit, J. (1863) *Etudes théoriques et pratiques sur le mouvement des eaux, 2e*, Dunod, Paris.

Duysings, J.J.H.M., J.M. Verstraten and L. Bruynzeel (1983) The identification of runoff sources of a forested lowland catchment: a chemical and statistical approach. *J. Hydrol.*, **64:** 357–75.

Dwyer, I.J. and D.W. Reed (1995) *Allowance for discretization in hydrological and environmental risk estimation*, Report 123, Institute of Hydrology, Wallingford, UK.

Eckis, R.P. (1934) South Coastal Basin investigation, geology and ground-water storage capacity of valley fill, *Bull. California Div. Water Res.*, **45**, 279 pp.

Edmunds, W.M., A.H. Bath and D.L. Miles (1982) Hydrochemical evolution of the East Midland Triassic sandstone aquifer, England, *Geochimica et Cosmochimica Acta*, **46:** 2069–81.

Eeles, C.W.O., M. Robinson and R.C. Ward (1990) Experimental basins and environmental models, in J.C. Hooghart, C.W.S. Posthumus and P.M.M. Warmerdam (eds), *Hydrological research basins and the environment*, TNO Committee on Hydrological Research, The Hague, pp. 3–12.

Eke, K.R., A.D. Barnden and D.J. Tester (1996) Impact of agricultural pesticides on water quality, in R.E. Hester and R.M. Harrison (eds), Issues in environmental science and technology, *Agricultural chemicals and the environment*, No. 5. Royal Society of Chemistry, London (Cambridge), 43–56.

Ellis, B. (ed) (1999) *Impacts of Urban Growth on Surface Water and Groundwater Quality*, IAHS Publ. No. 259, IAHS Press, Wallingford.

Ellis-Evans, J.C. and D. Wynn-Williams (1996) A great ice lake under the ice, *Nature*, **381:** 644–6.

Elliston, G.R. (1973) Water movement through the Gornergletscher, *Symposium on the Hydrology of Glaciers, Cambridge, 1969,* IASH Publ. No. **95:** 79–84.

Elsworth, D. and C.R. Mase (1993) Groundwater in rock engineering, in J.A. Hudson (ed), *Comprehensive Rock Engineering: Principles, practice and projects*, Pergamon, pp. 201–26.

Eltahir, E.A.B. and R.L. Bras (1994) Precipitation recycling in the Amazon basin, *QJRMS*, **120:** 861–80.

Engler, A. (1919) Untersuchungen uber den Einfluss des Waldes auf den Stand der Gewasser. *Mitt. des Schweiz Eidg. Anst. fur das Forlische Versuchswesen* **12,** 636 pp.

Engman, E.T. and R.J. Gurney (1991) *Remote Sensing in Hydrology*, Chapman & Hall, London, 225 pp.

Engman, E.T. and A.S. Rogowski (1974) A partial area model for storm flow synthesis, *WRR*, **10:** 464–72.

Ernst, L.F. (1978) Drainage of undulating sandy soils with high groundwater tables, *J. Hydrol.*, **39:** 1–30, 31–50.

Essenwanger, O.M. (1986) Elements of statistical analysis, *World Survey of Climatology*, vol. 1B, Elsevier, Amsterdam, 424 pp.

Farquharson, F.A.K., D. Mackney, M.D. Newson and A.J. Thomasson (1978) *Estimation of runoff potential of river catchments from soil survey*, Soil Survey Special Survey 11, Harpenden, 29 pp.

Farr, E. and W.C. Henderson (1986) *Land drainage*, Longman, London, 251 pp.

Faulkner, D.S. (1999) Rainfall frequency estimation, vol. 2, *Flood Estimation Handbook*, Institute of Hydrology, Wallingford, UK.

Feddes, R.A. (ed) (1995) *Space and Time Scale Variability and Interdependencies in Hydrological Processes*, International Hydrology Series, CUP, 420 pp.

Feddes, R.A., P. Kabat, P.J.T. van Bakel, J.J.B. Bronswijk and J. Halbertsma (1988) Modelling soil water dynamics in the unsaturated zone – state of the art, *J. Hydrol.*, **100:** 69–111.

Federer, C.A. (1975) Evapotranspiration, *Reviews of Geophysics and Space Physics*, **13:** 442–5.

Federer, C.A. (1979) A soil–plant–atmosphere model of transpiration and availability of soil water, *WRR*, **15:** 555–62.

Ferguson, P. and J.A. Lee (1983) Past and present sulphur pollution in the southern Pennines, *Atmos. Environ.*, **17:** 1131–7.

Ferguson, R. I. (1985) High densities, water equivalents, and melt rates of snow in the Cairngorm mountains, Scotland, *Weather*, **40:** 272–7.

Finney, H.J. (1984) The effect of crop covers on rainfall characteristics and splash detachment. *J. Agricultural Engg. Res.*, **29:** 337–43.

Finnigan, J.J. (1979) Turbulence in waving wheat, 11.Structure of momentum transfer, *Boundary Layer Met.*, **16:** 213–36.

Fleming, G. (1975) *Computer Simulation Techniques in Hydrology*, Environmental Science Series, Elsevier, New York, 333 pp.

Fogel, M.M. and L. Duckstein (1969) Point rainfall frequencies in convective storms. *WRR*, **5:** 1229–1237.

Folland, C.K., T.N. Palmer and D.E. Parker (1986) Sahel rainfall and worldwide sea temperatures, *Nature*, **320:** 602–7.

Forchheimer, P. (1914) *Hydraulik*, Teubner, Leipzig and Berlin.

Foster, S.S.D. (1975) The chalk groundwater tritium anomaly – a possible explanation, *J. Hydrol.*, **25:** 159–65.

Foster, S.S.D. and C.P. Young (1981) Effects of agricultural land use on groundwater quality with special reference to nitrate, in *A survey of British hydrogeology*, Royal Society, London, pp. 47–59.

Fowler, D. (1984) Transfer to terrestrial surfaces, *Proc. Phil. Trans. Roy. Soc. London, B*, **305:** 281–97.

Fowler, D. and J.N. Cape (1984) The contamination of rain samples by deposition on rain collectors, *Atmos. Environ.*, **18:** 183–9.

Fowler, D., J.N. Cape and I.D. Leith (1985) Acid inputs from the atmosphere in the United Kingdom, *Soil Use and Management*, **1:** 3–5.

Fowler, D., Cape, J.N., Leith, I.D., Paterson, I.S., Kinnaird, J.W. and I.A. Nicholson (1982) Rainfall acidity in northern Britain, *Nature*, **297:** 383–6.

Framji, K.K., B.C. Garg and S.D.L. Luthra (eds) (1982) *Irrigation and drainage in the world, a global review*, 3rd edn, International Commission on Irrigation and Drainage, New Delhi.

Freeze, R.A. and J. Banner (1970) The mechanism of natural groundwater recharge and discharge, 2. Laboratory column experiments and field measurements, *WRR*, **6:** 138–55.

Freeze, R.A. and J.A. Cherry (1979) *Groundwater*, Prentice-Hall, Englewood Cliffs, N.J., 604 pp.

Freeze, R.A. and P.A. Witherspoon (1966) Theoretical analysis of regional groundwater flow, 1. Analytical and numerical solutions to the mathematical model, *WRR*, **2:** 641–56.

Freeze, R.A. and P.A. Witherspoon (1967) Theoretical analysis of regional groundwater flow, 2. Effect of water-table configuration and subsurface permeability variation, *WRR*, **3:** 623–34.

Freeze, R.A. and P.A. Witherspoon (1968) Theoretical analysis of regional groundwater flow, 3. Quantitative interpretation, *WRR*, **4:** 581–90.

French, R.H. (1988) Effects of the length of record on estimates of annual and seasonal precipitation, in D. Ouzar, C.A. Brebia and V. de Kosinsky (eds), *Computational methods and water resources*, vol. 3, Computational Mechanics Publications, Southampton, pp. 3–13.

Fukushima, Y., O. Watanabe and K. Higuchi (1991) Estimation of streamflow change by global warming in a glacier-covered high mountain area of the Nepal Himalaya, in H. Bergmann, H. Lang, W. Frey, D. Issler and B. Salm (eds), *Snow, Hydrology and Forests in High Alpine Areas*, IAHS Publ. No. **205:** 181–8.

Gan, T.Y., E.M. Dlamini and G.F. Biftu (1997) Effects of model complexity and structure, data quality, and objective functions on hydrologic modeling, *J. Hydrol.*, **192**: 81–103.

Gardner, C.M.K. and M. Field (1983) An evaluation of the success of MORECS, a meteorological model, in estimating soil moisture deficits, *Agric. Met.*, **29:** 269–84.

Gardner, W.H. (1986) Water content, Ch. 21 in *Methods of soil analysis, I. Physical and mineralogical methods*, A. Klute (ed), ASA/SSSA, Madison, Wis., pp. 493–544.

Gardner, W.R. and M. Fireman (1958) Laboratory studies of evaporation from soil columns in the presence of a water table, *Soil Sci.*, **85:** 244–9.

Gardner, W.R., D. Hillel and Y. Benyamini (1970) Post irrigation movement of soil water, 2. Simultaneous redistribution and evaporation, *WRR*, **6:** 1148–53.

Garmouma, M., M.J. Teil, M. Blanchard and M. Chevreuil (1998) Spatial and temporal variations of herbicide (triazines and phenylureas) concentrations in the catchment basin of the Marne river (France), *The science of the total environment*, **224:** 93–107.

Garven, G. (1985) The role of regional fluid flow in the genesis of the Pine Point deposit, western Canada sedimentary basin, *Econ. Geol.*, **80:** 307–24.

Gash, J.H.C. (1979) An analytical model of rainfall interception by forests. *QJRMS*, **105:** 43–55.

Gash, J.H.C. (1986) A note on estimating the effect of a limited fetch on micro-meteorological evaporation measurements, *Boundary Layer Met.*, **35:** 409–13.

Gash, J.H.C. (1998) Personal communication, Institute of Hydrology.

Gash, J.H.C. and A.J. Morton (1978) An application of the Rutter model to the estimation of the interception loss from Thetford Forest. *J. Hydrol.*, **38:** 49–58.

Gash, J.H.C. and J.B. Stewart (1977) The evaporation from Thetford Forest during 1975, *J. Hydrol.*, **35:** 385–96.

Gash, J.H.C., C.R. Lloyd and G. Lachaud (1995) Estimating sparse forest rainfall interception with an analytical model. *J. Hydrol.*, **170:** 79–86.

Gee, G.W. and D. Hillel (1988) Groundwater recharge in arid regions: Review and critique of estimation methods, *Hydrol. Processes*, **2:** 255–66.

Germann, P.F. (1990) Macropores and hydrologic hillslope processes, in M.G. Anderson and T.P. Burt (eds) *Process Studies in Hillslope Hydrology*, Wiley, Chichester: 327–63.

Gillham, R. W. (1984) The capillary fringe and its effect on water-table response, *J. Hydrol.*, **67:** 307–24.

Gleick, P.H. (1993a) Water in the 21st century, in P.H. Gleick (ed), *Water in Crisis*, Oxford University Press, New York, pp. 105–13.

Gleick, P.H. (1993b) An introduction to global fresh water issues, in P.H. Gleick (ed), *Water in Crisis: A Guide to the World's Freshwater Resources*, Oxford University Press, New York, pp. 3–12.

Gleick, P.H. (1998) *The World's Water, 1998–99: The biennial report on freshwater resources*. Island Press, Washington D.C., 307 pp.

Glover, B.J. and P. Johnson (1974) Variations in the natural chemical concentrations of river water during flood flows, and the lag effect, *J. Hydrol.*, **22:** 303–16.

Gold, C.G. (1989) Surface interpolation, spatial adjacency and GIS, in J. Raper (ed), *Three dimensional applications in Geographical Information Systems*, Taylor and Francis, pp. 21–35.

Goodison, B.E., B. Sevruk and S. Klemm (1989) WMO solid precipitation measurement intercomparison: objectives, methodology, analysis, *IAHS Publ.*, **179:** 57–64.

Gorgens, A.H.M. and D.A. Hughes (1982) Synthesis of streamflow information relating to the semi-arid karoo biome of South Africa, *South African J. Science*, **78:** 58–68.

Gorham, E. (1958a) Atmospheric pollution by hydrochloric acid, *QJRMS*, **84:** 274–6.

Gorham, E. (1958b) The influence and importance of daily weather conditions in the supply of chloride, sulphate and other ions to fresh waters from atmospheric precipitation, *Proc. Phil. Trans. Roy. Soc. London, B*, **241:** 147–78.

Goss, M.J., K R. Howse and W. Harris (1978) Effects of cultivation on soil water retention and water use by cereals in clay soils, *J. Soil Sci.*, **29:** 475–88.

Gottschalk, L. and I. Krasovskaia (1994) Interpolation of runoff to a regular grid net: theoretical aspects, in P. Seuna, A. Gustard, N.W. Arnell and G.A. Cole (eds), *FRIEND: Flow regimes from experimental and network data*, IAHS Publ. No. **221:** 455–66, IAHS Press, Wallingford.

Gottschalk, L., L.M. Tallaksen and G. Perzyna (1997) Derivation of low flow distribution functions using recession curves, *J. Hydrol.*, **194:** 239–62.

Grace, J. (1983) *Plant–atmosphere relationships*, Chapman and Hall, London.

Grant, R.H., G.E. Bertolini and L.P. Herrington (1986) The intermittent vertical heat flux over a spruce forest canopy, *Boundary-Layer Met.*, **35:** 317–30.

Gray, W.M. (1990) Strong association between West African rainfall and U.S. landfall of intense hurricanes, *Science*, **249:** 1251–6.

Green, M.J. and P.R. Helliwell (1972) The effect of wind on the rainfall catch, *Proc. Symp. on the Distribution of Precipitation in Mountainous Areas*, vol. 2, World Meteorological Organization, pp. 27–46.

Green, W.H. and G.A. Ampt (1911) Studies in soil physics, part 1. The flow of air and water through soils, *J. Agric. Sci.*, **4:** 1–24.

Groisman, P.Y. and D.R. Easterling (1994) Variability and trends of total precipitation and snowfall over the United States and Canada, *J. Climate*, **7:** 184–205.

Groisman, P.Y. and D.R. Legates (1994) The accuracy of United States precipitation data, *Bull. Amer. Met. Soc.*, **75:** 215–26.

Guangxiao, D. and Z. Yiaoqi (1986) Land subsidence in China, *IAHS Publ.*, **151:** 405–14.

Guglielmi, Y. and L. Prieur (1997), Locating and estimating submarine freshwater discharge from an interstitial confined coastal aquifer by measurements at sea: example from the lower Var valley, France, *J. Hydrol.*, **190:** 111–22

Gunston, H.M. (1998) *Field hydrology in tropical countries—a practical introduction*, Intermediate Technology Publications, London, 110 pp.

Gunston, H.M. and C.H. Batchelor (1983) A comparison of the Priestley–Taylor and Penman methods for estimating reference crop evapotranspiration in tropical countries, *Agricultural Water Management*, **6:** 65–77.

Gurnell, A. M. and M. J. Clark (eds) (1987) *Glacio-fluvial sediment transfer*, John Wiley and Sons, Chichester, 524 pp.

Gurnell, A. M., K. J. Gregory, S. Hollis and C. T. Hill (1985) Detrended correspondence analysis of heathland vegetation: the identification of runoff contributing areas, *Earth Surf. Proc. and Landforms*, **10:** 343–51.

Gustafson, G. and J. Krazny (1993) Crystalline rock aquifers: their occurrence, use and importance, in *Hydrogeology of Hard Rocks*, Memoirs of the XXIVth Congress, Int. Assoc. Hydrogeologists, Oslo, 3–20.

Gustard, A. and K.M. Irving (1994) Classification of the low flow response of European soils, in P. Seuna, A. Gustard, N.W. Arnell and G.A. Cole (eds), *FRIEND: Flow regimes from international experimental and network data*, IAHS Publ. No. 221, IAHS Press, Wallingford, 113–17.

Gustard, A., A. Bullock and J.M. Dixon (1992) *Low flow estimation in the United Kingdom*, IH Rept. No. 108, Institute of Hydrology, Wallingford.

Gvirtzman, H., D. Ronen and M. Magaritz (1986) Anion exclusion during transport through the unsaturated zone, *J. Hydrol.*, **87:** 267–83.

Habermehl, M. A. (1985) Groundwater in Australia, in *Hydrogeology in the service of man*, Memoirs of the XVIIth Congress, Int. Assoc. Hydrogeologists, 31–52.

Hall, D.G. (1964) What is hydrology? How is it applied? *Proc. Inst. Civil Engrs.*, **27:** 662–4.

Hall, D.G. (1968) The assessment of water resources in Devon, England, using limited hydrometric data, *IAHS Publ.*, **76:** 110–20.

Hall, J.K., N.L. Hartwig and L.D. Hoffman (1983) Application mode and alternate cropping effects on atrazine losses from a hillside, *J. Environmental Quality*, **12:** 336–40.

Hall, R.L. (1985) Further interception studies of heather using a wet surface weighing lysimeter system, *J. Hydrol.*, **81:** 193–210.

Hall, R.L. (1987) Processes of evaporation from vegetation of the uplands of Scotland. *Trans. Roy. Soc. Edinburgh: Earth Sciences*, **78:** 327–34.

Hall, R.L. and R.J. Harding (1993) The water use of the Balquhidder catchments: a processes approach. *J. Hydrol.*, **145:** 285–314.

Hall, R.L. and R. Hopkins (1997) A net rainfall gauge for use with multi-stemmed trees. *Hydrology and Earth System Sciences*, **1:** 213–15.

Hall, R.L. and J.M. Roberts (1990) Hydrological aspects of new broadleaf plantations. *SEESOIL*, **6:** 2–38.

Hall, R.L., I.R. Calder, P.T.W. Rosier, M.H. Swaminath and J. Mumtaz (1992) Measurement and modelling of interception loss from a Eucalyptus plantation in southern India, in I.R. Calder, R.L. Hall and P.G. Adlard (eds), *Growth and water use in plantations*. J. Wiley, Chichester, pp. 270–89.

Hancock, N.H. and J.M. Crowther (1979) A technique for the direct measurement of water storage on a forest canopy. *J. Hydrol.*, **41:** 105–22.

Hansen, J.W., Hodges, A.W. and J.W. Jones (1998) ENSO influences on agriculture in the Southeastern United States. *Journal of Climate*, **11:** 404–11.

Hanshaw, B.B. and W. Back (1985) Deciphering hydrological systems by means of geochemical processes, *Hydrol. Sci. J.*, **30:** 257–71.

Harding, D.J.L. (ed) (1988) *Britain since 'Silent Spring': an update on the ecological effects of agricultural pesticides in the UK*, Proceedings of Symposium at Cambridge, 18 March 1988, Institute of Biology, London, 131 pp.

Harding, R.J. (1986) Exchanges of energy and mass associated with a melting snowpack, *IAHS Publ.*, **155:** 3–15.

Harding, R.J., C. Neal and P.G. Whitehead (1992) Hydrological effects of plantation forestry in North-Western Europe. In A. Teller, P. Mathy and J.N.R. Jeffers (eds), *Responses of Forest Ecosystems to Environmental Changes*. Elsevier Applied Science, London, pp. 445–55.

Harris, G.L., S.W. Bailey and D.J. Mason (1991) The determination of pesticide losses to water courses in an agricultural clay catchment with variable drainage and land management, in *Proceedings of Brighton Crop Protection Conference—Weeds, 1991*, British Crop Protection Council, Farnham, Surrey, **3:** 1271–8.

Harrison, G. (1985) *Drought '84*, Water Authorities Association, London, 27 pp.

Havas, M. (1986) Effects of acidic deposition on aquatic ecosystems, in A.C. Stern (ed), *Air pollutants, their transformation, transport and effects, 3e*, Air Pollution, vol. 6, Academic Press, New York, pp. 351–89.

Heath, R.C. (1982) Classification of groundwater systems of the United States, *Groundwater*, **20:** 393–401.

Heath, R. C. (1983) Basic groundwater hydrology, *USGS Wat. Sup. Pap.*, 2220, 84 pp.

Helvey, J.D. (1967) Interception by eastern white pine. *WRR*, **3:** 723–9.

Hem, J.D. (1985) Study and interpretation of the chemical characteristics of natural water, *USGS Wat. Sup. Pap.*, 2254, 3e, 263 pp.

Hendriks, M.R. (1993) Effects of lithology and land use on storm run-off in east Luxembourg, *Hydrol. Processes*, **7:** 213–26.

Hershfield, D.M. (1961) Estimating the probable maximum precipitation, *Proc. ASCE, J. Hydraul. Div.*, 87 (HY 5): 99–116.

Hertzler, R. A. (1939) Engineering aspects of the influence of forests on mountain streams, *Civil Engineering*, **9:** 487–9.

Herwitz, S.R. (1985) Interception storage capacities of tropical rainforest canopy trees. *J. Hydrol.*, **77:** 237–52.

Herzberg, B. (1901) Die Wasserversorgung einiger Nordseebader (The water supply to some North Sea resorts), *J. für Gasbeleuchtung und Wasserversorgung*, **44:** 815–19. Quoted in Todd (1980).

Hestnes, E. (1985) A contribution to the prediction of slush avalanches, *Annals of Glaciology*, **6:** 1–4.

Hewlett, J.D. (1961a) Watershed management, in *Report for 1961 Southeastern Forest Experiment Station*, US Forest Service, Ashville, N.C.

Hewlett, J.D. (1961b) Soil moisture as a source of baseflow from steep mountain watersheds, *Southeastern Forest Experiment Station, Paper* 132, US Forest Service, Ashville, N.C.

Hewlett, J.D. (1969) Tracing storm base flow to variable source areas on forested headwaters. *Technical Report* 2, School of Forest Resources, University of Georgia, Athens, Ga.

Hewlett, J.D. (1982a) Personal communication.

Hewlett, J.D. (1982b) *Principles of Forest Hydrology*, Univ. of Georgia Press, Athens.

Hewlett, J.D. and A.R. Hibbert (1961) Increase in water yield after several types of forest cutting. *Bull. Int. Assoc. Sci. Hydrology*, **6:** 5–17.

Hewlett, J.D. and A.R. Hibbert (1963) Moisture and energy conditions within a sloping soil mass during drainage. *JGR*, **68:** 1081–7.

Hewlett, J.D. and A.R. Hibbert (1967) Factors affecting the response of small watersheds to precipitation in humid areas, in *Forest hydrology*, W.E. Sopper and H.W. Lull (eds), Pergamon, Oxford, pp. 275–90.

Hibbert, A.R. (1967) Forest treatment effects on water yield. in W.E. Sopper and H.W. Lull (eds), *Forest hydrology*, Pergamon, Oxford, pp. 527–43.

Hibbert, A.R. (1971) Increases in streamflow after converting chaparral to grass. *WRR*, **7,** 71–80.

Hill, G. and R.B. Robertson (1987) The establishment and operation of an unmanned weather radar. Chapter 5 in Collinge, V.K. and C. Kirby (eds), *Weather Radar and Flood Forecasting*, J. Wiley and Sons, pp. 55–69.

Hillel, D. (1982) *Introduction to soil physics*, Academic Press, New York, 364 pp.

Hindley, D.R. (1973) The definition of dry weather flow in river flow measurement, *JIWE*, **27:** 438–40.

Hingston, F.J. and V. Gailitis (1976) The geographic variation of salt precipitated over western Australia, *Australian J. Soil Research*, **14:** 319–35.

Hitchon, B. and J. Hays (1971) Hydrodynamics and hydrocarbon occurrences Surat basin, Queensland, Australia, *WRR*, **7:** 658–76.

Hitschfeld, W. and J. Bordar (1954) Errors inherent in the radar measurement of rainfall at attenuating wavelengths. *Journal of Meteorology*, **2:** 58–67.

Hodgson, J.M. (ed) (1976) Soil survey field handbook, *Soil Survey Technical Monograph 5*, Soil Survey of England and Wales, Harpenden, 99 pp.

Hodnett, M.G. and J.P. Bell (1986) Soil moisture investigations of groundwater recharge through black cotton soils, in Madhya Pradesh, India, *Hydrol. Sci. J.*, **31:** 361–81.

Hodnett, M.G., I. Vendrame, A. De O. Marques Filho, M.D. Oyama and J. Tomasella (1997) Soil water storage and groundwater behaviour in a catenary sequence beneath forest in central Amazonia. II. Floodplain water table behaviour and implications for streamflow generation, *Hydrology and Earth System Sciences*, **1,** 279–90.

Hofer, T. (1993) Himalayan deforestation, changing river discharge, and increasing floods—myth or reality?, *Mountain Res. and Development*, **13:** 213–33.

Holko, L. and A. Lepistö (1997) Modelling the hydrological behaviour of a mountain catchment using TOPMODEL, *J. Hydrol.*, **196:** 361–77.

Hopmans, J. W. (1987) A comparison of various methods to scale soil hydraulic properties, *J. Hydrol.*, **93:** 241–56.

Hornberger, G.M., J.P. Raffensperger, P.L. Wiberg and K.N. Eshleman (1998) *Elements of Physical Hydrology*, Johns Hopkins University Press, Baltimore, 302 pp.

Hornberger, G.M., K.J. Beven, B.J. Sosby and D.E. Sappington (1985) Shenandoah watershed study: Calibration of a topography-based, variable contributing area hydrological model to a small forested catchment, *WRR*, **21:** 1841–50.

Horton, J.H. and R.H. Hawkins (1965) Flow path of rain from the soil surface to the water table, *Soil Sci.*, **100:** 377–83.

Horton, R.E. (1919) Rainfall interception. *Monthly Weather Review*, **47:** 603–23.

Horton, R.E. (1933) The role of infiltration in the hydrologic cycle, *Trans. AGU*, **14:** 446–60.

Horton, R.E. (1939) Analysis of runoff plot experiments with varying infiltration capacity, *Trans. AGU*, **20:** 693–711.

Hough, M.N. and D. Hollis (1997) Rare snowmelt estimation in the UK, *Meteorological Applications*, **5:** 127–38.

Hough, M.N. and R.J.A. Jones (1997) The UK Meteorological Office rainfall and evaporation calculation system: MORECS version 2.0—an overview, *Hydrology and Earth System Sciences*, **1:** 227–39.

Hsaio, T.C., E. Acevedo, E. Fereres and D.W. Henderson (1976) Water stress, growth and osmotic adjustment, *Proc. Phil. Trans. Roy. Soc., London, B*, **273:** 479–500.

Hubbard, R.K. and J.M. Sheridan (1983) Water and nitrate-nitrogen losses from a small, upland, coastal plain watershed, *J. Environmental Quality*, **12:** 291–5.

Hubbert, M.K. (1940) The theory of groundwater motion, *J. Geology*, **48:** 785–944.

Hubbert, M.K. (1956) Darcy's law and the field equations of the flow of underground fluids, *Trans. Amer. Institute of Mining Metal Engineers*, **207:** 222–39.

Huff, D.D., R.V. O'Neill, W.R. Emanuel, J.W. Elwood and J.D. Newbold (1982) Flow variability and hillslope hydrology, *Earth Surf. Proc. and Landforms*, **7:** 91–4.

Huff, F.A. (1970) Spatial distribution of rainfall rates, *WRR*, **6:** 254–60.

Humber, W. (1876) *A comprehensive treatise on the water supply of cities and towns*, Crosby Lockwood and Co., London, 378 pp.

Hurrell, J.W. (1995) Decadal trends in the North Atlantic Oscillation: regional temperatures and precipitation, *Science*, **269:** 676–9.

Hursh, C.R. (1944) Report of the sub-committee on subsurface flow. *Trans. AGU*, **25:** 743–6.

Hursh, C.R. and E.F. Brater (1941) Separating storm hydrographs from small drainage areas into surface and subsurface flow, *Trans. AGU*, **22,** 863–70.

Hutjes, R.W.A., Wierda, A. and A.W.L. Veen (1990) Rainfall interception in the Tai forest, Ivory Coast: application of two simulation models to a humid tropical system. *J. Hydrology*, **114:** 259–79.

IAHS (1973) *Symposium on the hydrology of glaciers*, IAHS Publ. 95.

IAHS (1975) *Snow and ice*, IAHS Publ. 104.

IAHS (1982) *Hydrological aspects of alpine and high mountain areas*, IAHS Publ. 138.

IAHS (1997) IAHS at Birmingham 1999, Newsletter, No. **61:** 18, International Association of Hydrological Sciences, IAHS Press, Wallingford.

IH (1980) *Low flow studies report*, Institute of Hydrology, Wallingford.

IH (1985) *Institute of Hydrology Research Report 1981–84*, NERC, Wallingford, 86 pp.

IH (1987) Report for 1985/86, in *The Natural Environment Research Council Report for 1985/86*, NERC, Swindon, pp. 61–78.

IH (1997) *Scientific Report 1996–97*, Institute of Hydrology, Wallingford, 62 pp.

IH (1998) *Broadleaf woodlands: The implications for water quantity and quality*. Report to the Environment Agency. Environment Agency Research and Development Publication No. 5, Stationery Office, London.

IH (1999) *Flood Estimation Handbook*, 5 vols., Institute of Hydrology, Wallingford.

IH/BGS (1988) *Hydrometric Register and Statistics 1981–85*, Hydrological data UK series, Institute of Hydrology/British Geological Survey, Wallingford, 178 pp.

IH/BGS (1993) *Hydrometric Register and Statistics 1986–90*, Hydrological data UK series, Institute of Hydrology/British Geological Survey, Wallingford, 190 pp.

IH/BGS (1994) *Hydrological Data UK, 1993 Yearbook*, Institute of Hydrology/British Geological Survey, Wallingford.

IH/BGS (1995) *Hydrological Data UK, 1994 Yearbook*, Institute of Hydrology/British Geological Survey, Wallingford.

IH/BGS (1996) *Hydrological Data UK, 1995 Yearbook*, Institute of Hydrology/British Geological Survey, Wallingford, 176 pp.

IH/BGS (1998) *Hydrometric Register and Statistics 1991–95*, Institute of Hydrology/British Geological Survey, Wallingford.

Ineson, J. (1956) Darcy's law and the evaluation of 'permeability', *IASH Symposia Darcy*, **2:** 165–72.

Ineson, J. (1963) Applications and limitations of pumping tests: (b) Hydrogeological significance, *JIWE*, **17:** 200–15.

Ineson, J. and R.A. Downing (1963) Changes in the chemistry of groundwaters of the Chalk passing beneath argillaceous strata, *Bulletin Geological Survey of Great Britain*, **20:** 176–92.

Innes, J.L. (1987) *Air pollution and forestry*, Forestry Commission Bulletin, 70, HMSO, London, 39 pp.

IPCC (1996) *Climate change 1995: The second assessment report*, Cambridge University Press, 3 Volumes.

ISSS (1976) Soil physics terminology. Report of the Terminology Committee (Chairman G. H. Bolt) of Commission I (Soil Physics), *Int. Soil Science Society Bull.*, **49:** 26–36.

Jackson, I.J. (1975) The relationships between rainfall parameters and interception by tropical forest. *J. Hydrol.*, **24:** 215–38.

Jacobs, A.F.G. and A. Verhoef (1997) Soil evaporation from sparse natural vegetation estimated from Sherwood Numbers, *J. Hydrol.*, **188:** 443–52.

Jacobson, R.L. and D. Langmuir (1974) Dissociation constants of calcite and $CaHCO_3^-$ from 0°C to 50°C, *Geochimica et Cosmochimica Acta*, **38:** 301–18.

Jaeger, L. (1983) Monthly and areal patterns of mean global precipitation. In A. Street-Perrot, M. Beran and R. Ratcliffe (eds), *Variations in the global water budget*, D. Reidel Publishing Co., Lancaster, pp. 129–40.

Jaeger, L. (1985) Eleven years of precipitation measurements above a small pole wood pine stand, in B. Sevruk (ed), *Correction of precipitation measurements*, Swiss Federal Institute of Technology, Zürich, pp. 101–3.

Jayatilaka, C.J. and R.W. Gillham (1996) A deterministic-empirical model of the effect of the capillary-fringe on near-stream area runoff, 1. Description of the model, *J. Hydrol.*, **184:** 299–315.

Jayatilaka, C.J., B. Storm and L.B. Mudgway (1998) Simulation of water flow on irrigation bay scale with MIKE-SHE, *J. Hydrol.*, **208:** 108–30.

Jaynes, D.B. (1985) Comparison of soil water hysteresis models, *J. Hydrol.*, **75:** 287–99.

Jensen, K.H., K. Bitsch and P.L. Bjerg (1993) Large scale dispersion experiments in a sandy aquifer in Denmark: observed tracer movements and numerical analysis, *WRR*, **29:** 673–96.

Jensen, M.E., R.D. Burman and R.G. Allen (1990) (eds) *Evaporation and irrigation water requirements*, Manuals and reports on engineering practice No. 70, American Society Civil Engineers, New York, 360 pp.

Jiaqi, C. (1987) The new stage of development of hydrology—water resources hydrology, in *Water for the future: hydrology in perspective*, IAHS Publ. **164:** 17–25.

Jobling, S., M. Nolan, C.R. Tyler, G. Brighty and J.P. Sumpter (1998) Widespread sexual disruption in wild fish, *Environmental Science and Technology*, **32:** 2498–2506.

Johnson, A.C., A.H. Haria, C.L. Bhardwaj, C. Volkner and A. Walker (1994) Water movement and isoproturon behaviour in a drained heavy clay soil, 2. Persistence and transport, *J. Hydrol.*, **163:** 217–31.

Johnson, A.H. and R.C. Reynolds (1977) Chemical character of headwater streams in Vermont and New Hampshire, *WRR*, **13:** 469–73.

Johnson, A.I. (ed) (1991) *Land Subsidence*, IAHS Publ. No. 200, IAHS, Wallingford, 690 pp.

Johnson, R.C. (1990) The interception, throughfall and stemflow in a forest in Highland Scotland and comparison with other upland forests in the UK. *J. Hydrol.*, **118:** 281–7.

Jones, H.G., T.D. Davies, A. Ohmura and E.M. Morris (eds) (1994) *Snow and Ice Covers: Interactions with the atmosphere and ecosystems*, IAHS Publ. No. 223, IAHS, Wallingford, 340 pp.

Jones, J.A.A. (1979) Extending the Hewlett model of stream runoff generation, *Area*, **11:** 110–14.

Jones, J.A.A. (1981) *The nature of soil piping—a review of research*, BGRG Research Monograph 2, GeoBooks, Norwich, 301 pp.

Jones, J.A.A. (1987) The effects of soil piping on contributing areas and erosion patterns, *Earth Surf. Proc. and Landforms*, **12:** 229–48.

Jones, J.A.A. (1997a) *Global Hydrology*, Longman, Harlow, 399 pp.

Jones, J.A.A. (1997b) Pipeflow contributing areas and runoff response, *Hydrol. Processes*, **11,** 35–41.

Jones, J.A.A. and F.G. Crane (1984) Pipeflow and pipe erosion in the Maesnant experimental catchment, in T.P. Burt and D.E. Walling (eds), *Catchment experiments in fluvial geomorphology*, GeoBooks, Norwich, pp. 55–72.

Jones, M.M. and N.C. Turner (1978) Osmotic adjustment in leaves of sorghum in response to water deficits, *Plant Physiology*, **61:** 122–6.

Joslin, J.D., P.A. Mays, M.H. Wolfe, J.M. Kelley, R.W. Garber and P.F. Brewer (1987) Chemistry of tension lysimeter water and lateral flow in spruce and hardwood stands, *J. Environmental Quality*, **16:** 152–60.

Junge, C.E. and W.T. Werby (1958) The concentration of chloride, sodium, potassium, calcium and sulphate in rain water over the United States, *J. Meteorol.*, **15:** 417–25.

Jungerius, P. D. (1985) Soils and geomorphology, *Catena, Suppl.* 6, 18 pp.

Jury, W.A. (1982) Simulation of solute transport using a transfer function model, *WRR*, **18:** 363–8.

Kabat, P., A.J. Dolman and J.A. Elbers (1997) Evaporation, sensible heat and canopy conductance of fallow savannah and patterned woodland in the Sahel, *J. Hydrol.*, **188:** 494–515.

Kalma, J.D. and M. Sivapalan (eds) (1995) *Scale Issues in Hydrological Modelling*, Wiley, Chichester, pp. 489.

Karl, T.R., P.Y. Groisman, R.W. Knight and R.H. Heim (1993) Recent variations of snow cover and snowfall in North America and their relation to precipitation and temperature variations, *J. Climate*, **6:** 1327–44.

Karl, T.R. and R.W. Knight (1998) Secular trends of precipitation amount, frequency and intensity in the United States, *Bull. Amer. Met. Soc.*, **79:** 231–41.

Karl, T.R., R.G. Quale and P.Y. Groisman (1993) Detecting variations and change: new challenges for observing and data management systems, *J. Climate*, **6:** 1481–94.

Kayane, I., M. Taniguchi and K. Sanjo (1985) Three dimensional groundwater flow system revealed by groundwater temperature, in H.E. Müller and K.R. Nippes (eds), *Problems of Regional Hydrology*, Beiträge zur Hydrologie, **2:** 791–802.

Keers, J.F. and P. Wescott (1977) *A computer based model for design rainfall in the United Kingdom*, Met. Office Scientific Paper, 36, HMSO, London, 14 pp.

Keller, H.M. (1988) European experiences in long-term forest hydrology research. In Swank, W.T. and Crossley, D.A. (eds) 'Forest Hydrology and Ecology at Coweeta', *Ecological Studies*, 66: Springer-Verlag, New York, pp. 407–59.

Keller, R. (1984) The world's fresh water: Yesterday, today, tomorrow, *Applied Geog. and Development*, **24:** 7–23.

Kelliher, F.M., Leuning, R., Raupach, M.R. and E.D. Schulze (1975) Maximum conductances for evaporation from global vegetation types, *Agricultural and Forest Meteorology*, **73:** 1–16.

Kerfoot, O. (1968) Mist precipitation on vegetation. *Forest Abstracts*, **29:** 8–20.

King, F.H. (1899) Principles and conditions of the movements of groundwater, *US Geological Survey 19th Annual Report, Pt. II*: 59–294.

Kirkby, M.J. (1985) Hillslope hydrology, in M.G. Anderson and T.P. Burt (eds), *Hydrological Forecasting*, Wiley, Chichester: 37–75.

Kirkby, M.J. and R.J. Chorley (1967) Throughflow, overland flow and erosion, *Bull. IASH*, **12:** 5–21.

Kittredge, J. (1948) *Forest influences*. McGraw-Hill, New York.

Klazura, G.E. and D.A. Imy (1993) A description of the initial set of analysis products available from the NEXRAD WSR-88D system, *Bull. Amer. Met. Soc.*, **74:** 1293–1311.

Klemes, V. (1988) A hydrological perspective, *J. Hydrol.*, **100:** 3–28.

Klute, A. (ed) (1986a) *Methods of soil analysis, I. Physical and mineralogical methods*, 2nd edn, Agronomy 9(1), American Society of Agronomy/Soil Science Society of America, Madison, Wis., 1188 pp.

Klute, A. (1986b) Water retention, laboratory methods, in A. Klute (ed), *Methods of soil analysis, I. Physical and mineralogical methods, 2e*, ASA/SSSA, Madison, Wis., pp. 635–62.

Kohout, F.A. and H. Klein (1967) Effect of pulse recharge on the zone of diffusion in the Biscayne aquifer, *IASH Symp. Haifa, Publ.*, **72:** 252–70.

Konovalov, V.G. (1990) Methods for the computations of onset date and daily hydrograph of the outburst from the Mertzbacher Lake, Tien-shan, in H. Lang and A. Musy (eds), *Hydrology in Mountainous Regions, I. Hydrological measurements, The water cycle*, IAHS Publ. No. **193**, 181–7.

Kontorshchikov, A.S. and K.A. Eremina (1963) Interception of precipitation by spring wheat during the growing season. *Soviet Hydrology*, **2:** 400–9.

Koorevar, P., G. Menelik and C. Dirksen (1983) *Elements of Soil Physics*, Developments in Soil Science 13, Elsevier, Amsterdam.

Koschmieder, H. (1934) Methods and results of definite rain measurements, *Mon. Weather Rev.*, **62:** 5–7.

Kosmas, C., N.G. Danalatos, J. Poesen and B. van Wesemael (1998) The effect of water vapour adsorption on soil moisture content under Mediterranean climatic conditions, *Agric. Water Management*, **36:** 157–68.

Kovar, K. and H.P. Nachtnebel (eds) (1996) *Application of Geographic Information Systems in Hydrology and Water Resources Management*, IAHS Publ. 235, IAHS, Wallingford, 712 pp.

Kramer, P.J. (1988) Changing concepts regarding plant water relations, *Plant, Cell and Environment*, **11:** 565–8.

Kramer, P.J. and J.S. Boyer (1995) *Water relations of plants and soils*, Academic Press, New York. 495 pp.

Krasovskaia, I. (1997) Entropy-based grouping of river flow regimes, *J. Hydrol.*, **202:** 173–91.

Kubota, J. and M. Sivapalan (1995) Towards a catchment-scale model of subsurface runoff generation based on synthesis of small-scale process-based modelling and field studies, in J.D. Kalma and M. Sivapalan (eds), *Scale Issues in Hydrological Modelling*, Wiley, Chichester, pp. 297–310.

Kudelsky, A.V. (1990) Principal characteristics of fold-mountain hydrogeology, in *Hydrology in Mountainous Regions, I. Hydrological Measurements; the Water Cycle*, Proceedings of two symposia held at Lausanne, Switzerland, August-September, 1990, IAHS Publ. No. **193:** 487–92.

Kuhn, M. (1996) The role of snow and ice in natural processes on local, regional and global scales. In V.M. Kotlyakov (ed) *Variations of snow and ice in the past and at present on a global and regional scale*, Technical Documents in Hydrology No. 1, Unesco, Paris, pp. 53–9.

Kuipers, H. and C. van Ouwerkerk (1963) Total pore-space estimations in freshly ploughed soil, *Neth. J. Agric. Sci.*, **11:** 45–53.

Kuittinen, R. (1986) Determination of areal snow-water equivalent values using satellite imagery and aircraft gamma-ray spectrometry, IAHS Publ. No. **160:** 181–9.

Kuittinen, R. (1989) Determination of snow water equivalents by using NOAA-satellite images, gamma ray spectrometry and field measurements, in A. Rango (ed), *Remote Sensing and Large-Scale Global Processes*, IAHS Publ. No. **186**, 151–9.

Kummerow, J. (1962) Quantitative measurements of fog in the Fray Jorge National Park. *Forest Abstracts*, **24:** 4576.

Kundzewicz, Z.W., L. Gottschalk and B. Webb (eds) (1987) *Hydrology 2000*, IAHS Publ. 171.

Kutiel, H., P. Maheras and S. Guika (1998) Singularity of atmospheric pressure in the eastern Mediterranean and its relevance to inter-annual variations of dry and wet spells, *Int. J. Climatology*, **18:** 317–27.

Kuusisto, E. (1986) The energy balance of a melting snow cover in different environments, IAHS Publ. No. **155:** 37–45.

Lamb, J.C. (1985) *Water quality and its control*, J. Wiley and Sons, New York, 384 pp.

Lamb, H.H. (1972) *Climate ... past, present and future I. Fundamentals and climate now*, Methuen and Co. Ltd, London, 613 pp.

Lamb, H.H. (1977) *Climate ... past, present and future II. Climatic history and the future*, Methuen and Co. Ltd, London, 835 pp.

Langbein, W.B. and S.A. Schumm (1958) Yield of sediment in relation to mean annual precipitation, *Trans. AGU*, **39:** 1076–84.

Lapidus, L. and N.R. Amundson (1952) Mathematics of adsorption in beds, *J. Physical Chemistry*, **56:** 984–95.

Laudon, H. and O. Slaymaker (1997) Hydrograph separation using stable isotopes, silica and electrical conductivity: an alpine example, *J. Hydrol.*, **201:** 82–101.

Lauren, J. G., R. J. Wagenet, J. Bouma and J. H. M. Wosten (1988) Variability of saturated hydraulic conductivity in a Glossaquic Hapludalf with macropores, *Soil Sci.*, **145(1):** 20–8.

Law, F. (1958) Measurement of rainfall, interception and evaporation losses in a plantation of Sitka spruce trees. *Proc. IASH Gen. Assoc. of Toronto*, **2:** 397–411.

Lawrence, A.R. and S.S.D. Foster (1987) *The pollution threat from agricultural pesticides and industrial solvents*, Hydrogeological Report, 87/2, British Geological Survey, Wallingford, 29 pp.

Lee, R. (1980) *Forest hydrology*, Columbia University Press, New York, 349 pp.

Leeks, G.J.L., C. Neal, H.P. Jarvie, H. Casey and D.V. Leach (1997) The LOIS river monitoring network: strategy and implementation, *The science of the total environment*, **194/195**, 101–9.

Legates, D.R. and C.J. Willmott (1990) Mean seasonal and spatial variability in gauge-corrected, global precipitation, *Int. J. Climatology*, **10:** 111–27.

Legrand, H. E. and V. T. Stringfield (1973) Karst hydrology - a review, *J. Hydrol.*, **20:** 97–120.

Leith, R.M. and S.I. Solomon (1985) Estimation of precipitation, evapotranspiration and runoff using GOES, *Advances in Evapotranspiration*, American Society Agricultural Engineers, pp. 366–76.

Leopold, L.B. and K.S. Davis (1970) *Water*, Time-Life International, 191 pp.

Lerner, D.N. (1997) Groundwater recharge, in O.M. Saether and P. de Caritat (eds), *Geochemical Processes, Weathering and Groundwater Recharge in Catchments*, Balkema, Rotterdam: 109–50.

Lerner, D.N. and M.H. Barrett (1996) Urban groundwater issues in the United Kingdom, *Hydrogeology J.*, **4:** 80–9.

Lester, J.E. (1990) Sewage and sewage sludge treatment, in *Pollution: causes, effects and control, 2e*, Royal Society of Chemistry, Cambridge, pp. 33–62.

Leyton, L., E.R.C. Reynolds and F.B. Thompson (1967) Rainfall interception in forest and moorland. In W.E.Sopper and H.W. Lull (eds), *Forest Hydrology*, Pergamon, Oxford, pp. 163–78.

Lhomme, J.P. (1997) Towards a rational definition of potential evaporation, *Hydrology and Earth System Sciences*, **1:** 257–64.

Linsley, R.K., M.A. Kohler and J.L. Paulhus (1982) *Applied hydrology*, McGraw-Hill, New York.

Linacre, E. (1992) *Climate data and resources*, Routledge, London, 366 pp.

Llorens, P. (1997) Rainfall interception by a Pinus sylvestris forest patch overgrown in a mediterranean mountainous abandoned area, II. Assessment of the applicability of Gash's analytical model. *J. Hydrol.*, **199:** 346–59.

Lloyd, C.R. (1990) The temporal distribution of Amazonian rainfall and its implications for forest interception, *QJRMS*, **116:** 1487–94.

Lloyd, C.R. and A. de O. Marques (1988) Spatial variability of throughfall and stemflow measurements in Amazonian rain forest. *Agricultural Forest Met.*, **42:** 63–73.

Lloyd, C.R., J.H.C. Gash, W.J. Shuttleworth and A. de O. Marques (1988) The measurement and modelling of rainfall interception by Amazonian rain forest. *Agricultural Forestry Met.*, **43**, 277–94.

Lloyd, J. G. (1968) River authorities and their work, *JIWE*, **22:** 343.

Loganathan, G. V., C. Y. Kuo and T. C. McCormick (1985) Frequency analysis of low flows, *Nordic Hydrol.*, **16:** 105–28.

Lohman, S. W. (1972) (Chairman) Definitions of selected groundwater terms—revisions and conceptual refinements. Report of the Committee on redefinition of ground-water terms, *USGS Wat. Sup. Pap.*, 1988, 21 pp.

Loye-Pilot, M.D. (1990) Isotopic and chemical separation for a forested headwater Mediterranean stream flood. A critical view, in J.C. Hooghart, C.W.S. Posthumus and P.M.M. Warmerdam (eds), *Hydrological Research Basins and the Environment*, TNO, The Hague, 189–98.

Lull, H.W. (1964) Ecological and silvicultural aspects. Sec. 6 in V.T. Chow (ed), *Handbook of Applied Hydrology*, McGraw-Hill, New York.

Lumadjeng, H.S. (1989) Modelling of hydrological processes, in A. Gustard, L.A. Roald, S. Demuth, H.S. Lumadjeng and R. Gross (eds), *Flow Regimes from Experimental and Network Data (FREND), I. Hydrological studies*, Institute of Hydrology, Wallingford, 254–70.

Lundberg, A., I.R. Calder and R. Harding (1998) Evaporation of intercepted snow: measurement and modelling. *J. Hydrol.*, **206:** 151–63.

Lvovich, M.I. (1973) The global water balance, *EOS*, **54:** 28–42.

McCuen, R.H. (1989) *Hydrologic analysis and design*, Prentice-Hall, New Jersey, 867 pp.

McCulloch, J.S.G. (1988) Hydrology—science or just technology?, *Research Report 1984–87*, Institute of Hydrology, Wallingford.

McGowan, M. and E. Tzimas (1985) Water relations of winter wheat: the root system, petiolar, resistance and development of a root abstraction equation, *Experimental Agriculture*, **21:** 377–88.

McGowan, M., P. Blanch, P.J. Gregory and D. Haycock (1984) Water relations of winter wheat, 5. The root system and osmotic adjustment in relation to crop evaporation, *J. Agric. Sci.*, **102:** 415–25.

McIlroy, I.C. (1971) An instrument for continuous recording of natural evaporation, *Agric. Met.*, **9:** 25–100.

McKeague, J. A., C. Wang and G. C. Topp (1982) Estimating saturated hydraulic conductivity from soil morphology, *Proc. SSSA*, **46:** 1239–44.

McMillan, W.D. and R.H. Burgy (1960) Interception loss from grass, *JGR*, **65:** 2389–94.

McNamara, J.P., D.L. Kane and L.D. Hinzman (1998) An analysis of streamflow hydrology in the Kuparuk River basin, arctic Alaska: A nested watershed approach, *J. Hydrol.*, **206:** 39–57.

McNaughton, K.G. (1976a) Evaporation and advection, I. Evaporation from extensive homogeneous surfaces, *QJRMS*, **102:** 181–91.

McNaughton, K.G. (1976b) Evaporation and advection, II. Evaporation downwind of a boundary separating region having different surface resistances and available energies, *QJRMS*, **102:** 193–202.

McNaughton, K.G. and T.A. Black (1973) A study of evapotranspiration from a Douglas fir forest using the energy balance approach, *WRR*, **9:** 1579–90.

McNaughton, K.G. and T.W. Spriggs (1989) An evaluation of the Priestley and Taylor equation and the complementary relationship using results from a mixed layer model of the convective boundary layer, *IAHS Publ.*, **177:** 89–104.

McNaughton, K.G., B.E. Clothier and J.P. Kerr (1979) Evaporation from land surfaces, in D.L. Murray and P. Ackroyd (eds), *Physical hydrology: New Zealand experience*, Hydrological Society, Wellington, N.Z., pp. 97–119.

Maddox, R.A. (1983) Large scale meteorological conditions associated with mid-latitude mesoscale convective complexes, *Mon. Weather Rev.*, **111:** 1475–93.

MAFF (1994) Floods in large basins, *Flood and Coastal Defence*, No. 5, Ministry of Agriculture, Fisheries and Food, London, p.4.

Marsh, P. and M.K. Woo (1984) Wetting front advance and freezing of meltwater within a snow cover, 1. Observations in the Canadian Arctic, *WRR*, **20:** 1853–64.

Marsh, P. and M.K. Woo (1985) Meltwater movement in natural heterogeneous snow covers, *WRR*, **21:** 1710–16.

Marsh, T.J. (1988) Personal communication.

Marsh, T.J. and P.A. Davies (1983) The decline and partial recovery of groundwater levels below London, *Proc. ICE*, **74:** 263–76.

Marsh, T.J. and I.G. Littlewood (1978) An estimate of annual runoff from England and Wales, 1728-1976, *Hydrol. Sci. Bull.*, **23:** 131–42.

Marsh, T.J. and M. Lees (1985) *Hydrological data UK, the 1984 drought*, Institute of Hydrology/British Geological Survey, Wallingford.

Marsh, T.J. and P.S. Turton (1996) The 1995 drought—a water resources perspective, *Weather*, **51:** 46–53.

Marsh, T.J., R.A. Monkhouse, N.W. Arnell, M.L. Lees and N.S. Reynard (1994) *The 1988–92 Drought*, Institute of Hydrology and British Geological Survey, Wallingford, 79 pp.

Marshall, J.S. and W.M. Palmer (1948) The distribution of raindrops with size, *J. Meteorol.*, **5:** 165–6.

Marshall, T.J., J.W. Holmes and C.W. Rose (1996) *Soil Physics, 3e*, Cambridge University Press.

Martinec, J. (1976) Snow and ice, in J.C. Rodda (ed), *Facets of hydrology*, vol. I, John Wiley and Sons, London, pp. 85–118.

Martinec, J. and A. Rango (1989) Effects of climate change on snowmelt runoff patterns, in A. Rango (ed), *Remote Sensing and Large-Scale Global Processes*, IAHS Publ. No. **186**, 31–8.

Martinec, J., H. Siegenthaler, H. Oescheger and E. Tongiorgi (1974) New insight into the runoff mechanism by environmental isotopes, *Proceedings of Symposium on Isotope Techniques in Groundwater Hydrology*, vol. 1, International Atomic Energy Agency, Vienna, pp. 129–43.

Martyn, D. (1992) *Climates of the world*, Developments in Atmospheric Science, **18**, Elsevier, Amsterdam, 435 pp.

Mason, B.J. (1971) *The physics of clouds, 2e*, Oxford University Press, London, 671 pp.

Mason, B.J. (1975) *Clouds, rain and rainmaking, 2e*, Cambridge University Press, Cambridge, 189 pp.

Massman, W.J. (1980) Water storage on forest foliage: a general model, *WRR*, **16:** 210–16.

Massman, W.J. (1983) The derivation and validation of a new model for the interception of rainfall by forests. *Agricultural Met.*, **28:** 261–86.

Matalas, N. C. (1982) *Reflections on hydrology*, 1st Chester C. Kisiel Memorial Lecture, University of Arizona, Department of Hydrology and Water Resources, 16 pp.

Mather, J.R. (ed) (1954) The measurement of potential evapotranspiration, *Publications in Climatology*, **7:** 225 pp.

Maxey, G.B. (1968) Hydrogeology of desert basins, *Groundwater*, **6:** 10–22.

Maxey, G.B. (1969) Subsurface water—groundwater, in *The Progress of Hydrology*, University of lllinois, Urbana, Ill., **2:** 787–815.

Maxey, G.B. and R.N. Farvolden (1965) Hydrogeologic factors in problems of contamination in arid lands, *Groundwater*, **3:** 29–32.

Mayer, R. and B. Ulrich (1974) Conclusions on the filtering action of forests from ecosystem analysis, *Oecologia Plantarum*, **9:** 157–68.

Mayes, J. (1996) Spatial and temporal fluctuations of monthly rainfall in the British Isles and variations in the mid-latitude western circulation, *Int. J. Climatology*, **16:** 585–96.

Meinzer, O.E. (1917) Geology and water resources of Big Smokey, Clayton, and Alkali Spring Valleys, Nevada, *USGS Wat. Sup. Pap.*, **423**.

Meinzer, O.E. (1923) Occurrence of groundwater in the United States, *USGS Wat. Sup. Pap.*, **489**, pp. 1–321.

Merriam, R.A. (1960) A note on the interception loss equation, *JGR*, **65:** 3850–1.

Metcalfe, S.E., J.D. Whyatt and R.G. Derwent (1995) A comparison of model and observed network estimates of sulphur deposition across Great Britain for 1990 and its likely source attribution. *Quarterly Journal Royal Met. Soc.*, **121:** 1387–1411.

Meteorological Office (1982) *Observer's handbook, 5e*, HMSO, London, 220 pp.

Meybeck, M. (1983) Atmospheric inputs and river transport of dissolved substances, *IAHS Publ.*, **141:** 173–92.

Meyboom, P. (1963) Patterns of groundwater flow in the prairie profile, in *Groundwater, Proc. Hydrology Symposium, No. 3*, National Research Council of Canada, Ottawa, pp. 5–20.

Meyboom, P. (1966) Unsteady groundwater flow near a willow ring in hummocky moraine, *J. Hydrol.*, **4:** 38–62.

Meyboom, P. (1967a) Groundwater studies in the Assiniboine River drainage basin, *Geological Survey Canadian Bull.*, **139**, 64 pp.

Meyboom, P. (1967b) Mass transfer studies to determine the groundwater regime of permanent lakes in hummocky moraine of western Canada, *J. Hydrol.*, **5:** 117–42.

Micklin, P.P. (1981) A preliminary systems analysis of impacts of proposed Soviet river diversions on Arctic sea ice, *EOS*, **62:** 489–93.

Miller, D.H. (1977) *Water at the surface of the earth*, International Geophysics Series, Vol. 21, Academic Press Inc., New York, 557 pp.

Miller, H.G. (1984) Deposition–plant–soil interactions, *Proc. Phil. Trans. Roy. Soc. London, B*, **305:** 339–52.

Miller, H.G. and J.D. Miller (1980) Collection and retention of atmospheric pollutants by vegetation, in D. Drablos and A. Tolian (eds), *Ecological impact of acid precipitation*, SNSF Conference, Oslo, pp. 33–40.

Miller, J.P. (1961) Solutes in small streams draining single rock types, Sangre de Cristo Range, New Mexico, *USGS Surv. Wat. Sup. Pap.*, 1535F, 23 pp.

Miller, R.J. and P.F. Low (1963) Threshold gradient for water flow in clay systems, *Proc. SSSA*, **27:** 605–9.

Mills, W.C. (1982) Stochastic modelling of rainfall for deriving distributions of watershed input, in V.P. Singh (ed), *Statistical analysis of rainfall and runoff*, Water Resources Publications, Littleton, Colo., pp. 103–18.

Miranda, A.C., P.G. Jarvis and J. Grace (1984) Transpiration and evaporation from heather moorland, *Boundary-Layer Met.*, **28:** 227–43.

Mitchell, J.F.B., S. Manabe, V. Meleshko and T. Tokioka (1990) Equilibrium climate change—and its implications for the future, in J.T. Houghton, B.A. Callender and S.K. Varney (eds) *Climate Change 1992*, Cambridge University Press, chapter 5.

Moncrieff, J.B. and 9 others (1997) A system to measure surface fluxes of momentum, sensible heat, water vapour and carbon dioxide, *J. Hydrol.*, **188:** 589–611.

Monteith, J.L. (1965) Evaporation and the environment, *Proc. Symposium on Experimental Biology*, **19:** 205–34.

Monteith, J.L. (1985) Evaporation from land surfaces: progress in analysis and prediction since 1948, in *Advances in Evapotranspiration*, American Society of Agricultural Engineers, pp. 4–12.

Monteith, J.L. (1995) Fifty years of potential evaporation, in T. Keane and E. Daly (eds), *The balance of water—present and future*, Proc. AGMET Conference, Dublin, Sept 7–9, 1994, pp. 29–45.

Monteith, J.L. and G. Szeicz (1961) The radiation balance of bare soil and vegetation, *QJRMS*, **87:** 159–70.

Monteith, J.L. and M.H. Unsworth (1990) *Principles of Environmental Physics, 2e*, Edward Arnold, London, 291 pp.

Moore, C.J. (1976) Eddy flux measurements above a pine forest, *QJRMS*, **102:** 913–18.

Moore, R.D. (1997) Storage-outflow modelling of streamflow recessions, with application to a shallow-soil forested catchment, *J. Hydrol.*, **198:** 260–70.

Moore, R.J. (1985) The probability-distributed and runoff production at point and basin scales, *Hydrol. Sci. J.*, **30:** 273–97.

Moore R.J. (1987) Towards more effective use of radar data for flood forecasting, In V.K. Collinge and C. Kirby (eds), *Weather radar and flood forecasting*, John Wiley and Sons, Chichester, pp. 223–38.

Moore, R.J. (1998) Personal communication, Institute of Hydrology.

Moran, M.S. and R.D. Jackson (1991) Assessing the spatial distribution of evapotranspiration using remotely sensed inputs, *J. Environmental Quality*, **20:** 725–37.

Morin, J. and H. S. Jarosch (1977) Runoff rainfall analysis for bare soils, *Soil Erosion Research Station Pamphlet* 164, Israel Ministry of Agriculture, Bet Dagan, 22 pp.

Morin, J., Y. Benyamini and A. Michaeli (1981) The effect of raindrop impact on the dynamics of soil surface crusting, *J. Hydrol.*, **52:** 321–35.

Morris, E.M. (1985) Snow and ice, in M.G. Anderson and T.P. Burt (eds), *Hydrological forecasting*, John Wiley and Sons, London, pp. 153–82.

Morris, S.E. and T.J. Marsh (1985) United Kingdom rainfall 1975–84: evidence of climatic instability?, *J. Meteorol.*, **10:** 324–32.

Morton, F.I. (1983) Operational estimates of areal evapotranspiration and their significance to the science and practice of hydrology, *J. Hydrol.*, **66:** 1–76.

Morton, F.I. (1985) The complementary relationship evapotranspiration model: how it works, in *Advances in Evapotranspiration*, American Society Agricultural Engineers, 377–84.

Morton, F.I. (1994) Evaporation research—A critical review and its lessons for the environmental sciences, *Critical Reviews in Environmental Science and Technology*, **24:** 237–80.

Moser, H., W. Rauert, G. Morgenschweis and H. Zojer (1986) Study of groundwater and soil moisture movement by applying nuclear, physical and chemical methods, in *Technical documents in hydrology*, UNESCO, Paris, 104 pp.

Mosley, M.P. (1979) Streamflow generation in a forested watershed, New Zealand, *WRR*, **15:** 795–806.

Mualem, Y. (1976) A new model for predicting the hydraulic conductivity of unsaturated porous media, *WRR*, **12(3):** 512–22.

Mulder, J.P.M. (1985) Simulating interception loss using standard meteorological data. In Hutchinson, B.A. and B.B. Hicks (eds) *The forest–atmosphere interaction.* D. Reidel, Dordrecht, pp. 177–196.

Munger, J.W. and S.J. Eisenreich (1983) Continental-scale variations in precipitation chemistry, *Environmental Science and Technology*, **17:** 32A–42A.

Murphy, C.E. and K.R. Knoerr (1975) The evaporation of intercepted rainfall from a forest stand: An analysis by simulation. *WRR*, **11:** 273–80.

Musgrave, G.W. (1938) Field research offers significant new findings. *Soil Conservation*, **3:** 210–14.

Naganna, C. and Y. Lingaraju (1990) A strategy for drought mitigation using groundwater: a case study in Kolar district, Karnataka State, India, in *Groundwater Monitoring and Management*, Proceedings of Dresden Symposium, March, 1987, IAHS Publ. No. **173:** 31–8.

Nagel, J.F. (1956) Fog precipitation on Table Mountain. *QJRMS*, **82:** 452–60.

Nakai, Y., Sakamoto, T., Terajima, T. Kitahara, H., and T. Saito (1993) Snow interception by forest canopies: weighing a conifer tree, meteorological observation and analysis by the Penman–Monteith formula, IAHS Publ. No. **233:** 227–36.

Nakamura, R. (1971) Runoff analysis by electrical conductance of water, *J. Hydrol.*, **14:** 197–212.

Narasimhan, T.N. (1998) Hydraulic characterization of aquifers, reservoir rocks and soils: A history of ideas, *WRR*, **34:** 33–46.

NERC (1975) *Flood Studies Report*, Natural Environment Research Council, 5 vols.

NERC (1991) Hydrogeology of hot dry rocks, *NERC News*, July, pp. 28–9.

Neuman, S.P. and P.A. Witherspoon (1970) Finite element method of analyzing steady seepage with a free surface, *WRR*, **6:** 889–97.

New Zealand Ministry of Works and Development (1985) SHE—model of the '80s, *Streamland*, No. 39, The Ministry of Works and Development, Wellington.

Nielsen, D.R., J.W. Biggar and K.T. Erh (1973) Spatial variability of field measured soil water properties, *Hilgardia*, **42: 21** 5–60.

Niemczynowicz, J. (1989) On the rainfall data for urban hydrological applications, in B. Sevruk (ed), *Precipitation measurement*, Swiss Federal Institute of Technology, Zürich, pp. 377–83.

Nieuwenhuis, G.J.A. (1981) Application of HCMM satellite and airplane reflection and heat maps in agrohydrology, *Advances in Space Res.*, **1:** 71–86.

NIH (1990) *Hydrology in ancient India*, National Institute of Hydrology, Roorkee, India, 103 pp.

Nilsson, J. and P. Grennfelt (1988) (eds) *Critical loads for sulphur and nitrogen*, Report 1988:15. Nordic Council of Ministers, Copenhagen.

Njitchoua, R., L. Dever, J.Ch. Fontes and E. Naah (1997) Geochemistry, origin and recharge mechanisms of groundwaters from the Garoua sandstone aquifer, northern Cameroon, *J. Hydrol.*, **190:** 123–40.

Nordin, C.F. (1985) The sediment loads of rivers, in J.C. Rodda (ed) *Facets of hydrology, 2*, J. Wiley and Sons, Chichester, pp. 183–204.

Nordstrum, D.K. and 18 others (1979) A comparison of computerized chemical models for equilibrium calculations in aqueous systems, in E.A. Jenne (ed) *Chemical modelling in aqueous systems*, Symposium Series 93, American Chemical Society, Washington, D.C., pp. 857–92.

Nortcliffe, S. (1988) Soil formation and characteristics of soil profiles, in A. Wild (ed), *Russell's soil conditions and plant growth*, Longman Scientific and Technical/Wiley, New York, pp. 168–212.

Nortcliffe, S. and J.B. Thornes (1984) Floodplain response of a small tropical stream, in T.P. Burt and D.E. Walling (eds), *Catchment experiments in fluvial geomorphology*, GeoBooks, Norwich, pp. 73–86.

NRC (1991) *Opportunities in the Hydrologic Sciences*, National Research Council, National Academy Press, Washington, D.C., pp. 90–104.

O'Brien, A.L. (1977) Hydrology of two small wetland basins in eastern Massachusetts, *Water Research Bull.*, **13:** 325–40.

O'Connell, P.E. (1991) A historical perspective, in D.S. Bowles and P.E. O'Connell (eds), *Recent Advances in the Modeling of Hydrologic Systems*, Kluwer, Dordrecht, 3–30.

O'Connell, P.E., R.J. Gurney, D.A. Jones, J.B. Miller, C.A. Nicholass and M.R. Senior (1978) *Rationalization of the Wessex Water Authority raingauge network*, Report 51, Institute of Hydrology, Wallingford, 179 pp.

O'Loughlin, E.M. (1981) Saturation regions in catchments and their relations to soil and topographic properties, *J. Hydrol.*, **53:** 229–46.

Ochsenkühn, K.M., J. Kontoyannakos and M. Ochsenkühn-Petropulu (1997) A new approach to a hydrochemical study of groundwater flow, *J. Hydrol.*, **194:** 64–75.

OECD (1986) *Water pollution by fertilizers and pesticides*, Organisation for Economic Cooperation and Development, Paris, 144 pp.

Ogallo, L.J. (1988) Relationships between seasonal rainfall in East Africa and the Southern Oscillation, *J. Climatology*, **8:** 31–43.

Oke, T.R. (1987) *Boundary layer climates, 2e*, Routledge, London, 435 pp.

Oki, T., K. Musiake, K. Masuda and H. Matsuyama (1993) Global runoff estimation by atmospheric water balance using ECMWF data set, in W.B. Wilkinson (ed), *Macroscale Modelling of the Hydrosphere*, IAHS Publ. No. **214:** 163–71, IAHS Press, Wallingford.

Oki, T., K. Musiake, H. Matsuyama and K. Masuda (1995) Global atmospheric water balance and runoff from large river basins, in J.D. Kalma and M. Sivapalan (eds), *Scale Issues in Hydrological Modelling*, Wiley, Chichester, pp. 411–34.

Oliver, H.R. (1983) The availability of evaporation data in space and time for use in water balance computations, *IAHS Publ.*, **148:** 21–31.

Olsen, H.W., E.N. Yearsley and K.R. Nelson (1989) Chemical causes of groundwater movement, in *Groundwater Contamination*, Proceedings of Baltimore Symposium, May, 1989, IAHS Publ. No. **185:** 65–72.

Onesti, L.J. (1985) Meteorological conditions that initiate slushflows in the central Brooks Range, Alaska, *Annals of Glaciology*, **6:** 23–5.

Ongley, E.D. (1996) *Control of water pollution from agriculture*. Irrigation and Drainage paper 55, Food and Agriculture Organization, Rome.

Oroud, I.M. (1998) The influence of heat conduction on evaporation from sunken pans in a hot, dry environment, *J. Hydrol.*, **210:** 1–10.

Packman, J.C. (1987) *Baluchistan daily rainfall*, Report to UK Overseas Development Administraion, Institute of Hydrology, Wallingford.

Pardé, M. (1955) *Fleuves et Rivières*, 3rd edn, Armand Colin, Paris.

Parsons, J. J. and W. A. Bowen (1966) Ancient ridged fields of the San Jorge River floodplain, Colombia, *Geographical Review*, **61:** 317–43.

Passerat de Silans, A., B.A. Monteny and J.P. Lhomme (1997) The correction of heat flux measurements to derive an accurate surface energy balance by the Bowen ratio method, *J. Hydrol.*, **189:** 453–65.

Passioura, J.B. (1988) Response to Dr P.J. Kramer's article 'Changing concepts regarding plant water relations', *Plant, Cell and the Environment*, **11:** 569–571.

Patric, J.H. (1966) Rainfall interception by mature coniferous forests of southeast Alaska. *J. Soil and Water Cons.*, **21:** 229–31.

Pazwash, H. and G. Mavrigian (1981) Millennial celebration of Karaji's hydrology, *Proc. ASCE, J. Hydraulics Div.*, 107, No. **HY3:** 303–9.

Pearce, A.J. and L.K. Rowe (1981) Rainfall interception in a multi-storied, evergreen mixed forest: estimates using Gash's analytical model. *J. Hydrol.*, **49:** 341–53.

Pearce, A.J., L.K. Rowe and J.B. Stewart (1980) Nighttime, wet canopy evaporation rates and the water balance of an evergreen mixed forest. *WRR*, **16:** 955–9.

Pearce, A.J., L.K. Rowe and C.L. O'Loughlin (1982) Hydrologic regime of undisturbed mixed evergreen forests, South Nelson, New Zealand. *J. Hydrol. (N.Z.)*, **21:** 98–116.

Pearce, A.J., M.K. Stewart and M.G. Sklash (1986) Storm runoff generation in humid headwater catchments, I. Where does the water come from? *WRR*, **22:** 1263–72.

Pearl, R.T., R.H. Mathews, L.P. Smith, H.L. Penman, E.R. Hoare and E.E. Skillman (1954) *The calculation of irrigation need*, Technical Bull. 4, Ministry of Agriculture and Fisheries, London.

Pecker, J.C. and S.K. Runcorn (eds) (1990) The Earth's climate and variability of the sun over recent millennia: geophysical, astronomical and archaeological aspects, *Proc. Phil. Trans. Roy. Soc., Series A*, **330:** 399–404, 692 pp.

Peixoto, J.P and A.H. Oort (1992) *Physics of clouds*, American Institute of Physics, New York. 520 pp.

Penman, H.L. (1948) Natural evaporation from open water, bare soil and grass, *Proc. Phil. Trans. Roy. Soc., Series A*, **193:** 120–45.

Penman, H.L. (1949) The dependence of transpiration on weather and soil conditions, *J. Soil Science*, **1:** 74–89.

Penman, H.L. (1952) Experiments on the irrigation of sugar beet, *J. Agric. Sci.*, **42:** 286–292.

Penman, H.L. (1954) Evaporation over parts of Europe, *IAHS Publ.*, **3:** 168–76.

Penman, H.L. (1956) Evaporation: an introductory survey, *Netherlands J. Agricultural Science*, **1:** 9–29.

Penman, H.L. (1963) *Vegetation and Hydrology*, Commonwealth Agricultural Bureau, Farnham Royal, 124 pp.

Penman, H.L. (1967) In discussion of J. Delfs, Interception and stemflow in stands of Norway spruce and beech in West Germany, in W.E. Sopper and H.W. Lull (eds), *Forest Hydrology*, Pergamon, Oxford, pp. 179–85.

Penman, H.L. and R.K. Schofield (1941) Drainage and evaporation from fallow soil at Rothamsted, *J. Agric. Sci.*, **31:** 74–109.

Penman, H.L. and R.K. Schofield (1951) Some physical aspects of assimilation and transpiration, *Proc. Symposium Society on Experimental Biology*, 5.

Periago, M.C., Lana, X., Fernandez Mills, G. and C. Serra (1998) Optimization of the pluviometric network of Catalonia (North-East Spain) for climatological studies. *International Journal of Climatology*, **18:** 183–98.

Perks, A., T. Winkler and B. Stewart (1996) *The adequacy of hydrological networks: a global assessment*, Technical reports in Hydrology and Water Resources, 52, World Meteorological Organisation, Geneva, 56 pp.

Persson, M. and R. Berndtsson (1998) Estimating transport parameters in an undisturbed soil column using time domain reflectometry and transfer function theory, *J. Hydrol.*, **205:** 232–47.

Peters, N.E. (1984) Evaluation of environmental factors affecting yields of major dissolved ions in streams in the United States, *USGS Wat. Sup. Pap.*, 2228, 39 pp.

Petts, G.E. and C. Amoros (1996) *The Fluvial Hydrosystem*, Chapman and Hall, London.

Petts, G.E. and C. Bradley (1997) Hydrological and ecological interactions within river corridors, in R.L. Wilby (ed) *Contemporary Hydrology*, Wiley, Chichester, pp. 241–71.

Philip, J. R. (1957) The theory of infiltration, 4. Sorptivity and algebraic infiltration equations, *Soil Sci.*, **84:** 257–64.

Philip, J. R. (1964) The gain, transfer and loss of soil water, in *Water resources use and management*, Melbourne University Press, pp. 257–75.

Pietrucien, C. (1985) Regional differentiation of dynamic and hydrochemical conditions of groundwater of the southern and eastern Baltic coast, in H.E. Müller and K.R. Nippes (eds), *Problems of Regional Hydrology*, Beiträge zur Hydrologie, **2:** 809–26.

Pilling, C., R.L. Wilby and J.A.A. Jones (1998) Downscaling of catchment hydrometeorology from GCM output using airflow indices in upland Wales, in H. Wheater and C. Kirby (eds) *Hydrology in a Changing Environment*, Wiley, Chichester, Vol. **1:** 191–208.

Pillsbury, A.F., R.E. Pelishek, J.F. Osborn and T.E. Szuszkiewicz (1962) Effects of vegetation manipulation on the disposition of precipitation on chaparral-covered watersheds. *JGR*, **67:** 695–702.

Pinder, G. F. and J. F. Jones (1969) Determination of the groundwater component of peak discharge from the chemistry of total runoff, *WRR*, **5:** 438–45.

Piper, A.M. (1944) A graphic procedure in the geochemical interpretation of water analyses, *Trans. AGU*, **25:** 914–23.

Pirt, J. (1983) *Low flow estimation in ungauged catchments*, Occasional Paper 6, Department of Geography, University of Technology, Loughborough.

Pirt, J. and J.R. Douglas (1982) A study of low flows using data from the Severn and Trent catchments, *JIWES*, **36:** 299–308.

Pirt, J. and C.M. Simpson (1982) A study of low flows using data from the Severn and Trent catchments—Part II: Flow frequency procedures, *JIWES*, **36:** 459–69.

Plant, J.A. and R. Raiswell (1983) Principles of environmental geochemistry, in I. Thornton (ed), *Applied environmental geochemistry*, Academic Press, London, pp. 1–39.

Poesen, J.W.A. (1986) Surface sealing as influenced by slope angle and position of simulated stones in the top layer of loose sediments, *Earth Surf. Proc. and Landforms*, **11:** 1–10.

Pointet, T. (ed) (1997) *Hard Rock Hydrosystems*, IAHS Publ., **224:** 168 pp.

Poiseuille, J.L.M. (1846) Recherches expérimentales sur le mouvement des liquides dans les tubes de très petit diamètre, *Roy. Acad. Sci. Inst. France Math. Phys. Sci. Mem.*, **9:** 433–543.

Poland, J.F. (1984) Guidebook to studies of land subsidence due to groundwater withdrawal, *Studies and Reports in Hydrology*, No. 40, UNESCO, Paris, 305 pp.

Preston-Whyte, R.A. and P.D. Tyson (1988) *The atmosphere and weather of Southern Africa*, Oxford University Press, Cape Town, 374 pp.

Price, A.G. and B.O. Bauer (1984) Small-scale heterogeneity and soil moisture variability in the unsaturated zone, *J. Hydrol.*, **70:** 277–93.

Price, D.J., I.R. Calder and R.C. Johnson (1995) *Modelling the effect of upland afforestation on water resources*, Report to the Scottish Office Environment Department, Institute of Hydrology, Wallingford, 55 pp.

Price, M. (1985) *Introducing groundwater*, George Allen and Unwin, London, 195 pp.

Price, M. (1987) Fluid flow of the chalk of England, in J.C. Goff and B.P.J. Williams (eds), *Fluid flow in sedimentary basins and aquifers*, Geology Society Special Publ. 34, pp. 141–56.

Price, M. (1996) *Introducing groundwater, 2e*, Stanley Thornes, Cheltenham, 278 pp.

Price, M., M.J. Bird and S.S.D. Foster (1976) Chalk pore-size measurements and their significance, *Water Services*, October, pp. 596–600.

Priestley, C.H.B. and R.J. Taylor (1972) On the assessment of surface heat flux and evaporation using large scale parameters, *Mon. Wea. Rev.*, **100:** 81–92.

Pruppacher, H.R. and J.D. Klett (1997) *Microphysics of clouds and precipitation*, Kluwer Academic Publishers, Dordrecht and London, 954 pp.

Querner, E.P. (1997) Description and application of the combined surface and groundwater model MOGROW, *J. Hydrol.*, **192:** 158–188.

Quisenberry, V. L. and R. E. Phillips (1976) Percolation of surface-applied water in the field, *Proc. SSSA*, **40:** 384–9.

Ragab, R. and J.D. Cooper (1993a) Variability of unsaturated zone water transport parameters: Implications for hydrological modelling, 1. In situ measurements, *J. Hydrol.*, **148:** 109–32.

Ragab, R. and J.D. Cooper (1993b) Variability of unsaturated zone water transport parameters: Implications for modelling, 2. Predicted versus in situ measurements and evaluation of methods, *J. Hydrol.*, **148:** 133–48.

Ragab, R., J. Finch and R. Harding (1997) Estimation of groundwater recharge to chalk and sandstone aquifers using simple soil models, *J. Hydrol.*, **190:** 19–41.

Ragan, R.M. (1968) An experimental investigation of partial area contributions, *Proceedings of Symposium of Berne*, IASH Publ., **76**, pp. 241–9.

Rakhmanov, V.V. (1966) *Role of forests in water conservation*, Goslesbumizdat, Moscow, 1962; translated and edited by A. Gourevitch and L. M. Hughes, Israel Program for Scientific Translations Ltd, Jerusalem.

Ramser, C.E. (1927) Runoff from small agricultural areas, *J. Agricultural Res.*, **34:** 797–823.

Rango, A. (1985) An international perspective on large-scale snow studies, *Hydrol. Sci. J.*, **30:** 225–38.

Rango, A. (1994) *Applications of remote sensing by satellite, radar and other methods to hydrology*, Operational Hydrology report No. 39, World Meteorological Organization, Geneva.

Rango, A. and V. van Katwijk (1990) Development and testing of a snowmelt-runoff forecasting technique, *Water Resources Bull.*, **26(1),** 135–44.

Rango, A., V. van Katwijk and J. Martinec (1990) Snowmelt runoff forecasts in Colorado with remote sensing, in H. Lang and A. Musy (eds), *Hydrology in Mountainous Regions, I. Hydrological measurements, The water cycle*, IAHS Publ. No. 193, 627–34.

Rao, N.H. (1998) Grouping water storage properties of Indian soils for soil water balance model applications, *Agric. Water Management*, **36:** 99–109.

Raschke, K. (1976) How stomata resolve the dilemma of opposing priorities, *Philosophical Transactions of the Royal of Society London*, Series B, **273:** 551–60.

Rawitz, E., E.T. Engman and G.D. Cline (1970) Use of the mass balance method for examining the role of soils in controlling watershed performance, *WRR*, **6:** 1115–23.

Rawls, W.J., D.L. Brakensiek and K.E. Saxton (1982) Estimation of soil water properties, *Trans. ASAE*, **25**(131)**:** 6–20.

Rawls, W.J., D.L. Brakensiek and N. Miller (1983) Green-Ampt infiltration parameters from soils data, *J. Hydraulic Engineering*, **109:** 62–70.

Reed, D.W. (1995) Rainfall assessment of drought severity and centennial events, Chap. 16, *Proceedings of CIWEM Centenary Conference*, Chartered Institution of Water and Environmental Management, London, 17 pp.

Refsgaard, J.-C. and B. Storm (1995) MIKE SHE, in V.P. Singh (ed), *Computer Models of Watershed Hydrology*, Water Resource Publications, Colorado, 809–46.

Reid, J.M., D.A. McLeod and M.S. Cresser (1981) Factors affecting the chemistry of precipitation and river water in an upland catchment, *J. Hydrol.*, **50:** 129–45.

Renard, K.G. (1979) Transmission losses, Paper prepared for SCS Unit Hydrologist Meeting, Brainerd, Minn. (cyclostyled).

Reynolds, B., C. Neal, M. Hornung and P.A. Stevens (1986) Baseflow buffering of streamwater acidity in five mid-Wales catchments, *J. Hydrol.*, **87:** 167–85.

Reynolds, E.R.C. and C.S. Henderson (1967) Rainfall interception by beech, larch and Norway Spruce. *Forestry*, **40:** 165–85.

Rhode, H. (1989) Acidification in a global perspective, *Ambio*, **18:** 155–9.

Richards, K. (1982) *Rivers: form and process in alluvial channels*, Methuen, London, 358 pp.

Richards, L.A. (1931) Capillary conduction of liquids through porous mediums, *Physics*, **1:** 318–33.

Richards, L.A. (1950) Laws of soil moisture, *Trans. AGU*, **31:** 750–6.

Rijtema, P.E. (1968) *On the relation between transpiration, soil physical properties and crop production as a basis for water supply plans*, Technical Bull. 58, Institute of Land and Water Management Research.

Ritchie, J.T. (1972) Model for predicting evaporation from a row crop with incomplete cover, *WRR*, **8:** 1204–13.

Ritchie, J.T. (1973) Influence of soil water status and meteorological conditions on evaporation from a canopy, *Agron. J.*, **65:** 893–7.

Roberts, G. (1987) Nitrogen inputs and outputs in a small agricultural catchment in the eastern part of the UK, *Soil Use and Management*, **3:** 148–54.

Roberts, G. and T.J. Marsh (1987) The effects of agricultural practices on the nitrate concentrations in the surface water domestic supply sources of western Europe, *IAHS Publ.*, **164:** 365–80.

Roberts, J.M. (1983) Forest transpiration: a conservative process? *J. Hydrol.*, **66:** 133–41.

Roberts, J.M. (1999) Plants and water in forests and woodlands, in A. Baird and R. Wilby (eds), *Ecohydrology: Plants and water in terrestrial and aquatic ecosystems*, Routledge, London, pp. 181–236.

Roberts, J.M., C.F. Pymar, J.S. Wallace and R.M. Pitman (1980) Seasonal changes in leaf area, stomatal conductance and transpiration from bracken below a forest canopy, *J. Applied Ecology*, **17:** 409–22.

Robinson, A.C. and J.C. Rodda (1969) Rain, wind and the aerodynamic characteristics of raingauges, *Met. Mag.*, **98:** 113–20.

Robinson, D.A., K.F. Dewey and R.H. Heim (1993) Global snow cover monitoring: an update, *Bull. Amer. Met. Soc.*, **74:** 1689–96.

Robinson, J.S. and M. Sivapalan (1995) Catchment-scale runoff generation model by aggregation and similarity analyses, in J.D. Kalma and M. Sivapalan (eds), *Scale Issues in Hydrological Modelling*, Wiley, Chichester, pp. 311–30.

Robinson, M. (1990) *Impact of improved land drainage on river flows*, IH Report No. 113, Institute of Hydrology, Wallingford.

Robinson, M. (1999) The consistency of long-term climate datasets: Two UK examples of the need for caution, *Weather*, **54:** 1–9.

Robinson, M. and A.C. Armstrong (1988) The extent of agricultural field drainage in England and Wales, 1971–80, *Trans. IBG*, **13:** 19–28.

Robinson, M. and K J. Beven (1983) The effect of mole drainage on the hydrological response of a swelling clay soil, *J. Hydrol.*, **64:** 205–23.

Robinson, M. and K. Blyth (1982) The effect of forestry drainage operations on upland sediment yields: a case study, *Earth Surf. Proc. and Landforms*, **7:** 85–90.

Robinson, M. and D.W. Rycroft (1999) The impact of drainage on streamflow. Chapter 23 in Skaggs, W. and J. van Schilfgaarde (eds), *Agricultural Drainage*. Agronomy Monograph 38, American Society of Agronomy/Crop Science Society of America/ Soil Science Society of America, Madison, Wisconsin, USA, pp. 753–786.

Robinson, M., E.L. Ryder and R.C. Ward (1985) Influence on streamflow of field drainage in a small agricultural catchment, *Agric. Water Management*, **10:** 145–58.

Robson, A.J. and C. Neal (1997) A summary of regional water quality for eastern UK rivers, *The science of the total environment*, 194/195, 15–37.

Robson, A.J., T.K. Jones, D.W. Reed and S.C. Bayliss (1998) A study of national trend and variation in UK floods, *Int. J. Climatology*, **18:** 165–82.

Rockström, J. and C. Valentin (1997) Hillslope dynamics of on-farm generation of surface water flows: The case of rain-fed cultivation of pearl millet on sandy soil in the Sahel, *Agric. Water Managt.*, **33:** 183–210.

Rodda, J.C. (1968) The rainfall measurement problem, *IASH Publ.*, **78:** 215–31.

Rodda, J.C., R.A. Downing and F.M. Law (1976) *Systematic Hydrology*, Newnes–Butterworth, London, 399 pp.

Rodda, J.C., A.V. Sheckley and P. Tan (1978) Water resources and climatic change, *JIWES*, **31:** 76–83.

Rodhe, A. (1981) Spring flood, melt water or ground water?, *Nordic Hydrol.*, **12:** 21–30.

Romkens, M.J., S.N. Prasad and F.D. Whisler (1990) Surface sealing and infiltration, in M.G. Anderson and T.P. Burt (eds), *Process Studies in Hillslope Hydrology*, Wiley, Chichester, pp. 127–72.

Rothlisberger, H. and H. Lang (1987) Glacial hydrology, in *Glacio-fluvial sediment transfer*, A.M. Gurnell and M.J. Clark (eds), John Wiley and Sons, Chichester.

Routledge, E.J., D. Sheahan, C. Desbrow, G. Brighty, M. Waldock and J.P. Sumpter (1998) Identification of estrogenic chemicals in sewage treatment effluent, 2. In vivo responses in trout and roach, *Environmental Science and Technology*, **32:** 1559–65.

Rowntree, P.R., J.M. Murphy and J.F.B. Mitchell (1993) Climate change and future rainfall predictions, *JIWE(M)*, **7:** 464–70.

Roxburgh, I.S. (1985) Thermal infrared detection of submarine springs associated with the Plymouth Limestone, *Hydrol. Sci. J.*, **30:** 185–96.

Royer, J. M. and G. Vachaud (1975) Field determination of hysteresis in soil water characteristics, *Proc. SSSA*, **39:** 221–3.

Rubin, J. (1966) Theory of rainfall uptake by soils initially drier than their field capacity and its applications, *WRR*, **2:** 739–94.

Rudloff, W. (1981) *World climates with tables of climatic data and practical suggestions*, Wissenschaftliche Verlagsgesellschaft mbH, Stuttgart, 632 pp.

Rutter, A.J. (1963) Studies in the water relations of Pinus sylvestris in plantation conditions, *J. Ecology*, **51:** 191–203.

Rutter, A.J. (1967) An analysis of evaporation from a stand of Scots pine. In W. E. Sopper and H. W. Lull (eds), *Forest Hydrology*, Pergamon, Oxford, pp. 403–17.

Rutter, A.J. (1968) Water consumption by forests. Chap. 2 in Kozlowski, T.T. (ed) *Water deficits and plant growth, II. Plant water consumption and response*, Academic Press, New York, pp. 23–84.

Rutter, A.J. and A.J. Morton (1977) A predictive model of rainfall interception in forests, III. Sensitivity of the model to stand parameters and meteorological variables, *J. Applied Ecology*, **14:** 567–88.

Rutter, A.J., K.A. Kershaw, P.C. Robins and A.J. Morton (1971) A predictive model of rainfall interception in forests, I. Derivation of the model from observations in a plantation of Corsican pine. *Agricultural Met.*, **9:** 367–84.

Rutter, A.J., A.J. Morton and P.C. Robins (1975) A predictive model of rainfall interception in forests, II. Generalization of the model and comparison with observations in some coniferous and hardwood stands. *J. Applied Ecology*, **12:** 367–80.

Salati, E. and P.B. Vose (1984) Amazon basin: a system in equilibrium, *Science*, **225:** 129–38.

Salby, M.L. (1992) The atmosphere, in K.E. Trenberth (ed), *Climate system modelling*, Cambridge University Press, pp. 53–115.

Sanderson, M. (1950) Some Canadian developments in agricultural climatology, *Weather*, **5:** 381–8.

Satterlund, D.R. and H.F. Haupt (1970) The disposition of snow caught by conifer crowns, *WRR*, **6:** 649–52.

Saulnier, G.-M., K. Beven and C. Obled (1997) Including spatially variable effective soil depths in TOPMODEL, *J. Hydrol.*, **202:** 158–72.

Saxena, R.K. (1984) Surface and groundwater mixing and identification of local recharge–discharge zones from seasonal fluctuations of Oxygen-18 in groundwater in fissured rock, in *Hydrochemical Balances of Freshwater Systems*, Proceedings Uppsala Symposium, IAHS Publ. No. 150: 419–28.

Schmugge, T.J., T.J. Jackson and H.L. McKim (1980) Survey of methods for soil moisture determination, *WRR*, **16:** 961–79.

Schnoor, J.L. (1996) *Environmental modelling: Fate and transport of pollutants in water, air and soil*, J. Wiley and Sons, Chichester, 682 pp.

Schulze, E.D., E. Streudle, T. Gollan and U. Schurr (1988) Response to Dr P.J. Kramer's article 'Changing concepts regarding plant water relations', *Plant, Cell and the Environment*, **11:** 573–6.

Scoging, H.M. and J.B. Thornes (1979) Infiltration characteristics in a semiarid environment, in *The hydrology of areas of low precipitation*, Proceedings of Canberra Symposium, December 1979, IAHS Publ. **128**, pp. 159–68.

Searcy, J.K. (1959) Flow-duration curves, *USGS Wat. Sup. Pap.*, 1542–A.

Seguin, B., J.C. Mandeville, Y. Kerr and J.P. Guinot (1985) A proposed methodology for daily ET mapping using thermal IR satellite imagery, in *Advances in Evapotranspiration*, Amer. Soc. Agric. Engineers, pp. 385–92.

Seip, H.M. and A. Tollan (1985) Acid deposition, in J.C. Rodda (ed), *Facets in hydrology, 2*, J. Wiley and Sons, Chichester, pp. 69–98.

Sellers, W.D. (1965) *Physical climatology*, University of Chicago Press.

Sevruk, B. (1982) *Methods of correction for systematic error in point precipitation measurement for operational use*, Operational Hydrology Report 21, World Meteorological Organization, Geneva, 91 pp.

Sevruk, B. and H. Geiger (1981) *Selection of distribution types for extremes of precipitation*, Operational Hydrology Report 15, World Meteorological Organization, Geneva, 64 pp.

Sevruk, B. and S. Klemm (1989) *Catalogue of national standard precipitation gauges, instruments and observing methods*, Report 39, World Meteorological Organization, Geneva, 50 pp.

Sevruk, B., I.A. Hertig and R. Spiess (1989) Wind field deformation above precipitation gauge orifices, *IAHS Publ.*, **179:** 65–70.

Sharkey, T.D. and T. Ogawa (1987) Stomatal responses to light, in E. Zeiger, G.D. Farquhar and I.R. Cowan (eds), *Stomatal function*, Stanford University Press, California, 503 pp.

Shaw, E.M. (1994) *Hydrology in Practice, 3e*, Chapman & Hall, London, 569 pp.

Shepherd, W. (1972) Some evidence of stomatal restriction of evaporation from well-watered plant canopies, *WRR*, **8:** 1092–5.

Shepherd, G.W., Cluckie, I.D., Collier, C.G., Yu, S. and P.K. James (1989) The identification of rainfall type from weather radar data. *Met. Mag.* **117:** 180–6.

Shiklomanov, I.A. (1993) World fresh water resources, in P.H. Gleick (ed), *Water in Crisis: A Guide to the World's Freshwater Resources*, Oxford University Press, New York, pp. 13–24.

Shiklomanov, I.A. (1997) *Assessment of Water Resources and Water Availability in the World*, WMO, 88 pp.

Shuttleworth, W.J. (1977) The exchange of wind-driven fog and mist between vegetation and the atmosphere. *Boundary Layer Met.*, **12:** 463–89.

Shuttleworth, W.J. (1978) A simplified one-dimensional theoretical description of the vegetation–atmosphere interaction, *Boundary Layer Met.*, **14:** 3–27.

Shuttleworth, W.J. (1988a) Evaporation from Amazonian rainforest, *Proc. Phil. Trans. Roy. Soc. London, B*, **233:** 321–46.

Shuttleworth, W.J. (1988b) Macrohydrology—the new challenge for process hydrology, *J. Hydrol.*, **100:** 31–56.

Shuttleworth, W.J. (1989) Micrometeorology of temperate and tropical forest. *Proc. Phil. Trans. Roy. Soc., London, B*, **324:** 299–334.

Shuttleworth, W.J. (1993) Evaporation, in D.R. Maidment (ed), *Handbook of hydrology*, McGraw-Hill, New York, pp. 4.1–4.53.

Shuttleworth, W.J. and I.R. Calder (1979) Has the Priestley–Taylor equation any relevance to forest evaporation? *J. Applied Met.*, **18:** 639–46.

Shuttleworth, W.J. and J.S. Wallace (1985) Evaporation from sparse crops—an energy combination approach, *QJRMS*, **111:** 839–55.

Shuttleworth, W.J., J.H.C. Gash, C.R. Lloyd, C.J. Moore and J.S. Wallace (1988) An integrated micrometeorological system for evaporation measurement, *Agricultural Forest Met.*, **143**, 295–317.

Silar, J. (1990) Time and its meaning in groundwater studies, in *Hydrology of Mountainous Areas*, Proceedings of the Strbske Pleso Workshop, Czechoslovakia, June 1988, IAHS Publ. No. **190:** 281–9.

Simons, M. (1969) Long-term trends in water use, in R.J. Chorley (ed), *Water, Earth and Man*, Methuen, London, 535–44.

Singh, B. and G. Szeicz (1979) The effect of intercepted rainfall on the water balance of a hardwood forest. *WRR*, **15:** 131–8.

Singh, P., G. Spitzbart, H. Hübl and H.W. Weinmeister (1997) Hydrological response of snowpack under rain-on-snow events: a field study, *J. Hydrol.*, **202:** 1–20.

Singh, V.P. (1989) *Hydrologic systems, vol. 2: Watershed modelling*. Prentice-Hall, New Jersey, 320 pp.

Siple, G. E. (1965) Saltwater encroachment in coastal South Carolina, *Proceedings of Conference on Hydrologic Activities in the South Carolina Region*, Clemson University, pp. 18–33.

Sivapalan, M. and J.D. Kalma (1995) Scale problems in hydrology: Contributions of the Robertson workshop, in J.D. Kalma and M. Sivapalan (eds), *Scale Issues in Hydrological Modelling*, Wiley, Chichester, pp. 1–8.

Sivapalan, M., K. Beven and E.F. Wood (1987) On hydrological similarity, II. A scaled model of storm runoff production, *WRR*, **23:** 2266–78.

Skartveit, A. (1982) Wet scavenging of sea salts and acid compounds in a rainy coastal area, *Atmos. Environ.*, **16:** 2715–24.

Skeffington, R.A. (1987) Do all forests act as sinks for air pollutants? In *Acidification and water pathways*, volume 2, Norwegian National Committee for Hydrology/UNESCO/WMO, pp. 85–94.

Sklash, M. G. and R. N. Farvolden (1979) The role of groundwater in storm runoff, *J. Hydrol.*, **43:** 45–65.

Sklash, M. G., M. K. Stewart and A. J. Pearce (1986) Storm runoff generation in humid headwater catchments, II. A case study of hillslope and low order stream response, *WRR*, **22:** 1273–82.

Skopp, J. (1986) Analysis of time-dependent chemical processes in soils, *J. Environmental Quality*, **15:** 205–13.

Slatyer, R.O. and I.C. McIlroy (1961) *Practical Microclimatology*, CSIRO and UNESCO, Melbourne.

Slichter, C.S. (1902) The motions of underground waters, *USGS Wat. Sup. Pap.*, 67.

Smedema, L.K. and D.W. Rycroft (1983) *Land drainage*, Batsford Academic and Educational Ltd, London, 376 pp.

Smettem, K.R.J. (1986) Solute movements in soils, in S.T. Trudgill (ed), *Solute processes*, J. Wiley and Sons, Chichester, pp. 141–65.

Smettem, K.R.J., Trudgill, S.T. and A.M. Pickles (1983) Nitrate loss in drainage waters in relation to bypassing flow and discharge on an arable site, *Journal Soil Science*, **34:** 499–509.

Smith, D.B., P.L. Wearn, H.J. Richards and P.C. Rowe (1970) Water movement in the unsaturated zone of high and low permeability strata by measuring natural tritium, *Isotope Hydrology 1970*, International Atomic Energy Authority, Vienna, pp. 73–81.

Smith, D.B., R.A. Downing, R.A. Monkhouse, R.L. Otlet and F.J. Pearson (1976) The age of groundwater in the Chalk of the London Basin, *WRR*, **12:** 392–404.

Smith, D.M. and S.J. Allen (1996) Measurement of sap flow in plant stems, *J. Experimental Botany*, **305:** 1833–44.

Smith, E.A. (1998) (ed) The second precipitation intercomparison project, Special Issue, *J. Atmospheric Sciences*, **55:** 1481–1729.

Smith, K. and R.C. Ward (1998) *Floods: Physical processes and human impacts*, Wiley, Chichester, 382 pp.

Smith, R.A. (1852) On the air and rain of Manchester, *Mem. Proceedings of Manchester Literary and Philosophical Society*, Series 2, **10**, 207–17.

Smith, R.A. (1872) *Air and rain: the beginnings of chemical climatology*, Longmans, London, 600 pp.

Smith, R.C.G., H.D. Barrs and J.L. Steiner (1985) Relationship between wheat yield and foliage temperature: theory and its application to infrared measurements, *Agricultural Forest Met.*, **36:** 129–43.

Soer, G.J.R. (1980) Estimation of regional evapotranspiration and soil moisture conditions using remotely sensed crop surface temperatures, *Remote Sensing of Environ.*, **9:** 27–45.

Soulsby, C., R.C. Helliwell, R.C. Ferrier, A. Jenkins and R. Harriman (1997) Seasonal snowpack influence on the hydrology of a sub-arctic catchment in Scotland, *J. Hydrol.*, **192:** 17–32.

Speidel, D.H. and A.F. Agnew (1988) The world water budget, in D.H. Speidel, L.C. Ruedisili and A.F. Agnew (eds), *Perspectives on Water*, Oxford University Press, New York, pp. 27–36.

Sposito, G. (1981) *The thermodynamics of soil solutions*, Oxford University Press, Oxford, 223 pp.

Starr, V.P. and J. Peixoto (1958) On the global balance of water vapor and the hydrology of deserts, *Tellus*, **10:** 189–94.

Steinich, B. and L.E. Marín (1997) Determination of flow characteristics in the aquifer of the Northwestern peninsula of Yucatan, Mexico, *J. Hydrol.*, **191:** 315–31.

Stevenson, K.R. and R.H. Shaw (1971) Effects of leaf orientation on leaf resistance to water vapour diffusion in soybean leaves, *Agron. J.*, **63:** 327–9.

Stevenson, T. (1842) Observations on the defects of rain gauges, with description of one of an improved form, *Edinburgh New Phil. J.*, **33:** 12–21.

Stewart, B.J., R. Srikanthan and A.J. Hall (1990) Assessment of the potential impact of climate change on rainfall in the Murray–Darling basin, Australia, in U. Shamir and C. Jiaqi (eds), *The Hydrological Basis for Water Resources Management*, IAHS Publ. **197:** 401–12, IAHS Press, Wallingford.

Stewart, E.J. (1989) Areal reduction factors for design storm construction: joint use of raingauge and radar data, *IAHS Publ.*, **181:** 31–40.

Stewart, J.B. (1977) Evaporation from the wet canopy of a pine forest, *WRR*, **13:** 915–21.

Stewart, J.B. (1988) Modelling surface conductance of pine forest, *Agricultural and Forest Met.*, **43:** 19–35.

Stewart, J.B. and A.S. Thom (1973) Energy budgets in pine forest, *QJRMS*, **99:** 154–70.

Stewart, J.B., E.T. Engman, R.A. Feddes and Y. Kerr (eds) (1996) *Scaling-up in Hydrology Using Remote Sensing*, Wiley, Chichester.

Stone, A.T. and J.J. Morgan (1990) Kinetics of chemical transformations in the environment, in W. Stumm (ed), *Aquatic chemical kinetics*, J. Wiley and Sons, Chichester, pp. 1–41.

Strahler, A.N. (1964) Quantitative geomorphology of drainage basins and channel networks, Sec. 4–11 in V.T. Chow (ed), *Handbook of applied hydrology*, McGraw-Hill, New York.

Streltsova, T.D. (1976) Hydrodynamics of groundwater flow in a fractured formation, *WRR*, **12:** 405–14.

Stringfield, V.T. and H.E. Legrand (1969) Relation of sea water to fresh water in carbonate rocks in coastal areas, with special reference to Florida. U.S.A. and Cephalonia (Kephallinia), Greece, *J. Hydrol.*, **9:** 387–404.

Stringfield, V.T. and H.E. Legrand (1971) Effects of karst features on circulation of water in carbonate rocks in coastal areas, *J. Hydrol.*, **14:** 139–57.

Stumm, W. and J.J. Morgan (1996) *Aquatic chemistry, 3e*, J. Wiley and Sons, New York.

Sud, Y.C. and M. Fennessy (1982) A study of the influence of surface albedo on July circulation in semi arid region using the GLAS General Circulation Model, *J. Climatology*, **2:** 105–25.

Sun, H. and D.J. Furbish (1997) Annual precipitation and river discharges in Florida in response to El Niño- and La Niña-sea surface temperature anomalies, *J. Hydrol.*, **199:** 74–87.

Sverdrup, H. and W. De Vries (1994) Calculating critical loads for acidity with the simple mass balance method, *Water, air, soil pollution*, **72:** 143–62.

Swank, W.T. and Crossley, D.A. (1988), (eds.) Forest Hydrology and Ecology at Coweeta. *Ecological Studies* **66:** Springer-Verlag, New York, 469 pp.

Swank, W.T. and N.H. Miner (1968) Conversion of hardwood-covered watersheds to white pine reduces water yield. *WRR*, **4:** 947–54.

Swanson, R.H. (1994) Significant historical developments in thermal methods for measuring sap flow in trees, *Agricultural and Forest Met.*, **72:** 113–32.

Swartzendruber, D. (1962) Non Darcy behaviour in liquid saturated porous media, *JGR*, **67:** 5205–13.

Swedish Ministry of Agriculture (1982) *Acidification today and tomorrow*, Stockholm, q230 pp.

Swinbank, W.C. (1951) The measurement of the vertical transfer of heat, *J. Meteorology*, **8:** 135–45.

Szeicz, G., G. Endrodi and S. Tajchman (1969) Aerodynamic and surface factors in evaporation, *WRR*, **5:** 380–94.

Szeicz, G., C.H.M. van Bavel and S. Takami (1973) Stomatal factor in the water use and dry matter production by sorghum, *Agric. Met.*, **12:** 361–89.

Tabony, R.C. (1977) *The variability of long-duration rainfall over Great Britain*, Scientific Paper No 37, Meteorological Office, HMSO.

Taha, A., J.M. Gresillon and B.E. Clothier (1998) Modelling the link between hillslope water movement and stream flow: application to a small Mediterranean forest watershed, *J. Hydrol.*, **203:** 11–20.

Tait, A.B. (1998) Estimation of snow water equivalent using passive microwave radiation data, *Remote sensing of the Environment*, **64:** 286–91.

Takhar, H.S. and A.J. Rudge (1970) Evaporation studies in standard catchments, *J. Hydrol.*, **11:** 329–62.

Tanaka, T. (1982) The role of subsurface water exfiltration in soil erosion processes, *Hydrol. Sci. J.*, **27:** 233 (abstract).

Taylor, C.M. and T. Lebel (1998) Observational evidence of persistent convective-scale rainfall patterns. *Monthly Weather Review*, **126:** 1597–607.

Taylor, R.J. and A.J. Dyer (1958) An instrument for measuring evaporation from natural surfaces, *Nature (London)*, **181:** 408–9.

Tebbutt, T.H.Y. (1977) *Principles of water quality control, 2e*, Pergamon, Oxford, 201 pp.

Teklehaimanot, Z. and P.G. Jarvis (1991) Direct measurement of evaporation of intercepted water from forest canopies. *J. Applied Ecology*, **28:** 603–18.

Teklehaimanot, Z., P.G. Jarvis and D.C. Ledger (1991) Rainfall interception and boundary layer conductance in relation to tree spacing. *J. Hydrol.*, **123:** 261–78.

Terzaghi, K. (1942) Soil moisture and capillary phenomena in soils, in *Hydrology*, O. E. Meinzer (ed), McGraw-Hill, New York, pp. 331–63.

Thiessen, A.H. (1911) Precipitation averages for large areas, *Mon. Weather Rev.*, **39:** 1082–4.

Thom, A.S. and H.R. Oliver (1977) On Penman's equation for estimating regional evaporation, *QJRMS*, **103:** 345–57.

Thompson, N., I.A. Barrie and M. Ayles (1981) *The Meteorological Office Rainfall Evaporation Calculations System: MORECS*, Hydrological Memorandum No. 45, Meteorological Office, Bracknell, 69 pp.

Thompson, N. (1982) A comparison of formulae for the calculation of water loss from vegetated surfaces, *Agric. Met.*, **26:** 265–72.

Thornthwaite, C.W. (1944) A contribution to the Report of the Committee on Transpiration and Evaporation, 1943–44, *Trans. AGU*, **25:** 686–93.

Thornthwaite, C.W. (1948) An approach towards a rational classification of climate, *Geographical Review*, **38:** 55–94.

Thornthwaite, C.W. (1954) A reexamination of the concept and measurement of potential evapotranspiration, *Publications in Climatology*, 7.

Thornthwaite, C.W. and F.K. Hare (1965) The loss of water to the air, *Meteorological Monographs*, **6:** 163–80.

Thornthwaite, C.W. and J.R. Mather (1955) The water balance, *Publications in Climatology*, **8:** 1–86.

Todd, D.K. (1980) *Groundwater hydrology*, John Wiley and Sons, New York, 535 pp.

Todorovic, P. and V. Yevyevich (1969) Stochastic process of precipitation, *Colorado State University, Hydrology Papers*, Fort Collins, Colo., Paper 35, 61 pp.

Topp, G.C. and J.L. Davis (1985) Measurement of soil water content using time-domain reflectometry (TDR): A field evaluation, *Soil Sci. Soc. Am. J.*, **49:** 19–24.

Tóth, J. (1962) A theory of groundwater motion in small drainage basins in central Alberta, Canada, *JGR*, **67:** 4375–87.

Tóth, J. (1963) A theoretical analysis of groundwater flow in small drainage basins, *JGR*, **68:** 4795–812.

Tóth, J. (1995) Hydraulic continuity in large sedimentary basins, *Hydrogeology J.*, **3:** 4–16.

Tóth, J. (1996) Reply to a comment by E. Mazor on Tóth (1995), *Hydrogeology J.*, **4:** 102–7.

Tranter, M., R. Armstrong, E. Brum, G. Jones, M. Sharp and M. Williams (eds) (1999) *Interactions between the Cryosphere, Climate and Greenhouse Gases*, IAHS Publ. No. 256, IAHS Press, Wallingford.

Travis, C.C. and E.L. Etnier (1981) A survey of sorption relationships for reactive solutes in soil, *J. Environmental Quality*, **10:** 8–17.

Trenberth, K.E. (1992) (ed) *Climate system modelling*, Cambridge University Press, Cambridge, 788 pp.

Troendle, C.A. (1985) Variable source area models, in M.G. Anderson and T.P. Burt (eds), *Hydrological forecasting*, John Wiley and Sons, pp. 347–403.

Truesdell, A.H. and B.F. Jones (1974) WATEQ, a computer program for calculating equilibrium of natural waters, *USGS Journal of Research*, **2:** 233–48.

Tsukamoto, Y., T. Ohta and H. Noguchi (1982) Hydrological and geomorphological studies of debris slides on forested hillslopes in Japan, *Hydrol. Sci. J.*, **27:** 234 (abstract).

Tufnell, L. (1984) *Glacier Hazards*, Longman, London.

Turner, N.C. (1986) Crop water deficits: a decade of progress, *Advances in Agronomy*, **39:** 1–51.

Turner, N.C. and J.E. Begg (1973) Stomatal behaviour and water status of maize, sorghum, and tobacco under field conditions. 1. At high soil water potential, *Plant Physiology*, **51:** 31–6.

Ubarana, V.N. (1996) Observations and modelling of rainfall interception at two experimental sites in Amazonia, in J.H.C. Gash, C.A. Nobre, J.M. Roberts and R.L. Victoria (eds), *Amazonian Deforestation and Climate*, John Wiley and Sons, Chichester, 611 pp.

UNEP (1995) *Water quality of world river basins*, Environment Library Series No. 14, United Nations Environment Programme, Nairobi, Kenya, 40 pp.

UNESCO (1987) Groundwater problems in coastal areas, *Studies and Reports in Hydrology* 45, UNESCO, Paris, 596 pp.

US Army (1956) *Snow hydrology*, US Army Corps of Engineers, Portland, 437 pp.

USSR IHD Committee (1979) *Atlas of the World Water Balance*, USSR Committee for the International Hydrological Decade, UNESCO, Paris.

Vachaud, G. and J. L. Thony (1971) Hysteresis during infiltration and redistribution in a soil column at different initial water contents, *WRR*, **7:** 111–27.

Vachaud, G., M. Vauclin, D. Khanji and M. Wakil (1973) Effects of air pressure on water flow in an unsaturated stratified vertical column of sand, *WRR*, **9:** 160–73.

Vaidhianathan, V.I. and C. Singh (1942) A new phenomenon in the movement of the free water-level in a soil and its bearing on the measurement of the water table, *Proc. Indian Academy of Science*, **15:** 264–80.

Valente, F., J.S. David and J.H.C. Gash (1997) Modelling interception loss for two sparse eucalypt and pine forests in central Portugal using reformulated Rutter and Gash analytical models. *J. Hydrol.*, **190:** 141–62.

Van de Griend, A. A. (1981) *A weather type hydrologic approach to runoff phenomena*, Rodopi, Amsterdam.

Van de Griend, A. A. and E. T. Engman (1985) Partial area hydrology and remote sensing, *J. Hydrol.*, **81:** 211–51.

Van de Ven, F.H.M., D. Gutknecht, D.P. Loucks and K.A. Salewicz (1991) *Hydrology for the Management of Large River Basins*, IAHS Publ. No. 201, IAHS Press, Wallingford, pp. 400.

Van den Assem, A. (1991) Calibration of weather radar data in the Netherlands, in I.D. Cluckie and C.G. Collier (eds), *Hydrological applications of weather radar*, Ellis Horwood, London, 15–24.

Van der Kloet, P. and H. S. Lumadjeng (1987) The development of an economic objective function for decision making in a water resource control problem, in A.J.

Carlsen (ed), *Decision making in water resources*, Proceedings of UNESCO Symposium, pp. 221–37.

Van der Leeden, F., F.L. Troise and D.K. Todd (1990) *The water encyclopedia*, Lewis Publishers, Michigan, 808 pp.

Van der Molen, W. H. (1983) Personal communication.

Van Genuchten, M.T. and P.J. Wierenga (1976) Mass transfer studies in sorbing porous media, 1. Analytical solutions, *Proc. SSSA*, **40**, 473–80.

Van Wijk, W.R. and D.A. de Vries (1954) Evapotranspiration. *Netherlands Journal of Agricultural Science,* **2:** 105–118.

Veihmeyer, F.J. (1972) The availability of soil moisture to plants: results of empirical experiments with fruit trees, *Soil Sci.*, **114:** 268–94.

Veihmeyer, F.J. and A.H. Hendrickson (1955) Does transpiration decrease as the soil moisture decreases?, *Trans. AGU*, **36:** 425–8.

Vidal, J. (1995) The water bomb, *The Guardian*, 8 August 1995.

Viessman, W. and G.L. Lewis (1996) *Introduction to Hydrology, 4e*, HarperCollins, London, pp. 784.

Villholth, K.G. and K.H. Jensen (1998) Flow and transport processes in a macroporous subsurface-drained glacial till soil—II: Model analysis, *J. Hydrol.*, 207: 121-35

Villholth, K.G., K.H. Jensen and J. Frederica (1998) Flow and transport processes in a macroporous subsurface-drained glacial till soil—I: Field investigations, *J. Hydrol.*, **207:** 98–120.

Vines, R.G. (1985) European rainfall patterns, *J. Climatology*, **5:** 607–16.

Vörösmarty, C.J., C.A. Federer and A. Schloss (1998) Potential evaporation functions compared on US watersheds: possible implications for global-scale water balance and terrestrial ecosystem modeling, *J.Hydrol.*, **207:** 147–69.

Wallace J.G. (1997) *Meteorological observations at the Radcliffe Observatory, Oxford: 1815–95*, School of Geography Research Paper No. 53, University of Oxford.

Wallace, J. M. and P. V. Hobbs (1997) *Atmospheric science: an introductory survey.* Academic Press, 467 pp.

Wallace, J.S. and C.J. Holwill (1997) Soil evaporation from tiger bush in south west Niger, *J. Hydrol.*, **188:** 426–42.

Wallace, J.S., J.M. Roberts and A.M. Roberts (1982) Evaporation from heather moorland in North Yorkshire, England, in *Hydrological research basins and their use in water resources planning*, Proceedings of International Symposium, Bern, September, pp. 397–405.

Wallace, J.S., J. Roberts and W.J. Shuttleworth (1984) A comparison of methods for estimating aerodynamic resistance of heather (Calluna vulgaris (L.) Hull) in the field, *Agricultural and Forest Met.*, **32:** 289–805.

Wallace, J.S., J.H.C. Gash, D.D. McNeil and M.V.K Sivakumar (1989) Evaporation from a sparse dryland millet crop in Niger, West Africa, in P.W. Unger, T.V. Sneed, W.R. Jordan and R. Jensen (eds), *Proc. Internat. Conference on dryland Farming*, Texas Agricultural Experimental station, pp. 325–7.

Wallen, C.C. (1970) *Climates of Northern and Western Europe*, World Survey of Climatology, 5, Elsevier, Amsterdam.

Wallick, E.I. and J. Tóth (1976) Methods of regional groundwater flow analysis with suggestions for the use of environmental isotopes, in *Interpretation of Environmental Isotope and Hydrochemical Data in Groundwater Hydrology*, IAEA, Vienna, pp. 37–64.

Walling, D.E. and T.P. Burt (1983) *Field experiments in fluvial geomorphology*, GeoBooks, Norwich.

Walling, D.E. and B.W. Webb (1983) The dissolved load of rivers: a global overview, *IAHS Publ.*, **141:** 3–20.

Walling, D.E. and B.W. Webb (1986) Solutes in river systems, in S.T. Trudgill (ed), *Solute processes*, J. Wiley and Sons, New York, pp. 251–327.

Wang, H.F. and M.P. Anderson (1982) *Introduction to Groundwater Modeling*, W.H. Freeman and Company, San Francisco.

Wang, H.F. and M.P. Anderson (1995) *Introduction to Groundwater Modeling*, Academic Press, New York, 256 pp.

Wankiewicz, A. C. (1978) Water pressure in ripe snowpacks, *WRR*, **14:** 593–600.

Ward, R.C. (1967) Design of catchment experiments for hydrological studies, *Geographical J.*, **133:** 495–502.

Ward, R.C. (1972) Checks on the water balance of a small catchment, *Nordic Hydrol.*, **3:** 44–63.

Ward, R.C. (1976) Evaporation, humidity and the water balance, in T.J. Chandler and S. Gregory (eds), *The climate of the British Isles*, Longman, London, pp. 183–98.

Ward, R.C. (1981) River systems and river regimes, in *British rivers*, J. Lewin (ed), Allen and Unwin, London, pp. 1–33.

Ward, R.C. (1984) Some aspects of river flow in northern New South Wales, Australia, *J. Hydrol.*, **71**, 31–51.

Ward, R.C. (in press) Hydrologic cycle, in *Encyclopedia of Global Change*, Oxford UP, New York.

Warner, R.F. (1977) Hydrology, in D.N. Jeans (ed), *Australia: a geography*, Routledge and Kegan Paul, London, pp. 53–84.

Warrick, A.W. and D.R. Nielsen (1980) Spatial variability of soil physical properties in the field, in D. Hillel (ed), *Applications of soil physics*, Academic Press, New York, pp. 319–44.

Warrick, A.W., P.J. Wierenga and L. Pan (1997) Downward water flow through sloping layers in the vadose zone: analytical solutions for diversions, *J. Hydrol.*, **192:** 321–37.

Washburn, A.L. (1980) *Geocryology: a survey of periglacial processes and environments*, 2nd edn, John Wiley and Sons, New York, 406 pp.

Watt Committee on Energy (1984) *Acid rain*, Report 14, London, 58 pp.

Watts, G. (1997) Hydrological modelling in practice, in R.L. Wilby (ed) *Contemporary Hydrology*, Wiley, Chichester, 151–93.

Waymire, E. and V.K. Gupta (1981) The mathematical structure of rainfall representations, *WRR*, **17:** 1261–94.

Weatherley, P.E. (1976) Water movement through plants, *Proc. Phil. Trans. Roy. Soc., London, Series B*, **273:** 435–44.

Weiss, L.L. and W.T. Wilson (1958) Precipitation gauge shields, *IASH Publ.*, **43:** 462–84.

Wellings, S.R. (1984a) Recharge of the upper chalk aquifer at a site in Hampshire, England, 1. Water balance and unsaturated flow, *J. Hydrol.*, **69:** 259–73.

Wellings, S.R. (1984b) Recharge of the upper chalk aquifer at a site in Hampshire, England, 2. Solute movement, *J. Hydrol.*, **69:** 275–85.

Wellings, S.R. and J.P. Bell (1982) Physical controls of water movement in the unsaturated zone, *QJEG*, **1**(6)**:** 235–41.

Wellings, S.R. and J.D. Cooper (1983) The variability of recharge of the English chalk aquifer, *Agric. Water Manag.*, **6:** 243–53.

Wellings, S.R., J.P. Bell and R.J. Raynor (1985) The use of gypsum resistance blocks for measuring soil water potential in the field, *Inst. Hydrology Rept.*, 92, Wallingford, 32 pp.

Weyman, D.R. (1973) Measurements of downslope flow of water in a soil, *J. Hydrol.*, **20:** 267–88.

Wheater, H. and C. Kirby (eds) (1998) *Hydrology in a Changing Environment*, Wiley, Chichester, 3 vols.

Whitaker, F.F. and P.L. Smart (1997) Groundwater circulation and geochemistry of a karstified bank-marginal fracture system, South Andros Island, Bahamas, *J. Hydrol.*, **197:** 293–315.

White, R.E. (1987) *Introduction to the principles and practices of soil science, 2e*, Blackwell Scientific Publications, 244 pp.

White, W.R. and J. Watts (eds) (1994) *River Flood Hydraulics*, Wiley, Chichester, 604 pp.

Whitehead, P.G. (1984) The application of mathematical models of water quality and pollution transport: an international survey, in *Technical documents in hydrology*, UNESCO, Paris, 50 pp.

Whitehead, P.G., C. Neal and R. Neale (1986) Modelling the effects of hydrological changes on stream water acidity, *J. Hydrol.*, **84:** 353–64.

Whiting, P.J. and M. Pomeranets (1997) A numerical study of bank storage and its contribution to streamflow, *J. Hydrol.*, **202:** 121–36.

WHO (1996) *Guidelines for drinking water quality, 2. Health criteria and other supporting information, 2e*, World Health Organization, Geneva.

Wiesner, C.J. (1970) *Hydrometeorology*, Chapman and Hall Ltd, London, 232 pp.

Wilby, R.L. (1997) Beyond the river catchment, in R.L. Wilby (ed) *Contemporary Hydrology: Towards holistic environmental science*, Wiley, Chichester, 317–46.

Wild, A. (ed) (1988) *Russell's soil conditions and plant growth*, 11th edn, Longman/Wiley, New York, 991 pp.

Wilhite, D.A. (1993) The enigma of drought, in D.A. Wilhite (ed), *Drought assessment, management and planning: theory and case studies*, Kluwer Academic Publishers, London, pp. 5–15.

Wilkinson, W.B. (ed) (1993) *Macroscale Modelling of the Hydrosphere*, IAHS Publ. No. 214, IAHS Press, Wallingford, pp. 193.

Williams, R.J., D.N. Brooke, P. Matthiessen, M. Mills, A. Turnbull and R.M. Harrison (1995) Pesticide transport to surface waters within an agricultural catchment, *JIWE(M)*, **9:** 72–81.

Wilson, J.W. and E.A. Brandes (1979) Radar measurement of rainfall—a summary, *Bull. Amer. Met. Soc.*, **60:** 1048–58.

Wind, G.P. (1961) Capillary rise and some applications of the theory of moisture movement in unsaturated soils, in *TNO Committee for Hydrological Research. Proceedings and Information No. 5*, Wageningen, pp. 186–99.

Winter, T.C. (1981) Uncertainties in estimating the water balance of lakes, *Water Resources Bulletin*, **17:** 82–115.

WMO (1975) *Manual on the observation of clouds and other meteors: International cloud atlas, Volume I*, Report No. 407, World Meteorological Organization, Geneva.

WMO (1986) *Manual for estimation of Probable Maximum Precipitation, 2e*, Operational Hydrology Report 1, World Meteorological Organization, Geneva, 269 pp.

WMO (1994) *Guide to hydrological practices*, Report No. 168, World Meteorological Organization, Geneva, 735 pp.

WMO (1995) *INFOHYDRO manual*, Operational Hydrology Report No. 28, World Meteorological Organization, Geneva.

WMO (1996) Water resources assessment makes progress, *World Climate News*, June, No. 9, World Meteorological Organization, Geneva.

WMO/UNESCO (1997) *The world's water: is there enough?*, WMO No. 857, Geneva, 22 pp.

Woodley, M.R. (1996) A review of two national rainfall series, *Int. J. Climatology*, **16:** 677–87.

Woods, T.L. and R.M. Garrels (1987) *Thermodynamic values at low temperature for natural inorganic materials*. Oxford University Press, Oxford, 242 pp.

Wright, E.P. (1992) The hydrogeology of crystalline basement aquifers in Africa, in E.P. Wright and W.G. Burgess (eds), *The Hydrogeology of Crystalline Basement Aquifers in Africa*, The Geological Society, London, pp. 1–27.

Wright, E.P., A.C. Benfield, W.M. Edmunds and R. Kitching (1982) Hydrogeology of the Kufra and Sirte basins, eastern Libya, *QJEG*, **15:** 83–103.

Yamanaka, T., A. Takeda and J. Shimada (1998) Evaporation beneath the soil surface: some observational evidence and numerical experiments, *Hydrol. Processes*, **12:** 2193–2203.

Yoshimoto, T. and T. Suetsugi (1990) Comprehensive flood disaster prevention measures in Japan, in H. Massing, J. Packman and F.C. Zuidema (eds), *Hydrological Processes and Water Management in Urban Areas*, IAHS Publ. No. 198, 175–181.

Young, G. J. (1985) *Techniques for the prediction of runoff from glacierized areas*, IAHS Publ. 149, 149 pp.

Youngs, E.G. (1991) Infiltration measurements—a review, *Hydrol. Processes*, **5:** 309–20.

Zaltsberg, E. (1987) Evaluation and forecasting of groundwater runoff in a small watershed in Manitoba, *Hydrol. Sci. J.*, **32:** 69–84.

Zaslavsky, D. and G. Sinai (1981) Surface hydrology, I. Explanation of phenomena, *Proc. ASCE, J. Hydraul. Div.*, **107**(HY1): 1–16.

Zekster, I.S. and R.G. Dzhamalov (1981) Groundwater discharge into the world oceans, *Nature and Resources*, **17:** 20–2.

Zhu, T.X., Q.G. Cai and B.Q. Zeng (1997) Runoff generation on a semi-arid agricultural catchment: field and experimental studies, *J. Hydrol.*, **196:** 99–118.

Zinke, P.J. (1967) Forest interception studies in the United States. In W.E. Sopper and H.W. Lull (eds), *Forest Hydrology*, Pergamon, Oxford, pp. 137–61.

Zuzel, J.F. and L.M. Cox (1975) Relative importance of meteorological variables in snowmelt, *WRR*, **11:** 174–6.

Reference abbreviations

The following abbreviations are used in the list of references:

Agric. Met.	Agricultural Meteorology
Agric. Water Manag.	Agricultural Water Management
Agron. J.	Agronomy Journal
Atmos. Environ.	Atmospheric Environment
Boundary-Layer Met.	Boundary-Layer Meteorology
Bull. Amer. Met. Soc.	Bulletin of the American Meteorological Society
Earth Surf. Proc. and Landforms	Earth Surface Processes and Landforms
Hydrol. Sci. J.	Hydrological Sciences Journal
IAHS Publ.	Publication of the International Association of Hydrological Sciences
J. Agric. Sci.	Journal of Agricultural Science
JGR	Journal of Geophysical Research
JIWE(M)	Journal of the Institution of Water Engineers (and Managers)
JIWE(S)	Journal of the Institution of Water Engineers (and Scientists)
J. Hydrol.	Journal of Hydrology
J. Meteorol.	Journal of Meteorology
J. Soil Sci.	Journal of Soil Science
Met. Mag.	Meteorological Magazine
Proc. ASCE	Proceedings American Society of Civil Engineers
Proc. ICE	Proceedings Institution of Civil Engineers (London)
Proc. Phil. Trans. Roy. Soc.	Proceedings Philosophical Transactions of the Royal Society (London)
Proc. SSSA	Proceedings Soil Science Society of America
QJEG	Quarterly Journal of Engineering Geology
QJRMS	Quarterly Journal of the Royal Meteorological Society
Soil Sci.	Soil Science
Trans. AGU	Transactions of the American Geophysical Union

Reference abbreviations

Trans. IBG	Transactions Institute of British Geographers
USGS Wat. Sup. Pap.	United States Geological Survey Water Supply Paper
WRR	Water Resources Research

Conversion factors and physical constants

International system of units (SI)

The Système Internationale has preferred base units which include the metre (m) for length, kilogram (kg) for mass, second (s) for time and degrees kelvin (K) for temperature. Since these are often of an inconvenient magnitude, derived and supplementary units are widely used.

The metric system uses prefixes to designate decimal multiples – normally using multiples of three, i.e. 10^3, 10^6 etc.

The most commonly used multipliers are shown below with examples:

10^6	mega	(M), 1 Ml = 10^6 l
10^3	kilo	(k), 1 kg = 10^3 g; 1 km = 10^3 m
10^{-2}	centi	(c), 1 cm = 10^{-2} m
10^{-3}	milli	(m), 1 mm = 10^{-3} m
10^{-6}	micro	(μ), 1 μm = 10^{-6} m

Useful conversion factors

Length	1 km = 0.6214 miles; 1 m = 3.281 feet
Area	1 km^2 = 100 hectares = 247.1 acres = 0.3861 sq mile
Volume	1 m^3 = 1000 litres = 35.31 ft^3 = 220.0 UK gallons = 264.22 US gallons
Mass	1 kg = 2.2046 pound; 1 g = 0.03527 ounce
	1 tonne = 1000 kg = 0.9842 UK ton
Velocity	1 km/h = 0.28 m/s
Flow rate	1 l/s = 86.4 m^3/day = 13.2 gal/minute = 791.9 gal/h.
Flow/area	1 l/s/km^2 = 0.09146 ft^3/ml^2
Force (Newton)	1 N = 1 kg m/s^2 = 0.102 kg force = 0.2248 pound force
Power (Watt)	1 W = 1 J/s = kg m^2/s^3 = 0.2388 cal/s
Pressure	1 Pa = 1 N/m^2 = 0.01 millibar; 1 mb = 0.75 mm Hg
	1 bar = 10^5 Pa = 1019.7 g/cm^2 = 0.987 atmospheres
Temperature °C	= 5/9 (°F – 32)

Basin area flow depths	$1\ \mathrm{mm/km^2} = 1000\ \mathrm{m^3}$
	mm/h = [Mean flow ($\mathrm{m^3/s}$) * 3.6]/[Area ($\mathrm{km^2}$)]

Physical constants

Standard acceleration due to gravity = $9.8066\ \mathrm{m/s^2}$, but the actual value varies from 9.832 at the poles to 9.78 at the equator.
Standard atmosphere = 101 325 Pa, but the actual atmospheric pressure fluctuates about this value (typically ±3 per cent).
Absolute zero (0 K) = −273.16°C

NB. Long numbers are often broken up into factors of one thousand. In Britain a comma is used, for example 1,000,000 (and a stop to denote the decimal point, for example 1.32). In many other European countries a space is used for thousands, for example 1 000 000 (and a comma to denote the decimal point, for example 1,32).

Metric conversion tables

*DISTANCE **

Inches		*Millimetres*
0.039	1	25.4
0.079	2	50.8
0.118	3	76.2
0.158	4	101.6
0.197	5	127.0
0.236	6	152.4
0.276	7	177.8
0.315	8	203.2
0.354	9	228.6

Feet		*Metres*
3.281	1	0.305
6.562	2	0.610
9.842	3	0.914
13.123	4	1.219
16.404	5	1.524
19.685	6	1.829
22.966	7	2.134
26.246	8	2.438
29.527	9	2.743

Yards		Metres
1.094	1	0.914
2.187	2	1.829
3.281	3	2.743
4.375	4	3.658
5.468	5	4.572
6.562	6	5.486
7.656	7	6.401
8.750	8	7.316
9.843	9	8.230

Miles		*Kilometres*
0.621	1	1.609
1.243	2	3.219
1.864	3	4.828
2.486	4	6.437
3.107	5	8.047
3.728	6	9.656
4.350	7	11.265
4.971	8	12.875
5.592	9	14.484

*VOLUME **

Cu. feet		*Cu. metres*
35.315	1	0.028
70.629	2	0.057
105.943	3	0.085
141.258	4	0.113
176.572	5	0.142
211.887	6	0.170
247.201	7	0.198
282.516	8	0.227
317.830	9	0.255

Imp. gallons		*Litres*
0.220	1	4.544
0.440	2	9.087
0.660	3	13.631
0.880	4	18.174
1.101	5	22.718
1.321	6	27.262
1.541	7	31.805
1.761	8	36.349
1.981	9	40.892

*AREA **

Sq. yards		*Sq. metres*
1.196	1	0.836
2.392	2	1.672
3.588	3	2.508
4.784	4	3.345
5.980	5	4.181
7.176	6	5.016
8.372	7	5.853
9.568	8	6.690
10.764	9	7.526

Sq. miles		*Sq. kms*
0.386	1	2.590
0.772	2	5.180
1.158	3	7.770
1.544	4	10.360
1.931	5	12.950
2.317	6	15.540
2.703	7	18.130
3.089	8	20.720
3.475	9	23.310

Acres		*Hectares*
2.471	1	0.405
4.942	2	0.809
7.413	3	1.214
9.884	4	1.619
12.355	5	2.023
14.826	6	2.428
17.297	7	2.833
19.768	8	3.237
22.239	9	3.642

* In the Distance, Area, and Volume conversion tables the figures in the central columns may be read as either metric or imperial units; for example, 1 cubic foot = 0.028 cubic metre; or 1 cubic metre = 35.315 cubic feet.

TEMPERATURE
(Celsius to Fahrenheit)

°C	0	1	2	3	4	5	6	7	8	9
40	104.0	105.8	107.6	109.4	111.2	113.0	114.8	116.6	118.4	120.2
30	86.0	87.8	89.6	91.4	93.2	95.0	96.8	98.6	100.4	102.2
20	68.0	69.8	71.6	73.4	75.2	77.0	78.8	80.6	82.4	84.2
10	50.0	51.8	53.6	55.4	57.2	59.0	60.8	62.6	64.4	66.2
0	32.0	33.8	35.6	37.4	39.2	41.0	42.8	44.6	46.4	48.2
0	32.0	30.2	28.4	26.6	24.8	23.0	21.2	19.4	17.6	15.8
−10	14.0	12.2	10.4	8.6	6.8	5.0	3.2	1.4	−0.4	−2.2
−20	−4.0	−5.8	−7.6	−9.4	−11.2	−13.0	−14.8	−16.6	−18.4	−20.2
−30	−22.0	−23.8	−25.6	−27.4	−29.2	−31.0	32.8	−34.6	−36.4	−38.2
−40	−40.0	−41.8	−43.6	−45.4	−47.2	−49.0	−50.8	−52.6	−54.4	−56.2

Author index

Subject index

Specific Learning Difficulties (Dyslexia)

Challenges and Responses